COMPUTER ORGANIZATION AND ARCHITECTURE,
FOURTH EDITION

A unified view of this broad field. Covers fundamentals such as CPU, control unit, microprogramming, instruction set, I/O, and memory. Also covers advanced topics such as RISC, superscalar, and parallel organization. **Awarded the Texty Award by the Text and Academic Authors Association for the best Computer Science and Engineering Textbook of 1996.**

LOCAL AND METROPOLITAN AREA NETWORKS, FIFTH EDITION

An in-depth presentation of the technology and architecture of local and metropolitan area networks. Covers topology, transmission media, medium access control, standards, internetworking, and network management. Provides an up-to-date coverage of LAN/MAN systems, including Fast Ethernet, ATM LANs, Fibre Channel and wireless LANs.

CRYPTOGRAPHY AND NETWORK SECURITY, SECOND EDITION

A tutorial and survey on network security technology. Each of the basic building blocks of network security, including conventional and public-key cryptography, authentication, and digital signatures, are covered. The book covers important network security tools and applications, including S/MIME, IP Security, Kerberos, SSL/TLS, SET, and X509v3. In addition methods for countering hackers and viruses are explored.

ISDN AND BROADBAND ISDN, with FRAME RELAY AND ATM:
FOURTH EDITION

An in-depth presentation of the technology and architecture of integrated services digital networks (ISDN). Covers the integrated digital network (IDN), xDSL, ISDN services, architecture, signaling system no. 7 (SS7) and detailed coverage of the ITU-T protocol standards. Also provides detailed coverage of protocols and congestion control strategies for both frame relay and ATM.

BUSINESS DATA COMMUNICATIONS, THIRD EDITION

A comprehensive presentation of data communications and telecommunications from a business perspective. Covers voice, data, image, and video communications and applications technology and includes a number of case studies.

ISDN AND BROADBAND ISDN WITH FRAME RELAY AND ATM

FOURTH EDITION

ISDN AND BROADBAND ISDN WITH FRAME RELAY AND ATM

FOURTH EDITION

William Stallings

Prentice Hall
Upper Saddle River, New Jersey 07458

Library of Congress Cataloging-in-Publication Data

Stallings, William.
    ISDN and broadband ISDN with frame relay and ATM /
    William Stallings. — 4th ed.
       p. cm.
    Includes bibliographical references and index.
    ISBN 0–13–973744–8
     1. Integrated services digital networks.   2. Broadband
    communication systems.   3. Frame relay (Data transmission).
    4. Asynchronous transfer mode.   I. Title.
    TK5103.75.S73   1998
    004.6'2—dc21   98–33694
                                       CIP

Publisher: Alan Apt
Acquisitions editor: Laura Steele
Editor-in-chief: Marcia Horton
Production editor: Rose Kernan
Managing editor: Eileen Clark
Art director: Heather Scott
Assistant to art director: John Christiana
Director of creative services: Paula Maylahn
Cover designer: Heather Scott
Manufacturing buyer: Pat Brown
Assistant vice president of production and manufacturing: David W. Riccardi

 © 1999, 1995, 1992, 1989 by Prentice-Hall, Inc.
Simon & Schuster / A Viacom Company
Upper Saddle River, New Jersey 07458

The author and publisher of this book have used their best efforts in preparing this book. These
efforts include the development, research, and testing of the theories and programs to determine
their effectiveness. The author and publisher make no warranty of any kind, expressed or
implied, with regard to these programs or the documentation contained in this book. The author
and publisher shall not be liable in any event for incidental or consequential damages in
connection with, or arising out of, the furnishing, performance, or use of these programs.

Printed in the United States of America

10 9 8 7 6 5 4 3 2 1

ISBN 0-13-973744-8

Prentice-Hall International (UK) Limited, *London*
Prentice-Hall of Australia Pty. Limited, *Sydney*
Prentice-Hall Canada, Inc., *Toronto*
Prentice-Hall Hispanoamericana, S. A., *Mexico*
Prentice-Hall of India Private Limited, *New Delhi*
Prentice-Hall of Japan, Inc., *Tokyo*
Simon & Schuster Asia Pte. Ltd., *Singapore*
Editora Prentice-Hall do Brasil, Ltda., *Rio de Janeiro*

As Always for A. T. S.
Compassionate
Caring
Charismatic
And Those Are Only The Cs

PREFACE

Perhaps the most important development in the computer-communications industry in the 1990s is the evolution of the integrated services digital network (ISDN) and its follow-on, the broadband ISDN (B-ISDN). The ISDN and B-ISDN have had a dramatic impact on the planning and deployment of intelligent digital networks providing integrated service for voice, data, and video. Further, the work on the ISDN and B-ISDN standards has led to the development of two major new networking technologies: frame relay and asynchronous transfer mode (ATM). Frame relay and ATM have become the essential ingredients in developing high-speed networks for local, metropolitan, and wider area applications.

INTENDED AUDIENCE

This book is intended for a broad range of readers who will benefit from an understanding of ISDN and B-ISDN concepts and the associated technologies of frame relay and ATM. This includes students and professionals in the fields of data processing and data communications, designers and implementers, and data communication and networking customers and managers. The book is designed to be self-contained. For the reader with little or no background in data communications, Part One and the appendices cover a number of basic topics

PLAN OF THE TEXT

The objective of this book is to provide a comprehensive technical survey of the protocols and architecture of ISDN and B-ISDN, including a detailed examination of frame relay and ATM.

The book divides into five parts. Part One deals with the fundamental technologies used in digital networks, including a discussion of digital transmission technology and a review of circuit switching and packet switching. Part Two is devoted to ISDN and examines the user–network interface architecture, protocols, and services. This part also describes Signaling System Number 7, a related facility. Part Three focuses on frame relay technology and protocols and examines the critical issue of congestion control in frame relay networks. Part Four covers B-ISDN architecture and protocols. Part Five examines ATM-related protocols and surveys various techniques for traffic and congestion control in ATM networks.

The book includes an extensive glossary, a list of frequently used acronyms, and a bibliography. Each chapter includes problems and suggestions for further reading.

Throughout, there is an emphasis on both technology and on standards. The book provides a comprehensive guide to understanding the many recommendations issued by the ITU Telecommunication Standardization Sector (ITU-T), formerly the CCITT.

INTERNET SERVICES FOR INSTRUCTORS AND STUDENTS

There is a Web page for this book that provides support for students and instructors. The page includes links to relevant sites, transparency masters of figures in the book in PDF (Adobe Acrobat) format, and sign-up information for the book's internet mailing list. The Web page is at http://www.shore.net/~ws/ISDN4e. An Internet mailing list has been set up so that instructors using this book can exchange information, suggestions, and questions with each other and with the author. As soon as typos or other errors are discovered, an errata list for this book will be available at http://www.shore.net/~ws.

WHAT'S NEW IN THE FOURTH EDITION

In the four years since the third edition of this book was published, the field has seen continued innovations and improvements. In this new edition, I try to capture these changes while maintaining a broad and comprehensive coverage of the entire field. To begin this process of revision, the third edition of this book was extensively reviewed by a number of professors who teach the subject. The result is that, in many places, the narrative has been clarified and tightened, and illustrations have been improved. Also, a number of new "field-tested" problems have been added; the solutions manual, available to instructors, includes solutions to all of the problems in the book.

Two noteworthy changes in this edition are the inclusion of xDSL and the expansion of the coverage of ATM. The term *xDSL* refers to a family of digital subscriber line technologies that provide high-speed access to ISDN and other wide area networks over ordinary twisted-pair lines from the network to a residential or business subscriber. The book surveys xDSL and especially asymmetric digital subscriber line (ADSL) technology. Another important change is the expansion of the coverage of ATM. This includes additional details on the ATM adaption layer

(AAL), treatment of the new available bit rate (ABR) service, and updated and expanded treatment of ATM traffic and congestion control.

Other changes permeate the book. The third edition was based on the ITU-T recommendations through mid-1994. Since that time, most of these older recommendations have been updated and new ones have been added. In addition, the ATM Forum has filled in many of the gaps in the ITU-T specification of ATM and related protocols. These changes are reflected throughout the book. To aid readers in keeping up with this evolving field, pointers to relevant Web sites are found in the Recommended Reading section of many chapters.

ACKNOWLEDGMENTS

This new edition has benefited from review by a number of people, who gave generously of their time and expertise. I would like to thank Pierre Catala, Texas A&M; Thomas Gannon, Worcester Polytechnic Institute; Elsa Valeroso, University of North Dakota; Subbarao Wunnava, Florida International University; Ibrahim Habib, City College of NY; Robert Blackshaw, GeoTrain Corporation; Tawfig Alrabiah, University of Pittsburgh; Teik Kheong Tan, TTK Consulting; Kenneth Molloy, KM Associates Inc.

CONTENTS

PART THREE FRAME RELAY, 309

Chapter 12 Frame Relay Protocols and Services, 311

Chapter 13 Frame Relay Congestion Control, 345

PART FOUR BROADBAND ISDN, 371

Chapter 14 Broadband ISDN Architecture, 373

ISDN AND BROADBAND ISDN WITH FRAME RELAY AND ATM

FOURTH EDITION

CHAPTER 1

INTRODUCTION

This book is a survey of ISDN and broadband ISDN (B-ISDN), together with the key networking technologies of frame relay and asynchronous transfer mode. Both the standardization of ISDN and B-ISDN and the development of frame relay and ATM have been driven by market pressures to reduce the cost of voice and data transmission and to expand networking services to provide high-speed data and video capability. In this chapter, we discuss some of the key factors driving the nature and pace of evolution in these areas.

1.1 THE ARRIVAL OF ISDN

Rapid advances in computer and communication technologies have resulted in the increasing merger of these two fields. The lines have blurred among computing, switching, and digital transmission equipment; and the same digital techniques are being used for data, voice, and image transmission. Merging and evolving technologies, coupled with increasing demands for efficient and timely collection, processing, and dissemination of information, have led to the development of integrated systems that transmit and process all types of data. The ultimate goal of this evolution is something that is referred to as the integrated services digital network (ISDN).

The ISDN is intended to be a worldwide public telecommunications network to replace existing public telecommunications networks and deliver a wide variety of services. The ISDN is defined by the standardization of user interfaces and implemented as a set of digital switches and paths supporting a broad range of traffic types and providing value-added processing services. In practice, there are multiple networks, implemented within national boundaries, but from the user's point of view, the eventual widespread deployment of ISDN will lead to a single, uniformly accessible, worldwide network.

The impact of ISDN on both users and vendors will be profound. To control ISDN evolution and impact, a massive effort at standardization is under way. Although ISDN standards are still evolving, both the technology and the emerging implementation strategy are well understood.

Even though ISDN has yet to achieve the universal deployment hoped for, it is already in its second generation. The first generation, sometimes referred to as **narrowband ISDN**, is based on the use of a 64-kbps channel as the basic unit of switching and has a circuit-switching orientation. The major technical contribution of the narrowband ISDN effort has been **frame relay**. The second generation, referred to as **broadband ISDN** (B-ISDN), supports very high data rates (100s of Mbps) and has a packet-switching orientation. The major technical contribution of the broadband ISDN effort has been **asynchronous transfer mode** (ATM), also known as cell relay.

A sample of the trends that are driving ISDN and B-ISDN is as follows:

- Computers are joining together instead of standing alone. The percentage of personal computers that have communications capability is rising. While yesterday's corporate computer was a stand-alone device, businesses today rely on a mix of small, medium, and large computers that can share resources (e.g., printers), share data, and exchange messages. Our analytical tools have sprouted wires; more and better wires are coming, and the wires will extend everywhere.
- Cellular radio is making communications mobile. Automobiles, taxis, and boats are becoming workstations. People can not only talk via cellular radio phones; they can also transmit data by linking up their portable computers. Look for the development of cellular phone/computer combinations. In time, automobiles will provide communication/computer systems as options. Any vehicle, then, will be a unit that can link up to the global information network.
- Computers for personal use will be ubiquitous. This will be especially so for students (from elementary school on up) and "knowledge workers," who deal primarily with paper—documents, reports, numbers. Many office workers have at least one workstation at the office and one at home. Furthermore, most people will own a powerful portable and possibly a wearable model—a very personal computer (VPC). The hotels you stay at in the future may have personal computers in their rooms as amenities; some hotels already do. Computing power will be at every hand; and, most important, each computer will tap into the network.
- The volume and richness of data are increasing dramatically. The first-generation personal computers have given way to the latest Windows and Macintosh systems, with color and high-quality graphics. New applications in the office environment are being developed that require much higher networking capacity, and desktop image processors will soon increase network data flow by an unprecedented rate. Examples of these applications include digital fax machines, document image processors, and graphics programs on personal computers. Resolutions as high as 400×400 per page are typical for these applications. Even with compression techniques, this will generate a tremendous data communications load. In addition, optical disks are beginning to reach technical maturity and are being developed toward realistic desktop capacities exceeding 1 Gbyte.
- Voice recognition and natural language processing technology will increase the intelligence of systems and networks. These have been two of the most difficult applications to develop, but they are now gradually emerging from

artificial-intelligence laboratories. Voice recognition is the ability to recognize spoken words. Natural language processing is the ability to extract the meaning of words and sentences. As these two applications develop, access to information banks and databases will become increasingly easier and therefore will create a greater demand. A user will be able to perform a transaction or access information with simple spoken or keyed commands. Interfacing with the worldwide network will be like talking with a very knowledgeable telephone operator, librarian, and universal expert rolled into one.

- Government use of computer systems will become more efficient. The government is the most prodigious producer and user of information in our society. ISDN will improve and disperse access and help to remove incompatibilities between different systems so that more can be done with less effort.

- National and global business activities will become easier to promote. The brokerage business has become almost a computer network in itself, depending on instant transmission of information and automated buy–sell orders. Banking today relies on more than automatic tellers and computerized accounting; money itself is becoming akin to information as fund transfers take place over growing data networks. And banks are beginning to sell online information services as adjuncts to electronic banking. Companies of all sizes are coming to depend on telecommunications for their daily business activities. Remote data entry, electronic mail, facsimile transmission, and decision support systems are just some of the operations that rely on communications. Multinational corporations and joint ventures between American and foreign firms depend on quick interchange of information. Communication networks are absolutely essential for the continued globalization of trade and industry.

- Office buildings are being wired for intelligence. The so-called smart building is beginning to appear. Such a building contains a network for voice, data, environmental control (heat, humidity, air conditioning), security (burglar, fire), and closed-circuit TV. Many of these services generate out-of-building transmission requirements.

- Person-to-person interaction will increase. Business is responding to the need for employees to interact and to avoid "telephone tag" with electronic mail, voice mail, file transfer, document exchange, and video teleconferencing facilities. All of these generate large data communications requirements.

- The fiber revolution will bring enormous capacity that will generate its own demand. In developed countries, fiber is rapidly replacing microwave and coaxial cable transmission paths. Fiber, together with satellite, is appearing more gradually elsewhere. The resulting quantum jump in capacity has permitted the planning and deployment of new applications on public and private networks.

1.2 THE COMPUTER-COMMUNICATIONS REVOLUTION

Ours has been called the postindustrial era. By that is meant that industrialization, which was the dominating factor and engine of change for over a century, no longer fulfills that role. To those societies that have experienced the industrial revolution, the social and economic changes have been profound. The postindustrial era is producing even greater and more rapid changes. Many trends are visible as threads making up the rope that is dragging humankind into a life and lifestyle dictated not by politicians and economists, but by the technologists. All of these threads, at bottom, depend on two major technologies: computers and communications.

Consider one example: biotechnology. One of the youngest technologies, biotechnology has already brought with it a number of firms in the business of producing commercially available products and some of the hottest action in the stock market in the 1980s. Biotechnology firms are doing research on substances that can combat cancer, eat oil spills, and solve many other problems facing society. All of the goods and ills of this technology are impossible without sophisticated use of computers. Computers are used to monitor and control the fabrication of new biological entities and to model the process of creating new substances so that the most promising direction of research can be followed. Extremely fast and powerful computer systems are needed for this purpose.

Another example is what is known as factory automation. General Motors, in particular, is convinced that the only way to compete with Japanese automakers is to reduce drastically the labor cost of producing cars. To do this, the factory environment must increasingly include microcomputers, programmable controllers, and robots. Computer technology must replace human labor on the assembly line. For the automated factory to work, sophisticated computer-controlled devices are required. Equally important, all of these devices must be interconnected with a local area network (LAN). The LAN ties together all of the equipment in the factory so that control signs can be sent to the automated devices on the assembly line, and data and alarm signals can be sent by these devices to computers that act in the role of foreman and supervisor.

As a final example, consider office automation, which can be defined as the incorporation of appropriate technology in the office to help people manage information. The key motivation for the move to office automation is, again, productivity. As the percentage of white-collar workers has increased, the information and paperwork volume has grown. In most installations, secretarial and other support functions are heavily labor intensive. Increased labor costs combined with low productivity and increasing workload have caused employers to seek effective ways of increasing their rather low capital investment in office-related work. At the same time, principals (managers, skilled information workers) are faced with their own productivity bind. Work needs to be done faster with less wait time and less waste time between segments of a job. This requires better access to information and better communication and coordination with others. As in the factory environment, the solution is a collection of computer-based equipment interconnected with a LAN.

It has become commonplace to talk about the dramatic pace of change in these two technologies, computers and communications. Rapid technological change has been characteristic of these two areas since the 1960s. What is new is that there has been a merger of these two technologies. This merger has been called the computer-communications revolution. It has had a profound impact on the providing industries and on the users—businesses and individuals. That merger, or revolution, was substantially accomplished by the late 1970s and early 1980s. We are now realizing the aftermath and logical conclusion of that revolution: ISDN.

1.3 FROM COMMUNICATIONS TO COMPUTERS

The communications facilities that provide voice, data, and video transmission services are increasingly relying on digital technology and computerized systems. The two driving forces here are the changing economics and regulatory focus of telephone networks and the increasing demand for terminal user services.

The Evolving Telephone Network

The U.S. public telephone network, once the almost exclusive property of AT&T and now fragmented among a number of companies, was originally an analog network. It is now in the slow process of evolving to what is being referred to as the integrated digital network (IDN), which is the subject of Part I of this book.

Increasingly, the choice of network designers is to use digital technology for transmission and switching. Despite its massive investment in analog equipment, AT&T is gradually converting to an all-digital network. Other long-distance transmission providers, such as MCI, are doing the same. The major reasons for this trend are as follows:

- **Component cost:** While the cost of analog components has remained fairly stable, the cost of digital components continues to drop. The use of large-scale integration (LSI) and very-large-scale integration (VLSI) decreases not only the size, but also the cost of virtually all equipment used to process digital signals.
- **Line sharing:** Over long distances, the signals from many telephone calls will share common transmission paths by means of multiplexing. Time-division multiplexing, using digital techniques, is more efficient than the analog-based frequency-division multiplexing. Thus, the voice input from the telephone is converted to digital for the long-distance links.
- **Network control:** Control signals that monitor the status and control the operation of networks are inherently digital. They can be more easily incorporated into an all-digital network.

Thus, more and more, digital technology is being applied to the telephone network. The techniques used are the same as those used in computer systems. So, increasingly, the major components of the telephone network are either computers themselves or computer controlled.

Teleprocessing and Telematics

Historically, and still today, telephone traffic has been the major reason for, and the major user of, long-distance communications facilities. Over the past 25 years, however, there has been a growing use of these facilities to transmit digital data. By far, the major component of this digital data requirement has been for communication between a user at a terminal and a computer remote from that user. The communications function that provides this remote terminal access is known as teleprocessing. More recently, additional services built on the basic teleprocessing function, known as telematics, have appeared.

To understand these trends, we need to say something about the way in which computer usage has evolved. In the 1950s, the typical computer was large and expensive. It was a limited resource that needed to be used efficiently. For this purpose, operating systems were developed. The original operating systems were batch, which controlled the execution of a sequence of user programs, called jobs. A user could submit a job, and that job would be queued up, waiting for the use of the computer. As soon as one job finished, the operating system would fetch the next job in line for execution.

As computers became more powerful and the demand for their use grew, batch operating systems became obsolete. The problem was that if only one program is executing, many of the system's resources are idle at any given time. For example, while data to be processed are being read in, those portions of the system that can perform arithmetic and logical functions are unused. To overcome this inefficiency, the time-sharing operating system was developed. With time sharing, many jobs can be active at any one time. The operating system orchestrates matters so that various resources are applied to particular jobs at any given time. And, whereas the user of a batch-oriented system would typically submit a job to a computer operator and come back sometime later for the results, the time-sharing user interacts directly with the operating system from a terminal.

The first time-sharing users used terminals that were in close proximity to the computer. But soon the demand for remote terminal access, known as teleprocessing, developed. A large organization (e.g., a bank or an insurance company) might have a central data processing facility but potential users in a number of satellite offices. Time-sharing services sprang up. Such a service "rented time" on its computer to users who could not afford their own system. More recently, transaction-processing systems have appeared. Point-of-sale systems, airline reservation systems, and so forth involve many terminal users who perform transactions that are recorded in a database on a remote computer.

Remote terminal access can be and is handled by the public telephone network. The digital data are converted to analog signals and transmitted just as the voice signals in an ordinary telephone call. But this is inefficient. When a call is placed, resources within the network are dedicated to setting up and maintaining the call. In effect, a circuit through the network is dedicated for the duration. Now, with a telephone call, generally one party or the other is talking most of the time, and good use is made of the circuit. But with a terminal-to-computer connection, much of the time the circuit is idle, when neither side is transmitting.

To improve efficiency, packet switching was developed. Terminal and computer data are sent out in small blocks, known as packets. These packets are routed through the network using paths and resources that are shared among a number of users sending packets. Thus, the network must know how to handle and process packets—another example of computerization of communications.

The demand for data communications and the use of packet switching continue to grow. In addition to the more traditional teleprocessing services, new telematic services are appearing. Telematic facilities provide a user at a terminal with access to a specific application or database. An example is a catalog-ordering service. The user is connected to the service and may select various items for viewing. Each catalog item is described on the user's terminal screen, and the user may place an order.

1.4 FROM COMPUTERS TO COMMUNICATIONS

While communications facilities have increasingly made use of computer technology, the opposite is also true. The hardware and software within a computer specifically devoted to the communications function have grown in size and importance. The reason for this is that, increasingly, data processing facilities are being implemented as a collection of cooperating computers rather than a single large computer. This is known as distributed processing, because the processing function is distributed among a number of computers. To follow what has happened, we need to look at three aspects:

- The economic forces that have made distributed processing possible
- The potential benefits of distributed processing that have encouraged its development
- The implications in terms of the communications function

Economic Forces and Potential Benefits

Two trends have combined to change the economic equation for distributed processing: the dramatic and continuing decrease in computer hardware costs, accompanied by an increase in computer hardware capability.

Today's microprocessors have speeds, instruction sets, and memory capacities comparable with those of minicomputers and even mainframes of just a few years ago. This trend has spawned a number of changes in the way information is collected, processed, and used in organizations. There is an increasing use of small, single-function systems, such as word processors and small business computers, and of general-purpose microcomputers, such as personal computers and workstations. These small, dispersed systems are more accessible to the user, more responsive, and easier to use than large central time-sharing systems.

As the number of systems increases, there is likely to be a desire to interconnect these systems for a variety of reasons, including

- Sharing expensive resources
- Exchanging data between systems

Sharing expensive resources, such as bulk storage and laser printers, is an important measure of cost containment. Although the cost of data processing hardware has dropped, the cost of such essential electromechanical equipment remains high. Even in the case of data that can be uniquely associated with a small system, economies of scale encourage the storage of those data on some sort of centralized server system. The cost per bit for storage on a microcomputer's floppy disk is orders of magnitude higher than that on a large disk or tape.

The ability to exchange data is an equally compelling reason for interconnection. Individual users of computer systems do not work in isolation and will want to retain some of the benefits provided by a central system, including the ability to exchange messages with other users and the ability to access data and programs from several sources in the preparation of a document or the analysis of data.

In addition to these benefits, several others are worth mentioning. A distributed system can be more reliable, more available to the user, and more able to survive failures. The loss of any one component should have minimal impact, and key components can be made redundant so that other systems can quickly take up the load after a failure. Finally, a distributed system provides the potential to connect devices from multiple vendors, which gives the customer greater flexibility and bargaining power.

The Computer's Communication Function

Distributed processing relies on a communications facility for interconnecting the computers that make up the distributed processing system. But more is involved. To achieve cooperative action, the computers themselves must incorporate functions traditionally thought of as communications functions.

Consider, for example, the transfer of a file between two computers. There must be a data path between the two computers, either directly or via a communication network. In addition, a number of functions must be provided, such as

1. The source system must either activate the direct data communication path or inform the communication network of the identity of the desired destination system.
2. The source system must ascertain that the destination system is prepared to receive data.
3. The file transfer application in the source system must ascertain that the file management program in the destination system is prepared to accept and store the file.
4. If the file formats used on the two systems are incompatible, one or the other system must perform a format translation function.

It is clear that there must be a high degree of cooperation between the two computer systems. The exchange of information between computers for the purpose of cooperative action is generally referred to as computer communications. Similarly, when two or more computers are interconnected via a communication network, the set of computers is referred to as a computer network. Because a similar level of cooperation is required between a user at a terminal and a computer, these terms are often used when some of the communicating entities are terminals.

These functions, which deal with control and cooperation, have been developed for use within the telephone network and are now finding application in the computers that make up a distributed processing system. Thus, just as the communications providers are increasingly using computer technology, the opposite is also occurring.

1.5 OUTLINE OF THE BOOK

This chapter serves as an introduction to the entire book. A brief synopsis of the remaining chapters follows.

Digital Transmission

All of the networks and technologies discussed in this book rely on digital transmission facilities for the transfer of voice, data, and video. Chapter 2 provides a survey of key digital transmission topics, including the encoding of all types of information and signals into digital form, multiplexing schemes, and the digital subscriber loop.

Line Coding and the Subscriber Line

Chapter 3 looks at techniques for digital transmission between the end user, or subscriber, and the network. High-speed digital transmission over the subscriber line is the most challenging aspect of digital network design. Chapter 3 examines techniques currently in use and discusses the emerging xDSL technology.

Communication Networks

Chapter 4 examines the two traditional approaches to wide area networking, both of which have influenced the evolution of ISDN and B-ISDN: circuit switching and packet switching. Chapter 4 also examines the standard user–network interface for packet-switched networks, X.25.

ISDN Overview

Chapter 5 serves as an overview to the following chapters on ISDN. The chapter examines the relationship between the integrated digital network (IDN) and ISDN. The overall structure of ISDN at the user–network interface is presented, and the standards defining ISDN are summarized.

ISDN Interfaces and Functions

Chapter 6 describes the architecture of ISDN at the user–network interface. ISDN includes a small set of standardized interfaces that supports a wide variety of services. These services are available through a transmission structure that provides various data rates over a multiplexed line. Two related issues are the addressing of subscribers over ISDN and the need for interworking between ISDNs and between an ISDN and a non-ISDN network.

ISDN Physical Layer

Chapter 7 discusses the ITU-T specifications for the physical layer of ISDN. These include a basic rate access at 192 kbps and a primary rate access at either 1.544 Mbps or 2.048 Mbps. All of these specifications deal with the interface between the subscriber's equipment and a network termination device on the subscriber's premises.

ISDN Data Link Layer

Chapter 8 discusses the ITU-T specifications for the data link layer of ISDN. The fundamental standard at this layer is LAPD, which is used to support call control signaling and user packet switching. Another standard, I.465/V.120, supports non-ISDN devices and provides a simple multiplexing capability for circuit-switched connections.

ISDN Network Layer

Chapter 9 discusses the ITU-T specifications for the network layer of ISDN. The focus of the chapter is Q.931, which specifies a user–network call control protocol. The protocol is used for setting up, maintaining, and terminating connections on user channels. In addition, Chapter 9 examines the call control protocol for requesting supplementary services.

ISDN Services

The reason for the existence of ISDN is the set of services that it provides. These services define the requirements for ISDN. Chapter 10 examines the general specification of services found in the ISDN standards. In these standards, services are defined in terms of attributes that can take on a range of values.

Signaling System Number 7

Signaling System Number 7 (SS7) is an elaborate set of recommendations that defines the protocols and mechanisms for the internal management of ISDN and other integrated digital networks. Chapter 11 introduces the overall architecture of SS7 and then examines the protocols at each layer of the SS7 protocol reference model.

Frame Relay Protocols and Service

Chapter 12 introduces the most important innovation to come out of the work on ISDN: frame relay. Frame relay provides a more efficient means of supporting packet switching than X.25 and is enjoying widespread use, not only in ISDN but in other networking contexts. This chapter looks at the data transfer protocol and call control protocol for frame relay and also looks at the related data link control protocol, LAPF.

Frame Relay Congestion Control

A critical component for frame relay is congestion control. Chapter 13 explains the nature of congestion in frame relay networks and both the importance and difficulty of controlling congestion. The chapter then describes a range of congestion control techniques that has been specified for use in frame relay networks.

Broadband ISDN Architecture

Although there are many similarities in the interface to narrowband ISDN and B-ISDN, the high data rates provided by B-ISDN lead to some notable differences. Chapter 14 examines some of the key technical developments that are driving the evolution of B-ISDN. The chapter then looks at the services that B-ISDN will support and the overall architecture of B-ISDN.

Broadband ISDN Protocols

Chapter 15 describes the overall protocol reference model for B-ISDN and then focuses on the physical layer specification. The other layers of the model deal with ATM, which is covered in later chapters. Chapter 15 includes an examination of the basic data rates and requirements for the B-ISDN physical layer. Then the principal means of organizing physical layer transmission for ISDN is examined. This is the high-speed synchronous digital transmission scheme known as synchronous optical network (SONET) or synchronous digital hierarchy (SDH).

ATM Protocols

Chapter 16 focuses on the transmission technology that is the foundation of B-ISDN: asynchronous transfer mode. As with frame relay, ATM is finding widespread application beyond its use as part of B-ISDN. This chapter begins with a description of the ATM protocol and format. Then the physical layer issues relating to the transmission of ATM cells are discussed. Finally, the ATM adaptation layer (AAL) is examined.

ATM Traffic and Congestion Control

Again, as with frame relay, congestion control is a vital component of ATM. This area, referred to as ATM traffic and congestion control, is one of the most complex aspects of ATM and is the subject of intensive ongoing research. Chapter 17 surveys those techniques that have been accepted as having broad utility in ATM environments.

Flow Control, Error Detection, and Error Control

A number of the protocols discussed in this book make use of some basic techniques for flow control, error detection, and error control. These include LAPD, LAPF, LAPB, X.25 level 3, and the Signaling Link layer of SS7. For readers unfamiliar with these techniques, Appendix A provides a brief description.

The OSI Model

The specifications for ISDN, B-ISDN, frame relay, and ATM all make use of the terminology and concepts of the open systems interconnection (OSI) model. The OSI model provides a framework within which protocol standards can be developed. In addition, the OSI model provides a terminology and architecture that are commonly used in networking discussions. For the reader unfamiliar with OSI, Appendix B provides an overview.

APPENDIX 1A INTERNET AND WEB RESOURCES

There are a number of resources available on the Internet and the Web to support this book and to help one keep up with developments in this field.

Web Sites for This Book

A special Web page has been set up for this book at http://www.shore.net/~ws/ISDN4e.html. The site includes the following:

- Links to other Web sites, including the sites listed in this book, provide a gateway to relevant resources on the Web.
- Online transparency masters are provided of most of the figures in this book in PDF (Adobe Acrobat) format.
- Sign-up information for the book's Internet mailing list is provided.
- I also hope to include links to home pages for courses based on the book; these pages may be useful to other instructors in providing ideas about how to structure their course.

As soon as any typos or other errors are discovered, an errata list for this book will be available at http://www.shore.net/~ws. The file will be updated as needed. Please e-mail any errors that you spot to ws@shore.net. Errata sheets for my other books are at the same Web site, as well as discount ordering information for the books.

Other Web Sites

There are numerous Web sites that provide some sort of information related to the topics of this book. In subsequent chapters, pointers to specific Web sites can be found in the "Recommended Reading" section. Because the URLs for Web sites tend to change frequently, I have not included these in the book. For all of the Web sites listed in the book, the appropriate link can be found at this book's Web site.

USENET Newsgroups

A number of USENET newsgroups are devoted to some aspect of ISDN, frame relay, or ATM. As with virtually all USENET groups, there is a high noise to signal ratio, but it is worth experimenting to see if any meet your needs. The most relevant are the following:

- **comp.dcom.cell-relay.:** The newsgroup for ATM discussions. Often quite good.
- **comp.dcom.frame-relay:** The newsgroup for frame relay discussions. Most of the entries are user oriented, but there are some technical discussions.
- **comp.dcom.isdn:** This newsgroup is primarily devoted to discussions about the use of ISDN, but there are occasional technical discussions.

PART ONE

Digital Communications Fundamentals

signals $\Rightarrow$ encoding of data
signalling $\Rightarrow$ propagating The signal

CHAPTER 2

DIGITAL TRANSMISSION

This chapter provides an overview of some of the key topics relating to digital transmission. The first section contrasts analog and digital transmission techniques. Then the encoding of analog signals into digital form for transmission is examined. This is followed by a discussion of approaches to multiplexing. The chapter concludes with a discussion of digital carrier systems, which form the backbone of a wide area digital network.

2.1 ANALOG AND DIGITAL DATA TRANSMISSION

The terms *analog* and *digital* correspond, roughly, to *continuous* and *discrete*, respectively. These two terms are used frequently in data communications in at least three contexts: data, signaling, and transmission.

Very briefly, we define data as entities that convey meaning. A useful distinction is that data have to do with the form of something; information has to do with the content or interpretation of those data. Signals are electric or electromagnetic encoding of data. Signaling is the act of propagating the signal along some suitable medium. Finally, transmission is the communication of data by the propagation and processing of signals. In what follows, we try to make these abstract concepts clear by discussing the terms *analog* and *digital* in these three contexts.

Analog and Digital Data

The concepts of analog and digital data are simple enough. **Analog data** take on continuous values on some interval. For example, voice and video are continuously varying patterns of intensity. Most data collected by sensors, such as temperature and pressure, are continuous valued. **Digital data** take on discrete values; examples are text and integers.

Analog and Digital Signaling

In a communications system, data are propagated from one point to another by means of electric signals. An **analog signal** is a continuously varying electromagnetic wave that may be propagated over a variety of media, depending on frequency; examples are copper wire media, such as twisted pair and coaxial cable; fiber optic cable; and atmosphere or space propagation (wireless). A **digital signal** is a sequence of voltage pulses that may be transmitted over a copper wire medium; for example, a constant positive voltage level may represent binary 1 and a constant negative voltage level may represent binary 0.

The principal advantages of digital signaling are that it is generally cheaper than analog signaling and is less susceptible to noise interference. The principal disadvantage is that digital signals suffer more from attenuation than do analog signals. Figure 2.1 shows a sequence of voltage pulses, generated by a source using two voltage levels, and the received voltage some distance down a conducting medium. Because of the attenuation, or reduction, of signal strength at higher frequencies, the pulses become rounded and smaller. It should be clear that this attenuation can rather quickly lead to the loss of the information contained in the propagated signal.

Both analog and digital data can be represented, and hence propagated, by either analog or digital signals. This is illustrated in Figure 2.2. Generally, analog data are a function of time and occupy a limited frequency spectrum. Such data can be directly represented by an electromagnetic signal occupying the same spectrum. The best example of this is voice data. As sound waves, voice data have frequency components in the range 20 Hz to 20 kHz. However, most of the speech energy is in a much narrower range. The standard spectrum of voice signals is 300 to 3400 Hz, and this is quite adequate to propagate speech intelligibly and clearly. The telephone instrument does just that. For all sound input in the range of 300 to 3400 Hz, an electromagnetic signal with the same frequency–amplitude pattern is produced. The process is performed in reverse to convert the electromagnetic energy back into sound. ⟶ signal ⟶ data

Digital data can also be represented by analog signals by use of a modem (modulator-demodulator). The modem converts a series of binary (two-valued) voltage pulses into an analog signal by modulating a carrier frequency. The resulting signal occupies a certain spectrum of frequency centered about the carrier and may be propagated across a medium suitable for that carrier. The most common modems represent digital data in the voice spectrum and hence allow those data to be propagated over ordinary voice-grade telephone lines. At the other end of the line, a modem demodulates the signal to recover the original data.

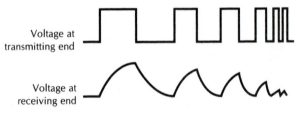

Voltage at transmitting end

Voltage at receiving end

Figure 2.1   Attenuation of Digital Signals.

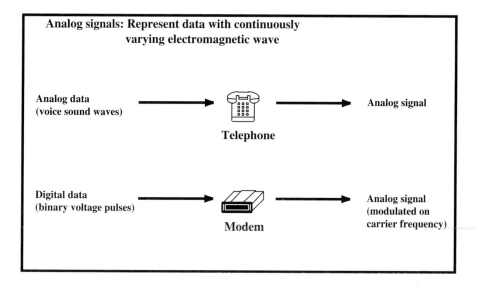

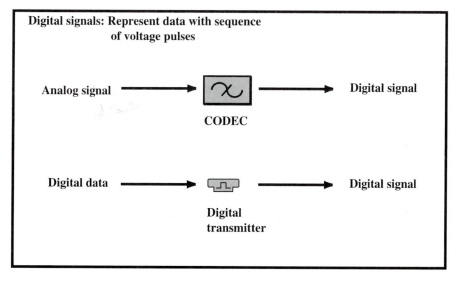

Figure 2.2 Analog and Digital Signaling of Analog and Digital Data.

In an operation very similar to that performed by a modem, analog data can be represented by digital signals. The device that performs this function for voice data is a codec (coder-decoder). In essence, the codec takes an analog signal that directly represents the voice data and approximates that signal by a bit stream. At the other end of the line, the bit stream is used to reconstruct the analog data. This topic is explored in Section 2.2.

Finally, digital data can be represented directly, in binary form, by two voltage levels. To improve propagation characteristics, however, the binary data are often encoded into a more complex form of digital signal; this topic is explored in Chapter 3.

Analog and Digital Transmission

Analog and digital signals may be transmitted on suitable transmission media. The way these signals are treated is a function of the transmission system. Table 2.1 summarizes the methods of data transmission. **Analog transmission** is a means of transmitting analog signals without regard to their content; the signals may represent analog data (e.g., voice) or digital data (e.g., data that pass through a modem). In either case, the analog signal will suffer attenuation that limits the length of the transmission link. To achieve longer distances, the analog transmission system includes amplifiers that boost the energy in the signal. Unfortunately, the amplifier also boosts the noise components. With amplifiers cascaded to achieve long distance, the signal becomes more and more distorted. For analog data, such as voice, quite a bit of distortion can be tolerated and the data remain intelligible. However, for digital data transmitted as analog signals, cascaded amplifiers will introduce errors.

Table 2.1   Analog and Digital Transmission

(a) Data and Signals

	Analog Signal	Digital Signal
Analog Data	Two alternatives: (1) signal occupies the same spectrum as the analog data; (2) analog data are encoded to occupy a different portion of spectrum.	Analog data are encoded using a codec to produce a digital bit stream.
Digital Data	Digital data are encoded using a modem to produce analog signal.	Two alternatives: (1) signal consists of a two voltage levels to represent the two binary values; (2) digital data are encoded to produce a digital signal with desired properties.

(b) Treatment of Signals

	Analog Transmission	Digital Transmission
Analog Signal	Is propagated through amplifiers; same treatment whether signal is used to represent analog data or digital data.	Assumes that the analog signal represents digital data. Signal is propagated through repeaters; at each repeater, digital data are recovered from inbound signal and used to generate a new analog outbound signal.
Digital Signal	Not used	Digital signal represents a stream of 1s and 0s, which may represent digital data or may be an encoding of analog data. Signal is propagated through repeaters; at each repeater, stream of 1s and 0s is recovered from inbound signal and used to generate a new digital outbound signal.

Digital transmission, in contrast, is concerned with the content of the signal. We have mentioned that a digital signal can be propagated only a limited distance before attenuation endangers the integrity of the data. To achieve greater distances, repeaters are used. A repeater receives the digital signal, recovers the pattern of ones and zeros, and retransmits a new signal. Thus, the attenuation is overcome.

The same technique may be used with an analog signal if the signal carries digital data. At appropriately spaced points, the transmission system has retransmission devices rather than amplifiers. The retransmission device recovers the digital data from the analog signal and generates a new, clean analog signal. Thus, noise is not cumulative.

The question naturally arises as to which is the preferred method of transmission. The answer being supplied by the telecommunications industry and customers is digital transmission, this despite an enormous investment in analog communications facilities. Both long-haul telecommunications facilities and intrabuilding services are being converted to digital transmission and, where possible, digital signaling techniques. The most important reasons are the following:

- **Cost:** The advent of very-large-scale-integration (VLSI) technology has caused a continuing drop in the cost and size of digital circuitry. Analog equipment has not shown a similar drop. Furthermore, maintenance costs for digital circuitry are a fraction of those for analog circuitry.
- **Data integrity:** With the use of digital repeaters rather than analog amplifiers, the effects of noise and other signal impairments are not cumulative. Thus, it is possible to transmit data longer distances and over lower-quality lines by digital means while maintaining the integrity of the data.
- **Capacity utilization:** It has become economical to build transmission links of very high bandwidth, including satellite channels and optical fiber. A high degree of multiplexing is needed to utilize such capacity effectively, and this is more easily and cheaply achieved with digital (time-division) rather than analog (frequency-division) techniques.
- **Security and privacy:** Encryption techniques can be readily applied to digital data and to analog data that have been digitized.
- **Integration:** By treating both analog and digital information digitally, all signals have the same form and can be treated similarly. Thus, economies of scale and convenience can be achieved by integrating voice, video, image, and digital data.

2.2 DIGITAL ENCODING OF ANALOG DATA

The evolution of public telecommunications networks to digital transmission requires that voice data be represented in digital form. It is important to note that this does not necessarily imply that the voice data be transmitted using digital signals. Figure 2.3 illustrates a common situation. Analog voice signals are digitized to produce a pattern of ones and zeros. As a digital signal, this pattern of ones and

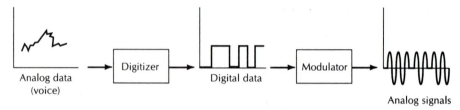

Figure 2.3   Digitizing Analog Data.

zeros may be fed into a modem so that an analog signal may be transmitted. However, this new analog signal differs significantly from the original voice signal, in that it represents an encoding of a binary stream. Hence, the digital transmission techniques discussed in Section 2.1 can be applied. In particular, retransmission devices rather than amplifiers are used to extend the length of a transmission link. Ultimately, of course, the new analog signal must be converted back to analog data that approximate the original voice input.

Pulse-Code Modulation

The best-known technique for voice digitization is pulse-code modulation (PCM). PCM is based on the sampling theorem, which states the following:

> If a signal f(t) is sampled at regular intervals of time and at a rate higher than twice the highest significant signal frequency, then the samples contain all the information of the original signal. The function f(t) may be reconstructed from these samples by the use of a low-pass filter.

A proof of this theorem can be found in [STAL97].

If voice data are limited to frequencies below 4000 Hz, a conservative procedure for intelligibility, then 8000 samples per second would be sufficient to characterize the voice signal completely. Note, however, that these are analog samples. To convert to digital, each of these analog samples must be assigned a binary code. Figure 2.4 shows an example in which each sample is approximated by being "quantized" into one of 16 different levels. Each sample can then be represented by 4 bits. But because the quantized values are only approximations, it is impossible to recover the original signal exactly. By using an 8-bit sample, which allows 256 quantizing levels, the quantity of the recovered voice signal is comparable with that achieved via analog transmission. Note that this implies that a data rate of 8000 samples per second × 8 bits per sample = 64 kbps is needed for a single voice signal.

Typically, the PCM scheme is refined using a technique known as nonlinear encoding, which means, in effect, that the 256 quantization levels are not equally spaced. The problem with equal spacing is that the mean absolute error for each sample is the same, regardless of signal level. Consequently, lower-amplitude values are relatively more distorted. By using a greater number of quantizing steps for signals of low amplitude, and a smaller number of quantizing steps for signals of large amplitude, a marked reduction in overall signal distortion is achieved.

PCM can, of course, be used for other than voice signals. For example, a color TV signal has a useful bandwidth of 4.6 MHz, and reasonable quality can be achieved with 10-bit samples for a data rate of 92 Mbps.

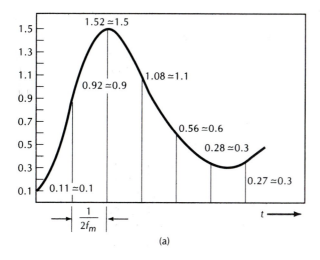

(a)

Digit	Binary equivalent	Pulse-code waveform
0	0000	
1	0001	
2	0010	
3	0011	
4	0100	
5	0101	
6	0110	
7	0111	
8	1000	
9	1001	
10	1010	
11	1011	
12	1100	
13	1101	
14	1110	
15	1111	

(b)

Figure 2.4 Pulse-Code Modulation.

Performance

Good voice reproduction via PCM can be achieved with 128 quantization levels, or 7-bit coding ($2^7 = 128$). A voice signal, conservatively, occupies a bandwidth of 4 kHz. Thus, according to the sampling theorem, samples should be taken at a rate of 8000 samples per second. This implies a data rate of $8000 \times 7 = 56$ kbps for the PCM-encoded digital data.

Consider what this means from the point of view of bandwidth requirement. An analog voice signal occupies 4 kHz. A 56-kbps digital signal will require on the order of at least 28 kHz. Even more severe differences are seen with higher-bandwidth signals. For example, a common PCM scheme for color television uses 10-bit codes, which works out to 92 Mbps for a 4.6-MHz bandwidth signal.

However, techniques have been developed to provide more efficient codes. In the case of voice, a reasonable goal appears to be in the neighborhood of 4 kbps. With video, advantage can be taken of the fact that from frame to frame, most picture elements will not change. Interframe coding techniques should allow the video requirement to be reduced to about 15 Mbps, and for slowly changing scenes, such as found in a video teleconference, down to 64 kbps or less.

2.3 MULTIPLEXING

In both local and wide area communications, it is almost always the case that the capacity of the transmission medium exceeds the capacity required for the transmission of a single signal. To make efficient use of the transmission system, it is desirable to carry multiple signals on a single medium. This is referred to as *multiplexing*.

Figure 2.5 depicts the multiplexing function in its simplest form. There are n inputs to a multiplexer. The multiplexer is connected by a single data link to a demultiplexer. The link is able to carry n separate channels of data. The multiplexer combines (multiplexes) data from the n input lines and transmits over a higher-capacity data link. The demultiplexer accepts the multiplexed data stream, separates (demultiplexes) the data according to channel, and delivers them to the appropriate output lines.

The widespread use of multiplexing in data communications can be explained by the following:

1. The higher the data rate, the more cost effective the transmission facility. That is, for a given application and over a given distance, the cost per kbps declines with an increase in the data rate of the transmission facility. Similarly,

n inputs — MUX — 1 link, *n* channels — DEMUX — *n* outputs

Figure 2.5 Multiplexing.

the cost of transmission and receiving equipment, per kbps, declines with increasing data rate.

2. Most individual data communicating devices require relatively modest data rate support. For example, for most client/server applications, a data rate of up to 64 kbps is generally more than adequate.

The preceding statements were phrased in terms of data communicating devices. Similar statements apply to voice communications. That is, the greater the capacity of a transmission facility, in terms of voice channels, the less the cost per individual voice channel, and the capacity required for a single voice channel is modest.

Two techniques for multiplexing in telecommunications networks are in common use: frequency-division multiplexing (FDM) and time-division multiplexing (TDM).

FDM exploits the fact that the useful bandwidth of the medium exceeds the required bandwidth of a given signal. A number of signals can be carried simultaneously if each signal is modulated onto a different carrier frequency, and the carrier frequencies are sufficiently separated so that the bandwidths of the signals do not overlap. Figure 2.6a depicts a simple case of FDM. Six signal sources are fed into a multiplexer that modulates each signal onto a different frequency ($f1, \ldots, f6$). Each signal requires a certain bandwidth centered around its carrier frequency, referred to as a *channel*. To prevent interference, the channels are separated by *guard bands*, which are unused portions of the spectrum (not shown in the figure).

An example is the multiplexing of voice signals. The useful spectrum for voice is 300 to 3400 Hz. Thus, a bandwidth of 4 kHz is adequate to carry the voice signal and provide a guard band. For both North America and internationally, a standard voice multiplexing scheme is twelve 4-kHz voice channels from 60 to 108 kHz. For higher-capacity links, larger groupings of 4-kHz channels are defined.

TDM takes advantage of the fact that the achievable bit rate (sometimes, unfortunately, called bandwidth) of the medium exceeds the required data rate of a digital signal. Multiple digital signals can be carried on a single transmission path by interleaving portions of each signal in time. The interleaving can be at the bit level or in blocks of octets or larger quantities. For example, the multiplexer in Figure 2.6b has six inputs that might each be, say, 9.6 kbps. A single line with a capacity of 57.6 kbps could accommodate all six sources. Analogously to FDM, the sequence of time slots dedicated to a particular source is called a *channel*. One cycle of time slots (one per source) is called a *frame*.

The TDM scheme depicted in Figure 2.6b is also known as *synchronous TDM*, referring to the fact that time slots are preassigned and fixed. Hence the timing of transmission from the various sources is synchronized. In contrast, asynchronous TDM allows time on the medium to be allocated dynamically. The digital carrier systems discussed in the next section, and SONET/SDH, discussed in Part Four, are examples of synchronous TDM.

TDM is not limited to digital signals. Analog signals can be interleaved in time. Also, with analog signals, a combination of TDM and FDM is possible. A transmission system can be frequency divided into a number of channels, each of which is further divided by TDM.

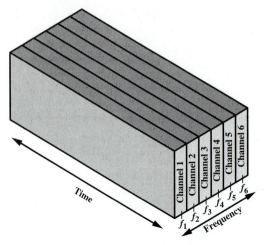

(a) Frequency-division multiplexing

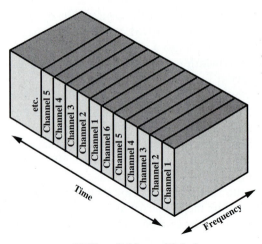

(b) Time-division multiplexing

Figure 2.6 FDM and TDM.

2.4 DIGITAL CARRIER SYSTEMS

A wide area circuit-switched network will involve a number of interconnected nodes. A link between a pair of nodes, referred to as a trunk, uses multiplexing to carry the traffic on a number of channels, or circuits. This multiplexing may be in the form of frequency-division multiplexing (FDM) or synchronous time-division multiplexing (TDM). As wide area telecommunication networks evolve toward an integrated digital network, synchronous TDM techniques are becoming dominant.

The long-distance carrier system provided in the United States and throughout the world was designed to transmit voice signals over high-capacity transmission

Table 2.2   North American and International TDM Carrier Standards

North American			International (ITU-T)		
Designation	Number of Voice Channels	Data Rate (Mbps)	Level	Number of Voice Channels	Data Rate (Mbps)
DS-1	24	1.544	1	30	2.048
DS-1C	48	3.152	2	120	8.448
DS-2	96	6.312	3	480	34.368
DS-3	672	44.736	4	1920	139.264
DS-4	4032	274.176	5	7680	565.148

links, such as optical fiber, coaxial cable, and microwave. Part of the evolution of these telecommunications networks to digital technology has been the adoption of synchronous TDM transmission structures. In the United States, AT&T developed a hierarchy of TDM structures of various capacities; this structure is used in Canada and Japan, as well as in the United States. A similar, but unfortunately not identical, hierarchy has been adopted internationally under the auspices of ITU[1] (Table 2.2). As we shall see, this dichotomy remains unresolved in the ISDN standards.

The basis of the North American TDM hierarchy is the DS-1 transmission format (Figure 2.7), which multiplexes 24 channels. Each frame contains 8 bits per channel plus a framing bit for $24 \times 8 + 1 = 193$ bits. For voice transmission, the following rules apply: Each channel contains one word of digitized voice data. The original analog voice signal is digitized using pulse-code modulation (PCM) at a rate of 8000 samples per second. Therefore, each channel slot and hence each frame must repeat 8000 times per second. With a frame length of 193 bits, we have a data rate of $8000 \times 193 = 1.544$ Mbps. For five of every six frames, 8-bit PCM samples are used. For every sixth frame, each channel contains a 7-bit PCM word plus a signaling bit. The signaling bits form a stream for each voice channel that contains network control and routing information. For example, control signals are used to establish a connection or terminate a call.

The same DS-1 format is used to provide digital data service. For compatibility with voice, the same 1.544-Mbps data rate is used. In this case, 23 channels of data are provided. The twenty-fourth channel position is reserved for a special sync byte, which allows faster and more reliable reframing following a framing error. Within each channel, 7 bits per frame are used for data, with the eighth bit used to indicate whether the channel, for that frame, contains user data or system control data. With 7 bits per channel, and because each frame is repeated 8000 times per second, a data rate of 56 kbps can be provided per channel. Lower data rates are provided using a technique known as subrate multiplexing. For this technique, an additional bit is robbed from each channel to indicate which subrate multiplexing rate is being provided. This leaves a total capacity per channel of $6 \times 8000 = 48$ kbps. This capacity is used to multiplex five 9.6-kbps channels, ten 4.8-kbps channels, or

---

[1]The International Telecommunications Union is an international standards-making organization; it is described in Appendix 5A.

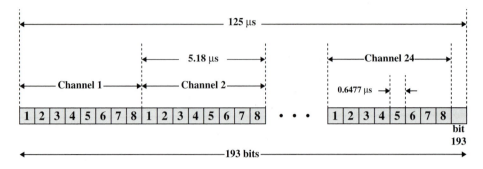

Notes:

1. Bit 193 is a framing bit, used for synchronization.
2. Voice channels:
    • 8-bit PCM used on five of six frames.
    • 7-bit PCM used on every sixth frame; bit 8 of each channel is a signaling bit.
3. Data channels:
    • Channel 24 is used for signaling only in some schemes.
    • Bits 1–7 used for 56 kbps service.
    • Bits 2–7 used for 9.6, 4.8, and 2.4 kbps service.

Figure 2.7   DS-1 Transmission Format.

twenty 2.4-kbps channels. For example, if channel 2 is used to provide 9.6-kbps service, then up to five data subchannels share this channel. The data for each subchannel appear as six bits in channel 2 every fifth frame.

Finally, the DS-1 format can be used to carry a mixture of voice and data channels. In this case, all 24 channels are utilized; no sync byte is provided.

Above this basic data rate of 1.544 Mbps, higher-level multiplexing is achieved by interleaving bits from DS-1 inputs. For example, the DS-2 transmission system combines four DS-1 inputs into a 6.312-Mbps stream. Data from the four sources are interleaved 12 bits at a time. Note that $1.544 \times 4 = 6.176$ Mbps. The remaining capacity is used for framing and control bits.

Each higher level of the TDM hierarchy is formed by multiplexing signals from the next lower level or by combination of those signals plus input at the appropriate data rate from other sources. First, the DS-1 transmission rate is used to provide both a voice and data service. The data service is known as the dataphone digital service (DDS). The DDS provides digital transmission service between customer data devices at data rates of from 2.4 to 56 kbps. The service is available at customer premises over two twisted-pair lines.

Various standardized multiplexers are employed to create higher-capacity transmission facilities. The most commonly used ones are listed in Table 2.2. The designations DS-1, DS-1C, and so on refer to the multiplexing scheme used for carrying information. AT&T and other carriers supply transmission facilities that support these various multiplexed signals, referred to as carrier systems. These are designated with a "T" label. Thus, the T1 carrier provides a data rate of 1.544 Mbps and is capable of supporting the DS-1 multiplex format and so on for higher data rates.

2.5 SUMMARY

Both analog and digital information can be encoded as either analog or digital signals. The particular encoding that is chosen depends on the media and communications facilities available and the requirements to be met. For example, to transmit digital information over an analog telephone line, a modem is used to convert the digital data into analog form. Similarly, there is an increasing use of digital facilities, and voice signals must be encoded in digital form to be transmitted on these digital facilities.

To make efficient use of high-speed telecommunications lines, some form of multiplexing is used. Multiplexing allows several transmission sources to share a larger transmission capacity. The two common forms of multiplexing are frequency-division multiplexing (FDM) and time-division multiplexing (TDM).

Public telephone and telecommunications networks have evolved from an all-analog technology to one that is increasingly digital. Digital carrier standards specify a time-division multiplexed structure for transmission within the network.

2.6 RECOMMENDED READING

[STAL97] covers all of the topics in this chapter in greater detail. A thorough treatment of both analog and digital communication is provided in [COUC97].

COUC97   Couch, L. *Digital and Analog Communication Systems.* Upper Saddle River, NJ: Prentice Hall, 1997.

STAL97   Stallings, W. *Data and Computer Communications,* 5th edition. Upper Saddle River, NJ: Prentice Hall, 1997.

2.7 PROBLEMS

2.1 Are the modem and codec functional inverses (i.e., could an inverted modem function as a codec, and vice versa)?

2.2 To paraphrase Lincoln: all of the channel some of the time, some of the channel all of the time. Relate this to Figure 2.6.

2.3 Bit 193 in the DS-1 transmission format is used for frame synchronization. Explain its use.

2.4 In the DS-1 transmission format, what is the control signal data rate for each voice channel?

2.5 What is the percentage of overhead in a T1 carrier (percentage of bits that are not user data)?

2.6 Find the number of the following devices that could be accommodated by a T1-type TDM line if 1% of the line capacity is reserved for synchronization purposes.
a. 110-bps teleprinter terminals
b. 300-bps computer terminals
c. 1200-bps computer terminals
d. 9600-bps computer terminals
e. 64-kbps PCM voice-frequency lines
How would these numbers change if each of the sources were operational an average of 10% of the time?

2.7 Assume that you are to design a TDM carrier, say DS-489, to support 30 voice channels using 6-bit samples and a structure similar to DS-1. Determine the required bit rate.

2.8 A digital transmission channel with a bit rate of $R = 36,000$ bps is available for PCM voice transmission. Assume each voice signal is limited to a maximum frequency of $f_M = 3.2$ kHz. Find the appropriate values of the sampling rate f_s, the number of quantization levels L, and the number of bits per sample n. *Hint:* First find a lower bound for f_s and an upper bound for n.

CHAPTER 3

LINE CODING AND THE SUBSCRIBER LINE

T he extension of digital links to network subscribers is an essential part of digital network evolution. It is not sufficient that the internal transmission and switching facilities of the network be digital. To provide the wide range of digital services planned for ISDN, the link between the network subscriber and the network switch, known as the **subscriber line, subscriber loop**, or **local loop**, must be digital.

We begin with a discussion of the basic subscriber line technology using twisted pair and optical fiber. Next, we explore the concept of digital line coding, which is an essential element in the design of digital subscriber line transmission schemes. We then look at the standard approach to providing high-speed subscriber line access for ISDN. This is followed by a look at a number of more recent schemes for digital subscriber line transmission, which are referred to as xDSL.

3.1 SUBSCRIBER LINE TECHNOLOGY

Currently, most of the subscriber lines to businesses and virtually all of the subscriber lines to homes makes use of twisted-pair cable. With the increasing demand for services that require high data rates, there is increasing interest in the use of optical fiber. We look at these two media for the subscriber line in turn.

Twisted Pair in the Subscriber Line

The simplest approach to providing digital service is the use of two twisted-pair wires between each subscriber and the local office or switch to which the subscriber attaches. One twisted-pair link would be used for transmission in each direction. However, the existing telephone network plant installed worldwide is based on the use of a single twisted-pair link between each subscriber and the local office. Thus, this approach would require the installation of a tremendous amount of new cable. Because of the economic impracticality of this approach, interest has focused on schemes that would allow full-duplex digital transmission over a single twisted-pair connection.

Approaches to Full-Duplex Transmission

The installed twisted-pair subscriber line system was intended for analog transmission. A simple means of achieving full-duplex transmission, then, is to use modems to convert the digital data into analog signals and to use a different frequency band in each direction.

An example of this approach is the 300-bps Bell 108 modem specification (Figure 3.1), which uses frequency-shift keying (FSK) to transmit digital data over an analog system. In FSK, the two binary values are represented by signals at two different frequencies. For transmission in one direction, the frequencies used to represent 1 and 0 are centered on 1170 Hz, with a shift of 100 Hz on either side. The effect of alternating between these two frequencies is to produce a signal spectrum, as indicated in the area on the left of Figure 3.1. Similarly, for transmission in the other direction, the modem uses frequencies shifted to 100 Hz to each side of a center frequency of 2125 Hz. The spectrum of this signal is indicated in the area on the right of Figure 3.1. Note that there is little overlap and thus little interference.

A difficulty with this approach is that only half of the bandwidth of the line is available for transmission in either direction. To satisfy ISDN requirements, the minimum data rate in each direction is 144 kbps. It is difficult to achieve these data rates with existing modem technology and with the installed twisted-pair plant.

The alternative is to dispense with modems and to transmit digital signals directly. For full-duplex operation, both stations transmit digital signals at the same time. In principle, the originating station is capable of sorting out an incoming signal from its own outgoing signal because the signal magnitude of its originating

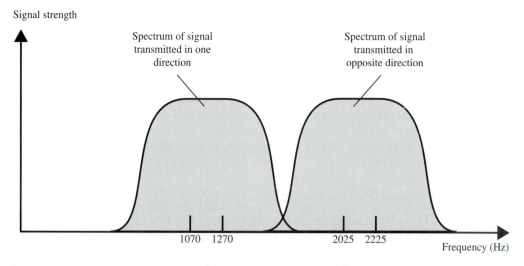

Figure 3.1 Full-Duplex FSK Transmission on a Voice-Grade Line.

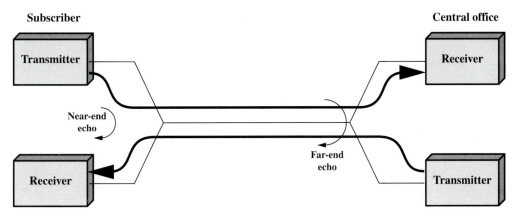

Figure 3.2   Echo in Twisted-Pair Subscriber Line.

signal is known. Unfortunately, due to irregularities in the electrical characteristics of the line, some portion of the originator's signal returns in the form of an echo.

Figure 3.2 illustrates the problem. Both transmitter and receiver are connected to the subscriber line through a hybrid, which is a device that allows signals to pass in both directions simultaneously. The echo is a reflection of the transmitted signal back to the sender, either from the sender's hybrid and the cable (near-end echo) or from the receiver's hybrid (far-end echo). The relative magnitude of the echo, compared with the true signal arriving from the other side, may be significant. This is because of the considerable difference in amplitude between transmitted and received signals at the ends of the wire pair, which may be as much as three orders of magnitude.

To overcome the problems associated with full-duplex digital transmission over a single twisted pair, two techniques have been developed: time-compression multiplexing and echo cancellation. Both techniques have been seriously considered for use in digital networks (Figure 3.3). At present, the consensus is that echo cancellation is the superior system. For example, this approach is favored in the United States; there is an American National Standard[1] for the subscriber line that uses echo cancellation (ANSI T1.601). Nevertheless, it is instructive to examine both approaches.

Time-Compression Multiplexing

In the technique of time-compression multiplexing (TCM), also known as the ping-pong method, data are transmitted in one direction at a time, with transmission alternating between the two directions. To achieve the desired subscriber data rate, the subscriber's bit stream is divided into equal segments, compressed in time to a higher transmission rate, and transmitted in bursts, which are expanded at the other end to the original rate. A short quiescent period is used between bursts going in opposite directions to allow the line to settle down. Thus, the actual

---

[1]American National Standards are issued by the American National Standards Institute (ANSI) and are widely used in the United States. Many ANSI standards subsequently become international standards.

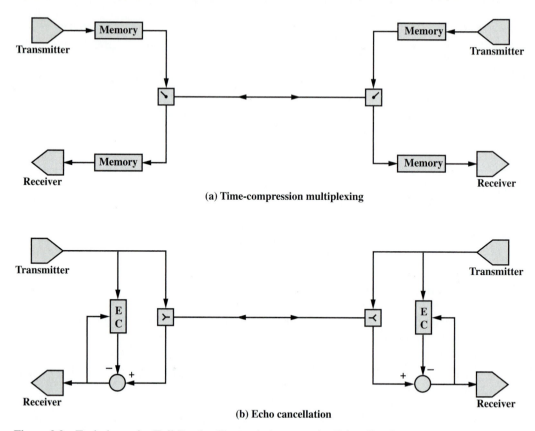

(a) Time-compression multiplexing

(b) Echo cancellation

Figure 3.3 Techniques for Full-Duplex Transmission over the Subscriber Loop.

data rate on the line must be greater than twice the data rate required by the subscriber and local office.

The timing implications are shown in Figure 3.4. The two sides alternate in the transmission of data. Each side sends blocks of some fixed length, which take a time T_b to transmit; this time is a linear function of the number of bits in a block. In addition, a time T_p is required for the propagation of a signal from one end to the other; this time is a linear function of the length of the subscriber line. Finally, a guard time T_g is introduced to turn the line around. Thus, the time to send one block is $(T_p + T_b + T_g)$. However, because the two sides must alternate transmissions, the rate at which blocks can be transmitted is only $1/2(T_p + T_b + T_g)$. We can relate this to the effective data rate, R, as seen by the two endpoints as follows. Let B be the size of a block in bits and R be the desired data rate in bits per second. Then the effective number of bits transmitted per second is

$$R = B/2(T_p + T_b + T_g)$$

The actual data rate, A, on the medium can easily be seen to be

$$A = B/T_b$$

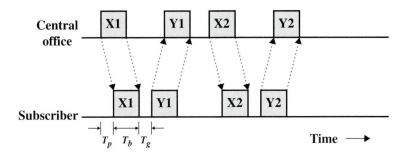

T_p = Propagation delay

T_b = Burst transmission time

T_g = Guard time

Figure 3.4   Transmission Using Time-Compression Multiplexing.

Combining the two, we have

$$A = 2R\left(1 + \frac{T_p + T_g}{T_b}\right)$$

Thus, the actual data rate on the link is more than double the effective data rate seen by the two sides. We will see that one of the basic data rates offered by ISDN is 144 kbps. To achieve this, it is necessary to transmit at over twice this rate, which would be something greater than 288 kbps. The actual value is in the neighborhood of 350 kbps. This is quite difficult to achieve on an ordinary twisted pair.

The choice of block size, B, is a compromise between competing requirements. If B is increased, there is a decrease in the actual data rate, A. This makes the task of implementation easier. On the other hand, this is accompanied by an increase in the signal delay due to buffering, which is undesirable for voice traffic. A block size of 16 to 24 bits seems reasonable [KADE81].

Figure 3.5 depicts the internal structure of a TCM unit. In both directions (transmit and receive) a buffer is needed that is equal to the block size, B. Data to be transmitted are entering into the buffer at a data rate of $R = B/2(T_p + T_b + T_g)$. The data are subsequently transmitted at a rate $A = B/T_b$. The reverse process occurs for reception. Transmission and reception alternate under a central timing control.

Echo Cancellation

With the echo cancellation method, digital transmission is allowed to proceed in both directions within the same bandwidth simultaneously. An estimate of the echo signal is generated at the transmitting end and is subtracted from the incoming signal. This effectively cancels the echo. Because the transmitted signal is known, the echo canceller can estimate the echo characteristics and produce an approximation. However, the exact behavior of the echo will depend on the physical characteristics and configuration of the copper wire. Not only is it difficult to measure these characteristics precisely, but they will vary over time. To enable more accurate approximation, a feedback circuit is included.

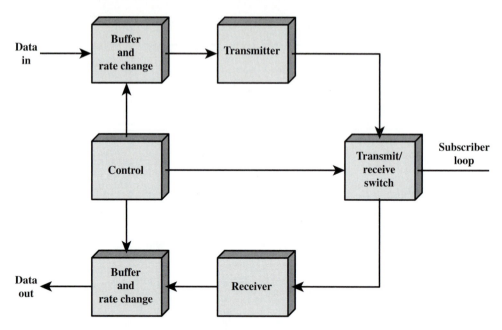

Figure 3.5 Internal Structure of TCM Unit.

A typical approach to echo cancellation is illustrated in Figure 3.6. Because the transmitted signal will be reflected at various points in the system, a number of signal elements, each delayed by a different amount, will contribute to the echo at any point in time. Furthermore, because the different contributing signal elements

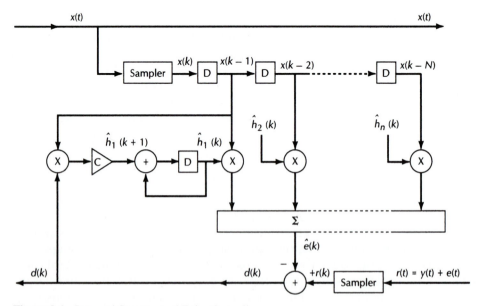

Figure 3.6 Internal Structure of Echo Canceller.

have traveled different distances, they will suffer different amounts of attenuation. This can be expressed in discrete time notation as follows:

$$e(k) = \sum_{n=1}^{k} h_n x(k - n)$$

where

$$
\begin{aligned}
e(k) &= \text{echo signal sampled at time k} \\
x(k - n) &= \text{signal transmitted at time } k - n \\
h_n &= \text{weighting factor for signal delayed by a time } n
\end{aligned}
$$

This echo signal can be estimated with

$$\hat{e}(k) = \sum_{n=1}^{N} \hat{h}_n(k) x(k - n)$$

where

$$\hat{h}_n(k) = \text{estimate of } h_n \text{ at time } k$$

If signal elements delayed longer than a time N make no measurable contribution to the echo, and if the $\hat{h}_n$ are exactly equal to the h_n, then the estimate will be equal to the actual echo. Of course, the $\hat{h}_n$ can only be approximations. In any case, this approximation is subtracted from the received signal to attempt to cancel the echo:

$$d(k) = r(k) - \hat{e}(k) = y(k) + e(k) - \hat{e}(k)$$

where

$$
\begin{aligned}
d(k) &= \text{signal resulting after cancellation} \\
r(k) &= \text{received signal} \\
y(k) &= \text{component of received signal due to transmission from other side}
\end{aligned}
$$

Again, assuming that only the first N components of the transmitted signal are significant, we can rewrite this as

$$d(k) = y(k) + \sum_{n=1}^{N} \left(h_n - \hat{h}_n(k) \right) x(k - n)$$

As Figure 3.6 illustrates, the outgoing signal, $x(t)$, is sampled periodically to produce $x(k)$ for various sampling times k ($k = 1,2,3, \ldots$). This sample is passed through a series of delays to retain delayed versions of the signal, $x(k - n)$. These delayed samples are then available at time k to produce the estimate $\hat{e}(k)$. The weighting factors, $\hat{h}_n(k)$, are updated at each sampling time by means of feedback:

$$\hat{h}_n(k + 1) = \hat{h}_n(k) + Cx(k - n)d(k)$$

where C is a scaling factor. This equation is somewhat easier to appreciate if we consider the case when there is no signal from the other side. In that case, we have

$$d(k) = \sum (h_n - \hat{h}_n(k))x(k - n)$$

In this case, the value of $d(k)$ would be zero if the echo estimate were exact. If the estimate is not exact, then each weighting factor, $\hat{h}_n(k)$, is adjusted by an amount proportional to $x(k - n)d(k)$. This procedure will result in a convergence of the weighting factor to the true values. Even in the presence of an actual signal, $y(t)$, the weighting factors converge, although more slowly [GERW84, FALC82].

The technique of echo cancellation avoids the necessity, found in TCM, of transmitting at more than double the subscriber rate. At the 144-kbps rate recommended by ITU-T for ISDN, this gives echo cancellation a distinct advantage over TCM. A careful analysis of the two systems indicates that for typical twisted-pair installations at a subscriber data rate of 144 kbps, a range of 2 km is practical for TCM, compared with a range of 4 km for echo cancellation [SZEC86]. Thus, the introduction of TCM into the subscriber line would require the extensive use of equipment such as concentrators and repeaters to overcome the poor range of the technique. Echo cancellation systems would require such equipment in far fewer cases.

Echo cancellation has the disadvantage of requiring complex digital signal processing circuitry. However, with the continuing advances in VLSI technology, the cost of echo cancellation is dropping, and it has become the preferred technique in achieving digital subscriber lines [MESS86, LECH86].

Optical Fiber in the Subscriber Line

Although optical fiber has enjoyed increased usage in the interexchange trunk portion of telecommunication networks, so far there has been little use of it in subscriber lines. As part of the planning for broadband ISDN, however, there has been significant effort devoted to design alternatives for bringing fiber to business and residential subscribers.

There has been a wide range of alternatives suggested for providing fiber in subscriber lines (e.g., see [MOCH94] and [OKAD92]). Fundamentally, all of these alternatives fall into two broad categories: those in which the subscriber interface appears as a simple direct link and those in which the subscriber interface must implement multiple-access logic.

To gain an understanding of these two approaches, let us begin with a simplified view of the existing twisted-pair arrangement, which is illustrated in Figure 3.7a. In this configuration, each subscriber accesses its central office (local switching center) via a single twisted pair. That is, there is a direct, point-to-point, twisted-pair link between each subscriber and the central office. In the United States, the average length of subscriber lines is about 3 km [REY83].

The physical layout of the collection of twisted pairs from the central office to all subscribers, referred to as the distribution network, is a star topology, with one link from the central office to each subscriber. For convenience, the actual installation involves collecting individual pairs into bundles that are encased in a cable.

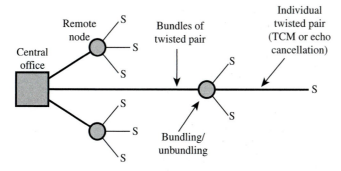

(a) Wire-based subscriber lines

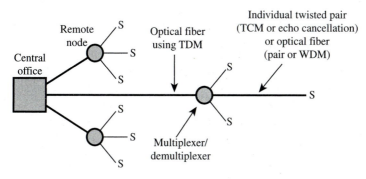

(b) Fiber-based active star

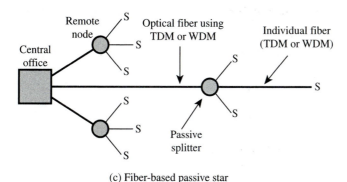

(c) Fiber-based passive star

Figure 3.7   Fiber Digital Subscriber Line Approaches.

At various points in the distribution network, the wires are unbundled for the final run to the subscriber.

The same installation layout can be used for a fiber-based digital subscriber line. Perhaps the simplest approach is illustrated in Figure 3.7b. In this layout, the central office is connected to a set of remote nodes by feeder cables. The feeder cable uses digital time-division multiplexing (TDM) to support multiple channels. A number of subscribers may be connected to a remote node, each with a single direct link. Thus, the remote node is a multiplexer that multiplexes traffic from a number of subscribers onto the feeder cable and demultiplexes traffic from the feeder cable to the subscribers. This approach is referred to as an active star, because each remote node serves as the base for a star layout, and each remote node is active, performing a multiplexing/demultiplexing function.

To provide full-duplex digital transmission on the feeder cable, two approaches are possible:

- **Two-fiber:** One optical fiber is used for transmission in each direction.
- **Wavelength-division multiplexing (WDM):** Two different signals are carried on the fiber at two different nonoverlapping frequency bands, one in each direction. In nonfiber systems, this would be referred to as frequency-division multiplexing (FDM), but the term *WDM* is preferred for fiber transmission.

This approach lends itself to a gradual evolution of the network. Typically, an initial deployment will involve optical fiber only for the feeder cables, with twisted pair used from the remote node to the subscriber. Either echo cancellation or time-compression multiplexing, as just discussed, can be used for this final link to the subscriber. Later on, the twisted pair can be replaced with fiber. To provide full-duplex digital transmission to the subscriber, either two-fiber or WDM is used in the final run to the subscriber.

The layout is not limited to a single layer of remote nodes but may actually involve a cascade of multiplexers, as illustrated in Figure 3.8. Here, the feeder cable from the central office supports N channels using a TDM structure. For example, a T1 cable would support 24 channels. At the first multiplexer, M lines are run to subscribers, and the remaining $N - M$ channels continue on to a second multiplexer. This arrangement allows the network to support many subscribers over a large area with a minimum of cable.

With the active star approach, the subscriber is not aware of the details of the implementation of the feeder and distribution network. In particular, the TDM structure of the feeder cable is of no concern to the subscriber equipment. An alternative structure, known as passive star, simplifies the remote nodes at the cost of additional logic at the subscriber equipment (Figure 3.7c).

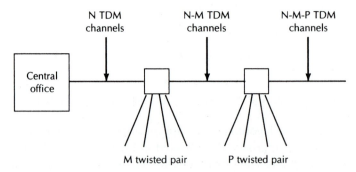

Figure 3.8 Use of Optical Fiber and Cascaded Multiplexers in the Local Loop.

With passive star, the feeder cable carries multiple channels as before. At the remote node, the signal is optically split onto a number of fibers going to the individual subscribers. Thus, all subscribers receive the same signal.

Two approaches to multiplexing are possible with the passive star arrangement:

- **Dense WDM:** Each subscriber is provided with a dedicated downstream (central office to subscriber) and dedicated upstream (subscriber to central office) wavelength. The term *dense* refers to the number of wavelengths supported. As many as 40 to 50 wavelengths may be possible with existing technology and components [LIN90], allowing the support of 20 to 25 subscribers per feeder cable.
- **TDM:** Capacity on the fiber is shared using time-division multiplexing. In the downstream direction, the TDM signal from the central office is broadcast to all of the subscribers on a feeder cable; each subscriber equipment copies the time slots assigned to it from the incoming signal. In the upstream direction, each subscriber is assigned time slots based on some fixed or dynamic multiple-access technique.

The passive star approach has the advantage that it does not require power at the remote node. Its disadvantage is that it requires more complex equipment at the subscriber end. Of the two multiplexing techniques considered for passive star, the TDM approach is less expensive at the present time. However, WDM component prices are falling, and this approach may soon be competitive with TDM techniques.

3.2 LINE CODING TECHNIQUES

In ISDN, both analog and digital data are transmitted using digital signals. A digital signal is a sequence of transmitted voltage pulses that is used to represent a stream of binary data. For example, a constant positive voltage level may represent binary 0, and a constant negative voltage level may represent binary 1. More complex encoding schemes may be used to improve performance or quality. In this section, we look at schemes that are used in ISDN; they are defined in Table 3.1 and depicted in Figure 3.9. First, we examine the criteria by which alternative schemes may be assessed.

Evaluation Criteria

There are two important tasks involved in interpreting digital signals at the receiver. First, the receiver must know the timing of each bit. That is, the receiver must know with some accuracy when a bit begins and ends. Second, the receiver must determine whether the signal level for each voltage pulse is high or low.

A number of factors determine how successful the receiver will be in interpreting the incoming signal: the signal-to-noise ratio (S/N), the data rate, and the bandwidth of the signal. With other factors held constant, the following statements are true:

Table 3.1 Definition of Digital Signal Encoding Formats

Nonreturn to Zero Level (NRZ-L)
0 = high level
1 = low level

Bipolar AMI
0 = no line signal
1 = positive or negative level, alternating for successive ones

Pseudoternary
0 = positive or negative level, alternating for successive zeros
1 = no line signal

B8ZS
Same as bipolar AMI, except that any string of eight zeros is replaced by a string with two code violations.

HDB3
Same as bipolar AMI, except that any string of four zeros is replaced by a string with one code violation.

- An increase in data rate increases bit error rate (the probability that a bit is received in error).
- An increase in S/N decreases bit error rate.
- Increased bandwidth allows increased data rate.

There is another factor that can be used to improve performance—the encoding scheme, which is simply the mapping from data bits to signal elements. A variety of approaches have been tried. Before describing some of these approaches, let us consider the ways of evaluating or comparing the various techniques. The following are among the important factors:

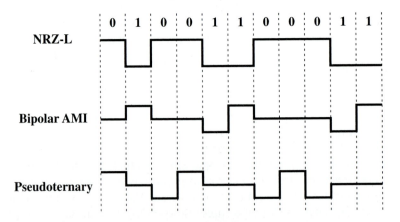

Figure 3.9 Digital Signal Encoding Formats.

- Signal spectrum
- Signal synchronization capability
- Error-detection capability
- Cost and complexity

Several aspects of the **signal spectrum** are important. A lack of high-frequency components means that less bandwidth is required for transmission. On the other hand, lack of a direct-current (DC) component is also desirable. With a DC component to the signal, there must be direct physical attachment of transmission components; with no DC component, AC coupling via the transformer is possible. This provides excellent electrical isolation, reducing interference. Finally, the magnitude of the effects of signal distortion and interference depend on the spectral properties of the transmitted signal. In practice, the transmission fidelity of a channel is usually worse near the band edges. Therefore, a good signal design should concentrate the transmitted power in the middle of the transmission bandwidth. In such a case, a smaller distortion should be present in the received signal. To meet this objective, codes can be designed with the aim of shaping the spectrum of the transmitted signal.

For successful reception of digital data, the receiver must know the timing of each bit. That is, the receiver must know with some accuracy when a bit begins and ends, so that the receiver may sample the incoming signal once per bit time to recognize the value of each bit. Thus, there must be some **signal synchronization capability** between transmitter and receiver. It is inevitable that there will be some drift between the clocks of the transmitter and receiver, and so some separate synchronization mechanism is needed. One approach is to provide a separate clock lead to synchronize the transmitter and receiver. This approach is rather expensive, because it requires an extra line, plus an extra transmitter and receiver. The alternative is to provide some synchronization mechanism that is based on the transmitted signal. This can be achieved with suitable encoding.

Error detection is the responsibility of a data link protocol that is executed on top of the physical signaling level. However, it is useful to have some **error-detection capability** built into the physical signaling scheme. This permits errors to be detected more quickly. Many signaling schemes have an inherent error-detection capability.

Finally, although digital logic continues to drop in price, the **cost and complexity** of the signaling scheme is a factor that should not be ignored.

Nonreturn to Zero

The most common, and easiest, way to transmit digital signals is to use two different voltage levels for the two binary digits. Codes that follow this strategy share the property that the voltage level is constant during a bit interval; there is no transition (no return to a zero voltage level). For example, the absence of voltage can be used to represent binary 0, with a constant positive voltage used to represent binary 1. More commonly, a negative voltage is used to represent one binary value and a positive voltage is used to represent the other. This latter code, known as **nonreturn to**

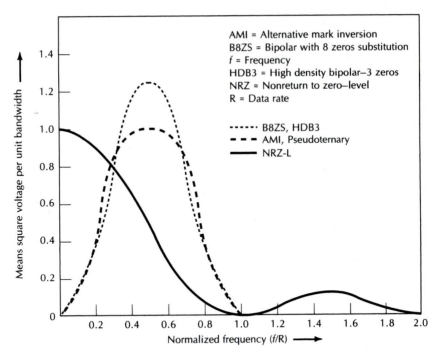

Figure 3.10 Spectral Density of Various Signal-Encoding Schemes.

zero level (NRZ-L), is illustrated[2] in Figure 3.9. NRZ-L is generally the code used to generate or interpret digital data by terminals and other devices. If a different code is to be used for transmission, it is typically generated from an NRZ-L signal by the transmission system.

The NRZ codes are the easiest to engineer and, in addition, make efficient use of bandwidth. This latter property is illustrated in Figure 3.10, which compares the spectral density of various encoding schemes. In the figure, frequency is normalized to the data rate. As can be seen, most of the energy in an NRZ signal is between DC and half the bit rate. For example, if an NRZ code is used to generate a signal with a data rate of 9600 bps, most of the energy in the signal is concentrated between 0 and 4800 Hz.

The main limitations of NRZ signals are the presence of a DC component and the lack of synchronization capability. To picture the latter problem, consider that with a long string of 1s or 0s for NRZ-L, the output is a constant voltage over a long period of time. Under these circumstances, any drift between the timing of transmitter and receiver will result in the loss of synchronization between the two.

Because of their simplicity and relatively low frequency response characteristics, NRZ codes are commonly used for digital magnetic recording. However, their limitations make these codes unattractive for signal transmission applications.

---

[2]In this figure, a negative voltage is equated with binary 1 and a positive voltage with binary 0. This is the opposite of the definition used in most other textbooks. However, the definition here conforms to the use of NRZ-L in data communications interfaces and the standards that govern those interfaces.

Multilevel Binary

A category of encoding techniques known as multilevel binary addresses some of the deficiencies of the NRZ codes. These codes use more than two signal levels. Two examples of this scheme are illustrated in Figure 3.9: bipolar AMI (alternate mark inversion) and pseudoternary.[3]

In the case of the **bipolar-AMI** scheme, a binary 0 is represented by no line signal, and a binary 1 is represented by a positive or negative pulse. The binary 1 pulses must alternate in polarity. There are several advantages to this approach. First, there will be no loss of synchronization if a long string of 1s occurs. Each 1 introduces a transition, and the receiver can resynchronize on that transition. A long string of 0s would still be a problem. Second, because the 1 signals alternate in voltage from positive to negative, there is no net DC component. Also, the bandwidth of the resulting signal is considerably less than the bandwidth for NRZ (Figure 3.10). Finally, the pulse alternation property provides a simple means of error detection. Any isolated error, whether it deletes a pulse or adds a pulse, causes a violation of this property.

The comments of the previous paragraph also apply to **pseudoternary**. In this case, it is the binary 1 that is represented by the absence of a line signal, and the binary 0 by alternating positive and negative pulses. There is no particular advantage of one technique versus the other, and each is the basis of some applications.

Although a degree of synchronization is provided with these codes, a long string of 0s in the case of AMI or 1s in the case of pseudoternary still presents a problem. Several techniques have been used to address this deficiency. One approach is to insert additional bits that force transitions. We will see that this technique is used in ISDN for relatively low-data-rate transmission. Of course, at a high data rate, this scheme is expensive, because it results in an increase in an already high signal transmission rate. To deal with this problem at high data rates, a technique that involves scrambling the data is used. We examine two examples of this technique later in this section.

Thus, with suitable modification, multilevel binary schemes overcome the problems of NRZ codes. Of course, as with any engineering design decision, there is a tradeoff. With multilevel binary coding, the line signal may take on one of three levels, but each signal element, which could represent $\log_2 3 = 1.58$ bits of information, bears only one bit of information. Thus, multilevel binary is not as efficient as NRZ coding. Another way to state this is that the receiver of multilevel binary signals has to distinguish between three levels ($+A$, $-A$, 0) instead of just two levels in the other signaling formats previously discussed. Because of this, the multilevel binary signal requires approximately 3 dB more signal power than a two-valued signal for the same probability of bit error. This is illustrated in Figure 3.11. Put another way, the bit error rate for NRZ codes, at a given signal-to-noise ratio, is significantly less than that for multilevel binary.

---

[3]These terms are not consistently used in the literature. In some books, these two terms are used for different encoding schemes than those defined here, and a variety of terms have been used for the two schemes illustrated in Figure 3.9. The nomenclature used here corresponds to the usage in various ITU-T recommendations.

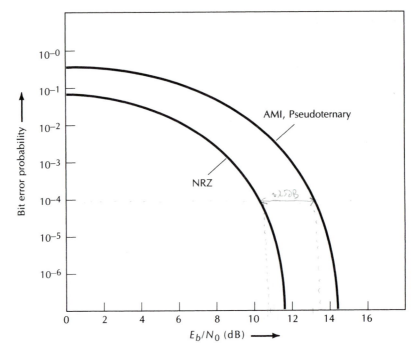

Figure 3.11 Theoretical Bit Error Rate for Various Digital Encoding Schemes.

Code Substitution Techniques

One approach to providing synchronization is the use of a code substitution scheme. The idea behind this approach is simple: Sequences that would result in a constant voltage level on the line are replaced by filling sequences that will provide sufficient transitions for the receiver's clock to maintain synchronization. The filling sequence must be recognized by the receiver and replaced with the original data sequence. The filling sequence is the same length as the original sequence, and so there is no data rate increase. The design goals for this approach can be summarized as follows:

- No DC component
- No long sequences of zero-level line signals
- No reduction in data rate
- Error-detection capability

Two techniques are in use in ISDN; these are illustrated in Figure 3.12.

A coding scheme that is commonly used in North America is known as **bipolar with 8 zeros substitution** (B8ZS). The coding scheme is based on a bipolar AMI. We have seen that the drawback of the AMI code is that a long string of zeros may result in loss of synchronization. To overcome this problem, the encoding is amended with the following rules:

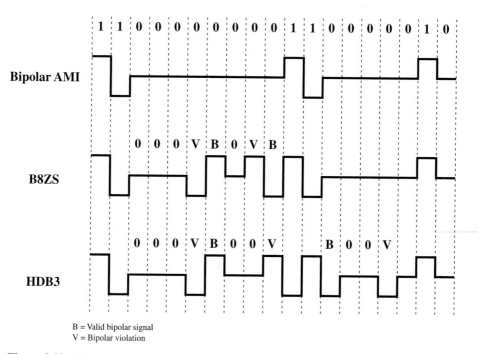

Figure 3.12 Encoding Rules for B8ZS and HDB3.

- If an octet of all zeros occurs and the last voltage pulse preceding this octet was positive, then the eight zeros of the octet are encoded as $0\,0\,0+\,-\,0\,-\,+$.
- If an octet of all zeros occurs and the last voltage pulse preceding this octet was negative, then the eight zeros of the octet are encoded as $0\,0\,0\,-\,+\,0\,+\,-$.

This technique forces two code violations of the AMI code, an event unlikely to be caused by noise or other transmission impairment. The receiver recognizes the pattern and interprets the octet as consisting of all zeros.

A coding scheme that is commonly used in Europe and Japan is known as the **high-density bipolar 3 zeros** (HDB3) code (Table 3.2). As before, it is based on the use of AMI encoding. In this case, the scheme replaces strings of four zeros with sequences containing one or two pulses. In each case, the fourth zero is replaced with a code violation. In addition, a rule is needed to ensure that successive violations are of alternate polarity so that no DC component is introduced. Thus, if

Table 3.2 HDB3 Substitution Rules

Polarity of Preceding Pulse	Number of Bipolar Pulses (ones) since Last Substitution	
	Odd	Even
−	000−	+00+
+	000+	−00−

the last violation was positive, this violation must be negative, and vice versa. Table 3.2 shows that this condition is tested for by knowing whether the number of pulses since the last violation is even or odd and knowing the polarity of the last pulse before the occurrence of the four zeros.

Figure 3.10 shows the spectral properties of these two codes. As can be seen, neither has a DC component. Most of the energy is concentrated in a relatively sharp spectrum around a frequency equal to one-half the data rate. Thus, these codes are well suited to high-data-rate transmission.

3.3 THE U INTERFACE

The ITU-T ISDN recommendations for ISDN do not include a complete specification for the ISDN subscriber line. However, ITU-T has issued Recommendation G.961,[4] which does address the interface between subscriber equipment and the subscriber line for basic rate access, which operates at 160 kbps. This interface is often referred to as the U reference point.

G.961 is only a partial specification. It specifies the use of either echo cancellation or time-compression multiplexing over a single twisted pair. Several alternative line coding techniques are defined in appendices. In the United States, work in this area has progressed much further. ANSI has issued a complete standard, T1.601,[5] for the basic access interface to the subscriber line. We examine the line coding for the ANSI standard in this section.

The line coding technique specified in T1.601 is known as **two binary, one quaternary** (2B1Q) coding. This code provides for more efficient use of bandwidth by having each signaling element represent two bits instead of one. Four different voltage levels are used. Because each signal element can take on one of four possible values, two bits of information are conveyed.

Table 3.3 shows the definition of 2B1Q. Two positive and two negative voltage levels are used. Corresponding to each voltage level is a pair of bits. The first

Table 3.3   Two Binary, One Quarternary (2B1Q) Signaling Levels

First Bit (polarity)	Second Bit (magnitude)	Quarternary Symbol	Voltage (volts)
1	0	+3	2.5
1	1	+1	0.833
0	1	−1	−0.833
0	0	−3	−2.5

[4]ITU-T Recommendation G.961, *Digital Transmission System for Metallic Local Lines for ISDN Basic Rate Access*, 1993.

[5]American National Standard ANSI T1.601, *Integrated Services Digital Network (ISDN)—Basic Access Interface for Use on Metallic Loops for Application on the Network Side of the NT (Layer 1 Specification)*, 1992.

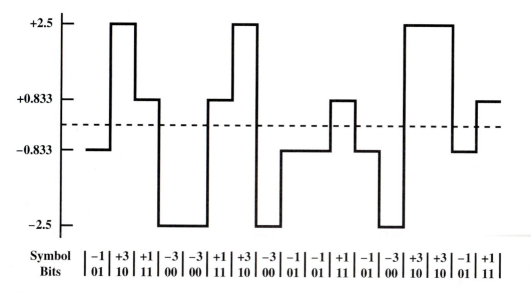

Figure 3.13   Example of 2B1Q Line Coding.

bit is one if the polarity of the pulse is positive and zero if the polarity is negative. The second bit is one if the magnitude of the pulse is 0.833 V and zero if the magnitude of the pulse is 2.5 V. Each of the four combinations of two bits is assigned a symbol. The four values listed under "quaternary symbol" in the table should be understood as symbol names, not numerical values.

Figure 3.13 is an example of 2B1Q coding.

With 2B1Q, we see a distinction between data rate and modulation rate. The data rate, expressed in bits per second (bps), is the rate at which bit values are transmitted. The modulation rate, expressed in bauds, is the rate at which signal elements are generated. In general,

$$D = R/b = R/\log_2 L$$

where

D = modulation rate, bauds
R = data rate, bps
L = number of different signal elements
b = number of bits per signal element

In the case of T1.601, the data rate is 160 kbps, and the modulation rate is therefore 80 kbaud.

The advantage of this type of encoding is that, in general, the bandwidth of the corresponding signal, compared with NRZ-L, is equal to the bandwidth of NRZ-L divided by the number of bits per signal element [COUC97]. Thus, 2B1Q should require only about half the bandwidth of NRZ-L. This code was chosen over other codes with higher baud rates for the U interface primarily because the lower baud rate minimized the two dominant transmission limitations in this application: intersymbol interference and near-end echo [LECH89].

A final note about the 2B1Q coding scheme. Prior to transmission the data are scrambled and then are subsequently descrambled at reception. This gives the data a pseudorandom nature that helps the receiver extract bit-timing information. It also improves the spectral characteristics of the signal, giving it a more uniform power distribution, as opposed to the potentially strong discrete spectral lines in non-scrambled data. See Appendix 3A for a discussion of scrambling.

3.4 QUADRATURE AMPLITUDE MODULATION

Quadrature amplitude modulation (QAM) is a popular analog signaling technique used in ADSL. We first provide a general introduction to analog signaling techniques and then look at QAM specifically.

Analog Signaling Techniques

The basis for analog signaling is a continuous constant-frequency signal known as the *carrier signal*. Digital information is encoded by means of a **modem** that modulates one of the three characteristics of the carrier: amplitude, frequency, or phase, or some combination of these. Figure 3.14 illustrates the three basic forms of modulation of analog signals for digital data:

- Amplitude-shift keying
- Frequency-shift keying
- Phase-shift keying

In all these cases, the resulting signal contains a range of frequencies on both sides of the carrier frequency, which is the *bandwidth* of the signal.

In **amplitude-shift keying (ASK)**, the two binary values are represented by two different amplitudes of the carrier frequency. In some cases, one of the amplitudes is zero; that is, one binary digit is represented by the presence, at constant amplitude, of the carrier, the other by the absence of the carrier. ASK is susceptible to sudden gain changes and is a rather inefficient modulation technique. ASK can be used with more than two amplitude levels. A four-level system would encode two bits with each signal burst.

The amplitude-shift keying technique is commonly used to transmit digital data over optical fiber. For light-emitting diode (LED) transmitters, binary one is represented by a short pulse of light and binary zero by the absence of light. Laser transmitters normally have a fixed "bias" current that causes the device to emit a low light level. This low level represents binary zero, while a higher-amplitude light-wave represents binary one.

In **frequency-shift keying (FSK)**, the two binary values are represented by two different frequencies near the carrier frequency. This scheme is less susceptible to error than amplitude-shift keying. On voice-grade lines, it is typically used up to 1200 bps. It is also commonly used for high-frequency (4 to 30 MHz) radio transmission. Figure 3.1 illustrates FSK.

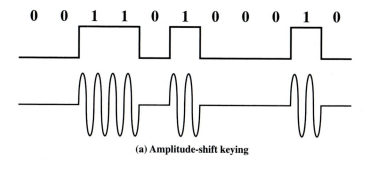

(a) Amplitude-shift keying

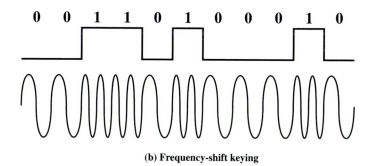

(b) Frequency-shift keying

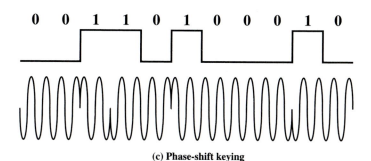

(c) Phase-shift keying

Figure 3.14   Modulation of Analog Signals for Digital Data.

In **phase-shift keying (PSK)**, the phase of the carrier signal is shifted to encode data. Figure 3.14c is an example of a two-phase system. In this system, a 0 is represented by sending a signal burst of the same phase as the preceding signal burst sent. A 1 is represented by sending a signal burst of opposite phase to the preceding one. PSK can use more than two phase shifts. A four-phase system would encode two bits with each signal burst. The phase-shift keying technique is more noise resistant and efficient than frequency-shift keying; on a voice-grade line, rates up to 9600 bps are achieved.

Finally, the techniques just discussed may be combined. A common combination is phase-shift keying and amplitude-shift keying, where some or all of the phase shifts may occur at one or two amplitudes. These techniques are referred to as *multilevel* signaling because each signal element represents multiple bits. Note that four-level ASK and four-phase PSK also fall into this category.

QAM Technique

QAM is a popular analog signaling technique that is used in ADSL. QAM takes advantage of the fact that it is possible to send two different signals simultaneously on the same carrier frequency, by using two copies of the carrier frequency, one shifted by 90° with respect to the other. For QAM, each carrier is ASK modulated. The two independent signals are simultaneously transmitted over the same medium. At the receiver, the two signals are demodulated and the results combined to produce the original binary input.

Figure 3.15 shows the QAM modulation scheme in general terms. The input is a stream of binary digits arriving at a rate of R bps. This stream is converted into two separate bit streams of $R/2$ bps each, by taking alternate bits for the two streams. In the diagram, the upper stream is ASK modulated on a carrier of frequency w_c by multiplying the bit stream by the carrier. Thus, a binary zero is represented by the absence of the carrier wave and a binary one is represented by the presence of the carrier wave at a constant amplitude. This same carrier wave is shifted by 90° and used for ASK modulation of the lower binary stream. The two modulated signals are then added together and transmitted. The transmitted signal can be expressed as follows:

$$s(t) = d_1(t)\cos w_c t + d_2(t)\sin w_c t$$

If two-level ASK is used, then each of the two streams can be in one of two states and the combined stream can be in one of $4 = 2 \times 2$ states. If four-level ASK is used (i.e., four different amplitude levels), then the combined stream can be in one of $16 = 4 \times 4$ states. Systems using 64 and even 256 states have been implemented. The greater the number of states, the higher the data rate that is possible within a given bandwidth. Of course, as discussed previously, the greater the number of states, the higher the potential error rate due to noise and attenuation.

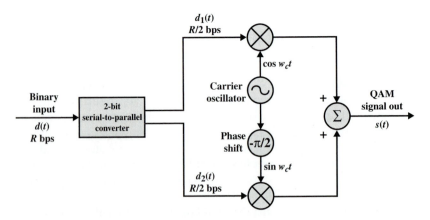

Figure 3.15 QAM Modulator.

3.5 ASYMMETRIC DIGITAL SUBSCRIBER LINE

In the implementation and deployment of a high-speed wide area public digital network, the most challenging part is the link between subscriber and network: the digital subscriber line. With billions of potential endpoints worldwide, the prospect of installing new cable for each new customer is daunting. Instead, network designers have sought ways of exploiting the installed base of twisted-pair wire that links virtually all residential and business customers to telephone networks. These links were installed to carry voice-grade signals in a bandwidth from zero to 4 kHz. However, the wires are capable of transmitting signals over a far broader spectrum—1 MHz or more.

ADSL is the most widely publicized of a family of new modem technologies designed to provide high-speed digital data transmission over ordinary telephone wire. ADSL is now being offered by a number of carriers and is defined in an ANSI standard. In this section, we first look at the overall design of ADSL and then examine the key underlying technology, known as DMT.

ADSL Design

The term *asymmetric* refers to the fact that ADSL provides more capacity downstream (from the carrier's central office to the customer's site) than upstream (from customer to carrier). ADSL was originally targeted at the expected need for video on demand and related services. This application has not materialized. However, since the introduction of ADSL technology, the demand for high-speed access to the Internet has grown. Typically, the user requires far higher capacity for downstream than for upstream transmission. Most user transmissions are in the form of keyboard strokes or transmission of short e-mail messages, whereas incoming traffic, especially Web traffic, can involve large amounts of data and include images or even video. Thus, ADSL provides a perfect fit for the Internet requirement.

ADSL uses frequency-division modulation (FDM) in a novel way to exploit the 1-MHz capacity of twisted pair. There are three elements of the ADSL strategy (Figure 3.16):

- Reserve lowest 25 MHz for voice, known as POTS (plain old telephone service). The voice is carried only in the 0–4 kHz band; the additional bandwidth is to prevent crosstalk between the voice and data channels.
- Use either echo cancellation or FDM to allocate two bands, a smaller upstream band and a larger downstream band.
- Use FDM within the upstream and downstream bands. In this case, a single bit stream is split into multiple parallel bit streams and each portion is carried in a separate frequency band.

When echo cancellation is used, the entire frequency band for the upstream channel overlaps the lower portion of the downstream channel. This has two advantages compared to the use of distinct frequency bands for upstream and downstream:

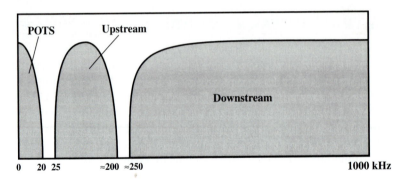

(a) Frequency-division multiplexing

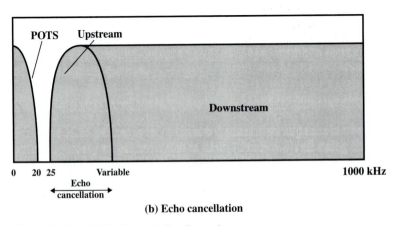

(b) Echo cancellation

Figure 3.16 ADSL Channel Configuration.

- The higher the frequency, the greater the attenuation. With the use of echo cancellation, more of the downstream bandwidth is in the "good" part of the spectrum.
- The echo cancellation design is more flexible for changing upstream capacity. The upstream channel can be extended upward without running into the downstream; instead, the area of overlap is extended.

The disadvantage of the use of echo cancellation is the need for echo cancellation logic on both ends of the line.

The ADSL scheme provides a range of up to 5.5 km, depending on the diameter of the cable and its quality. This is sufficient to cover about 95% of all U.S. subscriber lines and should provide comparable coverage in other nations.

Discrete Multitone

Discrete multitone (DMT) uses multiple carrier signals at different frequencies, sending some of the bits on each channel. The available transmission band (upstream or downstream) is divided into a number of 4-kHz subchannels. On initialization, the

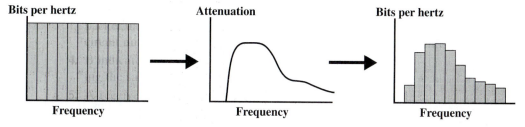

Figure 3.17   DMT Bits per Channel Allocation.

DMT modem sends out test signals on each subchannel to determine the signal-to-noise ratio. The modem then assigns more bits to channels with better signal transmission qualities and less bits to channels with poorer signal transmission qualities. Figure 3.17 illustrates this process. Each subchannel can carry a data rate of from 0 to 60 kbps. The figure shows a typical situation in which there is increasing attenuation and hence decreasing signal-to-noise ratio at higher frequencies. As a result, the higher-frequency subchannels carry less of the load.

Figure 3.18 provides a general block diagram for DMT transmission. After initialization, the bit stream to be transmitted is divided into a number of substreams, one for each subchannel that will carry data. The sum of the data rates of the substreams is equal to the total data rate. Each substream is then converted to an analog signal using QAM. This scheme works easily because of QAM's ability to assign

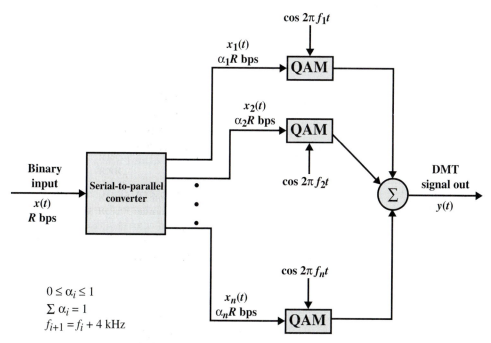

Figure 3.18   DMT Transmitter.

different numbers of bits per transmitted signal. Each QAM signal occupies a distinct frequency band, so these signals can be combined by simple addition to produce the composite signal for transmission.

Present ADSL/DMT designs employ 256 downstream subchannels. In theory, with each 4-kHz subchannel carrying 60 kbps, it would be possible to transmit at a rate of 15.36 Mbps. In practice transmission impairments prevent attainment of this data rate. Current implementations operate at from 1.5 to 9 Mbps, depending on line distance and quality.

3.6 xDSL

ADSL is one of a number of recent schemes for providing high-speed digital transmission of the subscriber line. Table 3.4 summarizes and compares some of the most important of these new schemes, which collectively are referred to as xDSL.

High-Data-Rate Digital Subscriber Line

HDSL was developed in the late 1980s by BellCore to provide a more cost-effective means of delivering a T1 data rate (1.544 Mbps). The standard T1 line uses alternate mark inversion (AMI) coding, which occupies a bandwidth of about 1.5 MHz. Because such high frequencies are involved, the attenuation characteristics limit the use of T1 to a distance of about 1 km between repeaters. Thus, for many subscriber lines one or more repeaters are required, which adds to the installation and maintenance expense.

Table 3.4 Comparison of xDSL Alternatives

	ADSL	**HDSL**	**SDSL**	**VDSL**
Bits/second	1.5 to 9 Mbps downstream	1.544 or 2.048 Mbps	1.544 or 2.048 Mbps	13 to 52 Mbps downstream
	16 to 640 kbps upstream			1.5 to 2.3 kbps upstream
Mode	Asymmetric	Symmetric	Symmetric	Asymmetric
Copper pairs	1	2	1	1
Range (24-gauge UTP)	3.7 to 5.5 km	3.7 km	3.7 km	1.4 km
Signaling	Analog	Digital	Digital	Analog
Line code	CAP/DMT	2B1Q	2B1Q	DMT
Frequency	1 to 5 MHz	196 kHz	196 kHz	≥ 10 MHZ
Bits/cycle	Varies	4	4	Varies

UTP = unshielded twisted pair

HDSL uses the 2B1Q coding scheme to provide a data rate of up to 2 Mbps over two twisted-pair lines within a bandwidth that extends only up to about 196 kHz. This enables a range of about 3.7 km to be achieved.

Single Line Digital Subscriber Line

Although HDSL is attractive for replacing existing T1 lines, it is not suitable for residential subscribers because it requires two twisted-pair lines, whereas the typical residential subscriber has a single twisted pair. SDSL was developed to provide the same type of service as HDSL but over a single twisted-pair line. As with HDSL, 2B1Q coding is used. Echo cancellation is used to achieve full-duplex transmission over a single pair.

Very High Data Rate Digital Subscriber Line

One of the newest xDSL schemes is VDSL. As of this writing, many of the details of this signaling specification remain to be worked out. The objective is to provide a scheme similar to ADSL at a much high data rate by sacrificing distance. The likely signaling technique is DMT/QAM.

VDSL does not use echo cancellation but provides separate bands for different services, with the following tentative allocation:

- POTS: 0–4 kHz
- ISDN: 4–80 kHz
- Upstream: 300–700 kHz
- Downstream: ≥ 1 MHz

3.7 SUMMARY

The last portion of telecommunications networks to convert to digital is the portion between the network and the business and residential subscribers, referred to as the subscriber line. With the existing twisted-pair facility, full-duplex digital transmission requires the use of either time-compression multiplexing or echo cancellation. The latter approach has proved the most popular. Ultimately, to support the higher data rates that will be demanded by customers, twisted pair will be replaced by optical fiber in the subscriber line or there will be a move to xDSL. Various techniques involving multiplexing, TDM, and WDM are being explored for optical fiber links. For xDSL, the ASDL version is currently the most popular.

3.8 RECOMMENDED READING

The best source of material on digital subscriber lines is [REEV95]. [MOCH94] is a worthwhile survey of optical fiber subscriber line technology.

A good analysis of line coding schemes can be found in [BERG96]. [SKLA88] also provides some insights, while [LECH89] specifically looks at line coding alternatives for the digital subscriber line. [HUAN91] is a detailed survey of the technical issues to be addressed at the U interface.

[CIOF97] provides an excellent a discussion of ADSL; another good paper on the subject is [MAXW96]. Recommended treatments of xDSL are [HAWL97] and [HUMP97]. The December 1995 issue of the *IEEE Journal on Selected Areas in Communications* is devoted to copper wire subscribe line technology, with extensive coverage of xDSL.

BERG96   Bergmans, J. *Digital Baseband Transmission and Recording.* Boston: Kluwer, 1996

CIOF97   Cioffi, J. "Asymmetric Digital Subscriber Lines." In Gibson, J., ed. *The Communications Handbook.* Boca Raton, FL: CRC Press, 1997.

HAWL97   Hawley, G. "Systems Considerations for the Use of xDSL Technology for Data Access." *IEEE Communications Magazine*, March 1997.

HUAN91   Huang, D., and Valenti, D. "Digital Subscriber Lines: Network Considerations for ISDN Basic Access." *Proceedings of the IEEE*, February 1991.

HUMP97   Humphrey, M., and Freeman, J. "How xDSL Supports Broadband Services to the Home." *IEEE Network*, January/March 1997.

LECH89   Lechleider, J. "Line Codes for Digital Subscriber Lines." *IEEE Communications Magazine,* September 1989.

MAXW96   Maxwell, K. "Asymmetric Digital Subscriber Line: Interim Technology for the Next Forty Years." *IEEE Communications Magazine*, October 1996.

MOCH94   Mochida, Y. "Technologies for Local-Access Fibering." *IEEE Communications Magazine*, February 1994.

REEV95   Reeve, W. *Subscriber Loop Signaling and Transmission Handbook.* Piscataway, NJ: IEEE Press, 1995.

SKLA88   Sklar, B. *Digital Communications: Fundamentals and Applications.* Englewood Cliffs, NJ: Prentice Hall, 1988.

Recommended Web sites are as follows:

- **ADSL Forum:** Includes a FAQ and technical information about ADSL Forum specifications.
- **Universal ADSL:** Home page of the Universal ADSL Working Group, an industry consortium promoting low-cost, high-speed residential ADSL access.

3.9 PROBLEMS

3.1 Develop a state diagram (finite state machine) representation of pseudoternary coding.

3.2 Consider the following signal-encoding technique. Binary data are presented as input, a_m, $m = 1, 2, 3, \ldots$. Two levels of processing occur. First, a new set of binary numbers is produced:

$$b_m = (a_m + b_{m-1}) \bmod 2$$

These are then encoded as

$$c_m = b_m - b_{m-1}$$

On reception, the original data are recovered by

$$a_m = c_m \quad \bmod 2$$

a. Verify that the received values of a_m equal the transmitted values of a_m.
b. What sort of encoding is this?

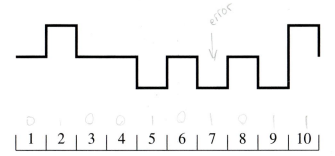

Figure 3.19 Waveform for Problem 3.5.

3.3 For the bit stream 01110010, sketch the waveforms for each of the codes of Table 3.1. Assume that the most recent preceding one bit (AMI) has a negative voltage and that the most recent preceding zero bit (pseudoternary) has a negative voltage.

3.4 Consider a stream of binary data consisting of a long sequence of 1s followed by a zero followed by a long string of 1s, with the same assumptions as Problem 3.3. Draw the waveform for this sequence using
   a. NRZ-L
   b. Bipolar AMI
   c. Pseudoternary

3.5 The bipolar-AMI waveform representing the binary sequence 0100101011 is transmitted over a noisy channel. The received waveform is shown in Figure 3.19; it contains a single error. Locate the position of this error and explain your answer.

3.6 Figure 3.20 shows the QAM demodulator corresponding to the QAM modulator of Figure 3.15. Show that this arrangement does recover the two signals $d_1(t)$ and $d_2(t)$, which can be combined to recover the original input.

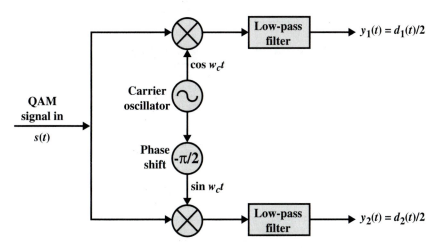

Figure 3.20 QAM Demodulator.

APPENDIX 3A   SCRAMBLING AND DESCRAMBLING

For some digital data-encoding techniques, a long string of binary zeros or ones in a transmission can make it difficult for the receiver to maintain synchronization with the transmitter. Also, other transmission properties are enhanced if the data are more nearly of a random nature rather than constant or repetitive. A technique commonly used to improve signal quality is scrambling and descrambling. The scrambling process tends to make the data appear more random.

The scrambling process consists of a feedback shift register, and the matching descrambler consists of a feedforward shift register. An example is shown in Figure 3.21. In this example, the scrambled data sequence may be expressed as follows:

$$B_m = A_m \oplus B_{m-3} \oplus B_{m-5}$$

where $\oplus$ indicates the exclusive or operation. The descrambled sequence is

$$
\begin{aligned}
C_m &= B_m \oplus B_{m-3} \oplus B_{m-5} \\
&= (A_m \oplus B_{m-3} \oplus B_{m-5}) \oplus B_{m-3} \oplus B_{m-5} \\
&= A_m .
\end{aligned}
$$

As can be seen, the descrambled output is the original sequence.

We can represent this process with the use of polynomials. Thus, for this example, the polynomial is $P = 1 \oplus X^{-3} \oplus X^{-5}$. The input is divided by this polynomial to produce the scrambled sequence. At the receiver, the received scrambled signal is multiplied by the same polynomial to reproduce the original output. Figure 3.22

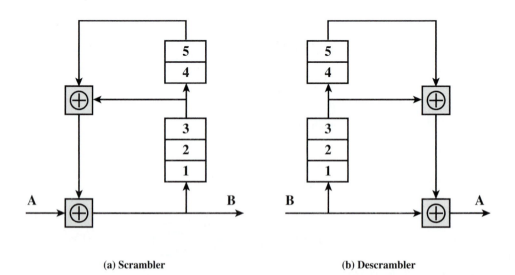

(a) Scrambler   (b) Descrambler

Figure 3.21   Scrambler and Descrambler.

```
                                    1 0 1 1 1 0 0 0 1 1 0 1 0 0 1 ← B
     P → 1 0 0 1 0 1 / 1 0 1 0 1 0 1 0 0 0 0 0 0 1 1 1              ← A
                       1 0 0 1 0 1
                       ─────────
                       1 1 1 1 1 0
                       1 0 0 1 0 1
                       ─────────
                         1 1 0 1 1 0
                         1 0 0 1 0 1
                         ─────────
                           1 0 0 1 1 0
                           1 0 0 1 0 1
                           ─────────
                                 1 1 0 0 1 1
                                 1 0 0 1 0 1
                                 ─────────
                                   1 0 1 1 0 1
                                   1 0 0 1 0 1
                                   ─────────
                                       1 0 0 0 0 0
                                       1 0 0 1 0 1
                                       ─────────
                                         1 0 1 0 0 0
```

(a) Scrambling

```
                              1 0 1 1 1 0 0 0 1 1 0 1 0 0 1 ← B
                                            1 0 0 1 0 1 ← P
                              ───────────────────────────
                              1 0 1 1 1 0 0 0 1 1 0 1 0 0 1
                        1 0 1 1 1 0 0 0 1 1 0 1 0 0 1
                  1 0 1 1 1 0 0 0 1 1 0 1 0 0 1
         C = A → 1 0 1 0 1 0 1 0 0 0 0 0 0 1 1 1
```

(b) Descrambling

Figure 3.22 Example of Scrambling with $P(X) = 1 + X^{-3} + X^{-5}$.

is an example using the polynomial P and an input of 101010100000111. The scrambled transmission, produced by dividing by P (100101), is 101110001101001. When this number is multiplied by P, we get the original input. Note that the input sequence contains the periodic sequence 10101010 as well as a long string of zeros. The scrambler effectively removes both patterns.

For the 2B1Q specification, in the network-subscriber direction, the polynomial is

$$1 \oplus X^{-5} \oplus X^{-23}$$

and in the subscriber-network direction it is

$$1 \oplus X^{-18} \oplus X^{-23}$$

CHAPTER 4

COMMUNICATION NETWORKS

This chapter provides an overview of the types of communication networks developed for metropolitan and wide area networking. The chapter begins with a survey of the spectrum of approaches that are used. Circuit switching and packet switching represent the two extreme ends of this spectrum and are the two traditional networking approaches. The remainder of the chapter, after Section 4.1, provides more detailed background on these two approaches.

4.1   SWITCHING TECHNIQUES

For transmission of data[1] beyond a local area, communication is typically achieved by transmitting data from source to destination through a network of intermediate switching nodes. These nodes are not concerned with the content of the data, but simply provide a switching facility that moves the data from node to node until they reach their destination. Figure 4.1 illustrates a simple network. The end devices that wish to communicate may be referred to as *stations*. The stations may be computers, terminals, telephones, or other communicating devices. We will refer to the switching devices whose purpose is to provide communication as *nodes*. Each station attaches to a node, and the collection of nodes is referred to as a *communications network*.

Figure 4.2 shows a spectrum of switching techniques available to transport information across a network. The two extreme ends of the spectrum represent the two traditional switching techniques: circuit switching and packet switching; the remaining techniques are of more recent vintage. In general,

---

[1]We use this term here in a very general sense, to include voice, image, and video, as well as ordinary data (e.g., numerical, text).

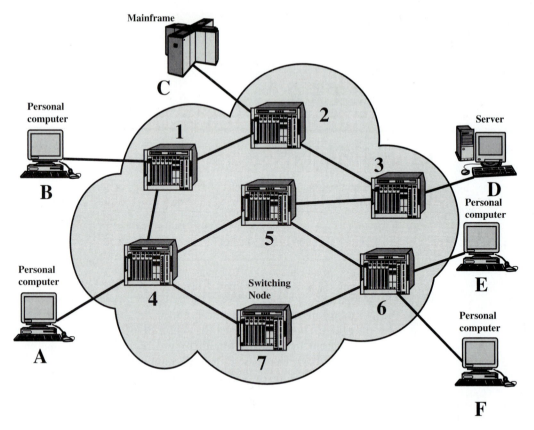

Figure 4.1 Simple Switching Network.

the techniques toward the left end of the line provide transmission with little or no variability and with minimal processing demands on attached stations, while techniques toward the right end provide increased flexibility to handle varying bit rates and unpredictable traffic at the expense of increasing processing complexity.

The bulk of this chapter provides a detailed look at the two most common switching techniques. The more advanced techniques will concern us later in the book and are examined briefly at the end of this chapter.

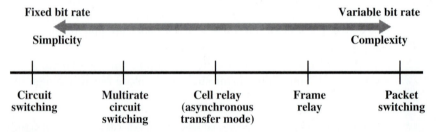

Figure 4.2 Spectrum of Switching Techniques (based on [PRYC93]).

4.2   CIRCUIT SWITCHING

Circuit switching is the dominant technology for both voice and data communications today and will remain so well into the ISDN era. Communication via circuit switching implies that there is a dedicated communication path between two stations. That path is a connected sequence of links between network nodes. On each physical link, a channel is dedicated to the connection. The most common example of circuit switching is the telephone network.

Communication via circuit switching involves three phases, which can be explained with reference to Figure 4.1.

1. **Circuit establishment.** Before any signals can be transmitted, an end-to-end (station-to-station) circuit must be established. For example, station A sends a request to node 4 requesting a connection to station E. Typically, the link from A to 4 is a dedicated line, so that part of the connection already exists. Node 4 must find the next leg in a route leading to node 6. Based on routing information and measures of availability and perhaps cost, node 4 selects the link to node 5, allocates a free channel (using frequency-division multiplexing, FDM, or time-division multiplexing, TDM) on that link, and sends a message requesting connection to E. So far, a dedicated path has been established from A through 4 to 5. Because a number of stations may attach to 4, it must be able to establish internal paths from multiple stations to multiple nodes. The remainder of the process proceeds similarly. Node 5 dedicates a channel to node 6 and internally ties that channel to the channel from node 4. Node 6 completes the connection to E. In completing the connection, a test is made to determine if E is busy or is prepared to accept the connection.

2. **Information transfer.** Information can now be transmitted from A through the network to E. The transmission may be analog voice, digitized voice, or binary data, depending on the nature of the network. As the carriers evolve to fully integrated digital networks, the use of digital (binary) transmission for both voice and data is becoming the dominant method. The path is as follows: A–4 link, internal switching through 4, 4–5 channel, internal switching through 5, 5–6 channel, internal switching through 6, 6–E link. Generally, the connection is full duplex, and signals may be transmitted in both directions simultaneously.

3. **Circuit disconnect.** After some period of information transfer, the connection is terminated, usually by the action of one of the two stations. Signals must be propagated to nodes 4, 5, and 6 to deallocate the dedicated resources.

Note that the connection path is established before data transmission begins. Thus, channel capacity must be reserved between each pair of nodes in the path and each node must have available internal switching capacity to handle the requested connection. The switches must have the intelligence to make these allocations and to devise a route through the network.

Circuit switching can be rather inefficient. Channel capacity is dedicated for the duration of a connection, even if no data are being transferred. For a voice connection, utilization may be rather high, but it still does not approach 100%. For a terminal-to-computer connection, the capacity may be idle during most of the time of the connection. In terms of performance, there is a delay prior to signal transfer for call establishment. However, once the circuit is established, the network is effectively transparent to the users. Information is transmitted at a fixed data rate with no delay other than the propagation delay through the transmission links. The delay at each node is negligible.

Circuit switching was developed to handle voice traffic but is now also used for data traffic. The best-known example of a circuit-switching network is the public telephone network. This is actually a collection of national networks interconnected to form the international service. Although originally designed and implemented to service analog telephone subscribers, it handles substantial data traffic via modem and is well on its way to being converted to a digital network. Another well-known application of circuit switching is the private branch exchange (PBX), used to interconnect telephones within a building or office. Circuit switching is also used in private networks. Typically, such a network is set up by a corporation or other large organization to interconnect its various sites. Such a network usually consists of PBX systems at each site interconnected by dedicated, leased lines obtained from one of the carriers, such as AT&T.

A public telecommunications network can be described using four generic architectural components (Figure 4.3):

- **Subscribers:** The devices that attach to the network. It is still the case that most subscriber devices to public telecommunications networks are telephones, but the percentage of data traffic increases year by year.
- **Subscriber line:** The link between the subscriber and the network, also referred to as the *subscriber loop* or *local loop*. Almost all subscriber line connections use twisted-pair wire. The length of a subscriber line is typically in a range from a few kilometers to a few tens of kilometers.
- **Exchanges:** The switching centers in the network. A switching center that directly supports subscribers is known as an *end office*. Typically, an end office will support many thousands of subscribers in a localized area. There are over 19,000 end offices in the United States, so it is clearly impractical for each end office to have a direct link to each of the other end offices; this would require on the order of 2×10^8 links. Rather, intermediate switching nodes are used.
- **Trunks:** The branches between exchanges. Trunks carry multiple voice-frequency circuits using either FDM or synchronous TDM. Earlier, these were referred to as carrier systems.

Circuit-switching technology has been driven by those applications that handle voice traffic. One of the key requirements for voice traffic is that there must be virtually no transmission delay and certainly no variation in delay. A constant signal transmission rate must be maintained, because transmission and reception occur at the same signal rate. These requirements are necessary to allow normal human conversation. Further, the quality of the received signal must be sufficiently high to provide, at a minimum, intelligibility.

Circuit switching achieved its widespread, dominant position because it is well suited to the analog transmission of voice signals. In today's digital world, its

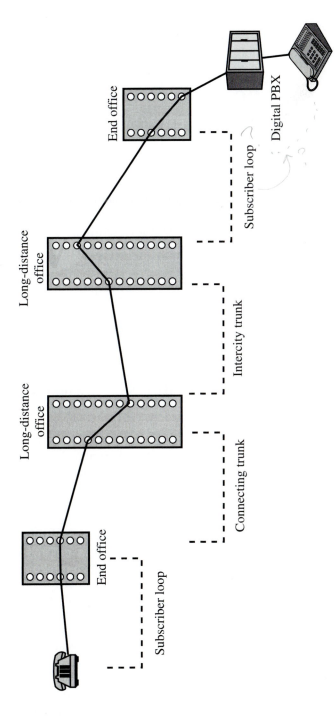

Figure 4.3 Example Connection over a Public Circuit-Switching Network.

inefficiencies are more apparent. However, despite the inefficiency, circuit switching is and will remain an attractive choice for both local area and wide area networking. One of its key strengths is that it is transparent. Once a circuit is established, it appears like a direct connection to the two attached stations; no special networking logic is needed at the station.

4.3 ROUTING FOR CIRCUIT-SWITCHING NETWORKS

In a large circuit-switched network, such as the AT&T long-distance telephone network, many of the circuit connections will require a path through more than one switch. When a call is placed, the network must devise a route through the network from calling subscriber to called subscriber that passes through some number of switches and trunks. There are two main requirements for the network's architecture that bear on the routing strategy: efficiency and resilience. First, it is desirable to minimize the amount of equipment (switches and trunks) in the network subject to the ability to handle the expected load. The load requirement is usually expressed in terms of a *busy-hour traffic load*, which is the average load expected over the course of the busiest hour of use during the course of a day. From a functional point of view, it is necessary to handle that amount of load. From a cost point of view, we would like to handle that load with minimum equipment. However, there is another requirement—namely, resilience. Although the network may be sized for the busy-hour load, it is possible for the traffic to surge temporarily above that level (for example, during a major storm). It will also be the case that, from time to time, switches and trunks will fail and be temporarily unavailable (unfortunately, maybe during the same storm). We would like the network to provide a reasonable level of service under such conditions.

The key design issue that determines the nature of the tradeoff between efficiency and resilience is the routing strategy. Traditionally, the routing function in public telecommunications networks has been quite simple. In essence, the switches of a network were organized into a tree structure, or hierarchy. A path was constructed by starting at the calling subscriber, tracing up the tree to the first common node, and then tracing down the tree to the called subscriber. To add some resilience to the network, additional high-usage trunks were added that cut across the tree structure to connect exchanges with high volumes of traffic between them. In general, this is a static approach. The addition of high-usage trunks provides redundancy and extra capacity, but limitations remain both in terms of efficiency and resilience. Because this routing scheme is not able to adapt to changing conditions, the network must be designed to meet some typical heavy demand. As an example of the problems raised by this approach, the busy hours for east-west traffic and north-south traffic do not coincide and place different demands on the system. It is difficult to analyze the effects of these variables, which leads to oversizing and therefore inefficiency. In terms of resilience, the fixed hierarchical structure with supplemental trunks may respond poorly to failures. Typically, in such designs the result of a failure is a major local congestion near the site of the failure.

To cope with the growing demands on public telecommunications networks, virtually all providers have moved away from the static hierarchical approach to a dynamic approach. A dynamic routing approach is one in which routing decisions are influenced by current traffic conditions. Typically, the circuit-switching nodes have a peer relationship with each other rather than a hierarchical one. All nodes are capable of performing the same functions. In such an architecture, routing is both more complex and more flexible. It is more complex because the architecture does not provide a "natural" path or set of paths based on hierarchical structure. But it is also more flexible, because more alternative routes are available.

As an example, we look at a form of routing in circuit-switching networks known as **alternate routing**. The essence of alternate routing schemes is that the possible routes to be used between two end offices are predefined. It is the responsibility of the originating switch to select the appropriate route for each call. Each switch is given a set of preplanned routes for each destination, in order of preference. If a direct trunk connection exists between two switches, this is usually the preferred choice. If this trunk is unavailable, then the second choice is to be tried, and so on. The routing sequences (sequence in which the routes in the set are tried) reflect an analysis based on historical traffic patterns and are designed to optimize the use of network resources.

If there is only one routing sequence defined for each source–destination pair, the scheme is known as a fixed alternate routing scheme. More commonly, a dynamic alternate routing scheme is used. In the latter case, a different set of preplanned routes is used for different time periods, to take advantage of the differing traffic patterns in different time zones and at different times of day. Thus, the routing decision is based both on current traffic status (a route is rejected if busy) and historical traffic patterns (which determines the sequence of routes to be considered).

A simple example is shown in Figure 4.4. The originating switch, X, has four possible routes to the destination switch, Y. The direct route (a) will always be tried first. If this trunk is unavailable (busy, out of service), the other routes will be tried in a particular order, depending on the time period. For example, during weekday mornings, route b is tried next.

A form of the dynamic alternate routing technique is employed by the Bell Operating Companies for providing local and regional telephone service [BELL90]; it is referred to as multialternate routing (MAR). This approach is also used by AT&T in its long-distance network [ASH90] and is referred to as dynamic non-hierarchical routing (DNHR).

4.4 CONTROL SIGNALING FOR CIRCUIT-SWITCHING NETWORKS

In a circuit-switched network, control signals are the means by which the network is managed and by which calls are established, maintained, and terminated. Both call management and overall network management require that information be exchanged between subscriber and switch, among switches, and between switch and network management center. For a large public telecommunications network, a relatively complex control-signaling scheme is required. In this section, we provide a brief overview of control-signal functionality and then look at the technique that is the basis of modern integrated digital networks, common channel signaling.

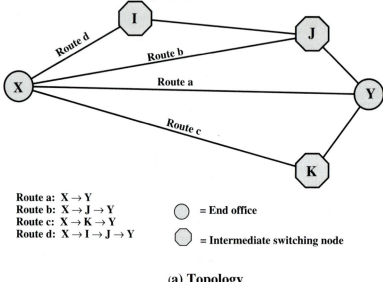

Route a: X → Y
Route b: X → J → Y
Route c: X → K → Y
Route d: X → I → J → Y

◯ = End office

⬡ = Intermediate switching node

(a) Topology

Time period	First route	Second route	Third route	Fourth and final route
Morning	a	b	c	d
Afternoon	a	d	b	c
Evening	a	d	c	b
Weekend	a	c	b	d

(b) Routing table

Figure 4.4 Alternate Routes from End Office X to End Office Y.

Signaling Functions

Control signals are necessary for the operation of a circuit-switched network and involve every aspect of network behavior, including both network services visible to the subscriber and internal mechanisms. As networks become more complex, the number of functions performed by control signaling necessarily grows. The following functions, listed in [MART90], are among the most important:

1. Audible communication with the subscriber, including dial tone, ringing tone, busy signal, and so on.
2. Transmission of the number dialed to switching offices, which will attempt to complete a connection.
3. Transmission of information between switches indicating that a call cannot be completed.

4. Transmission of information between switches indicating that a call has ended and that the path can be disconnected.
5. A signal to make a telephone ring.
6. Transmission of information used for billing purposes.
7. Transmission of information giving the status of equipment or trunks in the network. This information may be used for routing and maintenance purposes.
8. Transmission of information used in diagnosing and isolating system failures.
9. Control of special equipment such as satellite channel equipment.

As an example, consider a typical telephone connection sequence from one line to another in the same central office.

1. Prior to the call, both telephones are not in use (on hook). The call begins when one subscriber lifts the receiver (off hook), which is automatically signaled to switch.
2. The switch responds with an audible dial tone, signaling the subscriber that the number may be dialed.
3. The caller dials the number, which is communicated as a destination address to the switch.
4. If the called subscriber is not busy, the switch alerts that subscriber to an incoming call by sending a ringing signal, which causes the telephone to ring.
5. Feedback is provided to the calling subscriber by the switch:
   ¤ If the called subscriber is not busy, the switch returns an audible ringing tone to the caller while the ringing signal is being sent to the called subscriber.
   ¤ If the called subscriber is busy, the switch sends an audible busy signal to the caller.
   ¤ If the call cannot be completed through the switch, the switch sends an audible "reorder" message to the caller.
6. The called party accepts the call by lifting the receiver (off hook), which is automatically signaled to the switch.
7. The switch terminates the ringing signal and the audible ringing tone and establishes a connection between the two subscribers.
8. The connection is released when either subscriber hangs up.

When the called subscriber is attached to a different switch than the calling subscriber, the following switch-to-switch trunk signaling functions are required:

9. The originating switch seizes an idle interswitch trunk, sends an off-hook indication on the trunk, and requests a digit register at the far end, so that the address may be communicated.
10. The terminating switch sends an on-hook followed by an off-hook signal, known as a "wink." This indicates a register-ready status.
11. The originating switch sends the address digits to the terminating switch.

Table 4.1 Signaling Functions

SUPERVISORY
Supervisory signaling provides the mechanism for obtaining the resources to establish a call. It is used to initiate a call request, to hold or release an established connection, to initiate or terminate charging, to recall an operator on an established connection, to alert a subscriber, and to initiate custom calling. It involves the recognition of busy or idle states on subscriber lines and interoffice trunks, and the transmission of that information to the caller and switching system. This form of signaling involves both control and status functions.

Control
Supervisory signaling is used to control the use of resources. Switch and trunk capacity is assigned to a connection with supervisory signals. These resources, once seized, are held for the duration of the call and released upon call termination.
Status
Supervisory signaling also encompasses information concerning the status of a call or attempted call. This information is sent back through the network to the subscriber's switch.

ADDRESS
Address signaling provides the mechanism for identifying the subscribers participating in a call or call attempt. It conveys such information as the calling or called subscriber's telephone number and an area or country code or PBX trunk access code. It involves the transmission of digits of a called telephone number to a switching system from a subscriber or by one switching system to another. Address signaling includes both station-related and routing-related signals.

Station Related
Address signaling originates with the calling subscriber. From a telephone the signal is generated as a sequence of pulses (rotary dial) or a sequence of two-frequency tones (push button). For digital subscribers, a digital control signal may be used.
Routing Related
If more than one switch is involved in the call setup, signaling is required between switches. This includes address signaling, which supports the routing function, and supervisory signaling, which is involved in allocating resources.

CALL INFORMATION
Call information signals are transmitted to a caller to provide information to callers and operators relative to the establishment of a connection through a telephone network. A variety of audible tones is used for this purpose. These signals can be categorized as alerting and progress.

Alerting
Alerting signals are provided to a subscriber who is not placing a call. These include ringing a called telephone and alerting the subscriber that the phone is off the hook.
Progress
Call progress signals indicate the status of the call to the calling subscriber.

NETWORK MANAGEMENT
Network management signals include all those signals related to the ongoing operation and management of the network. They include signals that cause control to be exerted and signals that provide status.

Control
Network management control signals are used to control the overall routing selection process (e.g., to change the preplanned routes of a switch) and to modify the operating characteristics of the network in response to overload and failure conditions.
Status
Network management status signals are used by a switch to provide status information to network management centers and to other switches. Status information includes traffic volume, overload conditions, persistent error conditions, and failures.

This example gives some idea of the functions that are performed using control signals. A somewhat more detailed overview is given in Table 4.1. The functions performed by control signals can be roughly grouped into the categories of supervisory, address, call information, and network management. Figure 4.5, based on a figure in [FREE94], indicates the origin and destination of various control signals.

The term **supervisory** is generally used to refer to control functions that have a binary character (true/false; on/off), such as request for service, answer, alerting, and return to idle. They deal with the availability of the called subscriber and of the needed network resources. Supervisory control signals are used to determine if a needed resource is available and, if so, to seize it. They are also used to communicate the status of requested resources.

Address signals identify a subscriber. Initially, an address signal is generated by a calling subscriber when dialing a telephone number. The resulting address may be propagated through the network to support the routing function and to locate and ring the called subscriber's phone.

The term **call information** refers to those signals that provide information to the subscriber about the status of a call. This is in contrast to internal control signals between switches used in call establishment and termination. Such internal signals are analog or digital electrical messages. In contrast, call information signals are audible tones that can be heard by the caller or an operator with the proper phone set.

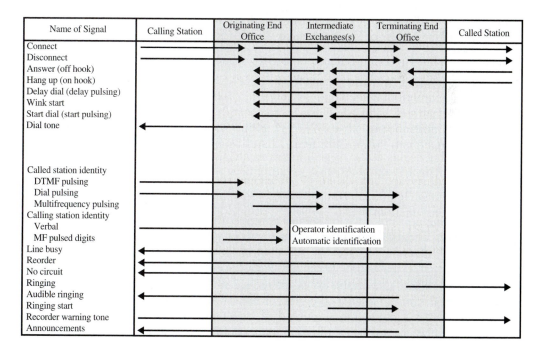

Note: A broken line indicates repetition of a signal at each office, whereas
a solid line indicates direct transmittal through intermediate offices.

Figure 4.5 Control Signaling through a Circuit-Switching Telephone Network.

Supervisory, address, and call information control signals are directly involved in the establishment and termination of a call. In contrast, **network management** signals are used for the maintenance, troubleshooting, and overall operation of the network. Such signals may be in the form of messages, such as a list of preplanned routes being sent to a station to update its routing tables. These signals cover a broad scope, and it is this category that will expand most with the increasing complexity of switched networks.

Location of Signaling

Control signaling needs to be considered in two contexts: (1) signaling between a subscriber and the network and (2) signaling within the network. Typically, signaling operates differently within these two contexts.

The signaling between a telephone or other subscriber device and the switching office to which it attaches is, to a large extent, determined by the characteristics of the subscriber device and the needs of the human user. Signals within the network are entirely computer-to-computer. The internal signaling is concerned not only with the management of subscriber calls but with the management of the network itself. Thus, for this internal signaling, a more complex repertoire of commands, responses, and set of parameters is needed.

Because two different signaling techniques are used, the local switching office to which the subscriber is attached must provide a mapping between the relatively less complex signaling technique used by the subscriber and the more complex technique used within the network. In Part Two, we will see a specific example of each technique as part of ISDN—namely, Q.931 for subscriber-to-network signaling and Signaling System Number 7 for internal network signaling.

Common-Channel Signaling

Traditional control signaling in circuit-switched networks has been on a per-trunk or inchannel basis. With **inchannel signaling**, the same channel is used to carry control signals as is used to carry the call to which the control signals relate. Such signaling begins at the originating subscriber and follows the same path as the call itself. This has the merit that no additional transmission facilities are needed for signaling; the facilities for voice transmission are shared with control signaling.

Two forms of inchannel signaling are in use: inband and out of band. **Inband signaling** uses not only the same physical path as the call it serves, it also uses the same frequency band as the voice signals that are carried. This form of signaling has several advantages. Because the control signals have the same electromagnetic properties as the voice signals, they can go anywhere that the voice signals go. Thus, there are no limits on the use of inband signaling anywhere in the network, including places where analog-to-digital or digital-to-analog conversion takes place. In addition, it is impossible to set up a call on a faulty speech path, because the control signals that are used to set up that path would have to follow the same path.

Out-of-band signaling takes advantage of the fact that voice signals do not use the full 4-kHz bandwidth allotted to them. A separate narrow signaling band within the 4 kHz is used to send control signals. The major advantage of this approach is that the control signals can be sent whether or not voice signals are on the line, thus allowing continuous supervision and control of a call. However, an out-of-band scheme needs extra electronics to handle the signaling band.

The information transfer rate is quite limited with inchannel signaling. With inband signals, the channel is only available for control signals when there are no voice signals on the circuit. With out-of-band signals, a very narrow bandwidth is available. With such limits, it is difficult to accommodate, in a timely fashion, any but the simplest form of control messages. However, to take advantage of the potential services and to cope with the increasing complexity of evolving network technology, a richer and more powerful control signal repertoire is needed.

A second drawback of inchannel signaling is the amount of delay from the time a subscriber enters an address (dials a number) to the time the connection is established. The requirement to reduce this delay is becoming more important as the network is used in new ways. For example, computer-controlled calls, such as with transaction processing, use relatively short messages; therefore, the call setup time represents an appreciable part of the total transaction time.

Both of these problems can be addressed with **common-channel signaling**, in which control signals are carried over paths completely independent of the voice channels (Table 4.2). One independent control signal path can carry the signals for a number of subscriber channels and hence is a common control channel for these subscriber channels.

The principle of common-channel signaling is illustrated and contrasted with inchannel signaling in Figure 4.6. As can be seen, the signal path for common-channel signaling is physically separate from the path for voice or other subscriber signals. The common channel can be configured with the bandwidth required to carry control signals for a rich variety of functions. Thus, both the signaling protocol and the network architecture to support that protocol are more complex than inchannel signaling. However, the continuing drop in computer hardware costs makes common-channel signaling increasingly attractive. The control signals are

Table 4.2 Signaling Techniques for Circuit-Switched Networks

	Description	Comment
Inchannel		
Inband	Transmits control signals in the same bank of frequencies used by the voice signals.	The simplest technique. It is necessary for call information signals and may be used for other control signals. Inband can be used over any type of subscriber line interface.
Out of band	Transmits control signals using the same facilities as the voice signal but a different part of the frequency band.	Unlike inband, out-of-band signaling provides continuous supervision for the duration of a connection.
Common Channel	Transmits control signals over signaling channels that are dedicated to control signals and are common to a number of voice channels.	Reduces call setup time compared with inchannel methods. It is also more adaptable to evolving functional needs.

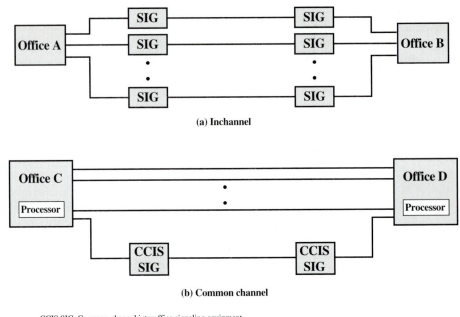

(a) Inchannel

(b) Common channel

CCIS SIG: Common-channel interoffice signaling equipment
SIG: Per-trunk signaling equipment

Figure 4.6 Inchannel and Common-Channel Signaling.

messages that are passed between switches and between a switch and the network management center. Thus, the control signaling portion of the network is, in effect, a distributed computer network carrying short messages.

Two modes of operation are used in common-channel signaling (Figure 4.7). In the **associated mode**, the common channel closely tracks along its entire length the interswitch trunk groups that are served between endpoints. The control signals are on different channels from the subscriber signals, and inside the switch, the control signals are routed directly to a control signal processor. A more complex, but more powerful, mode is the **disassociated mode**. With this mode, the network is augmented by additional nodes, known as signal transfer points. In effect, there are now two separate networks, with links between them so that the control portion of the network can exercise control over the switching nodes that are servicing the subscriber calls. Network management is more easily exerted in the disassociated mode because control channels can be assigned to tasks in a more flexible manner. The disassociated mode is used in ISDN.

With inchannel signaling, control signals from one switch are originated by a control processor and switched onto the outgoing channel. On the receiving end, the control signals must be switched from the voice channel into the control processor. With common-channel signaling, the control signals are transferred directly from one control processor to another, without being tied to a voice signal. This is a simpler procedure, and one that is less susceptible to accidental or intentional interference between subscriber and control signals. This is one of the main motivations for common-channel signaling. Another key motivation for common-channel signaling

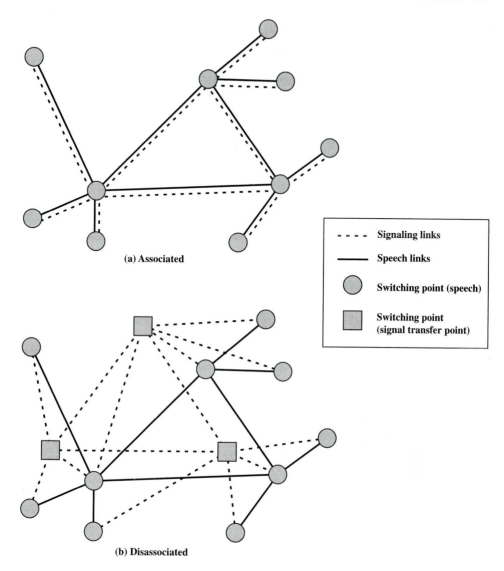

Figure 4.7 Common-Channel Signaling Modes [FREE96].

is that call setup time is reduced. Consider the sequence of events for call setup with inchannel signaling when more than one switch is involved. A control signal will be sent from one switch to the next in the intended path. At each switch, the control signal cannot be transferred through the switch to the next leg of the route until the associated circuit is established through that switch. With common-channel signaling, forwarding of control information can overlap the circuit-setup process.

With disassociated signaling, a further advantage emerges: One or more central control points can be established. All control information can be routed to a network control center where requests are processed and from which control signals are sent to switches that handle subscriber traffic. In this way, requests can be processed with a more global view of network conditions.

Of course, there are disadvantages to common-channel signaling. These primarily have to do with the complexity of the technique. However, the dropping cost of digital hardware and the increasingly digital nature of telecommunication networks make common-channel signaling the appropriate technology.

All of the discussion in this section has dealt with the use of common-channel signaling inside the network (that is, to control switches). Even in a network that is completely controlled by common-channel signaling, inchannel signaling is needed for at least some of the communication with the subscriber. For example, dial tone, ringback, and busy signals must be inchannel to reach the user. In general, the subscriber does not have access to the common-channel signaling portion of the network and does not employ the common-channel signaling protocol. However, we will see in Part Two that this statement is not true for ISDN.

4.5 PACKET SWITCHING

The long-haul circuit-switched telecommunications network was originally designed to handle voice traffic, and the majority of traffic on these networks continues to be voice. A key characteristic of circuit-switched networks is that resources within the network are dedicated to a particular call. For voice connections, the resulting circuit will enjoy a high percentage of utilization because, most of the time, one party or the other is talking. However, as the circuit-switched network began to be used increasingly for data connections, two shortcomings became apparent:

- In a typical data connection (e.g., client/server), much of the time the line is idle. Thus, with data connections, a circuit-switched approach is inefficient.
- In a circuit-switched network, the connection provides for transmission at constant data rate. Thus, both devices that are connected must transmit and receive at the same data rate. This limits the utility of the network in interconnecting a variety of host computers and terminals.

To understand how packet switching addresses these problems, let us briefly summarize packet-switching operation. Data are transmitted in short packets. A typical upper bound on packet length is 1000 octets (bytes). If a source has a longer message to send, the message is broken up into a series of packets (Figure 4.8). Each packet contains a portion (or all for a short message) of the user's data plus some control information. The control information, at a minimum, includes the information that the network requires to be able to route the packet through the network and deliver it to the intended destination. At each node en route, the packet is received, stored briefly, and passed on to the next node.

Let us return to Figure 4.1, but now consider that this is a simple packet-switched network. Suppose a packet is sent from station A to station E. The packet includes control information that indicates that the intended destination is E. The packet is sent from A to node 4. Node 4 stores the packet, determines the next leg

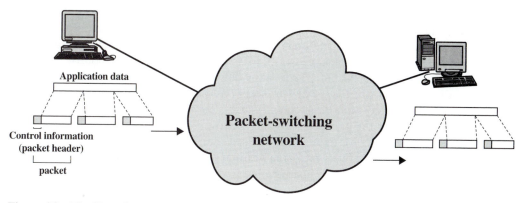

Figure 4.8 The Use of Packets.

of the route (say 5), and queues the packet to go out on that link (the 4–5 link). When the link is available, the packet is transmitted to node 5, which will forward the packet to node 6 and finally to E. This approach has a number of advantages over circuit switching:

- Line efficiency is greater, because a single node-to-node link can be dynamically shared by many packets over time. The packets are queued up and transmitted as rapidly as possible over the link. By contrast, with circuit switching, time on a node-to-node link is preallocated using synchronous time-division multiplexing. Much of the time, such a link may be idle because a portion of its time is dedicated to a connection that is idle.
- A packet-switched network can carry out data rate conversion. Two stations of different data rates can exchange packets, because each connects to its node at its proper data rate.
- When traffic becomes heavy on a circuit-switched network, some calls are blocked; that is, the network refuses to accept additional connection requests until the load on the network decreases. On a packet-switched network, packets are still accepted, but delivery delay increases.
- Priorities can be used. Thus, if a node has a number of packets queued for transmission, it can transmit the higher-priority packets first. These packets will therefore experience less delay than lower-priority packets.

Internal Operation

A station has a message to send through a packet-switched network that is of length greater than the maximum packet size. It therefore breaks the message up into packets and sends these packets, one at a time, to the network. A question arises as to how the network will handle this stream of packets as it attempts to route them through the network and deliver them to the intended destination. There are two approaches that are used in contemporary networks: datagram and virtual circuit.

In the **datagram** approach, each packet is treated independently, with no reference to packets that have gone before. Let us consider the implication of this approach. Suppose that station A in Figure 4.1 has a three-packet message to send to E. It transmits the packets, 1–2–3, to node 4. On each packet, node 4 must make a routing decision. Packet 1 arrives for delivery to E. Node 4 could plausibly forward this packet to either node 5 or node 7 as the next step in the route. In this case, node 4 determines that its queue of packets for node 5 is shorter than for node 7, and so it queues the packet for node 5. Ditto for packet 2. But for packet 3, node 4 finds that its queue for node 7 is now shorter and so queues packet 3 for that node. So the packets, each with the same destination address, do not all follow the same route. Because of this, it is just possible that packet 3 will beat packet 2 to node 6, and that the packets will be delivered to E in a different sequence from the one in which they were sent. It is up to E to figure out how to reorder them. Also, it is possible for a packet to be destroyed in the network. For example, if a packet-switched node crashes momentarily, all of its queued packets may be lost. If this were to happen to one of the packets in our example, node 6 has no way of knowing that one of the packets in the sequence of packets has been lost. Again, it is up to E to detect the loss of a packet and figure out how to recover it. In this technique, each packet, treated independently, is referred to as a datagram.

In the **virtual circuit** approach, a preplanned route is established before any packets are sent. For example, suppose that A has one or more messages to send to E. It first sends a special control packet, referred to as a Call Request packet, to 4, requesting a logical connection to E. Node 4 decides to route the request and all subsequent packets to 5, which decides to route the request and all subsequent packets to 6, which finally delivers the Call Request packet to E. If E is prepared to accept the connection, it sends a Call Accept packet to 6. This packet is passed back through nodes 5 and 4 to A. Stations A and E may now exchange data over the route that has been established. Because the route is fixed for the duration of the logical connection, it is somewhat similar to a circuit in a circuit-switching network and is referred to as a virtual circuit. Each packet now contains a virtual circuit identifier as well as data. Each node on the preestablished route knows where to direct such packets; no routing decisions are required. Thus, every data packet from A intended for E traverses nodes 4, 5, and 6; every data packet from E intended for A traverses nodes, 6, 5, and 4. Eventually, one of the stations terminates the connection with a Clear Request packet. At any time, each station can have more than one virtual circuit to any other station and can have virtual circuits to more than one station.

So the main characteristic of the virtual circuit technique is that a route between stations is set up prior to data transfer. But this route is not a dedicated path, as in circuit switching. A packet is still buffered at each node and queued for output over a line. In contrast to the datagram approach, with virtual circuits, the node need not make a routing decision for each packet. It is made only once for all packets using that virtual circuit.

For two stations that exchange data over an extended period of time, there are certain advantages to virtual circuits. First, the network may provide services related to the virtual circuit, including sequencing and error control. Sequencing refers to the fact that, because all packets follow the same route, they arrive in the original order. Error control is a service that assures not only that packets arrive in proper sequence, but that all packets arrive correctly. For example, if a packet in a sequence from node 4 to node 6 fails to arrive at node 6, or arrives with an error, node 6 can request a retransmission of that packet from node 4. Another advantage is that packets should transit the network more rapidly with a virtual circuit; it is not necessary to make a routing decision for each packet at each node.

One advantage of the datagram approach is that the call-setup phase is avoided. Thus, if a station wishes to send only one or a few packets, datagram delivery will be quicker. Another advantage of the datagram service is that, because it is more primitive, it is more flexible. For example, if congestion develops in one part of the network, incoming datagrams can be routed away from the congestion. With the use of virtual circuits, packets follow a predefined route, and thus it is more difficult for the network to adapt to congestion. A third advantage is that datagram delivery is inherently more reliable. With the use of virtual circuits, if a node fails, all virtual circuits that pass through that node are lost. With datagram delivery, if a node fails, subsequent packets may find an alternate route that bypasses that node.

Most currently available packet-switched networks make use of virtual circuits for their internal operation. To some degree, this reflects a historical motivation to provide a network that presents a service as reliable (in terms of sequencing) as a circuit-switched network. There are, however, several providers of private packet-switched networks that make use of datagram operation. From the user's point of view, there should be very little difference in the external behavior based on the use of datagrams or virtual circuits.

Packet Size

There is a significant relationship between packet size and transmission time, as shown in Figure 4.9. In this example, it is assumed that there is a virtual circuit from station X through nodes a and b to station Y. The message to be sent comprises 40 octets, and each packet contains 3 octets of control information, which is placed at the beginning of each packet and is referred to as a header. If the entire message is sent as a single packet of 43 octets (3 octets of header plus 40 octets of data), then the packet is first transmitted from station X to node a (Figure 4.9a). When the entire packet is received, it can then be transmitted from a to b. When the entire packet is received at node b, it is then transferred to station Y. Ignoring switching time, total transmission time is 129 octet-times (43 octets × 3 packet transmissions).

Suppose now that we break the message up into two packets, each containing 20 octets of the message and, of course, 3 octets each of header, or control, information. In this case, node a can begin transmitting the first packet as soon as it has arrived from X, without waiting for the second packet. Because of this overlap in transmission, the total transmission time drops to 92 octet-times. By breaking the message up into five packets, each intermediate node can begin transmission even sooner and the savings in time is greater, with a total of 77 octet-times for transmission. However, this process of using more and smaller packets eventually results in increased, rather than reduced, delay, as illustrated in Figure 4.9d. This is because each packet contains a fixed amount of header, and more packets mean more of these headers. Furthermore, the example does not show the processing and queuing delays at each node. These delays are also greater when more packets are handled for a single message. Thus, packet-switched network designers must consider these factors in attempting to find an optimum packet size.

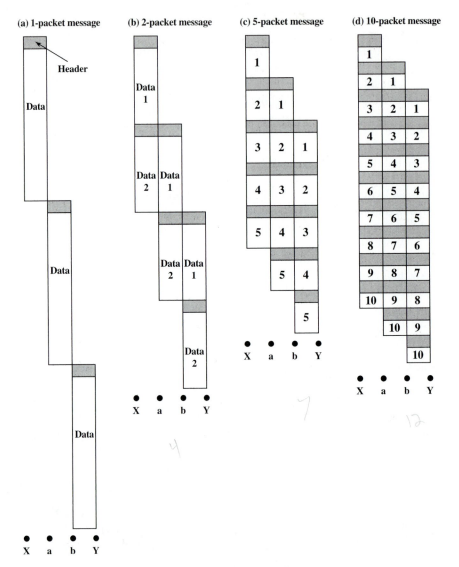

Figure 4.9 Effect of Packet Size on Transmission Time.

4.6 X.25

Perhaps the best-known and most widely used protocol standard is X.25. The standard specifies an interface between a host system and a packet-switched network. This standard is almost universally used for interfacing to packet-switched networks and is employed for packet switching in ISDN. The standard calls out three levels of protocols:

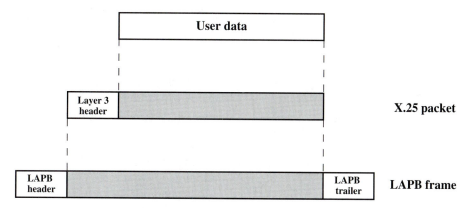

Figure 4.10 User Data and X.25 Protocol Control Information.

- Physical level
- Link level
- Packet level

These three levels correspond to the lowest three layers of the OSI model (see Appendix B). The physical level deals with the physical interface between an attached station (computer, terminal) and the link that attaches that station to the packet-switching node. It makes use of the physical-level specification in a standard known as X.21, but in many cases other standards, such as EIA-232, are substituted. The link level provides for the reliable transfer of data across the physical link, by transmitting the data as a sequence of frames. The link-level standard is referred to as LAPB (Link Access Protocol-Balanced). LAPB is a subset of a well-known data link control protocol, HDLC (high-level data link control). LAPB is very similar to the more recent LAPD, which is described in Chapter 8. The packet level provides a virtual circuit service and is described briefly in this section.

Figure 4.10 illustrates the relationship between the levels of X.25. User data are passed down to X.25 level 3, which appends control information as a header, creating a packet. The entire X.25 packet is then passed down to the LAPB entity, which appends control information at the front and back of the packet, forming a LAPB frame. Again, the control information in the frame is needed for the operation of the LAPB protocol.

Before examining the details of the packet level of X.25, it would be well to distinguish the concepts of internal operation and external service.

Internal Operation and External Service

One of the most important characteristics of a packet-switched network is whether it uses datagrams or virtual circuits. Actually, there are two dimensions of this characteristic, as illustrated in Figures 4.11 and 4.12. At the interface between a station and a network node, a network may provide either a connection-oriented or connectionless service. With a connection-oriented service, a station performs a call request to set up a logical connection to another station. All packets presented to the network are identified as belonging to a particular logical connection and are numbered sequentially. The network undertakes to deliver packets in sequence-number order. The logical connection is usually referred to as a virtual circuit, and the connection-oriented service is referred to as an **external virtual circuit service**; unfortunately, this external service is distinct from the concept of **internal virtual circuit operation**. With connectionless service, the network only agrees to handle packets independently and may not deliver them in order or reliably. This type of service is sometimes known as an **external datagram service**; again, this is a distinct concept from that of **internal datagram operation**. Internally, the network may actually construct a fixed route between endpoints (virtual circuit) or not (datagram). These internal and external design decisions need not coincide:

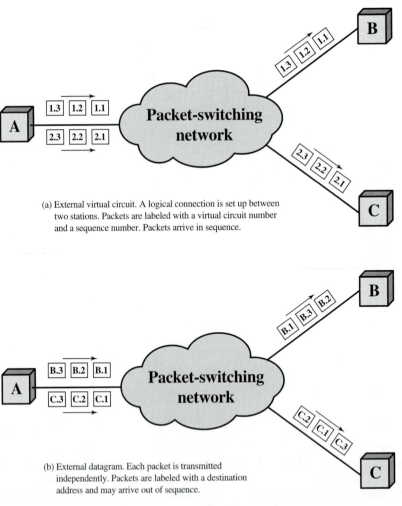

(a) External virtual circuit. A logical connection is set up between
two stations. Packets are labeled with a virtual circuit number
and a sequence number. Packets arrive in sequence.

(b) External datagram. Each packet is transmitted
independently. Packets are labeled with a destination
address and may arrive out of sequence.

Figure 4.11 External Virtual Circuit and Datagram Operation.

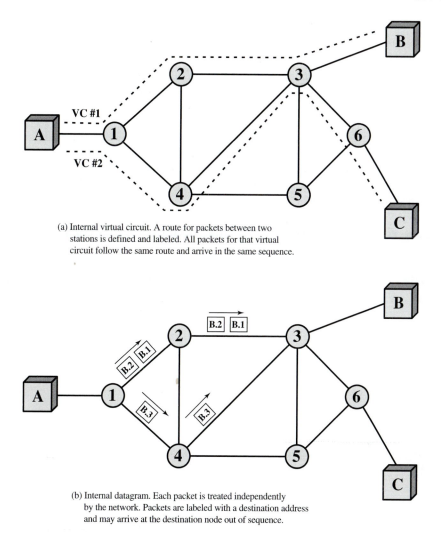

(a) Internal virtual circuit. A route for packets between two
    stations is defined and labeled. All packets for that virtual
    circuit follow the same route and arrive in the same sequence.

(b) Internal datagram. Each packet is treated independently
    by the network. Packets are labeled with a destination address
    and may arrive at the destination node out of sequence.

Figure 4.12   Internal Virtual Circuit and Datagram Operation.

- **External virtual circuit, internal virtual circuit:** When the user requests a virtual circuit, a dedicated route through the network is constructed. All packets follow that same route.
- **External virtual circuit, internal datagram:** The network handles each packet separately. Thus, different packets for the same external virtual circuit may take different routes. However, the network buffers packets at the destination node, if necessary, so that they are delivered to the destination station in the proper order.
- **External datagram, internal datagram:** Each packet is treated independently from both user's and the network's point of view.

- **External datagram, internal virtual circuit:** This combination makes little sense, because one incurs the cost of a virtual circuit implementation but gets none of the benefits.

The question arises as to the choice of virtual circuits or datagrams, both internally and externally. This will depend on the specific design objectives for the communication network and the cost factors that prevail. We have already made some comments concerning the relative merits of internal datagram versus virtual circuit operation. With respect to external service, we can make the following observations. The datagram service, coupled with internal datagram operation, allows for efficient use of the network; no call setup and no need to hold up packets while a packet in error is retransmitted. This latter feature is desirable in some real-time applications. The virtual circuit service can provide end-to-end sequencing and error control. This service is attractive for supporting connection-oriented applications, such as file transfer and remote terminal access. In practice, the virtual circuit service is much more common than the datagram service and will remain so for ISDN-related packet-switched networks. The reliability and convenience of a connection-oriented service is seen as more attractive than the benefits of the datagram service.

X.25 Packet Level

With the X.25 packet level, data are transmitted in packets over external virtual circuits. A variety of packet types is used (Table 4.3), all using the same basic format, with variations (Figure 4.13). The standard refers to user machines as data terminal equipment (DTE) and to a packet-switching node to which a DTE is attached as data circuit-terminating equipment (DCE).

The virtual circuit service of X.25 provides for two types of virtual circuit: virtual call and permanent virtual circuit. A **virtual call** is a dynamically established virtual circuit using a call setup and call-clearing procedure, explained subsequently. A **permanent virtual circuit** is a permanent, network-assigned virtual circuit. Data transfer occurs as with virtual calls, but no call setup or clearing is required.

Virtual Calls

Figure 4.14 shows a typical sequence of events in a virtual call. The left-hand part of the figure shows the packets exchanged between user machine A and the packet-switching node to which it attaches; the right-hand part shows the packets exchanged between user machine B and its node. The routing of packets inside the network is not visible to the user.

The sequence of events is as follows:

1. A requests a virtual circuit to B by sending a Call Request packet to A's DCE. The packet includes the source and destination addresses, as well as the virtual circuit number to be used for this new virtual circuit. Future incoming and outgoing transfers will be identified by this virtual circuit number.
2. The network routes this call request to B's DCE.

3. B's DCE receives the call request and sends an Incoming Call packet to B. This packet has the same format as the Call Request packet but a different virtual circuit number, selected by B's DCE from the set of locally unused numbers.

4. B indicates acceptance of the call by sending a Call Accepted packet specifying the same virtual circuit number as that of the Incoming Call packet.

5. A receives a Call Connected packet with the same virtual circuit number as that of the Call Request packet.

6. A and B send data and control packets to each other using their respective virtual circuit numbers.

Table 4.3 X.25 Packet Types and Parameters

Packet Type		Service		Parameters
From DTE to DCE	**From DCE to DTE**	**VC**	**PVC**	
Call Setup and Clearing				
Call Request	Incoming Call	X		Calling DTE address, called DTE address, facilities, call user data
Call Accepted	Call Connected	X		Calling DTE address, called DTE address, facilities, call user data
Clear Request	Clear Indication	X		Clearing cause, diagnostic code, calling DTE address, called DTE address, facilities, clear user data
Clear Confirmation	Clear Confirmation	X		Calling DTE address, called DTE address, facilities
Data and Interrupt				
Data	Data	X	X	—
Interrupt	Interrupt	X	X	Interrupt user data
Interrupt Confirmation	Interrupt Confirmation	X	X	—
Flow Control and Reset				
RR	RR	X	X	P(R)
RNR	RNR	X	X	P(R)
REJ		X	X	P(R)
Reset Request	Reset Indication	X	X	Resetting cause, diagnostic code
Reset Confirmation	Reset Confirmation	X	X	—
Restart				
Restart Request	Restart Indication	X	X	Restarting cause, diagnostic code
Restart Confirmation	Restart Confirmation	X	X	—
Diagnostic				
	Diagnostic	X	X	Diagnostic code, diagnostic explanation

(a) Data packet with 3-bit sequence numbers

Q	D	0	1	Group number
Channel number				
P(R)		M	P(S)	0
User data				

(b) Control packet for virtual calls with 3-bit sequence numbers

X	0	0	1	Group number
Channel number				
Packet type				1
Additional information				

(c) RR, RNR, and REJ packets with 3-bit sequence numbers

0	0	0	1	Group number
Channel number				
P(R)		Packet type		1

(d) Data packet with 7-bit sequence numbers

Q	D	1	0	Group number
Channel number				
P(S)				0
P(R)				M
User data				

(e) Control packet for virtual calls with 7-bit sequence numbers

X	0	1	0	Group number
Channel number				
Packet type				1
Additional information				

(f) RR, RNR, and REJ packets with 7-bit sequence numbers

0	0	1	0	Group number
Channel number				
Packet type				1
P(R)				0

(g) Data packet with 15-bit sequence numbers

0	0	1	0	0	0	0	Group number
Q	D	1	1	Group number			
Channel number							
P(S) —low order								0
P(S) —high order							
P(R) —low order								M
P(R) —high order							
User data							

(h) Control packet for virtual calls with 15-bit sequence numbers

0	0	1	1	0	0	0	Group number
X	0	1	1	Group number			
Channel number							
Packet type								1
Additional information							

(i) RR, RNR, and REJ packets with 15-bit sequence numbers

0	0	1	1	0	0	0	Group number
X	0	1	1	Group number			
Channel number							
Packet type								1
P(R) —low order								0
P(R) —high order							

Figure 4.13 X.25 Packet Formats.

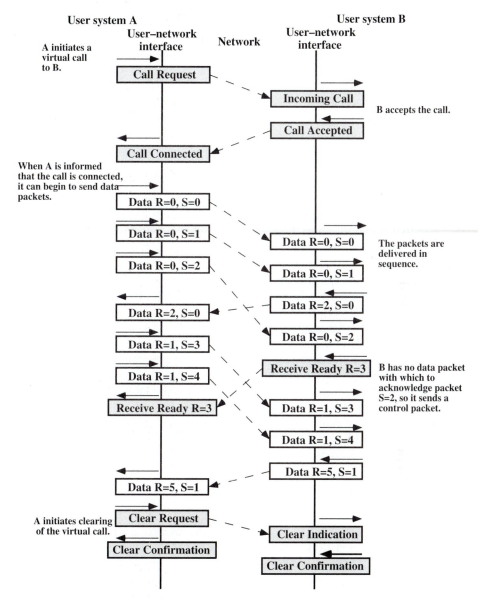

Figure 4.14 Sequence of Events: X.25 Protocol.

7. A (or B) sends a Clear Request packet to terminate the virtual circuit and receives a Clear Confirmation packet.

8. B (or A) receives a Clear Indication packet and transmits a Clear Confirmation packet.

We now turn to some of the details of the standard.

Packet Format

Figure 4.13 shows the basic packet formats used in X.25. For user data, the data are broken up into blocks of some maximum size, and a 24-bit or 32-bit header is appended to each block to form a data packet. For virtual circuits that use 15-bit sequence numbers, the header begins with a protocol identifier octet with the value 00110000. The header includes a 12-bit virtual circuit number (expressed as a 4-bit group number and an 8-bit channel number). The P(S) and P(R) fields support the functions of flow control and error control on a virtual circuit basis, as explained subsequently. The M, D, Q, and X bits support specialized functions, which will not be explored here (see [STAL97]).

In addition to transmitting user data, X.25 must transmit control information related to the establishment, maintenance, and termination of virtual circuits. Control information is transmitted in a control packet. Each control packet includes the virtual circuit number; the packet type, which identifies the particular control function; and additional control information related to that function. For example, a Call Request packet includes the calling and called address fields and a facilities field, used to request specific network services.

The way in which user data are encapsulated is as follows. The transmitting DTE must break its data up into units of some maximum length. X.25 specifies that the network must support a maximum user field length of at least 128 octets (i.e., the user data field may be some number of bits up to the maximum). In addition, the network may allow selection of some other maximum field length in the range 16 to 4096 octets. The DTE constructs control packets and encapsulates user data in data packets. These are then transmitted to the DCE via LAPB. Thus, the packet is encapsulated in a layer 2 frame (one packet per frame). The DCE strips off the layer 2 control fields and may encapsulate the packet according to some internal network protocol. The reader unfamiliar with the concept of encapsulation should consult Appendix B.

Multiplexing

Perhaps the most important service provided by X.25 is multiplexing. A DTE is allowed to establish up to 4095 simultaneous virtual circuits with other DTEs over a single physical DTE–DCE link. The DTE can internally assign these circuits in any way it pleases. Individual virtual circuits could correspond to applications, processes, or terminals, for example. The DTE–DCE link provides full-duplex multiplexing. That is, at any time, a packet associated with a given virtual circuit can be transmitted in either direction.

To sort out which packets belong to which virtual circuits, each packet contains a 12-bit virtual circuit number (expressed as a 4-bit logical group number plus an 8-bit logical channel number). Number zero is always reserved for diagnostic packets common to all virtual circuits. Then contiguous ranges of numbers are allocated for four categories of virtual circuits. Permanent virtual circuits are assigned numbers beginning with 1. The next category is one-way incoming virtual calls. This means that only incoming calls from the network can be assigned these numbers; the virtual circuit, however, is two way (full duplex). When a call request comes in, the DCE selects an unused number from this category.

One-way outgoing calls are those initiated by the DTE. In this case, the DTE selects an unused number from among those allocated for these calls. This separation of categories is intended to avoid the simultaneous selection of the same number for two different virtual circuits by the DTE and DCE.

Flow and Error Control

Flow control and error control in X.25 are implemented using sequence numbers. The flow control is the sliding-window mechanism, and error control is the go-back-N automatic-repeat-request (ARQ) mechanism. The basic operation of these mechanisms is explained in Appendix A. As a default, 3-bit sequence numbers are used. Optionally, a DTE may request, during call setup, the use of 7-bit or 15-bit sequence numbers.

The send sequence number, P(S), is used to number data packets uniquely on a virtual circuit basis; that is, the P(S) of each new outgoing data packet is one more than that of the preceding packet on the same virtual circuit, modulo 8 or modulo 128. The receive sequence number, P(R), contains the number of the next packet expected from the other side of a virtual circuit. When used in a data packet, this is known as piggybacked acknowledgment. If one side has no data to send, it may acknowledge incoming packets with the Receive Ready (RR) control packet, which contains the number of the next packet expected from the other side.

Flow control is provided by means of the Receive Not Ready (RNR) control packet; this packet acknowledges receipt of previous packets but indicates that the issuer is unable to receive additional packets. When such an indication is received, all transmission of data packets must cease; the busy side will notify the other side that it can resume transmission by means of an RR packet.

The basic form of error control is go-back-N ARQ (see Appendix A). Negative acknowledgment is in the form of a Reject (REJ) control packet. If a node receives a negative acknowledgment, it will retransmit the specified packet and all subsequent packets.

Reset and Restart

X.25 provides two facilities for recovering from errors. The reset facility is used to reinitialize a virtual circuit. This means that the sequence numbers on both ends are set to zero. Any data or interrupt packets in transit are lost. It is up to a higher-level protocol to recover from the loss of packets. A reset can be triggered by a number of error conditions, including loss of a packet, sequence number error, congestion, or loss of the network's internal virtual circuit. In this latter case, the two DCEs must rebuild the internal virtual circuit to support the still-existing X.25 DTE–DTE external virtual circuit. Either a DTE or DCE can initiate a reset, with a Reset Request or Reset Indication. The recipient responds with a Reset Confirmation. Regardless of who initiates the reset, the DCE involved is responsible for informing the other end.

A more serious error condition calls for a restart. The issuance of a Restart Request packet is equivalent to sending a Clear Request on all virtual calls and a Reset Request on all permanent virtual circuits. Again, either a DTE or DCE may initiate the action. An example of a condition warranting restart is temporary loss of access to the network.

4.7 COMPARISON OF CIRCUIT AND PACKET SWITCHING

A simple comparison of circuit switching and the two forms of packet switching is provided in Figure 4.15. The figure depicts the transmission of a message across four nodes, from a source station attached to node 1 to a destination station attached to node 4. In this figure, we are concerned with three types of delay:

- **Propagation delay.** The time it takes a signal to propagate from one node to the next. This time is generally negligible. The speed of electromagnetic signals through a wire medium, for example, is typically 2×10^8 m/s.
- **Transmission time.** The time it takes for a transmitter to send out a block of data. For example, it takes 1 s to transmit a 10,000-bit block of data onto a 10-kbps line.
- **Node delay.** The time it takes for a node to perform the necessary processing as it switches data.

For circuit switching, there is a certain amount of delay before the message can be sent. First, a Call Request signal is sent through the network, to set up a con-

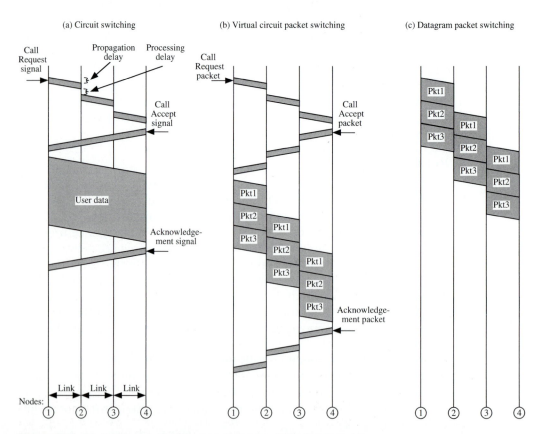

Figure 4.15 Event Timing for Circuit Switching and Packet Switching.

nection to the destination. If the destination station is not busy, a Call Accepted signal returns. Note that a processing delay is incurred at each node during the call request; this time is spent at each node setting up the route of the connection. On the return, this processing is not needed because the connection is already set up. After the connection is set up, the message is sent as a single block, with no noticeable delay at the switching nodes.

Virtual circuit packet switching appears quite similar to circuit switching. A virtual circuit is requested using a Call Request Packet, which incurs a delay at each node. The virtual circuit is accepted with a Call Accept packet. In contrast to the circuit-switching case, the call acceptance also experiences node delays, even though the virtual circuit route is now established. The reason is that this packet is queued at each node and must wait its turn for retransmission. Once the virtual circuit is established, the message is transmitted in packets. It should be clear that this phase of the operation can be no faster than circuit switching, for comparable networks. This is because circuit switching is an essentially transparent process, providing a constant data rate across the network. Packet switching involves some delay at each node in the path. Worse, this delay is variable and will increase with increased load.

Datagram packet switching does not require a call setup. Thus, for short messages, it will be faster than virtual circuit packet switching and perhaps circuit switching. However, because each individual datagram is routed independently, the processing for each datagram at each node may be longer than for virtual circuit packets. Thus, for long messages, the virtual circuit technique may be superior.

Figure 4.15 is intended only to suggest what the relative performance of the techniques might be; however, actual performance depends on a host of factors, including the size of the network, its topology, the pattern of load, and the characteristics of typical exchanges.

4.8 OTHER SWITCHING TECHNIQUES

Multirate Circuit Switching

One of the drawbacks of circuit switching is its inflexibility with respect to data rate. If a station attaches to an ordinary circuit-switching network, it is committed to operating at a particular data rate. This data rate must be used regardless of the application, whether it is digitized voice, or some data application. Thus, an application with a low data rate requirement would make inefficient use of the network link.

To overcome this inflexibility, an enhanced service, known as multirate circuit switching, was developed. This technique combines circuit switching with multiplexing. The basic concept is this: The station attaches to the network by means of a single physical link. That link is used to carry multiple fixed data rate channels between the station and a network node. The traffic on each channel can be switched independently through the network to various destinations.

For this technique, it is possible to develop a scheme in which all of the available channels operate at the same data rate, or a scheme that uses various data rates. For example, ISDN defines a variety of station–network interfaces, all of which employ multirate circuit switching. The simplest ISDN interface consists of two 64-kbps channels and one 16-kbps channel.

While this technique is more flexible than simple circuit switching, the same fundamental limitation exists. The user now has the choice of a number of data rates, but each data rate remains fixed and the likelihood of inefficient use of a particular channel remains.

Frame Relay

Packet switching was developed at a time when digital long-distance transmission facilities exhibited a relatively high error rate compared to today's facilities. As a result, there is a considerable amount of overhead built into packet-switching schemes to compensate for errors. The overhead includes additional bits added to each packet to enhance redundancy and additional processing at the end stations and the intermediate network nodes to detect and recover from errors.

With modern, high-speed telecommunications systems, this overhead is unnecessary and counterproductive. It is unnecessary because the rate of errors has been dramatically lowered and any remaining errors can easily be caught by logic in the end systems that operates above the level of the packet-switching logic. It is counterproductive because the overhead involved soaks up a significant fraction of the high capacity provided by the network.

To take advantage of the high data rates and low error rates of contemporary networking facilities, frame relay was developed. Whereas the original packet-switching networks were designed with a data rate to the end user of about 64 kbps, frame relay networks are designed to operate at user data rates of up to 2 Mbps. The key to achieving these high data rates is to strip out most of the overhead involved with error control.

Cell Relay

Cell relay, also known as asynchronous transfer mode (ATM), is in a sense a culmination of all of the developments in circuit switching and packet switching over the past 20 years. One useful way to view cell relay is as an evolution from frame relay. The most obvious difference between cell relay and frame relay is that frame relay uses variable-length packets and cell relay uses fixed-length packets, called cells. As with frame relay, cell relay provides minimum overhead for error control, depending on the inherent reliability of the transmission system and on higher layers of logic to catch and correct remaining errors. By using a fixed packet length, the processing overhead is reduced even further for cell relay compared to frame relay. The result is that cell relay is designed to work in the range of 10s and 100s of Mbps, compared to the 2 Mbps of frame relay.

Another way to view cell relay is as an evolution from multirate circuit switching. With multirate circuit switching, only fixed data rate channels are available to the end system. Cell relay allows the definition of virtual channels with data rates that are dynamically defined at the time that the virtual channel is created. By using small, fixed-size cells, cell relay is so efficient that it can offer a constant data rate channel even though it is using a packet-switching technique. Thus, cell relay extends multirate circuit switching to allow multiple channels, with the data rate of each channel dynamically set on demand.

4.9 SUMMARY

Circuit switching was designed to provide an efficient and high-quality facility for voice traffic. Key distinguishing features of circuit switching are that a circuit, once established, is transparent to the subscribers (equivalent to a direct connection) and that the delay across the circuit is nonvariable and small.

Several important aspects of circuit-switched networks have changed dramatically in the wake of the increasing complexity and digitalization of public telecommunications networks. Simple hierarchical routing schemes have been replaced with more flexible and powerful nonhierarchical schemes. This reflects a corresponding change in the underlying architecture, which leads to increased efficiency and resilience. Simple inchannel control signaling methods have been replaced with more complex and higher-speed common-channel signaling.

Packet switching was designed to provide a more efficient facility than circuit switching for bursty data traffic. A key distinguishing element of packet-switched networks is whether the internal operation is datagram or virtual circuit.

4.10 RECOMMENDED READING

As befits its age, circuit switching has inspired a voluminous literature. Two good books on the subject are [BELL91] and [FREE96]. The literature on packet switching is also enormous. Books with good treatments include [SPOH97], [BERT92], and [SPRA91].

All of the topics in this chapter are covered in greater detail in [STAL97].

BELL91   Bellamy, J. *Digital Telephony.* New York: Wiley, 1991.

BERT92   Bertsekas, D., and Gallager, R. *Data Networks.* Englewood Cliffs, NJ: Prentice Hall, 1992.

FREE96   Freeman, R. *Telecommunication System Engineering.* New York: Wiley, 1996.

SPOH97   Spohn, D. *Data Network Design.* New York: McGraw-Hill, 1997.

SPRA91   Spragins, J.; Hammond, J.; and Pawlikowski, K. *Telecommunications Protocols and Design.* Reading, MA.: Addison-Wesley, 1991.

STAL97   Stallings, W. *Data and Computer Communications, 5th edition.* Upper Saddle River, NJ: Prentice Hall, 1997.

4.11 PROBLEMS

4.1 Consider a simple telephone network consisting of two end offices and one intermediate switch with a 1-MHz full-duplex trunk between each end office and the intermediate switch. The average telephone is used to make four calls per eight-hour workday, with a mean call duration of six minutes. Ten percent of the calls are long distance. What is the maximum number of telephones an end office can support?

4.2 Explain the flaw in the following reasoning: Packet switching requires control and address bits to be added to each packet. This introduces considerable overhead in packet switching. In circuit switching, a transparent circuit is established. No extra bits are needed.

       a. Therefore, there is no overhead in circuit switching.

       b. Because there is no overhead in circuit switching, line utilization must be more efficient than in packet switching.

4.3 Assuming no malfunction in any of the stations or nodes of a network, is it possible for a packet to be delivered to the wrong destination?

4.4 Define the following parameters for a switching network:

N = number of hops between two given end systems
L = message length in bits
B = data rate, in bits per second (bps), on all links
P = fixed packet size, in bits
H = overhead (header) bits per packet
S = call setup time (circuit switching or virtual circuit) in seconds
D = propagation delay per hop in seconds

       a. For $N = 4$, $L = 3200$, $B = 9600$, $P = 1024$, $H = 16$, $S = 0.2$, $D = 0.001$, compute the end-to-end delay for circuit switching, virtual circuit packet switching, and datagram packet switching. Assume that there are no acknowledgments.

       b. Derive general expressions for the three techniques of part (a), taken two at a time (three expressions in all), showing the conditions under which the delays are equal.

4.5 What value of P, as a function of N, L, and H, results in minimum end-to-end delay on a datagram network? Assume that L is much larger than P, and D is zero.

4.6 Flow-control mechanisms are used at both levels 2 and 3 of X.25. Are both necessary or is this redundant? Explain.

4.7 There is no error-detection mechanism (frame-check sequence) in X.25. Isn't this needed to assure that all of the packets are delivered properly?

4.8 When an X.25 DTE and the DCE to which it attaches both decide to put a call through at the same time, a call collision occurs and the incoming call is canceled. When both sides try to clear the same virtual circuit simultaneously, the clear collision is resolved without canceling either request; the virtual circuit in question is cleared. Do you think that simultaneous resets are handled like call collisions or clear collisions? Why?

4.9 In X.25, why is the virtual circuit number used by one station of two communicating stations different from the virtual circuit number used by the other station? After all, it is the same full-duplex virtual circuit.

X.25 defines The interface between DTE and DCE not The neTwork.

PART TWO

Integrated Services Digital Networks

In Part One of this book, we looked at the underlying technology that supports the ISDN: that is, the technology of integrated digital networks (IDN). We are now in a position to turn to the ISDN itself. We begin, in Chapter 5, with an overview that provides a general description of the architecture of ISDN and looks at the standards that define ISDN.

Chapter 6 begins our detailed examination of ISDN architecture and protocols. The chapter includes a consideration of the multiplexed transmission structure, the possible configurations of ISDN at the user–network interface, the protocol architecture, and issues relating to addressing and interworking.

The next three chapters look at the protocols at the user–network interface for ISDN. Chapter 7 deals with the physical layer. After a review of line coding techniques, the two principal physical interfaces, basic and primary, are explored. The chapter also looks at details of the subscriber loop needed to support ISDN. Chapter 8 deals with the data link layer. The most important protocol at this level is LAPD. Chapter 9 deals with the network layer. The concern here is call control, which is provided by Q.931.

Chapter 10 examines the services to be provided by ISDN. These services, in effect, are the requirements that ISDN must satisfy.

Part Two closes with a discussion of Signaling System Number 7 (SS7) in Chapter 11. This system is an elaborate set of recommendations that define protocols for the internal management of an ISDN.

CHAPTER 5

ISDN OVERVIEW

W e begin this chapter with a look at the way in which public telephone and telecommunications networks have evolved to form integrated digital networks (IDNs). The IDN sets the stage for the development of the integrated services digital network (ISDN). Then we provide a general overview of ISDN. The next section of the chapter examines the standards that define the ISDN.

5.1 THE INTEGRATED DIGITAL NETWORK

Public telephone and telecommunications networks are rapidly evolving to the exclusive use of digital technology. The ways in which these networks employ digital technology are listed in Table 5.1. The movement toward digital technology has been pushed by the competitive desire to lower costs and improve the quality of voice transmission and networking services. As the use of distributed processing and data communications has grown, this evolution of an all-digital network has been pulled by the need to provide a framework for ISDN.

The evolution of the existing telecommunications networks and specialized carrier facilities to integrated digital networks is based on two technological developments: digital switching and digital transmission. The technology of digital transmission was discussed in Chapters 2 and 3. Both digital switching and digital transmission are, of course, well established. The first T-carrier system was introduced into commercial service by AT&T in 1962, and the first large-scale time-division digital switch, the Western Electric 4ESS, was introduced in 1976. More important than the benefits of either of these two technologies, however, was the revolutionary idea that the functions of transmission and switching could be integrated to form an integrated digital network (IDN). The idea was proposed as early as 1959 [VAUG59] and is in the process of being implemented worldwide.

Table 5.1 Use of Digital Technology in Public Telecommunications Networks

Switching
The circuit-switching nodes of the network make use of digital time-division switching techniques rather than analog space-division switching techniques.

Trunk (carrier) transmission
Digital transmission technology is used on the multiplexed trunks between switches, although either analog or digital signaling may be used. Each trunk carries multiple voice and/or data channels using synchronous time-division multiplexing.

Subscriber loop
Digital transmission technology may also be used between the subscriber and the switch to which the subscriber attaches over the "subscriber loop." This implies that digitized voice is employed and that full-duplex digital transmission over the subscriber loop is used.

Control signaling
Common-channel signaling over a packet-switched network embedded into the public telecommunications network is used. Packets contain messages used for routing, monitoring, and control.

To understand the implications of an IDN, consider Figure 5.1. Traditionally, the transmission and switching systems of an analog telephone network have been designed and administered by functionally separate organizations. The two systems are referred to by the operating telephone companies as outside plant and inside plant, respectively. In an analog network, incoming voice lines are modulated and multiplexed at the end office and sent out over a frequency-division multiplexed (FDM) line. Then the constituent signals may pass through one or more intermediate switching centers before reaching the destination end office. At each switching center, the incoming FDM carrier has to be demultiplexed and demodulated by an *FDM channel bank* before being switched by a space-division switch (Figure 5.1a). After switching, the signals have to be multiplexed and modulated again to be transmitted. This repeated process results in an accumulation of noise as well as cost.

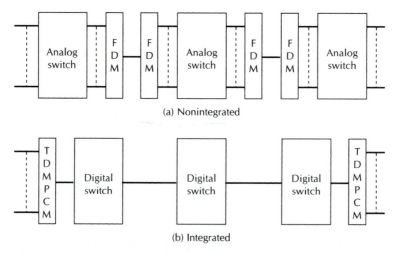

(a) Nonintegrated

(b) Integrated

Figure 5.1 The Integration of Transmission and Switching.

When both the transmission and switching systems are digital, integration as in Figure 5.1b can be achieved. Incoming voice signals are digitized using pulse-code modulation (PCM) and multiplexed using time-division multiplexing (TDM). Time-division digital switches along the way can switch the individual signals without decoding them. Furthermore, separate multiplex/demultiplex channel banks are not needed at the intermediate offices, because that function is incorporated into the switching system.

Figure 5.2 gives a simple example that suggests the architectures that are involved in the two approaches. Consider an intermediate switch in a circuit-switched network that has six voice channels (labeled A, B, C, D, E, F) of data coming in on one trunk (Figure 5.2a). Based on the calls that are currently established, three of the channels are to be switched out on one trunk (A, B, E) and three channels on another trunk (C, D, F). All three trunks link to other switches and are multiplexed to carry multiple channels of data. In the case of a digital system

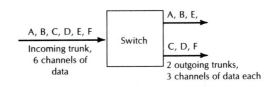

(a) General block diagram

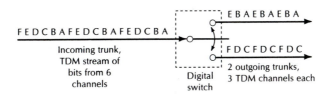

(b) Digital time-division switch

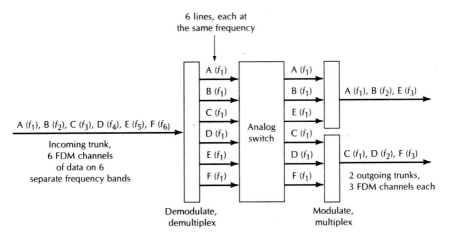

(c) Frequency-division switch

Figure 5.2   Example of Digital versus Analog Switching.

(Figure 5.2b), the voice signals are digitized and transmitted as a stream of bits. On a multiplexed trunk, bits from various voice signals are interleaved using time-division multiplexing (TDM). Thus, the incoming trunk has bits from six different voice channels interleaved in time. Inside the digital switch, each bit stream is routed and switched to the appropriate output line.

The architecture for the equivalent analog system is considerably more complex. Each voice signal occupies a frequency band of about 4 kHz. The incoming trunk requires a bandwidth of at least 24 kHz, and each voice signal occupies one channel centered on a unique frequency (f_1 for channel A, f_2 for channel B, etc.). These channels must be fed into a space-division analog switch. However, such a switch is only capable of switching signals from a collection of input lines to a collection of output lines. For general operation, any input line must be connectable to any output line; therefore, all inputs and outputs must be at the same frequency. Thus, the frequency-division multiplexed (FDM) input must be demultiplexed and each signal must be returned to the base voice frequency (f_1) to provide input to the switch. The switch routes the incoming data to the appropriate output lines, with each output line dedicated to a particular output trunk. For each trunk, the associated lines must pass through a modulator/multiplexer to produce an FDM signal for transmission over the outgoing trunk.

The conversion of telecommunications networks to digital transmission and digital switching is well under way. Much less well developed is the extension of digital service to the end user. Telephones are still sending analog voice signals to the end office, where they must be digitized. Lower-speed (< 56 kbps) end-user digital service is commonly available via leased lines at present, and higher-speed leased services are widely available to business customers.The provision of switched digital services over subscriber lines will eventually lead to an end-to-end switched digital telecommunications network.

The evolution from analog to digital has been driven primarily by the need to provide economic voice communications. The resulting network is also well suited to meet the growing variety of digital data service needs. Thus, the IDN will combine the coverage of the geographically extensive telephone network with the data-carrying capacity of digital data networks in a structure called the integrated services digital network (ISDN). In this latter context, the "integrated" of ISDN refers to the simultaneous carrying of digitized voice and a variety of data traffic on the same digital transmission links and by the same digital exchanges. The key to ISDN is the small marginal cost for offering data services on the digital telephone network, with no cost or performance penalty for voice services already carried on the IDN.

5.2 A CONCEPTUAL VIEW OF ISDN

ISDN is a massive undertaking in many ways, and it is difficult to provide a concise description of it. To begin to understand ISDN, we look in this section at the concept of ISDN from several different viewpoints:

- Principles of ISDN
- Evolution of the ISDN

- The user interface
- Objectives
- Benefits
- Services
- Architecture

Principles of ISDN

Standards for ISDN have been defined by ITU-T, a topic that we explore later in this chapter. Table 5.2, which is the complete text of one of the ISDN-related standards, states the principles of ISDN from the point of view of ITU-T. Let us look at each of these points in turn.

1. **Support of voice and nonvoice applications using a limited set of standardized facilities.** This principle defines both the purpose of ISDN and the means of achieving it. The ISDN will support a variety of services related to voice communications (telephone calls) and nonvoice communications (digital data exchange). These services are to be provided in conformance with standards (ITU-T recommendations) that specify a small number of interfaces and data transmission facilities. The benefit of standards will be explored later in this chapter. For now, we simply state that without such a limitation, a global interconnected ISDN is virtually impossible.

2. **Support for switched and nonswitched applications.** ISDN will support both circuit switching and packet switching. As we discussed in Part One, there is a place for both technologies. In addition, ISDN will support nonswitched services in the form of dedicated lines.

3. **Reliance on 64-kbps connections.** ISDN is intended to provide circuit-switched and packet-switched connections at 64 kbps. This is the fundamental building block of ISDN. This rate was chosen because, at the time, it was the standard rate for digitized voice and hence was being introduced into the evolving IDNs. Although this data rate is useful, it is unfortunately restrictive to rely solely on it. Future developments in ISDN will permit greater flexibility.

4. **Intelligence in the network.** An ISDN is expected to be able to provide sophisticated services beyond the simple setup of a circuit-switched call. In addition, network management and maintenance capabilities need to be more sophisticated than in the past. All of this is to be achieved by the use of Signaling System Number 7 and by the use of intelligent switching nodes in the network.

5. **Layered protocol architecture.** The protocols being developed for user access to ISDN exhibit a layered architecture and can be mapped into the OSI model. This has a number of advantages:
   - Standards already developed for OSI-related applications may be used on ISDN. An example is X.25 level 3 for access to packet-switching services in ISDN.
   - New ISDN-related standards can be based on existing standards, reducing the cost of new implementations. An example is LAPD, which is based on LAPB.

Table 5.2 ITU-T Recommendation I.120 (1993)

---

1 Principles of ISDN

1.1 The main feature of the ISDN concept is the support of a wide range of voice and non-voice applications in the same network. A key element of service integration for an ISDN is the provision of a range of services using a limited set of connection types and multipurpose user-network interface arrangements.

1.2 ISDNs support a variety of applications including both switched and non-switched connections. Switched connections in an ISDN include both circuit-switched and packet-switched connections and their concatenations.

1.3 As far as practicable, new services introduced into an ISDN should be arranged to be compatible with 64 kbit/s switched digital connections.

1.4 An ISDN will contain intelligence for the purpose of providing service features, maintenance and network management functions. This intelligence may not be sufficient for some new services and may have to be supplemented by either additional intelligence within the network, or possibly compatible intelligence in the user terminals.

1.5 A layered protocol structure should be used for the specification of the access to an ISDN. Access from a user to ISDN resources may vary depending upon the service required and upon the status of implementation of national ISDNs.

1.6 It is recognized that ISDNs may be implemented in a variety of configurations according to specific national situations.

2 Evolution of ISDNs

2.1 ISDNs will be based on the concepts for telephone IDNs and may evolve by progressively incorporating additional functions and network features, including those of any other dedicated networks such as circuit-switching and packet-switching for data so as to provide for existing and new services.

2.2 The transition from an existing network to a comprehensive ISDN may require a period of time extending over one or more decades. During this period arrangements must be developed for the networking of services on ISDNs and services on other networks.

2.3 In the evolution towards an ISDN, digital end-to-end connectivity will be obtained via plant and equipment used in existing networks, such as digital transmission; time-division multiplex switching and/or space-division multiplex switching. Existing relevant recommendations for these constituent elements of an ISDN are contained in the appropriate series of recommendations of CCITT and of CCIR.

2.4 In the early stages of the evolution of ISDNs, some interim user-network arrangements may need to be adopted in certain countries to facilitate early penetration of digital service capabilities. Arrangements corresponding to national variants may comply partly or wholly with I-Series Recommendations. However, the intention is that they not be specifically included in the I-Series.

2.5 An evolving ISDN may also include at later stages switched connections at bit rates higher and lower than 64 kbit/s.

◻ Standards can be developed and implemented independently for various layers and for various functions within a layer. This allows for the gradual implementation of ISDN services at a pace appropriate for a given provider or a given customer base.

6. **Variety of configurations.** More than one physical configuration is possible for implementing ISDN. This allows for differences in national policy (single-source versus competition), in the state of technology, and in the needs and existing equipment of the customer base.

Evolution of ISDN

As we discussed in Section 5.1, ISDN evolves from and with the integrated digital network (IDN). The evolution of the IDN has been driven by the need to provide economic voice communications. The resulting network, however, is also well suited to meet the growing variety of digital data service needs. Whereas the "I" in IDN refers to the integration of digital transmission and switching facilities, the "I" in ISDN refers to the integration of a variety of voice and data transmission services.

The second part of Table 5.2 gives the ITU-T view of the way in which ISDN will evolve. Let us look at each of these points in turn.

- **Evolution from telephone IDNs.** The intent is that the ISDN evolve from the existing telephone networks. Two conclusions can be drawn from this point. First, the IDN technology developed for and evolving within existing telephone networks forms the foundation for the services to be provided by ISDN. Second, although other facilities, such as third-party (not the telephone provider) packet-switched networks and satellite links, will play a role in ISDN, the telephone networks will have the dominant role. Although packet switching and satellite providers may be less than happy with this interpretation, the overwhelming prevalence of telephone networks dictates that these networks form the basis for ISDN.

- **Transition of one or more decades.** The evolution to ISDN will be a slow process. This is true of any migration of a complex application or set of applications from one technical base to a newer one. The introduction of ISDN services will be done in the context of existing digital facilities and existing services. There will be a period of coexistence in which connections and perhaps protocol conversion will be needed between alternative facilities and/or services.

- **Use of existing networks.** This point is simply an elaboration of point 2. For example, ISDN will provide a packet-switched service. For the time being, the interface to that service will be X.25. With the introduction of fast packet switching and more sophisticated virtual call control, there may need to be a new interface in the future.

- **Interim user–network arrangements.** Primarily, the concern here is that the lack of digital subscriber lines might delay introduction of digital services, particularly in developing countries. With the use of modems and other equipment, existing analog facilities can support at least some ISDN services.

- **Connections at other than 64 kbps.** The 64-kbps data rate was chosen as the basic channel for circuit switching. With improvements in voice digitizing technology, this rate is unnecessarily high. On the other hand, this rate is too low for many digital data applications. Thus, other data rates will be needed.

The details of the evolution of ISDN facilities and services will vary from one nation to another, and indeed from one provider to another in the same country. These points simply provide a general description, from ITU-T's point of view, of the process.

The User Interface

Figure 5.3 is a conceptual view of the ISDN from a user or customer point of view. The user has access to the ISDN by means of a local interface to a digital "pipe" of a certain bit rate. Pipes of various sizes will be available to satisfy differing needs. For example, a residential customer may require only sufficient capacity to handle a telephone and a personal computer. An office will typically wish to connect to the ISDN via an on-premise digital PBX or LAN and will require a much higher-capacity pipe.

That more than one size of pipe will be needed is emphasized in Figure 5.4, taken from Recommendation I.410. At the low end of demand would be a single terminal (e.g., a residential telephone) or multiple terminals in some sort of multi-drop arrangement (e.g., a residential telephone, personal computer, and alarm system). Offices are more likely to contain a network of devices attached to a LAN or PBX, with an attachment from that network acting as a gateway to the ISDN.

At any given point in time, the pipe to the user's premises has a fixed capacity, but the traffic on the pipe may be a variable mix up to the capacity limit. Thus, a user may access circuit-switched and packet-switched services, as well as other services, in a dynamic mix of signal types and bit rates. The ISDN will require rather complex control signals to instruct it how to sort out the time-multiplexed data and provide the required services. These control signals will also be multiplexed onto the same digital pipe.

An important aspect of the interface is that the user may, at any time, employ less than the maximum capacity of the pipe and will be charged according to the capacity used rather than "connect time." This characteristic significantly diminishes the value of current user design efforts that are geared to optimize circuit utilization by use of concentrators, multiplexers, packet switches, and other line-sharing arrangements.

Objectives

Activities currently under way are leading to the development of a worldwide ISDN. This effort involves national governments, data processing and communication companies, standards organizations, and others. Certain common objectives are, by and large, shared by this disparate group. The key objectives are as follows:

1. Standardization
2. Transparency
3. Separation of competitive functions
4. Leased and switched services
5. Cost-related tariffs
6. Smooth migration
7. Multiplexed support

Standardization is essential to the success of ISDN. Standards will provide for universal access to the network. ISDN-standard equipment can be moved from one location to another, indeed from one country to another, and be plugged into the network. The cost of such equipment will be minimized because of the competition

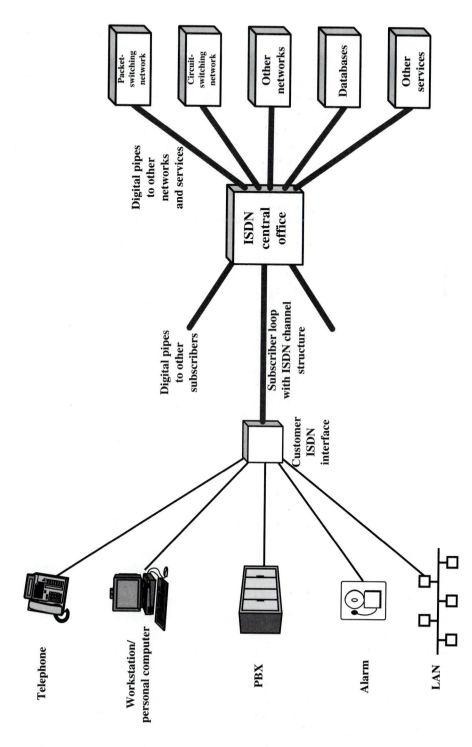

Figure 5.3 Conceptual View of ISDN Connection Features.

105

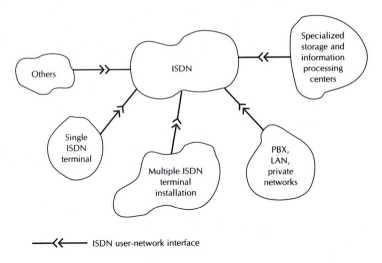

Figure 5.4   ISDN User–Network Interface Examples.

among many vendors to provide the same type of functionality. In addition, the use
of a layered protocol architecture and standardized interfaces allows users to select
equipment from multiple suppliers and allows changes to be made to a configuration in a gradual, piece-by-piece fashion.

It is also important that the digital transmission service have the property of
transparency; that is, the service is independent of, and does not affect, the content
of the user data to be transmitted. This permits users to develop applications and
protocols with the confidence that they will not be affected by the underlying ISDN.
Once a circuit or virtual circuit is set up, the user should be able to send information without the provider being aware of the type of information being carried. In
addition, user-provided encryption techniques can be employed to provide security
of user information.

The ISDN must be defined in a way that does not preclude the **separation of
competitive functions** from the basic digital transmission services. It must be possible to separate out functions that could be provided competitively as opposed to
those that are fundamentally part of the ISDN. In many countries, a single, govern-
ment-owned entity will provide all services. Some countries desire (in the case of
the United States, require) that certain enhanced services be offered competitively
(e.g., videotex, electronic mail).

The ISDN should provide both **leased** and **switched services**. This will give the
user the greatest range of options in configuring network services and allow the user
to optimize on the basis of cost and performance.

The price for ISDN service should be related to cost and independent of the
type of data being carried. Such a **cost-related tariff** will assure that one type of service is not in the position of subsidizing others. Price distinctions should be related
to the cost of providing specific performance and functional characteristics of a
service. In this way, distortions are avoided and providers can be driven by customer
need rather than some artificial tariff structure.

Because of the large installed base of telecommunications equipment in the
networks, and because of customer equipment with interfaces designed for those

networks, the conversion to ISDN will be gradual. Thus, for an extended period of time, the evolving ISDN must coexist with existing equipment and services. To provide for a **smooth migration** to ISDN, ISDN interfaces should evolve from existing interfaces, and interworking arrangements must be designed. Specific capabilities that will be needed include adapter equipment that allows pre-ISDN terminal equipment to interface to ISDN, internetwork protocols that allow data to be routed through a mixed ISDN/non-ISDN network complex, and protocol converters to allow interoperation of ISDN services and similar non-ISDN services.

In addition to providing low-capacity support to individual users, **multiplexed support** must be provided to accommodate user-owned PBX and local area network (LAN) equipment.

There are, of course, other objectives that could be named. Those just listed are certainly among the most important and widely accepted, and they help to define the character of the ISDN.

Benefits

The principal benefits of ISDN to the customer can be expressed in terms of cost savings and flexibility. The integration of voice and a variety of data on a single transport system means that the **user** does not have to buy multiple services to meet multiple needs. The efficiencies and economies of scale of an integrated network allow these services to be offered at lower cost than if they were provided separately. Further, the user needs to bear the expense of just a single access line to these multiple services. The requirements of various users can differ greatly in a number of ways: for example, in information volume, traffic pattern, response time, and interface types. The ISDN will allow the user to tailor the service purchased to actual needs to a degree not possible at present. In addition, customers enjoy the advantages of competition among equipment vendors. These advantages include product diversity, low price, and wide availability of services. Interface standards permit selection of terminal equipment and transport and other services from a range of competitors without changes in equipment or use of special adapters. Finally, because the offerings to the customer are based on the ISDN recommendations, which of necessity are slow to change, the risk of obsolescence is reduced.

Network providers, on a larger scale but in a similar way, profit from the advantages of competition, including the areas of digital switches and digital transmission equipment. Also, standards support universality and a larger potential market for services. Interface standards permit flexibility in selection of suppliers, consistent control signaling procedures, and technical innovation and evolution within the network without customer involvement.

Manufacturers can focus research and development on technical applications and be assured that a broad potential demand exists. In particular, the cost of developing VLSI implementations is justified by the potential market. Specialized niches in the market create opportunities for competitive, smaller manufacturers. Significant economies of scale can be realized by manufacturers of all sizes. Interface standards assure that the manufacturer's equipment will be compatible with the equipment across the interface.

Finally, **enhanced service providers** of, for instance, information-retrieval or transaction-based services, will benefit from simplified user access. End users will not be required to buy special arrangements or terminal devices to gain access to particular services.

Of course, any technical innovation comes with penalties as well as benefits. The main penalty here is the cost of migration. This cost, however, must be seen in the context of evolving customer needs. There will be changes in the telecommunications offerings available to customers, with or without ISDN. It is hoped that the ISDN framework will at least control the cost and reduce the confusion of migration. Another potential penalty of ISDN is that it will retard technical innovation. The process of adopting a standard is a long and complex one. The result is that by the time a standard is adopted and products are available, more advanced technical solutions have appeared. This is always a problem with standards. By and large, the benefits of standards outweigh the fact that they are always at least a little way behind the state of the art.

Services

The ISDN will provide a variety of services, supporting existing voice and data applications as well as providing for applications now being developed. Some of the most important applications are as follows:

- **Facsimile:** Service for the transmission and reproduction of graphics and handwritten and printed material. This type of service has been available for many years but has suffered from a lack of standardization and the limitations of the analog telephone network. Digital facsimile standards are now available and can be used to transmit a page of data at 64 kbps in 5 seconds.
- **Teletex:** Service that enables subscriber terminals to exchange correspondence. Communicating terminals are used to prepare, edit, transmit, and print messages. Transmission is at a rate of one page in 2 seconds at 9.6 kbps.
- **Videotex:** An interactive information retrieval service. A page of data can be transmitted in 1 second at 9.6 kbps.

These services fall into the broad categories of voice, digital data, text, and image. Most of these services can be provided with a transmission capacity of 64 kbps or less. This rate, as we have mentioned, is the standard rate offered to the user. Some services require considerably higher data rates and may be provided by high-speed facilities outside the ISDN (e.g., cable TV distribution plants) or in future enhancements to ISDN (see Part Four on broadband ISDN).

One of the key aspects of the ISDN will be that it is an "intelligent network." By use of a flexible signaling protocol, the ISDN will provide a variety of network facilities for each service.

Architecture

Figure 5.5 is an architectural depiction of ISDN. The ISDN will support a completely new physical connecter for users, a digital subscriber line, and a variety of transmission services.

The common physical interface provides a standardized means of attaching to the network. The same interface should be usable for telephone, personal computer,

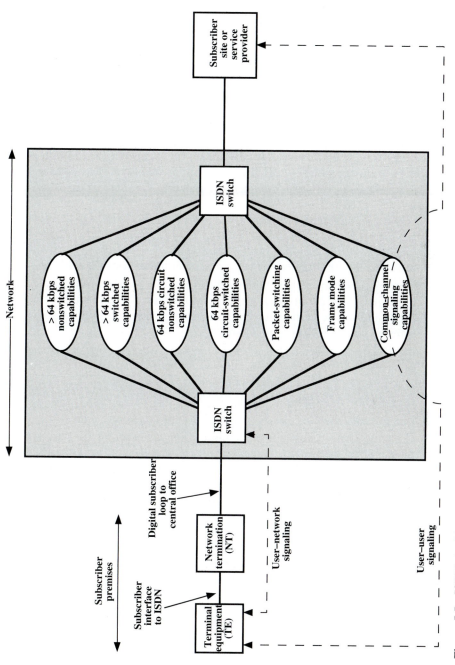

Figure 5.5 ISDN Architecture.

and videotex terminal. Protocols are required to define the exchange of control information between user device and the network. Provision must be made for high-speed interfaces to, for example, a digital PBX or a LAN. The interface supports a *basic* service consisting of three time-multiplexed channels, two at 64 kbps and one at 16 kbps. In addition, there is a *primary* service that provides multiple 64-kbps channels.

For both basic and primary service, an interface is defined between the customer's equipment, referred to generically as terminal equipment (TE), and a device on the customer's premises, known as a network termination (NT). The NT forms the boundary between the customer and the network.

The subscriber line is the physical signal path from the subscriber's NT to the ISDN central office. This line must support full-duplex digital transmission for both basic and primary data rates. Initially, much of the subscriber line plant will be twisted pair. As networks evolve and grow, optical fiber will be increasingly used.

The ISDN central office connects the numerous subscriber lines to the digital network. This provides access to a variety of lower-layer (OSI layers 1–3) transmission facilities, including the following:

- **Circuit-switched capabilities:** Operating at 64 kbps, this is the same facility provided by other digital-switched telecommunications networks.
- **Nonswitched capabilities:** One such facility offers a 64-kbps dedicated link. A nonswitched capability at a higher data rate is to be provided by broadband ISDN and will be in the nature of a permanent virtual circuit for asynchronous transfer mode (ATM) transmission.
- **Switched capabilities:** This refers to high-speed (> 64 kbps) switched connections using ATM as part of broadband ISDN.
- **Packet-switched capabilities:** This facility resembles packet-switched service provided by other data networks.
- **Frame-mode capabilities:** A service that supports frame relay.
- **Common-channel signaling capabilities:** These capabilities are used to control the network and provide call management. Internal to the network, Signaling System Number 7 (SS7) is used. The capability also includes user-to-network control dialogue. The use of control signaling for user-to-user dialogue is a subject for further study within ITU-T.

These lower-layer functions can be implemented with the ISDN. In some countries with a competitive climate, some of these lower-layer functions (e.g., packet switching) may be provided by separate networks that may be reached by a subscriber through ISDN.

5.3 ISDN STANDARDS

Although a number of standards organizations are involved in various aspects of ISDN, the controlling body is the ITU-T. In this section, we first look at the rationale for standards and then examine the ISDN-related standards from ITU-T. Appendix 5A of this chapter looks at ITU-T itself.

The Importance of Standards

It has long been accepted in the telecommunications industry that standards are required to govern the physical, electrical, and procedural characteristics of communication equipment. With the increasingly digital character of telecommunication networks, and with the increasing prevalence of digital transmission and processing services, the scope of what should be standardized has broadened. As we shall see, the functions, interfaces, and services embodied in ISDN that are subject to standardization cover an extremely broad range.

Although there is no widely accepted and quoted definition of the term *standard,* the following definition from the 1979 National Policy on Standards for the United States encompasses the essential concept [NSPA79]:

> A prescribed set of rules, conditions, or requirements concerning definition of terms; classification of components; specification of materials, performance, or operation; delineation of procedures; or measurement of quantity and quality in describing materials, product, systems, services, or practices.

[CERN84] lists the following advantages of standards:

- Increased productivity and efficiency in industry because of larger-scale, lower-cost production
- Increased competition by allowing smaller firms to market products, readily acceptable by the consumer, without the need for a massive advertising budget
- Dissemination of information and the transfer of technology
- Expansion of international trade because of the feasibility of exchange of products among countries
- Conservation of resources
- Increased opportunity for worldwide exchange of information, both voice and data

In the case of ISDN, because of the complexity of ISDN, and because its success depends on the capability of providing true interconnectivity and interoperability, standards are not only advantageous but essential in the introduction of such a network.

Historical Background

The development of ISDN is governed by a set of recommendations issued by ITU-T, called the I-series of recommendations. These recommendations, or standards, were first issued in 1984. A more complete set has since been issued.

It is enlightening to look at the history of ITU-T/CCITT's interest in ISDN. In 1968, CCITT established Special Study Group D (forerunner of today's Study Group XVIII, which has ISDN responsibility within CCITT) to look at a variety of issues related to the use of digital technology in the telephone network. At each plenary assembly, the study group was given assignments for the next four-year study period. The first and principal question assigned over this period is shown in Table 5.3. The titles of the first question reflect the evolution of CCITT interest. The focus shifts from digital technology, to integrated digital networks (IDNs), to ISDN.

Table 5.3 Question 1 As Assigned to Special Study Group D (1969–1976) and to Study Group XVIII (1977–1992)

Study Period	Title of Question 1
1969–1972	Planning of digital systems
1973–1976	Planning of digital systems and integration of services
1977–1980	Overall aspects of an ISDN
1981–1984	General network aspects of an ISDN
1985–1988	General question on ISDN
1989–1992	General aspects of ISDN

In 1968, Study Group D was set up to study all questions related to the standardization of transmission of pulse-code modulated (PCM) voice and to coordinate work going on in other groups relating to digital networking. Even at this early stage, there was a vision of an ISDN. Recommendation G.702, issued in 1972, contained the following definition of an integrated services digital network:

> An integrated digital network in which the same digital switches and digital paths are used to establish connections for different services, for example, telephony, data.

At this point, there was no information on the type of network that could integrate digital switches and paths, or how the network could integrate various services. Nevertheless, it was a recognition of the path that could be followed with digital technology.

During the next study period (1973–1976), there were continuing advances in digital transmission technology. In addition, digital switching equipment began to emerge from the laboratory. Thus, the construction of integrated digital networks became a real possibility. Accordingly, the 1976 set of recommendations included specifications dealing with digital switching as well as the specification of a new signaling system (Number 7) designed for use in the forthcoming digital networks. The first question for this period also specifically deals with the integration of services.

In planning for the 1977–1980 study period, CCITT recognized that the evolution toward a digital network was under way and was more important than the standardization of individual digital systems and equipment. Thus, the focus was on the integration aspects of the digital network and on the integration of services on an IDN. Two key developments that emerged during this study period were the following:

- The integration of services is based on providing a standardized user–network interface that allows the user to request various services through a uniform set of protocols.
- ISDN will evolve from the digital telephone network.

At the end of this period, the first ISDN standard emerged, entitled Integrated Services Digital Network (ISDN), G.705 (Table 5.4). No other standards on ISDN were issued in 1980; at this point, only the general concept of an ISDN had been developed.

Table 5.4   CCITT Recommendation G.705 (1980)

INTEGRATED SERVICES DIGITAL NETWORKS (ISDN)

The CCITT

considering

(a)   the measure of agreement that has so far been reached in the studies of Integrated Digital Networks (IDNs) dedicated to specific services such as telephony, data and also of an Integrated Services Digital Network (ISDN),
(b)   the need for a common basis for the future studies necessary for the evolution towards an ISDN

recommends
   that the ISDN should be based on the following conceptual principles:

(1)   The ISDN will be based on and evolve from the telephony IDN by progressively incorporating additional functions and network features including those of any other dedicated networks so as to provide for existing and new services.
(2)   New services introduced into the ISDN should be arranged to be compatible with 64-kbit/s switched digital connections.
(3)   The transition from the existing networks to a comprehensive ISDN may require a period of time extending over one or two decades.
(4)   During the transition period arrangements must be developed for the interworking of services on ISDNs and services on other networks.
(5)   The ISDN will contain intelligence for the purpose of providing service features, maintenance and network management functions. This intelligence may not be sufficient for some new services and may have to be supplemented by either additional intelligence within the network, or possibly compatible intelligence in the customer terminals.
(6)   A layered functional set of protocols appear desirable for the various access arrangements to the ISDN. Access from the customer to ISDN resources may vary depending upon the service required and on the status of evolution of national ISDNs.

As the next period began (1981–1984), ISDN was declared the major concern of CCITT for the upcoming study period. A set of recommendations, called the I-series, was published at the end of this period. This initial set of specifications was incomplete and, in some cases, internally inconsistent. Nevertheless, the specification of ISDN by 1984 was sufficient for manufacturers and service providers to begin to develop ISDN-related equipment and to demonstrate ISDN-related services and networking configurations. The 1984 series included this definition of ISDN, retained in the 1988 documents:

> An ISDN is a network, in general evolving from a telephony IDN, that provides end-to-end digital connectivity to support a wide range of services, including voice and non-voice services, to which users have access by a limited set of standard multi-purpose user-network interfaces.

Work on the I-series and related recommendations continued in the 1985–1988 period. At the beginning of this period, CCITT was significantly restructured to give a number of its study groups a part of future ISDN work. The dominant function of CCITT became the study of ISDN matters. The 1988 version of the I-series recommendations was sufficiently detailed to make preliminary ISDN implementations possible in the late 1980s.

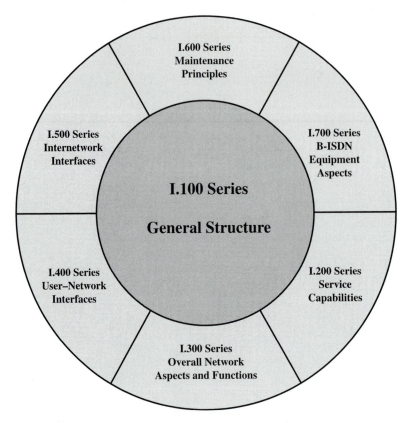

Figure 5.6   Structure of the I-Series Recommendations.

The I-Series Recommendations

The bulk of the description of ISDN is contained in the I-series of recommendations,[1] with some related topics covered in other recommendations. The characterization of ISDN contained in these recommendations is centered on three main areas:

1. The standardization of services offered to users, so as to enable services to be internationally compatible
2. The standardization of user–network interfaces, so as to enable terminal equipment to be portable, and to assist in (1)
3. The standardization of ISDN capabilities to the degree necessary to allow user–network and network–network interworking, and thus to achieve (1) and (2)

The current I-series recommendations related to ISDN (not including B-ISDN) are listed in Appendix 5B. Figure 5.6 illustrates the relationship among the various

---

[1]Some recommendations have two designations. For example, I.450 is also designated as Q.930.

I-series standards. The 1984 set contained recommendations in series I.100 through I.400. Some updates and expansions occurred in these series in the 1985–1988 study period. The I.500 and I.600 series were left for further study in 1984, a preliminary set of specifications was ready for 1988, and additional work has been done since then.

I.100 Series—General Structure

The I.100 series serves as a general introduction to ISDN. The general structure of the ISDN recommendations is presented as well as a glossary of terms. I.120, reproduced as Table 5.2, provides an overall description of ISDN and the expected evolution of ISDNs. Recommendation I.130 introduces terminology and concepts that are used in the I.200 series to specify services.

This chapter has covered much of what is in the I.100 series.

I.200 Series—Service Capabilities

The I.200 series is, in a sense, the most important part of the ISDN recommendations. Here, the services to be provided to users are specified. We may look on this as a set of requirements that the ISDN must satisfy. In the ISDN glossary (I.112), the term *service* is defined as follows:

> That which is offered by an Administration or RPOA to its customers to satisfy a specific telecommunication requirement.

Although this is a very general definition, the term *service* has come to have a very specific meaning in ITU-T, a meaning that is somewhat different from the use of that term in an OSI context. For ITU-T, a standardized service is characterized by [CERN84]

- Complete, guaranteed end-to-end comparability
- ITU-T-standardized terminals, including procedures
- Listing of the service subscribers in an international directory
- ITU-T-standardized testing and maintenance procedures
- Charging and accounting rules

There are three simple ITU-T services: telegraphy, telephony, and data. There are four newer ITU-T *telematic services*: teletex, facsimile, videotex, and message handling. The goal with all of these services is to ensure high-quality international telecommunications for the end user, regardless of the make of the terminal equipment and the type of network used nationally to support the service.

The I.200 series classifies services into lower-level bearer services and higher-level teleservices. For each service, various attributes are defined, constituting a "laundry list" that is configured by agreement between the subscriber and the provider. Chapter 10 is devoted to the topic of ISDN services.

I.300 Series—Overall Network Aspects and Functions

Whereas the I.200 series focuses on the user, in terms of the services provided to the user, the I.300 series focuses on the network, in terms of how the network goes about providing those services. A protocol reference model is presented that, while based on the seven-layer OSI model, attempts to account for the complexity of a connection that may involve two or more users (e.g., a conference call) plus a related common-channel signaling dialogue. Issues such as numbering and addressing are addressed. There is also a discussion of ISDN connection types.

Chapter 6 includes a discussion of ISDN network aspects.

I.400 Series—User–Network Interfaces

The I.400 series deals with the interface between the user and the network. Three major topics are addressed:

- **Physical configurations:** The issue of how ISDN functions are configured into equipment. The standards specify functional groupings and define reference points between those groupings.
- **Transmission rates:** The data rates and combinations of data rates to be offered to the user.
- **Protocol specifications:** The protocols at OSI layers 1 through 3 that specify the user–network interaction.

The first two of these topics are covered in Chapter 6. Chapters 7 through 9 deal with ISDN protocols.

I.500 Series—Internetwork Interfaces

ISDN supports services that are also provided on older circuit-switched and packet-switched networks. Thus, it is necessary to provide interworking between an ISDN and other types of networks to allow communications between terminals belonging to equivalent services offered through different networks. The I.500 series deals with the various network issues that arise in attempting to define interfaces between ISDN and other types of networks. Chapter 6 includes a discussion of I.500 issues.

I.600 Series—Maintenance Principles

This series provides guidance for maintenance of the ISDN subscriber installation, the network portion of the ISDN basic access, primary access, and higher-data-rate services. Maintenance principles and functions are related to the reference configuration and general architecture of ISDN. A key function that is identified in the series is loopback. In general, loopback testing is used for failure localization and verification.

I.700 Series—B-ISDN Equipment Aspects

This series was first introduced in 1996. It covers functional and characteristics of ATM equipment and various management aspects. Chapter 16 includes a discussion of ATM equipment functionality.

5.4 RECOMMENDED READING

A number of books on ISDN have been published in recent years. Perhaps the most useful for technical description are [KESS97] and [BLAC97].

BLAC97 Black, U. *ISDN and SS7: Architectures for Digital Signaling Networks.* Upper Saddle River, NJ: Prentice Hall, 1997.

KESS97 Kessler, G. *ISDN: Concepts, Facilities, and Services.* New York: McGraw-Hill, 1997.

Recommended Web sites are as follows:

- **ISDN Information Center:** Provided by Open Communication Networks, Inc. Good source of a variety of ISDN-related information.
- **Dan Kegel's ISDN Page:** Information on ISDN tariffs, standards status, and links to vendors.
- **International Telecommunication Union:** Home page of ITU.
- **American National Standards Institute:** Home page of ANSI.

5.5 PROBLEMS

5.1 Is an IDN necessary for an ISDN? Sufficient? Explain.

5.2 Elaborate on the statement in Section 5.1 that ISDN is virtually impossible without a limitation on the number of different user–ISDN interfaces and data transmission facilities.

5.3 It was mentioned in Section 5.1 that user-implemented multidrop lines and multiplexers may disappear. Explain why.

5.4 Compare recommendation G.705 (Table 5.4) of 1980 with I.120 (Table 5.2). What do the differences reveal about the evolution of CCITT/ITU thinking with respect to ISDN?

APPENDIX 5A ITU TELECOMMUNICATION STANDARDIZATION SECTOR

The ITU Telecommunications Standardization Sector (ITU-T) is a permanent organ of the International Telecommunication Union (ITU), which is itself a United Nations specialized agency. Hence the members of ITU-T are governments. The U.S. representation is housed in the Department of State. The charter of the ITU is that it "is responsible for studying technical, operating, and tariff questions and issuing Recommendations on them with a view to standardizing telecommunications on a worldwide basis." Its primary objective is to standardize, to the extent necessary, techniques and operations in telecommunications to achieve end-to-end compatibility of international telecommunication connections, regardless of the countries of origin and destination.

The ITU-T was created as of March 1, 1993, as one consequence of a reform process within the ITU. It replaces the International Telegraph and Telephone Consultative Committee (CCITT), which had essentially the same charter and objectives as the new ITU-T.

ITU-T is organized into 15 study groups that prepare recommendations:

1. Service Description
2. Network Operation
3. Tariff and Accounting Principles
4. Network Maintenance
5. Protection Against Electromagnetic Environment Effects
6. Outside Plant
7. Data Network and Open Systems Communications
8. Terminal Equipment and Protocols for Telematic Services
9. Television and Sound Transmission
10. Languages for Telecommunication Applications
11. Switching and Signaling
12. End-to-End Transmission Performance
13. General Network Aspects
14. Modems and Transmission Techniques for Data, Telegraph, and Telematic Services
15. Transmission Systems and Equipment

Work within ITU-T is conducted in four-year cycles. Every four years, a World Telecommunications Standardization Conference is held. The work program for the next four years is established at the assembly in the form of questions submitted by the various study groups, based on requests made to the study groups by their members. The conference assesses the questions, reviews the scope of the study groups, creates new or abolishes existing study groups, and allocates questions to them.

Based on these questions, each study group prepares draft recommendations. A draft recommendation may be submitted to the next conference, four years hence, for approval. Increasingly, however, recommendations are approved when they are ready, without having to wait for the end of the four-year study period. This accelerated procedure was adopted after the study period that ended in 1988. Thus, 1988 was the last time that a large batch of documents was published at one time as a set of recommendations.

APPENDIX 5B   ITU-T RECOMMENDATIONS ON ISDN

Number	Title	Date
I.112	Vocabulary of Terms for ISDNs	1993
I.114	Vocabulary of Terms for Universal Personal Telecommunications	1993
I.120	Integrated Services Digital Networks	1993
I.130	Method for the Characterization of Telecommunication Services Supported by an ISDN and Network Capabilities of an ISDN	1988

Number	Title	Date
I.140	Attribute Technique for the Characterization of Telecommunication Services Supported by an ISDN and Network Capabilities of an ISDN	1993
I.141	ISDN Network Charging Capabilities Attributes	1988
I.200	Guidance to the I.200 Series of Recommendations	1988
I.210	Principles of Telecommunication Services Supported by an ISDN and the Means to Describe Them	1993
I.220	Common Dynamic Description of Basic Telecommunication Services	1988
I.221	Common Specific Characteristics of Services	1993
I.230	Definition of Bearer Service Categories	1988
I.231	Circuit Mode Bearer Service Categories	1988
I.231.6	Circuit Mode 384 kbit/s 8 kHz Unrestricted 8 kHz Structured Bearer Service Category	1996
I.231.7	Circuit Mode 1536 kbit/s 8 kHz Unrestricted 8 kHz Structured Bearer Service Category	1996
I.231.8	Circuit Mode 1920 kbit/s 8 kHz Unrestricted 8 kHz Structured Bearer Service Category	1996
I.231.9	Circuit Mode 64 kbit/s 8 kHz Structured Multi-Use Bearer Service Category	1993
I.231.10	Circuit Mode Multiple-Rate Unrestricted 8 kHz Structured Bearer Service Category	1992
I.232	Packet Mode Bearer Services Categories	1988
I.232.3	User Signaling Bearer Service Category (USBS)	1993
I.240	Definition of Teleservices	1988
I.241	Teleservices Supported by an ISDN	1988
I.241.7	Telephony 7 kHz Teleservice	1993
I.241.8	Teleaction Stage One Service Description	1995
I.250	Definition of Supplementary Services	1988
I.251	Number Identification Supplementary Services	1988
I.251.1	Direct Dialing-In	1992
I.251.2	Multiple Subscriber Number	1992
I.251.3	Calling Line Identification Presentation	1992
I.251.4	Calling Line Identification Restriction	1992
I.251.5	Connected Line Identification Presentation	1995
I.251.6	Connected Line Identification Restriction	1995
I.251.7	Malicious Call Identification	1992
I.251.8	Sub-Addressing Supplementary Service	1992
I.251.9	Calling Name Identification Presentation	1996
I.251.10	Calling Name Identification Restriction	1996
I.252	Call Offering Supplementary Services	1988
I.252.2	Call Forwarding Delay	1992
I.252.3	Call Forwarding No Reply	1992
I.252.4	Call Forwarding Unconditional	1992
I.252.5	Call Deflection	1992

(*continued on next page*)

Number	Title	Date
I.252.7	Explicit Call Transfer	1997
I.253	Call Completion Supplementary Services	1988
I.253.1	Call Waiting Supplementary Services	1990
I.253.2	Call Hold	1992
I.253.3	Completion of Calls to Busy Subscribers (CCBS)	1996
I.253.4	Completion of Calls on No Reply (CCNR)	1996
I.254	Multiparty Supplementary Services	1988
I.254.2	Three-Party Supplementary Service	1992
I.254.5	Conference Call, Meet Me	1997
I.255	Community of Interest Supplementary Services	1988
I.255.1	Closed User Group	1992
I.255.2	Support of Private Numbering Plans (SPNP)	1996
I.255.3	Multi-Level Precedence and Preemption Service	1990
I.255.4	Priority Service	1990
I.255.5	Outgoing Call Barring	1992
I.256	Charging Supplementary Services	1988
I.256.2a	Advice of Charge: Charging Information at Call Set-up Time	1993
I.256.2b	Advice of Charge: Charging Information During the Call	1993
I.256.2c	Advice of Charge: Charging Information at the End of the Call	1993
I.256.3	Reverse Charging	1992
I.257	Additional Information Transfer	1988
I.257.1	User-to-User Signaling	1995
I.258.1	Terminal Portability	1995
I.258.2	Incall Modification	1995
I.259.1	Screening Supplementary Services: Address Screening	1996
I.310	ISDN—Network Functional Principles	1993
I.320	ISDN Protocol Reference Model	1993
I.324	ISDN Network Architecture	1991
I.325	Reference Configurations for ISDN Connection Types	1993
I.330	ISDN Numbering and Addressing Principles	1988
I.331	International Public Telecommunication Numbering Plan	1997
I.333	Terminal Selection in ISDN	1993
I.334	Principles Relating ISDN Numbers/Subaddresses to the OSI Reference Model Network Layer Addresses	1988
I.340	ISDN Connection Types	1992
I.350	General Aspects of Quality of Service and Network Performance in Digital Networks, Including ISDN	1993
I.351	Relationships Among ISDN Performance Recommendations	1997
I.352	Network Performance Objectives for Connection Processing Delays in an ISDN	1993
I.353	Reference Events for Defining ISDN Performance Parameters	1996
I.354	Network Performance Objectives for Packet Mode Communication in an ISDN	1993
I.355	ISDN 64 kbit/s Connection Type Availability Performance	1995

Number	Title	Date
I.410	General Aspects and Principles Relating to ISDN User–Network Interfaces	1988
I.411	ISDN User–Network Interfaces—Reference Configurations	1993
I.412	ISDN User–Network Interfaces—Interface Structures and Access Capabilities	1988
I.420	Basic User–Network Interface	1988
I.421	Primary Rate User–Network Interface	1988
I.430	Basic User–Network Interface—Layer 1 Specification	1995
I.431	Primary Rate User–Network Interface—Layer 1 Specification	1993
I.460	Multiplexing, Rate Adaptation, and Support of Existing Interfaces	1988
I.461	Support of X.21, X.21 *bis,* and X.20 *bis* Based DTEs by an ISDN	1993
I.462	Support of Packet Mode Terminal Equipment by an ISDN	1995
I.463	Support by an ISDN of DTEs with V-Series Type Interfaces	1996
I.464	Multiplexing, Rate Adaptation, and Support of Existing Interfaces for Restricted 64 kbit/s Transfer Capability	1991
I.465	Support by an ISDN of DTEs with V-Series Type Interfaces with Provisions for Statistical Multiplexing	1996
I.470	Relationship of Terminal Functions to ISDN	1988
I.500	General Structure of ISDN Interworking Recommendations	1993
I.501	Service Interworking	1993
I.510	Definitions and General Principles of ISDN Interworking	1993
I.511	ISDN-to-ISDN Layer 1 Internetwork Interface	1988
I.515	Parameter Exchange for ISDN Interworking	1993
I.520	General Arrangements for Network Interworking between ISDNs	1993
I.525	Interworking Between ISDN and Networks which Operate at Bit Rates of Less Than 64 kbit/s	1996
I.530	Network Interworking Between an ISDN and a PSTN	1993
I.540	General Arrangements for Interworking Between CSPDNs and ISDNs for the Provision of Data Transmission	1996
I.550	General Arrangements for Interworking Between PSPDNs and ISDNs for the Provision of Data Transmission	1996
I.560	Requirements to Be Met in Providing the Telex Service Within the ISDN	1993
I.570	Public/Private ISDN Internetworking	1993
I.571	Connection of VSAT Based Private Networks on the Public ISDN	1996
I.601	General Maintenance Principles of ISDN Subscriber Access and Subscriber Installation	1988
Q.920	ISDN User–Network Interface Data Link Layer—General Aspects	1993
Q.921	ISDN User–Network Interface Data Link Layer Specification	1993
Q.930	ISDN User–Network Interface Layer 3—General Aspects	1993
Q.931	ISDN User–Network Interface Layer 3 Specification for Basic Call Control	1993
Q.932	Generic Procedures for the Control of ISDN Supplementary Services	1993

CHAPTER 6

ISDN INTERFACES AND FUNCTIONS

This chapter looks at a variety of issues related to ISDN architecture as seen by the user. On the whole, the user need not be concerned with the internal functioning or mechanisms of an ISDN. However, the user is concerned with the nature of the interface and the way in which services are requested and provided.

Six areas are examined in this chapter:

- **Transmission structure:** The way in which logical channels providing bearer services are organized for transmission over the local loop
- **User–network interface configurations:** The way in which user–ISDN interactions are organized functionally and how this guides the actual equipment configuration and the definition of the user–ISDN interface
- **Protocol architecture:** The structure of user–network protocols and their relationship to the OSI model
- **ISDN connections:** The types of end-to-end connections that are supported by ISDN
- **Addressing:** The way in which a calling user specifies the called user so that the network can perform routing and delivery functions
- **Interworking:** The capability for an ISDN subscriber to establish a connection to a subscriber on a non-ISDN network

6.1 TRANSMISSION STRUCTURE

The digital pipe between the central office and the ISDN subscriber will be used to carry a number of communication channels. The capacity of the pipe, and therefore the number of channels carried, may vary from user to user.

The transmission structure of any access link will be constructed from the following types of channels:

- **B channel:** 64 kbps
- **D channel:** 16 or 64 kbps
- **H channel:** 384 (H_0), 1536 (H_{11}), or 1920 (H_{12}) kbps

The **B channel** is a user channel that can be used to carry digital data, PCM-encoded digital voice, or a mixture of lower-rate traffic, including digital data and digitized voice encoded at a fraction of 64 kbps. In the case of mixed traffic, all traffic of the B channel must be destined for the same endpoint; that is, the elemental unit of circuit switching is the B channel. If a B channel consists of two or more subchannels, all subchannels must be carried over the same circuit between the same subscribers. Three kinds of connections can be set up over a B channel:

- **Circuit-switched:** This is equivalent to switched digital service, available today. The user places a call and a circuit-switched connection is established with another network user. An interesting feature is that the call establishment does not take place over the B channel, but is done using common-channel signaling.
- **Packet-switched:** The user is connected to a packet-switching node, and data are exchanged with other users via X.25.
- **Semipermanent:** This is a connection to another user set up by prior arrangement and not requiring a call establishment protocol. This is equivalent to a leased line.

The designation of 64 kbps as the standard user channel rate highlights the fundamental disadvantage of standardization. The rate was chosen as the most effective for digitized voice, yet the technology has progressed to the point at which 32 kbps or even less will produce equally satisfactory voice reproduction. To be effective, a standard must freeze the technology at some defined point. Yet by the time the standard is approved, it may already be obsolete.

The **D channel** serves two main purposes. First, it carries common-channel signaling information to control circuit-switched calls on associated B channels at the user interface. In addition, the D channel may be used for packet-switching or low-speed (e.g., 100 bps) telemetry at times when no signaling information is waiting. Table 6.1 summarizes the types of data traffic to be supported on B and D channels.

H channels are provided for user information at higher bit rates. The user may use such a channel as a high-speed trunk or subdivide the channel according to the user's own TDM scheme. Examples of applications include fast facsimile, video, high-speed data, high-quality audio, and multiplexed information streams at lower data rates.

These channel types are grouped into transmission structures that are offered as a package to the user. The best-defined structures (Figure 6.1) are the basic channel structure (basic access) and the primary channel structure (primary access).

Basic access consists of two full-duplex 64-kbps B channels and a full-duplex 16-kbps D channel. The total bit rate, by simple arithmetic, is 144 kbps. However,

Table 6.1 ISDN Channel Functions

B Channel (64 kbps)	D Channel (16 kbps)
Digital voice	**Signaling**
64 kbps PCM	Basic
Low bit rate (32 kbps)	Enhanced
High-speed data	**Low-speed data**
Circuit switched	Videotex
Packet switched	Teletex
Other	Terminal
Facsimile	**Telemetry**
Slow-scan video	Emergency services
	Energy management

framing, synchronization, and other overhead bits bring the total bit rate on a basic access link to 192 kbps; the details of these overhead bits are presented in Chapter 7. The basic service is intended to meet the needs of most individual users, including residential subscribers and very small offices. It allows the simultaneous use of voice and several data applications, such as Internet access, a link to a central alarm service, facsimile, teletex, and so on. These services could be accessed through a single multifunction terminal or several separate terminals. In either case, a single physical interface is provided. Most existing two-wire local loops can support this interface [GIFF86].

In some cases, one or both of the B channels remain unused. This results in a B + D or D interface, rather than the 2B + D interface. However, to simplify the network implementation, the data rate at the interface remains at 192 kbps. Nevertheless, for those subscribers with more modest transmission requirements, there may be a cost savings in using a reduced basic interface.

Primary access is intended for users with greater capacity requirements, such as offices with a digital PBX or a LAN. Because of differences in the digital transmission hierarchies used in different countries, it was not possible to get agreement on a single data rate. The United States, Canada, and Japan make use of a transmission structure based on 1.544 Mbps; this corresponds to the T-1 transmission

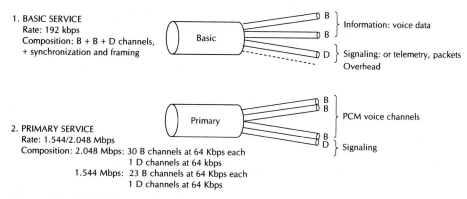

Figure 6.1 ISDN Channel Structures.

facility of AT&T. In Europe, 2.048 Mbps is the standard rate. Both of these data rates are provided as a primary interface service. Typically, the channel structure for the 1.544-Mbps rate will be 23 B channels plus one 64-kbps D channel and, for the 2.048-Mbps rate, 30 B channels plus one 64-kbps D channel. Again, it is possible for a customer with lesser requirements to employ fewer B channels, in which case the channel structure is $nB + D$, where n ranges from 1 to 23 or from 1 to 30 for the two primary services. Also, a customer with high data rate demands may be provided with more than one primary physical interface. In this case, a single D channel on one of the interfaces may suffice for all signaling needs, and the other interfaces may consist solely of B channels (24B or 31B).

The primary interface may also be used to support H channels. Some of these structures include a 64-kbps D channel for control signaling. When no D channel is present, it is assumed that a D channel on another primary interface at the same subscriber location will provide any required signaling. The following structures are recognized:

- **Primary rate interface H_0 channel structures:** This interface supports multiple 384-kbps H_0 channels. The structures are $3H_0 + D$ and $4H_0$ for the 1.544-Mbps interface and $5H_0 + D$ for the 2.048-Mbps interface.
- **Primary rate interface H_1 channel structures:** The H_{11} channel structure consists of one 1536-kbps H_{11} channel. The H_{12} channel structure consists of one 1920-kbps H_{12} channel and one D channel.
- **Primary rate interface structures for mixtures of B and H_0 channels:** These consist of zero or one D channel plus any possible combination of B and H_0 channels up to the capacity of the physical interface (e.g., $3H_0 + 5B + D$ or $3H_0 + 6B$ for the 1.544-Mbps interface).

6.2 USER–NETWORK INTERFACE CONFIGURATIONS

Reference Points and Functional Groupings

To define the requirements for ISDN user access, an understanding of the anticipated configuration of user premises equipment and of the necessary standard interfaces is critical. The first step is to group functions that may exist on the user's premises in ways that suggest actual physical configurations. Figure 6.2 shows the ITU-T approach to this task, using

- **Functional groupings:** Certain finite arrangements of physical equipment or combinations of equipment
- **Reference points:** Conceptual points used to separate groups of functions

An analogy with the OSI model might be useful at this point. The principal motivation for the seven-layer OSI architecture is that it provides a framework

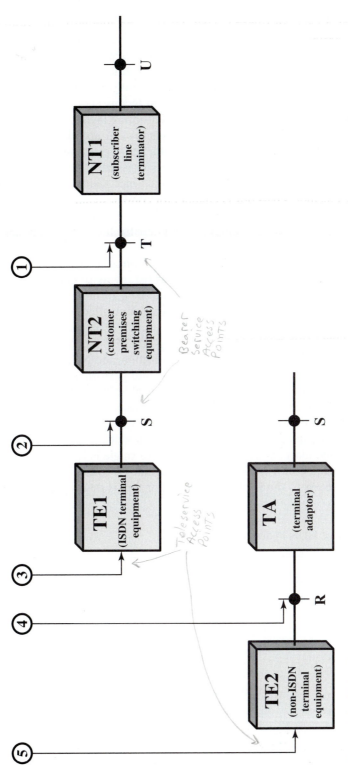

Figure 6.2 ISDN Reference Points and Functional Groupings.

127

for standardization. Once the functions to be performed in each layer are defined, protocol standards can be developed at each layer. This effectively organizes the standards work and provides guidance to software and equipment providers. Furthermore, by defining the services that each layer provides to the next higher layer, work in each layer can proceed independently. So long as the interface between two layers remains stable, new and different technical approaches can be provided within one layer without an impact on neighboring layers. In the case of ISDN, the architecture on the subscriber's premises is broken up functionally into groupings separated by reference points. This permits interface standards to be developed at each reference point. Again, this effectively organizes the standards work and provides guidance to the equipment providers. Once stable interface standards exist, technical improvements on either side of an interface can be made without impact on adjacent functional groupings. Finally, with stable interfaces, the subscriber is free to procure equipment from different suppliers for the various functional groupings, so long as the equipment conforms to the relevant interface standards.

Let us consider first the functional groupings. **Network termination 1** (NT1) includes functions that may be regarded as belonging to OSI layer 1—that is, functions associated with the physical and electrical termination of the ISDN on the user's premises (Table 6.2). The NT1 may be controlled by the ISDN provider and forms a boundary to the network. This boundary isolates the user from the transmission technology of the subscriber loop and presents a new physical connector interface for user device attachment. In addition, the NT1 will perform line maintenance functions such as loopback testing and performance monitoring. The NT1 supports multiple channels (e.g., at the physical level, the bit streams of these channels are multiplexed together, using synchronous time-division multiplexing). Finally, the NT1 interface might support multiple devices in a multidrop arrangement. For example, a residential interface might include a telephone, personal computer, and alarm system, all attached to a single NT1 interface via a multidrop line. For such a configuration, the NT1 includes a contention resolution algorithm to control access to the D channel; this algorithm is described in Chapter 7.

Table 6.2   Functions of ISDN Functional Groupings

NT1	NT2	TE
Line transmission termination	Layers 2 and 3 protocol handling	Protocol handling
Line maintenance and performance monitoring	Layers 2 and 3 multiplexing	Maintenance functions
Timing	Switching	Interface functions
Power transfer	Concentration	Connection functions to other equipment
Layer 1 multiplexing	Maintenance functions	
Interface termination, including multidrop termination employing layer 1 contention resolution	Interface termination and other layer 1 functions	

Network termination 2 (NT2) is an intelligent device that may include, depending on the requirement, up through OSI layer 3 functionality. NT2 can perform switching and concentration functions. Examples of NT2 are a digital PBX, a terminal controller, and a LAN. For example, a digital PBX can provide NT2 functions at layers 1, 2, and 3. A simple terminal controller can provide NT2 functions at only layers 1 and 2. A simple time-division multiplexer can provide NT2 functions at only layer 1. An example of a switching function is the construction of a private network using semipermanent circuits among a number of sites. Each site could include a PBX that acts as a circuit switch or a host computer that acts as a packet switch. The concentration function simply means that multiple devices, attached to a digital PBX, LAN, or terminal controller, may transmit data across ISDN.

Terminal equipment refers to subscriber equipment that makes use of ISDN. Two types are defined. **Terminal equipment type 1** (TE1) refers to devices that support the standard ISDN interface. Examples are digital telephone, integrated voice/data terminals, and digital facsimile equipment. **Terminal equipment type 2** (TE2) encompasses existing non-ISDN equipment. Examples are terminals with a physical interface, such as RS-232, and host computers with an X.25 interface. Such equipment requires a **terminal adaptor** (TA) to plug into an ISDN interface.

The definitions of the functional groupings also define, by implication, the reference points. **Reference point T** corresponds to a minimal ISDN network termination at the customer's premises. It separates the network provider's equipment from the user's equipment. **Reference point S** corresponds to the interface of individual ISDN terminals. It separates user terminal equipment from network-related communications functions. **Reference point R** provides a non-ISDN interface between user equipment that is not ISDN compatible and adaptor equipment. Typically, this interface will comply with an X series or V series ITU-T recommendation. The final reference point, illustrated in Figure 6.2, is **reference point U.** This interface describes the full-duplex data signal on the subscriber line. At present, this reference point is not defined in I.411, which states that "there is no reference point assigned to the transmission line, because an ISDN user–network interface is not envisaged at this location."

Earlier drafts of I.411, up through 1981, defined such a reference point. In 1981, this definition was dropped without explanation, to be replaced by the flat assertion just noted, which survived into the 1984 final version of I.411 and has not subsequently been removed. However, it may be useful to define a U-interface standard to give the customer the option of having equipment from different vendors on the two sides of the interface.

There has been considerable work within the U.S. standards groups affiliated with ITU-T to develop a U-interface standard based on echo cancellation techniques. This work has resulted in a U.S. standard (described in Chapter 7). At this time, it is not clear whether this standard will be adopted by ITU-T.

Service Support

The structure defined in Figure 6.2 can be related to the ISDN services. This helps to clarify further the distinction between bearer services and teleservices, while also clarifying the implications of the functional groupings and reference points.

Bearer services supported by ISDN are accessed at points 1 and/or 2 (reference points T and S). In both cases, the basic service concept is identical. Thus, for example, a bearer service of *circuit-mode 64-kbps 8-kHz structure unrestricted* can be supplied at either reference point. The choice between access points 1 and 2 depends on the configuration of the communications equipment at the customer premises.

At access point 4 (reference point R), other standardized services (e.g., X series and V series interfaces) may be accessed. This allows terminals not conforming to the ISDN interface standards to be used in conjunction with the bearer services. For such terminals, a terminal adapter is required to adapt the existing standard to the ISDN standard. Such adaption can include data rate, analog-to-digital, or other interface characteristics.

Access points 3 and 5 provide access to teleservices. ISDN teleservices incorporating terminals that conform to ISDN standards are accessed at access point 3. Teleservices that make use of terminals based on existing non-ISDN standards are accessed at point 6. For these services, as with the bearer services, a terminal adapter may be required.

Access Configurations

Based on the definitions of functional groupings and reference points, various possible configurations for ISDN user–network interfaces have been proposed by ITU-T. These are shown in Figure 6.3. Note that on the customer's premises there may be interfaces at S and T, at S but not T, at T but not S, or at a combined S–T interface. The first case (S and T) is the most straightforward; one or more pieces of equipment correspond to each functional grouping. Examples were given previously when the functional groupings were defined.

In the second case (S but not T), the functions of NT1 and NT2 are combined. In this case, the line termination function is combined with other ISDN interface functions. Two possible situations are reflected by this arrangement. The ISDN provider can provide the NT1 function. If that same provider also offers computer, LAN, and/or digital PBX equipment, the NT1 functions can be integrated into this other equipment. Alternatively, the NT1 function need not be an integral part of the ISDN offering and can be supplied by a number of vendors. In this case, a LAN or digital PBX vendor might integrate the NT1 function into its equipment.

In the third case (T but not S), the NT2 and terminal (TE) functions are combined. One possibility here is a host computer system that supports users but also acts as a packet switch in a private packet-switching network that uses ISDN for trunking. Another possibility is that terminal equipment is supported by non-ISDN-standard interfaces. This latter possibility is illustrated in Figure 6.3f and discussed subsequently.

The final configuration (combined S–T interface) illustrates a key feature of ISDN interface compatibility: An ISDN subscriber device, such as a telephone, can connect directly to the subscriber loop terminator or into a PBX or LAN, using the same interface specifications and thus ensuring portability.

Figure 6.4 provides examples of the ways in which a customer may implement the NT1 and NT2 functions. These examples illustrate that a given ISDN function can be implemented using various technologies and that different ISDN functions

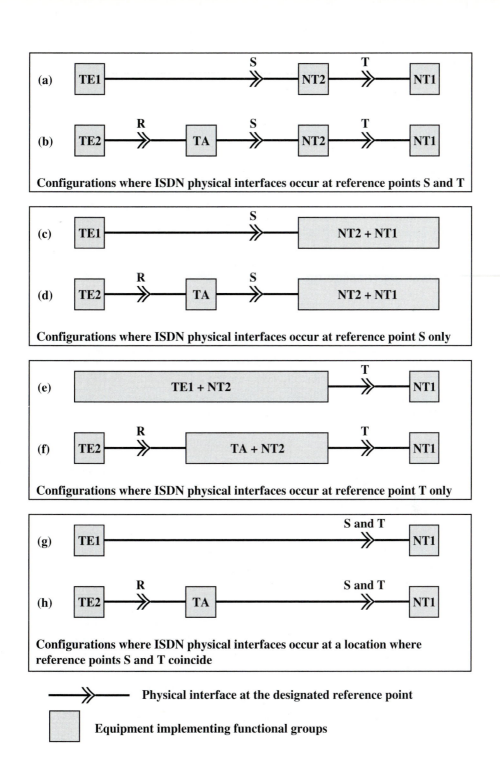

Figure 6.3 Examples of Physical Configurations for ISDN User–Network Interfaces.

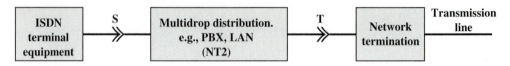

(a) **An implementation where ISDN physical interfaces occur at reference points S and T (see Figure 6.3a)**

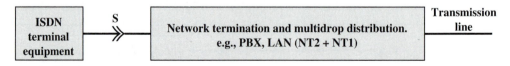

(b) **An implementation where an ISDN physical interfaces occurs at reference point S but not T (see Figure 6.3c)**

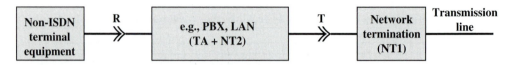

(c) **An implementation where an ISDN physical interfaces occurs at reference point T but not S (see Figure 6.3f)**

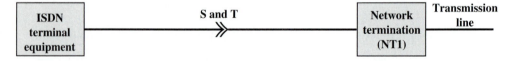

(d) **An implementation where a single ISDN physical interface occurs at a location where reference points S and T coincide (see Figure 6.3g)**

Figure 6.4 Examples of Implementations of NT1 and NT2 Functions.

can be combined in a single device. For example, Figure 6.4c illustrates that a LAN can interface to ISDN using a primary or basic access interface, while the user devices make use of a very different interface (e.g., a token-ring LAN interface).

One additional set of configurations is suggested by ITU-T. These configurations cover cases in which the subscriber has more than one device at a particular interface point, but not so many devices that a separate PBX or LAN is warranted. In these cases, it is possible to have multiple physical interfaces at a single reference point. Examples are shown in Figure 6.5. Figures 6.5a and 6.5b show multiple terminals connected to the network, either through a multidrop line or through a multiport NT1. These cases are not intended to require that individual terminals can talk to each other, as in a LAN, but rather that each terminal can communicate with the network.

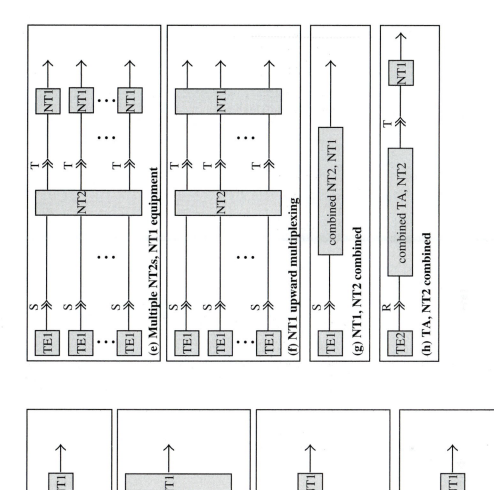

Figure 6.5 Possible Configurations for ISDN User–Network Interfaces.

133

Figures 6.5c and 6.5d provide multiple connections between TE1s and NT2. The two figures more or less correspond to PBX and LAN, respectively. Figure 6.5e shows the case of multiple NT1 equipment, whereas Figure 6.5f shows a case in which NT1 provides a layer 1 multiplexing of multiple connections.

The final two configurations indicate that either S or T, but not both, need not correspond to a physical interface in a particular configuration. We have already referred to the combination of NT1 and NT2. In addition, an NT2 can be equipped with the capability to attach TE2 equipment directly.

6.3 ISDN PROTOCOL ARCHITECTURE

The development of standards for ISDN includes the development of protocols for interaction between an ISDN user and the network, and between two ISDN users. It would be desirable to fit these new ISDN protocols into the open systems interconnection (OSI) model. This would enable critical protocol architectural issues to be identified readily and facilitate the development of ISDN protocols.

Although general purpose in nature, the OSI model does not serve to represent all of the protocol functions required in an ISDN. In particular, a simple seven-layer stack does not capture the relationship between a control-signaling protocol on the D channel being used to set up, maintain, and terminate a connection on the B or H channel. To accommodate this type of functionality, ITU-T has developed a more complex protocol reference model, defined in I.320 and illustrated in Figure 6.6. In this model, there are two layered stacks of protocol entities within a single functional grouping:

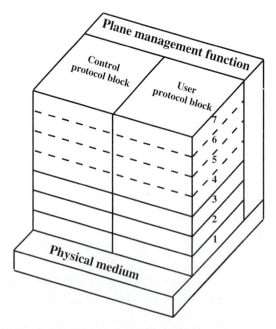

Figure 6.6 Global View of Protocol Architecture.

- **User protocol block:** Has the exclusive task of transparent transfer of user information
- **Control protocol block:** Has the exclusive task of supporting ISDN signaling

User protocols are the traditional protocols, such as X.25, that are modeled by the OSI model. Control protocols perform the following functions:

- Controlling a network connection (such as establishing and terminating)
- Controlling multimedia calls
- Controlling the use of an already established connection (e.g., change in service characteristics during a call)
- Providing supplementary services

Finally, the ISDN protocol reference model includes a plane management function that cuts across all of the protocol layers. The term *plane* refers to the cooperative interaction among protocols at the same layer on different systems. The plane management function includes a variety of network management functions that enable a network management system to control the parameters and operation of remote systems and that enable a local system to collect configuration and operational data to be reported to a network management system.

Figure 6.7 depicts the ISDN-related protocols discussed in this part of the book in the context of the OSI model. Note that control signaling is essentially a D channel function but that user data may also be transferred across the D channel. ·

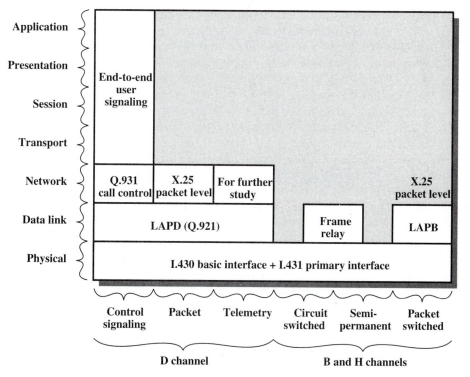

Figure 6.7 ISDN Protocols at the User–Network Interface.

ISDN is essentially unconcerned with user layers 4–7. These are end-to-end layers employed by the user for the exchange of information. Network access is concerned only with layers 1–3. Layer 1, defined in I.430 and I.431, defines the physical interface for basic and primary access, respectively. Because the B and D channels are multiplexed over the same physical interface, these standards apply to both types of channels. Above this layer, the protocol structure differs for the two channels.

For the D channel, a new data link layer standard, LAPD (link access protocol, D channel), has been defined. This standard is based on HDLC, modified to meet ISDN requirements. All transmission on the D channel is in the form of LAPD frames that are exchanged between the subscriber equipment and an ISDN switching element. Three applications are supported: control signaling, packet switching, and telemetry. For **control signaling,** a call control protocol has been defined (Q.931). This protocol is used to establish, maintain, and terminate connections on B channels. Thus, it is a protocol between the user and the network. Above layer 3, there is the possibility for higher-layer functions associated with user-to-user control signaling. These are a subject for further study. The D channel can also be used to provide **packet-switching** services to the subscriber. In this case, the X.25 level 3 protocol is used, and X.25 packets are transmitted in LAPD frames. The X.25 level 3 protocol is used to establish virtual circuits on the D channel to other users and to exchange packetized data. The final application area, **telemetry,** is a subject for further study.

The B channel can be used for circuit switching, semipermanent circuits, and packet switching. For **circuit switching,** a circuit is set up on a B channel on demand. The D channel call control protocol is used for this purpose. Once the circuit is set up, it may be used for data transfer between the users. Recall from Chapter 2 that a circuit-switched network provides a transparent data path between communication stations.

A **semipermanent circuit** is a B channel circuit that is set up by prior agreement between the connected users and the network. As with a circuit-switched connection, it provides a transparent data path between end systems.

With either a circuit-switched connection or a semipermanent circuit, it appears to the connected stations that they have a direct full-duplex link with each other. They are free to use their own formats, protocols, and frame synchronization. Hence, from the point of view of ISDN, layers 2–7 are not visible or specified. In addition, however, ITU-T has standardized I.465/V.120, which does provide a common link-control functionality for ISDN subscribers.

In the case of **packet switching,** a circuit-switched connection is set up on a B channel between the user and a packet-switched node using the D channel control protocol. Once the circuit is set up on the B channel, the user employs X.25 levels 2 and 3 to establish a virtual circuit to another user over that channel and to exchange packetized data.

6.4 ISDN CONNECTIONS

Narrowband ISDN provides six types of service for end-to-end communication:

- Circuit-switched calls over a B or H channel
- Semipermanent connections over a B or H channel

- Packet-switched calls over a B or H channel
- Packet-switched calls over a D channel
- Frame relay calls over a B or H channel
- Frame relay calls over a D channel

Circuit Switching

The network configuration and protocols for circuit switching involve both the B and D channels. The B channel is used for the transparent exchange of user data. The communicating users may use any protocols they wish for end-to-end communication. The D channel is used to exchange control information between the user and the network for call establishment and termination and access to network facilities.

Figure 6.8 depicts the protocol architecture that implements circuit switching (see Table 6.3 for a key to Figures 6.8, 6.11, and 6.12). The B channel is serviced by an NT1 or NT2 using only layer 1 functions. The end users may employ any protocol, although generally layer 3 will be null. On the D channel, a three-layer network access protocol is used and is explained subsequently. Finally, the process of establishing a circuit through ISDN involves the cooperation of switches internal to ISDN to set up the connection. These switches interact using Signaling System Number 7.

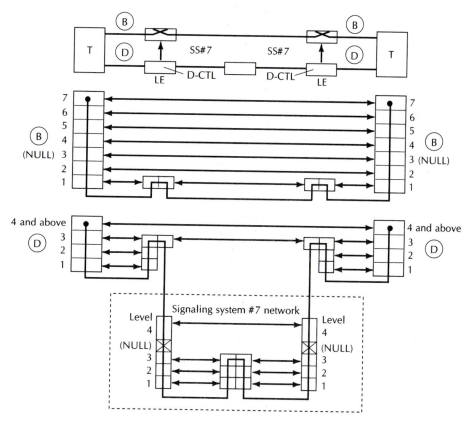

Figure 6.8 Network Configuration and Protocols for Circuit Switching.

Table 6.3 Key to Figures 6.8, 6.11, and 6.1

B	=	An ISDN B channel
D	=	An ISDN D channel
T	=	Terminal
D-CTL	=	D channel controller
SS 7	=	ITU-T Signaling System 7
STP	=	Signaling transfer point
(Null)	=	Channel not present
7, 6, 5, 4, 3, 2, 1	=	Layers in ISO basic reference model
LEVEL	=	Levels in SS 7
LE	=	Local exchange
TE	=	Transit exchange
PSF	=	Packet-switching facility
Horizontal line	=	Peer-to-peer protocol
Vertical line	=	Layer-to-layer data flow

Semipermanent Connections

A semipermanent connection between agreed points may be provided for an indefinite period of time after subscription, for a fixed period, or for agreed periods during a day, week, or other interval. The upper protocol structure depicted in Figure 6.8 is also valid in this case. That is, only layer 1 functionality is provided by the network interface; the call control protocol is not needed, because the connection already exists.

Packet Switching

The ISDN must also permit user access to packet-switched services for data traffic (e.g., interactive) that is best serviced by packet switching. There are two possibilities for implementing this service: Either the packet-switching capability is furnished by a separate network, referred to as a packet-switched public data network (PSPDN), or the packet-switching capability is integrated into ISDN.

PSPDN Service

When the packet-switching service is provided by a separate PSPDN, the access to that service is via a B channel. Both the user and the PSPDN must therefore be connected as subscribers to the ISDN. In the case of the PSPDN, one or more of the packet-switching network nodes, referred to as packet handlers, are connected to ISDN. We can think of each such node as a traditional X.25 DCE supplemented by the logic needed to access ISDN. Any ISDN subscriber can then communicate, via X.25, with any user connected to the PSPDN, including

- Users with a direct, permanent connection to the PSPDN
- Users of the ISDN that currently enjoy a connection, through the ISDN, to the PSPDN

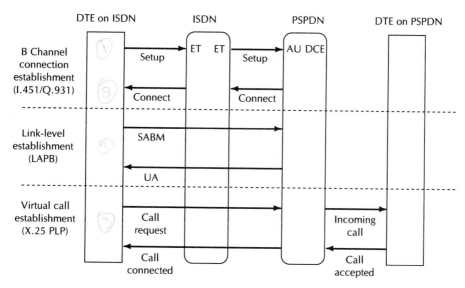

Figure 6.9 Virtual Call Setup.

The connection between the user (via a B channel) and the packet handler with which it communicates may be either semipermanent or circuit switched. In the former case, the connection is always there, and the user may freely invoke X.25 to set up a virtual circuit to another user. In the latter case, the D channel is involved, and the following sequence of steps occurs (Figure 6.9):

1. The user requests, via the D channel call control protocol (Q.931), a circuit-switched connection on a B channel to a packet handler.
2. The connection is set up by ISDN, and the user is notified via the D channel call control protocol.
3. The user sets up a virtual circuit to another user via the X.25 call establishment procedure on the B channel (described in Chapter 3). This requires that first a data link connection, using LAPB, must be set up between the user and the packet handler.
4. The user terminates the virtual circuit using X.25 on the B channel.
5. After one or more virtual calls on the B channel, the user is done and signals via the D channel to terminate the circuit-switched connection to the packet-switching node.
6. The connection is terminated by ISDN.

Figure 6.10 shows the configuration involved in providing this service. In the figure, the user is shown to employ a DTE device that expects an interface to an X.25 DCE. Hence, a terminal adapter is required. Alternatively, the X.25 capability can be an integrated function of an ISDN TE1 device, dispensing with the need for a separate TA.

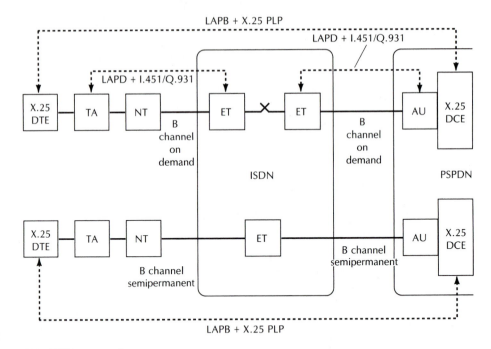

AU = ISDN access unit
TA = Terminal adapter
NT = Network termination 2 and/or 1
ET = Exchange termination
PLP = Packet-level procedure
PSPDN = Packet-switched public data network

Figure 6.10 Access to PSPDN for Packet-Mode Service.

ISDN Service

When the packet-switching service is provided by ISDN, the packet-handling function is provided within the ISDN, either by separate equipment or as part of the exchange equipment. The user may connect to a packet handler either by a B channel or the D channel. On a B channel, the connection to the packet handler may be either switched or semipermanent, and the same procedures described previously apply for switched connections. In this case, rather than establish a B channel connection to another ISDN subscriber that is a PSPDN packet handler, the connection is to an internal element of ISDN that is a packet handler. Figure 6.11 illustrates the protocol implications.

In addition, packet-switching service can also be obtained on the D channel. For D channel access, ISDN provides a semipermanent connection to a packet-switching node within the ISDN. The user employs the X.25 level 3 protocol, as is done in the case of a B channel virtual call. Here, the level 3 protocol is carried by LAPD frames. Because the D channel is also used for control signaling, some means is needed to distinguish between X.25 packet traffic and ISDN control traffic. This is accomplished by means of the link layer addressing scheme explained in Chapter 8. Figure 6.12 illustrates the protocol implications.

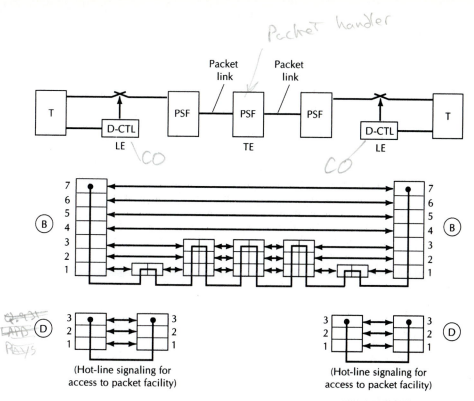

Packet handler

Figure 6.11 Network Configuration and Protocols for Packet Switching Using B Channel with Circuit-Switched Access.

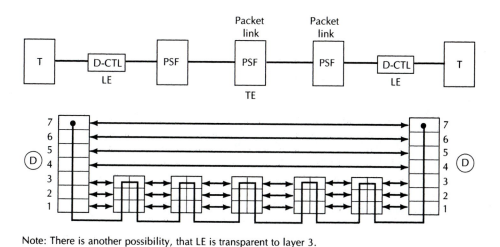

Note: There is another possibility, that LE is transparent to layer 3.

Figure 6.12 Network Configuration and Protocols for Packet Switching.

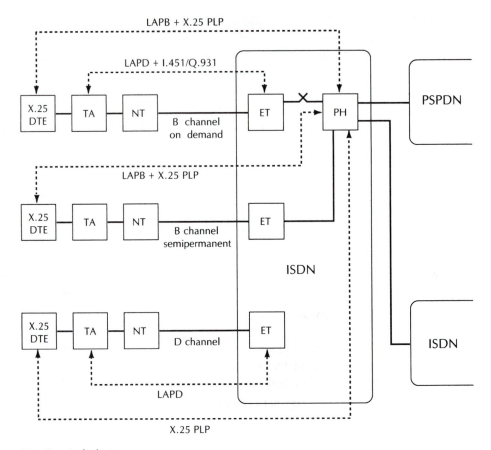

TA = Terminal adapter
NT = Network termination 2 and/or 1
ET = Exchange termination
PLP = Packet-level procedure
PSPDN = Packet-switched public data network
PH = Packet handling function

Figure 6.13 Access to ISDN for Packet-Mode Service.

Figure 6.13 shows the configuration for providing packet switching within ISDN. Note that any ISDN user can engage in an X.25 virtual circuit with any other ISDN user over either the B or D channels. In addition, it will be typical also to provide access to X.25 users on other ISDNs and PSPDNs by appropriate interworking procedures. One common approach is the use of X.75, which specifies an interworking scheme between two public X.25 networks.

6.5 ADDRESSING

In the worldwide public telephone network, calls are placed based on the telephone number of the called party. For worldwide telephone connectivity, each subscriber must have a unique telephone number, and the network must be able to determine the location of the subscriber based on that number. A telephone number supports two important functions:

- It routes the call.
- It activates the necessary procedures for proper call charging.

Similarly, a numbering plan is needed for ISDN. The numbering scheme for ISDN should be based on the following requirements:

- It should be easily understood and used by the subscriber.
- It should be compatible with existing and planned switching equipment.
- It should allow for expansion of the size of the subscriber population.
- It should facilitate interworking with existing public network numbering schemes.

As work on ISDN proceeded through the early 1980s, there was considerable sentiment that ISDN numbering should be based on the current numbering plan for telephony, embodied in ITU-T E.164. However, E.164 allows for only 12 decimal digits and was felt to be inadequate for the large number of subscribers anticipated for ISDN. ISDN must accommodate not only telephones but a large population of data devices. The result was the adoption of a numbering scheme that is an enhancement of E.164. This scheme embodies the following principles:

- As mentioned, it is an enhancement of E.164. In particular, the telephone country code specified in E.164 is used to identify countries in the ISDN numbering plan.
- It is independent of the nature of the service (e.g., voice or data) or the performance characteristics of the connection.
- It is a sequence of decimal digits (not alphanumeric).
- Interworking between ISDNs requires only the use of the ISDN number.

ISDN Address Structure

ITU-T makes a distinction between a number and an address. An **ISDN number** is one that relates to the ISDN network and ISDN numbering plan. It contains sufficient information for the network to route a call. Typically, but not always, an ISDN number corresponds to the subscriber attachment point to the ISDN (i.e., to the T reference point). An **ISDN address** comprises the ISDN number and any mandatory and/or optional additional addressing information. This additional information is not needed by the ISDN to route the call but is needed at the subscriber site to distribute the call to the appropriate party. Typically, but not always, an ISDN address corresponds to an individual terminal (i.e., to the S reference point). This situation is illustrated in Figure 6.14a, which shows a number of terminals connected to an NT2 (e.g., a PBX or LAN). The NT2 as a whole has a unique ISDN number, while each individual terminal has an ISDN address. Another way to express the distinction between ISDN numbers and addresses is that an ISDN number is associated with a D channel, which provides common-channel signaling for a number of subscribers, each of which has an ISDN address.

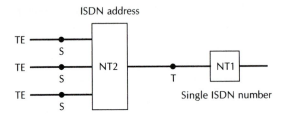

(a) Single ISDN number at T interface

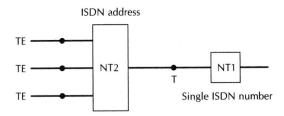

(b) Direct dialing-in

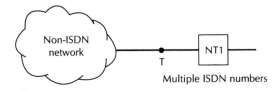

(c) Non-ISDN network

Figure 6.14 ISDN Addressing.

Other correspondences between reference points and ISDN numbers and addresses are possible; these are discussed subsequently.

Figure 6.15 shows the format of the ISDN address. An address in this format would appear in call setup messages communicated in common-channel signaling protocols such as Signaling System Number 7. The elements of the address are as follows:

- **Country code:** Specifies the destination country (or geographic area) of the call. It is composed of a variable number of decimal digits (1 to 3) and is defined in Recommendation E.164 (existing telephony numbering plan).

- **National destination code:** Is of variable length and a portion of the national ISDN number. If subscribers within a country are served by more than one ISDN and/or public switched telephone network (PSTN), it can be used to select a destination network within the specified country. It can also be used in a trunk code (area code) format to route the call over the destination network to a particular region of the network. The NDC code can, where required, provide a combination of both of these functions.

- **ISDN subscriber number:** Is also of variable length and constitutes the remainder of the national ISDN number. Typically, the subscriber number is the

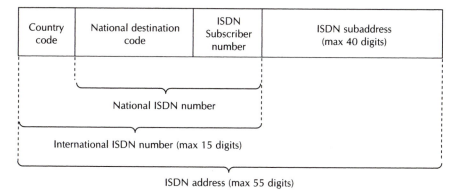

Figure 6.15 Structure of the ISDN Address.

number to be dialed to reach a subscriber in the same local network or numbering area.

- **ISDN subaddress:** Provides additional addressing information and is a maximum of 40 digits in length. The subaddress is not considered part of the numbering plan but constitutes an intrinsic part of the ISDN addressing capability.

The national destination code plus the ISDN subscriber number form a unique national ISDN number within a country. This plus the country code form the international ISDN number, which is at present limited to a maximum of 15 digits. ITU-T is considering expanding this to 16 or 17 digits. The ISDN subaddress is added to the international ISDN number to form an ISDN address with a maximum of 55 digits.

Address Information

Figure 6.14a shows the most straightforward way of employing ISDN numbers and addresses: Each T reference point is assigned an ISDN number, and each S reference point is assigned an ISDN address. The last field of the ISDN address, known as the subaddress, allows multiple subscribers to be discriminated at the subscriber site in a fashion that is transparent to the network. As an example, consider a site consisting of a digital PBX supporting some number of telephones. The national ISDN number for the PBX could be 617-543-7000. To address a local telephone with extension number 678, a remote caller would need to dial 617-543-7000-678. The ISDN would route the call based on the first 10 digits; the remaining 3 digits would be used by the PBX to connect the call to the appropriate extension.

An alternative use of numbers and addresses is suggested by Figure 6.14b. In this case, a number of terminals each have their own ISDN number. This feature is referred to as **direct dialing-in** (DDI). With DDI, the numbering scheme for local terminals is built into the national scheme. For example, again suppose a digital PBX with a main number of 543-7000, with an extension to that PBX of 678. To dial the extension directly from the outside, a user would dial 543-7678, and the 543-7XXX block would be lost for use except for 999 extension possibilities for that

PBX. DDI is simpler for the subscriber than subaddressing, because fewer digits are needed to place a call. With DDI, the ISDN still routes on the basis of the ISDN number. In addition, the last few digits forming the end of the ISDN number are transferred to the called subscriber's installation. The number of digits used varies and depends upon the requirement of the called subscriber's equipment and the capacity of the numbering plan used. DDI must be used sparingly to assure that sufficient ISDN numbers are available to support all subscribers.

It is possible to combine DDI and subaddressing. This would allow direct dialing-in to certain intermediate equipment on site, such as terminal concentrators, with the subaddress used to discriminate devices attached to the intermediate equipment.

Another alternative is to assign multiple ISDN numbers to a single reference point. For example, at an ISDN interface, a user might have an attachment to a non-ISDN network, such as a private packet-switching network (Figure 6.14c). Although physically there is only a single attachment point to the ISDN, it might be desirable to provide visibility to ISDN of a number of the devices on the private network by assigning a unique ISDN number to each.

Numbering Interworking

For some extended transition period, there will be a number of public networks in addition to ISDN, including public switched telephone networks (PSTN) and public data networks, such as X.25 packet-switching networks and telex networks. A variety of standards have been issued that deal with the address structure and address assignment for these various networks. Unfortunately, although these standards have been developed with knowledge of the others, they are not compatible with each other or with the ISDN numbering plan. This creates the problem of how addressing can be performed between an ISDN subscriber and a subscriber on another network that has a connection to ISDN.

Other Address Structures

Figure 6.16 illustrates the address structure for the major international public network standards. The international PSTN standard, E.164, makes use of a 12-digit number. The country code is the same as the country code used in ISDN. The national significant number of the PSTN corresponds to the national ISDN number, although the latter may contain three more digits. Thus, E.164 and the ISDN standard are reasonably compatible.

X.121 provides a standard for public data networks. As can be seen, there are a number of variations, depending on the network. If a data terminal is accessed through a public data network, then the E.164 number, prefixed by a 9, is used. For public data networks, a data country code is used, which unfortunately is not the same as a telephone country code. Nor is the national data number related in any way to the national telephone number. The telex numbering scheme also bears no relation to E.164.

Finally, ISO has developed an international numbering scheme in the context of the OSI model. The authority and format identifier (AFI) portion of the ISO address confines one of six subdomains of the global network addressing domain:

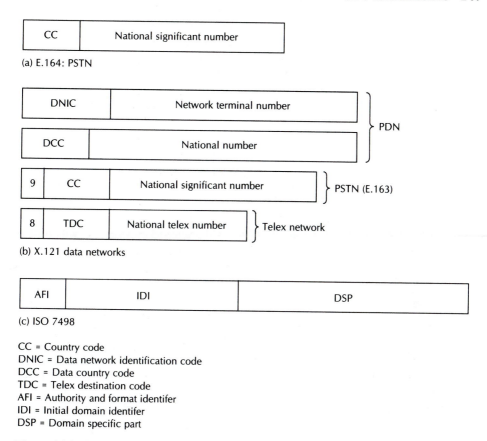

(a) E.164: PSTN

(b) X.121 data networks

(c) ISO 7498

CC = Country code
DNIC = Data network identification code
DCC = Data country code
TDC = Telex destination code
AFI = Authority and format identifer
IDI = Initial domain identifer
DSP = Domain specific part

Figure 6.16   International Network Numbering.

- A set of four domains, each of which corresponds to a type of public telecommunications network (i.e., packet-switched, telex, PSTN, and ISDN), all of which are administered by ITU-T.
- An ISO geographic domain that is allocated and corresponds to individual countries. ISO member bodies within each country are responsible for assigning these addresses.
- An ISO international organization domain that is allocated and corresponds to different international organizations (e.g., NATO).

In addition, the AFI specifies the format of the IDI part and the structure of the DSP part. The initial domain identifier is the initial (and perhaps only) part of the actual address and is interpreted according to the value of the AFI. Finally, the DSP part, if any, provides additional addressing information.

For ISDN networks, the AFI has a value of 44 for ISDN numbers expressed as decimal digits and 45 for ISDN numbers expressed as binary numbers. The latter is not standard ISDN procedure, but may be employed by a user in an OSI context; in that case, the number would have to be converted to decimal for use by ISDN. In general, the international ISDN number is identical to the initial domain identifier, and the ISDN subaddress is identical to the domain-specific part of the ISO address.

Interworking Strategies

From the point of view of ISDN addressing, interworking is defined as a procedure whereby an ISDN subscriber can set up a call to subscribers or services terminated on other public networks. Two general approaches are possible: single-stage and two-stage selection.

With the **single-stage approach,** the calling party designates the address of the called party in the call setup procedure. This address contains sufficient information for

- ISDN to route the call to a point at which the called network attaches to ISDN
- The called network to route the call to the called party

ITU-T suggests two ways in which single-stage addresses could be constructed. In the first method, the address begins with a prefix that identifies the particular network to be accessed; the remainder of the address is in the format used by that network (Figure 6.17a). In this approach, the calling address would have to identify the called numbering plan as part of the calling procedure. An example of such a prefix is the authority and format indicator of the ISO address structure. In the ISDN signaling protocol (Q.931), to be discussed in Chapter 8, there is, in fact, a place in the call setup address field for such a code, known as the numbering plan identification field.

An alternative address structure for the single-stage approach is one that conforms to the ISDN address structure. In this case, some national destination codes (NDCs; see Figure 6.15) could be specially assigned for interworking purposes. This is a less general solution than the prefix approach, as the number of available NDCs is limited.

With the **two-stage approach,** the first stage of selection provides the calling party access via ISDN to an interworking unit (IWU) associated with the point of attachment of the called network to the ISDN. The calling party uses an ISDN number to set up a connection to the IWU. When a connection is established, the IWU responds. The necessary address information for the called party on that particular network is then forwarded, as a second stage of selection, through the ISDN and the IWU to complete the call in the non-ISDN network (Figure 6.17b).

The main disadvantages of the two-stage approach are as follows:

- Additional digits must be dialed by the caller.
- The caller must employ two numbering plans.
- A delimiter or pause is necessary between the two stages (e.g., a second dial tone).

For these reasons, ITU-T prefers the one-stage approach but allows the two-stage approach.

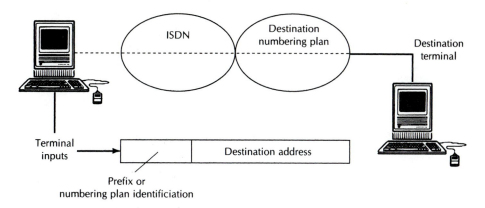

(a) Single-stage interworking

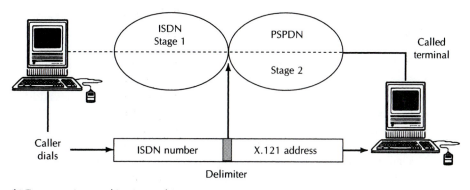

(b) Two-stage interworking (example)

Figure 6.17 Strategies for Numbering Interworking.

6.6 INTERWORKING

It is clear that there is never likely to be a single, monolithic, worldwide ISDN. In the near term, there will be a variety of non-ISDN public networks operating, with the need for the subscribers on these networks to connect to subscribers on ISDN networks. Even in the case of different national ISDNs, differences in services or the attributes of services may persist indefinitely. Accordingly, ITU-T has addressed the issue of the interworking of other networks with ISDN.

One issue related to interworking, that of interworking between numbering plans, was discussed in the preceding section. The interworking of numbering plans allows an ISDN subscriber to identify a non-ISDN subscriber for the purpose of establishing a connection and using some service. However, for successful communication to take place there must be agreement on, and the capability to provide, a common set of services and mechanisms. To provide compatibility between ISDN and existing network components and terminals, a set of interworking functions must be implemented. Typical functions include the following:

- Provide interworking of numbering plans.
- Match physical-layer characteristics at the point of interconnection between the two networks.
- Determine if network resources on the destination network side are adequate to meet the ISDN service demand.
- Map control signal messages such as services identification, channel identification, call status, and alerting between the ISDN's common-channel signaling protocol and the called network's signaling protocol, whether the latter is inchannel or common channel.
- Ensure service and connection compatibility.
- Provide transmission structure conversion, including information modulation technique and frame structure.
- Maintain synchronization (error control, flow control) across connections on different networks.
- Collect data required for proper billing.
- Coordinate operation and maintenance procedures to be able to isolate faults.

Thus, interworking may require the implementation of a set of interworking functions, either in ISDN or the network attached to ISDN. The approach identified by ITU-T for standardizing the interworking capability is to define additional reference points associated with interworking and to standardize the interface at that reference point. This is a sound strategy that should minimize the impact both on ISDN and on other networks. The inclusion of these additional reference points is illustrated in Figure 6.18. As before, ISDN-compatible customer equipment attaches to ISDN via the S or T reference point. The following additional reference points are defined:

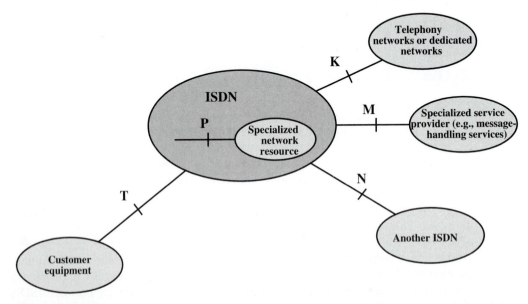

Figure 6.18   Reference Points Associated with the Interconnection of Customer Equipment and Other Networks to an ISDN.

- **K:** Interface with an existing telephone network or other non-ISDN network requiring interworking functions. The functions are performed by ISDN.
- **M:** A specialized network, such as teletex or MHS. In this case, an adaption function may be needed, to be performed in the specialized network.
- **N:** Interface between two ISDNs. Some sort of protocol is needed to determine the degree of service compatibility.
- **P:** There may be some specialized resource that is provided by the ISDN provider but that is clearly identifiable as a separate component or set of components.

In I.510, ITU-T identifies five other types of networks that support telecommunication services, that are also supported by an ISDN, and that are candidates, therefore, for interworking with an ISDN:

- Another ISDN
- Public-switched telephone network (PSTN)
- Circuit-switched public data network (CSPDN)
- Packet-switched public data network (PSPDN)
- Telex

Table 6.4, from I.510, depicts the type of interworking functions that may be required for each interworking configuration. In this context, a connection is a network-oriented function relating to the establishment of an information transfer path through the network, while a communication is a user-oriented function relating to the end-to-end protocols needed for the exchange of information between subscribers.

Table 6.4 ISDN Support of Telecommunication Services in an Interworking Configuration (I.510)

Services Supported by ISDN	ISDN Interconnected with					
	ISDN	**PSTN**	**CSPDN**	**PSPDN**	**TELEX**	**Other Dedicated Network**
Telephony	O	N	—	—	—	N
Data transmission	(L)	N, L	N, (L)	N, (L)	—	N, (L)
Telex	O	—	—	—	N, L	N, L
Teletex	O	N, L	N, L	N, L	—	N, L, H
Facsimile	O	N, L	N, L	N, L	—	N, L, H

O   No interworking function foreseen
N   Connection-dependent interworking needed
L   Lower-layer communication-dependent interworking needed
H   Higher-layer communication-dependent interworking needed
(X)   X may be needed

ISDN–ISDN Interworking

The simplest case of interworking involves two ISDNs. If the two ISDNs provide identical bearer services and teleservices, then no interworking capabilities are required. However, it may be the case that the two networks differ in the attribute values that they support for one or more services. In that case, interworking is needed. The interworking would occur in two phases. In the *control phase,* a service negotiation takes place in order to reach a service agreement. A service agreement can be reached if the maximum common service that can be provided across the two networks equals or exceeds the minimum service that the caller will accept. If agreement is reached, then the connection is established, which involves splicing together connections from the two ISDNs to form a single connection from the user's point of view. User-to-user communication can then take place in the *user phase.*

Figure 6.19 illustrates the call negotiation procedure used to reach service agreement. The following steps are involved:

1. A call from TEx to ISDN2 is routed to IWF1.
2. IWF1 communicates with IWF2 and determines whether the requested service (indicated by bearer capability) of the calling user is supported by ISDN2, using a service list in IWF2. If the compatibility is satisfied, network interworking between ISDN1 and ISDN2 begins.
3. If the service compatibility does not exist, IWF2 (or IWF1) negotiates with the calling user to change or abandon the service request.
4. With a changed service request, step 2 or 3 is repeated until service compatibility is satisfied or the effort abandoned.
5. When the connection between TEx and TEy is established, low-level compatibility (bearer) and high-level compatibility (teleservice) is examined on an end-to-end basis. The network does not participate in this procedure, but agreement between ISDNs concerning user-to-user information transfer method might be required.

Thus, it is first necessary to determine if the two ISDNs can support the required attributes of the caller's requested bearer service. Then the end-to-end compatibility between the two users is determined.

ISDN–PSTN Interworking

In many countries, digitization of the existing public switched telephone network (PSTN) has been ongoing for a number of years, including implementation of digital transmission and switching facilities and the introduction of common-channel signaling. The availability of digital subscriber loops has lagged behind the introduction of these other digital aspects. In any case, such networks exhibit some overlap with the capabilities of a full ISDN but lack some of the services that an ISDN will support. Thus, it will be necessary for some time to provide interworking between ISDN and PSTN facilities.

Table 6.5 (from I.530) identifies the key characteristics of an ISDN and a PSTN, indicating possible interworking functions to accommodate dissimilar

Table 6.5 Key ISDN and PSTN Characteristics

	ISDN	PSTN	Interworking Functions
Subscriber interface	Digital	Analog	a
User–network signaling	Out of band (I.441/I.451)	Mainly inband (e.g., DTMF)	b, e
User terminal equipment supported	Digital TE (ISDN NT, Te1 or TE2 + TA)	Analog TE (e.g., dial pulse telephones, PBXs, modem-equipped DTEs)	c
Interexchange signaling	SS7 ISDN User Part (ISUP)	Inband (e.g., R1, R2, SS4, SS 5) or out of band (e.g., SS 6, SS7 TUP)	d, e
Transmission facilities	Digital	Analog/digital	a
Information transfer mode	Circuit/packet	Circuit	f
Information transfer capability	Speech, digital unrestricted, 3.1-kHz audio, video, etc.	3.1-kHz audio (voice/voiceband data)	f

a = Analog-to-digital and digital-to-analog conversion on transmission facilities.
b = Mapping between PSTN signals in the subscriber access and I.451 messages for intra-exchange calls.
c = Support of communication between modem-equipped PSTN DTEs and ISDN terminals.
d = Conversion between the PSTN signaling system and Signaling System No. 7 ISDN user part.
e = Mapping between signals in the ISDN subscriber (I.441, I.451) access and PSTN inband interexchange signaling (e.g., R1).
f = Further study required.

characteristics. Some sort of negotiation procedure, similar to that depicted in Figure 6.19, will be needed to establish connections.

The interworking between an ISDN and a PSTN is reasonably straightforward. The number plan of the telephone network is the same as that used for ISDN, so no conversion is required. The interworking function must include a mapping between the control signaling used in ISDN and that used in the telephone network. Finally, a conversion is needed between digital and analog forms of user information.

ISDN–CSPDN Interworking

A circuit-switched public data network, as the name implies, provides a digital transmission service using circuit switching. The interface for DTEs to this type of network is X.21. Like X.25, X.21 is actually a three-layer set of protocols that includes inband control signaling for setting up and terminating connections. In the case of X.21, the connections are actual rather than virtual circuits.

The interworking functions for this case have not been fully worked out; much has been left for further study. A mapping is required between the call control protocol of X.21 and that used in ISDN. For addressing, ISDNs and CSPDNs utilize

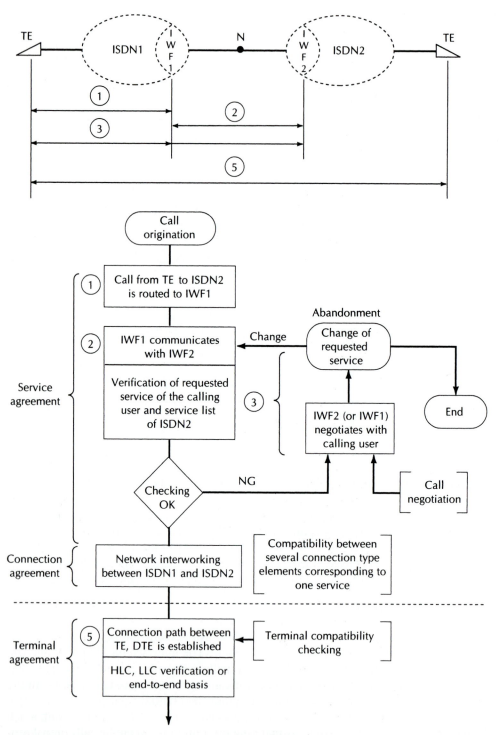

Figure 6.19 Call Negotiation Procedure in ISDN–ISDN Interworking.

differing numbering plans (i.e., E.164 and X.121, respectively). A one-stage address translation, as described in the previous section, is specified.

ISDN–PSPDN Interworking

A packet-switched public data network provides a packet-switching service using an X.25 interface. There are two interworking cases:

- A circuit-mode bearer service is used on ISDN.
- A packet-mode bearer service is used on ISDN.

In the first case, interworking is achieved by means of a circuit-mode connection across ISDN from an ISDN subscriber to a packet handler in the PSPDN (see Figure 6.10). In the second case, the ISDN functions as a packet-switching network (Figure 6.13). For this case, there is an established interworking protocol to be used between two public packet-switching networks: X.76. In essence, X.75 acts as a splicing mechanism to tie together two virtual circuits in the two networks in such a way that it appears as a single virtual circuit to the two end DTEs.

6.7 SUMMARY

The functions performed by an ISDN can be defined by the services that it supports and the functions visible at the user–network interface. Among the most important defining characteristics of ISDN are the following:

- **Transmission structure:** ISDN offers a service structured as a set of channels. The B channel is a user channel that supports circuit-switched, semipermanent, and packet-switched use. The D channel supports user–network control signaling and packet switching. The two standard transmission offerings are the basic service, consisting of two B channels and one D channel, and the primary service, consisting of 24 or 31 B channels and one D channel.
- **User–network interface configurations:** The user–network interface is defined in terms of reference points and functional groupings. This approach provides for standardized interfaces that facilitate the use of equipment from multiple vendors and that simplify access to ISDN.
- **Protocol architecture:** The interaction between ISDN and a subscriber can be described within the context of the OSI protocol reference model. Essentially, the ISDN recommendations deal with layers 1 to 3 of that model. A physical layer specification covers both basic and primary access for all channels. For the D channel, LAPD is defined at the data link layer, and Q.931 (call control) and the X.25 packet level (packet-mode service on the D channel) are specified for the network level. For the B channel, ISDN supports the use of X.25 and LAPB for packet-mode service and also provides I.465/V.120 as a common optional data link mechanism.

- **ISDN connections:** ISDN provides four types of service for end-to-end communication: circuit-switched calls over a B or H channel, semipermanent connections over a B or H channel, packet-switched calls over a B or H channel, and packet-switched calls over the D channel.

- **Addressing:** Addressing refers to the way in which a calling user specifies the called user so that the network can perform routing and delivery functions. ISDN makes use of a number scheme based on E.164 and can interwork with non-ISDN numbers to allow interworking of ISDN with other networks.

- **Interworking:** Interworking refers to the capability for an ISDN subscriber to establish a connection to a subscriber on a non-ISDN network. The most important such networks are public switched telephone networks (analog networks), circuit-switched public data networks (X.21 networks), and packet-switched public data networks (X.25 networks).

6.8 RECOMMENDED READING

[KESS97] and [VERM90] provide good coverage of most of the topics in this chapter. [PAND90] looks at interworking issues, with an emphasis on ISDN–PSTN interworking.

KESS97   Kessler, G. *ISDN: Concepts, Facilities, and Services.* New York: McGraw-Hill, 1993.

PAND90   Pandya, R., and Cullum, M. "Planning for Circuit-Switched Data Services in the ISDN Era: Interworking Solutions and Standards." *Computer Networks and ISDN Systems,* December 1990.

VERM90   Verma, P., ed. *ISDN Systems: Architecture, Technology, and Applications.* Englewood Cliffs, NJ: Prentice Hall, 1990.

6.9 PROBLEMS

6.1 An ISDN customer has offices at a number of sites. A typical office is served by two 1.544-Mbps digital pipes. One provides circuit-switched access to ISDN; the other is a semipermanent connection to another user site. The on-premises equipment consists of a digital PBX plus a host computer system with an X.25 capability. The user has three requirements:
- Telephone service
- A private packet-switched network for data
- Video teleconferencing at 1.544 Mbps

How might the user allocate capacity optimally to meet these requirements?

6.2 What is the percentage overhead on the basic channel structure?

6.3 In Figure 6.4, there is no access point defined for reference point U. One reason for this is that ITU-T has not yet recognized this interface. However, if and when this interface is incorporated in the ITU-T recommendations, is it appropriate to talk about accessing services (bearer or teleservices) at this reference point, or is this a primitive level of interfacing below the level at which services become available to the subscriber?

6.4 What is the difference between direct dialing-in (Figure 6.14b), in which there are multiple ISDN numbers, one for each of multiple S reference points, and the use of multiple ISDN numbers at a single T reference point?

APPENDIX 6A   ISDN ELEMENTARY FUNCTIONS

In I.310, ITU-T specifies a set of elementary functions for ISDN. The objective is to provide a functional description of ISDN that lists those functions required to support ISDN services while at the same time leaving implementers free to implement and configure these functions in the network as they see fit. The functions required to support ISDN services are classified into the following categories:

- **Connection handling:** Functions that enable the establishment, holding, and release of connections (e.g., user-to-network signaling)
- **Routing:** Functions that determine a suitable connection for a particular call request (e.g., called number analysis)
- **Resources handling:** Functions that enable the control of the resources necessary for the use of connections (e.g., transmission equipment, switching resources, data storage equipment)
- **Supervision:** Functions that check the resources used to support the connections, to detect and signal possible problems, and to solve them if possible (e.g., transmission error detection and correction)
- **Operations and maintenance:** Functions that control the correct working of the services/network for the subscriber as well as for the network administration
- **Charging:** Functions for charging subscribers
- **Interworking:** Functions that provide for both service and network interworking

Table 6.6 lists the elementary functions defined in I.310.

Table 6.6   ISDN Elementary Functions (I.310)

Connection Handling
Characteristics of Services-Requested Examination
Determine the required service characteristics of a call by means of information sent by the terminal.
Connection Elements Type Determination
Determine connection types and connection elements necessary to provide requested service.
User Access Resources Reservation
Determine type of user–network access (basic, primary) and channel availability; reserve needed channels.
Transit Resources Reservation
Reserve transit connection element, based on the state of resources.
Communication References Handling
Assign a local reference to the call and an internal reference to the connection, and clear these references when the call/connection is cleared/released.
Establishment Control
Set up a connection.
Release Control
Release a connection.
Service-Related Authorization Examination
Determine the authorization (calling or called user) relating to basic and supplementary services that have been subscribed to.
User–Network Signaling Handling
Support layer 3 protocol of the user–network signaling system.

Table 6.6 ISDN Elementary Functions (I.310) *(continued)*

Interexchange Signaling Handling (User Part)
Support the user part of the interexchange signaling system.
Supplementary Services Compatibility Checking
Check the compatibility of requested supplementary services with requested bearer service or teleservice and with other requested supplementary services; verify coherence of associated parameters.
Building Up and Maintaining Dynamic Information Related to the Call/Connection
Compile information related to the call/connection (e.g., resources needed, details of call in progress, supplementary services, and associated parameters).
Signaling Interworking
Support interworking functions between signaling systems.
Priority
Handle specific calls with priority (e.g., in the case of overload or degraded mode of operation).
Queue Handling
Store requests in a queue in order to handle request later in a predefined order.

Routing

ISDN Number Identification
Identify the ISDN number of the user–network interface.
Called Number Analysis
Analyze called ISDN number sent by the calling terminal in the call setup phase.
Routing Information Examination
Analyze routing information that may be sent by the calling terminals and that has an effect on path selection.
Predetermined Specific Routing
Select a specific routing according to the information received from the calling terminal (e.g., routing toward operators, access points, an interworking unit, and operational or maintenance unit).
Connection Path Selection
Select the transit outgoing part relating to connection types used and the overall path through the network.
Rerouting
Select a new connection path through the network depending on changed conditions during call setup or information transfer phases.

Resources Handling

Hold and Release of Channels
Hold channel(s) reserved to support a communication and release it at the end of this communication.
Hold and Release of Circuits
Hold the circuit(s) reserved to support a communication and release it at the end of this communication.
Insertion and Suppression of Specific Equipment
Insert or remove specific equipment to satisfy the service request invoked by the user (e.g., echo suppressors, A–μ law conversion units, interworking unit, storage unit).
Tones, Announcements, and Display Information
Provide call progress information as a tone, a recorded announcement, or visual display information.
User–Network Signaling Handling
Support layers 1 and 2 of the user–network signaling system.
Interexchange Signaling Handling (Message Transfer)
Support the message-transfer part of the interexchange signaling system.
Path Search Inside Switching Unit
Select an internal connection inside the switching unit.
Synchronization Handling
Provide synchronization between different functional entities and provide internal synchronization.
Timing Handling
Provide timing between time instances involved in calls.

Table 6.6   ISDN Elementary Functions (I.310) *(continued)*

Line Service Marking
Store for each customer information on the bearer services, teleservices, and supplementary services subscribed to.
Real-Time Clock
Provide real-time information.

Supervision
User–Network Access Resources Monitoring
Check the correct operation of subscriber access resources.
Transit Resource Monitoring
Check the correct operation of the transit resources.
Continuity Checking
Check the correct operation of the transit resources.
Detection of Congestion
Detect congestion during the selection of a connection path.
Semipermanent Connection Checking
Check the availability of a given semipermanent connection.

Operation and Maintenance
Management of Subscriber Data
Manage subscriber data related to services (e.g., in/out of service, number translation, changing of subscriber data).
Fault Report
Register the cause if an attempt to set up a call fails.

Charging
Charging Management
Determine the charging mode (free, ordinary, peak, reduced rate).
Charging Registering
Register the details of the call.
Charging Recording
Format the charging details in a standardized way.
Billing
Calculate the variable charges that depend on the use of a service and the fixed costs of the subscription.
Accounting
Analyze, store, and forward information relating to the use of internetwork resources, between the different administrations involved in a call.
Charging Information
Indicate to the user the amount of the charge involved in the use of a service.

Interworking
Rate Adaption
Adapt the user/dedicated network bit rates to the ISDN bit rates.
Protocol Conversion
Support mapping functions between interfaces.
Handling of Signaling for Interworking
Handle signaling information for interworking.
Numbering Interworking
Support interworking functions between numbering plans.

CHAPTER 7

ISDN PHYSICAL LAYER

The ISDN physical layer is presented to the user at either reference point S or T (Figure 6.2). In either case, the following functions are included as physical layer (OSI layer 1) functions:

- Encoding of digital data for transmission across the interface
- Full-duplex transmission of B channel data
- Full-duplex transmission of D channel data
- Multiplexing of channels to form basic or primary access transmission structure
- Activation and deactivation of physical circuit
- Power feeding from network termination to the terminal
- Terminal identification
- Faulty terminal isolation
- D channel contention access

The last function is needed when there is a multipoint configuration for basic access; this is described subsequently.

The nature of the physical interface and functionality differs for basic and primary user–network interfaces. We examine each interface in turn. Finally, we look at the U reference point, which is not standardized as part of the ITU-T I-series but which is an ANSI standard.

7.1 BASIC USER–NETWORK INTERFACE

The layer 1 specification for the basic user–network interface is defined in Recommendation I.430. Recall that the basic interface supports a 2B + D channel structure at 192 kbps. In this section, we examine four key aspects of the basic interface:

- Line coding
- Physical connector
- Framing and multiplexing
- Contention resolution for multidrop configurations

Line Coding

At the interface between the subscriber and the network terminating equipment (T or S reference point), digital data are exchanged using full-duplex transmission. A separate physical line is used for the transmission in each direction. Hence, we need not concern ourselves with echo cancellation or time-compression multiplexing techniques to achieve full-duplex operation. Because the distances are relatively short, and because all of the equipment is on the subscriber's premises, it is far easier to use two separate physical circuits than to use any other technique for full-duplex operation.

The electrical specification for the interface dictates the use of a pseudoternary coding scheme (Figure 3.9). Binary one is represented by the absence of voltage; binary zero is represented by a positive or negative pulse of 750 mV $\pm$ 10%. The data rate is 192 kbps.

Basic Access Physical Connector

The actual physical connection between a TE and an NT at the S or T reference point for the basic access interface is specified not in an ITU-T recommendation but in an ISO standard (ISO 8887).[1] This standard specifies an eight-pin physical connector (Figure 7.1).

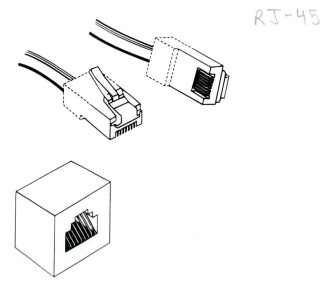

RJ-45

Figure 7.1 ISDN Physical Connector.

---

[1]ISO Standard ISO 8887, *Interface Connector and Contact Assignments for ISDN Basic Access Interface Located at Reference Points S and T,* 1992.

The physical connection terminates in matching plugs that provide for four, six, or eight contacts. The number of contacts provided depends on usage, as is explained subsequently.

Table 7.1 lists the contact assignments for each of the eight pins on both the NT and TE sides. Two pins each are needed to provide balanced transmission in each direction. These contact points are used to connect twisted-pair leads coming from the NT and TE devices.

The specification provides for the capability to transfer power across the interface. The direction of power transfer depends on the application. In a typical application, it may be desirable to provide for power transfer from the network side toward the terminals (for example, to maintain a basic telephony service in the event of failure of the locally provided power). Two possibilities are seen for the transfer of power from an NT to a TE (Figure 7.2):

- Using the same access leads used for the bidirectional transmission of the digital signal (power source and sink 1)
- On additional wires, using access leads g–h

The remaining two leads are not used in the ISDN configuration but may be useful in other configurations. Thus, the ISDN physical interface consists of just six leads.

Framing and Multiplexing

The basic access structure consists of two 64-kbps B channels and one 16-kbps D channel. These channels, which produce a load of 144 kbps, are multiplexed over a 192-kbps interface at the S or T reference point. The remaining capacity is used for various framing and synchronization purposes.

Table 7.1 Contact Assignments for Plugs and Jacks of ISDN Physical Connector (ISO 8887)

Contact	TE	NT
a	Power Source 3	Power Sink 3
b	Power Source 3	Power Sink 3
c	Transmit	Receive
f	Receive	Transmit
e	Receive	Transmit
d	Transmit	Receive
g	Power Sink 2	Power Source 2
h	Power Sink 2	Power Source 2

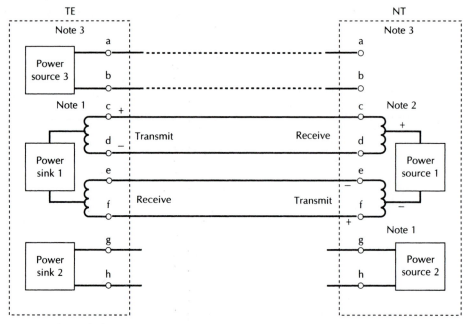

Note 1 — This symbol refers to the polarity of framing pulses.
Note 2 — This symbol refers to the polarity of power during normal power conditions (reversed for restricted conditions).
Note 3 — The access lead assignments indicated in this figure are intended to provide for direct interface cable wiring; i.e., each interface pair is connected to pair of access leads having the same two letters at TEs and NTs.

Figure 7.2 Reference Configuration for Signal Transmission and Power Feeding in Normal Operating Mode.

Frame Format

As with any synchronous time-division multiplexed (TDM) scheme, basic access transmission is structured into repetitive, fixed-length frames. In this case, each frame is 48 bits long; at 192 kbps, frames must repeat at a rate of one frame every 250 μs. Figure 7.3 shows the frame structure; the upper frame is transmitted from the subscriber's terminal equipment (TE) to the network (NT1 or NT2); the lower frame is transmitted by the NT1 or NT2 to the TE. Frame synchronization is such that each frame transmitted from a TE toward the NT is later than the frame in the opposite direction by two bit-times.

Each frame of 48 bits includes 16 bits from each of the two B channels and 4 bits from the D channel. The remaining bits have the following interpretation. Let us first consider the frame structure in the TE-to-NT direction. Each frame begins with a framing bit (F) that is always transmitted as a positive pulse. This is followed by a DC balancing bit (L) that is set to a negative pulse to balance the voltage. The F–L pattern thus acts to synchronize the receiver on the beginning of the frame. The specification dictates that, following these first two bit positions, the first occurrence of a zero bit will be encoded as a negative pulse. After that, the pseudoternary rule is observed. The next eight bits (B1) are from the first B channel. This is followed

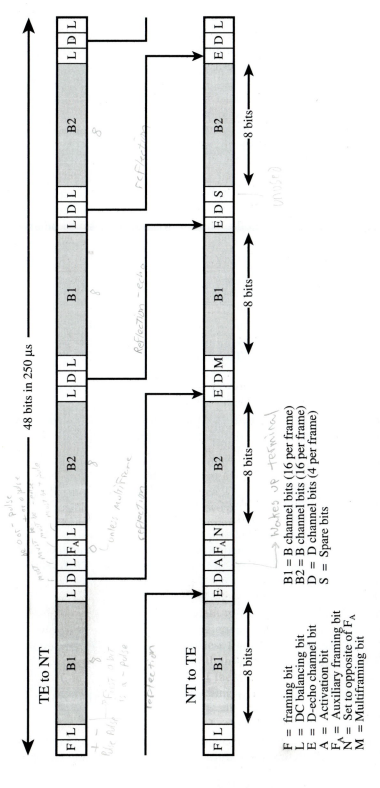

F = framing bit
L = DC balancing bit
E = D-echo channel bit
A = Activation bit
F_A = Auxiliary framing bit
N = Set to opposite of F_A
M = Multiframing bit

B1 = B channel bits (16 per frame)
B2 = B channel bits (16 per frame)
D = D channel bits (4 per frame)
S = Spare bits

Figure 7.3 Frame Structure at Reference Points S and T for ISDN Basic Rate Access.

165

by another DC balancing bit (L). Next comes a bit from the D channel, followed by its balancing bit. This is followed by the auxiliary framing bit (F_A), which is set to zero unless it is to be used in a multiframe structure, as explained subsequently. There follows another balancing bit (L), eight bits (B2) from the second B channel, and another balancing bit (L). This is followed by bits from the D channel, first B channel, D channel again, second B channel, and the D channel yet again, with each group of channel bits followed by a balancing bit.

The frame structure in the NT-to-TE direction is similar to the frame structure for transmission in the TE-to-NT direction. The following new bits replace some of the DC balancing bits. The D channel echo bit (E) is a retransmission by the NT of the most recently received D bit from the TE; the purpose of this echo is explained subsequently. The activation bit (A) is used to activate or deactivate a TE, allowing the device to come on line or, when there is no activity, to be placed in low power-consumption mode. The N bit is normally set to binary one. The N and M bits may be used for multiframing, as explained subsequently. The S bit is reserved for other future standardization requirements.

Frame Alignment

To assure that the transmitter (NT or TE) and receiver (TE or NT) do not get out of alignment, the frame structure includes deliberate violations of the pseudoternary code. The receiver looks for these violations to assure that frame alignment is being maintained. Two violations are included:

- **The first F bit:** This bit is always a positive zero. The frame is structured so that the last zero bit of the frame is positive.
- **The first zero bit after the first L bit:** Both of these bits are of negative polarity. This second violation occurs at the F_A bit at the latest.

Multiframe Structure

A recently added feature of the basic interface specification is the provision for an additional channel for traffic in the TE-to-NT direction, called the Q channel. At present, the use of the Q channel is for further study. However, the current version of I.430 provides the structure for the Q channel (Table 7.2). To implement the Q channel, a multiframe structure is established by setting the M bit (NT-to-TE direction) to binary one on every twentieth frame. In the TE-to-NT direction, the F_A bit in every fifth frame is a Q bit. Thus, in each 20-frame multiframe there are four Q bits.

Normally, in the NT-to-TE direction the F_A bit is set to binary zero, with the following N bit set to binary one. To identify the Q-bit positions in the TE-to-NT direction, the corresponding F_A /N bits in the NT-to-TE direction are inverted (F_A = binary one, N = binary zero).

Contention Resolution for Multidrop Configurations

Multidrop Configurations

With the basic access interface, it is possible to have more than one TE device in a passive bus configuration. Figure 7.4 shows the allowable configurations. The

Table 7.2   Q-bit Position Identification and Multiframe Structure

Frame number	NT-to-TE M bit	NT-to-TE F_A bit position	TE-to-NT F_A bit position
1	1	1	Q1
2	0	0	0
3	0	0	0
4	0	0	0
5	0	0	0
6	0	1	Q2
7	0	0	0
8	0	0	0
9	0	0	0
10	0	0	0
11	0	1	Q3
12	0	0	0
13	0	0	0
14	0	0	0
15	0	0	0
16	0	1	Q4
17	0	0	0
18	0	0	0
19	0	0	0
20	0	0	0
1	1	1	Q1
2	0	0	0
etc.			

simplest is a point-to-point configuration, with only one TE. In this configuration, the maximum distance between the NT equipment and the TE is on the order of 1 km. The second configuration is an ordinary passive bus, which has traditionally been referred to as a multidrop line. This kind of configuration imposes limitations on the distances involved. This has to do with the way in which signal strength is determined.

When two devices exchange data over a link, the signal strength of the transmitter must be adjusted to be within certain limits. The signal must be strong enough so that, after attenuation and signal impairment across the medium, it meets the receiver's minimum signal strength requirements and maintains an adequate signal-to-noise ratio. On the other hand, the signal must not be so strong as to overload the circuitry of the transmitter, which creates harmonics and nonlinear effects. With a point-to-point link, the principal factor to take into account is the length of the medium. With a multidrop link, each tap into the bus creates losses and distortions. Accordingly, for a given data rate and transmission medium, a multidrop line will need to be shorter than a point-to-point line. In the case of the basic access interface, ITU-T specifies a maximum distance of between 100 and 200 m, with a maximum of eight TEs connected at random points along the interface cable.

The length of the short passive bus is also limited by the differential round-trip delay in signal propagation. Because the devices are connected at various points, the

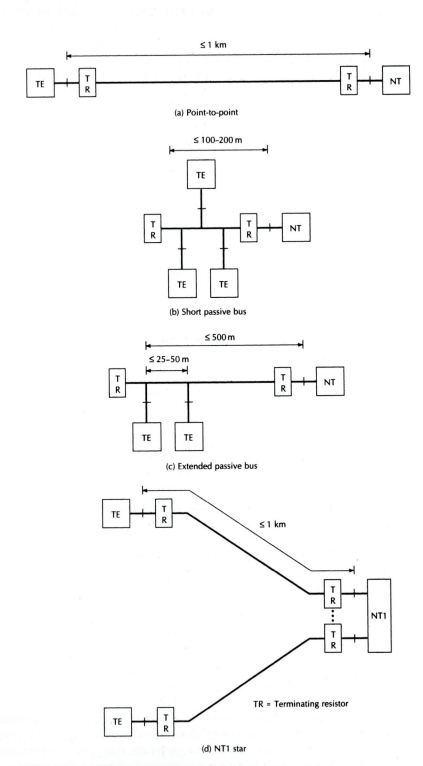

Figure 7.4 Basic Interface Wiring Configurations.

NT receiver must cater to pulses arriving with different delays from various terminals. To maintain receiver synchronization, the limit of 100 to 200 m is needed. A greater length can be achieved if all of the devices are clustered together at the far end of the line (Figure 7.4c). With this extended bus configuration, a maximum length of 500 m, with a maximum differential distance between terminals of 25–50 m, is possible.

The final configuration, illustrated in Figure 7.4d, is the star configuration. This configuration permits multiple TEs but requires only point-to-point wiring. In this configuration, the NT1 must include digital logic to provide for the operation of the D channel echo. The NT1 must transmit the same echo bit over all NT1-to-TE lines. The value of the echo bit is 0 if any of the incoming D bits is 0; otherwise, it is 1. On the network side, the NT1 must merge the transmissions from all of the TEs to form a single 192-kbps stream.

Contention Resolution

The contention resolution function is required when multiple TE1 terminals share a single physical line (Figures 7.4b and 7.4c). There are three types of traffic to consider:

- **B channel traffic:** No additional functionality is needed to control access to the two B channels, because each channel is dedicated to a particular TE at any given time.
- **Incoming D channel traffic:** The D channel is available for use by all the devices for both control signaling and for packet transmission, and so the potential for contention exists. The LAPD addressing scheme, described in the next chapter, is sufficient to sort out the proper destination for each data unit. That is, each LAPD frame includes the explicit address of the destination TE; all TEs at the subscriber site can read this address and determine whether the frame of data is for them.
- **Outgoing D channel traffic:** Access must be regulated so that only one device at a time transmits. This is the purpose of the contention resolution algorithm.

The contention resolution algorithm regulates transmission over the D channel so that signaling information is given priority (priority class 1) over all other types of information (priority class 2). The D channel contention resolution algorithm has the following elements:

1. When a subscriber device has no LAPD frames to transmit, it transmits a series of binary ones on the D channel. Using the pseudoternary encoding scheme, this corresponds to the absence of line signal.
2. The NT, on receipt of a D channel bit, reflects back the binary value as a D channel echo bit (Figure 7.5), called an E bit.
3. When a terminal is ready to transmit an LAPD frame, it listens to the stream of incoming D channel echo bits. If it detects a string of 1-bits of length equal to a threshold value X_i, where i = priority class for this LAPD frame, it may transmit. Otherwise, the terminal must assume that some other terminal is transmitting, and wait.

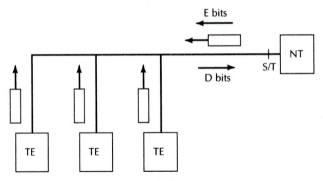

Figure 7.5 Contention Resolution.

4. It may happen that several terminals are monitoring the echo stream and begin to transmit at the same time, causing a collision. To overcome this condition, a transmitting TE monitors the echo bits and compares them with its transmitted bits. If a discrepancy is detected, the terminal ceases to transmit and returns to a listen state.

The electrical characteristics of the interface (i.e., 1 bit = absence of signal) are such that any user equipment transmitting a 0 bit will override user equipment transmitting a 1 bit at the same instant. This arrangement ensures that one device will be guaranteed successful completion of its transmission.

The priority mechanism is based on the threshold value X_i. Signaling information is given priority over packet information. Within each of these two priority classes, a station begins at normal priority and then is reduced to lower priority after a transmission. It remains at the lower priority until all other terminals have had an opportunity to transmit. The values of X_i are as follows:

- **Signaling information**
  - Normal priority $X_1 = 8$
  - Lower priority $X_1 = 9$
- **Nonsignaling information**
  - Normal priority $X_2 = 10$
  - Lower priority $X_2 = 11$

Figure 7.6 shows an example of contention resolution. The figure shows the transmission of D bits from TE to NT and the transmission of E bits from NT to TE; other bits are ignored and the time sequence is compressed to show only the D and E bits. Three TEs (A, B, and C) are all attempting to use the D channel. As long as all binary zeros and ones from all sources are identical, all continue to transmit. As soon as a source notes a binary zero on the E channel when it has transmitted a binary one on the D channel in the corresponding bit position, the source drops out.

To summarize, each TE maintains two priority values, X_1 and X_2, corresponding to signaling and nonsignaling information to be transmitted on the D channel. Each of these values is initialized to a normal priority level. When a TE has D channel information of class i to transmit, it waits until it sees a string of 1 bits on

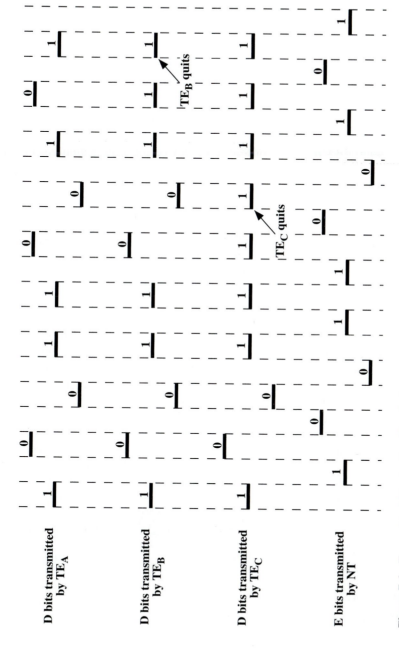

Figure 7.6 Example of Contention Resolution.

171

the E channel equal to X_i and then transmits. This causes the corresponding priority value to be placed at lower priority.

To recover to normal priority, a TE listens for consecutive E bits equal to 1. When the TE observes a string of 1 bits on the E channel equal to the value of the lower level of priority (i.e., the larger value), it changes the priority for that class back to the value for the normal level of priority.

7.2 PRIMARY RATE USER–NETWORK INTERFACE

The primary interface, like the basic interface, multiplexes multiple channels across a single transmission medium. In the case of the primary interface, only a point-to-point configuration is allowed. Typically, the interface exists at the T reference point with a digital PBX or other concentration device controlling multiple TEs and providing a synchronous TDM facility for access to ISDN. Two data rates are defined for the primary interface: 1.544 Mbps and 2.048 Mbps.

Interface at 1.544 Mbps

The ISDN interface at 1.544 Mbps is based on the North American DS-1 transmission structure, which is used on the T1 transmission service. Figure 7.7a illustrates the frame format for this data rate. The bit stream is structured into repetitive 193-bit frames. Each frame consists of 24 8-bit time slots and a framing bit. The same time slot repeated over multiple frames constitutes a channel. At a data rate of 1.544 Mbps, frames repeat at a rate of one every 125 μs, or 8000 frames per second. Thus, each channel supports 64 kbps. Typically, the transmission structure is used to support 23 B channels and 1 D channel. As discussed in Chapter 6, other assignments can be made, including 24 B channels and various combinations of H channels.

The framing bit is used for synchronization and other management purposes. A multiframe structure of 24 193-bit frames is imposed, and Table 7.3 shows the assignment of values to the 24 framing bits across the 24-frame multiframe. Six of the bits form a frame-alignment signal (FAS), with the code 001011, which repeats every multiframe. The purpose is to provide a form of synchronization. If for some reason the receiver becomes one or more bits out of alignment with the transmitter, it will fail to detect the alignment signal and hence will detect the misalignment.

The bits designated as e_i bits can be used as a 6-bit cyclic redundancy check (CRC) of the framing bits (see Appendix A for a discussion of CRC).

The remaining bits, labeled m bits, are used for various operations and maintenance functions.

The line coding for the 1.544-Mbps interface is AMI using B8ZS.

Interface at 2.048 Mbps

The ISDN interface at 2.048 Mbps is based on the European transmission structure of the same data rate. This scheme is defined in detail in G.704.[2]

---

[2]ITU-T Recommendation G.704, *Synchronous Frame Structures Used at Primary and Secondary Hierarchical Levels,* 1991.

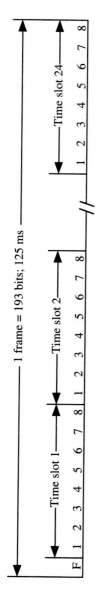

(a) Interface at 1.544 Mbps

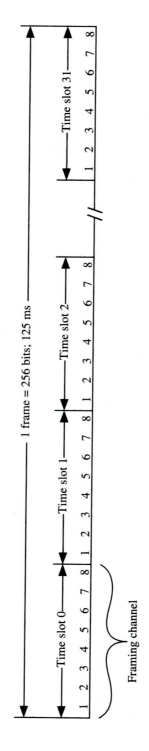

(b) Interface at 2.048 Mbps

Figure 7.7 ISDN Primary Access Frame Formats.

Table 7.3 Multiframe Structure for 1.544-Mbps Interface

Multiframe frame number	Multiframe bit number	F bits		
		Assignments		
		FAS	O&M	CRC
1	1	—	m	—
2	194	—	—	e_1
3	387	—	m	—
4	580	0	—	—
5	773	—	m	—
6	966	—	—	e_2
7	1159	—	m	—
8	1352	0	—	—
9	1545	—	m	—
10	1738	—	—	e_3
11	1931	—	m	—
12	2124	1	—	—
13	2317	—	m	—
14	2510	—	—	e_4
15	2703	—	m	—
16	2896	0	—	—
17	3089	—	m	—
18	3282	—	—	e_5
19	3475	—	m	—
20	3668	1	—	—
21	3861	—	m	—
22	4054	—	—	e_6
23	4247	—	m	—
24	4440	1	—	—

FAS = frame-alignment signal
O&M = operations and maintenance
CRC = cyclic redundancy check

Figure 7.7b illustrates the frame format for this data rate. The bit stream is structured into repetitive 256-bit frames. Each frame consists of 32 8-bit time slots. The first time slot is used for framing and synchronization purposes; the remaining 31 time slots support user channels. At a data rate of 2.048 Mbps, frames repeat at a rate of one every 125 μs, or 8000 frames per second. Thus, each channel supports 64 kbps. Typically, the transmission structure is used to support 30 B channels and 1 D channel. As discussed in Chapter 6, other assignments can be made, such as 31 B channels and various combinations of H channels.

Table 7.4 shows the use of the bits in time slot 0. The frame-alignment signal occupies positions 2 to 8 in channel time slot 0 of every other frame. This signal, which is 0011011, is used for alignment in the same fashion as the frame-alignment signal on the 1.544-Mbps interface. The S_1 bits may be used for a 4-bit CRC procedure, explained in the next paragraph. The A bit can be used for a remote alarm indication; in an alarm condition, it would be set to 1. The S_{ai} bits are spare bits with no current defined use.

Where there is a need for enhanced error-monitoring capability, a multiframe structure, illustrated in Table 7.5, may be used. The 4-bit CRC value is carried

Table 7.4 Allocation of Bits 1 to 8 of the Frame in 2.048-Mbps Interface

Bit Number / Alternate Frames	1	2	3	4	5	6	7	8
Frame containing the frame-alignment signal	S_1 / Note 1	0	0	1	1	0	1	1
		Frame-alignment signal						
Frame not containing the frame-alignment signal	S_1 / Note 1	1 / Note 2	A / Note 3	S_{a4}	S_{a5}	S_{a6}	S_{a7}	S_{a8}
				Note 4				

Note 1: S_1 = bits reserved for international use. One specific use is for CRC.
Note 2: This bit is fixed at 1 to assist in avoiding simulation of the frame-alignment signal.
Note 3: A = remote alarm indication.
Note 4: S_{a4} to S_{a8} = additional spare bits.

in the first bit position of alternate frames. The two E bits are used to signal back to the other side that a CRC error has been detected, by setting the binary value of one E bit from 1 to 0 for each errored sub-multiframe.

The line coding for the 2.048-Mbps interface is AMI using HDB3.

Table 7.5 Multiframe Structure for 2.048-Mbps Interface

Multiframe	Sub-multiframe (SMF)	Frame Number	1	2	3	4	5	6	7	8
Multiframe	I	0	C_1	0	0	1	1	0	1	1
		1	0	1	A	S_{a4}	S_{a5}	S_{a6}	S_{a7}	S_{a8}
		2	C_2	0	0	1	1	0	1	1
		3	0	1	A	S_{a4}	S_{a5}	S_{a6}	S_{a7}	S_{a8}
		4	C_3	0	0	1	1	0	1	1
		5	1	1	A	S_{a4}	S_{a5}	S_{a6}	S_{a7}	S_{a8}
		6	C_4	0	0	1	1	0	1	1
		7	0	1	A	S_{a4}	S_{a5}	S_{a6}	S_{a7}	S_{a8}
	II	8	C_1	0	0	1	1	0	1	1
		9	1	1	A	S_{a4}	S_{a5}	S_{a6}	S_{a7}	S_{a8}
		10	C_2	0	0	1	1	0	1	1
		11	1	1	A	S_{a4}	S_{a5}	S_{a6}	S_{a7}	S_{a8}
		12	C_3	0	0	1	1	0	1	1
		13	E	1	A	S_{a4}	S_{a5}	S_{a6}	S_{a7}	S_{a8}
		14	C_4	0	0	1	1	0	1	1
		15	E	1	A	S_{a4}	S_{a5}	S_{a6}	S_{a7}	S_{a8}

E = CRC-4 error indication bits
S_{a4} to S_{a8} = Spare bits
C_1 to C_4 = Cyclic Redundancy Check—4 (CRC-4) bits
A = Remote alarm indication

7.3 U INTERFACE

In this section, we look at the ANSI T1.601 Standard for the U interface to support basic rate ISDN access; see Section 3.3 for a discussion of the line coding technique for this interface.

The basic access structure consists of two 64-kbps B channels and one 16-kbps D channel. These channels, which produce a load of 144 kbps, are multiplexed over a 160-kbps interface at the U reference point. The remaining capacity is used for various framing and synchronization purposes.

Frame Format

2B1Q line code

As with any synchronous time-division multiplexed (TDM) scheme, basic access transmission is structured into repetitive, fixed-length frames. In this case, each frame is 240 bits long; at 160 kbps, frames must repeat at a rate of one frame every 1.5 ms. Figure 7.8 shows the frame structure; the structure consists of three parts:

→ 2 bits/symbol

- **Synchronization word:** The first nine symbols (18 bits) of the frame form a synchronization word, with the quaternary symbols in the sequence (+3 +3 −3 −3 −3 +3 −3 +3 +3), except as noted subsequently. This word allows the receiver to synchronize easily on the beginning of each frame.

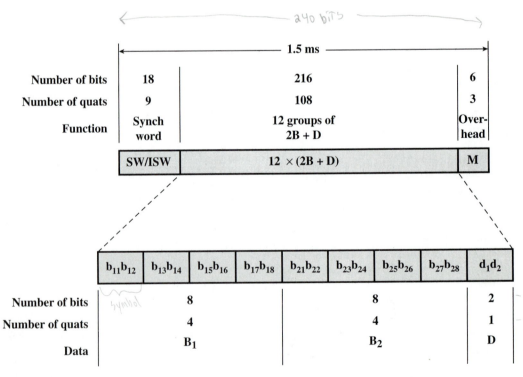

Figure 7.8 2B1Q Transmission Frame.

- **User data:** The next 12 groups of 18 bits each carry B and D channel data, as illustrated in the lower portion of Figure 7.8.
- **M channel:** The last 6 bits of the frame form a 4-kbps M channel for maintenance and other purposes.

Note that the interleaving of B and D bits is different at the U reference points (8 B1, 8 B2, 2 D) than at the S and T reference points (8 B1, D, 8 B2, D). Because the channel data rates are the same at all three reference points, this presents only a minor buffering problem. The NT1 is responsible for the conversion between the two different frame formats.

Multiframe Structure

The basic frame structure is organized into superframes consisting of eight frames each, as shown in Table 7.6. The first frame in the superframe is identified by inverting the polarity of the synchronization word in that frame, with the pattern (-3 -3 $+3$ $+3$ $+3$ -3 $+3$ -3 -3). Within the superframe, there are 48 M bits, and these are used for a variety of purposes. The most notable use is to form a 12-bit CRC for error checking.

Table 7.7 provides a comparison of the basic rate interface at the U and S/T reference points.

Table 7.6 2B1Q Superframe Technique and Overhead Bit Assignments (Network to NT Direction)

		Framing	2B+D	Overhead Bits ($M_1 - M_6$)					
Quad positions		1–9	10–117	188s	118m	119s	119m	120s	120m
Bit positions		1–18	19–234	235	236	237	238	239	240
Superframe #	Basic frame #	Synch word	2B+D	M_1	M_2	M_3	M_4	M_5	M_6
A	1	ISW	2B+D	eoc_{a1}	eoc_{a2}	eoc_{a3}	act	1	1
A	2	SW	2B+D	eoc_{dm}	eoc_{11}	eoc_{12}	dea	1	fbe
A	3	SW	2B+D	eoc_{13}	eoc_{14}	eoc_{15}	1	crc_1	crc_2
A	4	SW	2B+D	eoc_{16}	eoc_{17}	eoc_{18}	1	crc_3	crc_4
A	5	SW	2B+D	eoc_{a1}	eoc_{a2}	eoc_{a3}	1	crc_5	crc_6
A	6	SW	2B+D	eoc_{dm}	eoc_{11}	eoc_{12}	1	crc_7	crc_8
A	7	SW	2B+D	eoc_{13}	eoc_{14}	eoc_{15}	1	crc_9	crc_{10}
A	8	SW	2B+D	eoc_{16}	eoc_{17}	eoc_{18}	1	crc_{11}	crc_{12}
B, C, ...									

act = activation bit

crc = cyclic redundancy check; covers 2B+D & M_4

dea = deactivation bit

eoc = embedded operations channel

Table 7.7 Comparison of Basic Rate Interface
Physical Layer Standards [KESS97]

	CCITT I.430	ANSI T1.601
Reference point	S or T	U
Devices	TE1/TA to NT	NT1 to LE
Distance	1 km	5.5 km
Physical configuration	Point-to-point or point-to-multipoint	Point-to-point
Bit Rate	192 kbps	160 kbps
User data rate	144 kbps	144 kbps
Line code	Pseudoternary	2B1Q
Signaling rate	192 kbaud	80 kbaud
Maximum voltage	± 750 mV	± 2.5 V
Timing source	NT	LE
Number of wire pairs	2	1
Full-duplex method	One wire pair for each direction	Echo cancellation
Interleaving scheme*	$B1_8D_1B2_8D_1$ (twice per frame)	$B1_8B2_8D_2$ (12 times per frame)
Number of bits per frame	48	240
Number of bits user data	36	216
Number of bits overhead	12	24
Number of frames/s	4,000	666.666…

*Subscript indicates the number of contiguous bits that are sent on B1, B2, and D channels.

7.4 SUMMARY

The physical layer specification for ISDN is divided into two principal parts: one for basic access and one for primary access.

The basic-rate access supports 2 B channels and 1 D channel for a user data rate of 144 kbps. At the S and T reference points, the interface provides a frame structure operating at 192 kbps that supports the three user channels plus some overhead and maintenance bits. The pseudoternary coding scheme is used. An eight-pin physical connector is specified.

The primary rate operates at 1.544 and 2.048 Mbps. The 1.544-Mbps interface uses AMI coding with B8ZS. The 2.048-Mbps interface uses AMI coding with HDB3.

Although ITU-T has not issued an ISDN recommendation for the U interface, ANSI has issued a standard that uses echo cancellation and the 2B1Q line code at 160 kbps to support the basic rate interface.

7.5 PROBLEMS

7.1 With the exception of the first occurrence of the L bit in a basic rate frame, all subsequent L bits have either zero voltage or a positive voltage, but not a negative voltage. Why?

7.2 Demonstrate that the last nonzero pulse of a basic rate frame is always positive. Note that the first pulse of the following frame is also positive. Is there an advantage to that?

7.3 What is the data rate on the Q channel?

7.4 In the discussion of D channel contention resolution, it was stated that a station remains at lower priority until all other terminals have had a chance to transmit. In the standard (I.430) it states that the value of the lower level of priority is changed back to the value of the higher level of priority when the TE observes a string of 1 bits on the echo stream of length equal to the value of the lower level of priority. Does this in fact guarantee that all other terminals have had a chance to transmit?

7.5 What is the percentage overhead for each of the two primary rate interfaces?

CHAPTER 8

ISDN DATA LINK LAYER

Above the physical layer, a data link control protocol is needed for communication. ITU-T has defined a data link control protocol for the D channel, known as LAPD, that is used for communication between the subscriber and the network. All D channel traffic employs the LAPD protocol. For B channel traffic, the situation is somewhat different. For a packet-switched connection, LAPB is used to connect the subscriber to a packet-switching node. For a circuit-switched connection, there is an end-to-end circuit between two subscribers, and they are free to use any protocol at the link level for end-to-end data link control. However, two ISDN-related data link control protocols are available. I.465/V.120 is a recommendation for terminal adaptation that is based on the use of a data link control protocol similar to LAPD. This protocol allows the multiplexing of multiple logical connections over a single B channel circuit between two end users. I.465/V.120 is also part of a series of standards dealing with terminal adaption. These standards define the way in which ISDN provides support for non-ISDN devices.

The other data link protocol that has been developed is LAPF, which supports the frame-mode bearer service. A discussion of LAPF is deferred until Chapter 12.

8.1 LAPD

All traffic over the D channel employs a link-layer protocol known as LAPD (link access protocol—D channel), defined in Q.921. We look first at the services that LAPD provides to the network layer, and then at various elements of the LAPD protocol.[1]

---

[1]The basic link control functions of flow control, error detection, and error control, which are part of the LAPD protocol, are discussed in Appendix A.

Services

The purpose of LAPD is to convey user information between layer 3 entities across ISDN using the D channel. The LAPD service will support

- Multiple terminals at the user–network installation (e.g., see Figure 7.4)
- Multiple layer 3 entities (e.g., X.25 level 3, Q.931)

↳ D channel control signalling

The LAPD standard provides two forms of service to LAPD users: the unacknowledged information-transfer service and the acknowledged information-transfer service. The **unacknowledged information-transfer service** simply provides for the transfer of data link frames containing user data with no acknowledgment. The service does not guarantee that data presented by one user will be delivered to another user, nor does it inform the sender if the delivery attempt fails. The service does not provide any flow-control or error-control mechanism. This service supports both point-to-point (deliver to one user) or broadcast (deliver to a number of users). This service allows for fast data transfer and is useful for management procedures such as alarm messages and messages that need to be broadcast to multiple users.

The **acknowledged information-transfer service** is the more common one and is similar to the service offered by LAPB and HDLC. With this service, a logical connection is established between two LAPD users. Three phases occur: connection establishment, data transfer, and connection termination. During the *connection establishment phase*, the two users agree to exchange acknowledged data. One user issues a connection request to the other. If the other is prepared to engage in a logical connection, then the request is acknowledged affirmatively, and a logical connection is established. In essence, the existence of a logical connection means that the LAPD service provider at each end of the connection will keep track of the frames being transmitted and those being received, for the purposes of error control and flow control. During the *data-transfer phase*, LAPD guarantees that all frames will be delivered in the order that they were transmitted. During the *connection termination phase*, one of the two users requests termination of the logical connection.

LAPD Protocol: Basic Characteristics

The LAPD protocol is modeled after the LAPB protocol used in X.25 and on HDLC. Both user information and protocol-control information and parameters are transmitted in frames. Corresponding to the two types of service offered by LAPD, there are two types of operation:

- **Unacknowledged operation:** Layer 3 information is transferred in unnumbered frames. Error detection is used to discard damaged frames, but there is no error control or flow control.
- **Acknowledged operation:** Layer 3 information is transferred in frames that include sequence numbers and that are acknowledged. Error-control and flow-control procedures are included in the protocol. This type of service is also referred to in the standard as multiple-frame operation.

These two types of operations may coexist on a single D channel. With the acknowledged operation, it is possible simultaneously to support multiple logical LAPD connections. This is analogous to the ability in X.25 level 3 to support multiple virtual circuits.

Frame Structure

All user information and protocol messages are transmitted in the form of frames. Figure 8.1 depicts the structure of the LAPD frame. Let us examine each of these fields in turn.

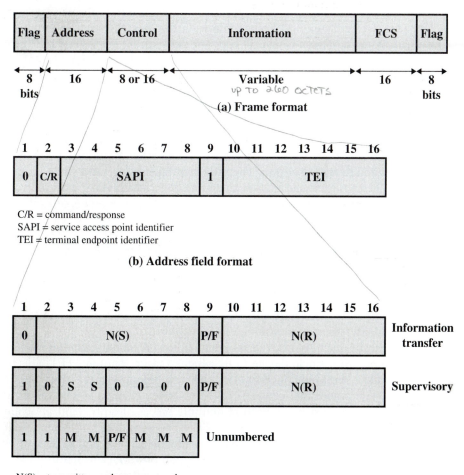

(a) Frame format

C/R = command/response
SAPI = service access point identifier
TEI = terminal endpoint identifier

(b) Address field format

N(S) = transmitter send sequence number
N(R) = transmitter receive sequence number
S = supervisory function bit
M = modifier function bit
P/F = poll/final bit

(c) Control field formats

Figure 8.1 LAPD Formats.

in BRI
which is
Provdotener-1 P0l5
=> P0l5, 51 00,

Flag Fields

Flag fields delimit the frame at both ends with the unique pattern 01111110. A single flag may be used as the closing flag for one frame and the opening flag for the next. On both sides of the user–network interface, receivers are continuously hunting for the flag sequence to synchronize on the start of a frame. While receiving a frame, a station continues to hunt for that sequence to determine the end of the frame. Because the protocol allows the presence of arbitrary bit patterns (i.e., there are no restrictions on the content of the various fields imposed by the link protocol), there is no assurance that the pattern 01111110 will not appear somewhere inside the frame, thus destroying synchronization. To avoid this problem, a procedure known as *bit stuffing* is used. Between the transmission of the starting and ending flags, the transmitter will always insert an extra 0 bit after each occurrence of five 1s in the signal unit. After detecting a starting flag, the receiver monitors the bit stream. When a pattern of five 1s appears, the sixth bit is examined. If this bit is 0, it is deleted. If the sixth bit is a 1 and the seventh bit is a 0, the combination is accepted as a flag. If the sixth and seventh bits are both 1, the sender is indicating an abort condition.

Bit stuffing
in The
LAPD Frame
alleviates
restrictions on
data carried
↓
data
Transparency

Because of the use of bit stuffing, arbitrary bit patterns can be inserted into the data field of the frame. This property is known as *data transparency*.

Figure 8.2 shows an example of bit stuffing. Note that in the first two cases, the extra 0 is not strictly necessary for avoiding a flag pattern but is necessary for the operation of the algorithm. The pitfalls of bit stuffing are also illustrated in this figure. When a flag is used as both an ending and a starting flag, a 1-bit error merges two frames into one. Conversely, a 1-bit error inside a frame could split it in two.

Address Field

LAPD has to deal with two levels of multiplexing. First, at a subscriber site, there may be multiple user devices sharing the same physical interface. Second, within each user device, there may be multiple types of traffic: specifically, packet-switched data and control signaling. To accommodate these levels of multiplexing, LAPD employs a two-part address, consisting of a terminal endpoint identifier (TEI) and a service access point identifier (SAPI).

Typically, each user device is given a unique **terminal endpoint identifier**. It is also possible for a single device to be assigned more than one TEI. This might be the case for a terminal concentrator. TEI assignment occurs either automatically when the equipment first connects to the interface or manually by the user. In the latter case, care must be taken that multiple pieces of equipment attached to the same interface do not have the same TEI. The advantage of the automatic procedure is that it allows the user to change, add, or delete equipment at will without prior notification to the network administration. Without this feature, the network would be obliged to manage a database for each subscriber that would need to be updated manually. Table 8.1a shows the assignment of TEI numbers.

The **service access point identifier** identifies a layer 3 user of LAPD and thus corresponds to a layer 3 protocol entity within a user device. Four specific values have been assigned, as shown in Table 8.1b. An SAPI of 0 is used for call-control procedures for managing B channel circuits; the value 16 is reserved for packet-mode communication on the D channel using X.25 level 3; and a value of 63 is used

Original pattern:

11111111111101111101111110

After bit stuffing

11111011111011011111010111110010

(a) Example

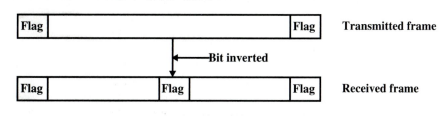

(b) An inverted bit splits a frame in two

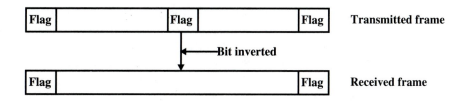

(c) An inverted bit merges two frames

Figure 8.2 Bit Stuffing.

for the exchange of layer 2 management information. The most recent assignment is the value of 1 for packet-mode communication using Q.931. This could be used for user–user signaling. Finally, values in the range 32 to 61 are reserved to support frame relay connections.

The SAPI values are unique within a TEI. That is, for a given TEI, there is a unique layer 3 entity for a given SAPI. Thus, the TEI and the SAPI together uniquely identify a layer 3 user at subscriber site. The TEI and SAPI together are also used to uniquely identify a logical connection; in this context, the combination of TEI and SAPI is referred to as a **data link connection identifier** (DLCI). At any one time, LAPD may maintain multiple logical connections, each with a unique

Table 8.1 SAPI and TEI Assignments

(a) TEI Assignments

[margin note: TEI identifies user devices]

TEI Value	User Type
0–63	Nonautomatic TEI assignment user equipment
64–126	Automatic TEI assignment user equipment
127	Used during automatic TEI assignment *[annotation: broadcast]*

(b) SAPI Assignments

[margin note: SAPI identifies layer 3 users]

SAPI Value	Related Protocol or Management Entity
0	Call control procedures *[annotation: managing B ch circuits]*
16	Packet communication conforming to X.25 level 3
32–61	Frame relay communication
63	Layer 2 management procedures
All others	Reserved for future standardization

[margin notes: Q931 / For Packet mode]

DLCI. Thus, at any one time, a layer 3 entity may have only one LAPD logical connection. Figure 8.3 provides an example. It shows six independent logical connections over a single D channel interface, terminating in two TEs on the user side of the interface.

The address field format is illustrated in Figure 8.1b. The SAPI and TEI fields refer to the address of the subscriber layer 3 entity. On transmission, the layer 3 entity includes this address in the frame. Frames arriving from the network have this address, and the LAPD entity uses the address to deliver the user data to the appropriate layer 3 entity. In addition, the address field includes a **command/response** (C/R) bit. As explained subsequently, all LAPD messages are categorized as either commands or responses, and this bit is used to indicate which type of message is contained in the frame.

Control Field

LAPD defines three types of frames, each with a different control field format. **Information-transfer frames** (I-frames) carry the data to be transmitted for the user. Additionally, flow- and error-control data, using the go-back-N ARQ mechanism (see Appendix A), are piggybacked on an information frame. **Supervisory frames** (S-frames) also provide the ARQ mechanism. **Unnumbered frames** (U-frames) provide supplemental link-control functions and are also used to support unacknowledged operation. The first one or two bits of the control field serve to identify the frame type. The remaining bit positions are organized into subfields, as indicated in Figure 8.1c. Their use is explained in the subsequent discussion of LAPD operation.

All of the control field formats contain the poll/final (P/F). In command frames, it is referred to as the P bit and is set to 1 to solicit (poll) a response frame from the peer LAPD entity. In response frames, it is referred to as the F bit and is set to 1 to indicate the response frame transmitted as a result of a soliciting command.

[margin note: what are command Frames]

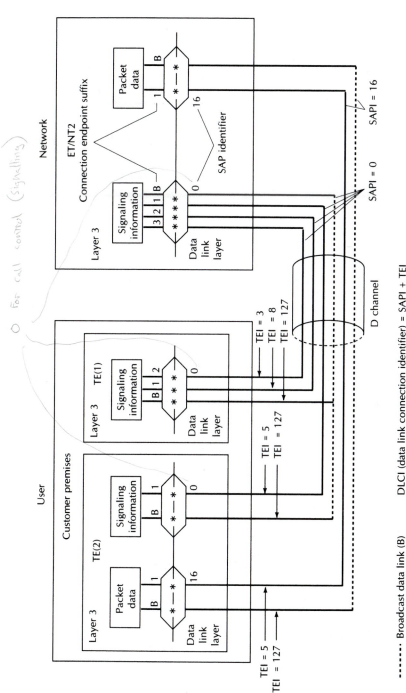

Figure 8.3 Overview Description of the Relation between SAPI, TEI, and Data Link Endpoint Identifier (I.440).

- - - - - Broadcast data link (B)
———— Point-to-point link

DLCI (data link connection identifier) = SAPI + TEI
Connection endpoint identifier = SAPI + connection endpoint suffix

NOTE: The management entity is not shown in this figure.

187

Table 8.2 LAPD Commands and Responses

Name	Command/ Response	Description
Information (I)	C/R	Exchange user data
Supervisory (S)		
Receive ready (RR)	C/R	Positive acknowledgment; ready to receive I-frame
Receive not ready (RNR)	C/R	Positive acknowledgment; not ready to receive
Reject (REJ)	C/R	Negative acknowledgment; go back N
Unnumbered (U)		
Set asynchronous balanced mode extended (SABME)	C	Request logical connection
Disconnected mode (DM)	R	Unable to establish or maintain logical connection
Unnumbered information (UI)	C/R	Used to unacknowledged information transfer service
Disconnect (DISC)	C	Terminate logical link connection
Unnumbered acknowledgment (UA)	R	Acknowledge SABME or DISC
Frame reject (FRMR)	R	Report receipt of unacceptable frame
Exchange identification (XID)	C/R	Exchange identification information

Information Field

The information field is present only in I-frames and some unnumbered frames. The field can contain any sequence of bits but must consist of an integral number of octets. The length of the information field is variable up to some system-defined maximum. In the case of both control signaling and packet information, Q.921 specifies a maximum length of 260 octets.

Frame-Check Sequence Field

The frame-check sequence (FCS) is an error-detecting code calculated from the remaining bits of the frame, exclusive of flags. The code used is the CRC-CCITT code defined in Appendix A.

Acknowledged Operation

The acknowledged operation of LAPD consists of the exchange of I-frames, S-frames, and U-frames between a subscriber TE and the network over the D channel. The various commands and responses defined for these frame types are listed in Table 8.2. In describing LAPD operation, we will discuss these three types of frames.

Connection Establishment

A logical connection may be requested by either the network or the subscriber by transmitting a SABME[2] frame. Generally, this will be in response to a

---

[2]This stands for Set Asynchronous Balanced Mode Extended. It is used in HDLC to choose the ABM mode, which involves two peer entities (as opposed to a primary and one or more secondaries), and to

request from a layer 3 entity. The SABME frame contains the TEI and the SAPI of the layer 3 entity to which connection is requested. The peer LAPD entity receives the SABME frame and passes up a connection request indication to the appropriate layer 3 entity. If the layer 3 entity responds with an acceptance of the connection, then the LAPD entity transmits a UA frame back to the other side. When the UA is received, signifying acceptance, the LAPD entity passes a confirmation up to the requesting user. If the destination user rejects the connection request, its LAPD entity returns a DM frame, and the receiving LAPD entity informs its user of the rejection.

Data Transfer

When the connection request has been accepted and confirmed, the connection is established. Both sides may begin to send user data in I-frames, starting with sequence number 0. The N(S) and N(R) fields of the I-frame are sequence numbers that support flow control and error control. A LAPD entity sending a sequence of I-frames will number them sequentially, modulo 128, and place the sequence number in N(S). N(R) is the piggybacked acknowledgment for I-frames received; it enables the LAPD entity to indicate which number I-frame it expects to receive next.

The S-frames are also used for flow control and error control. Sliding-window flow control and go-back-N ARQ error control are used. The Receive Ready (RR) frame is used to acknowledge the last I-frame received by indicating the next I-frame expected. The RR is used when there is no reverse user traffic to carry a piggybacked acknowledgment. Receive Not Ready (RNR) acknowledges an I-frame, as with RR, but also asks the peer entity to suspend transmission of I-frames. When the entity that issued RNR is again ready, it sends an RR. REJ initiates the go-back-N ARQ. It indicates that the last I-frame received has been rejected and that retransmission of all I-frames beginning with number N(R) is required.

Disconnect

Either LAPD entity can initiate a disconnect, either on its own initiative if there is some sort of fault or at the request of its layer 3 user. The LAPD entity issues a disconnect on a particular logical connection by sending a DISC frame to the peer entity on the connection. The remote entity must accept the disconnect by replying with a UA and informing its layer 3 user that the connection has been terminated. Any outstanding unacknowledged I-frames may be lost, and their recovery is the responsibility of higher layers.

Frame-Reject Frame

The frame-reject (FRMR) frame is used to indicate that an improper frame has arrived—one that somehow violates the protocol (Figure 8.4). One or more of the following conditions have occurred:

---

select extended sequence number length of 7 bits (as opposed to the default of 3 bits). Both ABM and 7-bit sequence numbers are mandatory in LAPD acknowledged operation. Thus, this is simply a connection request command, but the HDLC terminology is retained for consistency.

| | 17 | 25 | 33 | 40 |

| Rejected frame control field | 0 | V(S) | C/R | V(R) | W | X | Y | Z | 0 | 0 | 0 | 0 |

V(S) = Current send sequence number
V(R) = Current receive sequence number
C/R = 1 if the rejected frame was a response
    = 0 if the rejected frame was a command
  W = 1 if control field is invalid
  X = 1 if frame contained an information field not permitted with this frame or is a
      supervisory or unnumbered frame with incorrect length
  Y = 1 information field exceeded maximum allowable length
  Z = 1 if received N(R) value invalid

Figure 8.4   Frame Reject (FRMR) Information Field.

- The receipt of a control field that is undefined (not one of the control field encodings listed in Table 8.2) or not implemented.
- The receipt of an S-frame or U-frame with incorrect length.
- The receipt of an invalid N(R). The only valid N(R) is in the range from the sequence number of the last acknowledged frame to the sequence number of the last transmitted frame.
- The receipt of an I-frame with an information field that exceeds the maximum established length.

The effect of the FRMR is to abort the connection. Upon receipt of an FRMR, the receiving entity may try to reestablish the connection using the connection establishment procedure described earlier.

The exchange identification (XID) frame is used for two stations to exchange information relating to connection management. When a peer entity receives an XID command, it responds with an XID response. The actual information exchanged is beyond the scope of the standard.

Examples of Acknowledged Operation

To understand better the acknowledged operation, several examples are presented in Figure 8.5. The examples all make use of the vertical time sequence diagram. It has the advantages of showing time dependencies and illustrating the correct send–receive relationship. Each arrow represents a single frame transiting a data link between TE and NT. Each arrow includes a legend that specifies the frame name, the setting of the P/F bit, and, where appropriate, the values of N(R) and N(S). The setting of the P or F bit is 1 if the designation is present and 0 if absent.

Figure 8.5a shows the frames involved in link setup and disconnect. In the example, the TE is requesting the connection; a similar sequence occurs if the NT requests the connection. The data link entity for the TE issues an SABME command to the other side and starts a timer, T200 (see Table 8.3). The other LAPD entity, upon receiving the SABME, returns a UA response and sets local variables and counters to their initial values. The initiating entity receives the UA response, sets its variables and counters, and stops the timer. The logical connection is now

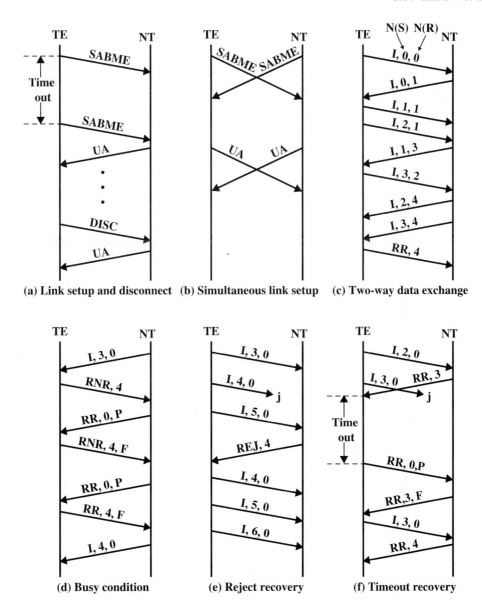

Figure 8.5 Examples of LAPD Operation.

active, and both sides may begin transmitting frames. Should the T200 expire without a response, the originator will repeat the SABME, as illustrated. This would be repeated until a UA or DM is received or until, after a given number of tries (N200), the entity attempting initiation gives up and reports failure to a management entity. In this case, higher-layer intervention is necessary. The same figure (Figure 8.5a) shows the disconnect procedure. One side issues a DISC command, and the other responds with a UA response.

Table 8.3 LAPD System Parameters

Parameter	Default Value	Definition
T200	1 second	Time to wait for an acknowledgment before initiating recovery
T201	= T200	Minimum time between TEI identity check messages
T202	2 seconds	Minimum time between TEI identity request messages
T203	10 seconds	Maximum time with no frames exchanged
N200	3	Maximum number of retransmissions of a frame
N201	260 octets	Maximum length of information field
N202	3	Maximum number of retransmissions of TEI identity request message
k	1 for 16-kbps signaling; 3 for 16-kbps packet; 7 for 64 kbps	Maximum number of outstanding I-frames

LAPD is a balanced mode of operation, meaning that the NT and TE entities have equal status. Thus, it is possible that both sides may attempt to set up a logical connection involving the same two TEI/SAPI users at about the same time. Figure 8.5b illustrates that this situation is resolved by having both sides respond to the incoming SABME and then setting up the logical connection.

Figure 8.5c illustrates the full-duplex exchange of I-frames. When an entity sends a number of I-frames in a row with no incoming data, then the receive sequence number is simply repeated (e.g., I,1,1; I,2,1 in the TE-to-NT direction). When an entity receives a number of I-frames in a row with no outgoing frames, then the receive sequence number in the next outgoing frame must reflect the cumulative activity (e.g., I,1,3 in the NT-to-TE direction). Note that, in addition to I-frames, data exchange may involve supervisory frames.

Figure 8.5d shows an operation involving a busy condition. Such a condition may arise because a LAPD entity is not able to process I-frames as fast as they are arriving, or the intended user is not able to accept data as fast as they arrive in I-frames. In either case, the entity's receive buffer fills up and it must halt the incoming flow of I-frames using an RNR command. In this example, the TE issues an RNR, which requires the NT to halt transmission of I-frames. The station receiving the RNR will usually poll the busy station at some periodic interval by sending an RR with the P bit set. This requires the other side to respond with either an RR or an RNR. When the busy condition has cleared, the TE returns an RR, and I-frame transmission from the NT can resume.

An example of error recovery using the REJ command is shown in Figure 8.5e. In this example, the TE transmits I-frames numbered 3, 4, and 5. Number 4 suffers an error. The NT detects the error and discards the frame. When the NT receives I-frame number 5, it discards this frame because it is out of order and sends an REJ with an N(R) of 4. This causes the TE entity to initiate retransmission of all I-frames sent, beginning with frame 4. It may continue to send additional frames after the retransmitted frames.

An example of error recovery using a timeout is shown in Figure 8.5f. In this example, the TE transmits I-frame number 3 as the last in a sequence of I-frames. The frame suffers an error. The NT detects the error and discards it. However, the NT cannot send an REJ. This is because there is no way to know on which logical connection the damaged frame was sent or, indeed, whether or not it was even an I-frame. If an error is detected in a frame, all of the bits of that frame are suspect, and the receiver has no way to act upon it. The transmitter, however, started a timer (T200) as the frame was transmitted. This timer has a duration long enough to span the expected response time. When the timer expires, the station initiates recovery action. This is usually done by polling the other side with an RR command with the P bit set, to determine the status of the other side. Because the poll demands a response, the entity will receive a frame containing an N(R) field and be able to proceed. In this case, the response indicates that frame 3 was lost, which the TE retransmits.

These examples are not exhaustive. However, they should give the reader a good feel for the behavior of LAPD.

Unacknowledged Operation

Unacknowledged operation provides for the exchange of user data without error control or flow control. The unnumbered information (UI) frame is used to transmit user data. When a LAPD user wishes to send data, it passes the data to its LAPD entity, which passes the data in the information field of a UI frame. When this frame is received, the information field is passed up to the destination user. There is no acknowledgment returned to the other side. However, error detection is performed and frames in error are discarded.

Management Functions

There are two functions related to link management that apply to the LAPD entity as a whole, rather than to a particular connection or user of LAPD. These are for TEI management and for parameter negotiation.

TEI Management

The TEI management capability provides for automatic TEI assignment procedures. These procedures may be invoked for newly connected TE equipment at a specific user–network interface, so that no manual setting of a TEI value is necessary. The initiation of TEI assignment is triggered by one of two events. First, if equipment is connected to the user–network interface, and the user attempts either unacknowledged data transfer or the establishment of a logical connection, the LAPD entity suspends action on the request until a TEI assignment takes place. Or, second, the user-side layer management entity may initiate the TEI assignment procedures for its own reasons. In either case, the user LAPD entity transmits a UI frame with an SAPI of 63, a TEI of 127, and an information field that contains two subfields: message type and reference number. The message type is *identity request*. The reference number is a random number used to differentiate among a number of simultaneous identity requests by different user equipment. If the network side is able to assign an unused TEI value in the range

Table 8.4 Messages for TEI Management Procedures

Message Name	Direction	Parameters	Description
Identity request	User → network	Ri = random Ai = 127	Request automatic TEI assignment
Identity assigned	Network → user	Ri = match identity request value Ai = TEI assignment (64–126)	Assigns TEI value
Identity denied	Network → user	Ri = match identity request value Ai = Denied TEI value (64–126) Ai = 127 (no TEI value available)	Denies an identity request
Identity check request	Network → user	Ai = TEI value to be checked (64–126) Ai = 127 (check all values)	Allows network to either establish the TEI value is in use or verify duplicate TEI assignment
Identity check response	User → network	Ai = TEI value (0–126) Ri = random	Response by user equipment with matching TEI value
Identity remove	Network → user	Ai = TEI value (0–126) Ai = 127 (remove all TEI values)	Removes a TEI value
Identity verify	User → network	Ai = TEI value to be checked (0–126) Ri = 0	Allows the user side to request that the network invoke the identity check procedure for verification of duplicate TEI assignment

Ri = reference number
Ai = action indicator

194

64 to 126, then it responds with a UI frame with an SAPI of 63, a TEI of 127, and an information field that contains three subfields: message type, reference number, and action indicator. The reference number is equal to the value received from the user, the message type is *identity assigned,* and the action indicator is the assigned TEI value. If the network is unable to assign a TEI, it returns a UI with a message type of identity denied.

In addition to automatic TEI assignment, there are procedures for checking the value of an existing TEI assignment and removing a TEI assignment. These procedures also make use of UI frames.

Table 8.4 summarizes the messages used for TEI management. The first three messages have already been discussed. The identity check request message is used in TEI audit and recovery procedures. It allows the network side to establish that a particular TEI value is in use or to discover the existence of multiple user equipment assigned the same TEI value. When an identity check message is issued by the network, the TE or TEs with the matching TEI respond with an identity check response message. If the identity check request is issued with an action indicator of 127, then all TEs respond. This check procedure may also be invoked as a response to an identity verify request message from the user equipment.

If the network side determines that a TEI value should be discontinued, it issues an identity remove message, and the appropriate user equipment will remove its TEI and enter a state of TEI unassigned. The network may issue such a command if it determines that a duplicate TEI assignment exists.

Figure 8.6 illustrates the format of the information field of a UI LAPD frame for carrying a TEI management message.

Parameter Negotiation

Associated with LAPD operation are certain key parameters. Each parameter is assigned a default value in the standard, but provisions are made for the negotiation of other values. The parameters and their default values are listed in Table 8.3. If a LAPD entity wishes to use a different set of values for a particular logical connection, it may issue an XID frame, with the desired values contained in subfields of the information field. The other side responds with an XID containing the list of parameter values that the peer can support. Each value must be in the range between the default value and the requested value.

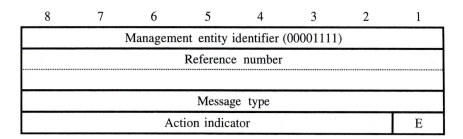

8	7	6	5	4	3	2	1
Management entity identifier (00001111)							
Reference number							
Message type							
Action indicator							E

Figure 8.6   UI Information Field for TEI Management Messages.

8.2 TERMINAL ADAPTION

Terminal
Adaptors

Much of the existing data communications equipment is not compatible with the interfaces, protocols, and data rates of ISDN. In the long run, equipment will be built with ISDN interfaces, but this existing equipment must be accommodated during the transition period. This is the function of the terminal adapter (TA). In essence, a terminal adapter maps a non-ISDN terminal, personal computer, multiplexer, or modem into an ISDN interface. Analog telephones and facsimile machines can also be accommodated. In most cases, the adaption is to the basic rate (2B + D) interface.

There is actually a family of terminal adapters, one type for each type of non-ISDN interface. All of these devices map the characteristics and functions of a particular device to the ISDN characteristics and functions. In general terms, the following functions are performed:

- **Rate adaption:** A data stream of less than 64 kbps is mapped into a 64-kbps data stream.
- **Signaling conversion:** The signaling protocol of the device is mapped into the ISDN signaling protocol, Q.931. For example, many devices support interfaces, such as X.21 or EIA-232-D, which provide an inband signaling protocol. These inband messages must be converted to D channel Q.931 messages.
- **X.25 conversion:** The functions of non-ISDN X.25 devices are converted to operate on the B and/or D channels. This involves both rate adaption and signaling conversion.
- **Physical interface conversion:** The ISDN interface consists of two twisted pairs at the S or T interface. The non-ISDN interface must be mapped onto this physical interface.
- **Digitization:** In the case of analog devices, analog-to-digital conversion is required.

To accommodate the wide variety of existing equipment and the need to support both circuit-switching and packet-switching applications, ITU-T has developed a complex set of capabilities that are defined primarily in the I.460 series of recommendations. Table 8.5 summarizes the procedures defined in the I.460 series, and Table 8.6 compares the features of the various approaches.

Table 8.5 Summary of TA Procedures

ISDN Service	TA Procedures	R Interface(s)	ISDN Channel(s)
Circuit switched	I.465/V.120 (U.S.) I.463/V.110 (Europe, Japan) I.461/X.30	V.24, V.35 V.24, V.35 X.21	B, H B B
Packet switched	I.462/X.31 circuit mode I.462/X.31 packet mode	X.25 X.25	B B, D, H

Table 8.6   Comparison of TA Standards [WEIS89]

	I.463/V.110 & I.461/X.30	I.465/V.120	I.462/X.31
ISDN bearer service	Circuit	Circuit	Circuit/packet
Rate adaption	1–3 stages	Flag stuffing	Flag stuffing
Multiple destinations	No	No	Yes
HDLC-based	No	Yes	Yes
B channel multiplexing	No	Yes—LLI	Yes—VCN
D channel operation	No	No	Yes, with packet bearer service
Error detection	None	CRC—V.41	CRC—V.41
Error correction	None	Retransmission	Retransmission
Flow control	Limited (X bit)	Yes—sliding window	Yes—sliding window
Type of DTE at R	Async/sync (bit transparent)	Async/HDLC/bit transparent	X.25 sync

CRC = cyclic redundancy check
DTE = data terminal equipment
VCN = virtual circuit number
LLI = logical link ID
PAD = packet assembler/disassembler
TA = terminal adapter

The terminal adapter may be either a stand-alone device or a personal computer circuit card. In either case, the TA supports D channel signaling (Q.931 and Q.921) and a procedure on the B channel that indicates the nature of the adaption. The TA allows the terminal equipment (TE2 in Figure 6.2) to communicate across ISDN with another TE2 attached to a TA. A TE2 may also communicate across ISDN with a TE1. In both cases, the two partners must use the same B channel procedure, such as V.110 or V.120, to communicate.

Rate Adaption

The principal means of transmitting user data is the B channel, which operates at a data rate of 64 kbps. However, it is desirable to be able to support subscriber devices on the B channel that operate at data rates of less than 64 kbps. There are two reasons for this. First, much existing equipment, such as terminals and personal computers, operates at data rates of less than 64 kbps.

The second reason has to do with the advantages of multiplexing. As we have pointed out, in the current version of the ISDN standards, the entire B channel is the fundamental unit of circuit switching. That is, even if a B channel is logically divided into a number of subchannels, all of the subchannels must be carried on a single circuit between the same pair of subscribers. Even so, a subscriber may have several devices attached to an ISDN interface and wish to connect two or more of them to the same destination. For example, a residential user might want to connect to his or her office and make use of a personal computer and a facsimile at the same time. It will be cheaper if all of this traffic can be carried on one B channel. Furthermore, if all of the data traffic to the office is multiplexed on one B channel, the other B channel of the resident's basic interface is free for sending and receiving telephone calls.

We examine rate adaption in this subsection and then look at multiplexing in the next subsection.

Rate adaption is the function of adapting a terminal with a data rate of less than 64 kbps to a data rate of 64 kbps. Figure 8.7 summarizes the techniques that are specified in I.460.

The initial distinction made in I.460 is whether the bit stream to be carried on the B channel is exactly 8, 16, or 32 kbps or whether it is some other data rate.

Data Rate of 8, 16, or 32 kbps

The first case is illustrated in Figure 8.8. Bits are transmitted on the B channel as a stream of octets at a rate of 64 kbps or, equivalently, 8000 octets per second.

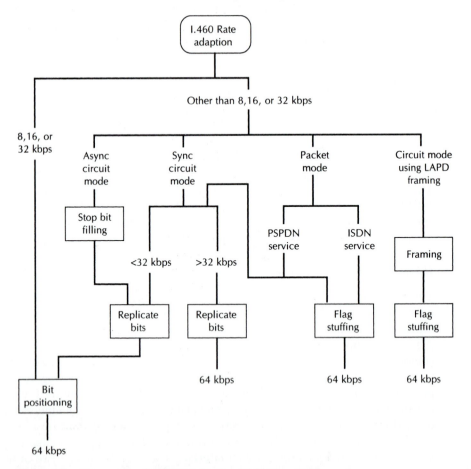

Figure 8.7 Alternatives for Rate Adaption to 64-kbps B Channel.

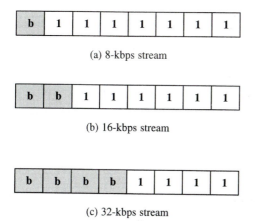

(a) 8-kbps stream

(b) 16-kbps stream

(c) 32-kbps stream

Figure 8.8 Allocation of Bits in B Channel Octet for Rate Adaption.

For an 8-kbps subscriber device, a terminal adapter (TA) works as follows. Data from the subscriber arrive at the TA at a rate of 8 kbps. Each incoming bit is transmitted in an octet in which the first bit of the octet is a user data bit, and the remaining 7 bits are each set to binary one. For data arriving from the ISDN side, the first bit of each incoming octet is passed on to the terminal and the remaining 7 bits are discarded. A similar adaption procedure is followed for terminals operating at 16 kbps and 32 kbps. For 16-kbps streams, the first 2 bits of each octet are used, and for 32-kbps streams, the first 4 bits of each octet are used.

Synchronous Circuit-Mode Devices

The second case listed in I.460 (rates other than 8, 16, or 32 kbps) breaks down into a number of subcases, several of which are broken down even further. Let us consider next the case of a synchronous device using the B channel circuit-mode service; procedures for this case are defined in I.461/X.30 (terminals that use the X.21, X.21 *bis,* and X.20 *bis* interfaces) and I.463/V.110 (terminals that use the V-series interfaces). If the terminal data rate is less than 32 kbps, then a two-stage adaption function is used; this is illustrated in Figure 8.9. The allowable input rates are shown in Table 8.7a. The user data rate is first converted to an intermediate rate of 8, 16, or 32 kbps and then converted from this intermediate rate to 64 kbps. The advantage of using a two-stage technique is that the second stage could be reversed (e.g., from 64 kbps to 8 kbps) somewhere in the network for the purpose of conserving loop or trunk capacity. As a service offering, this could carry a lower tariff rate.

The second stage of the rate adaptation, labeled RA2 in Figure 8.9, is the same as that just described for adapting 8, 16, or 32 kbps to 64 kbps. The first stage, labeled RA1, involves the creation of a frame, with only some of the bits in the frame carrying user data. As a specific example, consider the adaptation of a user rate of 2400 bps to an intermediate ISDN rate of 8 kbps, which is illustrated in Table 8.8. The conversion is implemented by means of an 80-bit frame structure. Although the data transmitted out of the RA1 module is a constant bit stream, it is considered to consist of a sequence of 80-bit frames. The bits of the frame are as follows:

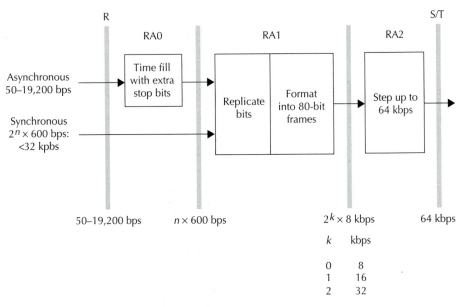

Figure 8.9 Rate Adaption (I.463/V.110).

- The first octet is all zeros. The first bit of the remaining nine octets is one. These 17 bits constitute a frame-alignment pattern that provides a means of synchronization.
- The sixth octet contains a one followed by a set of "E bits," E1, E2, ..., E7. These bits are used to indicate the user data rate. At present only the first three bits are used for this purpose; the remaining bits are reserved for future use. The code 110 for E1, E2, E3 indicates that the user data rate is 2400 bps.
- The S bits are status bits that convey channel-associated status information. The exact nature of these bits depends on the physical interface between the subscriber terminal and the terminal adapter.
- The X bits are unused and reserved for future use.
- Each data bit is repeated. This repetition is not strictly necessary; it acts to fill in unneeded bit positions. These positions could also have been filled in with arbitrary bits.

Each frame contains 24 user data bits. Because we have an 8-kbps output data rate and 80-bit frames, the rate of transmission of frames is 100 frames per second; therefore, the rate of transmission of user data is 2400 bps, as required. In general, we can summarize the function of the RA1 module in Figure 8.9 as follows. Define

F = the number of bits in the frame
F_u = the number of data bits in the frame
R_u = the user data rate
R_f = the desired rate of transmission, in frames per second
R = the desired rate of transmission, in bits per second

Two formulas must be satisfied:

$$F \times R_f = R$$

and

$$R_u / R_f = F_u \quad \text{with no remainder}$$

When the data rate to be adapted is between 32 kbps and 64 kbps, only the RA1 stage of Figure 8.9 is needed.

Table 8.7   Terminal Rates Supported by V.110

(a) Synchronous User Rates	
Synchronous data rate (bps)	RA1 synchronous rate (kbps)
600	8
1200	8
2400	8
4800	8
7200	16
9600	16
12,000	32
14,400	32
19,200	32
24,000	64
28,800	64
38,400	64

(b) Asynchronous User Rates		
Asynchronous data rate (bps)	RA0/RA1 synchronous rate (bps)	RA1 synchronous rate (kbps)
50	600	8
75	600	8
110	600	8
150	600	8
200	600	8
300	600	8
600	600	8
1200	1200	8
2400	2400	8
3600	4800	8
4800	4800	8
7200	9600	16
9600	9600	16
12,000	19,200	32
14,400	19,200	32
19,200	19,200	32
24,000	38,000	64
28,800	38,000	64
38,400	38,400	64

Table 8.8   Adaption of 2400-bps User Rate to 8-kcs Intermediate Rate

Octet	Bits							
1	0	0	0	0	0	0	0	0
2	1	D1	D1	D2	D2	D3	D3	S
3	1	D4	D4	D5	D5	D6	D6	X
4	1	D7	D7	D8	D8	D9	D9	S
5	1	D10	D10	D11	D11	D12	D12	S
6	1	1	1	0	E4	E5	E6	E7
7	1	D13	D13	D14	D14	D15	D15	S
8	1	D16	D16	D17	D17	D18	D18	X
9	1	D19	D19	D20	D20	D21	D21	S
10	1	D22	D22	D23	D23	D24	D24	S

D = data bits
S = status bits
E = user data rate indication
X = reserved for future use

So far, we have discussed the case of circuit-switched connections. With this type of connection, there is a transparent transmission of data between the two subscribers. With rate adaption, it is still necessary that the two subscribers operate at the same data rate. For example, a terminal operating at 2400 bps can be rate adapted to 64 kbps. One could attempt to connect this terminal through ISDN to a 4800-bps, computer port that is also rate adapted to 64 kbps. However, the computer will transmit data at 4800 bps, and the terminal's adapter expects and requires that the incoming 64-kbps stream contain only user data at a rate of 2400 bps. Thus, the traditional circuit-switching requirement, that the data rate of both users connected to the same circuit must be the same, applies in ISDN.

One final point about the circuit-switching rate adaption. The user data rate is identified during the call setup, which takes place via common-channel signaling on the D channel. During the call setup phase, the network will assure that the data rate of the two subscribers is the same; otherwise, the connection request is rejected.

Asynchronous Circuit-Mode Devices

I.463/V.110 also specifies TA functions for handling asynchronous devices. To accommodate these devices, a three-stage method is employed. The second and third stages are the RA1 and RA2 functional modules defined for the synchronous case. The first stage, labeled RA0, converts an asynchronous character stream to one of the acceptable synchronous data rates. Table 8.7b lists the asynchronous data rates supported.

The technique used in the RA0 stage is simply to add additional stop bits between characters to step up the data rate to the nearest intermediate rate that can be accepted by the RA1 module. Because asynchronous transmission allows multiple stop bits between characters, the asynchronous receiver can accept the padded character stream directly. If the receiver is to match the data rate of the asynchronous transmitter, then the additional stop bits can be stripped off by the TA at the receiving end.

Packet-Mode Support

Recommendation I.462/X.31 specifies the support of packet-mode equipment over ISDN. Recall that there are two cases: packet switching done by an external network (Case A) and packet switching done within ISDN (Case B). In either case, the subscriber does not have a direct circuit to another subscriber. Rather, the subscriber has a circuit connection to a packet-switched node and communicates with other packet-switching subscribers via X.25. Here again, we may be faced with the case of a preexisting subscriber device that operates at a data rate of less than 64 kbps.

Consider first Case A, connection to an external packet-switching node via a circuit over a B channel. Recall from Figure 4.10 that X.25 packets are transmitted in LAPB frames. If the data rate of the subscriber device is less than 64 kbps, then a terminal adapter can function as follows. LAPB frames are accepted from the subscriber at the subscriber's data rate and buffered in the TA. Each frame is then transmitted onto the B channel at 64 kbps. Because frames are being transmitted faster than they are generated, there will be gaps. These gaps are filled with additional flag octets (01111110). When frames are received from the network at 64 kbps, they are buffered and delivered to the subscriber at the subscriber's data rate. Excess flag octets between frames are discarded. This process is known as *interframe flag stuffing*. With this procedure, the network cannot distinguish between packet-mode devices operating at 64 kbps and those operating at less than 64 kbps. Therefore, the D channel signaling used to connect a device to a packet-switching node indicates a data rate of 64 kbps.

The alternative approach is the *two-stage rate adaption* of Figure 8.9 (RA1 and RA2). In this case, the bits transmitted by the subscriber are embedded into the 80-octet structure described earlier, and the D channel signaling indicates the user data rate. With this technique, the packet-switching node to which the subscriber is linked must match the data rate of the subscriber. This is clearly less flexible than the interframe flag stuffing approach, and the latter is recommended by ITU-T.

In Case B, ISDN offers an internal packet-switching service over both the B channel and the D channel. X.25 packets are carried in LAPB frames for the B channel and LAPD frames for the D channel. Rate adaption to 64 kbps for the B channel and to 16 kbps for the D channel is accomplished via flag stuffing.

Circuit-Mode Support Using LAPD Framing

An alternative method of supporting synchronous circuit-mode equipment is defined in I.465/V.120. In essence, an incoming synchronous bit stream is encapsulated into LAPD frames and then adapted to 64 kbps by flag stuffing. Unlike the other techniques discussed so far, I.465/V.120 may also be used on H_0 (384 kbps), H_{11} (1.536 Mbps), and H_{12} (1.92 Mbps) channels.

The terminal adaption function is based on a modification of LAPD that supports connections between subscribers using the I.465/V.120 protocol. This protocol provides a consistent method for carrying different types of data streams. In this section, we provide a brief introduction to I.465/V.120 and focus on its rate adaption functions. The protocol is examined in more detail in the next section.

I.465/V.120 provides support for three R-interface terminal types:

- Asynchronous protocol sensitive
- HDLC synchronous protocol sensitive
- Bit transparent

The **asynchronous protocol sensitive** case refers to communication between an asynchronous terminal and a host that expects asynchronous input or between two asynchronous terminals. For transmission, the start and stop bits of each character are removed and the incoming characters are buffered in the terminal adapter. The length of the buffer equals the maximum information field size that may be transmitted in a frame. When the buffer is full, a LAPD frame is created and transmitted. In addition, a partially full buffer of characters may be sent when a carriage return is received or when a timeout occurs. When a frame is received, the characters are recovered and sent to the destination TE with the appropriate start and stop bits.

The **HDLC synchronous protocol sensitive** case refers to communication between entities that are using HDLC as a link-control protocol for end-to-end operation. For transmission, most of the HDLC frame is encapsulated in a LAPD frame. Several inessential fields are discarded. On reception, the HDLC frame is recovered, the missing fields are added, and the reconstituted frame is passed on to the destination entity. The details of this frame processing are examined in the next section.

The **bit transparent** case will accommodate any synchronous device. The TA encapsulates the bits from the R interface into fixed-size LAPD frames as they are received. The TA takes data from frames received and sends them to the TE2.

The advantage of the I.465/V.120 approach compared with the I.461/V.110 approach is that the data are transmitted in I.465/V.120 using a data link control protocol. This provides for the benefits of flow control and error control that are inherent in a link-control protocol (see Appendix A).

Multiplexing

Multiplexing, in the context of this section, is the function of combining traffic from multiple terminals, each with a data rate of less than 64 kbps, onto a single B channel at 64 kbps. Figure 8.10 summarizes the techniques that are specified in I.460. As in the case of rate adaption, the initial distinction made in I.460 is whether the bit stream to be carried on the B channel is exactly 8, 16, or 32 kbps or whether it is some other data rate.

Data Rate of 8, 16, or 32 kbps

In this case, there are multiple bit streams of 8, 16, and/or 32 kbps with an aggregate data rate that is less than or equal to 64 kbps. For this case, bits from different streams, up to a total of 64 kbps, are interleaved within each octet.

Two approaches to multiplexing are defined. With **fixed-format multiplexing**, the following rules are observed:

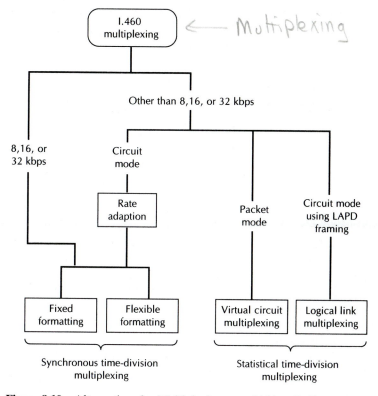

Figure 8.10 Alternatives for Multiplexing on a 64-kbps B Channel.

1. An 8-kbps bit stream may occupy any bit position; a 16-kbps bit stream may occupy bit positions (1, 2), (3, 4), (5, 6), or (7, 8); a 32-kbps bit stream may occupy bit positions (1, 2, 3, 4) or (5, 6, 7, 8).
2. A subrate stream occupies the same bit position(s) in each successive B channel octet.
3. All unused bit positions are set to binary one.

If this procedure is used and the data substreams are added one at a time, it is possible that the 64-kbps capacity will not be utilized effectively. For example, if bit positions 1 and 8 are used to support two 8-kbps substreams, then a 32-kbps substream cannot be added even though the capacity is available. An approach that avoids this is **flexible-format multiplexing**. The following rules are observed:

1. An attempt is made to accommodate a new subrate stream using the fixed-format procedure.
2. If this attempt fails, the new subrate stream is added by inserting each successive bit of the new stream into the earliest available bit position in the B channel octet.

3. A subrate stream occupies the same bit position(s) in each successive B channel octet.

4. All unused bit positions are set to binary one.

This procedure always allows subrate streams to be multiplexed up to the 64-kbps limit of the B channel. The fixed-format procedure is simpler to implement and should be used if the mixture of subrate streams is known in advance. When the mixture is dynamic, ITU-T recommends the use of the more complex flexible-format procedure.

Note that both of these approaches are examples of synchronous time-division multiplexing.

Circuit-Mode Devices

The second case listed in I.460 (rates other than 8, 16, or 32 kbps) breaks down into a number of subcases. Let us consider next the case of a device using the B channel circuit-mode service. In this case, a two-stage approach is used. First, each stream is rate adapted to 8, 16, or 32 kbps. Second, the resulting streams are multiplexed as described previously.

As with the previous case, the approach described here is an example of synchronous time-division multiplexing.

Packet-Mode Support

For packet-mode devices, the multiplexing function is automatically provided by the layer 3 virtual circuit mechanism of X.25. Recall that in X.25, a DTE is allowed to establish up to 4095 simultaneous virtual circuits (Chapter 3). Thus, once a connection is made via a B channel or D channel to a packet-switching node, multiple virtual circuits can be set up across that connection. Furthermore, the virtual circuits need not all terminate at the same destination. A virtual circuit can be established with any subscriber to the same packet-switching network service.

Finally, this multiplexing capability exists whether the packet switching is provided by an external packet-switching network that is reached via a B channel circuit (Case A) or is supported internal to the ISDN (Case B).

Circuit-Mode Support Using LAPD Framing

As described previously, I.465/V.120 specifies that all data be transmitted in modified LAPD frames. One of the fields of the frame is a 13-bit logical link identifier (LLI). The LLI functions much as the X.25 virtual circuit number but operates in this case at the link layer. With the use of the LLI, the subscriber can simultaneously establish multiple logical links over a single B channel circuit. The LLI enables the recipient to sort out the incoming traffic and route it to the appropriate user.

One limitation of this approach, compared with the X.25 approach, is that all the multiplexing occurs between the same two endpoints. That is, a single-channel circuit, defined between two subscribers, supports multiple logical channels between those two subscribers.

8.3 BEARER CHANNEL DATA LINK CONTROL USING I.465/V.120

In the preceding section, we introduced I.465/V.120, which provided a technique for supporting non-ISDN terminals over an ISDN B channel using a data link control protocol that is a modified form of LAPD. I.465/V.120 provides a consistent method for carrying different types of data streams, including

- **Asynchronous protocol sensitive:** Asynchronous terminal-computer traffic
- **HDLC synchronous protocol sensitive:** Synchronous transmission between devices using HDLC
- **Bit transparent:** Arbitrary synchronous data streams

As just described, I.465/V.120 defines techniques for mapping from each of these data stream types into a common transmission technique using the I.465/V.120 data link control protocol. Thus, two TE2s that share one of the preceding transmission techniques can communicate over ISDN via I.465/V.120. But more is implied in this recommendation, as shown in Figure 8.11. A TE2 can also communicate with a TE1. In this case, the TA maps the TE2 traffic into I.465/V.120 traffic, and the TE1 must include logic for transmitting and receiving I.465/V.120 traffic. Finally, because this is a general-purpose data link control protocol, it can be used by two TE1s to communicate with each other. Thus, I.465/V.120 provides a flexible and useful data link control protocol for the B channel.

The V.120 standard may be used either in a circuit-switching or a frame relay environment. Specifically, it provides for operation

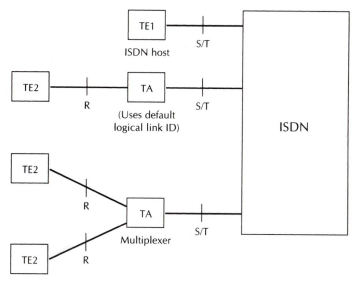

Figure 8.11   Types of I.465/V.120 TE Connections [WEIS89].

- Over either circuit-mode or frame-mode connections
- Using either demand or semipermanent establishment of communications
- Over any of the following types of access channel:
    - ¤ for circuit-mode connections: B, H0, H10, or H11.
    - ¤ for frame-mode connections: B, H0, H10, or H11, or D.

The bulk of this section is devoted to a discussion of circuit-mode operation. At the end of the section, we briefly discuss the frame-mode case. We begin with an examination of the frame structure that is used in the data link protocol and then examine connection control procedures.

I.465/V.120 Frame Structure for Circuit-Mode Connections

Figure 8.12a shows the overall I.465/V.120 frame format. The flag, control, and frame-check sequence (FCS) fields are the same as those of LAPD. The only differences are in the address and information fields.

Address Field

The address field includes a 13-bit logical link identifier (LLI). The LLI makes it possible simultaneously to support multiple logical connections, or links, over the same B channel. This is analogous to the ability in X.25 level 3 to support multiple virtual circuits. The limitation here, compared with X.25, is that all of the communicating pairs must be on the two ends of a single B channel. One example of an application of this multiplexing capability is the support of multiple terminals through a TA that acts as a statistical multiplexer (Figure 8.13). All of the terminal traffic is multiplexed over a single B channel to a host computer. The data streams of the various terminals are individually identified by their LLI.

Table 8.9a shows the assignment of LLI values. A value of 0 is used for inchannel signaling. This has to do with setting up and managing logical link connections, as explained later. There is a default value of LLI = 256, which eliminates the LLI management procedure and thereby simplifies I.465/V.120 implementation for terminal adaptation of a single non-ISDN terminal. Values between 257 and 2047 are used for individual logical links; thus a total of 1791 logical links can be carried simultaneously on a single B channel. The value of 8191 is used for inchannel management procedures that are not part of the standard.

Information Field

As usual, the information field is used to carry user information. In addition, it may contain a one- or two-octet header. The first header octet, referred to as the terminal adaptation header, is mandatory for protocol-sensitive modes (asynchronous and HDLC synchronous) and is optional for bit transparent modes. The second header octet, referred to as the control state information octet, may be present if the first octet is present.

The bits of the terminal adaption header (Figure 8.12d) are as follows:

(text continues on page 211)

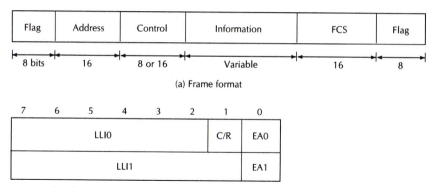

(a) Frame format

LLI0 = High-order 6 bits of logical link identifier
LLI1 = Low-order 7 bits of logical link identifier
C/R = Command/response
EA0 = Octet 2 address extension bit—set to 0
EA1 = Octet 3 address extension bit—set to 1 (for 2-octet address field)

(b) Address field

H = Terminal adaption header (optional for bit transparent mode)
CS = Optional header extension for control state information

(c) Information field

E	BR	res	res	C2	C1	B	F

E = Extension bit
BR = Break/HDLC idle bit
C1, C2 = Error-control bus
B, F = Segmentation bits
res = Reserved for future standardization

(d) Terminal adaption header

E	DR	SR	RR	res	res	res	res

E = Extension bit
DR = Data ready
SR = Send ready
RR = Receive ready
res = Reserved for future standardization

(e) Optional header extension

Figure 8.12   I.465/V.120 for Circuit-Mode Bearer Services.

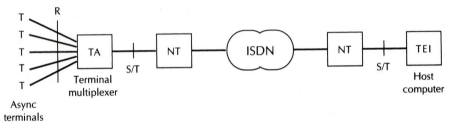

Figure 8.13 I.465/V.120 Assignments.

Table 8.9 I.465/V.120 Assignments

(a) Reserved LLI values

LLI	Function
0	Inchannel signaling
1–255	Reserved for future standardization
256	Default LLI
257–2047	For LLI assignment
2048–2190	Reserved for future standardization
8191	Inchannel layer management

(b) Coding of C1 and C2 bits

C1	C2	Synchronous mode	Asynchronous mode	Bit transparent mode
0	0	No error detected	No error detected	No error detected
0	1	FCS error (interface at R)	Stop-bit error	Not applicable
1	0	Abort	Parity error on the last character in frame	Not applicable
1	1	TA overrun (interface at R)	Both stop-bit and parity error	Not applicable

(c) Coding of B and F bits

B	F	Synchronous mode	Asynchronous mode	Bit transparent mode
0	0	Begin frame	Not applicable	Not applicable
0	1	Middle frame	Not applicable	Not applicable
1	0	Final frame	Not applicable	Not applicable
1	1	Single frame	Required	Required

210

- **Extension bit (E):** Allows for extension of the header to provide additional control state information. A zero indicates that a control state octet follows.
- **Break/HDLC idle bit (BR):** In asynchronous mode, this bit indicates the invocation of the break function by the TE2. In HDLC mode, it indicates an HDLC idle condition at the R referent point.
- **Error-control bits (C1, C2):** Used for TA error detection and transmission. Table 8.9b indicates the coding of these bits.
- **Segmentation bits (B, F):** Used in HDLC synchronous mode for segmentation and reassembly. This allows the TA to segment a single HDLC frame into multiple segments, which are reassembled at the receiver. Table 8.9c indicates the coding of these bits.

The bits of the control state information octet (Figure 8.12e) are as follows:

- **Extension bit (E):** Allows for further extension of the header; currently, no such extension is defined.
- **Data Ready bit (DR):** Indicates whether the interface at the R reference point is activated.
- **Send Ready bit (SR):** This bit set to 1 indicates that the TE is ready to send data.
- **Receive Ready bit (RR):** This bit set to 1 indicates that the TE is ready to receive data.

The last three bits just listed correspond to leads commonly found on modem interfaces for terminals. This allows the setting of these leads to be transmitted across ISDN.

Connection Control for Circuit-Mode Connections

The first step in using the I.465/V.120 data link control protocol is to establish a B channel circuit across ISDN. This is done using the Q.931 call-control protocol over the D channel, which is described in Chapter 8. —This is chapter 8
Once a circuit is established, the data link control protocol can be used in either connectionless or connection-oriented mode. For connectionless data transfer, an LLI of 256 is used and information is exchanged using UI frames, as in LAPD.
For connection-oriented data link control, it is necessary to proceed in three stages:

1. Establish a logical link between two peer entities at the two ends of the B channel circuit, and assign a unique LLI to the connection.
2. Exchange information in I-frames. The LLI field is used to allow multiplexing of a number of logical links.
3. Release the logical link.

Ultimately, when no more connections are active, one side or the other may choose to terminate the B channel circuit. Again, this is done using the Q.931 call-control protocol on the D channel. Now let us return to a consideration of the management of logical links on an existing B channel circuit.

Table 8.10   I.465/V.120 Connection Control Messages

(a) SETUP Message Content

Information Element	Type
Protocol discriminator	M
Call reference	M
Message type	M
Logical link identifier	O^1
Called party subaddress	O^2
Calling party subaddress	O^3
Low-layer compatibility	O^4

1: Included if the calling user assigns LLI for that connection.
2: Included if the calling user wishes to select a specific physical interface associated with this terminal adaptor.
3: Included if it is desired to identify the specific physical interface associated with the terminal adaptor of the calling user.
4: Included when the calling user want to pass low-layer compatibility information to the called user.

(b) CONNECT Message Content

Information Element	Type
Protocol discriminator	M
Call reference	M
Message type	M
Logical link identifier	O^1
Low-layer compatibility	O^2

1: Included if the called user is assigning LLI.
2: Included to allow the called user to negotiate low-layer compatibility information with the calling user.

(c) RELEASE Message Content

Information Element	Type
Protocol discriminator	M
Call reference	M
Message type	M
Cause	O

(d) RELEASE COMPLETE Message Content

Information Element	Type
Protocol discriminator	M
Call reference	M
Message type	M
Cause	O

The management of logical links is accomplished by an exchange of four messages (Table 8.10): SETUP, CONNect, RELease, and RELease COMPlete.[3] These messages can be exchanged between the peer data link control protocol entities in one of two ways:

1. In a B channel I.465/V.120 information frame with LLI = 0
2. In a D channel Q.931 user-to-user information message, if provided by the network

The choice of method is a terminal equipment option and is partially determined by the availability of end-to-end user signaling capability on the D channel. In both cases the message consists of a sequence of fields, as illustrated in Figure 8.14. If logical links are managed via the D channel, then these messages are embedded in a LAPD frame with an SAPI of 1 (see Table 8.1). If logical links are managed via the B channel, then these messages are embedded in an I.465/V.120 frame with an LLI of 0.

Three fields are common to all messages:

---

[3]These message types are the same as four of the messages in Q.931, with roughly the same meaning. The parameters are different for the two protocols, and the semantics are somewhat different.

- **Protocol discriminator:** Used to distinguish the protocol for I.465/V.120 logical link control from other protocols. Other protocols so far defined include Q.931, the X.25 packet-level protocol, and the protocol for frame relay connection control.
- **Call reference:** Identifies the B channel call to which this message refers. This parameter is discussed in Chapter 9.
- **Message type:** Identifies which I.465/V.120 message is being sent. The contents of the remainder of the message depend on the message type.

Following these three common fields, the remainder of the message consists of a sequence of zero or more information elements, or parameters. These are described subsequently, as we consider the individual message types. Each of these information elements consists of three fields: an identifier specifying which parameter this is, a length field, and a value.

Logical Link Establishment

Either side may request the establishment of a logical link by sending a SETUP message. The other side, upon receiving the SETUP message, must reply with a CONNect message if it accepts the connection; otherwise, it responds with a RELease COMPlete message.

If the side sending the SETUP message assigns the LLI, it chooses an unused value in the range 257–2047 and includes this value in the SETUP message. Otherwise, the LLI value is assigned by the accepting side in the CONNect message.

The two sides must agree on the type of terminal adaption support that is being provided. Unless this is arranged by prior agreement, the calling side should specify the relevant parameters in the low-layer compatibility element of the SETUP message. These parameters include the mode of operation (asynchronous protocol sensitive, HDLC synchronous protocol sensitive, bit transparent), the data

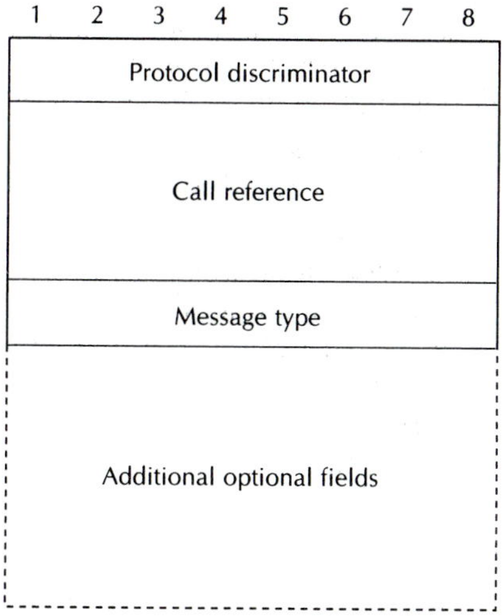

Figure 8.14 I.465/V.120 Message Format.

- TA uses Q.931 on D channel to establish circuit on B channel to TE1; use of I.465/V.120 on B channel is specified.
- TA issues I.465/V.120 messages (SETUP, CONNect) on D channel to establish a logical connection from one of its terminals to the TE1. Protocol discriminator field distinguishes these messages from Q.931 messages. LLI field used to assign unique LLI to this logical connection.
- TA may establish logical connections for other terminals using D channel I.465/V.120 messages. Each connection is assigned a unique LLI.
- Information is exchanged on the B channel using I.465/V.120 frames. The LLI field supports multiplexing.
- TA issues I.465/V.120 messages (RELease, RELease COMPlete) on D channel to terminate a logical connection from one of its terminals to the TE1.
- When all logical connections have been terminated, TA uses Q.931 on D channel to terminate circuit on B channel to TE1.

(a) Logical link establishment via D channel

- TA uses Q.931 on D channel to establish circuit on B channel to TE1; use of I.465/V.120 on B channel is specified.
- TA issues I.465/V.120 messages (SETUP, CONNect) on B channel to establish a logical connection from one of its terminals to the TE1. LLI field used to assign unique LLI to this logical connection.
- TA may establish logical connections for other terminals using B channel I.465/V.120 messages. Each connection is assigned a unique LLI.
- Information is exchanged on the B channel using I.465/V.120 frames. The LLI field supports multiplexing.
- TA issues I.465/V.120 messages (RELease, RELease COMPlete) on B channel to terminate a logical connection from one of its terminals to the TE1.
- When all logical connections have been terminated, TA uses Q.931 on D channel to terminate circuit on B channel to TE1.

(b) Logical link establishment via B channel

Figure 8.15 Alternative Connection Control Procedures for Scenario of Figure 8.13.

214

rate in each direction, and other details of the terminals supported. The called side may alter any of these parameters by including a revised low-layer compatibility element in the CONNect message.

Logical Link Clearing

Either side may request to clear a logical link by sending a RELease message. The other side, upon receipt of this message, must respond with a RELease COMPlete message. The Cause parameter is currently used only to specify whether this is a normal clearing or a call-rejected action.

As an example of the use of these messages, consider the configuration of Figure 8.13. A terminal adapter (TA) acts as a multiplexer to support multiple terminals. In this scenario, a B channel circuit is set up between the TA and a host computer across ISDN. When any terminal is to be connected to the host, it is assigned a separate logical link. Figure 8.15 shows the sequence of steps involved.

Frame–Mode Connections

The terminal adaption protocol defined in I.465/V.120 may be supported by a frame-mode bearer service. In this case, the protocol operates over a logical frame-mode connection rather than over a circuit-switched connection.

Frame Structure

The frame structure for the frame-mode case depends on whether the service is frame relay or frame switching. These services are described in detail in Chapter 11. In essence, a frame relay bearer service does not guarantee delivery of frames and provides no facilities for flow control and error control. The frame-switching bearer service does provide flow- and error-control capabilities and guarantees frame delivery. In the frame-switching case, the frame format is the same as shown in Figure 8.12, with the exception of the address field. A different address structure, described in Chapter 12, is used. In the case of the frame relay bearer service, the frame format is the same as that of Figure 8.12, except that there is no control field.

Connection Control

For demand establishment of frame-mode bearer connections for I.465/V.120, the frame-mode signaling protocol, defined in Q.933, is used. This protocol is discussed in Chapter 12 and is similar to the connection control protocol used on circuit-switched connections for I.465/V.120.

8.4   SUMMARY

LAPD defines the data link control protocol to be used on the D channel. This single protocol carries higher-layer protocol information for control signaling (Q.931), for X.25 packet switching, and for frame-mode connections. LAPD is based on LAPB, which is part of the X.25 standard, with modifications to the address field.

LAPB constitutes layer 2 of the X.25 packet-switching interface standard. It is used in conjunction with X.25 layer 3 on B channels to provide packet-switching support for ISDN users. When X.25 is used over the D channel, LAPD replaces LAPB as the layer 2 protocol.

I.465/V.120 is a terminal adaption procedure that provides a general-purpose data link control protocol for use over B and H channels. The chief feature of this protocol is that it allows multiple logical connections to be set up on a single circuit between two end users. This is part of the I.460 family of recommendations that specify support for existing non-ISDN terminals. Key functions are rate adaption and control-signaling adaption.

8.5 RECOMMENDED READING

Data link control protocols are discussed in greater detail in [STAL97]. The V-series of protocols, including V.110 and V.120 are discussed in some detail in [BLAC95].

BLAC95 Black, U. *The V Series Recommendations.* New York: McGraw-Hill, 1995.

STAL97 Stallings, W. *Data and Computer Communications, 5th edition.* Upper Saddle River, NJ: Prentice Hall, 1997.

8.6 PROBLEMS

8.1 It is clear that bit stuffing is needed for user data fields in LAPD frames, since we wish to accommodate arbitrary user data. Is it needed for the other fields? Specify which ones.

8.2 Suggest improvements to the bit-stuffing algorithm to overcome the problems of a single-bit error.

8.3 It was pointed out that some of the stuffed bits in Figure 8.2 were not strictly necessary. Consider the following rule: A 0 is stuffed by the transmitter only after the appearance of 011111.
   a. Describe the destuffing rule.
   b. Apply the rules to the bit stream in Figure 8.2.

8.4 Using the example bit string of Figure 8.2, show the signal pattern on the line using NRZ-L coding. Does this suggest a side benefit of bit stuffing?

8.5 Construct tables similar to Table 8.8 for the following data rate adaptions:
   a. 600 bps to 8 kbps
   b. 1200 bps to 8 kbps
   c. 4800 bps to 8 kbps
   d. 9600 bps to 16 kbps
   e. 19.2 kbps to 32 kbps
   f. 48 kbps to 64 kbps
   g. 56 kbps to 64 kbps

8.6 In the discussion of rate adaption, it was suggested that the two-stage procedure could save network capacity, since a conversion of, say, 8 kbps to 64 kbps could be reversed in the network. Since all of the subchannels of a single B channel must be carried on the same ISDN circuit between the same pair of subscribers, what opportunity for such savings is possible?

8.7 Subscriber X sets up a 64-kbps circuit-switched connection to subscriber Y over a B channel. Over time, various subchannels of traffic are carried between X and Y on the B channel. The pattern of traffic is as follows: add 8 kbps; add 32 kbps; add 16 kbps; subtract 32 kbps; add 16 kbps; subtract 8 kbps; add 32 kbps. Using flexible format multiplexing, show the assignment of B channel octet bits over time.

CHAPTER 9

ISDN NETWORK LAYER

→ D channel

For ISDN a new network-layer protocol, Q.931, has been developed that provides out-of-band call control for B and H channel traffic. This protocol, which makes use of the D channel, operates at the network level of the OSI model. It is used for both circuit-mode and packet-mode communication. A related recommendation, Q.932, provides additional functionality for controlling supplementary services. Both the basic protocol and the supplementary service facility are examined in this chapter.

9.1 OVERVIEW

The ISDN network layer includes a D channel protocol used to establish, maintain, and terminate network connections on B and H channels. The protocol also provides generic procedures for the invocation and operation of supplementary services. The ISDN specification for call control is contained in six recommendations:

- **Q.930—ISDN User–Network Interface Layer 3—General Aspects:** Describes in general terms the D channel layer 3 functions and protocol employed across an ISDN user–network interface.

- **Q.931—Specification for Basic Call Control:** Specifies the procedures for establishing, maintaining, and clearing network connections at the ISDN user–network interface.

- **Q.932—Generic Procedures for the Control of ISDN Supplementary Services:** Defines the generic procedures used for the invocation and operation of supplementary services in association with existing calls or outside any existing calls.

- **Q.933—Specification for Frame-Mode Basic Call Control:** Specifies procedures for establishing, maintaining, and clearing frame-mode connections at the ISDN user–network interface.

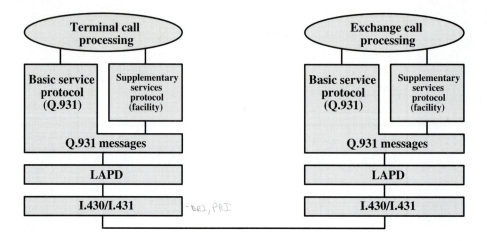

Figure 9.1   Modeling of Basic and Supplementary Services.

- **Q.939—Typical DSS 1 Service Indicator Codings for ISDN Telecommunications Services:** Provides specific codings for telecommunications services.
- **Q.950—Supplementary Service Protocols—Structure and General Principles:** Provides detailed procedures applicable to individual supplementary services.

The collection of capabilities for providing call control signaling over the D channel is referred to as Digital Subscriber Signaling System Number 1 (DSS 1). The general architecture is depicted in Figure 9.1. The physical layer, defined in I.430 (basic access) and I.431 (primary access), supports all B channel and D channel traffic. At the data link layer, LAPD supports all D channel traffic, including call control signaling. At the network layer, basic call control procedures and supplementary services procedures are both supported by messages defined in the Q.931 protocol. Thus, there is not a separate protocol for requesting and controlling supplementary services. Rather, some Q.931 messages define supplementary service control procedures.

9.2   BASIC CALL CONTROL

Q.931 specifies procedures for establishing connections on B and H channels that share the same interface to ISDN as the D channel. It also provides user-to-user control signaling over the D channel. In OSI terms, Q.931 is a layer 3, or network layer, protocol. As Figure 9.2 indicates, this protocol relies on LAPD to transmit messages over the D channel. Each Q.931 message is encapsulated in a link-layer frame. This link-layer frame is transmitted on the D channel, which is multiplexed at the physical layer with other channels according to I.430 or I.431.

ITU-T specifies the following as basic functions to be performed at the network layer for call control:

- Interaction with the data link layer (LAPD) to transmit and receive messages
- Generation and interpretation of layer 3 messages
- Administration of timers and logical entities (e.g., call references) used in the call control procedures
- Administration of access resources, including B channels and packet-layer logical channels (X.25)
- Verification that services provided are consistent with user requirements (e.g., as expressed by bearer capability, addresses, and low-layer and high-layer compatibilities)

In addition to these basic functions, a number of other functions may be required in certain network configurations to support certain services. ITU-T cites the following:

- **Routing and relaying:** For end systems connected to different subnetworks, routing and relaying functions are required to establish an end-to-end network connection.
- **Network connection control:** Includes mechanisms for providing network connections making use of data link connections.
- **Conveying user-to-network and network-to-user information:** This function may be carried out with or without the establishment of a circuit-switched connection.
- **Network connection multiplexing:** Layer 3 provides multiplexing of call control information for multiple calls onto a single data link (LAPD) connection.
- **Segmenting and reassembly:** It may be necessary to segment Q.931 messages on transmission and reassemble these messages upon reception for transfer across particular local user–network interfaces.
- **Error detection:** Error-detection functions check for procedural errors in the layer 3 protocol.
- **Error recovery:** This function includes mechanisms for recovering from detected errors.

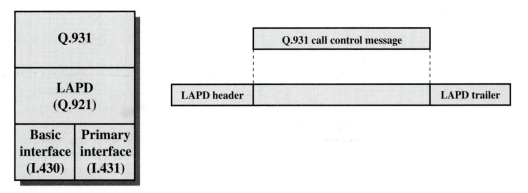

Figure 9.2   Call Control Protocol Architecture.

- **Sequencing:** This function provides mechanisms for sequenced delivery of layer 3 information when requested.
- **Congestion control and user data flow control:** Congestion control may dictate temporary denial of a connection establishment request. Flow control for user-to-user signaling may be provided.
- **Restart:** This function is used to return channels and interfaces to an idle condition to recover from certain abnormal conditions.

Terminal Types

Two basic types of user terminals are supported by ISDN: functional and stimulus. **Functional terminals** are considered to be intelligent devices and can employ the full range of Q.931 messages and parameters for call control. All signaling information is sent in a single control message (en bloc sending). **Stimulus terminals** are devices with a rudimentary signaling capability. A simple digital telephone is an example of a stimulus terminal. Messages sent to the network by a stimulus terminal are usually generated as a direct result of actions by the terminal user (e.g., handset lifted, key depression) and in general do little more than describe the event that has taken place at the human–machine interface. Thus, stimulus terminals transmit signaling information one event or one digit at a time (overlap sending). Signaling messages sent by the network to a stimulus terminal contain explicit instruction regarding the operations to be performed by the terminal (e.g., connect B channel, start alerting). For stimulus terminals, control functions are centralized in the exchange, and functional expansion, if any, will be realized by changes in the exchange.

Messages

The process of establishing, controlling, and terminating a call, as well as the process of selecting supplementary services, occurs as a result of control signaling messages exchanged between the user and the network over a D channel. A common format is used for all messages defined in Q.931, illustrated in Figure 9.3.

Common Fields

The first three fields are common to all messages:

- **Protocol discriminator:** Used to distinguish messages for user–network call control from other message types. As Table 9.1 suggests, other protocols may share the D channel.
- **Call reference:** Identifies the B or H channel call to which this message refers.
- **Message type:** Identifies which Q.931 or Q.932 message is being sent. The contents of the remainder of the message depend on the message type.

The protocol identifier used for Q.931 is binary 00001000. Other protocol identifier values are shown in Table 9.1. Other types of layer 3 messages that may be carried in a LAPD frame are assigned other numbers. Note that a large subset of the possible 8-bit numbers is available for use by X.25. The reason for this is that the X.25 layer 3 format does not include a specific protocol identifier field. However, all X.25 packets begin with an octet in which the third and fourth bits are either 10 or 01 (see Figure 4.13). Accordingly, non-X.25 traffic can be discriminated from X.25 traffic by the presence of either 00 or 11 in those bit positions.

The call reference field comprises three subfields. The *length* subfield specifies the length of the remainder of the field in octets. This length is one octet for a basic rate interface and two octets for a primary rate interface. The *call reference value* is the number assigned to this call. It uniquely identifies a connection and is used by future messages (e.g., a Disconnect message) to specify that connection. This number is assigned by the TE if it is requesting a connection and by the NT if it is announcing an incoming call. The *flag* indicates which end of the LAPD logical connection initiated the call: The value is 0 if the message is from the side that originated this call reference, and the value is 1 if the message is to the side that originated this call reference. The flag is needed to prevent a conflict in the event that both the NT and TE simultaneously select the same unused call reference value for a new connection.

The call reference value has only local significance. The call reference value assigned to the other end of the connection is determined locally at that other end.

There are two special cases of the call reference value to note. A dummy call reference has a length subfield value of 0 and hence is one octet long (all zeros). This is reserved for Q.932 supplementary service procedures, discussed later. The second case is a call reference value of zero (i.e., the length subfield has a value of 1, indi-

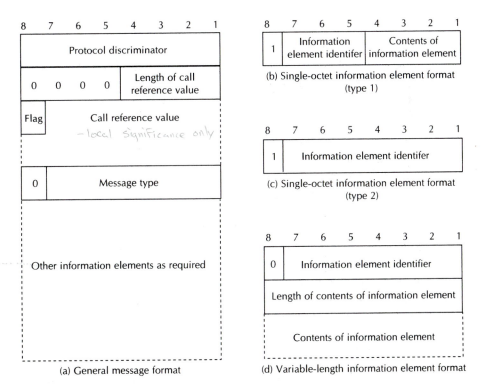

(a) General message format

(b) Single-octet information element format (type 1)

(c) Single-octet information element format (type 2)

(d) Variable-length information element format

Figure 9.3 Q.931 Formats.

Table 9.1   Protocol Discriminator Values

```
0 0 0 0 0 0 0 0     User-specific protocol          ⎫
0 0 0 0 0 0 0 1     OSI high layer protocols        ⎪
0 0 0 0 0 0 1 0     X.25 call user data             ⎪
0 0 0 0 0 0 1 1     system management               ⎬  user-user signaling
0 0 0 0 0 1 0 0     IA5 characters                  ⎪
0 0 0 0 0 1 0 1     ASN.1/BER coded information     ⎪
0 0 0 0 0 1 1 0     reserved for future use         ⎪
0 0 0 0 0 1 1 1     V.120 rate adaption             ⎭


0 0 0 0 1 0 0 0     Q.931 user-network call control messages


0 0 0 1 0 0 0 0     ⎫
    through         ⎬   reserved for other network layer
0 0 1 1 1 1 1 1     ⎭   or layer 3 protocols, including X.25


0 1 0 0 0 0 0 0     ⎫
    through         ⎬   national use
0 1 0 0 1 1 1 1     ⎭


0 1 0 1 0 0 0 0     ⎫
    through         ⎬   reserved for other network layer
1 1 1 1 1 1 1 0     ⎭   or layer 3 protocols, including X.25
```

All other values are reserved

cating the presence of a second octet in the call reference field, and the numerical value of the call reference value subfield is zero). This case is a global call reference, used for data link restart procedures; the messages are applicable to all call references associated with the data link connection identifier (DLCI).

Following these three common fields, the remainder of the message consists of a sequence of zero or more information elements, or parameters. These contain additional information to be conveyed with the message. Thus, the message type specifies a command or response, and the details are provided by the information elements. Some information elements must always be included with a given message (mandatory), and others are optional. Three formats for information elements are used, as indicated in Figures 9.3b through 9.3d.

Types of Messages

Q.931 messages can be grouped along two dimensions: the applications they support and the functions they perform. Messages apply to one of four applications:

- **Circuit-mode connection control:** Refers to the functions needed to set up, maintain, and clear a circuit-switched connection on a B channel. This function corresponds to call control in existing circuit-switching telecommunications networks.
- **Packet-mode access connection control:** Refers to the functions needed to set up a circuit-switched connection (called an access connection in this context) to an ISDN packet-switching node; this connects the user to the packet-switching network provided by the ISDN provider.

- **User-to-user signaling not associated with circuit-switched calls:** Allows two users to communicate without setting up a circuit-switched connection. A temporary signaling connection is established and cleared in a manner similar to the control of a circuit-switched connection. Signaling takes place over the D channel and thus does not consume B channel resources.
- **Messages used with the global call reference:** Refers to the functions that enable the user or network to return one or more channels to an idle condition.

In addition, messages perform functions in one of four categories:

- **Call establishment:** Used initially to set up a call. This group includes messages between the calling terminal and the network and between the network and the called terminal. These messages support the following services: Set up a B channel call in response to user request; provide particular network facilities for this call; inform calling user of the progress of the call establishment process.
- **Call information:** Sent between the user and network once a call has been set up, but prior to the disestablishment (termination) phase. One of the messages in this group allows the network to relay, without modification, information between the two users of the call. The nature of this information is beyond the scope of the standard, but it is assumed that it is control-signaling information that cannot or should not be sent directly over the B channel circuit. The remainder of the messages allow users to request the suspension and later resumption of a call. When a call is suspended, the network remembers the identity of the called parties and the network facilities supporting the call, but it deactivates the call so that no additional charges are incurred and so that the corresponding B channel is freed. Presumably, the resumption of a call is quicker and cheaper than the origination of a new call.
- **Call clearing:** Sent between the user and network to terminate a call.
- **Miscellaneous:** May be sent between the user and network at various stages of the call. Some may be sent during call setup; others may be sent even though no calls exist. The primary function of these messages is to negotiate network features (supplementary services).

Circuit–Mode Connection Control

Table 9.2 lists, with a brief definition, the messages used for circuit-mode connection control. Each entry includes an indication of the direction of the message:

- Only user to network (u → n)
- Only network to user (n → u)
- Both directions

  Each entry also specifies whether the message has

- **Local significance:** Relevant only in the originating or terminating access (i.e., the user–network interface for the user that originated the call or the user that accepted the call) to the network by the user

Table 9.2 Q.931 Messages for Circuit-Mode Connection Control

Message	Significance	Direction	Function
Call establishment messages			
ALERTING	Global	Both	Indicates that user alerting has begun
CALL PROCEEDING	Local	Both	Indicates that call establishment has been initiated
CONNECT	Global	Both	Indicates call acceptance by called TE
CONNECT ACKNOWLEDGE	Local	Both	Indicates that user has been awarded the call
PROGRESS	Global	Both	Reports progress of a call
SETUP	Global	Both	Initiates call establishment
SETUP ACKNOWLEDGE	Local	Both	Indicates that call establishment has been initiated but requests more information
Call information phase messages			
RESUME	Local	$u \rightarrow n$	Requests resumption of previously suspended call
RESUME ACKNOWLEDGE	Local	$n \rightarrow u$	Indicates requested call has been reestablished
RESUME REJECT	Local	$n \rightarrow u$	Indicates failure to resume suspended call
SUSPEND	Local	$u \rightarrow n$	Requests suspension of a call
SUSPEND ACKNOWLEDGE	Local	$n \rightarrow u$	Call has been suspended
SUSPEND REJECT	Local	$n \rightarrow u$	Indicates failure of requested call suspension
Call clearing messages			
DISCONNECT	Global	Both	Sent by user to request connection clearing; sent by network to indicate connection clearing
RELEASE	Local	Both	Indicates intent to release channel and call reference
RELEASE COMPLETE	Local	Both	Indicates release of channel and call reference
INFORMATION	Local	Both	Provides additional information
NOTIFY	Access	Both	Indicates information pertaining to a call
STATUS	Local	Both	Sent in response to a STATUS ENQUIRY or at any time to report an error
STATUS ENQUIRY	Local	Both	Solicits STATUS message

- **Access significance:** Relevant in the originating and terminating access, but not in the network
- **Global significance:** Relevant in the originating and terminating access and in the network

Tables 9.3 through 9.6 list the parameters associated with each circuit-mode connection control message for call establishment, call information phase, call clearing, and miscellaneous functions, respectively. Parameters are designated as mandatory (M) or optional (O). Table 9.7 provides a brief definition of these parameters.

Bearer Capability Information Element

One key parameter, the bearer capability information element (Figure 9.4), warrants elaboration. This parameter is used in the SETUP message to request a bearer service as specified in I.231. Unlike many of the message parameters, which are passed through from source to destination, this one is used by the network in establishing the connection. The parameter actually carries two types of information:

- The selection of bearer service from the choice of bearer services offered by the network to which the calling user is connected. An example is unrestricted digital information. This information is coded in octets 3 and 4 of the bearer capability information element when the circuit mode is requested and in octets 3, 4 (including 4.1 if necessary), 6, and 7 for packet mode.
- Information about the terminal or intended call that is used to decide destination terminal compatibility and possibly to facilitate interworking with other ISDNs or other non-ISDN networks. An example is A-law encoding. This information is encoded in octet 5 of the bearer capability information element.

Octet 3 includes an indication of whether the bearer capability is an ITU-T standard or not. If it is, then the information-transfer capability field specifies one of the following: speech, unrestricted digital information, restricted digital information, 3.1-kHz audio, 7-kHz audio, or video.

Octet 4 indicates whether circuit mode or packet mode is requested and the user channel data rate (64 kbps, 2×64 kbps, 384 kbps, 1.536 Mbps, 1.92 Mbps, or $N \times 64$ kbps). If the selected rate in octet 4 is $N \times 64$ kbps, then octet 4.1 is present and indicates the value of N.

Octet 5 is used to indicate the coding rule followed for the information transfer capability (for example, V.110 or V.120 rate adaption, X.31 flag stuffing, A-law, μ-law). Octet 5a includes an indication of synchronous or asynchronous transfer and a negotiation indication used with V.110. The user rate shows the base rate from which rate adaption occurs. Octet 5b deals with the details of the chosen rate-adaption technique and takes two forms, one used with V.110 and one used with V.120. For V.110 the fields are as follows:

- **Intermediate rate:** Not used, 8 kbps, 16 kbps, 32 kbps
- **Network-independent clock on transmission:** Required, not required
- **Network-independent clock on reception:** Can be supported, cannot be supported

(text continues on page 229)

Table 9.3 Information Elements for Q.931 Call Establishment Messages for Circuit-Mode Connection Control

Information Elements	Alerting	Call Proceeding	Connect	Connect Acknowledge	Progress	Setup	Setup Acknowledge
Sending complete						O	
Repeat indicator						O	
Bearer capability	O	O	O		O	M	
Channel identification	O	O	O			O	O
Cause					O		
Progress indicator	O	O	O		M	O	O
Network-specific facilities						O	
Display	O		O	O	O	O	O
Date/time			O				
Keypad facility						O	
Signal	O		O	O		O	
Calling party number						O	
Calling party subaddress						O	
Called party number						O	
Called party subaddress						O	
Transit network selection						O	
Low-layer compatibility			O			O	
High-layer compatibility	O	O	O		O	O	

Table 9.4 Information Elements for Q.931 Call Information Phase Messages for Circuit-Mode Connection Control

info elements / messages →	Resume	Resume Acknowledge	Resume Reject	Suspend	Suspend Acknowledge	Suspend Reject
Call identity	O			O		
Channel identification		M				
Cause			M			M
Display		O	O		O	O

Table 9.5 Information Elements for Q.931 Call-Clearing Messages for Circuit-Mode Connection Control

info elements / messages	Disconnect	Release	Release Complete
Cause	M	O	O
Progress indicator	O		
Display	O	O	O
Signal	O	O	O

Table 9.6 Information Elements for Q.931 Miscellaneous Messages for Circuit-Mode Connection Control

	Information	Notify	Status	Status Enquiry
Cause			M	
Bearer capability		O		
Notification indicator		M		
Call state			M	
Sending complete	O			
Display	O	O	O	O
Keypad facility	O			
Signal	O			
Called party number	O			

Table 9.7 Definition of Information Elements for Q.931 Messages

Bearer Capability

Indicates provision, by the network, of one of the bearer capabilities defined in I.231 and I.232. It contains detailed information on protocol options at each layer to construct the desired service.

Call Identity

Identifies a suspended call. It is assigned at the start of call suspension.

Call State

Describes the current state of a call, such as active, detached, or disconnect.

Called/Calling Party Number

Identifies the ISDN address of the called or calling party.

Called/Calling Party Subaddress

Identifies the subaddress of the called or calling party.

Cause

Describes the reason for generating certain messages, to provide diagnostic information in the event of procedural errors, and to indicate the location of the cause originator. The location is specified in terms of which network originated the cause.

Channel Identification

Identifies the channel/subchannel within the interface (e.g., which B channel) that is controlled by these signaling procedures.

Date/Time

Indicates when the message was generated by the network.

Display

Supplies additional information coded in IA5 (International Alphabet 5, which is the same as ASCII) characters. Intended for display on user terminal.

High-Layer Compatibility

Specifies the terminal type or application that is on the user side of an S/T interface (e.g., telephony, Teletex, X.400 message-handling system). The network transports this information transparently end-to-end to enable the remote user to perform compatibility checking.

Keypad Facility

Conveys IA5 characters entered by means of a terminal input.

Low-Layer Compatibility

Used for end-to-end compatibility checking. It includes information-transfer capability, information-transfer rate, and protocol identification at layers 1 through 3.

Network-Specific Facilities

Specifies facilities peculiar to a particular network.

Notification Indicator

Provides information pertaining to a call. The values currently defined are user suspended, user resumed, and bearer service charge.

Progress Indicator

Describes an event that has occurred during the life of a call.

Repeat Indicator

Indicates that one possibility should be selected from repeated information elements.

Sending Complete

Indicates completion of called party number.

Signal

Conveys information causing a stimulus mode terminal to generate tones and alerting signals. Example values are dial tone on, ring back tone on, busy tone on, and tones off.

Transit Network Selection

Identifies network that connection should use to get to final destination. This information element may be repeated within a message to select a sequence of networks through which a call must pass.

8	7	6	5	4	3	2	1	Octet
Bearer capability information element identifier								
0	0	0	0	0	1	0	0	1
Length of the bearer capability contents								2
1	Coding standard		Information transfer capability					3
1	Transfer mode		Information transfer rate					4
1	Rate multiplier							4.1
0/1	Layer 1 identity		User information layer 1 protocol					5
0/1	Synch/ asynch	Negoti- ation	User Rate					5a
0/1	Intermediate rate		NIC on Tx	NIC on Rx	Flow control on Tx	Flow control on Rx	0 Spare	5b (if V.110)
0/1	Hdr/no hdr	Multi- frame	Mode	LLI negot.	Assign- or/ee	In-band negot.	0 Spare	5b (if V.121)
0/1	Number of stop bits		Number of data bits		Parity			5c
1	Duplex mode	Modem type						5d
1	Layer 2 identity		User information layer 2 protocol					6
1	Layer 3 identity		User information layer 3 protocol					7

Figure 9.4 Bearer Capability Information Element.

- **Flow control on transmission:** Required, not required
- **Flow control on reception:** Can be supported, cannot be supported

For V.120, the fields are as follows:

- **Header:** Rate adaption header included, not included
- **Multiple-frame establishment support:** Supported, not supported
- **Mode:** Bit transparent, protocol sensitive
- **Logical link identifier negotiation:** Whether default LLI (256) will be used
- **Assignor/assignee:** Default assignor or assignee only
- **Inband/outband negotiation:** Negotiation with USER INFORMATION messages on D channel or inband using LLI = 0

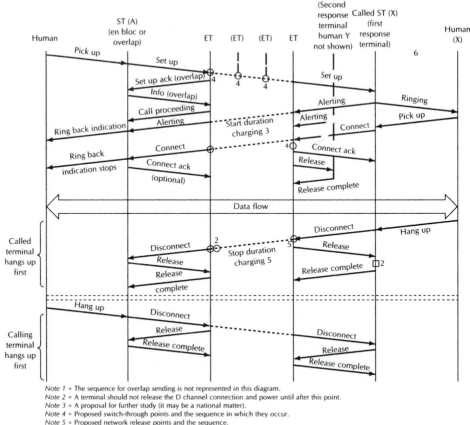

Figure 9.5 Procedure for a Simple Circuit-Switched Call (Example).

Octets 5c and 5d contain additional physical layer characteristics. Octet 6 covers layer 2 use (I.441/Q.921 or X.25 layer 2). Octet 7 covers layer 3 use (Q.931 or X.25 layer 3).

Circuit-Mode Example

Figure 9.5 is an example of the use of the protocol to set up a B channel circuit-switched telephone call. We will follow this example through to give the reader an idea of the use of the Q.931 protocol. The example is for the placement of a telephone call, but the sequence would be similar for a computer-to-computer or terminal-to-computer data call.

The process begins when a calling subscriber lifts the handset. The ISDN-compatible telephone ensures that the D channel is active before itself generating a dial tone (not shown). When the subscriber keys in the called number (not shown), the telephone set accumulates the digits and, when all are keyed in, sends a SETUP message over the D channel to the exchange. The SETUP message includes the destination number; a channel identification, which specifies the B channel to be used; and any requested network services or facilities (e.g., reverse charging).

The SETUP message triggers two activities at the local exchange. First, using internal control signaling, the local exchange sends a message through the network that results in designating a route for the requested call and allocating resources for that call. Second, the exchange sends back a CALL PROC message, indicating that call setup is underway. The exchange may also request more information from the caller (via SETUP ACK and INFO). When the internal control message reaches the remote exchange, it sends a SETUP message to the called telephone. The called telephone accepts the call by sending an ALERT message to the network and generating a ringing tone. The ALERT message is transmitted all the way back to the calling telephone set. When the called party lifts the handset, the telephone sends a CONN message to the network. The local exchange sends a CONN ACK message to its subscriber and forwards the CONN message to the calling exchange, and it in turn forwards it to the calling telephone. The B channel circuit is now available for the called and calling telephones.

Because the call setup process makes use of common-channel signaling, other channels are undisturbed, and the fact that all of the B channels are engaged does not prevent the D channel dialogue. For example, even if all of a user's channels are assigned to circuits, an incoming call request will be presented to the user via the D channel; the user can, if desired, put a call in progress on hold to use the corresponding B channel for the new call.

Once the circuit is set up, full-duplex 64-kbps data streams are exchanged via the B channel between the two end users. Additional signaling messages, such as call information phase messages, may be transmitted during this period.

Call termination begins when one of the telephone users hangs up. This causes a DISC message to be sent from the telephone to the exchange. The exchange responds with a REL message, and when the telephone sends REL COM, the B channel is released. The complementary action takes place at the other telephone–network interface.

Packet-Mode Connection Control

When packet-mode communication is used over ISDN, the possible configurations are more complex than for circuit-mode communication. The possibilities are discussed in some detail in Section 6.4. To summarize, three alternatives for packet-mode communication are possible:

- Circuit-switched access to a packet-switched public data network (PSPDN) over a B channel
- Packet-switched access to an ISDN virtual circuit service over a B channel
- Packet-switched access to an ISDN virtual circuit service over the D channel

In all three cases, the user is connected to a packet-handling node that is part of a packet-switched network, rather than to an end user. In each case, the user then uses the X.25 call control procedure to set up virtual circuits to other end users that are connected to the same packet-switched network.

Circuit-Switched Access to a PSPDN

In this case, a B channel circuit-mode connection is set up to a packet handler external to the ISDN. Thus, the procedures are essentially the same as for setting up a circuit-mode connection to any other external user. However, because the remote user is a packet handler, only a subset of Q.931 is required.

Table 9.8 lists, with brief definitions, the messages used for connection control for circuit-switched access to a PSPDN. As can be seen, these are a subset of the messages used for general circuit-mode connection control (Table 9.2). The following are the differences:

1. For the call establishment phase, the SETUP ACKNOWLEDGE message is not used to request more information. The circuit required for packet-switched access is sufficiently standardized that no additional information is required.

2. No call information phase messages are supported. This means it is not possible to suspend and resume circuit-mode connections to a PSPDN.

3. The INFORMATION and NOTIFY messages are not supported, again, because this information is not needed.

Table 9.8 Q.931 Messages for Packet-Mode Access Connection Control

Message	Significance	Direction	Function
Access connection establishment messages			
ALERTING	Local	u → n	Indicates that user alerting has begun
CALL PROCEEDING	Local	Both	Indicates that access connection establishment has been initiated
CONNECT	Local	Both	Indicates access connection acceptance by called TE
CONNECT ACKNOWLEDGE	Local	Both	Indicates that user has been awarded the access connection
PROGRESS	Local	u → n	Reports progress of an access connection in the event of interworking with a private network
SETUP	Local	Both	Initiates access connection establishment
Access connection clearing messages			
DISCONNECT	Local	Both	Sent by user to request connection clearing; sent by network to indicate connection clearing
RELEASE	Local	Both	Indicates intent to release channel and call reference
RELEASE COMPLETE	Local	Both	Indicates release of channel and call reference
Miscellaneous messages			
STATUS	Local	Both	Sent in response to a STATUS ENQUIRY or at any time to report an error
STATUS ENQUIRY	Local	Both	Solicits STATUS message

B Channel Access to the ISDN Virtual Circuit Service

The procedures and messages for this form of access are essentially the same as those for access to a PSPDN. In this case, the user is establishing a connection to a packet handler that is internal to the ISDN.

D Channel Access to the ISDN Virtual Circuit Service

In this case, no Q.931 procedures are required. The user has access to the D channel virtual circuit service simply by sending X.25 packets inside of LAPD frames over the D channel.

User–Signaling Bearer Service Control

This facility supports signaling connections between end users without setting up a B channel circuit-switched connection. A temporary signaling connection over the D channel is established and cleared in a manner similar to the control of a circuit-switched connection.

Table 9.9 lists, with brief definitions, the Q.931 messages used for user-to-user signaling. As can be seen, these are a subset of the messages used for circuit-mode connection control (Table 9.2). The following are the differences:

- **Call establishment phase:** The PROGRESS messages may be used during circuit-switched connection establishment if the call leaves the ISDN environment, to report the progress of the call as it attempts to interwork with other networks. This feature is not provided for signaling connections.

- **Call information phase:** The only message provided for this phase is the USER INFORMATION message. The two end users can transfer information between themselves by exchanging these messages.

- **Call-clearing phase:** The DISCONNECT message, which requests a connection clearing, is not used for signaling connections. Instead, either side may abruptly close the connection with a RELEASE message.

- **Miscellaneous messages:** The CONGESTION CONTROL message enables the end users to control the flow of data between them. If the message includes a *receive not ready* indication, the receiving user should suspend sending USER INFORMATION messages. The user may resume transfer of such messages upon receipt of a CONGESTION CONTROL message with a *receive ready* indication.

Global Call Reference

Table 9.10 lists, with brief definitions, the messages used for global call reference. Only three messages are used. The STATUS message is the same as that used in other contexts to report an error condition. The RESTART and RESTART ACKNOWLEDGE messages are only used for global call reference. These messages are used to return a given channel or all channels to a predefined state after a fault condition.

Table 9.9 Q.931 Messages for User-to-User Signaling Not Associated with Circuit-Switched Calls

Message	Significance	Direction	Function
Call establishment messages			
ALERTING	Global	Both	Indicates that user alerting has begun
CALL PROCEEDING	Local	Both	Indicates that call establishment has been initiated
CONNECT	Global	Both	Indicates call acceptance by called TE
CONNECT ACKNOWLEDGE	Local	Both	Indicates that user has been awarded the call
SETUP	Global	Both	Initiates call establishment
SETUP ACKNOWLEDGE	Local	Both	Indicates that call establishment has been initiated but requests more information
Call information phase messages			
USER INFORMATION	Access	Both	Transfers information from one user to another
Call clearing messages			
RELEASE	Local	Both	Indicates intent to release channel and call reference
RELEASE COMPLETE	Local	Both	Indicates release of channel and call reference
Miscellaneous messages			
CONGESTION CONTROL	Local	Both	Sets or releases flow control on USER INFORMATION messages
INFORMATION	Local	Both	Provides additional information
STATUS	Local	Both	Sent in response to a STATUS ENQUIRY or at any time to report an error
STATUS ENQUIRY	Local	Both	Solicits STATUS message

Table 9.10 Q.931 Messages Used with the Global Call Reference

Message	Significance	Direction	Function
RESTART	Local	Both	Requests the recipient to restart the indicated channel(s) or interface
RESTART ACKNOWLEDGE	Local	Both	Indicates that the requested restart is complete
STATUS	Local	Both	Reports an error condition

234

9.3   CONTROL OF SUPPLEMENTARY SERVICES

Recommendation Q.932 defines the generic procedures applicable for the control of supplementary services. These procedures may be associated with a particular call or outside any existing call.

Q.932 identifies three major methods by which supplementary services may be controlled:

- Keypad protocol
- Feature key management protocol
- Functional protocol

The first two methods are appropriate for stimulus terminals, as defined earlier in this section, where individual keystrokes (keypad) or button pressing (feature key management) are used to trigger service operation. The functional protocol allows more sophisticated use of supplementary services for functional terminals, using Q.931 messages.

Keypad Protocol

The keypad protocol supports supplementary service invocation in the user-to-network direction. It makes use of the following:

- Keypad facility information element in SETUP and INFORMATION Q.931 messages in the user–network direction
- Display information element in any Q.931 message in the network–user direction

The terminal uses the keypad facility information element for the invocation of individual supplementary services; these are network dependent. Typically, a terminal user enters a service request at a keypad, and this request is translated into a keypad facility information element. The network uses the display information element to give an indication to the local user (or by the remote network to the remote user) regarding a supplementary service being invoked. Typically, display information from the network is displayed on a user terminal or causes an audible output.

A terminal user may invoke a supplementary service at call establishment time using the SETUP message. A supplementary service may be subsequently invoked using the INFORMATION message. If the network requests additional information, using the display information element, the terminal user responds with additional information conveyed in an INFORMATION message.

Feature Key Management Protocol

As with the keypad protocol, the feature key management protocol enables a user to invoke network supplementary services. In this case, it is assumed that the user terminal has function keys or a similar facility that allows the user to select services. This protocol makes use of the following information elements:

- Feature activation information element in SETUP and INFORMATION Q.931 messages in the user–network direction
- Feature indication information element in any Q.931 message in the network–user direction

Associated with each terminal, the network maintains a user's service profile. When the user presses a function key, a numeric identifier is passed to the network in a feature activation information element. The network then maps this to the corresponding supplementary service as indicated by that user's service profile.

The network responds to a supplementary service request with a response message that includes a feature indication information element, which indicates the status of a requested supplementary service. Status values are as follows: deactivated, activated, prompt (waiting for user input), and pending. The user's equipment may convey this information to the user in a manner appropriate for its human–machine interface.

Functional Protocol

The functional protocol approach to controlling supplementary services makes use of a number of specific messages designed for the purpose. The control of supplementary services by either the network or the user includes the following cases:

- The invocation of supplementary services during the establishment of a call
- The invocation of supplementary services during the clearing of a call
- The invocation of call-related supplementary services during the active state of a call
- The activation, deactivation, interrogation, or registration of supplementary services independent from an active call
- The invocation of multiple, different supplementary services within a single message
- The invocation of supplementary services related to different calls
- Cancellation of invoked supplementary services and notification to the initiator of the supplementary service

The functional protocol is divided into two categories of procedures: the separate message approach and the common information element procedure. Table 9.11 lists the messages used for each category.

Separate Message Approach

This approach uses specific message types to indicate a desired function. So far the only messages defined in this category deal with call holding. A user or network may request that a call be held. The requested party may either accept or reject the request. Once a call is on hold, either side may request that the call be returned to an active state (retrieved), and the requested party may either accept or reject the request.

Table 9.11   Q.932 Messages for Supplementary Services Functional Protocol

Message	Direction	Function	Information Elements
Separate Message Approach			
HOLD	Both	Requests the hold function for an existing call	Display
HOLD ACKNOWLEDGE	Both	Indicates that the hold function has been successfully performed	Display
HOLD REJECT	Both	Indicates the denial of a request to hold a call	Cause, Display
RETRIEVE	Both	Requests the retrieval of a held call	Channel identification, Display
RETRIEVE ACKNOWLEDGE	Both	Indicates that the retrieve function has been successfully performed	Channel identification, Display
RETRIEVE REJECT	Both	Indicates the inability to perform the requested retrieve function	Cause, Display
Common Information Element Procedure			
FACILITY	Both	Requests or acknowledges a supplementary service	Facility, Display
REGISTER	Both	Assigns a new call reference for non-call-associated transactions	Facility, Display

Common Information Element Procedure

This approach uses the facility information element to reference one or more supplementary services. This element may be carried in an existing Q.931 message or in a REGISTER or FACILITY message. These latter two messages are used when the only purpose of the messages is to reference one or more supplementary services.

The advantages of this procedure are the following:

- It allows new services to be introduced easily.
- It allows multiple supplementary service invocations within one message.
- It supports supplementary services with a large number of variants without a proliferation of new messages.
- It supports non-call-associated supplementary services.

The facility information element identifies a specific supplementary service and includes one of the following indications:

- **Invoke:** To invoke the service
- **Return result:** To return the result of the service request
- **Return error:** To indicate that the service request is in error
- **Reject:** To reject a service request

9.4 SUMMARY

For call-control signaling, the D channel layer 3 interface is defined in recommendations Q.930 and Q.931. It specifies procedures for establishing a connection on the B and H channels that share the same interface to ISDN as the D channel. It provides both circuit-switched and packet-switched connections. It also provides user-to-user control signaling over the D channel.

Q.932 defines a variety of procedures for invoking supplementary services associated with existing connections as well as services unrelated to a specific connection.

9.5 RECOMMENDED READING

[HARM89] is a good survey of Q.931.

HARM89 Harman, W., and Newman, C. "ISDN Protocols for Connection Control." *IEEE Journal on Selected Areas in Communications,* September 1989.

9.6 PROBLEMS

9.1 X.25 and most other layer 3 protocols provide techniques for flow control and error control. Why are such features not provided in Q.931?

bearer services — convey information without alteration of content
↳ lower 3 layers of OSI model

Tele services — combine transportation and information processing functions
↳ employ bearer services plus higher layer functions

CHAPTER 10

ISDN SERVICES

ISDN provides a variety of services, supporting existing voice and data applications as well as providing for applications now being developed. This chapter begins by looking at the service capabilities defined in the ITU-T ISDN recommendations. These are general in nature and define network capabilities needed to support anticipated user requirements. Based on these general service capabilities, a number of specific ISDN services have been defined. There are two ways to classify these services. One way is to classify them into bearer services and teleservices; another way is to classify them into basic services and supplementary services. These two classifications are examined in the second and third sections of this chapter.

10.1 SERVICE CAPABILITIES

The I.200 series of ITU-T recommendations, referred to as *service capabilities,* provides a classification and method of description of the telecommunication services supported by ISDN. These services encompass existing services and define additional ones. The purpose of the recommendations is to provide a unifying framework for viewing these services and to set forth the user requirements for ISDN. The series, however, does not impose implementation or configuration guidelines. That is, the way in which the service is to be provided is left open. For example, the description of a teletex service does not presuppose which organization (user, private network, public network, information service provider, etc.) provides the various elements that make up a complete teletex service.

Three types of services are defined by ITU-T: bearer services, teleservices, and supplementary services. Bearer services provide the means to convey information (speech, data, video, etc.) between users in real time and without alteration of the content of the message. These services correspond to the lower three layers of the OSI model. Teleservices combine the transportation function with the information processing function. They employ bearer services to transport data and, in addition, provide a set of higher-layer functions. These higher-layer functions correspond to OSI layers

4 through 7. Whereas bearer services define requirements for, and are provided by, network functions, teleservices include terminal as well as network capabilities. Examples of teleservices are telephony, teletex, videotex, and message handling. Both bearer services and teleservices may be enhanced by supplementary services. A supplementary service is one that may be used in conjunction with one or more of the bearer or teleservices. It cannot be used alone. An example is reverse charging. This can be used to reverse charges on a circuit-switched call or a packet-switched virtual call. Reverse charging can also be used with a teleservice, such as the message-handling service, to create a "collect message."

In each of these three categories (bearer, teleservice, supplementary), there are a number of specific services defined by ITU-T. To characterize and differentiate these various services, a collection of attributes has been defined. Each service is characterized by specific values assigned to each descriptive attribute. This method makes it easy to define a service precisely and to compare different services.

Table 10.1 lists the attributes that have so far been defined by ITU-T (in I.140). Table 10.2 provides a brief definition of the attributes together with the values that

Table 10.1   Service and Network Attributes

Service Attributes	Network Attributes
Bearer Services	**Connection Types**
1 Information-transfer mode	1 Information-transfer mode
2 Information-transfer rate	2 Information-transfer rate
3 Information-transfer capability	3 Information-transfer capability
4 Structure	4 Establishment of communication
5 Establishment of communication	5 Symmetry
6 Symmetry	6 Connection configuration
7 Communication configuration	7 Structure
8 Access channel and rate	8 Channel (rate)
9-1 Signaling access protocol layer 1	9 Connection control protocol
9-2 Signaling access protocol layer 2	10 Information-transfer coding/protocol
9-3 Signaling access protocol layer 3	11 Network performance
9-4 Information access protocol layer 1	12 Network interworking
9-5 Information access protocol layer 2	13 Operations and management
9-6 Information access protocol layer 3	
10 Supplementary services provided	**Connection Elements**
11 Quality of service	1 through 13, as above
12 Interworking possibilities	
13 Operational and commercial	
Teleservices	
1 through 9-6, as above	
10 Type of user information	
11 Layer 4 protocol	
12 Layer 5 protocol	
13 Layer 6 protocol	
14 Layer 7 protocol	
15 Supplementary services provided	
16 Quality of servicez	
17 Interworking possibilities	
18 Operational and commercial	

Table 10.2 Attributes and Their Values

Attribute	Definition	Values
Information-transfer mode	Mode for transferring user information	Circuit, packet, ATM
Information-transfer rate	Bit rate (circuit mode) or throughput (packet mode) between two access points	Appropriate bit rate or throughput
Information-transfer capability	Used to characterize the transfer of different types of information through ISDN	Unrestricted digital information:sequence of bits with specified bit rate without alteration Speech: digitized speech with a specific encoding rule 3.1-kHz audio: digitized audio with a bandwidth of 3.1 kHz with a specific encoding rule 7-kHz audio: unrestricted 15-kHz audio Video: digitized video with a specific encoding rule
Structure	Capability to deliver information retaining data integrity	8-kHz integrity: all bits transmitted in a single 125-μs interval are delivered in a corresponding 125-μs interval Service data unit integrity: all bits submitted as a block are delivered in a corresponding block Time slot sequence integrity: information is delivered in the same order as sent Restricted differential time delay: information is delivered within 50 ms Unstructured: no structure is implied
Establishment of communication	Mode of establishing and releasing a communication	Demand: in response to user request Reserved: connection and release times reserved via user request Permanent: preestablished connection
Symmetry	Relationship of information flow between two or more access or reference points	Unidirectional: only one direction Bidirectional symmetric: flow characteristics are the same in both directions Bidirectional asymmetric: flow characteristics may differ in the two directions
Communication configuration	Spatial arrangement for transferring information between two or more access points	Point-to-point: only two access points Multipoint: more than two access points Broadcast: for further study

Table 10.2 Attributes and Their Values *(continued)*

Attribute	Definition	Values
Access channel and rate	Channels and rates used to transfer user and/or signaling information	Name of channel and corresponding bit rate
Signaling access protocol layer 1–3	Protocols on the signaling channel	Appropriate protocols
Information access protocol layer 1–3	Protocols on the information transfer channel	Appropriate protocols
Supplementary services provided	Supplementary services associated with a given telecommunications service	Appropriate services
Quality of service	A group of specific subattributes (e.g., service reliability)	For further study
Interworking possibilities	To be defined	
Operational and commercial	To be defined	
Type of user information	Type of user information	Speech; sound; text; facsimile; text-facsimile; videotex; video; text-interactive
Layer 4–7 protocol	Protocols on the information transfer channel	Appropriate protocols
Information transfer susceptance	Identifies equipment that may restrict types of information	Speech processing equipment; echo suppression equipment; multisatellite hops
Establishment of connection	Mode of establishment and release of a connection that supports a communication	Demand: set up on demand Semipermanent: provided for a definite period, pass through a switched network Permanent: preestablished connection
Connection configuration	Spatial arrangement for transferring information on a connection	Appropriate topology and timing of connection establishment and release
Network performance	Network performance that relates to a connection	Error and slip performance
Network interworking	To be defined	
Operation and management	To be defined	

they can take on. Most of these terms are self-explanatory; some of the others will be discussed later in this section, in the context of a specific service. One additional comment may be useful. A distinction is made between a communication and a connection. These terms are defined as follows in I.112:

> **Communication:** The transfer of information according to agreed conventions.
> **Connection:** A concatenation of transmission channels or telecommunication circuits, switching, and other functional units set up to provide for the transfer of signals between two or more points in a telecommunication network, to support a single communication.

Thus, a communication is a user-oriented concept, and a connection is a network-oriented concept. Those attributes that refer to communication are used to characterize ISDN service, while those attributes that refer to connections are used to characterize ISDN connections. This latter topic will be discussed in the next chapter.

In addition to service attributes, I.140 defines associated network attributes. These attributes relate to connections. For a given communication over a given connection, the connection attributes must be such as to support the attributes of the communication.

10.2 BEARER SERVICES AND TELESERVICES

So far, ITU-T has defined a total of 10 circuit-mode bearer services and 3 packet-mode bearer services; these are listed in Table 10.3. Table 10.4 lists possible values for service attributes for these bearer services. More bearer services, especially at higher data rates, will be defined in the future. However, this mix of services so far defined provides the capability of meeting a wide variety of user requirements and is sufficient for initial implementations of ISDN.

Circuit–Mode Bearer Services

Circuit-mode bearer services are typically characterized by the provision of user information transfer over a B channel and signaling over the D channel.

Table 10.3   ISDN Bearer Services

Circuit-Mode Bearer Services	Packet-Mode Bearer Services
• 64 kbps unrestricted, 8 kHz structured	• Virtual call and permanent virtual circuit
• 64 kbps, 8 kHz structured, usable for speech information transfer	• Connectionless (further study)
• 64 kbps, 8 kHz structured, usable for 3.1 kHz audio information transfer	• User signaling
• Alternate speech/unrestricted 64 kbps, 8 kHz structured	
• 64 kbps, 8 kHz structured multiuse	
• 2 × 64 kbps unrestricted, 8 kHz structured	
• 384 kbps unrestricted, 8 kHz structured	
• 1536 kbps unrestricted, 8 kHz structured	
• 1920 kbps unrestricted, 8 kHz structured	
• Multiple-rate unrestricted, 8 kHz structured	

Table 10.4 Values for Each Bearer Service Attribute

Attributes	Possible Values of Attributes								
	Circuit						Packet		
Information-transfer attributes									
1. Information-transfer mode	Circuit						Packet		
2. Information-transfer rate *(Bit rate (kbps) / Throughput)*	64	2 × 64	384	1536	1920	Others for further study	Options for further study		
3. Information-transfer capability	Unrestricted digital information		Speech	3.1-kHz audio	7-kHz audio	15-kHz audio	Video	Others for further study	
4. Structure	8-kHz integrity		Service data unit integrity			Unstructured			
5. Establishment of communication	Demand		Reserved			Permanent			
6. Symmetry	Unidirectional		Bidirectional symmetric			Bidirectional asymmetric			
7. Communication configuration	Point-to-point		Multipoint			Broadcast			
Access attributes									
8. Access channel and rate	D(16)	D(64)	B	H_0	H_{11}	H_{12}	Others for further study		
9.1 Signaling access protocol layer 1	I.430/I.431	I.461	I.462	I.463	I.465	Others for further study			
9.2 Signaling access protocol layer 2	I.440/I.441		I.462	X.25	Others for further study				
9.3 Signaling access protocol layer 3	I.450/I.451	I.461	I.462	X.25	I.463	Others for further study			
9.4 Information access protocol layer 1	I.430/I.431	I.460	I.461	I.462	I.463	I.465	G.711	G.722	For further study
9.5 Information access protocol layer 2	HDLC	I.440 I.441	X.25	I.462	Others for further study				
9.6 Information access protocol layer 3	T.70-3	X.25	I.462	I.463	Others for further study				
General attributes	Under study								

64-kbps Unrestricted, 8-kHz Structured

This is the most general-purpose service defined for this data rate. The term *unrestricted* means that the information is transferred without alteration and that there is no restriction on the bit pattern to be transferred; this is also known as a *transparent* bearer service. Users may employ this service for any application that requires a data rate of 64 kbps. Figure 10.1 illustrates two possible applications. In the first, the user is connecting digital PBX systems and using them to transport voice digitized at 32 kbps. Although 64 kbps is the ISDN standard data rate for dig-

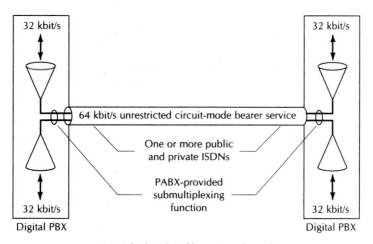

(a) Multiplexed 32-kbps voice channels

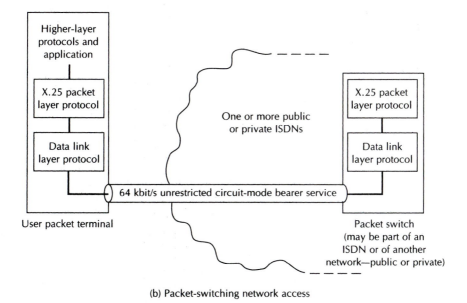

(b) Packet-switching network access

Figure 10.1   Example Uses of the 64-kbps, 8-kHz Structured, Unrestricted Services [SCAC86].

itized voice, sophisticated encoding algorithms enable high-quality voice transmission at 32 kbps. Thus, the user is saving on data transmission capacity by employing a private encoding algorithm. However, the basic unit of switching within ISDN is 64 kbps; consequently, the two 32-kbps voice channels must be connected to the same pair of subscribers. That is, it is not possible to use this service to set up two 32-kbps circuits going to two different destinations. Figure 10.1b shows another use of this service. In this case, the 64-kbps circuit is used to connect a host system to a non-ISDN packet-switched network.

The term *8-kHz structured* means that, in addition to bit transmission, a structure is transferred between customers. When one user transmits information to another user, the transmission is accompanied by 8-kHz timing information, which delimits the data in 8-bit units. This 8-kHz structural integrity implies that octets are preserved within the corresponding time interval; that is, an octet is never split across a time interval boundary. This applies in particular to speech, which requires the 8-kHz structure in addition to the 64-kbps information flow to recognize the octets, which are formed by speech encoding, at the receiving side. In text transmission, character boundaries are preserved. Thus, there is no need for the user to provide an inband, user-to-user synchronization scheme.

64-kbps, 8-kHz Structured, Usable for Speech Information

This service defines a specific structure for the digital signal—namely, pulse-code modulation (PCM) as defined in ITU-T recommendation G.711. Because the network may assume that the encoded data are speech, it may use processing techniques appropriate for speech, such as analog transmission, echo cancellation, and low-bit-rate voice encoding. Because these transformations may not be precisely reversible, bit integrity is not guaranteed. However, the received signal should produce a high-quality reproduction of the transmitted voice signal. In other respects, this service is the same as the unrestricted service. The restriction to speech allows the use of processing techniques in the network that may optimize the transmission. Furthermore, the network may perform conversions between digital encoding laws. For example, the G.711 standard specifies two versions of the PCM algorithm, μ-law and A-law. The former is used in North America and Japan; the latter is used in the rest of the world. Thus, the voice signal on a connection that crosses these geographic boundaries is automatically converted.

Because of the transformations that may take place on this service, it is not appropriate for data transfer using a modem. The bit pattern generated by the demodulator may not exactly match that presented to the modulator.

64-kbps, 8-kHz Structured, Usable for 3.1-kHz Audio Information

This service assumes that digitized audio information is being transmitted. This permits routing over analog circuits using codecs, as in the previous service. However, other forms of processing peculiar to speech signals are prohibited. For example, a form of multiplexing known as time-assigned speech interpolation (TASI) exploits the bursty character of speech to multiplex speech channels. Thirty speech calls can be squeezed into a T1 24-channel system with no noticeable degradation.

However, this technique is not appropriate for nonspeech signals that happen to occupy the voice frequency band, such as digital data that have been passed through a voice-grade modem.

Alternate Speech/Unrestricted 64-kbps, 8-kHz Structured

This service involves the alternate transfer of speech and unrestricted signals. The service is intended for user terminals with multiple capabilities. The request for this alternate capability, and the initial mode desired by the user, must be identified at call setup time. There is a requirement for a short (as yet undefined) changeover time when the user requests a change from one service to the alternate service.

The speech mode of this bearer service is the same as the bearer service identified as 64-kbps, 8-kHz structured, usable for speech information transfer. The unrestricted mode of this bearer service is the same as the bearer service identified as 64-kbps unrestricted, 8-kHz structured.

64-kbps, 8-kHz Structured Multiuse

This service provides the transfer of circuit-mode, 64-kbps unrestricted digital information between terminals. In addition, it enables a multiuse terminal to be connected to other terminal types, with ISDN automatically invoking the appropriate bearer service. In particular, a multiuser terminal may interoperate with the following using this service:

- Speech terminal, using speech information transfer bearer service
- 3.1-kHz audio terminal, using 3.1-kHz audio information transfer service
- Public switched telecommunications network (PSTN), using the alternate speech/unrestricted bearer service

2 × 64-kbps Unrestricted, 8-kHz Structured

This service provides for the use of two 64-kbps channels that bear some relationship to each other. It is intended for terminals that require greater than 64-kbps data rate but can be accommodated with 128 kbps. The user information is transferred in two 64-kbps B channels and must be reassembled into a single 128-kbps stream at the receiving end.

384/1536/1920-kbps Unrestricted, 8-kHz Structured

These three services provide for high-speed digital transfer, at rates of 384, 1536, and 1920 kbps. These services could be used for a variety of applications, including video, private networking between PBXs, and links between other networks. The following ISDN primary rate channels are used:

- H_0 for 384 kbps
- H_{11} for 1536 kbps
- H_{12} for 1920 kbps

Multiple-Rate Unrestricted, 8-kHz Structured

This service allows users to request from the ISDN on a demand basis the establishment and release of circuit-mode connections supporting unrestricted information transfer rates at integer multiples of 64 kbps up to the maximum rate of the interface (1.536 Mbps or 1.92 Mbps).

As with the 2×64-kbps service, multiple B channels are used. When this service is requested, ISDN will attempt to place the call. If the service is supported at the called user, then the network determines if sufficient B channels are available at the called end to set up the circuit.

Multiple-rate (or multirate) ISDN is one of the newest of the ISDN services. It is attractive to users that have high-capacity applications that may not need the exact data rates offered by the H channels. See [KOVA94] for a discussion of multiple-rate services and the network technology needed to support them.

Packet–Mode Bearer Services

Packet-mode bearer services involve packet-handling functions. These services may be provided over B or D channels:

- **Virtual call and permanent virtual circuit:** This service is the traditional packet–network interface allowing both switched and permanent virtual circuits. The user attaches to ISDN in the same manner as attaching to a packet-switched network, using X.25.
- **Connectionless:** This service provides for a datagram style of packet service. It might be provided to support applications such as telemetry, alarm, and transaction services, which do not need the connection-oriented service. The access protocol would differ from X.25 and is a subject for further study.
- **User signaling:** This service is intended to support the transfer of packets via the D channel between end users. It is to be used in applications in which limited amounts of information are to be exchanged. Examples of such applications include support of user management protocols and transfer of control information between any kind of user equipment, such as digital PBXs.

Teleservices

The area of teleservices in ISDN is significantly less well developed than that of bearer services. Teleservices are intended to cover a wide variety of user applications over ISDN. The list of services so far defined in I.241 is shown in Table 10.5. In general, the services cover applications that are in the nature of terminal-service applications, most of which have been defined by ITU-T. This can be contrasted with what might be considered computer-to-computer applications. These latter applications have mostly been defined by ISO and include file transfer and document architecture.

Table 10.6 is a list of the possible values for service attributes for the teleservices. The lower-layer (OSI layers 1–3) attributes are essentially the same as for the

Table 10.5   ISDN Teleservices

Service	Description
Telephony	Provides 3.1-kHz speech communication. The digital signal follows the agreed encoding laws for speech, and the network may use digital signal processing techniques, such as echo cancellation. User information is provided over a B channel; signaling is provided over the D channel.
Teletex	Provides end-to-end text communication using standardized character sets, presentation formats, and communication protocols. The high-layer attributes are based on those of the ITU-T standardized teletex service (F.200). User information is provided over a B channel; signaling is provided over the D channel.
Telefax	Provides end-to-end facsimile communication using standardized picture coding, resolution, and communication protocols. The high-layer attributes are based on the facsimile Group 3 and Group 4 recommendation of ITU-T. User information is provided over a B channel; signaling is provided over the D channel.
Videotex	An enhancement of the existing videotex service with retrieval and mailbox functions for text (alpha) and graphic (mosaic, geometric, photographic) information.
Telex	Provides interactive text communication. The digital signal follows the internationally agreed recommendations for telex above the ISDN physical layer. User information is transferred over circuit- or packet-mode bearer channels; signaling is provided over the D channel.
Teleconference	Provides the necessary arrangements for real-time conferencing among single individuals or groups of individuals at two or more locations. The exchange of speech signals is always provided; the use of supplementary facilities, for the exchange of signals other than speech, is to be determined by the conference participants.
Videotelephony	A symmetrical, bidirectional, real-time, audiovisual teleservice in which speech and moving pictures are communicated; the picture information transmitted is sufficient for the adequate representation of fluid movements of persons.
7-kHz audio	Enables a user to communicate with high-quality speech or by interchanging sounds with higher quality than that provided by 3.1-kHz telephony. User information is provided over a B channel; signaling is provided over the D channel.

bearer services. This is because a teleservice relies on a bearer service for information transport across the ISDN. The upper-layer attributes form a protocol architecture that maps into OSI layers 4 through 7; this topic is addressed in the next section.

One service conspicuously absent from Table 10.5 is the message-handling service (MHS), defined by the X.400 series of recommendations. This is one of the most important and widely available of the ITU-T-defined teleservices and will be included in future revisions to I.240.

Table 10.6 Possible Values for Each Teleservice Attribute

Attributes	Possible Values of Attributes					
Information-transfer attributes						
1. Information-transfer mode	Circuit			Packet		
2. Information-transfer rate	64		Others for further study	Bit rate (kbps) / Throughput	Options for further study	
3. Information-transfer capability	Unrestricted digital information	Speech	3.1-kHz audio	7-kHz audio	Others for further study	
4. Structure	8-kHz integrity	Service data unit integrity	Unstructured	Others for further study		
5. Establishment of communication	Demand	Reserved	Permanent			
6. Symmetry	Unidirectional	Bidirectional symmetric	Bidirectional asymmetric			
7. Communication configuration	Point-to-point	Multipoint	Broadcast			
Access attributes						
8. Access channel and rate	D(16)	D(64)	B	Others for further study		
9.1 Signaling access protocol layer 1	I.430/I.431	I.461	I.462	I.463	I.465	Others for further study
9.2 Signaling access protocol layer 2	I.440/I.441	I.462	X.25	Others for further study		

Table 10.6 Possible Values for Each Teleservice Attribute (*continued*)

Attributes	Possible Values of Attributes								
Access Attributes									
9.3 Signaling access protocol layer 3	I.450/I.451				I.463			Others for further study	
9.4 Information access protocol layer 1	I.430/I.431	I.460	I.461	I.462	I.463	I.465	G.711	Others for further study	
9.5 Information access protocol layer 2	HDLC		I.440/I.441	X.75 SLP	X.25 LAPB			Others for further study	
9.6 Information access protocol layer 3	ISO 8208		X.25 PLP					Others for further study	
10. Type of user information	Speech	Sound	Text	Fax	Text-fax	Videotex	Video	Teletex	Other
11. Layer 4 protocol	X.224		T.70					Others for further study	
12. Layer 5 protocol	X.225		T.62					Others for further study	
13. Layer 6 protocol	T.400 series		G.711	T.70	T.6			Others for further study	
Resolution	200 ppi	240 ppi	300 ppi	400 ppi				Others for further study	
Graphic mode	Alpha-mosaic	Geometric		Photographic				Others for further study	
14. Layer 7 protocol	T.60		T.500 series					Others for further study	
General attributes	Under study								

10.3 BASIC AND SUPPLEMENTARY SERVICES

Classification of ISDN services into basic and supplementary services is based on whether a service can be offered to a user on its own on a stand-alone basis (basic) or not (supplementary). Thus, all of the bearer services discussed in Section 10.2 are basic services.

Each teleservice is defined, and could be implemented, in a manner independent from the bearer services and teleservices with which it might be used. This allows each supplementary service to be used in a uniform fashion, regardless of the bearer service or teleservice that it supports. For example, the methods of requesting and authorizing reverse charging should be the same for a circuit-switched call or an MHS message.

Table 10.7 lists the supplementary services that have been defined so far. All of these originated in the telephone world. However, most of them can also be applied to packet-mode bearer services and to some teleservices.

Table 10.7 ISDN Supplementary Service

<table>
<tr><td colspan="1" align="center">**Number Identification**</td></tr>
</table>

Direct dialing-in
    Enables a user to call directly to another user on an ISDN-compatible PBX or Centrex, without attendant intervention, or to call a terminal on a passive bus selectively.

Multiple subscriber number
    Allows multiple ISDN numbers to be assigned to a single interface (e.g., multiple telephone numbers at the same residence).

Calling line identification presentation
    Service offered to the called party that provides the ISDN number of the calling party.

Calling line identification restriction
    Service offered to the calling party to restrict presentation of the calling party's ISDN number to the called party.

Connected line identification presentation
    Service offered to the calling party that provides the ISDN number of the party to whom the caller is connected.

Connected line identification restriction
    Service offered to the connected party to restrict presentation of the connected party's ISDN number to the calling party.

Malicious calls identification
    Enables a called party to request that a calling party be identified to the network and be registered in the network. This would be used by the called party on calls considered to be malicious. The network provider could retain the information for later use.

Subaddressing
    Allows the called user to expand the user's addressing capacity beyond the ones given by the ISDN number. The subaddress could be used to select a specific terminal or to invoke a specific process in a terminal.

Calling name identification presentation
    Service to the called party that provides name information associated with the calling party.

Call Offering

Call transfer
    Enables a user to transfer an established call to a third party. This service is different from the call forwarding service since, in this case, the call to be transferred must have an established end-to-end connection prior to the transfer.

Table 10.7   ISDN Supplementary Service *(continued)*

Call forwarding busy
Permits a served user to have the network send incoming calls (or just those associated with a specified basic service) addressed to the served user's ISDN number to another number when this user's line is busy. The served user's originating service is unaffected.

Call forwarding no reply
Permits a served user to have the network send incoming calls (or just those associated with a specified basic service) addressed to the served user's ISDN number to another number when there is no answer on this user's line. The served user's originating service is unaffected.

Call forwarding unconditional
Permits a served user to have the network send all incoming calls (or just those associated with a specified basic service) addressed to the served user's ISDN number to another number. The served user's originating service is unaffected.

Call deflection
Permits a user, in real time, to request that the network redirect an incoming call addressed to the served user's ISDN number to another number. This service is provided on a per access basis.

Line hunting
Enables incoming calls to a specific ISDN number (or numbers) to be distributed over a group of interfaces or terminals.

Call Completion

Call waiting
Enables a terminal equipment, which is already active in a communication, to notify its user of an incoming call. The user then has the choice of accepting, rejecting, or ignoring the waiting call.

Call hold
Allows a user to interrupt communications on an existing call and then subsequently reestablish the connection.

Completion of calls to busy subscribers
Enables a calling user, encountering a busy destination, to be notified when the busy destination becomes free and to have the provider reinitiate the call to that destination if the calling user still desires.

Completion of calls on no reply
Enables a calling user, encountering a destination that does not answer the call, to be notified when the destination becomes free after having terminated an activity and to have the provider reinitiate the call to that destination if the calling user still desires.

Multiparty

Conference calling
Allows multiple users to communicate simultaneously with one another.

Three party service
Allows a subscriber to hold an existing call and make a call to a third party. The following arrangements may then be possible: the ability to switch between the two calls, the introduction of a common speech path among the three parties, and the connection of the other two parties.

Community of Interest

Closed user group
Allows a group of users to intercommunicate only among themselves or, as required, one or more users may be provided with incoming/outgoing access to users outside the group.

Private numbering plan
Allows a subscriber to use a private numbering plan for communication across one or more networks between nominated user access interfaces. This service provides a group of users the capability to place calls by using digit sequences having different structures and meanings than provided by the public numbering plan.

Table 10.7 ISDN Supplementary Service *(continued)*

Multilevel precedence and preemption service

Provides prioritized call handling service. Precedence involves assigning a priority level to a call. Preemption involves the seizing of resources, which are in use by a call of lower precedence, by a higher-level precedence call in the absence of idle resources.

Priority service

Provides for preferential treatment in the network to calls originating from and/or addressed to certain numbers in the order of path selection.

Outgoing call barring

Enables a user to bar calls that are originating from this user's access. The user may bar all outgoing calls or a special group of calls.

Charging

Credit card calling

For further study.

Advice of charge

Provides the user paying for a call with usage-based charging information. This service may be provided at call setup time, during the call, and/or at the completion of the call.

Reserve charging

Allows the called user to be charged for the entire call or part of the call. Only usage-based charges can be charged to the called user.

Additional Information Transfer

User-to-user signaling

Allows an ISDN user to send/receive a limited amount of information to/from another ISDN user over the signaling channel in association with a call to the other ISDN user.

Incall Modification

Enables a user to change within an established call from one type of call characterized by one set of bearer capabilities, low-layer and/or high-layer capabilities, to another type of call with another set without changing the end-to-end connection from a user/network-access point of view.

10.4 SUMMARY

The requirements that guide the design and implementation of ISDN can be expressed in terms of telecommunications services. These services are the reason for the existence of ISDN or any network. Thus, it is important to be clear about what services are to be provided and, in detail, what characteristics and attributes that the user expects to have associated with these services. Once this is known, the network capabilities needed to support the services can be determined.

ITU-T has specified these services as part of the I-series of recommendations. Two types of services are defined: bearer services and teleservices. Bearer services are the lower-level functions responsible for transferring data between subscribers across ISDN. These services correspond to layers 1 through 3 of the OSI model. ITU-T has defined these services quite explicitly. Teleservices are the actual user-visible services that are supported across ISDN. These services correspond to layers 4 through 7 of the OSI model and make use of the bearer services. Strictly speaking, the protocols that are part of the teleservices are not part of and are not visible to a communications network, including ISDN. However, there are several reasons for addressing teleservices in the context of ISDN. First, both teleservices and bearer services make use of a common set of supplementary services (e.g., reverse charging), and a uniform means of specifying and invoking those services is useful. Second, the nature of a teleservice will determine the nature of the bearer service used, and standards on the interrelationships are useful.

10.5 PROBLEMS

10.1 In the United States, there has been considerable thought given to the types of telecommunication services that should be subject to government regulation of price and quality and those that should be offered competitively with little or no regulation. Two important efforts in this regard are the Computer Inquiry II by the Federal Communications Commission (FCC) and the Modification of Final Judgment (MFJ), which resulted in the break-up of AT&T. In Computer Inquiry II, the FCC defined the following terms:

> **Basic Service:** limited to the common-carrier offering of transmission capacity for the movement of information.
> **Enhanced Service:** any offering over the telecommunications network that is more than a basic transmission service. Such services employ computer processing applications that act on the format, content, code, protocol, or similar aspects of the subscriber's transmitted information; provide the subscriber additional, different, or restructured information; or involve subscriber interaction with stored information.

The MFJ produced the following definitions:

> **Telecommunication Service:** the transmissions, between or among points specified by the user, of information of the user's choosing, without change in the form or content of the information as seen and received, by means of electromagnetic transmission, with or without benefit of any closed transmission medium, including all instrumentalities, facilities, apparatus, and services (including the collection, storage, forwarding, switching, and delivery of such information) essential to such transmission.
> **Information Service:** a capability for generating, acquiring, storing, transforming, processing, retrieving, utilizing, or making available information that may be conveyed via telecommunications, except that such service does not include any use of such capability for the management, control, or operation of a telecommunications system or the management of a telecommunications service.

Compare these two pairs of definitions with these definitions from I.112:

> **Bearer Service:** a type of telecommunication service that provides the capability for the transmission of signals between user-network interfaces.
> **Teleservice:** a type of telecommunication service that provides the complete capability, including terminal equipment functions, for communication between users according to protocols established by agreement between Administrations and/or RPOAs.

CHAPTER 11

SIGNALING SYSTEM NUMBER 7

In Chapter 4, we discussed the transition of network control signaling from an inchannel to a common-channel approach. Common-channel signaling is more flexible and powerful than inchannel signaling and is well suited to support the requirements of integrated digital networks. The culmination of this transition is Signaling System Number 7 (SS7), first issued by CCITT in 1980, with revisions in 1984, 1988, and 1992. SS7 is designed to be an open-ended common-channel signaling standard that can be used over a variety of digital circuit-switched networks. Furthermore, SS7 is specifically designed to be used in ISDNs. SS7 is the mechanism that provides the internal control and network intelligence essential to an ISDN.

The overall purpose of SS7 is to provide an internationally standardized general-purpose common-channel signaling system with the following primary characteristics:

- Optimized for use in digital telecommunication networks in conjunction with digital stored program-control exchanges, utilizing 64-kbps digital channels
- Designed to meet present and future information transfer requirements for call control, remote control, management, and maintenance
- Designed to be a reliable means for the transfer of information in the correct sequence without loss or duplication
- Suitable for operation over analog channels and at speeds below 64 kbps
- Suitable for use on point-to-point terrestrial and satellite links

The scope of SS7 is immense, because it must cover all aspects of control signaling for complex digital networks, including the reliable routing and delivery of control messages and the application-oriented content of those messages. Appendix 11B, which lists the ITU-T recommendations that comprise SS7, should give the reader some feel for the complexity of the standard. In this chapter, we provide an overview of SS7 and highlight key aspects of it.

11.1 SS7 ARCHITECTURE

Functional Architecture

With common-channel signaling, control messages are routed through the network to perform call management (setup, maintenance, termination) and network management functions. These messages are short blocks or packets that must be routed through the network. Thus, although the network being controlled is a circuit-switched network, the control signaling is implemented using packet-switching technology. In effect, a packet-switched network is overlaid on a circuit-switched network to operate and control the circuit-switched network.

SS7 defines the functions that are performed in the packet-switched network but does not dictate any particular hardware implementation. For example, all of the SS7 functions could be implemented in the circuit-switching nodes as additional functions; this approach is the associated signaling mode depicted in Figure 4.7. Alternatively, separate switching points that carry only the control packets and are not used for carrying circuits can be used, as depicted in Figure 4.7b. Even in this case, the circuit-switching nodes would need to implement portions of SS7 so that they could receive control signals.

Signaling Network Elements

SS7 defines three functional entities: signaling points, signal transfer points, and signaling links. A **signaling point** (SP) is any point in the signaling network capable of handling SS7 control messages. It may be an endpoint for control messages and incapable of processing messages not directly addressed to itself. The circuit-switching nodes of the network, for example, could be endpoints. Another example is a network control center. A **signal transfer point** (STP) is a signaling point that is capable of routing control messages; that is, a message received on one signaling link is transferred to another link. An STP could be a pure routing node or could also include the functions of an endpoint. Finally, a signaling link is a data link that connects signaling points.

Figure 11.1 highlights the distinction between the packet-switching signaling function and the circuit-switching information transfer function, in the case of a nonassociated signaling architecture. We can consider that there are two planes of operation. The **control plane** is responsible for establishing and managing connections. These connections are requested by the user over the D channel using Q.931. The Q.931 dialogue is between the user and the local exchange. For this purpose, the local exchange acts as a signaling point, because it must convert between the dialogue with the user (Q.931) and the control messages inside the network that actually perform user-requested actions (SS7). Internal to the network, SS7 is used to establish and maintain a connection; this process may involve one or more signaling

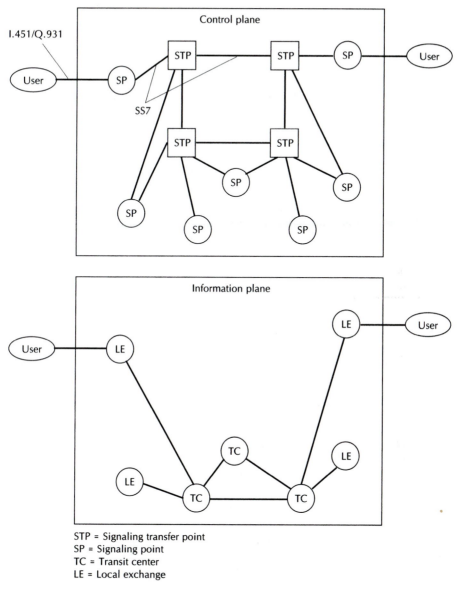

STP = Signaling transfer point
SP = Signaling point
TC = Transit center
LE = Local exchange

Figure 11.1 Signaling and Information Transfer Networks.

points and signal transfer points. Once a connection is set up, information is transferred from one user to another, end-to-end, in the **information plane**. A circuit is
set up from the local exchange of one user to that of another, perhaps being routed
through one or more other circuit-switching nodes, referred to as transit centers. All
of these nodes (local exchanges, transit centers) are also signaling points, because
they must be able to send and receive SS7 messages to establish and manage the
connection.

Signaling Network Structures

A complex network will typically have both signaling points (SPs) and signal transfer points (STPs). A signaling network that includes both SP and STP nodes could be considered as having a hierarchical structure in which the SPs constitute the lower level and the STPs represent the higher level. The latter may further be divided into several STP levels. Figure 11.1 is an example of a network with a single STP level.

Several parameters could influence the decisions concerning design of the network and the number of levels to be implemented:

- **STP capacities:** Includes the number of signaling links that can be handled by the STP, the signaling message transfer time, and the message throughput capacity.
- **Network performance:** Includes the number of SPs and the signaling delays.
- **Availability and reliability:** Measures the ability of the network to provide service in the face of STP failures.

When considering the network constraints in terms of performance, one STP level seems preferable. However, considerations of reliability and availability may dictate a solution with more than one level. The following guidelines are suggested by ITU-T:

- In a hierarchical signaling network with a single STP level,
  - □ Each SP that is not an STP at the same time is connected to at least two STPs.
  - □ The meshing of STPs is as complete as possible (full mesh: every STP has a direct link to every other STP).
- In a hierarchical signaling network with two STP levels (e.g., Figure 11.2),
  - □ Each SP that is not an STP at the same time is connected to at least two STPs of the lower level.

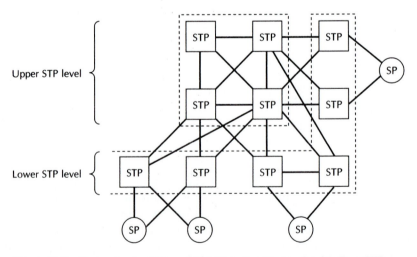

Figure 11.2 Example of a Hierarchical Signaling Network with Two STP Levels.

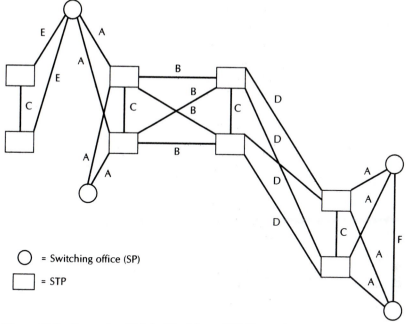

Figure 11.3 Example of Links Used in an SS7 Network.

◻ Each STP in the lower level is connected to at least two STPs of the upper level.
◻ The STPs in the upper level are fully meshed.

The two-level STP hierarchical design would be typically designed such that the lower level is dedicated to traffic in a particular geographic region of the network, and the higher level handles interregion traffic.

One possible realization of an SS7 architecture is depicted in Figure 11.3, which shows the approach taken by AT&T [PHEL86, DONO86]. SPs and STPs are connected by links that are defined by function (Table 11.1). STPs are configured in pairs for redundancy and linked by cross (C) links. Circuit-switching nodes hook into the SS7 packet-switching network by means of access (A) links to paired STPs. Bridge (B) links are provided between STP pairs in different regions and D links between STP pairs at different hierarchical levels. The remaining link types (E and F) provide additional paths to and from circuit-switching nodes to reflect particular high traffic demands.

It can be seen that this design combines good performance with high availability. Between any pair of signaling points, messages must ordinarily traverse only one or two STPs. This provides low message transit delay. At the same time, the loss of a critical STP or signaling link does not prevent communication, although a somewhat longer route may need to be followed.

Protocol Architecture

So far, we have been discussing SS7 architecture in terms of the way in which functions are organized to create a packet-switching control network. The term *archi-*

Table 11.1 Signaling Links

Designation	Connection	Use
A	SP TO STP	Provides access to the signaling network from a switching office.
B	STP to STP at same level of a hierarchy	Primary routing of messages from one SP to another via multiple STPs.
C	STP to mated STP	Communication between paired STPs; also provides alternate route around failed B links.
D	STP to STP at different levels of a hierarchy	Routing of messages up or down in a hierarchy.
E	SP to STP	Provides direct connection to nonhome STP from a switching office.
F	SP to SP	Provides direct access between switching offices with a high community of interest.

tecture can also be used to refer to the structure of protocols that specify SS7. As with the open systems interconnection (OSI) model, the SS7 standard is a layered architecture. Figure 11.4 shows the current structure of SS7 and relates it to OSI.

The SS7 architecture consists of four levels. The lowest three levels of the SS7 architecture, referred to as the **message transfer part** (MTP), provide a reliable but connectionless (datagram style) service for routing messages through the SS7 network. The lowest level, the **signaling data link**, corresponds to the physical layer of the OSI model and is concerned with the physical and electrical characteristics of the signaling links. These include links between STPs, between an STP and an SP, and control links between SPs. The signaling link level is a data link control protocol that provides for the reliable sequenced delivery of data across a signaling data link; it corresponds to layer 2 of the OSI model. The top level of the MTP, referred to as the **signaling network level** or function, provides for routing data across multiple STPs from control source to control destination. These three levels together do not provide the complete set of functions and services specified in the OSI layers 1–3, most notably in the areas of addressing and connection-oriented service. In the 1984 version of SS7, an additional module was added, which resides in level 4, known as the **signaling connection control part** (SCCP). The SCCP and MTP together are referred to as the **network service part** (NSP). A variety of different network-layer services are defined in SCCP, to meet the needs of various users of NSP. The remainder of the modules of SS7 are considered to be at level 4 and comprise the various users of NSP. NSP is simply a message delivery system; the remaining parts deal with the actual contents of the messages. The **ISDN user part** (ISUP) provides for the control signaling needed in an ISDN to deal with ISDN subscriber calls and related functions. The **transaction capabilities application part** (TCAP), first introduced in 1988, provides the mechanisms for transaction-oriented (as opposed to connection-oriented) applications and functions. The **operations, maintenance, and administra-**

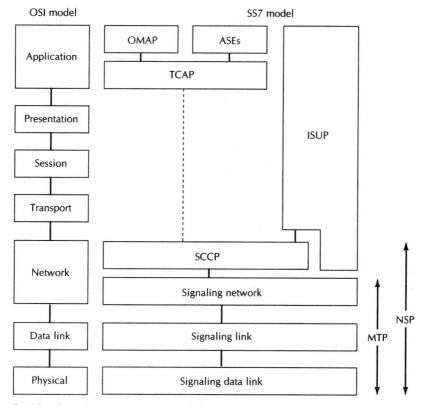

OMAP = Operations, maintenance, and administration
ASE = Application service element
TCAP = Transaction capabilities application part
ISUP = ISDN user part
SSCP = Signaling connection control part
MTP = Message transfer part
NSP = Network service part

Figure 11.4   SS7 Protocol Architecture.

tion part (O&MAP) specifies network management functions and messages related to operations and maintenance. In addition, other modules, referred to as **application service elements** (ASEs), may be defined to support other applications.

The MTP was developed prior to SCCP and was tailored to the real-time needs of telephony applications. The connectionless nature of MTP provides a low-overhead facility tailored to the requirements of telephony. In the context of ISDN, it became clear that there were other applications, such as network management, that needed the full services of the OSI network layer, such as expanded addressing capability and reliable message transfer. SCCP was designed to meet these requirements. The resulting split in OSI network functions between the signaling network layer and SCCP has the advantage that the higher-overhead SCCP services can be used only when required, with the more efficient MTP used for other applications.

11.2 SIGNALING DATA LINK LEVEL

The signaling data link is a full-duplex physical link dedicated to SS7 traffic. SS7 is optimized for use over 64-kbps digital links. However, the recommendations allow for the use of circuit-switched connections to the data link, lower speeds, and analog links with modems. The link can be routed via a satellite.

11.3 SIGNALING LINK LEVEL

The signaling link level corresponds to the data link control layer of the OSI model. Thus, its purpose is to turn a potentially unreliable physical link into a reliable data link. Reliability implies that

- All transmitted blocks of data are delivered with no losses or duplications.
- Blocks of data are delivered in the same order in which they were transmitted.
- The receiver is capable of exercising flow control over the sender.

The last point assures that blocks of data are not lost after delivery because of buffer overflow.

Many of the techniques found in better-known data link control protocols, such as LAPD and LAPB, are used in the SS7 signaling link level. However, the formats and some of the procedures are different. The differences in some cases are matters of style rather than substance. In other cases, they arise from the performance needs of signaling that require the network to respond quickly to system or component-failure events.

Signal Unit Formats

We begin our discussion of the signaling link protocol with a description of the formats of the basic elements of the protocol. The blocks of data transmitted at the signaling link level are referred to as signal units. As Figure 11.5 illustrates, there are three types of signal units:

- **Message signal unit (MSU):** Carries user data from level 4.
- **Level status signal unit (LSSU):** Carries control information needed at the signaling link level.
- **Fill-in signal unit (FISU):** Transmitted when no other signal units are available. This allows for a consistent error-monitoring method (described subsequently) so that faulty links can be quickly detected and removed from service even when traffic is low.

The MSU begins and ends with a **flag** field, which delimits the signal unit at both ends with the unique pattern 01111111. As with LAPB and LAPD, bit stuffing is used to avoid the appearance of the flag pattern in the body of the frame.

The next four fields are used to implement the typical flow-control and error-control mechanisms found in many layer 2 and layer 3 protocols. The flow control

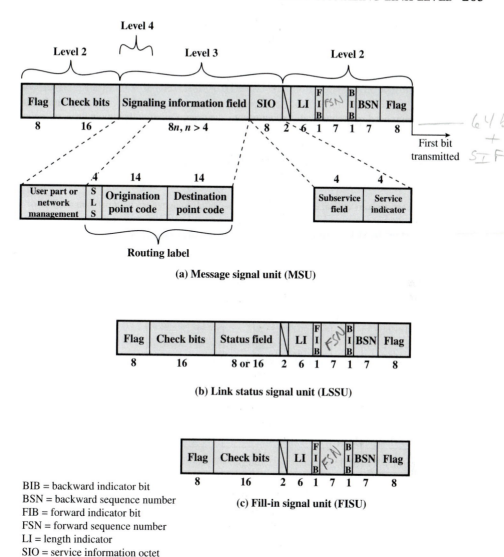

Figure 11.5 Signal Unit Formats.

is the sliding-window mechanism, and error control is the go-back-N automatic-repeat-request (ARQ) mechanism. The basic operation of these mechanisms is explained in Appendix A. The **backward sequence number** (BSN) contains the number of the last MSU successfully received from the other side; this provides for piggybacked acknowledgment. Negative acknowledgment associated with this BSN is indicated by inverting the **backward indicator bit** (BIB). The new value of the BIB will be maintained in all subsequent signal units to indicate positive acknowledgment until another error is detected. When this occurs, the BIB is again inverted on the next outgoing signal unit. The **forward sequence number** (FSN) is used to number MSUs uniquely, modulo 128. The FSN of each new MSU is one more than the preceding MSU. The **forward indicator bit** (FIB) is used to indicate whether the MSU containing it is a new MSU or a retransmission due to receipt of a negative acknowledgment. For a retransmission, the FIB is inverted; all succeeding signal units maintain the same value of FIB until another negative acknowledgment is received.

The **length indicator** (LI) field specifies the length in octets of the following upper-level fields. This provides a cross-check on the closing flag. It also serves as a signal unit type indicator, because the three types of signal units carry upper-level data of different lengths. The FISU has no user data field; the LSSU has a single user data field of one octet; and the MSU has a data portion that is longer than two octets. Thus, a value of 0 indicates an FISU; a value of 1 or 2 indicates an LSSU; and a value of 3 to 63 provides for various lengths of the MSU.

The next two fields contain information of use to higher levels and are simply treated as data to be transferred across the link. The **service information octet** (SIO) indicates the nature of the MSU. This octet consists of two subfields, the service indicator and the subservice field (Table 11.2). The service indicator specifies the user of the MTP: what type of message is being carried. The subservice field indicates whether the message relates to a national or international network. Some of the bits in the subservice field are either unused, reserved for future use, or available for national use. The **signaling information field** (SIF) contains information of interest to both the signaling network level and level 4 of SS7. This field consists of two subfields, the routing label and user data. The routing label is a 32-bit address field, containing 14-bit source and destination node addresses and a 4-bit signaling link selection field that is used to distribute the traffic among alternative routes. The second part of the SIF contains user data from some SS7 application or network management data. For example, an ISDN user part would be contained here.

The **check bits** (CK) field contains an error-detecting code used to enable the receiver to determine if there have been any transmission errors. The check bits are calculated from the remainder of the bits in the signal unit exclusive of flags, using a cyclic redundancy check (CRC). The CRC is calculated by the transmitter and inserted into the signal unit. The same calculation is performed by the receiver. If there is a discrepancy between the received CRC and the CRC calculated by the receiver, then an error is assumed. The 16-bit CRC-CCITT formula is used. This formula and the error-detection process are examined in Appendix A.

The link status signal unit (LSSU) shares many of the same fields as the MSU. The only difference is that instead of the two user fields (SIO and SIF) in the MSU, there is a single **status field** (SF) that is carried as user data in the LSSU. Again, this field is simply treated as data to be transferred across the link. The field is used to indicate the sender's view of the actual status of the link. This information may be used for network management purposes.

Finally, the fill-in signal unit (FISU) contains no new fields. It has the same structure as the MSU and the LSSU, but with no user fields.

Operation

The key functions performed by the signaling link protocol are flow control, error control, and error monitoring.

Table 11.2 Service Information Octet and Status Field Codes

(a) Service Information Octet

Service Indicator	
Code	**Indication**
0000	Signaling network management messages
0001	Signaling network testing and maintenance messages
0010	Spare
0011	Signaling connection control part (SCCP)
0100	Telephone user part
0101	ISDN user part
0110	Data user part (call- and circuit-related messages)
0111	Data user part (facility registration and cancellation)
1000	MTP testing user part
1001	Broadband ISDN user part
1010	Satellite ISDN user part
1011 to 1111	Spare

Subservice Field	
Code	**Meaning**
00XX	International network
01XX	Spare
10XX	National network
11XX	Reserved for national use

(b) Status Field

Code	**Indication**
000	Out of alignment
001	Normal alignment
010	Emergency alignment
011	Out of service
100	Processor outage
101	Busy

Flow Control

Both flow control and error control employ a sliding-window technique (see Appendix A), in which each message signal unit (MSU) is numbered sequentially. Each new MSU is given a new forward sequence number (FSN) that is one more (modulo 128) than the preceding sequence number. Link status signal units (LSSUs) and fill-in signal units (FISUs) are not numbered separately but carry the FSN of the last transmitted MSU. All three types of signal units carry piggybacked acknowledgments and negative acknowledgments, in the form of backward sequence numbers (BSNs). Figure 11.6 provides an example of an error-free exchange of signal

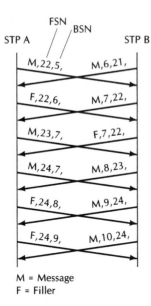

M = Message
F = Filler

Figure 11.6 Error-Free
Signal Unit Exchange.

units. Note that when both sides have data to send via the MSU, then the MSU is used to provide a piggybacked acknowledgment. When one side has no data to send, it transmits FISUs, which provide acknowledgment.

Flow control is provided by the LSSU. When one side is unable to keep up with the flow of data from the other side, it transmits an LSSU with a busy indication in the status field. When such an indication is received, all transmission of MSUs must cease; the busy side will notify the other side that it can resume transmission by means of another LSSU. This activity is generally invisible to the next higher level (signaling network level), which may simply notice that throughput has declined. However, if a congestion condition persists and is not reported to the signaling network level, then the performance of the entire signaling network may be degraded. If the network level is aware of a congestion problem, then control packets can be routed around the point of congestion. For this purpose, tight timer control on the allowable duration of the busy condition is imposed. Three rules specify the time constraints:

- If a receiver becomes overloaded, it must send a busy signal to stop transmission from the other side. The receiver withholds acknowledgment of the MSU that triggered the congestion-control condition and of subsequent MSUs received during the busy condition. If the overload condition persists, the node must repeatedly send a busy indication at intervals of T5 time units (suggested value 80–120 ms). The other side suspends transmission of MSUs while the busy condition persists.
- When congestion abates at the receiver, the receiver signals the end of the busy condition by resuming the positive acknowledgment of incoming MSUs.

- Even if repeated busy indications are received every T5 time units, a node will report to the network level that a link is *out of service* after a time interval of T6 (suggested value 3–6 seconds).

Error Control

Two forms of error control are defined:

- **Basic method:** Applies for signaling links where the one-way propagation delay is less than 15 ms.
- **Preventive cyclic retransmission method:** Applies for signaling links with a one-way propagation delay greater than or equal to 15 ms; this would include signaling links established via satellite.

The **basic method** of error control is go-back-N ARQ (see Appendix A). If a node receives a negative acknowledgment in an MSU, LSSU, or FISU, it will retransmit the specified signal unit and all subsequent signal units. Figure 11.7 illustrates this algorithm.

The alternative to go-back-N for long-delay links is **preventive cyclic retransmission**. For a link with a relatively long propagation delay, each message unit is

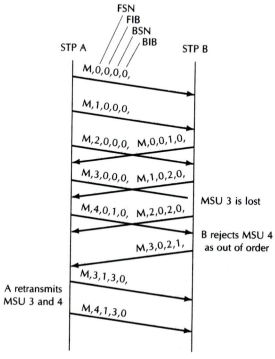

Figure 11.7 Transmission of MSUs with Error Correction.

comparatively short, and the link may be idle most of the time. In such a circumstance, it is not efficient to wait for a negative acknowledgment before retransmitting. Instead, whenever a node has no MSUs to send, it automatically retransmits unacknowledged MSUs, without waiting for a positive or negative acknowledgment. Only positive acknowledgments are sent by the other side.

Because only positive acknowledgments are sent by the other side, there is a danger that a unit in error may go undetected and uncorrected for a considerable period of time. This is particularly true when the flow of traffic is heavy. In that case, one side may be so occupied sending new units that it rarely performs voluntary retransmission. Accordingly, when a predetermined number of outstanding, unacknowledged signal units exist, the transmission of new units is interrupted and the retained signal units are retransmitted cyclically until the number of unacknowledged signal units is reduced. This feature is known as the *forced retransmission procedure.*

Error Monitoring

Two types of signaling link error-rate monitoring are provided: signaling unit error-rate monitor and alignment error-rate monitor.

Signaling unit error-rate monitoring is employed while the signaling link is in service and provides a means for detecting when a link should be taken out of service due to excessive errors. A counter is maintained that is initialized to zero and manipulated based on two parameters:

T = threshold above which an error is signaled to level 3
$1/D$ = the lowest error rate (ratio of signal unit errors to signal units) that will eventually cause an error to be signaled to level 3

For each signal unit received in error, the counter is incremented by 1. The counter is decremented by 1 (but not below 0) for every sequence of D received signal units, whether in error or not. The link is considered unreliable whenever the count reaches the threshold T. For 64-kbps links, the parameter values are set at T = 64 and D = 256 (error rate = $1/D$ = 0.004). This technique is known as a "leaky bucket" algorithm. It will ultimately detect a consistent error rate at or above the rate of $1/D$, but it will not be triggered by an occasional surge of errors, such as might be caused by a noise burst.

Alignment error-rate monitoring is employed while the signaling link is being initialized and aligned. Alignment simply means that transmitter and receiver are aligned with respect to the opening flag field of each transmitted frame. The alignment error-rate monitoring procedure provides the criteria for rejecting a signaling link for service due to an excessive error rate. For this purpose a counter is used that is initialized to zero and is incremented by one for each signal unit received in error. If the counter exceeds a threshold before the end of an initial "proving period," the proving period is aborted. In the event of failure, the proving-period procedure may be tried up to five times. Five successive failures result in the link being declared unreliable.

11.4 SIGNALING NETWORK LEVEL

The signaling network level provides the functions and procedures for the transfer of SS7 messages between signaling points. As Figure 11.8 illustrates, the signaling network level includes functions related to message handling and functions related to network management.

Signaling Message-Handling Functions

The message-handling functions are performed at every signaling point (including signal transfer points). They are based on the parts of the message signal unit known as the routing label and the service information octet (Figure 11.5a).

The message-handling functions fall into three categories:

- **Discrimination:** Determines if a message is at its destination or is to be relayed to another node. This decision is based on analysis of the destination code in the routing label of the message. If this is the destination, the signal unit is delivered to the distribution function; otherwise, it is delivered to the routing function. The discrimination function is only needed in signal transfer points (STPs).

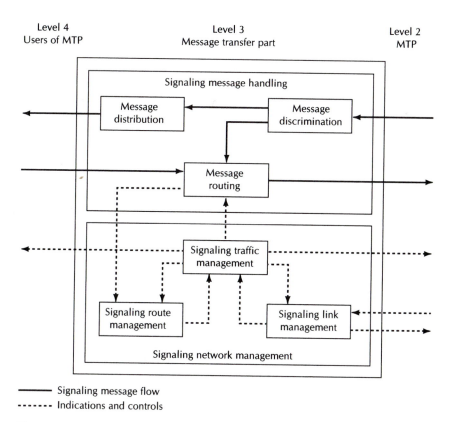

Figure 11.8   Message Transfer Part—Level 3.

- **Routing:** Determines the signaling link to be used in forwarding a message. The message may have been received from the discrimination function or from a local level 4 entity.
- **Distribution:** Determines the user part to which a message should be delivered. The decision is based on analysis of the service indicator portion of the service information octet.

The routing decision is based on the value of the signaling link selection (SLS) field, which is assigned by a user part in level 4. For a given source/destination pair, several alternate routes may be possible; the value of the SLS field specifies which particular route is to be followed. With a 4-bit field, a total of 16 different routes through the network may be defined. These different routes are, in effect, different internal virtual circuits. In general, all of the control signals associated with a single call will follow the same route; this guarantees that they will arrive in sequence. However, the MTP needs to distribute traffic uniformly. This requirement can be satisfied if the user part varies the route selection from one call to the next.

Signaling Network Management Functions

The other main component of the signaling network level is signaling network management. The main objective of this component is to overcome link degradations (failures or congestion). To meet this objective, the signaling management function is concerned with monitoring the status of each link, with dictating alternate routes to overcome link degradation and communicating the alternate routes to the affected nodes, and with recovering from the loss of messages due to link failure. The goal for SS7 is no more than 10 minutes of unavailability per year for any route. This goal is achieved through redundancy of links and dynamic rerouting.

This emphasis on the internal management of the network is rare; virtually all other network protocols make no mention of network management. In most cases, it is preferable to leave network management details to the provider, so that the provider can pursue the most cost-effective approach and be responsive to changes both in customer expectations and advances in technology. However, in the case of SS7, there are strong reasons for the emphasis on network management:

1. The function being specified is critical. The performance of a network's control signaling architecture affects all subscribers to the network.
2. The various networks involved must support international traffic. Degradations in one nation's signaling system will have repercussions beyond that nation's borders. Thus, some international agreement on the degree of reliability of national networks is indicated.
3. Recovery and restoration actions may involve multiple networks (e.g., in the case of international calls). If SS7 did not include failure and congestion recovery procedures, it would be necessary for the administration of each public network to enter into bilateral agreements with a number of other networks.

As Figure 11.8 indicates, signaling network management functions fall into three categories:

- Signaling traffic management
- Signaling link management
- Signaling route management

Table 11.3 summarizes the functions performed in each category. As can be seen, the signaling network management component as a whole is quite complex. In

Table 11.3   Signaling Network Management Procedures

Signaling Traffic Management

Changeover
Divert traffic to one or more alternative links in the event of a link unavailability.

Changeback
Reestablish traffic on a signaling link that becomes available.

Forced rerouting
Divert traffic to an alternate route when a route becomes unavailable.

Controlled rerouting
Divert traffic to a route that has been made available.

Signaling point restart
When a signaling point becomes available and when signaling traffic is diverted to or through this point, update the network routing status and control.

Management inhibiting
Link is made unavailable to user-part-generated traffic for maintenance or testing purposes.

Signaling traffic flow control
Limit signaling traffic at its source when the signaling network is not capable of transferring all signaling traffic offered by the user because of network failures or congestion.

Signaling Link Management

Signaling link activation, restoration, and deactivation
Restore failed links, activate new links, and deactivate links.

Link set activation
Activate a link set not having any links in service.

Automatic allocation of signaling terminals and signaling data links
Allocate terminals to links.

Signaling Route Management

Transfer-controlled procedure
Performed at an STP in the case of link congestion. Message sources are told to stop sending messages having a congestion priority less than the congestion level of the link.

Transfer-prohibited procedure
Performed at an STP to inform adjacent signaling points that they must no longer route to a particular destination via this STP.

Transfer-allowed procedure
Informs adjacent signaling points that routing to a given destination is now normal.

Transfer-restricted procedure
If possible, adjacent signaling points should no longer route to a particular destination via this STP.

Signaling-route-set test procedure
Used by signaling points receiving transfer-prohibited and transfer-restricted messages to recover the signaling route information that may not have been received due to some failure.

Signaling-route-set congestion test procedure
Used to update the congestion status associated with a route toward a particular destination.

the remainder of this section, we attempt only to give the reader a feel for the kinds of procedures contained within each category.

The functions listed in Table 11.3 are actually performed by the exchange of level 3 messages between signaling points. These messages are carried in the signaling information field (SIF) of an MSU (Figure 11.5a). Each message consists of an 8-bit field that identifies the particular message and a message value of 0, 8, 16, or 24 bits.

All of the procedures relating to signaling network management involve the monitoring and control of the status of various entities, including signaling links, signaling routes, signaling points, and signaling route sets. This latter entity refers to a collection of alternative routes between a source and destination. Table 11.4 summarizes the status values that each of these entities may have.

Signaling Traffic Management

Signaling traffic management is used to divert signaling traffic, without causing message loss or duplication, from unavailable signaling links or routes to one or more alternative signaling links or routes, or to reduce traffic in the case of congestion.

As an example of the functions performed in the category of signaling traffic management, let us consider the changeover procedure. The objective of the

Table 11.4 Status Values for the Signaling Network Level

Signaling Link Status	
Available	Messages may be transmitted over this link.
Unavailable	
Failed	Unable to perform transmission function within acceptable performance parameters.
Deactivated	Removed from service by signaling link management or external management function.
Blocked	Processor outage exists at one end of the link.
Inhibited	Link unavailable to user-part-generated traffic.
Signaling Route Status	
Available	Signaling traffic toward a particular destination can be transferred via this signaling transfer point.
Restricted	Signaling traffic toward a particular destination is being transferred with some difficulty via this signaling transfer point.
Unavailable	Signaling traffic toward a particular destination cannot be transferred via this signaling transfer point.
Signaling Point Status	
Available	Signaling traffic may be transferred to this signaling point.
Unavailable	Signaling traffic may not be transferred to this signaling point.
Signaling Route Set Status	
Congested	Indicates that the buffer occupancy rate of a link exceeds a given threshold.
Uncongested	The buffer occupancy rate of a link is within predetermined limits.

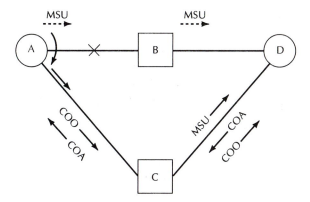

Figure 11.9 Example of Changeover Procedure.

changeover procedure is to ensure that signaling traffic carried by a link that becomes unavailable is diverted to the alternative signaling link(s) as quickly as possible while avoiding message loss, duplication, or missequencing.

Figure 11.9 shows an example of the changeover procedure for messages traveling along a route between signaling points A and D. Changeover is initiated when a signaling link is recognized as unavailable. This might occur, for example, if the link error-rate monitoring function of layer 2 reports the failure. The following actions are then performed:

1. Transmission and acceptance of MSUs on the concerned signaling link are terminated.
2. Alternative links are determined to construct an alternative route.
3. Those messages in the retransmission buffer of the unavailable link that have not been received by the far end are identified.
4. The identified messages are transferred to the transmission buffer of the alternate link.

Steps 3 and 4 are accomplished in the following way: A signaling point that recognizes the unavailability of a link sends a changeover order (COO) message to the remote signaling point over some available alternate route. The message value field contains the forward sequence number of the last message accepted from the unavailable signaling link. When the other side receives the COO, it responds with a changeover acknowledgment (COA) message, which contains the forward sequence number of its last accepted MSU. The two sides are now able to resume the exchange of MSUs containing user-part information over an alternate route, maintaining the proper sequence with no losses or duplications. The new route is decided by the signaling message-handling function of the two endpoints.

In our example, traffic between signaling points A and D is initially carried via signaling point B. When the link between A and B becomes unavailable, A sends a COO message to D via signal transfer point C. C responds along the same route with a COA. Subsequently, all MSUs follow the route through C.

Signaling Link Management

Signaling link management is used to restore failed signaling links, activate new signaling links, and deactivate aligned signaling links. There is a basic set of mandatory functions that perform signaling link management for links directly connected to a signaling point. There are additional, optional functions that allow for more efficient use of signaling equipment when signaling terminal devices have switched access to signaling data links.

Signaling Route Management

Signaling route management is used to distribute information about the signaling network status to block or unblock signaling routes.

As an example of the functions performed by signaling route management, we consider the signaling-route-set congestion procedure. This procedure is used by STPs to control congestion. Whereas congestion occurring between signaling points can easily be handled by flow control at level 2, when congestion occurs on a link emanating from an STP, the source SPs that send messages through that link must be controlled.

Each outgoing link of each signaling transfer point has a transmit buffer with three threshold levels: congestion onset (T), congestion abatement (A), and discard (D), where A < T < D. The discard threshold is equivalent to the buffer capacity. The set of routes through the link in question is either congested or uncongested, depending on the buffer occupancy history. When the link is uncongested and the arrival of incoming message units causes the portion of the buffer that is filled to exceed T, then the link is considered to be congested, and a choking message, the transfer controlled (TFC) message, is sent to the source of the node that caused the threshold to be reached and to the source of all subsequent messages while the link is congested. When the buffer occupancy level decreases below A, transmission of choking messages ceases and the link is considered uncongested. Thus, the status of the link when the occupancy of the buffer is between A and T can be in either state, depending on buffer occupancy history. This is a "hysteresis" effect, which prevents frequent changes of the link status.

When a signaling point receives a choking message, it stops generating messages for the route involved. Two timers are used to determine when to resume normal routing. When a node receives a choking message, it starts a timer with a duration of T_{15} seconds. When the timer expires, the node sends a signaling route set congestion test (RCT) message to the same destination along the normal route and waits for a time period T_{16} to see if another choking message is returned in response to this RCT message. If a choking message is received within T_{16}, the T_{15} timer is reset and the process begins again. If T_{16} expires, then the node assumes that the congestion has abated and resumes normal routing.

Figure 11.10 illustrates the operation of the algorithm at a signaling point. At time $t = 0$, the SP receives a TFC message. The SP stops generating user-part messages for the indicated destination and starts the T_{15} timer. When this timer expires, the SP sends an RCT message and prepares to wait for time T_{16}. Before this timer expires, another TFC message is received, and the process begins again. In this example, after the second RCT message, timer T_{16} expires and the SP resumes normal transmission.

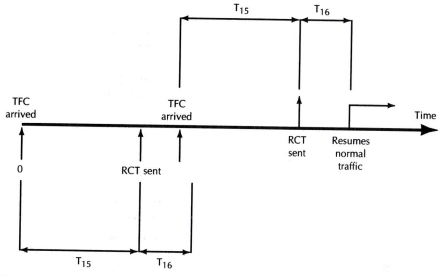

TFC = Transfer controlled message
RCT = Signaling route set congestion test message
T_{15} = Timer: waiting to start signaling route set congestion test
T_{16} = Timer: waiting for route set congestion status update

Figure 11.10   Example Behavior of an SP for the SS7 Congestion Control Scheme [LEE89].

11.5 SIGNALING CONNECTION CONTROL PART

The signaling connection control part (SCCP) was developed as it became apparent that SS7 would have to support more than signaling and needed more explicit addressing and more sophisticated services between remote signaling points. The signaling network level does not provide all of the routing and addressing capabilities that the OSI model dictates for the network layer. As an example, the message distribution function provides only a limited addressing capability. For newer user-part applications, a more complex specification of the user of a message at a node is necessary; this can be provided by the signaling connection control part (SCCP). The SCCP enhances the connectionless sequenced transmission service provided by the MTP, to meet the needs of those user parts requiring enriched connectionless or connection-oriented service to transfer signaling information between nodes. Classic circuit-switched telephone-call-related signaling does not use SCCP. For this application and those user parts for which MTP suffices, the extra overhead of SCCP can be avoided.

Thus, the enhancements provided by SCCP over those available in just the message transfer part are in the areas of addressing and message-transfer services. The **addressing** capabilities of SCCP extend those found in MTP, which is limited to delivering a message to a specified node and using a 4-bit service indicator (Table

11.2a) to distribute messages within a node. SCCP supplements this capability by providing addressing that uses destination point codes (DPCs; see Figure 11.5) plus subsystem numbers (SSNs). The SSN is local addressing information that identifies each of the SCCP users at a node. Another addressing enhancement is the ability to address messages with global titles, such as dialed digits, that are not in a form usable by MTP for routing. SCCP provides a mapping facility for translating global titles into an address of the form DPC + SSN.

SCCP also provides enhanced **message-transfer services**, two connectionless and two connection oriented. The four classes are as follows:

0—Basic connectionless

1—Sequenced (MTP) connectionless class

2—Basic connection oriented

3—Flow-control connection oriented

In Class 0 service, a user provides a block of data, referred to as a network service data unit (NSDU), to SCCP for delivery to a user at another node. The NSDUs are transported independently and may be delivered out of sequence. This is a pure connectionless, or datagram, service.

For Class 1 service, Class 0 is enhanced with the ability to specify that a particular stream of NSDUs should be delivered in sequence. SCCP does this by assigning a sequence number to each member NSDU and giving all messages in the stream the same signaling link code (Figure 11.5).

The remaining two classes of service operate over logical connections, called signaling connections. These connections are equivalent to virtual circuits through the signaling network. Each logical connection is given a unique signaling link code. Class 2 provides this basic connection-oriented service.

For Class 3 service, Class 2 is enhanced with the ability to perform flow control over a logical connection. Also, the detection of message loss and missequencing is provided. In the event of lost or missequenced messages, the signaling connection is reset and notification is given to higher layers.

As with most standards at the various layers of the OSI model, SCCP can be specified in terms of the services that it provides to higher layers and the protocol between peer SCCP entities in different nodes. Both of these aspects are summarized in Figure 11.11, which shows the internal structure of SCCP (which is implemented as a set of protocol elements) and the interface to upper and lower layers (which is defined by a service specification). The structure consists of four functional blocks:

- **Connection-oriented control:** Controls the establishment and release of signaling connections and provides for data transfer on signaling connections.
- **Connectionless control:** Provides for connectionless transfer of data units.
- **Management:** Provides capabilities beyond those of MTP to handle the congestion or failure of either the SCCP user or the signaling route to the SCCP user. With this capability, SCCP can route messages to backup systems in the event that failures prevent routing to the primary system.

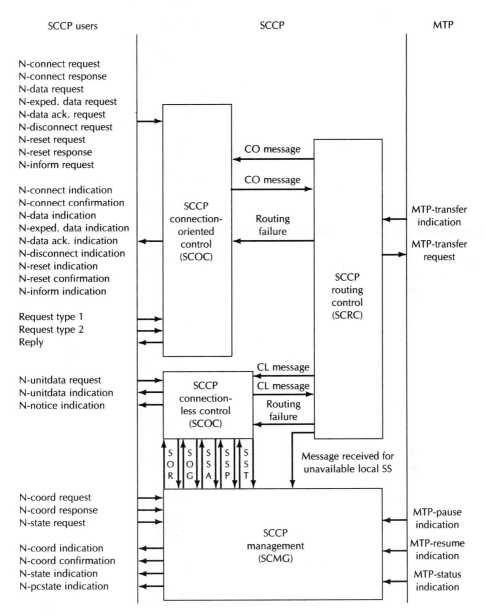

Figure 11.11 SCCP Overview.

- **Routing control:** Upon receipt of a message from MTP or from functions (1) or (2), SCCP routing provides the necessary routing functions either to forward the message to MTP for transfer or pass the message to (1) or (2). A message whose "called party address" is a local user is passed to (1) or (2), while one destined for a remote user is forwarded to the MTP for transfer to a distant SCCP user.

We examine SCCP services and protocol in turn.

SCCP Services

As with any protocol service, SCCP can be expressed in terms of primitives, which can be viewed as commands or procedure calls, with parameters. Each type of primitive appears in one or more variations (request, indication, response, confirm), depending on the requirements of the service. See Appendix 10B for a discussion of the standard conventions used for primitives and parameters.

Connection-Oriented Services

The connection-oriented service provided by SCCP is based on the OSI network service, which is defined in ISO 8348 and ITU-T X.213.1 Key characteristics of the network service, as listed in the standard, are as follows:

- **Independence of underlying communications facility:** Network service users need not be aware of the details of the subnetwork facilities used.
- **End-to-end transfer:** All routing and relaying are performed by the network layer and are not of concern to the network service user.
- **Transparency:** The network service does not restrict the content, format, or coding of the user data.
- **Quality-of-service selection:** The network service user has some ability to request a given quality of service.
- **User addressing:** A system of addressing is used that allows network service users to refer unambiguously to one another.

Table 11.5 lists the primitives and parameters for the connection-oriented service; the parameters are defined in Table 11.6. Figure 11.12 displays the sequences in which primitives may be used.

Connection establishment begins with a user request, contained in an N-CONNECT.request primitive. In addition to specifying the called and calling user, the primitive can request certain services to be provided for the requested connection:

- **Receipt confirmation selection:** Ordinarily, the network service will not confirm that data have been delivered to the other side; it is assumed that the data are delivered. However, the user may request that explicit confirmation be provided.
- **Expedited data selection:** The user may also request that an expedited data service be available.
- **Quality of service:** The user may specify two quality-of-service parameters. First, the user proposes one of the four classes to be used for the connection. If appropriate, the user also proposes a flow-control window size.

The remainder of the connection establishment process involves confirming the setup of a connection and the negotiation of quality-of-service parameters. The negotiation proceeds as follows:

Table 11.5 Network Service Primitives for Connection-Oriented Service

Primitive	Parameters
N-CONNECT.request N-CONNECT.indication N-CONNECT.response N-CONNECT.confirmation	Called address, Calling address, Responding address, Receipt confirmation selection, Expedited data selection, Quality of Service parameter selection, User data, Connection identification
N-DATA.request N-DATA.indication	Confirmation request, User data, Connection identification
N-EXPEDITED-DATA.request N-EXPEDITED-DATA.indication	User data, Connection identification
N-DATA-ACKNOWLEDGE.request N-DATA-ACKNOWLEDGE.indication	Connection identification
N-DISCONNECT.request N-DISCONNECT.indication	Originator, Reason, User data, Responding address, Connection identification
N-RESET.request N-RESET.indication N-RESET.response N-RESET.confirmation	Originator, Reason, Connection identification

1. The calling user specifies Class 3 or Class 2 in the quality-of-service parameter of the N-CONNECT.request. If Class 3 is selected, a flow-control window size is specified.

2. The SCCP at the calling user's node, at any intermediate STPs, or at the called user's node may downgrade a Class 3 request to a Class 2 request. If Class 3 was requested and is not downgraded, any of these nodes may reduce the window size.

3. An N-CONNECT.indication is issued to the called user with the resulting quality of service.

4. The called user responds with an N-CONNECT.response. The called user may downgrade the class or reduce the flow-control window size.

5. The final quality of service is conveyed to the calling user in an N-CONNECT.confirm.

The preceding actions describe a successful connection establishment. A connection request may also be denied, in one of several ways. When the called user receives the N-CONNECT.indication, it may not have resources available for the call. In that case, the called user responds with an N-DISCONNECT.request. This results in an N-DISCONNECT.indication being passed to the calling user, which is a refusal of the request. Similarly, if the network cannot support the new connection, an N-DISCONNECT.indication is issued by SCCP to the calling user.

Table 11.6 Parameters for SCCP Service Primitives

Affected DPC
Identifies a signaling point that is failed, congested, or allowed.

Affected Subsystem
An address that identifies a user that is failed, withdrawn, congested, or allowed.

Called Address
Identifies the destination of a communication. Address may be a global title, subsystem number, or signaling point code.

Calling Address
Identifies the destination of a communication. Address may be a global title, subsystem number, or signaling point code.

Confirmation Request
Used in an N-DATA primitive to indicate the need to confirm the receipt of the N-DATA primitive by the remote SCCP user.

Connection Identification
Used to allocate a primitive to a certain connection.

Expedited Data Selection
May be used to indicate during setup whether expedited data can be transferred via the connection. A negotiation will be performed between SCCP users, local and remote.

Originator
Indicates the source of a reset or disconnect and can be any of the following:
•Network service provider.
•Network service user.
•Unidentified.

Quality-of-Service Parameter Set
Parameters used during call setup to negotiate the protocol class for the connection and, if applicable, the flow-control window size.

Reason
Gives information about the cause of a reset, disconnect, or connection refusal.

Reason for Return
Identifies the reason that a message was not able to be delivered to its final destination.

Receipt Confirmation Selection
Indicates the use/availability of the receipt confirmation service. The need for such a service is a subject for further study.

Responding Address
Indicates to which destination the connection has been established or refused.

Return Option
Used in the connectionless service to determine the handling of messages encountering transport problems. The possible values are discard message on error and return message on error.

Signaling Point Status
Used to inform a user of the status of an affected DPC. Values are inaccessible, congested, and accessible.

Sequence Control
For connectionless service, indicates to the SCCP whether the user wishes the service sequence guaranteed or sequence not guaranteed.

Subsystem Multiplicity Indicator
Identifies the number of replications of a subsystem.

User Data
Data passed transparently by SCCP from one end user to the other.

User Status
Used to inform an SCCP user of the status of an affected subsystem. Possible values are in service and out of service.

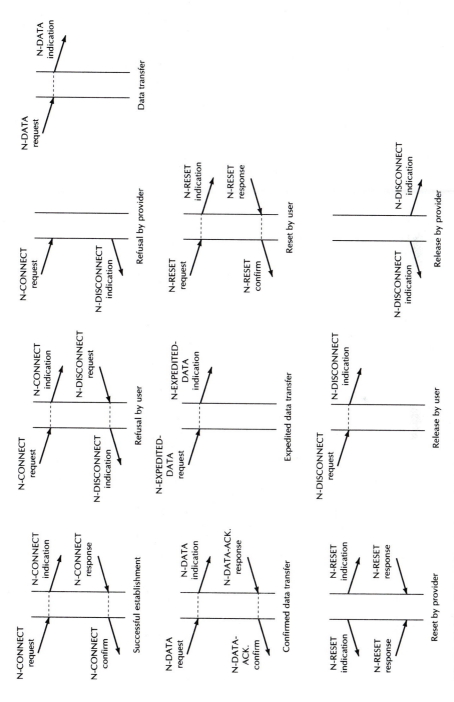

Figure 11.12 Connection-Oriented Service: Primitive Sequences.

283

Once a logical connection is set up between two SCCP users, the **data-transfer** phase is entered. User data are conveyed in an N-DATA primitive. Note that there are only request and indication primitives defined. The reason that there is no need for a confirmation back to the user that sent the data is that the connection-oriented service guarantees to deliver all data in the proper order, with no losses. However, if the user requires acknowledgment, then the N-DATA-ACKNOWLEDGE primitives are used.

The N-EXPEDITED-DATA primitive may be used if previously requested for this connection. The expedited data service provides a means for expediting the delivery of occasional urgent data. Examples are an interrupt, an alarm, or an abrupt connection termination at a higher layer. The network service will endeavor to have the expedited data transmitted across the network as rapidly as possible, perhaps overtaking some previously transmitted ordinary data. Normal flow-control mechanisms are bypassed.

The N-RESET primitive can occur with Class 3 transfer. N-RESET overrides all other activities and causes SCCP to start a reinitialization procedure for sequence numbering. During this process, some outstanding data units may be lost. SCCP may need to perform a reset if for some reason it becomes out of synchronization with the other side. A user may need to perform a reset because it wishes to abort the current exchange without losing the connection.

The N-DISCONNECT primitive is used for the connection release phase and also for connection refusal during the connection establishment phase. Parameters are included to notify the reason for connection release/refusal and the initiator of the release/refusal procedure.

Connectionless Services

The connectionless service provided by SCCP is based on the OSI connectionless network service, which is defined in ISO 8348 and ITU-T X.213. Table 11.7 lists the primitives and parameters for the connectionless service; the parameters are defined in Table 11.6.

The connectionless service provides the SCCP user with the ability to transfer signaling messages via the signaling network without the setup of a signaling connection. The basic enhancement provided over the MTP service is the ability to map the called address to the signaling point code of the MTP service.

The transfer of data is achieved with the N-UNITDATA primitives. Under certain conditions of congestion and unavailability of subsystems and/or signaling

Table 11.7 Primitives of the Connectionless Service

Primitive	Parameters
N-UNITDATA.request N-UNITDATA.indication	Called address, Calling address, Sequence control, Return option, User data
N-NOTICE.indication	Called address, Calling address, Reason for return, User data

points, connectionless messages could be discarded instead of being delivered. If the user wishes to be informed of the nondelivery of messages, the return option parameter is set to "return message on error" in the N-UNITDATA.request. The sequence control parameter is used to select one of two data transfer modes:

- **With sequence control:** MTP guarantees an in-sequence delivery of messages that contain the same signaling link code (SLC). The SCCP user employs this service by including the sequence control parameter. SCCP will put the same SLC code into the primitive to MTP for all primitives from the SCCP user with the same sequence control value.
- **Without sequence control:** SCCP inserts SLCs randomly, or with respect to the load sharing within the signaling network.

If the user has selected the return message option, the SCCP will use the N-NOTICE primitive to notify the originating user of a failure to deliver a message.

SCCP Management

Table 11.8 lists the primitives and parameters for SCCP management; the parameters are defined in Table 11.6. SCCP management is used to maintain network performances by rerouting or throttling traffic in the event of failure or congestion in the network. These procedures apply to both connection-oriented and connectionless services of the SCCP.

The N-COORD primitive is used to coordinate the withdrawal of one of the SCCP users when multiple replications of a user at a node are employing SCCP. This informs SCCP that a particular user is no longer available.

The two N-STATE primitives allow a user and SCCP to exchange status information. The N-PCSTATE primitive is used to inform a user about the status of a signaling point.

SCCP Protocol

The SCCP protocol is subdivided into four protocol classes, one for each SCCP service class:

Table 11.8 Primitives of the SCCP Management

Primitive	Parameters
R-COORD.request R-COORD.indication R-COORD.response R-COORD.confirmation	Affected subsystem, Subsystem multiplicity indicator
N-STATE.request N-STATE.indication	Affected subsystem, User status, Subsystem multiplicity indicator
N-PCSTATE.indication	Affected DPC, Signaling point status

0—Basic connectionless

1—Sequenced (MTP) connectionless class

2—Basic connection oriented

3—Flow-control connection oriented

In effect, SCCP consists of four distinct services, each with its own protocol. The formats and many of the procedures are shared among the four protocol classes.

Protocol Formats

The SCCP protocol makes use of 16 types of messages, which are listed and defined in Table 11.9. Table 11.10 shows the mandatory (M) and optional (O) parameters associated with each message, with the exception of management-related messages.

Table 11.9 SCCP Messages

Connection-Oriented (Protocol Classes 2 and 3)

Connection request (CR)
Sent by a calling SCCP to a called SCCP to request the setting up of a signaling connection between the two entities.

Connection confirm (CC)
Sent by the called SCCP to the calling SCCP to indicate to the calling SCCP that it has performed the setup of the signaling connection.

Connection refused (CREF)
Sent by the called SCCP or an intermediate node SCCP to indicate to the calling SCCP that the connection setup has been refused.

Data form 1 (DT1)
Sent by either end of a signaling connection to pass transparently SCCP user data between two SCCP nodes. Protocol class 2 only.

Data form 2 (DT2)
Sent by either end of a signaling connection to pass transparently SCCP user data between two SCCP nodes and to acknowledge messages flowing in the other direction. Protocol class 3 only.

Data acknowledgment (AK)
Controls the window flow-control mechanism. Protocol class 3 only.

Expedited data (ED)
Functions as a DT2 message but includes the ability to bypass the flow-control mechanism that has been selected for the data transfer phase. Protocol class 3 only.

Expedited data acknowledgment (EA)
Used to acknowledge an EA message. Protocol class 3 only.

Inactivity test (IT)
May be sent periodically by either end of a signaling connection to check if this connection is active at both ends.

Protocol data unit error (ERR)
Sent on detection of any protocol errors.

Released (RLSD)
Indicates that the sending SCCP wants to release a signaling connection and that the associated resources at the sending SCCP have been brought into the disconnect pending condition. It also indicates that the receiving node should release the connection and any other associated resources as well.

Table 11.9 SCCP Messages *(continued)*

Release complete (RLC)
> Sent in response to an RLSD to acknowledge the RLSD and to indicate that the appropriate procedures have been completed.

Reset request (RSR)
> Indicates that the sending SCCP wants to initiate a reset procedure (reinitialization of sequence numbers) with the receiving SCCP.

Reset confirm (RSC)
> Sent in response to an RSR to acknowledge the RSRC and to indicate that the appropriate procedures have been completed.

Connectionless (Protocol Classes 0 and 1)

Unitdata (UDT)
> Used by an SCCP to send data in connectionless mode.

Unitdata service (UDTS)
> Indicates to the originating SCCP that a UDT it sent cannot be delivered to its destination.

Subsystem (User) Management

Subsystem allowed (SSA)
> Sent to concerned destinations to inform those destinations that a subsystem that was formally prohibited is now allowed.

Subsystem out-of-service request (SOR)
> Allows subsystems to go out of service without degrading the performance of the network. When a subsystem wishes to go out of service, the request is transferred by means of an SOR between the SCCP at the subsystem's node and the SCCP at the duplicate subsystem's node.

Subsystem out-of-service grant (SOG)
> Sent in response to an SOR to the requesting SCCP if both the requested SCCP and the backup of the affected subsystem agree to the request.

Subsystem prohibited (SSP)
> Sent to concerned destinations to inform SCCP management at those destinations of the failure of a subsystem.

Subsystem status test (SST)
> Sent to verify the status of a subsystem marked prohibited.

Figure 11.13 shows the format of an SCCP message. The routing label identifies a particular signaling connection for connection-oriented protocols (Class 2 and 3) and may be used for sequencing and load leveling for connectionless protocols. The message type field identifies one of the 16 messages. The remainder of the message carries the parameters for the given message type. Some of these parameters are mandatory (must be included with every instance of the message) and some are optional. Of the mandatory parameters, some are of fixed length and can be represented in a compact form that consists of the value of the parameter. The remaining mandatory parameters and all of the optional parameters are of variable length. Hence, the length of each such parameter must also be included. In the case of optional parameters, each parameter must also be labeled, because it is not known ahead of time if the parameter is included.

Table 11.10 Inclusion of Fields in Messages

Parameter Field	CR	CC	CREF	RLSD	RLC	DT1	DT2	AK	ED	EA	RSR	RSC	ERR	IT	UDT	UDTS
Destination local reference number	m	m	m	m	m	m	m	m	m	m	m	m	m	m	m	m
Source local reference number	m	m		m	m						m	m		m		
Called party address	m	o	o												m	m
Calling party address	o	m													m	m
Protocol class	m	m												m	m	
Segmenting/reassembly						m										
Receive sequence number								m								
Sequencing/segmenting							m							m		
Credit	o	o						m								
Release cause				m												
Return cause																m
Reset cause											m					
Error cause													m			
User data	o	o	o	o		m	m		m						m	m
Refusal cause			m													
End of optional parameters	o	o	o	o												

Messages

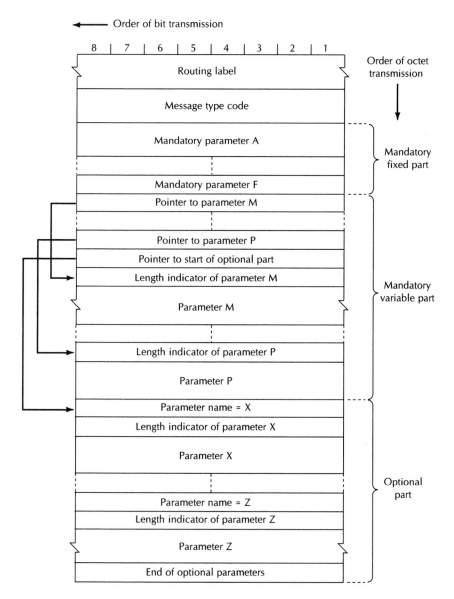

Figure 11.13 General SCCP Message Format.

Connectionless Data Transfer

For classes 0 and 1, only two message types are used: unitdata (UDT) and unitdata service (UDTS). SCCP constructs and sends a UDT in response to an N-UNITDATA.request from an SCCP user. The way in which the UDT is "sent" is to pass it down as MTP user data to MTP.

For Class 0 operation, SCCP translates the called address parameter in the N-UNITDATA.request into a destination point code (DPC) that can be understood by MTP. It selects a route through the network and requests that MTP transmit the message. If the message is successfully delivered to the called SCCP, this triggers an N-UNITDATA.indication up to the destination SCCP user. If the message is discarded, and if the return option has been selected, a UDTS message is returned to the calling SCCP, which in turn generates an N-NOTICE.indication.

For Class 1 operation, all of the procedures in the previous paragraph are followed. In addition, the sequence control parameter in the N-UNITDATA.request is used by SCCP. SCCP uses the same signaling link code for all messages that are to be sequenced.

Connection Establishment

For connection-oriented service, the connection establishment phase requires, at minimum, the exchange of a CR and a CC message.

The purpose of this phase is to establish a signaling connection with an agreed protocol class, and if Class 3 is selected, an agreed flow-control window size.

The operation begins when an SCCP user issues an N-CONNECT.request. SCCP generates a corresponding CR message with the appropriate called party address. The protocol class parameter in the message indicates the requested protocol class (Class 2 or 3). If Class 3 is selected, the credit parameter indicates the requested flow-control window size. The source local reference number is the way in which this logical connection is to be identified at the calling end; it is equivalent to an X.25 virtual circuit number.

At the called end, SCCP receives the CR message and issues an N-CONNECT. indication to the appropriate user. If the call is accepted, an N-CONNECT.response is issued back to SCCP. SCCP then returns a CC message with the appropriate protocol class and flow-control parameters. When this message is received at the calling SCCP, an N-CONNECT.confirm is issued to the calling user. If the call is not accepted, an N-DISCONNECT.request is issued by the called user, which generates a CREF message, which ultimately generates an N-DISCONNECT.indication to the calling user.

Connection-Oriented Data Transfer

Normal data transfer over a signaling connection is accomplished using data form 1 (DT1) or data form 2 (DT2) messages for Classes 2 and 3, respectively. Let us consider DT1 first.

Each DT1 may contain all of the user data, the NSDU, contained in an N-DATA.request. Alternatively, if the DT1 would exceed the maximum message size by transferring all of the NSDU, SCCP may segment the NSDU and send it out as a sequence of DT1 messages. In that case, each member of the sequence except the last has the segmenting/reassembly parameter set to 1, to indicate that more data follow. The last message in the sequence has this parameter set to 0. When all of the data have arrived, the destination SCCP passes the NSDU up to the user in an N-DATA.indication.

For Class 3 operation, the DT2 message is used. In this case, the sequencing/segmenting parameter is used, which has the following components:

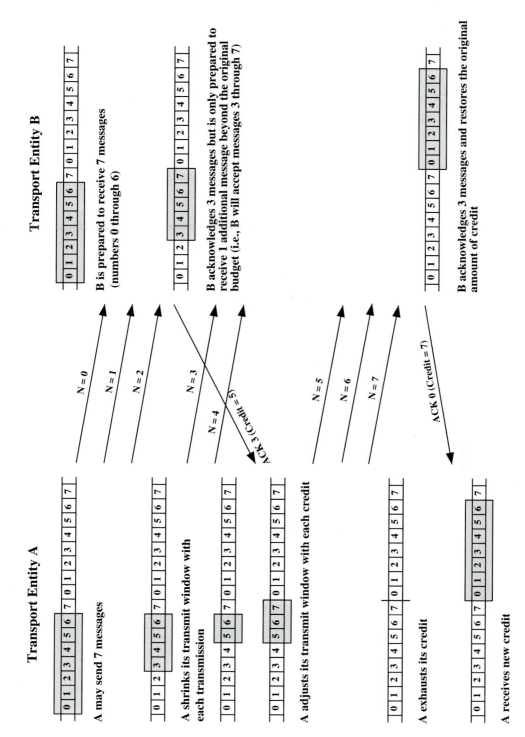

Figure 11.14 Example of Credit Allocation Mechanism

291

- **P(S):** A 7-bit send sequence number
- **P(R):** A 7-bit receive sequence number
- **M:** A 1-bit more indicator

The P(S) and P(R) fields operate the same way as send and receive sequence numbers in LAPD and X.25 to provide flow control. The M bit is used for segmentation and reassembly.

For Class 3, a flow-control scheme based on credit allocation is used. The initial credit is set in the CR and CC messages. Subsequent credit is granted in the AK message.

The credit allocation scheme decouples acknowledgment from flow control, in contrast to fixed sliding-window flow-control schemes, such as X.25 and LAPD, where the two mechanisms are coupled. The credit allocation scheme provides a greater degree of control over data flow. In a message scheme, a message may be acknowledged without granting new credit, and vice versa. Figure 11.14 illustrates the protocol (compare Figure A.3 in Appendix A). For simplicity, we show a data flow in one direction only. In this example, too, messages are numbered sequentially modulo 8 for simplicity. Initially, through the connection establishment process, the send and receive sequence numbers are synchronized and A is granted a credit allocation of 7. A advances the trailing edge of its window each time that it transmits and advances the leading edge when it is granted additional credit.

Expedited data transfer uses the ED and EA messages. Only one ED may be outstanding at a time. The sender must receive an EA before sending another ED.

Connection Termination

A connection is terminated by the exchange of RLSD and RLC messages.

11.6 ISDN USER PART

The ISDN user part (ISUP) of Signaling System Number 7 defines the functions, procedures, and interexchange signaling information flows required to provide circuit-switched services and associated user facilities for voice and nonvoice calls over ISDN. We can state three requirements for the ISUP:

- It must rely on the message-transfer part or network service part of SS7 for the transmission of messages.
- Its design must be flexible to accommodate future enhancements of ISDN capabilities.
- It must interwork with the user–network Q.931 call control protocol.

This last point highlights the distinction between the ISUP, which is defined in ITU-T recommendations Q.761–Q.764 and Q.931. The call control protocol defined in Q.931 refers to common-channel control-signaling facilities open to use by the ISDN subscriber. Q.931 is used by the subscriber to set up calls to other subscribers, with associated user facilities. ISUP refers to signaling facilities employed by the network provider on behalf of the ISDN user. Thus, ISDN communicates with the ISDN user (subscriber) via Q.931 for the purpose of call control and uses ISUP internal to the network to implement subscriber call control requests. The term *user part* is unfortunate, because this does not refer to the ISDN user; rather, it refers to the fact that the ISUP is a user of the lower layers of SS7.

Messages

The network procedures for establishing, controlling, and terminating a call occur as a result of ISUP messages exchanged between exchanges and signal transfer points within the network. A common format is used for all messages defined in ISUP, illustrated in Figure 11.15. The message consists of fields organized into the following parts:

- **Routing label:** This is actually part of the MTP header, as shown in Figure 11.5a. This label indicates the source and destination points of the message. The label also includes a signaling link code field, used in load sharing across multiple physical links. This field is shown in Figure 11.15 to highlight the fact that for each individual circuit connection the same routing label must be used in all messages associated with that connection.
- **Circuit identification code:** Specifies the circuit to which this message relates.
- **Message type:** Identifies which ISUP message is being sent. The contents of the remainder of the message depend on the message type.
- **Mandatory fixed part:** Contains those parameters that are mandatory for a particular message type and of fixed length. The position, length, and order of the parameters are uniquely defined by the message type.
- **Mandatory variable part:** Contains those parameters that are mandatory for a particular message type and of variable length. Each parameter requires a pointer and a length indicator as well as a parameter value.
- **Optional part:** Contains those parameters that may or may not occur for a particular message type. Each parameter requires a name and length indicator as well as a parameter value.

Table 11.11 lists all of the ISUP messages, together with a brief definition. The messages can be divided into nine categories. **Forward setup messages** are used to set up a circuit. In addition to identifying the exchange endpoints, these messages allow for the specification of the desired characteristics of the call. These messages propagate in a forward direction, from the exchange originating the call to the exchange that is the destination point. **General setup messages** are used during the call establishment phase. They provide a means of transferring any additional information required during call setup, plus a means for checking that a circuit that straddles more than one ISDN maintains the desired characteristics across all networks. **Backward setup messages** support the call setup process and initiate accounting and charging procedures. **Call supervision messages** are additional messages that might be needed in the process of call establishment. This group includes indications of whether the call was answered or not and the capability to support manual intervention between ISDNs that cross national boundaries. **Circuit supervision messages** relate to an already established circuit. Three key functions are supported. A circuit may be released, which terminates the call. A circuit may be suspended and later resumed. Finally, a circuit that is not

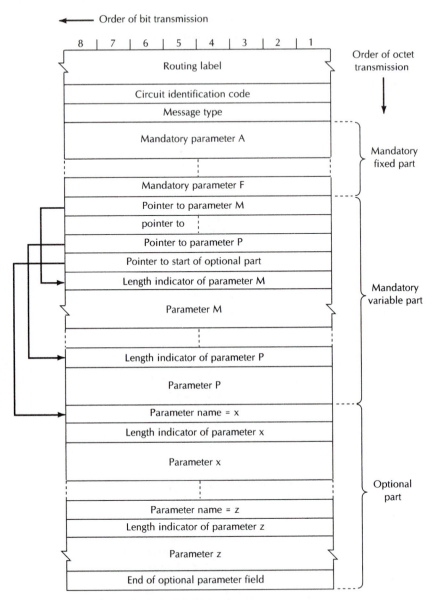

Figure 11.15 Message Format for ISDN User Part.

currently being used for a call may be established. In this case, it is possible to block the circuit so that outgoing calls on the circuit are prevented, saving the circuit for incoming calls. In the case of a group of circuits that is treated as a single unit for control, **circuit group supervision messages** perform similar functions. **Incall modification messages** are used to alter characteristics or associated network facilities of an active call, two quite different facilities. Finally, the category of **end-to-end messages** includes pass-along and end-to-end user information capabilities, explained subsequently.

(text continues on page 297)

Table 11.11   ISDN User-Part Messages

Forward Setup

Initial address
Sent in forward direction to initialize seizure of an outgoing circuit and to transmit address and related information.

Subsequent address
May be sent following initial address message to convey additional calling party address information.

General Setup

Information request
Requests additional call-related information.

Information
Conveys additional call-related information.

Continuity
Sent in forward direction to indicate continuity of the preceding speech circuit to the following international exchange.

Backward Setup

Address complete
Sent in backward direction to indicate that all the address information required for routing the call to the called party has been received.

Connect
Sent in backward direction to indicate that all the address information required for routing the call to the called party has been received and that the call has been answered.

Call progress
Indicates that an event has occurred during call setup that should be relayed to the calling party.

Call Supervision

Answer
Sent in backward direction to indicate that the call has been answered.

Forward transfer
Sent in the forward direction on semiautomatic calls when the outgoing international exchange operator wants the help of an operator at the incoming international exchange.

Release
Indicates that the circuit identified in the message is being released.

Circuit Supervision

Delayed release
Indicates that the subscriber has disconnected but that the network is holding the connection.

Release complete
Sent in response to a release message when the circuit concerned has been brought into the idle condition.

Continuity check request
Sent by an exchange for a circuit on which a continuity check is to be performed to the exchange at the other end of the circuit, requesting that continuity checking equipment be attached.

Reset circuit
Sent to release a circuit when, because of a fault, it is unknown whether a release or release complete message is appropriate. If, at the receiving end, the circuit is blocked, reception of this message should cause the condition to be removed.

Loopback acknowledgment
Sent in the backward direction in response to a continuity check request message, indicating that a loop has been connected.

Table 11.11 ISDN User-Part Messages *(continued)*

Blocking
> Sent for maintenance purposes to the exchange at the other end of the circuit, to cause subsequent outgoing calls on that circuit to be blocked.

Unblocking
> Sent to the exchange at the other end of a circuit to cancel, in that exchange, the blocked condition caused by a previous blocking or circuit group blocking message.

Unequipped circuit identification code
> Sent from one exchange to another when it receives an unequipped circuit identification code.

Blocking acknowledgment
> Response to a blocking message, indicating that the circuit has been blocked.

Unblocking acknowledgment
> Response to an unblocking message, indicating that the circuit has been unblocked.

Overload
> Sent in a backward direction, on nonpriority calls, in response to an initial address message, to invoke a temporary trunk blocking of the circuit concerned when the exchange generating the message is subject to load control.

Suspend
> Indicates that the subscriber's terminal has been temporarily disconnected.

Resume
> Indicates that the subscriber, after having sent a suspend message, is reconnected.

Confusion
> Sent in response to any message for which the exchange does not recognize the message or a part of the message.

Circuit Group Supervision

Circuit group blocking
> Sent for maintenance purposes to the exchange at the other end of a group of circuits to cause subsequent outgoing calls on that group of circuits to be blocked.

Circuit group unblocking
> Sent to the exchange at the other end of a group of circuits to cancel, in that exchange, the blocked condition caused by a previous circuit group blocking message.

Circuit group blocking acknowledgment
> Response to a circuit group blocking message, indicating that the group of circuits has been blocked.

Circuit group unblocking acknowledgment
> Response to a circuit group unblocking message, indicating that the group of circuits has been unblocked.

Circuit group reset
> Sent to release a group of circuits when, because of a fault, it is unknown which of the clearing signals is appropriate for each of the circuits in the group. Circuits that are blocked at the receiving end should be unblocked on receiving this message.

Circuit group reset acknowledgment
> Response to a reset circuit group message, indicating either that the group of circuits has been reset or that resetting has been started and that the resulting status will be reported.

Circuit group query
> Requests that the far-end exchange give the state of all circuits in a particular group.

Circuit group query response
> Sent in response to a circuit group query message to indicate the state of all circuits in a particular range.

In-Call Modification

Call modification request
> Indicates a calling or called party request to modify the characteristics of an established call (e.g., from data to voice).

Table 11.11 ISDN User-Part Messages *(continued)*

Call modification completed

Response to a call modification request message, indicating that the requested call modification has been completed.

Call modification reject

Response to a call modification request message, indicating that the request has been rejected.

Facility request

Sent from an exchange to another exchange or to a database to request activation of a facility.

Facility accepted

Sent to an exchange from an exchange or database indicating that the requested facility has been invoked.

Facility reject

Sent to an exchange from an exchange or database indicating that the facility request has been rejected.

End-To-End

Pass-along

Sent to transfer information between two signaling points along the same signaling path as that used to establish a physical connection between those two points.

User-to-user information

Used for the transport of user-to-user signaling independent of call-control messages.

Example

Figure 11.16 is an example of the use of the protocol to set up a B channel circuit-switched telephone call. We will follow this example through to give the reader an idea of the use of the ISUP protocol.

Call Establishment

The process within the ISDN is triggered by a Q.931 SETUP message on the D channel between an ISDN user and an exchange, which becomes the originating exchange for this call. The SETUP message contains the information about the characteristics of the requested call and the associated network facilities required. If the exchange determines that the called party is on another exchange, then the first hop on the route to that exchange is determined, and an initial address message is sent to this intermediate exchange. This message contains the ISDN number of the called party, the type of connection required (e.g., 64-kbps transparent), the identity of the selected physical circuit to the succeeding exchange, and its characteristics. The initial address message is then sent to the exchange on which the selected outgoing link terminates. At each transit, or intermediate, exchange, the initial address message is received and analyzed. Based on the destination address and other routing information, the transit exchange makes a routing decision, selects the appropriate outgoing link, and transmits the initial address message to the next exchange. A connection is set up between the incoming and outgoing paths. This process continues until the initial address message reaches the terminating, or destination, exchange. If the terminating exchange requires additional information, it sends a backward setup message. For example, the calling party address may be required at the destination exchange but not be included in the initial address message. The terminating exchange will determine the identity of the party to be connected. If the

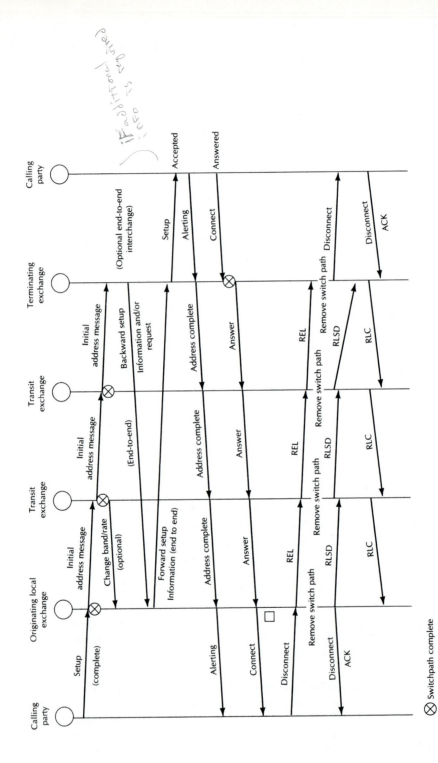

Figure 11.16 Successful Ordinary Call (En Bloc Operation).

⊗ Switchpath complete

☐ Charging begins (optionally charging may begin prior to receipt of answer)

connection is allowed, the exchange notifies the called party of the incoming call with a Q.931 SETUP message on a D channel, containing any information received in the initial address message that is relevant to the called party.

When the terminal device begins alerting the user, it returns a Q.931 ALERT message. When this is received by the local exchange, it sends an address complete message back through the ISDN to the originating exchange. This message serves several purposes:

- It is an acknowledgment to the originating exchange that a connection has been established.
- It indicates that the called party was found to be idle and is being alerted.
- It may carry charging information.
- It may contain a request to the originating exchange to forward additional call-related information.

When the address complete message is received by the originating exchange, that exchange sends a Q.931 ALERT message to the calling party.

When the called party answers, a Q.931 CONN message is sent to the terminating exchange, which sends an answer message back through the ISDN to the originating exchange, which issues a Q.931 CONN to the calling party. At both ends, the user–network B channel is connected to the internal ISDN circuit. Charging, if applicable, begins.

Call Release

The release procedures are based on a three-message (release, released, release complete) approach in which the release message is transmitted through the network as quickly as possible. In this example we show a release initiated by the calling party. The same procedures are used whether the release is initiated by the called or calling party.

The process is triggered by a Q.931 DISC message on the D channel between the calling party and the local exchange. On receipt of this message, the exchange immediately starts the release of the switched path that supports the B channel circuit and, at the same time, sends a release message to the succeeding exchange. This message is passed through the network to all intermediate exchanges and the terminating exchange. The release message is intended to inform the exchanges involved in the call as quickly as possible that the call-related circuit connections are to be released.

Meanwhile, at the originating exchange, when the path has been fully disconnected, three actions are taken:

- Send a Q.931 REL message to the calling subscriber to indicate that the B channel circuit has been released.
- Send a released message to the succeeding exchange to indicate that the circuit has been released.
- Start a timer T_1 to ensure that a release complete message is received within a specified time.

At each intermediate exchange, the receipt of a release message causes the following actions:

- Start a timer T_{12} to ensure that a released message is received from the preceding exchange.
- Send a release message to the succeeding exchange.
- Disconnect the switched path.
- When the path has been fully disconnected, send a released message to the succeeding exchange.
- Start a timer T_1 to ensure receipt of a release complete message.
- When a released message is received from the preceding exchange, return a release complete message to the preceding exchange.

At the terminating exchange, the receipt of a release message causes the following actions:

- Issue a Q.931 DISC message to the called subscriber.
- Start a timer T_{12} to ensure receipt of a released message.
- Disconnect the switched path.
- When a released message is received from the preceding exchange, return a release complete message to the preceding exchange.

The timers are used in the following way: If a release complete message is not received within T_1, the exchange will repeat the released message. If repeated transmissions of released messages are not acknowledged, the exchange sends a reset circuit message and alerts maintenance personnel. If a released message is not received within T_{12}, the exchange sends a reset circuit message and alerts maintenance personnel.

The use of the three messages satisfies the requirements for both speed and reliability. The release message is sent through the network as quickly as possible so that all exchanges can begin to release the resources dedicated to the circuit. The released and release complete messages ensure that the circuit is in fact released throughout the network.

End-to-End Signaling

End-to-end signaling is defined as the capability to transfer signaling information directly between the endpoints of a circuit-switched connection or between signaling points that are not interconnected by a circuit-switched connection. End-to-end signaling is used typically between the ISUPs located in call originating and terminating exchanges. It can be used to request or respond to requests for additional call-related information or to transfer user-to-user information transparently through the network.

If the end-to-end signaling relates to an existing connection, it may be achieved by the **pass-along method**. With this method, signaling information is sent along the signaling path of a previously established physical connection. The message is passed along the route of transit exchanges that constitute the circuit path. No information processing occurs at a transit exchange, which simply forwards the information to the next exchange. With this method, the ISUP makes direct use of the message-transfer part of SS7.

The pass-along method makes use of an end-to-end connection, which is set up whenever a circuit is established between two subscribers. The end-to-end connection consists of a number of connection sections, which run in parallel with and use the same identification code as the circuit sections that comprise the user's circuit. Thus, when a call is placed, two connections are established across ISDN. One is a circuit that supports the user's B channel traffic, and the other is an SS7 end-to-end connection. These two connections follow the same route through the network but are separate dedicated connections.

An alternative method for end-to-end signaling is the **signaling connection control part (SCCP) method**. This method, which makes use of the SCCP protocol of SS7, can be used whether or not there is a circuit established between the message originating and terminating exchanges. In this case, the route taken by end-to-end signaling messages is determined by SCCP and may not relate to any user circuit.

Services

The basic service provided by the ISDN user part is the setup and release of a simple circuit-switched call. In addition, the following supplementary services are supported:

- Calling line identification
- Call forwarding
- Closed user groups
- Direct dialing-in
- User-to-user signaling

Calling line identification consists of two related supplementary services: presentation and restriction. Calling line identification presentation is a service that enables a subscriber to be informed on incoming calls of the address of the calling party, unless the calling party restricts access to this information. The information may be contained in the initial address message. If not, the terminating exchange requests the information either by setting an appropriate indication in the address complete message or by generating an information request message. In either case, the originating exchange returns the requested information in an information message.

The **call forwarding** service redirects incoming calls addressed to a particular number to an alternate number. The redirection occurs only when the facility is activated by the subscriber at the called number. Three types of call forwarding have been defined:

- **Call forwarding busy:** Forward calls that encounter busy.
- **Call forwarding no reply:** Forward calls that meet no reply for a specified period of time.
- **Call forwarding unconditional:** Forward all calls.

The **closed user group** service enables a subscriber to belong to one or more closed user groups. In its basic form, a closed user group permits the subscribers belonging to the group to communicate with each other but precludes communication with all other subscribers. Thus, the members of the group are protected from unauthorized access (into or out of the group). A subscriber may belong to zero, one, or more closed user groups. In addition to the basic service, there are extensions that may be defined:

- **Closed user group with outgoing access:** This enables the subscriber in a closed user group to make outgoing calls to the open part of the network (i.e., subscribers not belonging to any closed user group) and to subscribers belonging to other closed user groups with the incoming access capability.
- **Closed user group with incoming access:** This enables the subscriber in a closed user group to receive incoming calls from the open part of the network and from subscribers belonging to other closed user groups with the outgoing access capability.
- **Incoming calls barred within a closed user group:** This enables the subscriber in a closed user group to originate calls to subscribers in the same group but precludes the reception of incoming calls from subscribers in the same group.
- **Outgoing calls barred within a closed user group:** This enables the subscriber in a closed user group to receive calls from subscribers in the same group but prevents the subscriber from originating calls to subscribers in the same group.

When this facility is in use, the originating and terminating exchanges must verify that a call is allowable before establishing that call, either by accessing information stored locally in the exchange or by access to some sort of centralized database. In the latter case, the closed user group selection and validation request and response messages are used to communicate with the database.

Direct dialing-in enables a user to call another user on a digital PBX or other private system without attendant intervention.

User-to-user signaling provides a means of communication between two end users through the signaling network for the purpose of exchanging information of end-to-end significance. Three services are provided:

- **Service 1:** Allows the transfer of user-to-user information (UUI) during the setup and clearing phases of a call, with UUI embedded within ISUP call-control messages.
- **Service 2:** Allows the transfer of user-to-user information (UUI) during the setup phase of a call, transferred independently of call-control messages. The ISUP user-to-user information message is used.
- **Service 3:** Allows the transfer of user-to-user information (UUI) during the active phase of a call. The ISUP user-to-user information message is used.

11.7 SUMMARY

Signaling System Number 7 is a set of specifications of services and protocols for use in the internal control and network intelligence of a digital network. It is based on the use of common-channel signaling and is designed specifically for ISDN.

The **signaling data link level** is the lowest level of SS7 and corresponds to OSI layer 1. It specifies a full-duplex physical link dedicated to SS7 traffic. The principal option is a 64-kbps digital link.

The **signaling link level** corresponds to OSI layer 2. This protocol uses the same principles as LAPD and LAPB. However, the formats and some of the procedures are different.

The **signaling network level** embodies some of the functions of OSI layer 3. It includes functions relating to message handling, such as discrimination, routing, and distribution, and functions relating to network management, such as traffic management, route management, and link management.

The **signaling connection control part (SCCP)** completes the set of functions normally associated with OSI layer 3. SCCP provides enhanced addressing capability over the signaling network level and supports reliable, connection-oriented data transfer.

The **ISDN user part (ISUP)** defines the functions, procedures, and interexchange signaling information flows required to provide user-channel services and associated user facilities for voice and nonvoice calls over ISDN.

11.8 RECOMMENDED READING

The April 1992 issue of the *Proceedings of the IEEE* contains a special section of six papers on SS7, including an excellent tutorial paper. Another good tutorial paper is [JABB91]. The July 1990 issue of *IEEE Communications Magazine* is devoted to SS7.

[BLAC97] and [RUSS95] are more detailed treatments of the topics covered in this chapter. [BHAT97] also provides a detailed technical treatment, with emphasis on practical implementation issues.

A detailed performance study of the error-control methods of the signaling link level is provided in [FUJI90]. [RAMA93] analyzes the link-error-monitoring protocols. [RUMS95] and [MANF93] provide analyses of SS7 congestion-control techniques.

BHAT97   Bhatnagar, P. *Engineering Networks for Synchronization, CCS 7 and ISDN.* New York: IEEE Press, 1997.

BLAC97   Black, U. *ISDN and SS7: Architectures for Digital Signaling Networks.* Upper Saddle River, NJ: Prentice Hall, 1997.

FUJI90   Fujioka, M.; Ikeda, Y.; and Norigoe, M. "Error Control Criteria in the Message Transfer Part of CCITT Signaling System No. 7." *IEEE Transactions on Communications,* September 1990.

JABB91   Jabbari, B. "Common Channel Signaling System Number 7 for ISDN and Intelligent Networks." *Proceedings of the IEEE,* February 1991.

MANF93   Manfield, D., Millsteed, G., and Zukerman, M. "Congestion Controls in SS7 Signaling Networks." *IEEE Communications Magazine,* June 1993.

RAMA93   Ramaswami, V., and Wang, J. "Analysis of the Link Error Monitoring Protocols in the Common Channel Signaling Network." *IEEE Transactions on Networking,* February 1993.

RUMS95   Rumsewicz, M., and Smith, D. "A Comparison of SS7 Congestion Control Options During Mass Call-In Situations." *IEEE/ACM Transactions on Networking,* February 1995.

RUSS95   Russell, R. *Signaling System #7.* New York: McGraw-Hill, 1995.

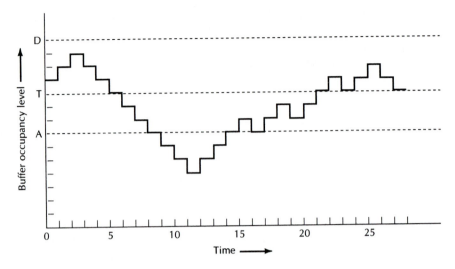

Figure 11.17 Example History of Buffer Occupancy Level.

11.9 PROBLEMS

11.1 Would it be possible to provide a circuit-switched rather than a packet-switched implementation of SS7? What would be the relative merits of such an approach?

11.2 Is something like SS7 needed to provide control signaling in a packet-switched network? If so, why not use SS7?

11.3 A proposed refinement to the basic method of error control at the signaling link level is referred to as the basic method with double transmission (BDT). In this method, each unit is transmitted twice consecutively. A retransmission is requested by the receiver only when both copies of a unit are hit by errors, causing two identical copies to be sent again. Compare this method with the basic method and with the preventive cyclic retransmission method in terms of procedural complexity and performance.

11.4 Ignoring the effects of bit stuffing, calculate the message information capacity of an SS7 signaling link, assuming all messages consist of 2 octets and only MSUs are sent.

11.5 Figure 11.17 shows an example of the buffer occupancy history of a link. For the congestion-control strategy at the network signaling level, indicate the periods when the link is considered congested and uncongested.

11.6 Why is there not an N-DATA.response or an N-DATA.confirm primitive in Table 11.5?

11.7 In a credit flow-control scheme, what provision can be made for credit allocations that are lost in transit?

APPENDIX 11A SERVICE PRIMITIVES AND PARAMETERS

In a communications architecture, such as the OSI model or the SS7 protocol architecture, each layer is defined in two parts: the protocol between peer (at the same layer) entities in different systems, and the services provided by one layer to the next higher layer in the same system.

We have seen a number of examples of protocols, which are defined in terms of the formats of the protocol data units that are exchanged and the rules governing the use of those protocol data units. The services between adjacent layers are expressed in terms of primitives and parameters. A primitive specifies the function to be performed, and the parameters are used to pass data and control information. The actual form of a primitive is implementation dependent. An example is a procedure call.

Four types of primitives are used in standards to define the interaction between adjacent layers in the architecture. These are defined in Table 11.12. The layout of Figure 11.18a suggests the time ordering of these events. For example, consider the transfer of a connection request from SCCP user A to a peer entity B in another system. The following steps occur:

1. A invokes the services of SCCP with an N-CONNECT.request primitive. Associated with the primitive are the parameters needed, such as the called address.

2. The SCCP entity in A's system prepares an SCCP message to be sent to its peer SCCP entity in B.

3. The destination SCCP entity delivers the data to B via an N-CONNECT.indication, which includes the calling address and other parameters.

4. B issues an N-CONNECT.response to its SCCP entity.

5. B's SCCP entity conveys the acknowledgment to A's SCCP entity in a message.

6. The acknowledgment is delivered to A via an N-CONNECT.confirm.

This sequence of events is referred to as a **confirmed service**, as the initiator receives confirmation that the requested service has had the desired effect at the other end. If only request and indication primitives are involved (corresponding to steps 1 through 3), then the service dialogue is a **nonconfirmed service**; the initiator receives no confirmation that the requested action has taken place (Figure 11.18b).

Table 11.12 Primitive Types

REQUEST	A primitive issued by a service user to invoke some service and to pass the parameters needed to specify the requested service.

INDICATION	A primitive issued by a service provider to either
	    1. indicate that a procedure has been invoked by the peer service user on the connection and to provide the associated parameters, or
	    2. notify the service user of a provider-initiated action.

RESPONSE	A primitive issued by a service user to acknowledge or complete some procedure previously invoked by an indication to that user.
CONFIRM	A primitive issued by a service provider to acknowledge or complete some procedure previously invoked by a request by the service user.

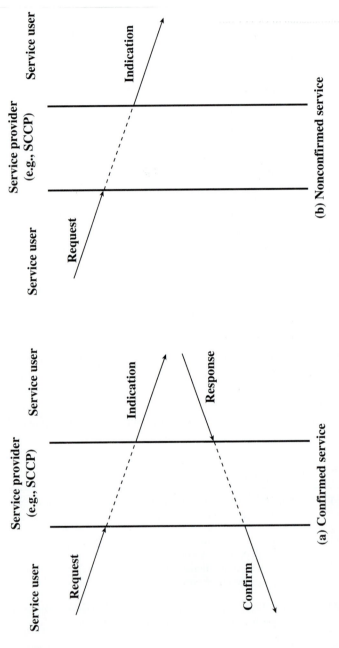

Figure 11.18 Time Sequence Diagrams for Service Primitives.

APPENDIX 11B   ITU-T RECOMMENDATIONS ON SS7

Number	Title	Date
Q.700	Introduction to CCITT SS7	1993
Q.701	Functional Description of the Message Transfer Part (MTP) of SS7	1993
Q.702	Signaling Data Link	1988
Q.703	Signaling Link	1996
Q.704	Signaling Network Functions and Messages	1996
Q.705	Signaling Network Structure	1993
Q.706	Message Transfer Part Signaling Performance	1993
Q.707	Testing and Maintenance	1988
Q.708	Numbering of International Signaling Point Codes	1993
Q.709	Hypothetical Signaling Reference Connection	1993
Q.710	Simplified MTP Version for Small Systems	1988
Q.711	Function Description of the Signaling Connection Control Part (SCCP)	1996
Q.712	Definition and Functions of SCCP Messages	1996
Q.713	SCCP Formats and Codes	1996
Q.714	SCCP Procedures	1996
Q.715	SCCP User Guide	1996
Q.716	SCCP Performances	1993
Q.721	Functional Description of the SS7 Telephone User Part (TUP)	1988
Q.722	General Function of Telephone Messages and Signals	1988
Q.723	Formats and Codes	1988
Q.724	Signaling Procedures	1988
Q.725	Signaling Performance in the Telephone Application	1993
Q.730	ISDN Supplementary Services	1993
Q.731.1	Direct Dialing-in	1996
Q.731.3	Calling Line Identification Presentation	1993
Q.731.8	Sub-addressing	1992
Q.732.2	Call Offering Supplementary Services	1996
Q.732.7	Explicit Call Transfer	1996
Q.733.1	Call Waiting	1992
Q.733.2	Call Hold	1993
Q.734.1	Conference Calling	1993
Q.734.2	Three-party Service	1996
Q.735.1	Closed User Group	1993
Q.735.6	Global Virtual Network Service	1996
Q.736.1	International Telecommunication Charge Card	1995
Q.736.3	Reverse Charging	1995
Q.737.1	User-to-user Signaling	1993
Q.750	Overview of SS7 Management	1993
Q.751.1	Network Element Management Information Model for MTP	1995

Number	Title	Date
Q.752	Monitoring and Measurements for SS7 Networks	1997
Q.753	SS7 Management Functions MRVT, SRVT, and CVT and Definition of the OMASE-User	1997
Q.754	Operations, Maintenance and Administration Part (OMAP)	1997
Q.755	SS7 Protocol Tests	1993
Q.756	Guide Book to OMAP	1997
Q.761	Functional Description of the ISDN User Part of SS7	1993
Q.762	General Function of Messages and Signals	1993
Q.763	Formats and Codes	1993
Q.764	Signaling Procedures	1993
Q.766	Performance Objectives in the ISDN Application	1993
Q.767	Application of ISUP for International ISDN Interconnections	1991
Q.768	Signaling Interface Between an International Switching Center and an ISDN Satellite Subnetwork	1995
Q.771	Functional Description of Transaction Capabilities	1993
Q.772	Transaction Capabilities Information Element Definitions	1993
Q.773	Transaction Capabilities Formats and Encoding	1993
Q.774	Transaction Capabilities Procedures	1993
Q.775	Guidelines for Using Transaction Capabilities	1997
Q.780	SS7 Test Specification General Description	1995
Q.781	MTP Level 2 Test Specification	1996
Q.782	MTP Level 3 Test Specification	1996
Q.783	TUP Test Specification	1988
Q.784	ISUP Basic Call Test Specification	1991
Q.785	ISUP Protocol Test Specification for Supplementary Services	1991
Q.786	SCCP Test Specification	1992
Q.787	Transaction Capabilities Test Specification	1993
Q.788	User-network-interface to User-network-interface Compatibility Test Specifications	1997

PART THREE

Frame Relay

The most important technical innovation to come out of the standardization work on narrowband ISDN is frame relay. Frame relay is a streamlined technique for packet switching that operates at the data link layer and that has significantly less overhead than traditional packet switching with an X.25 interface.

Although conceived as a service and switching mechanism for narrowband ISDN, frame relay has gained broad acceptance and is used in a number of networking contexts outside of ISDN. Because of its importance, Part Three of this book is devoted to frame relay.

Chapter 12 covers the key elements of frame relay: the protocol for exchange of user data and the call control protocol for establishing, maintaining, and terminating frame relay connections. The chapter also describes LAPF, which is a data link protocol that may be used on top of frame relay to provide end-to-end error and flow control.

One of the most difficult technical issues associated with frame relay is congestion control. Chapter 13 examines the nature and importance of the problem and presents a variety of approaches to congestion control.

CHAPTER 12

FRAME RELAY PROTOCOLS AND SERVICE

The 1988 I.122 recommendation, entitled *Framework for Providing Additional Packet Mode Bearer Services,* introduced a new form of packet transmission that has become one of the most significant contributions of the narrowband ISDN work.[1] This new technique is now generally referred to as frame-mode bearer service, or frame relay. The former term emphasizes the service being offered to the user, while the latter emphasizes the protocol that implements the service.

Since 1988, significant progress has been made on frame relay. Both ITU-T and ANSI have been active in this area, with ANSI often publishing standards that have later been incorporated into ITU-T recommendations. Table 12.1 is a list of relevant documents from the two organizations.

It is anticipated that the ITU-T recommendations will remain aligned with the current ANSI standards. This chapter draws on all of these documents. We begin with an overview of frame relay that discusses the motivation for the use of this technology. Next, we look at the protocol architecture defined to support the frame-mode bearer service. Then we define the call control signaling aspects. Finally, we discuss the data link protocol that supports user data transfer.

---

[1]The title of this recommendation changed with the release of the 1993 version to *Framework for Frame Mode Bearer Services.* The new edition of the recommendation is just a list of other recommendations related to frame-mode bearer service.

Table 12.1 Standards for Frame Relay

(a) ITU-T Recommendations on Frame Relay

Number	Title	Date
I.122	Framework for Frame Mode Bearer Services	1993
I.233	Frame Mode Bearer Services	1992
I.370	Congestion Management for the ISDN Frame Relaying Bearer Service	1991
I.372	Frame Relay Bearer Service Network-to-Network Interface Requirements	1993
I.555	Frame Mode Bearer Service Interworking	1993
Q.922	ISDN Data Link Layer Specification for Frame Mode Bearer Services	1992
Q.933	Signaling Specifications for Frame Mode Call Control	1995

(b) ANSI Standards on Frame Relay

Number	Title	Date
T1.606	Architectural Framework and Service Description for Frame-Relaying Bearer Service	1993
T1.617	Signaling Specification for Frame Relay Bearer Service for DSS1	1994
T1.618	Core Aspects of Frame Protocol for Use with Frame Relay Bearer Service	1991

12.1 BACKGROUND

The traditional approach to packet switching, as was discussed in Chapter 3, is X.25. There are several key features of the X.25 approach:

- Call control packets, used for setting up and clearing virtual circuits, are carried on the same channel and same virtual circuit as data packets. In effect, inband signaling is used.
- Multiplexing of virtual circuits takes place at layer 3.
- Both layer 2 and layer 3 include flow-control and error-control mechanisms.

This approach results in considerable overhead. Figure 12.1a indicates the flow of data across a packet-switching network through just three nodes between source and destination.[2] Data are taken from the source device and stored to make retransmission possible. The data are organized as a sequence of blocks. For each block, an X.25 header is added to form a packet. Then routing calculations are made. Finally, the packet is enclosed in a LAPB frame by adding a LAPB header and trailer. The frame is then transmitted over a data link to the next packet-switching

---

[2]To simplify the picture, the processing between each end system and the packet-switching node to which it is attached is ignored.

ADD IP header

Inspect IP header

Remove IP header

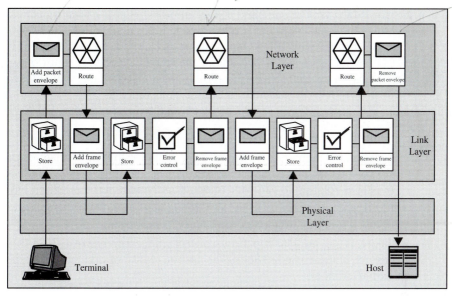

(a) Packet switching

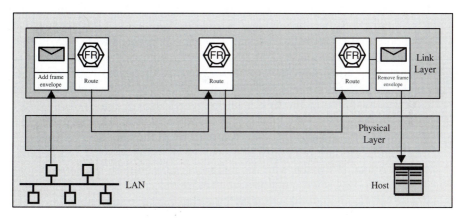

(b) Frame relay

Figure 12.1 Packet Switching and Frame Relay Operation.

node. The node performs flow- and error-control functions at the data link layer, which involves sending an acknowledgment back across the link and may require retransmission. Then the node removes the data link layer fields to examine the packet header for routing purposes. This entire process is repeated at each hop across the network.

All of this overhead may be justified when there is a significant probability of error on any of the links in the network. This approach may not be the most appropriate for ISDN. On the one hand, ISDN employs reliable digital transmission technology over high-quality, reliable transmission links, many of which are optical fiber. On the other hand, with ISDN, high data rates can be achieved, especially with the use of H channels. In this environment, the overhead of X.25 is not only unnecessary, but degrades the effective utilization of the high data rates available with ISDN.

Frame relaying is designed to eliminate as much as possible of the overhead of X.25. The key differences of frame relaying from a conventional X.25 packet-switching service are as follows:

Frame relay vs X.25

- Call control signaling is carried on a separate logical connection from user data. Thus, intermediate nodes need not maintain state tables or process messages relating to call control on an individual per-connection basis.
- Multiplexing and switching of logical connections takes place at layer 2 instead of layer 3, eliminating one entire layer of processing.
- There is no hop-by-hop flow control and error control. End-to-end flow control and error control are the responsibility of a higher layer, if they are employed at all.

Figure 12.1b indicates the operation of frame relay, in which a single user data frame is sent from source to destination through three frame relay nodes. The frame contains the addressing information necessary to route the data through the frame relay network. No flow or error control is performed between frame relay nodes.

Let us consider the advantages and disadvantages of this approach. The principal potential disadvantage of frame relaying, compared with X.25, is that we have lost the ability to do link-by-link flow and error control. (Although frame relay does not provide end-to-end flow and error control, this is easily provided at a higher layer.) In X.25, multiple virtual circuits are carried on a single physical link, and LAPB is available at the link level for providing reliable transmission from the source to the packet-switching network and from the packet-switching network to the destination. In addition, at each hop through the network, the link-control protocol can be used for reliability. With the use of frame relaying, this hop-by-hop link control is lost. However, with the increasing reliability of transmission and switching facilities, this is not a major disadvantage.

The advantage of frame relaying is that we have streamlined the communications process. The protocol functionality required at the user–network interface is reduced, as is the internal network processing. As a result, lower delay and higher throughput can be expected. One study indicates a reduction in frame processing time of an order of magnitude [BUSH89], and the ITU-T recommendation (I.233) indicates that frame relay is to be used at access speeds up to 2 Mbps. Thus, we can expect to see frame relaying supplant X.25 as ISDN matures.

ANSI standard T1.606 lists four examples of applications that would benefit from the frame relay service used over a high-speed H channel:

- **Block-interactive data applications:** An example of a block-interactive application would be high-resolution graphics (e.g., high-resolution videotex, CAD/CAM). The pertinent characteristics of this type of application are low delays and high throughput.

- **File transfer:** The file-transfer application is intended to cater to large file-transfer requirements. Transit delay is not as critical for this application as it is, for example, in the first application. High throughput might be necessary to produce reasonable transfer times for large files.
- **Multiplexed low bit rate:** The multiplexed low-bit-rate application exploits the multiplexing capability of the frame-relaying service to provide an economical access arrangement for a large group of low-bit-rate applications. An example of one such low-bit-rate application is given in the next bullet item. The low-bit-rate sources may be multiplexed onto a channel by an NT function.
- **Character-interactive traffic:** An example of a character-interactive traffic application is text editing. The main characteristics of this type of application are short frames, low delays, and low throughput.

Frame relay can be viewed as a streamlined version of X.25 that accomplishes the key functions of X.25 using only two layers. Another way of viewing frame relay is that it is an enhanced version of I.465/V.120. That latter standard allows for multiple logical connections to be multiplexed on a single circuit between two subscribers. Frame relay supports not only multiplexing but switching: Multiple logical connections from one subscriber over one channel can be set up to multiple subscribers across the network.

12.2 FRAME-MODE PROTOCOL ARCHITECTURE

Before describing the protocol architecture to support the frame-mode bearer service, we need to distinguish between two forms of that service. We then look at the protocol architecture for each form.

Frame-Mode Bearer Services

ITU-T I.233 makes a distinction between two different frame-mode bearer services: frame relaying and frame switching.

The frame-relaying bearer service is a basic network service for the transfer of data link frames over a D, B, or H channel. The service has the following characteristics:

- The user–network interface allows for the establishment of multiple virtual calls and/or permanent virtual circuits to multiple destinations.
- In the case of virtual calls, the control signaling is performed in a logically separate manner via a D channel signaling protocol.
- User data are transmitted in the form of frames, using a data link protocol referred to as LAPF (Link Access Procedure for Frame-Mode Bearer Services).
- The network preserves the order of frames transmitted at one S or T reference point when they are delivered at the other end.
- The network detects transmission, format, and operational errors and discards the affected frames.

The frame-switching bearer service is an enhanced network service for the transfer of data link frames over a D, B, or H channel. It exhibits all of the characteristics of the frame-relaying bearer service just listed, plus it has the following characteristics:

- Frames are transmitted with acknowledgments returned to the transmitting user.
- Flow control is supported across the user–network interface in both directions.
- The network detects and recovers from transmission, format, and operational errors.
- The network detects and recovers from lost or duplicated frames.

In essence, the frame-relaying service is an unreliable multiplexed service. It is an unacknowledged service in which it is possible that frames may be lost by the network and in which there is no mechanism for flow control across the user–network interface. However, the frame-relaying service does provide that frames are delivered in the order in which they are transmitted. The frame-switching service is a reliable multiplexed service. It provides flow control and error control and thus is more analogous to X.25 in functionality.

Frame-relaying services are now widely available, whereas at the time of this writing there are no commercially available frame-switching services. Given the inherent reliability of contemporary networks, plus the existence of higher layers of software to provide end-to-end reliability, frame switching is unlikely to enjoy much use. The bulk of this chapter is devoted to frame relay; features and functions specific to frame switching are discussed when they occur in this chapter.

Protocol Architecture at the User–Network Interface

Figure 12.2 depicts the protocol architecture to support the frame-mode bearer service. As in other areas of ISDN, we need to consider two separate planes of operation: a control (C) plane, which is involved in the establishment and termination of logical connections, and a user (U) plane, which is responsible for the transfer of user data between subscribers. Thus, C-plane protocols are between a subscriber and the network, while U-plane protocols provide end-to-end functionality.

Control Plane

The control plane for frame-mode bearer services is similar to that for the control of packet-mode and circuit-switching services. Control signaling is done over the D channel, to control the establishment and termination of frame-mode virtual calls on the D, B, and H channels.

At the data link layer, LAPD (Q.921) is used to provide a reliable data link control service, with error control and flow control, between user (TE) and network (NT) over the D channel. This data link service is used for the exchange of Q.931/Q.933 control signaling messages. As was mentioned earlier (Table 8.1), an SAPI value of 0 in the address field of the LAPD frame indicates that the LAPD frame is carrying a Q.931/Q.933 message.

Figure 12.3 shows explicitly which protocols are implemented in the TE and NT equipment for control signaling over the D channel for frame-mode bearer services.

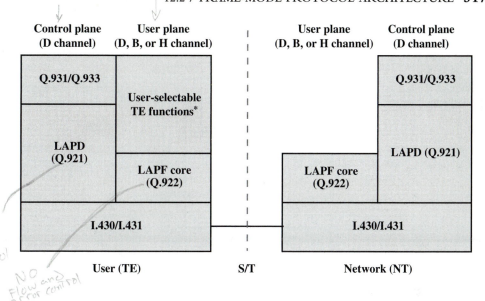

Between The user and The network

Provide end To end Functionality

Flow and error control

No Flow and error control

* Additional functions to support flow and error control may be provided. LAPF control is one protocol that may be used.

Figure 12.2   User–Network Interface Protocol Architecture.

User Plane

For the actual transfer of information between end users, the user-plane protocol is LAPF (Link Access Procedure for Frame-Mode Bearer Services), which is defined in Q.922. Q.922 is an enhanced version of LAPD (Q.921). Only the core functions of LAPF are used for frame relay:

- Frame delimiting, alignment, and transparency
- Frame multiplexing/demultiplexing using the address field
- Inspection of the frame to ensure that it consists of an integer number of octets prior to zero bit insertion or following zero bit extraction
- Inspection of the frame to ensure that it is neither too long nor too short
- Detection of transmission errors
- Congestion control functions

The last function listed is new to LAPF and is discussed in Section 12.4. The remaining functions listed are also functions of LAPD.

The core functions of LAPF in the user plane constitute a sublayer of the data link layer. This provides the bare service of transferring data link frames from one subscriber to another, with no flow control or error control. Above this, the user may choose to select additional data link or network-layer end-to-end functions. These are not part of the ISDN frame relay service. Based on the core functions, ISDN offers frame relaying as a connection-oriented link layer service with the following properties:

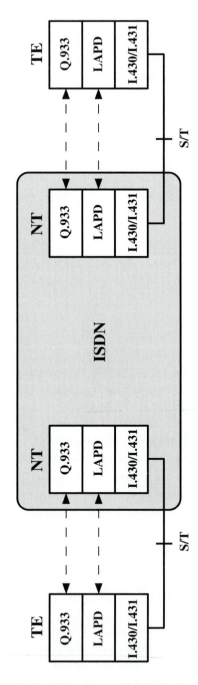

Figure 12.3 Connection Establishment and Release Phase (frame relay and frame switching).

- Preservation of the order of frame transfer from one edge of the network to the other
- A small probability of frame loss

Figure 12.4 shows which protocols are implemented in the TE and NT equipment for user data transfer for frame-mode bearer services. This protocol architecture is valid for D, B, and H channels. For the frame relay service, the NT devices only implement up through the core functions of LAPF. The end systems (TE devices) implement higher-layer protocols above this. One possibility, illustrated in Figure 12.4a, is to include the control functions of LAPF. Alternative protocols are also possible.

For the frame-switching service, both the network (NT) and user (TE) sides implement the full LAPF protocol (Figure 12.4b). The upper sublayer of LAPF, referred to as the control portion of LAPF, implements flow- and error-control procedures, similar to those found in LAPB and LAPD.

Comparison with X.25

As can be seen, this architecture minimizes the amount of work accomplished by the network. User data are transmitted in frames with virtually no processing by

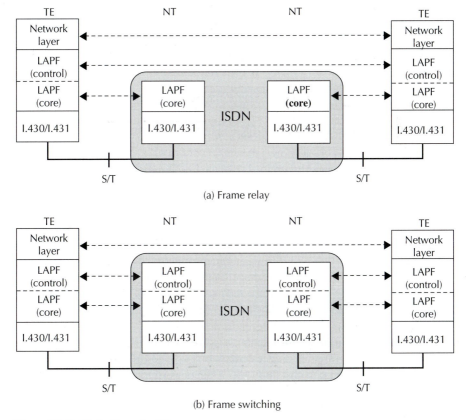

Figure 12.4 Data Transfer Phase.

the intermediate network nodes, other than to check for errors and to route based on connection number. A frame in error is simply discarded, leaving error recovery to higher layers.

Figure 12.5 compares the protocol architecture of frame-mode bearer service with that of X.25. The packet-handling functions of X.25 operate at layer 3 of the OSI model. At layer 2, either LAPB or LAPD is used, depending on whether the protocol is operating on a B channel or D channel. Table 12.2 provides a functional comparison of X.25 and frame relay, and Figure 12.6 illustrates the differences. As can be seen, the processing burden on the network for X.25 is considerably higher than for frame relay.

The relationship between LAPB and the packet level in X.25 is illustrated in Figure 12.7a. Between the subscriber device (DTE) and the packet-switching node to which it is attached (DCE), a LAPB protocol is used to assure reliable transfer of frames. Each frame contains a packet that includes a virtual circuit number in its header. Thus, a number of different virtual circuits can be supported through the LAPB "pipe." As Figure 12.7a also shows, these virtual circuits can have different routes through the network going to different destinations. Thus, a subscriber can maintain a number of virtual circuits to different other subscribers on the network. As with X.25, frame relay involves the use of logical connections, in this case called virtual connections rather than virtual circuits. Figure 12.7b emphasizes that the frames transmitted over these virtual connections are not protected by a data link control pipe with flow and error control. Another difference between X.25 and frame relay is that the latter devotes a separate virtual connection to call control. The setting up and tearing down of virtual connections is done over this permanent control-oriented virtual connection.

12.3 FRAME-MODE CALL CONTROL

This section examines the various approaches for setting up frame relay connections and then describes the protocol used for connection control.

Call Control Alternatives

The call control protocol for frame relay must deal with a number of alternatives. First, let us consider two cases for the provision of frame-handling services. For frame relay operation, a user is not connected directly to another ISDN user, but rather to a frame handler in the network. Just as for X.25, an ISDN user is connected to a packet handler. There are two cases (Figure 12.8):

- **Case A:** The local exchange does not provide the frame-handling capability. In this case, switched access must be provided from the TE to the frame handler elsewhere in the network. This can either be a demand connection or a semipermanent connection. In either case, the frame relay service is provided over a B or H channel.

(text continues on page 326)

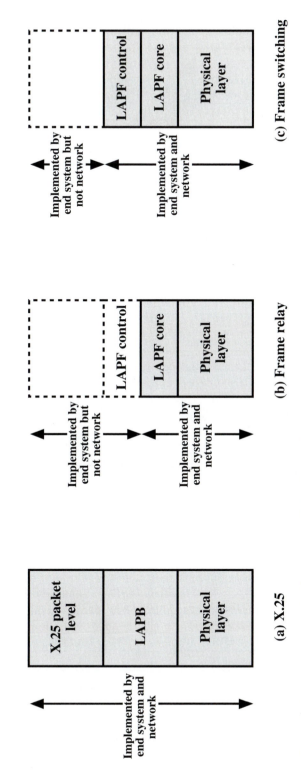

Figure 12.5 Comparison of X.25 and Frame Relay Protocol Stacks.

Table 12.2   Comparison of X.25 Packet Switching and Frame Relay

Function	X.25 in ISDN (X.31)	Frame Relay
Flag generation/recognition	X	X
Transparency	X	X
FCS generation/recognition	X	X
Recognize invalid frames	X	X
Discard incorrect frames	X	X
Address translation	X	X
Fill interframe time	X	X
Multiplexing of logical channels	X	X
Manage V(S) state variable	X	
Manage V(R) state variable	X	
Buffer packets awaiting acknowledgment	X	
Manage retransmission timer T1	X	
Acknowledge received I-frames	X	
Check received N(S) against V(R)	X	
Generation of REJ (rejection message)	X	
Respond to P/F (poll/final) bit	X	
Keep track of number of retransmissions	X	
Act upon reception of REJ	X	
Respond to RNR (receiver not ready)	X	
Respond to RR (receiver ready)	X	
Management of D bit	X	
Management of M bit	X	
Management of Q bit	X	
Management of P(S)	X	
Management of P(R)	X	
Detection of out-of-sequence packets	X	
Management of network layer RR	X	
Management of network layer RNR	X	

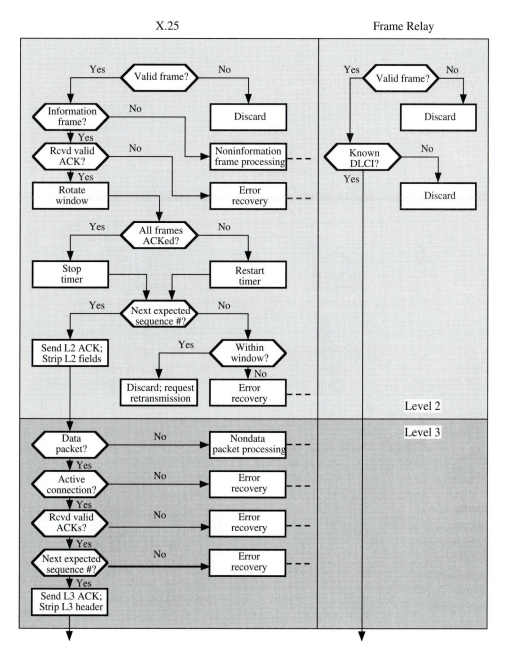

Figure 12.6 Simplified Model of X.25 and Frame Relay Processing.

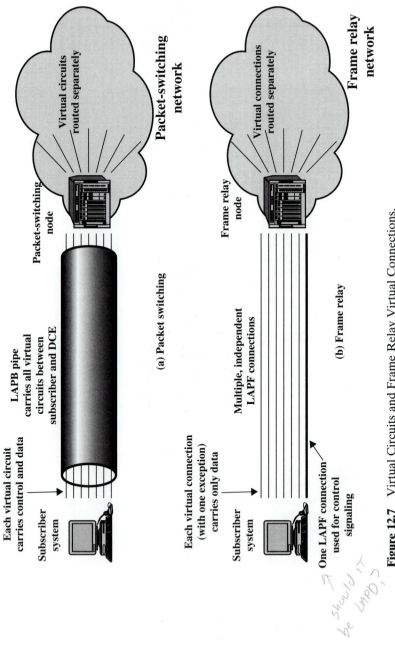

Figure 12.7 Virtual Circuits and Frame Relay Virtual Connections.

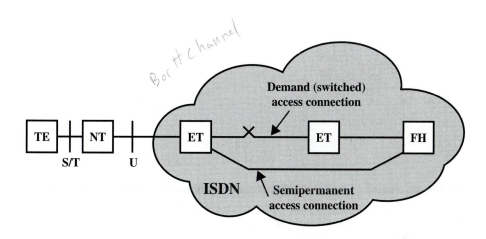

B or H channel

(a) Case A: switched access

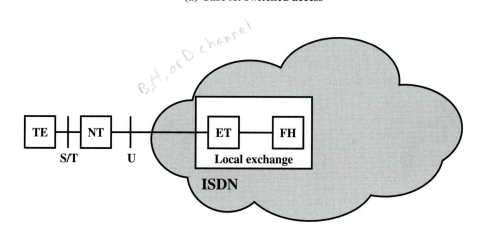

B, H, or D channel

(b) Case B: integrated access

TE = terminal equipment
NT = network equipment
ET = exchange termination
FH = frame handler

Figure 12.8 Frame Relay Access Modes.

- **Case B:** The local exchange does provide the frame-handling capability. In this case, the frame relay service may be provided on a B or H channel or on the D channel. For B or H channel service, a demand connection must be used to dedicate a B or H channel to frame relay unless a semipermanent assignment already exists. For D channel service, this point has not been finally specified, but it appears that both a demand service and a semipermanent service via the D channel may be options.

All of the previous considerations have to do with the connection between the subscriber and the frame handler, which we refer to as the access connection. Once this connection exists, it is possible to multiplex multiple logical connections, referred to as frame relay connections, over this access connection. Such logical connections may be either on demand or semipermanent.

Table 12.3 summarizes these call control alternatives. First let consider the establishment of an access connection. If the connection is semipermanent, then no call control protocol is required. If the connection is to be set up on demand, then there are two alternatives:

- **Case A:** The access connection is to be set up on a B or H channel to a remote frame handler. The normal ISDN call-control protocol, Q.931, is used on the D channel to set up the access connection. This is the same strategy used to support X.25 on a B channel.
- **Case B:** The access connection is to be set up to the local exchange. If the connection is to be set up on a B or H channel, then the normal ISDN call control protocol, Q.931, is used on the D channel to set up the access connection. If the D channel is to be used and the access connection is on demand rather than semipermanent (for X.25, the connection is always semipermanent), then again Q.931 is used on the D channel to set up the access connection.

Now consider the establishment of a frame relay connection. For this purpose an access connection must already exist. For a semipermanent frame relay connection, no call control protocol is required; note that this requires the existence of a semipermanent access connection. If the frame relay connection is to be set up on demand over an existing access connection, there are again two alternatives:

- **Case A:** It is possible to use Q.933 call control messages on frame relay connection DLCI = 0. As with I.465/V.120, these messages are carried in the information field of the data link frame.
- **Case B:** Alternatively, again as with I.465/V.120, it is possible to use the same call control messages embedded in LAPD frames on the D channel. For this purpose, SAPI 0 is used, as for Q.931 messages.

In either case, the call control messages are actually a subset of the messages used in Q.931, with some new parameters tailored to the frame relay application.

Table 12.3   Establishment of Connection for Frame Relay Services

		Access connection/frame relay connection		
		Demand/demand	Semipermanent/ demand	Semipermanent/ semipermanent
Case A: Switched access to frame handler	**Establishment of access connection**	I.451/Q.931 on D channel to set up connection on B or H channel *to The Frame handler*	Semipermanent	
	Establishment of frame relay connection	Inchannel frame relay messages on B or H channel, DLCI = 0 *Q.933 → LAPF*		Semipermanent
Case B: Integrated access to frame handler	**Establishment of access connection**	I.451/Q.931 on D channel to set up connection on D, B or H channel	Semipermanent	
	Establishment of frame relay connection	Frame relay messages on D channel, SAPI = 0		Semipermanent

Call Control Protocol

The call control protocol involves the exchange of messages between the user and a frame handler over a previously created access connection. The messages are transmitted in one of two ways:

- **Case A:** Switched access to frame handler. Call control messages are transmitted in frame relay frames over the same channel (B or H) as the frame relay connections, using the same frame structure, with a data link connection identifier of DLCI = 0. The DLCI is explained later. *DLCI implies LAPF*
- **Case B:** Integrated access to frame handler. Call control messages are transmitted in LAPD frames with SAPI = 0 over the D channel.

In either case, the set of messages, which is defined in Q.933, is a subset of those used in Q.931. For frame relay, however, these messages are used to set up and manage logical frame relay connections rather than actual circuits. Accordingly, some of the parameters used for frame relay call control differ from those used in Q.931.

Figure 12.9 provides an example of the types of exchanges involved for switched access to a frame handler. First, the calling user must establish a circuit-switched connection to a frame handler that is one of the nodes of the frame relay network. This is done with the usual SETUP, CONNECT, and CONNECT ACK messages, exchanged at the local user–network interface and at the interface between the network and a frame handler. The procedures and parameters for this exchange are carried out on the D channel and are defined in Q.931. In the figure, it is assumed that the access connection is created for a B channel.

Once the access connection is established, an exchange takes place directly between the end user and the frame-handling node for each frame-mode connection that is set up. Again, the SETUP, CONNECT, and CONNECT ACK messages are used. In this case, the procedures and parameters for this exchange are defined in Q.933, and the exchange is carried out on the same B channel that will be used for the frame-mode connection.

The set of messages used for frame relay call control is, in fact, identical with those used for packet-mode access connection control. These were listed, with brief definitions, in Table 9.8. Tables 12.4 through 12.6 show the information elements used with these messages for frame relay call control. Most of these information elements are defined in Table 9.7. Several of the information elements warrant further elaboration.

Data Link Connection Identifier

The data link connection identifier (DLCI) is used to identify the logical connection that is the subject of the message. The use of DLCIs allows multiple logical connections to be multiplexed over the same channel.

(text continues on page 331)

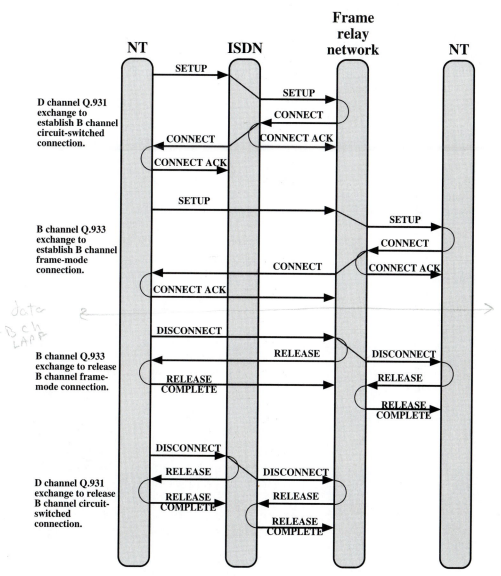

Figure 12.9 Example of Frame-Mode Control Signaling.

Table 12.4 Information Elements for Q.933 Call Establishment Messages for Frame-Mode Connection Control

	Alerting	Call Proceeding	Connect	Connect Acknowledge	Progress	Setup
Bearer capability						M
Channel identification	O	O	O			O
Cause					O	
Progress indicator	O	O	O		M	O
Network-specific facilities						O
Display	O	O	O	O	O	O
Calling party number						O
Calling party subaddress						O
Called party number						O
Called party subaddress						O
Transit network selection						O
Low-layer compatibility			O			O
High-layer compatibility						O
Data link connection identifier	O	O	O			O
User-user	O		O			O
End-to-end transit delay			O			O
Packet layer binary parameters			O			O
Link layer core parameters			O			O
Link layer protocol parameters			O			O
Connected number			O			
Connected subaddress			O			
X.213 priority			O			O
Repeat indicator						O

Table 12.5 Information Elements for Q.933 Call-Clearing Messages for Frame-Mode Connection Control

	DISCONNECT	RELEASE	RELEASE COMPLETE
Cause	M	O	O
Display	O	O	O
Connected number	O	O	O
Connected subaddress	O	O	O
User-user	O	O	O

Bearer Capability

This information element is used in the SETUP message to request a bearer service as specified in I.133, to be provided by the network (Figure 12.10). Unlike many of the message's information elements, which are passed through from source to destination, this one is used by the network in establishing the connection.

The format of this parameter conforms to the general bearer capability parameter in Q.931. In the current version of the standard, only one value is allowed in each field; all other values are reserved for future use.

Octet 3 includes an indication of whether the bearer capability is an ITU-T standard or not. If it is, then the information-transfer capability field specifies unrestricted digital information. Octet 4 indicates that the transfer mode is frame mode. The remainder of the octet is normally used in Q.931 to specify a transfer rate; this subfield is reserved for future use. Octet 6 specifies the use of either the core aspects of LAPF or the full LAPF protocol.

Table 12.6 Information Elements for Q.933 Miscellaneous Messages for Frame-Mode Connection Control

	STATUS	STATUS INQUIRY
Cause	M	
Call state	M	
Display	O	O

8	7	6	5	4	3	2	1	Octet
Bearer capability information element identifier								
0	0	0	0	0	0	0	0	1
Length of the bearer capability contents								2
1	Coding standard		Information transfer capability					3
1	Transfer mode		Reserved					4
Layer 2 identity			User information layer 2 protocol					6
1	0	0						

Notes: Octet 5 is omitted; the configuration is assumed to be point-to-point, and the method of establishment is on demand.
Octet 6 is used to select between frame-relaying and frame-switching bearer services.

Figure 12.10 LAPF Bearer Capability Information Element.

End-to-End Transit Delay

This information element is used to request and indicate the nominal maximum permissible transit delay applicable on a per-call basis. The end-to-end delay is the time it takes to send a frame containing user data from one end user to another, including the total frame relay processing time in the end user systems.

Link-Layer Core Parameters

This information element indicates requested parameters related to the core data link service (LAPF core). This information is exchanged between each end user and the network. The format of this information element is shown in Figure 12.11. Note that each parameter consists of a parameter identifier field followed by one or more octets of parameter value. The following parameters are included:

- **Maximum frame-mode information field size:** The maximum size of the information field of a frame in octets; determined independently in each direction. The default value is 262 octets for the D channel and 4096 octets for the B and H channels. The two end users and the network may negotiate a smaller maximum size.
- **Throughput:** The average number of frame-mode information field bits transferred per second. The value is expressed in the form $A \times 10B$ bps, where A is the multiplier and B is the magnitude.
- **Minimum acceptable throughput:** The lowest throughput value that the calling user is willing to accept for the call. If the network or the called user is unable to sustain this throughput, the call shall be cleared.
- **Committed burst size:** The maximum amount of data that the network agrees to transfer, under normal conditions, over a measurement interval T.
- **Excess burst size:** The maximum amount of uncommitted data that the network will attempt to transfer, under normal conditions, over a measurement interval T.

8	7	6	5	4	3	2	1	Octet
Link-layer core parameters information element identifier								1
0	1	0	0	1	0	0	0	1
Length of link-layer core parameters contents								2
Maximum frame-mode information field (FMIF) size								3
0	0	0	0	1	0	0	1	3
0	Outgoing maximum FMIF size							3a
0/1	Outgoing maximum FMIF size (cont)							3b
0	Incoming maximum FMIF size							3c*
1	Incoming maximum FMIF size (cont)							3d*
Throughput								4*
0	0	0	0	1	0	1	0	4*
0	Outgoing magnitude			Outgoing multiplier				4a*
0/1	Outgoing multiplier (cont)							4b*
0	Incoming magnitude			Incoming multiplier				4c*
0/1	Incoming multiplier (cont)							4d*
Minimum acceptable throughput								5*
0	0	0	0	1	0	1	0	5*
0	Outgoing magnitude			Outgoing multiplier				5a*
0/1	Outgoing multiplier (cont)							5b*
0	Incoming magnitude			Incoming multiplier				5c*
1	Incoming multiplier (cont)							5d*
Committed burst size								6*
0	0	0	0	1	1	0	1	6*
0	Outgoing committed burst size value							6a*
0/1	Outgoing committed burst size value (cont)							6b*
0	Incoming committed burst size value							6c*
1	Incoming committed burst size value (cont)							6d*
Excess burst size value								7*
0	0	0	0	1	1	1	0	7*
0	Outgoing excess burst size value							7a*
0/1	Outgoing excess burst size value (cont)							7b*
0	Incoming excess burst size value							7c*
1	Incoming excess burst size value (cont)							7d*

Figure 12.11   Link-Layer Core Parameters Information Element.

The measurement interval is determined according to the following table:

Throughput	Committed Burst Size (B_c)	Excess Burst Size (B_e)	Measurement Interval (T)
>0	>0	>0	$T = B_c/$Throughput
>0	>0	=0	$T = B_c/$Throughput
=0	=0	>0	$T = B_e/$Access Rate

The concepts of committed and excess burst size are explored in Chapter 13.

Link-Layer Protocol Parameters

This information element indicates requested parameters related to the data link control protocol. In the case of the frame relay bearer service, this information is exchanged between a pair of end users and is carried transparently by the network. In the case of the frame-switching bearer service, the information is exchanged between user and network.

The format of this information element is shown in Figure 12.12. The following parameters are included:

- **Transmit window value:** The maximum size of the sliding-window flow-control window; may take on a value from 1 to 127.

8	7	6	5	4	3	2	1	Octet
Link-layer core parameters information element identifier								
0	1	0	0	1	0	0	1	1
Length of link-layer core protocol parameters contents									2
Transmit window size identifier								3
0	0	0	0	0	1	1	1	
1	Transmit window value							3a
Retransmission timer identifier								4*
0	0	0	0	1	0	0	1	
0	Retransmission timer value							4a*
1	Retransmission timer value (cont)							4b*
Mode of operation								5*
1	0	0	0	1	1	1	1	
1	Spare						Mode indication	5a*

Figure 12.12 Link-Layer Protocol Parameters Information Element.

- **Retransmission timer value:** The amount of time that a sender will wait for acknowledgment before retransmission, expressed in units of tenths of a second.
- **Mode of operation:** Indicates whether 3-bit or 7-bit sequence numbers will be used.

12.4 LAPF

The frame-mode bearer service is supported by a new data link control protocol, LAPF (Link Access Procedure for Frame-Mode Bearer Services), which is defined in Q.922. LAPF is based on and is an extension of LAPD. The LAPF frame format is used for frame transfer on all user channels (B, D, and H).

For the frame-relaying bearer service, a subset of LAPF, known as the core protocol, provides a streamlined data link service. The full LAPF protocol, also known as the control protocol, is required for the frame-switching bearer service.

LAPF Core Protocol

Frame Format

The operation of frame relay for user data transfer is best explained by beginning with the frame format, illustrated in Figure 12.13. The format is similar to that

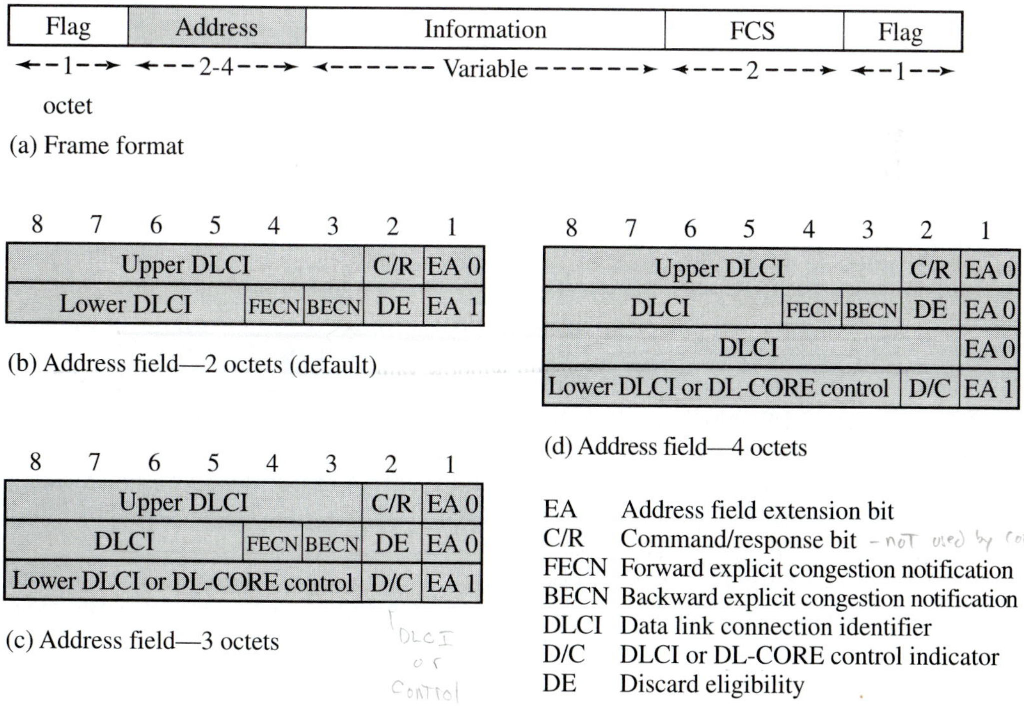

NO CONTROL FIELD

Flag	Address	Information	FCS	Flag
←–1–→	←––2-4––→	←–––––– Variable –––––→	←–––2–––→	←–1–→

octet

(a) Frame format

(b) Address field—2 octets (default)

8	7	6	5	4	3	2	1
Upper DLCI						C/R	EA 0
Lower DLCI			FECN	BECN	DE	EA 1

(c) Address field—3 octets

8	7	6	5	4	3	2	1
Upper DLCI						C/R	EA 0
DLCI			FECN	BECN	DE	EA 0
Lower DLCI or DL-CORE control						D/C	EA 1

DLCI or control

(d) Address field—4 octets

8	7	6	5	4	3	2	1
Upper DLCI						C/R	EA 0
DLCI			FECN	BECN	DE	EA 0
DLCI							EA 0
Lower DLCI or DL-CORE control						D/C	EA 1

EA   Address field extension bit
C/R   Command/response bit *– not used by core protocol*
FECN Forward explicit congestion notification
BECN Backward explicit congestion notification
DLCI Data link connection identifier
D/C   DLCI or DL-CORE control indicator
DE   Discard eligibility

Figure 12.13   LAPF-Core Formats.

of LAPD and LAPB with one obvious omission: There is no control field. This has the following implications:

- There is only one frame type, used for carrying user data. There are no control frames.
- It is not possible to use inband signaling; a logical connection can only carry user data.
- It is not possible to perform flow control and error control, because there are no sequence numbers.

[margin handwritten note: Can do In channel Signalling (DLCI=0)]

The flag and frame-check sequence (FCS) fields function as in LAPD and LAPB. The information field carries higher-layer data. If the user selects to implement additional data link control functions end to end, then a data link frame can be carried in this field. For example, in a local area network context, the logical link control (LLC) protocol could be used on top of the LAPF core protocol. This is similar to the approach taken in I.465/V.120, in which an HDLC frame is carried in the information field of an I.465/V.120 frame. Note that the protocol implemented in this fashion is strictly between the end subscribers and is transparent to frame relay. Another alternative is to extend the LAPF frame to employ the LAPF control protocol; this latter approach is discussed in the next subsection.

The length of the address field, and hence of the DLCI, is determined by the address field extension (EA) bits. The address field has a default length of 2 octets and may be extended to 3 or 4 octets. It carries a data link connection identifier (DLCI) of 10, 16, 17, or 23 bits. The DLCI serves the same function as the virtual circuit number in X.25: It allows multiple logical frame relay connections to be multiplexed over a single channel. As in X.25, the connection identifier has only local significance: Each end of the logical connection assigns its own DLCI from the pool of locally unused numbers, and the network must map from one to the other. The alternative, using the same DLCI on both ends, would require some sort of global management of DLCI values. Table 12.7 summarizes the assignments that have been made for DLCI values.

For D channel frame relay, a 2-octet address field is assumed, and the DLCI values are limited to the range 512 to 991. This is equivalent to an SAPI of 32–61. Thus, frame relay frames can be multiplexed with LAPD frames on the D channel, and the two types of frames are distinguished on the basis of bits 8 to 3 in the first octet of the address field. Figure 12.14 illustrates this distinction. The 16-bit pattern in Figure 12.14b corresponds to an SAPI of 16 and a TEI of 66. For the 16-bit pattern of Figure 12.14d, if this is interpreted as a LAPD address field, then the SAPI is 32. Because this is one of the SAPI values reserved for frame relay, we interpret this as a LAPF address field. Therefore, this address value yields a DLCI of 520.

[margin handwritten note: SAPI 32-61 implies Relay Frame → interpret as → LAPF]

In the 3- and 4-octet address formats, the D/C bit indicates whether the remaining six usable bits of that octet are to be interpreted as the lower DLCI bits or as data link core control protocol bits. So far, no additional core control functions have been identified for which these bits are needed.

The C/R bit is application specific and not used by the data link core control protocol. The remaining bits in the address field have to do with congestion control and are discussed in Chapter 13.

Table 12.7 LAPF DLCI Assignments

(a) Values for B channel and H channel applications

10-bit format (2 octet field or 3-octet field with D/C = 1)	16-bit format (3 octet field with D/C = 0)	17-bit format (4 octet field with D/C = 1)	23-bit format (4 octet field with D/C = 0)	Function
		DLCI range		
0	0	0	0	Inchannel signaling
1–15	1–1023	1–2047	1–131,071	Reserved
16–991	1024 (16×2^6)–63,487	2048 (16×2^7)–126,975	131,072 (16×2^{13})–4,194,303	Assigned using frame relay connection procedures
992–1007	63,488 (992×2^6)–64,511	126,976 (992×2^7)–129,023		Layer 2 management of frame mode bearer service
1008–1022	64,512 (1008×2^6)–65,534	129,024 (1008×2^7)–131,070		Reserved
1023	65,535	131,071		Inchannel layer 2 management

(b) Values for D channel applications

DLCI range	Function
512–991	Assigned using frame relay connection procedures

Not used 4-1
The CISO Protocol

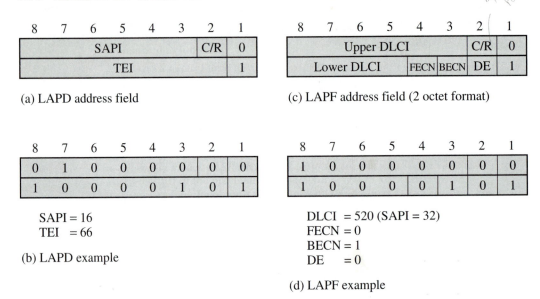

(a) LAPD address field

(c) LAPF address field (2 octet format)

SAPI = 16
TEI = 66

(b) LAPD example

DLCI = 520 (SAPI = 32)
FECN = 0
BECN = 1
DE   = 0

(d) LAPF example

Figure 12.14   LAPF and LAPF Address Field Formats.

Network Function

The frame-relaying function performed by ISDN, or any network that supports frame relaying, consists of the routing of frames with the format of Figure 12.13a, based on their DLCI values.

Figure 12.15 suggests the operation of a frame handler in a situation in which a number of users are directly connected to the same frame handler over different physical channels. The operation could just as well involve relaying a frame through two or more frame handlers. In this figure, the decision-making logic is shown conceptually as a separate module, the frame relay control point. This module is responsible for making routing decisions.

Typically, routing is controlled by entries in a connection table based on DLCI that map incoming frames on one channel to another. The frame handler switches a frame from an incoming channel to an outgoing channel based on the appropriate entry in the connection table and translates the DLCI in the frame before transmission. For example, incoming frames from TE B on logical connection 306 are retransmitted to TE D on logical connection 342. This technique has been referred to as chained-link path routing [LAI88]. The figure also shows the multiplexing function: Multiple logical connections to TE D are multiplexed over the same physical channel.

Note also that all of the TEs have a logical connection to the frame relay control point with a value of DLCI = 0. These connections are reserved for inchannel call control, to be used when Q.931 on the D channel is not used for frame relay call control.

As part of the frame relay function, the FCS of each incoming frame is checked. When an error is detected, the frame is simply discarded. It is the responsibility of the end users to institute error recovery above the frame relay protocol.

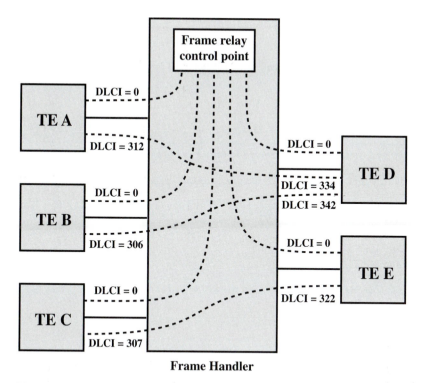

Figure 12.15 Frame Handler Operation.

LAPF Control Protocol

For the frame-switching bearer service, the LAPF control protocol, which is the full Q.922 protocol, is used. This protocol is implemented in the end systems and in the frame handlers as well (Figure 12.5).

Figure 12.16 shows the format of the LAPF control protocol frame. The only difference between this format and that of the LAPF core protocol frame is the inclusion of a control field. The control field is, in fact, the same format as used for LAPD, with the same interpretation. The address field is the same as shown in Figure 12.13 for the core protocol. Thus, the control protocol provides the functions of error control and flow control that are missing from the LAPF core protocol.

It is important to note that with frame switching, the control field in the LAPF frame is used between user and network for flow and error control and is not an end-to-end function. Recall from Figure 12.5 that the LAPF control protocol may also be used in a frame-relaying bearer service for end-to-end use only. This point is clarified in Figure 12.17. As Figure 12.17a shows, with the frame-relaying bearer service, the LAPF core protocol frame is used. The information field of that frame may contain a (protocol data unit) PDU for a higher-layer protocol, such as LLC, that provides end-to-end flow and error control.

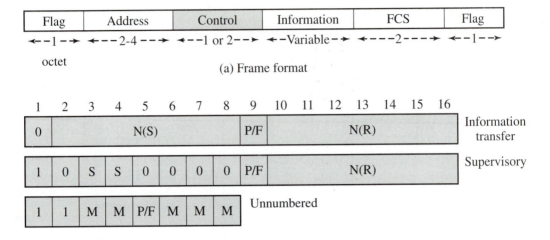

N(S) Transmitter send sequence number
N(R) Transmitter receive sequence number
P/F   Poll/final bit
S   Supervisory function bit
M   Modifier function bit

(b) Control field formats

Figure 12.16 LAPF-control Formats.

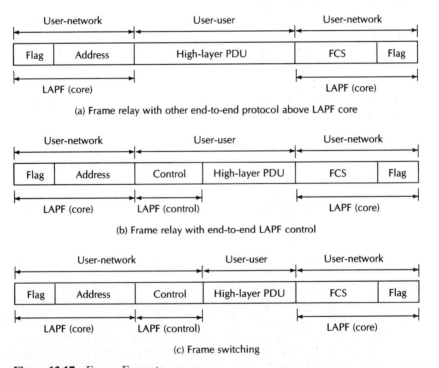

(a) Frame relay with other end-to-end protocol above LAPF core

(b) Frame relay with end-to-end LAPF control

(c) Frame switching

Figure 12.17 Frame Formats.

In addition, one possible option for end-to-end flow and error control is the full LAPF control protocol. In this case, we do not place an entire LAPF control protocol frame in the information field of the LAPF core protocol frame. Rather, we simply add the control field. The resulting layout is shown in Figure 12.17b. Note that the control field is transparent to the frame relay network and is only used by the two end systems. The information field of this frame may contain a higher-level PDU, such as for a network or transport protocol.

The same layout appears for a frame-switching bearer service, as shown in Figure 12.17c. The difference is not in the format but in the way in which the bits are handled. For the frame-switching service, the LAPF control field is visible to the network. Thus, flow and error control is exercised across the user–network interface. End-to-end flow and error control, if desired, must be provided by a higher-layer protocol.

12.5 SUMMARY

Frame relay was developed as an alternative to X.25 and provides a streamlined packet-switching interface and mechanism. By reducing the considerable overhead associated with X.25, frame relay provides a means for exploiting the high data rates available on contemporary networks. Although the standards for frame relay are being developed in the context of ISDN, frame relay is enjoying widespread acceptance in a number of non-ISDN environments.

The frame relay specifications cover two major areas: call control and data transfer. Frame relay connections may be permanent, in which case call control is not required. For switched frame relay connections, a separate call control connection is used, providing efficient out-of-band signaling.

The data-transfer portion of the frame relay specification calls for a two-layer protocol architecture, the physical and data link layers. End-system addressing and connection multiplexing are done at layer 2, using LAPF, eliminating one layer of processing.

Table 12.8 summarizes the four data link protocols that are relevant to ISDN.

12.6 RECOMMENDED READING

[BLAC96] is a good survey of frame relay, with an emphasis on the technical and protocol aspects. Another good technical treatment is contained in [SPOH97]. Another comprehensive description, which includes a good technical treatment as well as product and implementation considerations, is [DORL96].

BLAC96   Black, U. *Frame Relay Networks: Specifications and Implementations.* New York: McGraw-Hill, 1996.

DORL96   Dorling, B.; Pieters, P.; and Valenzuela, E. IBM Frame Relay Guide. IBM Publication SG24-4463-01, 1996. Available at www.redbooks.ibm.com.

SPOH97   Spohn, D. *Data Network Design.* New York: McGraw-Hill, 1997.

Table 12.8 Comparison of ISDN Data Link Layer Specifications

	I.441/Q.921 (LAPD)	LAPB (Layer 2 of X.25)	I.465/V.120	Frame Mode Bearer Service
User Data Channel	D	B	B + H	D + B + H
Call Control for Logical Connections	N/A	N/A (X.25-3 uses inchannel call control)	I.451/Q.931 on D or LLI = 0 on bearer channel	I.451/Q.931 on D or DLCI = 0 on bearer channel
Multiplexing	Multiple TEs (TEI) Multiple Layer 3 Users (SAPI)	None (X.25-3 supports multiple virtual circuits)	Multiple users (LLI)	Multiple users (DLCI)
Logical Connections	N/A	N/A (X.25-3 supports multiplexing and switching)	Multiplexing	Multiplexing and switching
Peer Entities	Network	Multiple users on network	Multiple users on same circuit	Multiple users on network

Recommended Web sites are as follows:

- **Frame Relay Forum:** An association of corporate members comprised of vendors, carriers, users, and consultants committed to the implementation of frame relay in accordance with national and international standards. Site includes list of technical and implementation documents for sale.
- **Frame relay resources:** A collection of pointers to frame relay information on the Web.

12.7 PROBLEMS

12.1 Q.933 recommends a procedure for negotiating the sliding-window flow-control window, which may take on a value from 1 to 127. The negotiation makes use of a variable k that is calculated from the following parameters:

L_d = data frame size in octets
R_u = throughput bits/s
T_{td} = end-to-end transit delay in seconds
k = window size (maximum number of outstanding I-frames)

The procedure is described as follows:

> The window size should be negotiated as follows. The originating user should calculate k using the preceding formula substituting maximum end-to-end transit delay and outgoing maximum frame size for T_{td} and L_d, respectively. The SETUP message shall include the link layer protocol parameters, the link layer core parameters, and the end-to-end transit delay information elements. The destina-

tion user should calculate its own k using the preceding formula substituting cumulative end-to-end transit delay and its own outgoing maximum frame size for T_{td} and L_d, respectively. The CONNECT message shall include the link layer core parameters and the end-to-end transit delay information element so that the originating user can adjust its k based on the information conveyed in these information elements. The originating user should calculate k using the preceding formula substituting cumulative end-to-end transit delay and incoming maximum frame size for T_{td} and L_d, respectively.

Suggest a formula for calculating k from the other variables and justify the formula.

$$R_v \left(\frac{bits}{sec}\right) * T_{rd} (se) = \text{length of Path in bits}$$

$$\frac{\text{length of path}}{L_d (octets) * 8 \frac{bits}{octet}} = \text{\# of frames in path (each way)}$$

This must be doubled to fill link and ensure that there is no stopping and waiting

$$\Rightarrow \quad \left[\frac{R_v T_{+d}}{L_d \cdot 8} + 2 \right] * 2 = K$$

CHAPTER 13

FRAME RELAY CONGESTION CONTROL

With the frame relay bearer service, there is no mechanism for flow control and error control between user and network: The LAPF frame does not contain a control field and therefore there are no sequence numbers to work with. While this streamlined protocol provides for efficient data transfer, it lays the network open to the possibility of congestion. To deal with this problem, ITU-T and ANSI have proposed a variety of congestion control techniques. Because the number of techniques, which can be used alternatively or in conjunction with one another, is large, and because the specifications are scattered through various documents in no particular order, this is the most confusing aspect of frame relay.

The purpose of this chapter is to provide a systematic overview of frame relay congestion control. We begin with a discussion of the need for congestion control. Next we look at the explicit congestion control techniques proposed for the frame relay bearer service. We then turn to what are referred to as implicit congestion control techniques.

13.1 CONGESTION IN FRAME RELAY NETWORKS

A frame relay network is a form of packet-switching network in which the "packets" are layer 2 frames. As in any packet-switching network, one of the key areas in the design of a frame relay network is congestion control. To understand the issue involved in congestion control, we need to look at some results from queuing theory. In essence, a frame relay network is a network of queues. At each frame handler, there is a queue of frames for each outgoing link. If the rate at which frames arrive and queue up exceeds the rate at which frames can be transmitted, the queue size grows without bound and the delay experienced by a frame goes to infinity. Even if the frame arrival rate is less than the frame transmission rate, queue length will grow dramat-

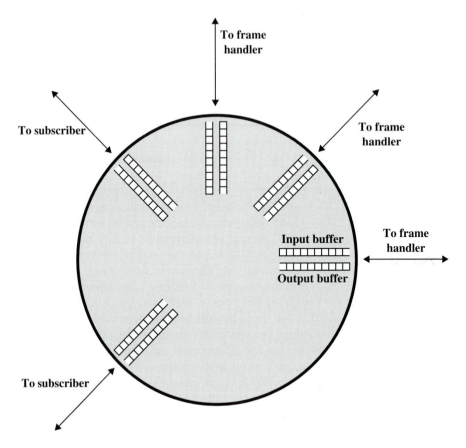

Figure 13.1 Input and Output Queues at Frame Handler.

ically as the arrival rate approaches the transmission rate. As a rule of thumb, when the line for which frames are queuing becomes more than 80% utilized, the queue length grows at an alarming rate.

Consider the queuing situation at a single frame handler, such as is illustrated in Figure 13.1. Any given node has a number of transmission links attached to it: one or more to other frame handlers, and zero or more to ISDN subscribers. On each link, frames arrive and depart. We can consider that there are two buffers at each link, one to accept arriving frames, and one to hold frames that are waiting to depart. In practice, there might be two fixed-size buffers associated with each link, or there might be a pool of memory available for all buffering activities. In the latter case, we can think of each link having two variable-size buffers associated with it, subject to the constraint that the sum of all buffer sizes is a constant.

In any case, as frames arrive, they are stored in the input buffer of the corresponding link. The node examines each incoming frame to make a routing decision and then moves the frame to the appropriate output buffer. Frames queued up for output are transmitted as rapidly as possible. If frames arrive too fast for the node to process them (make routing decisions), or faster than frames can be cleared from

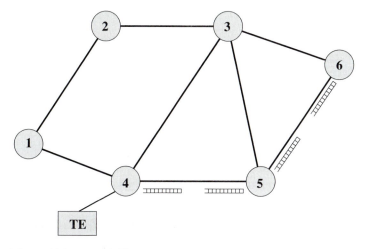

Figure 13.2 Interaction of Queues in a Frame Relay Network.

the outgoing buffers, then eventually frames will arrive for which no memory is available.

When such a saturation point is reached, one of two general strategies can be adopted. The first such strategy is simply to discard any incoming frame for which there is no available buffer space. This approach is self-defeating, because the discarded frames will have to be retransmitted, adding to network congestion. The other alternative is for some mechanism to be used that restricts the rate at which new frames are inserted into the network. In its simplest version, such a strategy would consist of enabling each node that is experiencing queue saturation to exercise some sort of flow control over its neighbors so that the traffic flow remains manageable. But as Figure 13.2 illustrates, each of a node's neighbors is also managing a number of queues. If node 6 restrains the flow of frames from node 5, this causes the output buffer in node 5 for the link to node 6 to fill up. Thus, congestion at one point in the network can quickly propagate throughout a region or all of the network. This leads to a requirement to employ a strategy that will control the flow of frames into the network, both globally and in local regions. This latter approach is referred to as congestion control.

Ideal Performance

Figure 13.3 suggests the ideal goal for network utilization. The top graph plots the steady-state total throughput (number of frames delivered to destination end systems) through the network as a function of the offered load (number of frames transmitted by source end systems), both normalized to the maximum theoretical throughput of the network. For example, if a network consists of a single node with two 1-Mbps links, then the theoretical capacity of the network is 2 Mbps, consisting of a 1-Mbps flow in each direction. In the ideal case, the throughput of the network increases to accommodate load up to an offered load equal to the full capacity of the network; then normalized throughput remains at 1.0 at higher input loads. Note, however, what happens to the end-to-end delay experienced by the average frame

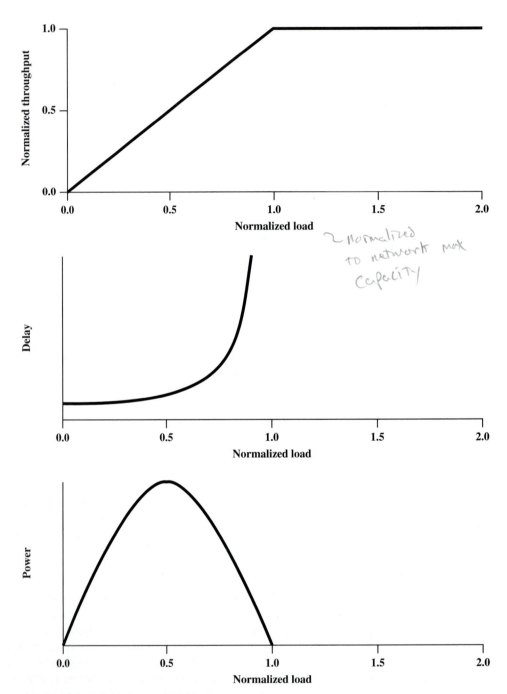

Normalized to network max capacity

Figure 13.3 Ideal Network Utilization.

even with this assumption of ideal performance. At negligible load, there is some small constant amount of delay that consists of the propagation delay through the network from source to destination plus processing delay at each node. As the load on the network increases, queuing delays at each node are added to this fixed amount of delay. When the load exceeds the network capacity, delay becomes infinite in the steady state.

Here is a simple intuitive explanation of why delay must go to infinity. Suppose that each node in the network is equipped with buffers of infinite size and suppose that the input load exceeds network capacity. Under ideal conditions, the network will continue to sustain a normalized throughput of 1.0. Therefore, the rate of frames leaving the network is 1.0. Because the rate of frames entering the network is greater than 1.0, internal queue sizes grow. In the steady state, with input greater than output, these queue sizes grow to infinity and therefore queuing delays grow to infinity.

It is important to grasp the meaning of Figure 13.3 before looking at real-world conditions. This figure represents the ideal, but unattainable, goal of all traffic and congestion control schemes. No scheme can exceed the performance depicted in Figure 13.3.

You will sometimes see the term *power* used in network performance literature. Power is defined as the ratio of throughput to delay, and this is depicted for the ideal case in the bottom graph of Figure 13.3. It has been shown that, typically, a network configuration and congestion control scheme that results in higher throughput also results in higher delay [JAIN91], and that power is a concise metric that can be used to compare different schemes.

Practical Performance

The ideal case reflected in Figure 13.3 assumes infinite buffers and no overhead related to frame transmission or congestion control. In practice, buffers are finite, leading to buffer overflow, and attempts to control congestion consume network capacity in the exchange of control signals.

Let us consider what happens in a network with finite buffers if no attempt is made to control congestion or to restrain input from end systems. The details will, of course, differ depending on network configuration and on the statistics of the presented traffic. However, the graphs in Figure 13.4 depict the devastating outcome in general terms.

At light loads, throughput and hence network utilization increases as the offered load increases. As the load continues to increase, a point is reached (point A in the plot) beyond which the throughput of the network increases at a rate slower than the rate at which offered load is increased. This is due to network entry into a moderate congestion state. In this region, the network continues to cope with the load, although with increased delays. The departure of throughput from the ideal is accounted for by a number of factors. First, unless the flow of frames is uniform, with no variation, queuing theory tells us that queing delays will arise at each node due to the ebb and flow of traffic. Also, the load is unlikely to be spread uniformly throughout the network. Therefore, while some nodes may experience moderate congestion, others may be experiencing severe congestion and may need to discard traffic. In addition, as the load increases, the network will attempt to balance the load by routing

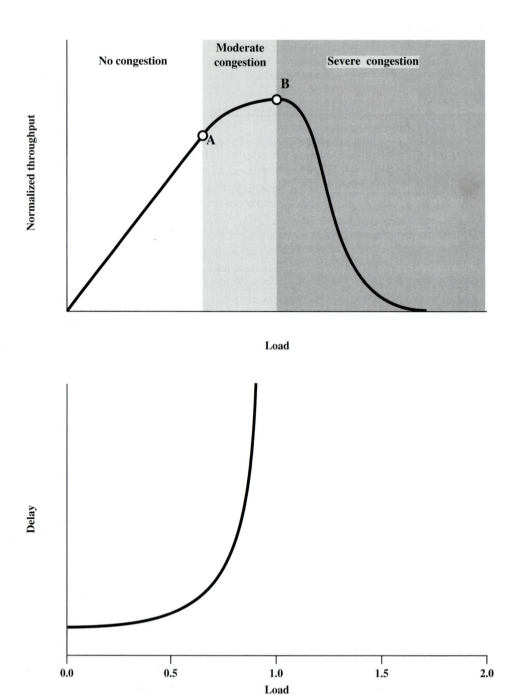

Figure 13.4   The Effects of Congestion.

frames through areas of lower congestion. For the routing function to work, an increased number of routing messages must be exchanged between nodes to alert each other to areas of congestion; this overhead reduces the capacity available for data frames.

As the load on the network continues to increase, the queue lengths of the various frame handlers grow. Eventually, a point is reached (point B in the plot) beyond which throughput actually drops with increased offered load. The reason for this is that the buffers at each node are of finite size. When the buffers at a frame handler become full, it must discard frames. Thus, the sources must retransmit the discarded frames in addition to new frames. This only exacerbates the situation: As more and more frames are retransmitted, the load on the system grows, and more buffers become saturated. While the system is trying desperately to clear the backlog, users are pumping old and new frames into the system. Even successfully delivered frames may be retransmitted because it take too long, at a higher layer (e.g., transport layer), to acknowledge them: The sender assumes the frame did not get through. Under these circumstances, the effective capacity of the system is virtually zero.

It is clear that these catastrophic events must be avoided, which is the task of congestion control. The object of all congestion control techniques is to limit queue lengths at the nodes so as to avoid throughput collapse.

13.2 APPROACHES TO CONGESTION CONTROL

I.370 defines the objectives for frame relay congestion control to be the following:

- Minimize frame discard.
- Maintain, with high probability and minimum variance, an agreed quality of service.
- Minimize the possibility that one end user can monopolize network resources at the expense of other end users.
- Be simple to implement, and place little overhead on either end user or network.
- Create minimal additional network traffic.
- Distribute network resources fairly among end users.
- Limit spread of congestion to other networks and elements within the network.
- Operate effectively regardless of the traffic flow in either direction between end users.
- Have minimum interaction or impact on other systems in the frame-relaying network.
- Minimize the variance in quality of service delivered to individual frame relay connections during congestion (e.g., individual logical connections should not experience sudden degradation when congestion approaches or has occurred).

Congestion control is particularly difficult for a frame relay network because of the limited tools available to the frame handlers. The frame relay protocol has been streamlined to maximize throughput and efficiency. A consequence of this is that a frame handler cannot control the flow of frames coming from a subscriber or

Table 13.1   Frame Relay Congestion Control Techniques

Technique	Type	Function	Key Elements
Discard control	Discard strategy	Provides guidance to network concerning which frames to discard	DE bit
Backward explicit Congestion Notification	Congestion avoidance	Provides guidance to end systems about congestion in network	BECN bit or CLLM message
Forward explicit Congestion Notification	Congestion avoidance	Provides guidance to end systems about congestion in network	FECN bit
Implicit congestion notification	Congestion recovery	End system infers congestion from frame loss	Sequence numbers in higher-layer PDU

an adjacent frame handler using the typical sliding-window flow control protocol, such as is found in LAPD.

Congestion control is the joint responsibility of the network and the end users. The network (i.e., the collection of frame handlers) is in the best position to monitor the degree of congestion, while the end users are in the best position to control congestion by limiting the flow of traffic.

Table 13.1 lists the congestion control techniques defined in the various ITU-T and ANSI documents. **Discard strategy** deals with the most fundamental response to congestion: When congestion becomes severe enough, the network is forced to discard frames. We would like to do this in a way that is fair to all users.

Congestion avoidance procedures are used at the onset of congestion to minimize the effect on the network. Thus, these procedures would be initiated at or prior to point A in Figure 13.4, to prevent congestion from progressing to point B. Near point A, there would be little evidence available to end users that congestion is increasing. Thus, there must be some **explicit signaling** mechanism from the network that will trigger the congestion avoidance.

Congestion recovery procedures are used to prevent network collapse in the face of severe congestion. These procedures are typically initiated when the network has begun to drop frames due to congestion. Such dropped frames will be reported by some higher layer of software (e.g., LAPF control protocol or TCP) and serve as an **implicit signaling** mechanism. Congestion recovery procedures operate around point B and within the region of severe congestion, as shown in Figure 13.4.

ITU-T and ANSI consider congestion avoidance with explicit signaling and congestion recovery with implicit signaling to be complementary forms of congestion control in the frame relaying bearer service.

13.3 TRAFFIC RATE MANAGEMENT

As a last resort, a frame relaying network must discard frames to cope with congestion. There is no getting around this fact. Because each frame handler in the network has finite memory available for queuing frames (Figure 13.2), it is possible for a queue to overflow, necessitating the discard of either the most recently arrived frame or some other frame.

The simplest way to cope with congestion is for the frame relaying network to discard frames arbitrarily, with no regard to the source of a particular frame. In that case, because there is no reward for restraint, the best strategy for any individual end system is to transmit frames as rapidly as possible. This, of course, exacerbates the congestion problem.

Network Use of CIR and DE Bit

To provide for a fairer allocation of resources, the frame relay bearer service includes the concept of a committed information rate (CIR). This is a rate, in bits per second, that the network agrees to support for a particular frame-mode connection. Any data transmitted in excess of the CIR is vulnerable to discard in the event of congestion. Despite the use of the term *committed*, there is no guarantee that even the CIR will be met. In cases of extreme congestion, the network may be forced to provide a service at less than the CIR for a given connection. However, when it comes time to discard frames, the network will choose to discard frames on connections that are exceeding their CIR before discarding frames that are within their CIR.

In theory, each frame-relaying node should manage its affairs so that the aggregate of CIRs of all the connections of all the end systems attached to the node does not exceed the capacity of the node. In addition, the aggregate of the CIRs should not exceed the physical data rate across the user–network interface, known as the access rate. The limitation imposed by access rate can be expressed as follows:

$$\sum_i \text{CIR}_{i,j} \leq \text{AccessRate}_j \tag{13.1}$$

where

$\text{CIR}_{i,j}$ = Committed information rate for connection i on channel j
AccessRate_j = Data rate of user access channel j (D, B, or H)

Considerations of node capacity may result in the selection of lower values for some of the CIRs.

For permanent frame relay connections, the CIR for each connection must be established at the time the connection is agreed between user and network. For switched connections, the CIR parameter is negotiated. Recall from Chapter 12 that the Link Layer Core Parameters Information Element includes throughput and minimum acceptable throughput parameters. When present in the SETUP message from a user, the throughput parameter represents the throughput requested by the calling user. Either the network or the called user may reduce this parameter, so that its value in the CONNECT message returned to the called user represents the CIR. However, the CIR may not be less than the minimum acceptable throughput declared by the calling user. If this level of throughput cannot be supported, the connection request is rejected.

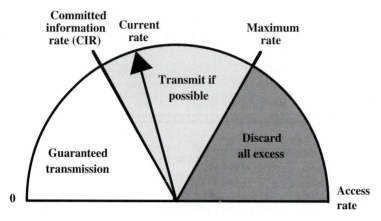

Figure 13.5   Operation of the CIR.

The CIR provides a way of discriminating among frames in determining which frames to discard in the face of congestion. Discrimination is indicated by means of the discard eligibility (DE) bit in the LAPF frame (Figure 12.13). The frame handler to which the user's station attaches performs a metering function (Figure 13.5). If the user is sending data at less than the CIR, the incoming frame handler does not alter the DE bit. If the rate exceeds the CIR, the incoming frame handler will set the DE bit on the excess frames and then forward them; such frames may get through or may be discarded if congestion is encountered. Finally, a maximum rate is defined, such that any frames above the maximum are discarded at the entry frame handler.

The CIR, by itself, does not provide much flexibility in dealing with traffic rates. In practice, a frame handler measures traffic over each logical connection for a time interval specific to that connection and then makes a decision based on the amount of data received during that interval. Two additional parameters, assigned on permanent connections and negotiated on switched connections, are needed:

- **Committed burst size (B_c):** The maximum amount data that the network agrees to transfer, under normal conditions, over a measurement interval T. These data may or may not be contiguous (i.e., they may appear in one frame or in several frames).

- **Excess burst size (B_e):** The maximum amount of data in excess of B_c that the network will attempt to transfer, under normal conditions, over a measurement interval T. These data are uncommitted in the sense that the network does not commit to delivery under normal conditions. Put another way, the data that represent B_e are delivered with lower probability than the data within B_c.

The quantities B_c and CIR are related. Because B_c is the amount of committed data that may be transmitted by the user over a time T, and CIR is the rate at which committed data may be transmitted, we must have

$$T = \frac{B_c}{\text{CIR}}$$
(13.2)

Figure 13.6, based on a figure in I.370, illustrates the relationship among these parameters. On each graph, the solid line plots the cumulative number of information bits transferred over a given connection since time $T = 0$. The dashed line labeled Access Rate represents the data rate over the channel containing this connection. The dashed line labeled CIR represents the committed information rate over the measurement interval T. Note that when a frame is being transmitted, the solid line is parallel to the Access Rate line; when a frame is transmitted on a channel, that channel is dedicated to the transmission of that frame. When no frame is being transmitted, the solid line is horizontal.

Part (a) of the figure shows an example in which three frames are transmitted within the measurement interval, and the total number of bits in the three frames is less than B_c. Note that during the transmission of the first frame, the actual transmission rate temporarily exceeds the CIR. This is of no consequence because the frame handler is only concerned with the cumulative number of bits transmitted over the entire interval. In part (b) of the figure, the last frame transmitted during the interval causes the cumulative number of bits transmitted to exceed B_c. Accordingly, the DE bit of that frame is set by the frame handler. In part (c) of the figure, the third frame exceeds B_c and so is labeled for potential discard. The fourth frame exceeds $B_c + B_e$ and is discarded.

This scheme is an example of a leaky bucket algorithm, and a mechanism for implementing it is illustrated in Figure 13.7. The frame handler records the cumulative amount of data sent over a connection in a counter C. The counter is decremented at a rate of B_c every T time units. Of course, the counter is not allowed to become negative, so the actual assignment is $C \leftarrow \text{MIN} \, [C, B_c]$. Whenever the counter value exceeds B_c but is less than $B_c + B_e$, incoming data are in excess of the committed burst size and are forwarded with the DE bit set. If the counter reaches $B_c + B_e$, all incoming frames are discarded until the counter has been decremented.

CIR Levels

The use of CIR values for rate enforcement allows priority to be allocated to different traffic streams multiplexed over the same access channel. An application with higher throughput requirements can be assigned a larger CIR than an application with a lower throughput requirement. The only constraint is that the total data rate allocated must not exceed the access rate of the channel (Equation 13.1).

It is also possible to establish a frame relay connection with a CIR of zero. This simply means that the network makes no commitment to deliver frames for this connection, but will use any surplus capacity to do so. A typical scenario might have a number of high-priority connections with CIRs to suit their application requirements multiplexed with a set of lower-priority virtual channels with a CIR of zero.

With the CIR set to zero, it is not possible to use Equation 13.2 to define the measurement interval for that connection. Instead the following equation is used:

$$T = \frac{B_e}{\text{Access Rate}} \tag{13.3}$$

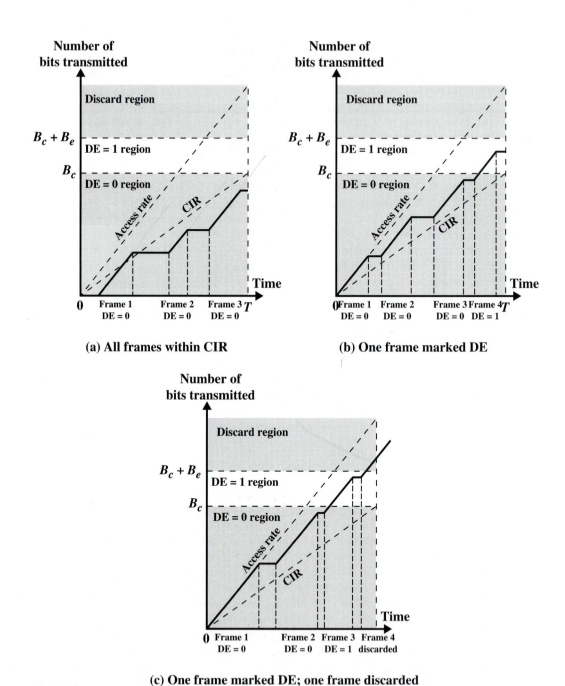

(a) All frames within CIR

(b) One frame marked DE

(c) One frame marked DE; one frame discarded

Figure 13.6 Illustration of Relationships among Congestion Parameters.

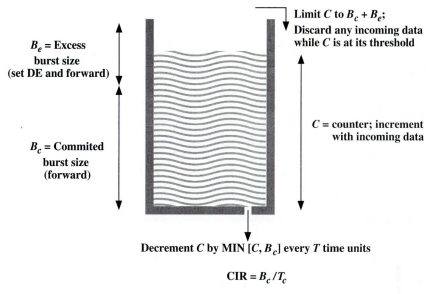

B_e = Excess
burst size
(set DE and forward)

B_c = Commited
burst size
(forward)

Limit C to $B_c + B_e$;
Discard any incoming data
while C is at its threshold

C = counter; increment
with incoming data

Decrement C by MIN $[C, B_c]$ every T time units

$$CIR = B_c / T_c$$

Figure 13.7   Leaky Bucket Algorithm.

End-User Control of DE Bit

The DE bit may also be set by the end system that originates the frame transmission. This allows the user to decide which frames are less important and therefore should be more vulnerable to discard. Figure 13.7 cannot be used to illustrate this case very well. In essence, when a user marks a frame with the DE bit, the network considers the frame to be within B_e but not part of the CIR.

13.4 EXPLICIT CONGESTION AVOIDANCE

It is desirable to use as much of the available capacity in a frame relay network as possible but still react to congestion in a controlled and fair manner. This is the purpose of explicit congestion avoidance techniques. In general terms, for explicit congestion avoidance, the network alerts end systems to growing congestion within the network and the end systems take steps to reduce the offered load to the network.

As the standards for explicit congestion avoidance were being developed, two general strategies were considered [BERG91]. One group believed that congestion always occurred slowly and almost always in the network egress nodes. Another group had seen cases in which congestion grew very quickly in the internal nodes and required quick decisive action to prevent network congestion. We will see that these two approaches are reflected in the forward and backward explicit congestion avoidance techniques, respectively.

With congestion avoidance techniques, the network, when it detects increasing congestion, signals this fact to those end users with frame relay connections that

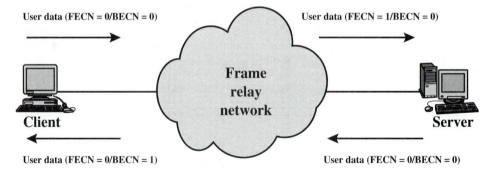

Figure 13.8 Example of Use of FECN/BECN Bits (mild congestion in the direction of server).

are affected by the congestion. This explicit signaling may make use of one of two bits in the LAPF address field of each frame or a special message in an XID LAPF frame. Either bit may be set by any frame handler that detects congestion. If a frame handler receives a frame in which one or both of these bits are set, it must not clear the bits before forwarding the frame. Thus, the bits constitute signals from the network to the end user. The two bits are as follows:

- **Backward explicit congestion notification (BECN) bit:** Notifies the user that congestion avoidance procedures should be initiated where applicable for traffic in the opposite direction of the received frame. It indicates that the frames that the user transmits on this logical connection may encounter congested resources.
- **Forward explicit congestion notification (FECN) bit:** Notifies the user that congestion avoidance procedures should be initiated where applicable for traffic in the same direction as the received frame. It indicates that this frame, on this logical connection, has encountered congested resources.

In addition, a frame handler may use a message:

- **Consolidated link layer management (CLLM) message:** Notifies the user that congestion avoidance procedures should be initiated where applicable for traffic in the opposite direction of the received frame. It indicates that the frames that the user transmits on a set of logical connections may encounter congested resources.

In all of these cases, the network usually supplies the notification (Figure 13.8).[1] The actual protocol for responding to the notification is supplied by layers above the frame-relaying bearer service. The ITU-T and ANSI documents define some suggested protocols. In this section, we look first at the network decision to send notifications and then at the details of the suggested protocols.

---

[1]In some cases, the notification may be sent by the end stations as well. For example, in some of IBM's products, the end system sets the BECN bit in the first frame transported after a frame with FECN = 1 has been received. This informs the other end of the connection about the congestion, allowing it to decrease its transfer rate to help the network relieve the congestion [DORL96].

Network Notification of Congestion

For the network to be able to detect and then signal congestion, it is necessary for each frame handler to monitor its queuing behavior. If queue lengths begin to grow to a dangerous level, then either forward or backward explicit notification or a combination should be set to try to reduce the flow of frames through that frame handler. The choice of forward or backward may be determined by whether the end users on a given logical connection are prepared to respond to one or the other of these notifications. This may be determined at configuration time. In any case, the frame handler has some choice as to which logical connections should be alerted to congestion. If congestion is becoming quite serious, all logical connections through a frame handler might be notified. In the early stages of congestion, the frame handler might just notify users for those connections that are generating the most traffic.

In an appendix to ANSI T1.618, a procedure for monitoring queue lengths is suggested. The frame handler monitors the size of each of its queues. A cycle begins when the outgoing circuit goes from idle (queue empty) to busy (nonzero queue size, including the current frame). The average queue size over the previous cycle and the current cycle is calculated. If the average size exceeds a threshold value, then the circuit is in a state of incipient congestion, and the congestion avoidance bits should be set on some or all logical connections that use that circuit. By averaging over two cycles instead of just monitoring current queue length, the system avoids reacting to temporary surges that would not necessarily produce congestion.

The average queue length may be computed by determining the area (product of queue size and time interval) over the two cycles and dividing by the time of the two cycles. This algorithm is illustrated in Figure 13.9.

Forward Explicit Congestion Notification

The FECN bit is set to notify the receiving end system that the marked frame has encountered congestion. In response to this, the receiving system should try to reduce the flow of data from the sending system on this frame relay connection. The mechanism for doing so must be above the level of the frame relay bearer service, which provides no direct flow control facilities.

In general terms, the receiving end system should use the following strategy for each connection:

1. Compute the fraction of frames for which the FECN bit is set over some measurement interval.
2. If more frames have the FECN bit set than have a FECN bit of zero, then reduce the flow of frames from the sending system.
3. If the congestion condition persists, institute additional reductions.
4. When the congestion condition ends, gradually increase the flow of frames.

This strategy reacts slowly to congestion notifications for two reasons: First, the end system does not react immediately to a particular FECN bit but waits until the average behavior of the system over an interval indicates congestion. Second, the end system does not immediately reduce its outgoing flow but rather signals its peers to reduce the incoming flow. All of this is consistent with a belief that congestion occurs slowly.

The algorithm makes use of the following variables:

t = current time

t_i = time of ith arrival or departure event

q_i = number of frames in the system after the event

T_0 = time at the beginning of the previous cycle

T_1 = time at the beginning of the current cycle

The algorithm consists of three conponents:

1. Queue length update: Beginning with $q_0 := 0$

   If the ith event is an arrival event, $q_i := q_{i-1}+1$

   If the ith event is a departure event, $q_i := q_{i-1}-1$

2. Queue area (integral) update:

   Area of the previous cycle $= \sum_i q_{i-1}(t_i - t_{i-1})$

   $$t_i \in [T_0, T_1)$$

   Area of the current cycle $= \sum_i q_{i-1}(t_i - t_{i-1})$

   $$t_i \in [T_1, t)$$

3. Average queue length update:

   Average queue length over the two cycles

   $$= \frac{\text{Area of the two cycles}}{\text{Time of the two cycles}} = \frac{\text{Area of the two cycles}}{t - T_0}$$

Figure 13.9 Queue Length Averaging Algorithm.

The details of the algorithm depend on whether the end system has actual control of the information rate from the source system or uses some sort of sliding-window flow-control scheme (e.g., LAPF control protocol or TCP). A rate-based system can provide a more precise control of information flow because it is based on the actual information rate in bits per second. Because frame relay does not require the use of fixed-size frames, a window-based system can provide only an approximate control over information rate. Such control is reasonably precise only if the statistical variance of the frame size is small.

Rate-Based Control

For rate-based control, it is assumed that a destination system has a means of regulating the data rate at the source end system. Let us refer to current data rate as the rate R. On each connection, the end system maintains two counters: FECN0 is the number of LAPF frames with FECN = 0 and FECN1 is the number of LAPF frames with FECN = 1. These counts are accumulated over a measurement interval δ. The standards suggests a value of δ approximately equal to four times the end-to-end transit delay. Recall that this is one of the information elements in the SETUP message.

The algorithm is as follows. Initially, set R = CIR or less in the receive direction. This is referred to as a slow start and is intended to avoid an impulse load on the network at the time the user begins transmitting. Then, at the beginning of each measurement interval, set FECN0 = FECN1 = 0. At the end of each measurement interval,

1. If FECN1 ≥ FECN0, then set $R = 0.875 \times R$.

$$R_{i+1} = 0.875 R_i$$

2. If FECN1 < FECN0, then set $R = 1.0625 \times R$.

In addition, if a connection has been idle for a long time, then R should be set to CIR for that connection.

Note that when congestion is detected, the rate reduction is by 1/8, whereas the recovery is by a factor of 1/16. This slower recovery strategy is intended to avoid oscillations between congested and noncongested states.

Window-Based Control

For window-based flow control, we assume that sliding-window flow control is used and that the destination system can adjust the receive window size W between 1 and some maximum value W_{max}. Again the counters FECN0 and FECN1 are accumulated over a measurement interval δ. If the current window size is W, then δ is defined to be twice the interval during which W frames are transmitted and acknowledged (i.e., two window turns).

The algorithm is as follows. Initially, set $W = 1$. Again, this provides a slow start. Then, at the beginning of each measurement interval, set FECN0 = FECN1 = 0. At the end of each measurement interval,

1. If FECN1 ≥ FECN0, then set $W = \lfloor MAX[0.875 \times W, 1] \rfloor$.
2. If FECN1 < FECN0, then set $W = MIN[W + 1, W_{max}]$.

In addition, if a connection has been idle for a long time, then W should be set to 1 for that connection.

Backward Explicit Congestion Notification

Backward explicit congestion notification can be achieved with either the BECN bit in the LAPF address field or a consolidated link layer management (CLLM) message carried in a LAPF frame. We consider the BECN bit first.

The BECN bit is set to notify the receiving end system that the frames it transmits on this connection may encounter congestion. In response to this, the receiving system should reduce the flow of data transmitted on that connection.

In general terms, the receiving end system should use the following strategy for each connection:

1. When the first frame with the BECN bit set is received, reduce the information rate to CIR.
2. If additional consecutive frames with the BECN bit set are received, then institute additional reductions.
3. If a consecutive sequence of frames with the BECN bit set to zero are received, then gradually increase the flow of frames.

This strategy reacts rapidly to congestion notifications for two reasons: First, the end system reacts immediately to a single BECN bit. Second, the end system immediately reduces its outgoing flow rather than signaling its peers to reduce the incoming flow. All of this is consistent with a belief that congestion occurs quickly.

As with the response to forward explicit congestion notification, the details of the algorithm depend on whether control is rate based or window based.

Rate-Based Control

For rate-based control, the standards define a step count S that is used to determine when the transmitter may increase or decrease its rate. Figure 13.10 provides the definition. The IR terms specify the maximum information rate that this connection can generate; the terms are divided by 8 to yield a result in octets per second. In the definition of S, the two terms in parentheses specify the number of maximum-length frames that may be in transit in the network for this connection.[2]

The algorithm is as follows. Initially, set IR = CIR or less in the transmit direction. Then

1. If a frame with BECN set to 1 is received, and the user's offered rate, R, is greater than CIR, then reduce the offered rate to CIR.
2. If S consecutive frames are subsequently received with the BECN bit set to 1, the user should reduce its rate to the next lower "step." Further rate reductions should not occur until an additional S consecutive frames are received with the BECN bit set. The step rates are as follows:

$$R = 0.675 \times CIR$$

$$R = 0.5 \times CIR$$

$$R = 0.25 \times CIR$$

3. After the user has reduced its rate due to receipt of BECN signals, it may increase its rate by a factor of 0.125 after any $S/2$ consecutive frames are received with the BECN bit clear. That is, $R = 1.125 \times R$.

---

[2]In the Q.922 definition of this algorithm, the maximum information field length is identified by the name N202. However, elsewhere in the document, the maximum information field is referred to by N203 for the core protocol. ANSI T1.618 exhibits the same discrepancy. The only other use of N202 in ITU-T documents is in Q.921 (LAPD), where it refers to the maximum number of transmissions of the TEI identity request message. Accordingly, Figure 13.8 uses N203.

$$IR_f = \frac{Th_f}{8} + \left(\frac{Be_f}{Be_f + Bc_f}\right)\frac{AR_f}{8}$$

$$IR_b = \frac{Th_b}{8} + \left(\frac{Be_b}{Be_b + Bc_b}\right)\frac{AR_b}{8}$$

$$S = \frac{F_b}{F_f}\left(IR_f\frac{TD}{N203_f} + IR_b\frac{TD}{N203_b}\right)$$

where

IR_f	=	Maximum information rate in the forward direction
IR_b	=	Maximum information rate in the backward direction
Th_f	=	Throughput (CIR) in the forward direction
Th_b	=	Throughput (CIR) in the backward direction
Be_f	=	Excess burst size forward
Be_b	=	Excess burst size backward
Bc_f	=	Committed burst size forward
Bc_b	=	Committed burst size backward
AR_f	=	Access rate forward
AR_b	=	Access rate backward
S	=	Step function count
F_b/F_f	=	Ratio (either expected or measured over some implementation-dependent period of time) of frames received to frames sent
TD	=	End-to-end transit delay
$N203_f$	=	Maximum information field length in the forward direction
$N203_b$	=	Maximum information field length in the backward direction

Figure 13.10 Calculation of Step Function Count.

In addition, if a connection has been idle for a long time, then R should be set to CIR for that connection.

Window-Based Control

For window-based control, the step count S is defined to be the interval during which one frame is transmitted and acknowledged. The algorithm is as follows. Initially, set the window size W to some small value such as 1 or 0.5 × last window size. Then

1. If a frame with BECN set to 1 is received, then set $W = \lfloor \text{MAX}[0.625 \times W, 1]\rfloor$.
2. If S consecutive frames are subsequently received with the BECN bit set to 1, the user should repeat the reduction.

3. After the user has reduced its window size due to receipt of BECN signals, it may increase its window size by one after any $S/2$ consecutive frames are received with the BECN bit clear. That is, $W = \text{MIN}[W + 1, W_{\text{max}}]$.

In addition, if a connection has been idle for a long time, then W should be set to its initial value for that connection.

Consolidated Link Layer Management

CLLM is a variation of backward explicit congestion notification that uses a message rather than the BECN bit to signal congestion. The CLLM technique can be used when congestion occurs at a network node, but no reverse traffic is available to carry the BECN indication. CLLM messages carry a list of congested DLCIs to reduce the traffic load on the network. The end station is expected to relieve the congestion by limiting the data transfer on the DLCIs identified.

The CLLM is a message carried in the information XID LAPF frame. Figure 13.11 shows the general format, and Figure 13.12 illustrates the corresponding bit pattern. Note that the LAPF header contains a control field. This is so despite the fact that, for the frame relay bearer service, the network implements only

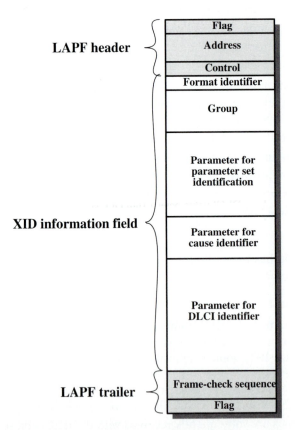

Figure 13.11 General CLLM Format for Congestion Control.

Octet	8	7	6	5	4	3	2	1	Field name
1	0	1	1	1	1	1	1	0	Flag
2	1	1	1	1	1	0	R	0	Address octet 1 (R indicates response)
3	1	1	1	1	0	0	0	1	Address octet 2
4	1	0	1	0	1	1	1	1	XID control field
5	1	0	0	0	0	0	1	0	Format identifier (130)
6	0	0	0	0	1	1	1	1	**Group identifier = 15 (private parameter negotiation)**
7									Group length octet 1
8									Group length octet 2
9	0	0	0	0	0	0	0	0	**Parameter identifier = 0 (parameter set identification)**
10	0	0	0	0	0	1	0	0	Parameter length = 4
11	0	1	1	0	1	0	0	1	Parameter value = 105 (IA5 character "I")
12	0	0	1	1	0	0	0	1	Parameter value = 49 (IA5 character "1")
13	0	0	1	1	0	0	1	0	Parameter value = 50 (IA5 character "2")
14	0	0	1	1	0	0	1	0	Parameter value = 50 (IA5 character "2")
15	0	0	0	0	0	0	1	0	**Parameter identifier = 2 (cause identifier)**
16	0	0	0	0	0	0	0	1	Parameter length = 1
17									Cause value
18	0	0	0	0	0	0	1	1	**Parameter identifier = 3 (DLCI identifiers)**
19									Parameter length = 2n
20									DLCI value octet 1 (1st DLCI)
21									DLCI value octet 2 (1st DLCI)
•									•
•									•
•									•
2n + 17									DLCI value octet 1 (nth DLCI)
2n + 18									DLCI value octet 2 (nth DLCI)
2n + 19									FCS octet 1
2n + 20									FCS octet 2
2n + 21	0	1	1	1	1	1	1	0	Flag

Figure 13.12   CLLM Message for B or H Channel.

the LAPF core protocol, which does not include a control field. The end system can recognize that this is an XID LAPF control frame containing a CLLM by the address used. The DLCI address used is decimal 1007. On the D channel, this is equivalent to SAPI = 62.

The body of the XID frame, which is the CLLM, begins with a format identifier that marks this as a CLLM message. The remainder of the information field consists of four fields. Each field consists of an identifier subfield that identifies a particular parameter, the length of the parameter value, and finally the value itself. The CLLM consists of the following fields:

- **Group:** Indicates that this information field is "private" in the sense that it contains parameters beyond the scope of the HDLC-specific parameters defined in the HDLC standard (ISO 8885). The length field indicates the length of all of the following parameters.
- **Parameter set identification:** Indicates that this message contains parameters for I.122, which is the frame-mode bearer service.
- **Cause identifier:** Identifies the cause of this message as determined by the congested network node that originated the message.
- **DLCI identifier:** A list of the DLCIs of the frame relay bearer connections that are congested.

The following cause values are recognized:

- Network congestion due to excessive traffic—short term
- Network congestion due to excessive traffic—long term
- Facility or equipment failure—short term
- Facility or equipment failure—long term
- Maintenance action—short term
- Maintenance action—long term
- Unknown—short term
- Unknown—long term

Short term indicates that the condition is anticipated to have a duration of seconds or minutes; otherwise the designation is long term.

13.5 IMPLICIT CONGESTION CONTROL

Implicit signaling occurs when the network discards a frame, and this fact is detected by the end user at a higher, end-to-end layer, such as the Q.922 control protocol. When this occurs, the end user software may deduce that congestion exists.

For example, in a data link control protocol such as the Q.922 control protocol, which uses a sliding-window flow- and error-control technique, the protocol detects the loss of an I-frame in one of two ways:

1. When a frame is dropped by the network, the following frame will generate a REJ frame from the receiving endpoint.
2. When a frame is dropped by the network, no acknowledgment is returned from the other end system. Eventually, the source end system will time out and transmit a command with the P bit set to 1. The subsequent response with the

F bit set to 1 should indicate that the receive sequence number N(R) from the other side is less than the current send sequence number.

Once congestion is detected, the protocol uses flow control to recover from the congestion. Q.922 suggests that a user that is capable of varying the flow-control window size use this mechanism in response to implicit signaling. Let us assume that the layer 2 window size, W, can vary between the parameters W_{min} and W_{max} and is initially set to W_{max}. In general, we would like to reduce W as congestion increases to throttle gradually the transmission of frames. Three classes of adaptive window schemes based on response to one of the two aforementioned conditions have been suggested [CHEN89a, DOSH88]:

1.1 Set $W = Max[W - 1, W_{min}]$.
1.2 Set $W = W_{min}$.
1.3 Set $W = Max[\alpha W, W_{min}]$, where $0 < \alpha < 1$.

Successful transmissions (measured by receipt of acknowledgments) may indicate that the congestion has gone away and window size should be increased. Two possible approaches are as follows:

2.1 Set $W = Min[W + 1, W_{max}]$ after N consecutive successful transmissions, for some fixed value N.
2.2 Set $W = Min[W + 1, W_{max}]$ after W consecutive successful transmissions.

A study reported in [CHEN89a] suggests that the use of strategy 1.3 with $\alpha = 0.5$ plus strategy 2.2 provides good performance over a wide range of network parameters and traffic patterns. This is the strategy recommended in Q.922.

13.6 SUMMARY

The lack of flow- and error-control mechanisms in the LAPF core protocol complicates the task of congestion control in frame relay networks. A variety of complementary approaches to congestion control have been outlined in the ITU-T and ANSI documents:

- **Discard strategy:** The use of the DE bit enables the network to discriminate among frames in making the discard decision.
- **Explicit congestion notification:** Several bits in the address field of LAPF frames plus the CLLM message can be used by the network to alert end users to potential congestion on specific frame relay connections. The end system can then take steps at higher layers to reduce the flow in the forward or backward direction on those connections.
- **Implicit congestion control:** If the network is discarding frames, this fact will become evident at a higher layer that is using flow and error control. Information rates can then be reduced at that higher layer.

13.7 RECOMMENDED READING

Interesting examinations of frame relay congestion control issues are found in [GOLD91], [BERG91], [CHEN89a], [CHEN89b], and [DOSH88].

BERG91   Bergman, W. "Narrowband Frame Relay Congestion Control." *Proceedings, Tenth Annual Phoenix Conference on Computers and Communications*, March 1991.

CHEN89a   Chen, K., and Rege, K. "A Comparative Performance Study of Various Congestion Controls for ISDN Frame Relay Networks." *Proceedings, IEEE INFOCOM '89*, April 1989.

CHEN89b   Chen, K.; Ho, K.; and Saksena, V. "Analysis and Design of a Highly Reliable Transport Architecture for ISDN Frame Relay Networks." *IEEE Journal on Selected Areas in Communications*, October 1989.

DOSH88   Doshi, B., and Nguyen, H. "Congestion Control in ISDN Frame-Relay Networks." *AT&T Technical Journal*, November/December 1988.

GOLD91   Goldstein, F. "Congestion Control in Frame Relay Networks Using Explicit Binary Feedback." *Proceedings, Tenth Annual Phoenix Conference on Computers and Communications*, March 1991.

13.8 PROBLEMS

13.1 A proposed congestion control technique is known as isarithmic control. In this method, the total number of frames in transit is fixed by inserting a fixed number of permits into the network. These permits circulate at random through the frame relay network. Whenever a frame handler wants to relay a frame just given to it by an attached user, it must first capture and destroy a permit. When the frame is delivered to the destination user by the frame handler to which it attaches, that frame handler reissues the permit. List three potential problems with this technique.

13.2 Consider the frame relay network depicted in Figure 13.13. C is the capacity of a link in frames per second. Node A presents a constant load of 0.8 frames per second destined for A'. Node B presents a load λ destined for B'. Node S has a common pool of buffers that it uses for traffic both to A' and B'. When the buffer is full, frames are discarded and are later retransmitted by the source user. S has a throughput capacity of 2. Plot the total throughput (i.e., the sum of A–A' and B–B' delivered traffic) as a function of λ. What fraction of the throughput is A–A' traffic for λ > 1?

13.3 Explicit congestion control may be triggered if the source end system times out waiting for an acknowledgment to a previous protocol data unit (PDU). This raises the question at what value should the timer be set. If the value is too small, there will be many unnecessary retransmissions, wasting network capacity, and unnecessary imposition of congestion control. If the value is too large, the protocol will be sluggish in responding to a lost PDU and in signaling congestion. Because the delay across the network is variable, it may be preferable to use a dynamically calculated timer instead of a fixed value.

One approach would be simply to take the average of observed round-trip times over a number of segments, and then set the retransmission timer equal to a value slightly greater than the average. If the average accurately predicts future round-trip delays, then the resulting retransmission timer will yield good performance. The simple averaging method can be expressed as follows:

$$ARTT(K + 1) = \frac{1}{K + 1}\sum_{i=1}^{K+1} RTT(i)$$

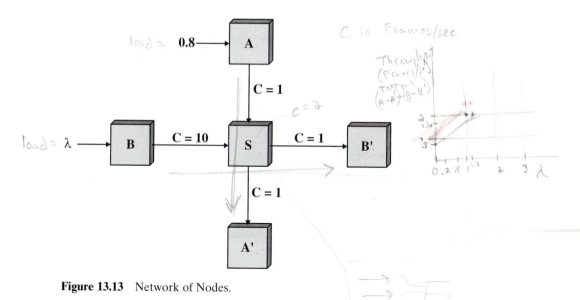

Figure 13.13 Network of Nodes.

where $RTT(K)$ is the round-trip time observed for the Kth transmitted segment, and $ARTT(K)$ is the average round-trip time for the first K segments. This expression can be rewritten as follows:

$$ARTT(K + 1) = \frac{K}{K + 1}ARTT(K) + \frac{1}{K + 1}RTT(K + 1)$$

a. The TCP standard recommends the following formulas for estimating round-trip time and setting the retransmission timer:

$$SRTT(K+1) = \alpha \times SRTT(K) + (1 - \alpha) \times RTT(K+1)$$
$$RXT(K+1) = MIN(UBOUND, MAX(LBOUND, \beta \times SRTT(K + 1)))$$

where $SRTT$ is referred to as the smoothed round-trip time, $RXT(K)$ is the retransmission timer value assigned after the first K segments, UBOUND and LBOUND are prechosen fixed upper and lower bounds on the timer value, and α and β are constants. The recommended initial values for a new connection are $RTT = 0$ seconds and $RXT = 3$ seconds.

Now consider that the observed round-trip times for the first 20 segments on a connection have the following values: 1, 2, 3, 4, 5, 6, 7, 8, 9, 10, 10, 10, 10, 10, 10, 10, 10, 10, 10, 10. Show the values for $ARRT(K)$, $SRTT(K)$, and $RXT(K)$ for this sequence. For the latter two parameters, include results for $\alpha = 0.25, 0.75,$ and 0.875, and $\beta = 1.0$ and 1.25. Ignore UBOUND and LBOUND for this calculation.

b. Repeat part (a) for the sequence 20, 19, 18, 17, 16, 15, 14, 13, 12, 11, 10, 10, 10, 10, 10, 10, 10, 10, 10, 10.

c. What function do α and β perform, and what is the effect of higher and lower values of each? Compare $SRTT$ with $ARTT$.

13.4 The technique specified in the TCP standard and described in the previous problem enables a TCP entity to adapt to changes in round-trip time. However, it does not cope well with a situation in which the round-trip time exhibits a relatively high variance. To cope with this, Von Jacobsen proposed a refinement to the standard algorithm that has now been officially adopted for use with TCP. The algorithm can be summarized as follows:

$$SRTT(K + 1) = (1 - \gamma) \times SRTT(K) + \gamma \times RTT(K + 1)$$
$$ERR(K + 1) = RTT(K + 1) - SRTT(K)$$
$$SDEV(K + 1) = SDEV(K) + \gamma \times (|ERR(K + 1)| - SDEV(K))$$
$$= (1 - \gamma) \times SDEV(K) + \gamma \times |ERR(K + 1)|$$
$$RXT(K + 1) = SRTT(K + 1) + 2 \times SDEV(K + 1)$$

where *SDEV* is the smoothed estimate of deviation of round-trip time, and *ERR* is the difference between the predicted and observed values of round-trip time.

a. Show the values of $SRTT(K)$ and $RXT(K)$ for the same sequences used in parts (a) and (b) of the preceding problem, for $\gamma = 0.75, 0.25$, and 0.125.

b. Compare Von Jacobsen's algorithm with the original TCP algorithm. What does the Von Jacobsen algorithm do? How is it superior to the original algorithm?

13.5 The Von Jacobsen algorithm is quite effective in tracking the round-trip time until there is a period in which the variability of round-trip times is high or until there is a need to retransmit segments due to timer expiration.

a. What problem does retransmission cause in estimating round-trip time?

b. Suggest and justify a way to compensate for retransmissions. *Hint:* The approach mandated for TCP, known as Karn's algorithm, is as follows: Follow the Von Jacobsen algorithm until a timer expires, necessitating retransmission. Then use a different strategy until an acknowledgment arrives before a timer expires. Now all you need to do is come up with this alternative strategy.

Broadband ISDN

Although some work still continues on the recommendations for narrowband ISDN, especially in the area of frame relay, the structure and most of the details for narrowband ISDN are now in final form. Since 1988, the attention of ITU-T has focused on a far more ambitious undertaking, broadband ISDN (B-ISDN).

Chapter 14 provides an overview of B-ISDN, beginning with an examination of the variety of services that this high-speed network is designed to support. The chapter also discusses the requirements at the user–network interface and the functional architecture at that interface.

Chapter 15 surveys the protocols associated with the B-ISDN user–network interface. Following a discussion of the overall protocol reference model, the chapter focuses on the physical layer aspects. The chapter also discusses SONET/SDH, which is a separate set of standards that are also used at the B-ISDN physical layer.

CHAPTER 14

BROADBAND ISDN ARCHITECTURE

As we saw in Chapter 5, the planning for ISDN began as far back as 1976 and has only in recent years moved from the planning stage to prototypes and actual implementations. It will be a number of years before the full spectrum of ISDN services is widely available, and there will continue to be refinements of and improvements to ISDN services and network facilities. Nevertheless, with the publication of the 1988 "Blue Book" set of recommendations from CCITT, the bulk of the work on ISDN is complete. To be sure, future versions of the standards will provide refinements and enhancements to ISDN. But since 1988, much of the planning and design effort has become directed toward a network concept that is more revolutionary than ISDN itself. This new concept is broadband ISDN (B-ISDN).

ITU-T modestly defines B-ISDN as "a service requiring transmission channels capable of supporting rates greater than the primary rate." Behind this innocuous statement lie plans for a network and set of services that will have far more impact on business and residential customers than ISDN. With B-ISDN, services, especially video services, requiring data rates orders of magnitudes beyond those that can be delivered by ISDN will become available. These include support for image processing, video, and high-capacity workstations and local area networks (LANs). To contrast this new network and these new services to the original concept of ISDN, that original concept is now referred to as narrowband ISDN.

The primary triggers for evolving toward the B-ISDN include an increasing demand for high-bit-rate services, especially image and video services, and the evolution of technology to support those services. The key developments in technology are as follows:

- Optical fiber transmission systems that can offer low-cost, high-data-rate transmission channels for network trunks and for subscriber lines
- Microelectronic circuits that can offer high-speed, low-cost building blocks for switching, transmission, and subscriber equipment

- High-quality video monitors and cameras that can, with sufficient production quantities, be offered at low cost

These advances in technology will result in the integration of a wide range of communications facilities and the support of, in effect, universal communications with the following key characteristics:

- Worldwide exchange between any two subscribers in any medium or combination of media
- Retrieval and sharing of massive amounts of information from multiple sources, in multiple media, among people in a shared electronic environment
- Distribution, including switched distribution, of a wide variety of cultural, entertainment, and educational materials to home or office, virtually on demand

We begin our examination of B-ISDN in this chapter. First, we look at the standards that are being developed by ITU-T and others for B-ISDN. Next we discuss the services that B-ISDN is intended to provide, and then we look at the requirements these services impose on B-ISDN. Finally, we discuss the B-ISDN architecture at the user–network interface.

14.1 B-ISDN STANDARDS

In 1988, as part of its I-series of recommendations on ISDN, CCITT issued the first two recommendations relating to B-ISDN: I.113, *Vocabulary of Terms for Broadband Aspects of ISDN,* and I.121, *Broadband Aspects of ISDN.* These documents represented the level of consensus reached among the participants concerning the nature of the future B-ISDN, as of late 1988. They provided a preliminary description and a basis for future standardization and development work. Some of the important notions developed in these documents are presented in Table 14.1. Table 14.2 lists the factors that are guiding ITU-T work on B-ISDN.

Since 1988, the work within CCITT (now ITU-T) has been guided by the concepts outlined in Tables 14.1 and 14.2. The result, so far, has been the publication of a number of recommendations in the I-series that specifically relate to B-ISDN. These are listed in Table 14.3.

Mention should be made at this point of the ATM Forum, which is playing a crucial role in the development of ISDN standards. In the ITU and the constituent member bodies from the participating countries, the process of developing standards is characterized by wide participation by government, users, and industry representatives and by consensus decision making. This process can be quite time-consuming. While ITU-T has streamlined its efforts, the delays involved in developing standards are particularly significant in the area of B-ISDN, which is dominated by the rapidly evolving asynchronous transfer mode (ATM) technology. Because of the strong level of interest in ATM technology, the ATM Forum was

Table 14.1 Noteworthy Statements in I.113 and I.121

Broadband: A service or a system requiring transmission channels capable of supporting rates greater than the primary rate.

The term *B-ISDN* is used for convenience in order to refer to and emphasize the broadband aspects of ISDN. The intent, however, is that there be one comprehensive notion of an ISDN that provides broadband and other ISDN services.

Asynchronous transfer mode (ATM) is the transfer mode for implementing B-ISDN and is independent of the means of transport at the physical layer.

B-ISDN will be based on the concepts developed for ISDN and may evolve by progressively incorporating directly into the network additional B-ISDN functions enabling new and advanced services.

Since the B-ISDN is based on overall ISDN concepts, the ISDN access reference configuration is also the basis for the B-ISDN reference configuration.

Table 14.2 Factors Guiding ITU-T Work on B-ISDN (I.121)

The emerging demand for broadband services

The availability of high-speed transmission, switching, and signal-processing technologies

The improved data- and image-processing capabilities available to the user

The advances in software application processing in the computer and telecommunications industries

The need to integrate both interactive and distribution services

The need to integrate both circuit- and packet-transfer mode into one universal broadband network

The need to provide flexibility in satisfying the requirements of both user and operator

The need to cover broadband aspects of ISDN in ITU-T recommendations

created with the goal of accelerating the development of ATM standards. The ATM Forum has seen more active participation from computing vendors than has been the case in ITU-T. Because the forum works on the basis of majority rule rather than consensus, it has been able to move rapidly to define some of the needed details for the implementation of ATM [PRAS93]. This effort, in turn, has fed into the ITU-T standardization effort.

Table 14.3 ITU-T Recommendations on Broadband ISDN

Number	Title	Date
I.113	Vocabulary of Terms for Broadband Aspects of ISDN	1997
I.121	Broadband Aspects of ISDN	1991
I.150	B-ISDN ATM Functional Characteristics	1995
I.211	B-ISDN Service Aspects	1993
I.311	B-ISDN General Network Aspects	1996
I.321	B-ISDN Protocol Reference Model and Its Application	1991
I.327	B-ISDN Functional Architecture	1993
I.356	B-ISDN ATM Layer Cell Transfer Performance	1993
I.357	B-ISDN Semipermanent Connection Availability	1996
I.361	B-ISDN ATM Layer Specification	1995
I.363	B-ISDN ATM Adaptation Layer (AAL) Specification	1993
I.363.1	B-ISDN ATM Adaptation Layer (AAL) Specification: Type 1 AAL	1996
I.363.3	B-ISDN ATM Adaptation Layer (AAL) Specification: Type 3/4 AAL	1996
I.363.5	B-ISDN ATM Adaptation Layer (AAL) Specification: Type 5 AAL	1996
I.364	Support of Broadband Connectionless Data Service on B-ISDN	1995
I.371	Traffic Control and Congestion Control in B-ISDN	1996
I.413	B-ISDN User–Network Interface	1993
I.414	Overview of Recommendations on Layer 1 for ISDN and B-ISDN Customer Access	1993
I.432.1	B-ISDN UNI Physical Layer Specification: General Characteristics	1996
I.432.2	B-ISDN UNI Physical Layer Specification: 155.520 Mbps and 622.080 Mbps Operation	1996
I.432.3	B-ISDN UNI Physical Layer Specification: 1.544 Mbps and 2.048 Mbps Operation	1996
I.432.4	B-ISDN UNI Physical Layer Specification: 51.840 Mbps Operation	1996
I.432.5	B-ISDN UNI Physical Layer Specification: 25.600 Mbps Operation	1997
I.580	General Arrangements for Interworking Between B-ISDN and 64 kbit/s Based ISDN	1995
I.610	B-ISDN Operation and Maintenance Principles and Functions	1995
I.731	Types and General Characteristics of ATM Equipment	1996
I.732	Functional Characteristics of ATM Equipment	1996
I.751	ATM Management of the Network Element View	1996

14.2 BROADBAND SERVICES

When the capacity available to the ISDN user is increased substantially, the range of services that ISDN can support also increases substantially. ITU-T classifies the services that could be provided by a B-ISDN into interactive services and distribution services (Figure 14.1). Interactive services are those in which there is a two-way exchange of information (other than control-signaling information) between two

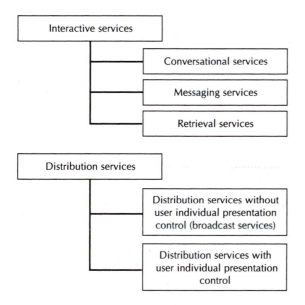

Figure 14.1 Broadband Services.

subscribers or between a subscriber and a service provider. These include conversational services, messaging services, and retrieval services. Distribution services are those in which the information transfer is primarily one way, from service provider to B-ISDN subscriber. These include broadcast services, for which the user has no control over the presentation of the information, and cyclical services (explained subsequently), which allow the user some measure of presentation control.

Conversational Services

Conversational services provide the means for bidirectional dialogue communication with bidirectional, real-time (not store-and-forward), end-to-end information transfer between two users or between a user and a service provider host. These services support the general transfer of data specific to a given user application. That is, the information is generated by and exchanged between users; it is not "public" information.

This category encompasses a wide range of applications and data types, including moving pictures (video), data, and document. In the long run, perhaps the most important category of B-ISDN service is video conversational services, and perhaps the most important of these services is video telephony. Video telephony simply means that the telephone instrument includes a video transmit and receive/display capability so that dial-up calls include both voice and live picture. The first use of this service is likely to be the office environment. It can be used in any situation where the visual component of a call is advantageous, including sales, consulting, instruction, negotiation, and the discussion of visual information, such as reports, charts, advertising layouts, and so on. As the cost of videophone terminals declines, it is likely that this will be a popular residential service as well.

Another video conversational service is videoconference. The simplest form of this service is a point-to-point capability, which can be used to connect conference rooms. This differs from videophone in the nature of the equipment used. Accordingly, the service must specify the interface and protocols to be used to assure compatible equipment between conference rooms. A point-to-point videoconference would specify additional features, such as facsimile and document transfer and the use of special equipment such as electronic blackboards. A different sort of videoconference is a multipoint service. This would allow participants to tie together single videophones in a conference connection, without leaving their workplaces, using a video conference server within the network. Such a system would support a small number (e.g., five) of simultaneous users. Either one participant would appear on all screens at a time, as managed by the video conference server, or a split-screen technique could be used.

A third variant of video conversational service is video surveillance. This is not a distribution service, because the information delivery is limited to a specific intended subscriber. This form of service can be unidirectional; if the information is simple video images generated by a fixed camera, then the information flow is only from video source to subscriber. A reverse flow would come into play if the user had control over the camera (change orientation, zoom, etc.). The final example listed in the table is video/audio information transmission service. This is essentially the same capability as video telephony. The difference is that a higher-quality image may be required. For example, computer animation that represents a detailed engineering design may require much higher resolution than ordinary human-to-human conversation.

Another type of conversational service is for data. In this context, the term *data* means arbitrary information whose structure is not visible to ISDN. Examples of applications that would use this service include the following:

- File transfer in a distributed architecture of computer and storage systems (load sharing, back-up systems, decentralized databases, etc.)
- Large-volume or high-speed transmission of measured values or control information
- Program downloading
- Computer-aided design and manufacturing (CAD/CAM)
- Connection of local area networks (LANs) at different locations

Finally, there is a conversational transfer of documents. This could include very high resolution facsimile or the transfer of mixed documents that might include text, facsimile images, voice annotation, and/or a video component. Two types of applications are likely here: a document-transfer service for the exchange of documents between users at workstations and a document storage system, based on the document-transfer service, which provides document servers for the filing, update, and access of documents by a community of users.

Messaging Services

Messaging services offer user-to-user communication between individual users via storage units with store-and-forward, mailbox, and/or message-handling (e.g., information editing, processing, and conversion) functions. In contrast to conversational services, messaging services are not in real time. Hence, they place lesser demands on the network and do not require that both users be available at the same time. Analogous narrowband services are X.400 and teletex.

One new form of messaging service that could be supported by ISDN is video mail, analogous to today's electronic mail (text/graphic mail), and voice mail. Just as electronic mail replaces the mailing of a letter, so video mail replaces mailing a video cassette. This may become one of the most powerful and useful forms of message communication. Similarly, a document mail service allows the transmission of mixed documents, containing text, graphics, voice, and/or video components.

Retrieval Services

Retrieval services provide the user with the capability to retrieve information stored in information centers that is, in general, available for public use. This information is sent to the user on demand only. The information can be retrieved on an individual basis; that is, the time at which an information sequence is to start is under the control of the user.

An analogous narrowband service is Videotex. This is an interactive system designed to service both home and business needs. It is a general-purpose database retrieval system that can use the public switched telephone network or an interactive metropolitan cable TV system. Figure 14.2 depicts a typical system. The Videotex provider maintains a variety of databases on a central computer. Some of these are public databases provided by the Videotex system. Others are vendor-supplied services, such as a stock market advisory. Information is provided in the form of pages of text and simple graphics.

Broadband videotex is an enhancement of the existing Videotex system [SUGI88]. The user would be able to select sound passages, high-resolution images of TV standard, and short video scenes, in addition to the current text and simplified graphics. Examples of broadband videotex services include the following:

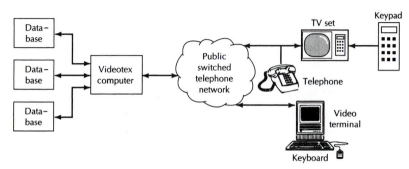

Figure 14.2 A Typical Videotex System.

- Retrieval of encyclopedia entries
- Results of quality tests on consumer goods
- Computer-supported audiovisual entries
- Electronic mail-order catalogs and travel brochures with the option of placing a direct order or making a direct booking

Another retrieval service is video retrieval. With this service, a user could order full-length films or videos from a film/video library facility. Because the provider may have to satisfy many requests, bandwidth considerations dictate that only a small number of different video transmissions can be supported at any one time. A realistic service would offer perhaps 500 movies/videos for each two-hour period. Using a 50-Mbps video channel, this would require a manageable 25-Gbps transmission capacity from video suppliers to distribution points. The user would be informed by the provider at what time the film will be available to be viewed or transmitted to the subscriber's video recorder.

Of greater interest to business, educational, and medical organizations, the envisioned broadband retrieval service would also allow the retrieval of high-resolution images such as X-ray or computerized axial tomography (CAT) scans, mixed-media documents, and large data files. This service could also be used for remote education and training.

Distribution Services without User Presentation Control

Services in this category are also referred to as broadcast services. They provide a continuous flow of information, which is distributed from a central source to an unlimited number of authorized receivers connected to the network. Each user can access this flow of information but has no control over it. In particular, the user cannot control the starting time or order of the presentation of the broadcasted information. All users simply tap into the flow of information.

The most common example of this service is broadcast television. Currently, broadcast television is available from network broadcast via radio waves and through cable television distribution systems. With the capacities planned for B-ISDN, this service can be integrated with the other telecommunications services. In addition, higher resolutions can now be achieved, and it is anticipated that these higher-quality services will also be available via B-ISDN.

An example of a nonvideo service is an electronic newspaper broadcast service. This would permit the transmission of facsimile images of newspaper pages to subscribers who had paid for the service.

Distribution Services with User Presentation Control

Services in this class also distribute information from a central source to a large number of users. However, the information is provided as a sequence of information entities (e.g., frames) with cyclical repetition. So the user has the ability of individual access to the cyclical distributed information and can control start and order of presentation. Due to the cyclical repetition, the information entities, selected by the user, will always be presented from the beginning.

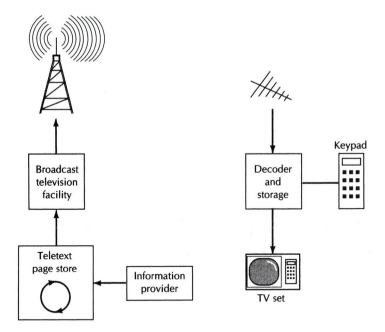

Figure 14.3 A Typical Teletext System.

An analogous narrowband service is Teletext, which is depicted in Figure 14.3. Teletext is a simple one-way system that uses unallocated portions of the bandwidth of a broadcast TV signal. At the transmission end, a fixed set of pages of text is sent repeatedly in round-robin fashion. The receiver consists of a special decoder and storage unit, a keypad for user entry, and an ordinary TV set. The user keys in the number of the page desired. The decoder reads that page from the incoming signal, stores it, and displays it continuously until instructed to do otherwise. Typically, pages of Teletext form a tree pattern, with higher-level pages containing menus that guide the selection of lower-level pages. Thus, although the system appears inter-active to the user, it is actually a one-way broadcast of information. Because only a small portion of the TV signal bandwidth is used for this purpose, the number of pages is limited by a desire to reduce access time. A typical system will support a few hundred pages with a cycle time of a few tens of seconds.

Teletext is oriented primarily to the home market, with different sets of pages offered on different channels. Examples of information presented by such a system are stock market reports, weather reports, news, leisure information, and recipes.

With B-ISDN, an enhancement to Teletext known as cabletext can be pro-vided. Whereas Teletext uses only a small portion of an analog TV channel, cable-text would use a full digital broadband channel for cyclical transmission of pages with text, images, and possible video and audio passages. As an electronic newspa-per that uses public networks, or as an in-house information system for trade fairs, hotels, and hospitals, cabletext will provide low-cost access to timely and frequently requested information. A typical system might allow access to 10,000 pages with a cycle time of 1 second [ARMB87].

Table 14.4 Applications Having Good Prospects for Broadband ATM-Based Services [DEMA93]

(a) Business	(b) Residential
High-Speed Image Networking —Design automation (CAD/CAM/CAE) —Medical imaging/consultation —Photographic editing —Scientific visualization —High-resolution graphics/image rendering	Distribution Video —Broadcast TV/HDTV —Broadcast distance learning —Enhanced pay-per-view (near video-on-demand) —Video-on-demand —Video catalog/advertising —Teleshopping
Interactive Multimedia —Interactive teletraining —Work-at-home/telecommuting —Executive (desktop) teleconferencing —Print/publishing collaboration —Subject-matter-expert consultation —Virtual reality —Multimedia telephony	Interactive Multimedia —Multimedia electronic mail —Multimedia 700, 800, and 900 services —Sports event simulcasting/telewagering —Interactive distance learning —Multimedia videotext/"Yellow Pages" —Interactive TV/games —Multimedia telephony and virtual reality
Wide Area Network Distributed Computing —LAN backbone/interconnect —Host-to-host channel networking —Disaster recovery/information vaulting —Load sharing	

Business and Residential Services

A different way of organizing the types of services that can be supported by a B-ISDN is to group those services into business and residential categories. Table 14.4 lists services that are likely to be supported with B-ISDN and its related ATM technology.

In the business world, the changes both in organizational structure and in the degree of reliance on high-capacity, high-speed networked computing suggest an increasing demand for high-capacity broadband communications. In particular, in many organizations, some or all of the following factors will come into play:

- Increasing use of applications involving high volumes of data, including high-resolution graphics and image processing
- A distributed client/server architecture, with communication across an internet
- Increasing reliance on multiple-LAN, multiple-site configuration

In the residential category, nonbusiness consumers want more advanced telecommunications services that build on their familiarity with telephone and cable TV services. Entertainment and "useful" applications, at the right price, will dominate this market.

14.3 REQUIREMENTS

To get some sense of what is required for a broadband ISDN, we need to look at the requirements it must satisfy. As a first step, the B-ISDN services presented in Section 14.2 provide a qualitative description of requirements. To decide on the

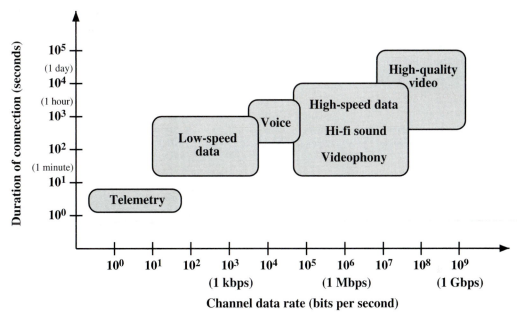

Figure 14.4 Data Rate and Duration of Potential Broadband ISDN Services [PRYC93b].

transmission structure, we need some ideas of the data rate requirements of the subscriber. Figure 14.4 provides an estimate. As can be seen, the potential range of data rates is wide. The figure also gives estimated durations of calls, which is also a factor in network design.

Another estimate of data rate requirements is shown in Table 14.5. Note that the values here differ from those in Figure 14.4. In both cases, the numbers can only be estimates for the projected services, and the differences point out the uncertainty in planning that will face B-ISDN designers. The column labeled CBR/VBR refers to whether support for this service requires a constant-bit-rate or a variable-bit-rate transmission facility. The table also includes the useful parameter of burst ratio, the ratio of the time for which the channel is occupied to the time during which information is sent. This quantity provides guidance on the type of switching technology (circuit switching versus packet switching) appropriate for BISDN. The last two columns in the table deal with error and delay characteristics when ATM cell transmission is used; this topic is explored in Part Five.

It is worth elaborating briefly on the data rate requirements for video transmission, because it is video that will drive the overall data rate requirement. The transmission of an analog video signal requires on the order of 6 MHz bandwidth. Using straightforward digitization techniques, the data rate required for digital video transmission can be as much as 1 Gbps. This is clearly too high even for a network based on optical fiber and high-speed switches. Two complementary approaches are used to reduce bit rate requirements:

- Use data-compression techniques that remove redundancy or unnecessary information.
- Allow for distortions that are least objectionable to the human eye.

Table 14.5 Characteristics of Various Traffic Types [DUBO92]

Service Type	Service Category	Bandwidth Range	CBR/ VBR	Burst Lengths	Burst Ratio	Cell Loss Tolerance	Cell Delay Tolerance
Voice	PCM voice	64 kbps	CBR	1	N/A	10^{-4} to 10^{-6}	10–150 ms
	ADPCM voice	32 kbps	CBR	1	N/A	10^{-4} to 10^{-6}	10–150 ms
	Predictive coding	16 kbps	VBR	5–15	2–3 KB	10^{-6} to 10^{-8}	10–150 ms
	High-quality voice	192–384 kbps	CBR	1	N/A	10^{-5} to 10^{-6}	10–150 ms
	Voice mail	16–64 kbps	CBR/ VBR	1–3	N/A	10^{-6}	500 ms–5 s
	CD-quality voice	1.4 Mbps	CBR	1	N/A	10^{-6}	500 ms–25 s
	Video teleconferencing/voice part	64–192 kbps	CBR	1	N/A	10^{-7} to 10^{-9}	10–150 ms
Data	LAN interconnection	1.5–100 Mbps	VBR	vary	100–1000 B	10^{-12}	10–100 ms
	Host-host file transfer	64 kbps–1.5 Mbps	VBR	1	12 KB–10 MB	10^{-12}	1–500 s
	PC file transfer	9.6–64 kbps	VBR	1	1 KB–1 MB	10^{-9}	10–100 s
	Client/server system	10–100 Mbps	VBR	1000	1–500 KB	10^{-9}	10–500 ms
	Remote database access	1–10 Mbps	VBR	1000	100 B–100 KB	10^{-9}	1m–10 s
	Remote procedure call	6–60 Mbps	VBR	15–20	60–1000 B	10^{-9}	100 µs–100 ms
	Electronic mail	9.6 kbps–1.5 Mbps	CBR	1	50–5000 B	10^{-9}	1–10 s
	Workstation CAD/CAM	64 kbps–1.5 Mbps	VBR	5	40–100 KB	10^{-9}	1–10 s
	Mainframe CAD/CAM	1.5–36 Mbps	VBR	10–100	100 KB–1 MB	10^{-9}	10–60 s
	Transaction processing	64 kbps–5 Mbps	VBR	40	100–300 B	10^{-9}	1–3 s
	Time sharing	2.4–64 kbps	VBR	30–100	20–4000 B	10^{-9}	100 ms–10 s
Video	Video telephony	64 kbps–2 Mbps	CBR/ VBR	2–5	2–10 KB	10^{-9}	150–350 ms
	Videoconferencing	128 kbps–14 Mbps	CBR/ VBR	2–5	1.6–40 KB	10^{-9}	150–350 ms
	Video/image mail	1–4 Mbps	CBR	1	64 KB–1 MB	10^{-10}	1–5 s
	Broadband videotex	64 kbps–10 Mbps	VBR	10	> 1 MB	10^{-7} to 10^{-10}	0.1–2 s
	NTSC-quality TV	15–44 Mbps	VBR	2–5	0.5–1.3 MB	10^{-10}	40 ms
	HDTV-quality TV	150 Mbps	VBR	2–5	5–14 MB	10^{-12}	40 ms
	Video browsing	2–40 Mbps	CBR	1	0.5–40 MB	10^{-9}	0.1–2 s
	Group 4 fax (400 × 400)	64 kbps	CBR	1	256–640 KB	10^{-8}	4–10 s
	Medical X-ray (14 × 17 in)	1.5–10 Mbps	CBR/ VBR	25	5–8 MB	10^{-12}	2 s
	Medical MRI/ CAT scan	10–200 Mbps	CBR/ VBR	25	250 kb–3 MB	10^{-12}	2 s
	High-resolution graphics	100 Mbps–10 Gbps	VBR	25	1–100 MB	10^{-12}	10–500 ms

Table 14.6 Applications of Compressed Video [ACKL93]

Market	Data rate	Standard	Resolution (pixels × lines)	Frame rate (frames per second)
Analog videophone	5–10 kbps	none*	170 × 128	2–5
Basic-rate video telephony	56–128 kbps	P×64	176 × 144	5–10
Business conferencing	≥ 384 kbps	P×64	352 × 288	15–30
Interactive multimedia	1–2 Mbps	MPEG	up to 352 × 288	15–30
Digital NTSC	3–10 Mbps	NTSC	720 × 480	30
High-definition television	> 15 Mbps	FCC	1200 × 800	60

* Several standards initiatives are in progress:

P×64: a set of standards established by ITU-T for video telephony and conferencing

MPEG: Motion Picture Experts Group, which sets ISO standards for video, particularly CD-ROM

FCC: Federal Communications Commission

NTSC: National Television Systems Committee, which sets standards for television and video playback and recording in the United States.

Knowing what information is necessary and the types of acceptable distortion requires an in-depth understanding of the image source to be coded and of human vision. With this knowledge, one can apply various coding techniques and engineering tradeoffs to achieve the best image possible.

What is acceptable image quality and data rate is a function of application. For example, videophone and videoconferencing require both transmission and reception. To limit the engineering requirements at the subscriber site, we would like to limit drastically the video transmission data rate. Fortunately, in the case of videophone, the resolution required, especially for residential applications, is modest, and in the case of both videoconference and videophone, the rate of change of the picture is generally low. This latter property can be exploited with interframe redundancy-compression techniques, as opposed to merely the intraframe compression techniques used in systems such as facsimile.

Table 14.6 indicates the relationship between the quality of the video image and the data rate required. At the low end of the spectrum is the use of ordinary analog telephone lines to support video transmission. The compressed-video data rate is limited to about 10 kbps, in turn limiting the picture resolution and frame rate, thereby limiting the picture quality.

The first four categories are often referred to as low-bit-rate encoding systems, which are defined as systems that transmit at data rates of about 2 Mbps or less [HASK87]. For business conferencing and interactive multimedia, there is reduced resolution compared with broadcast television and reduced ability to track movement. In general, this produces acceptable quality. However, if there is rapid movement in the scene being televised, this will appear as jerky, discontinuous movement on the viewer's screen. Furthermore, if there is a desire to transmit a high-resolution graphics image (e.g., during a presentation at a videoconference), then the resolution on the screen may be inadequate. To overcome this latter problem, the transmitter should be capable of switching between a full-motion, lower-resolution transmission and a freeze-frame, higher-resolution transmission at the same data rate.

At present, a data rate of 64 kbps produces a noticeably inferior picture. This data rate may be acceptable for videophone. However, the distinction among the first four categories may disappear as advances in coding technology continue.

Digital NTSC coding corresponds to the quality of analog broadcast television today.

Finally, the highest-quality standard is known as high-definition television (HDTV). This system is comparable in resolution with 35-mm film projection and will put the quality of TV reception in the home and office at the level of the cinema. With HDTV, not only is the resolution greater, but the system will support wider screens, more along the lines of cinema screens in height–width ratio.

Table 14.6 provides a rather large range of data rates within most of the categories. This is for two reasons. First, the technology of digital video coding is evolving rapidly, and this table attempts to predict the rates needed. Second, a distinction is made between two types of signals:

- Contribution, where the signal is transferred between studios and is subject to postproduction studio processing.
- Distribution, where the signal is distributed for viewing and is not subject to such processing.

Generally, a higher degree of compression can be applied for distribution than for contribution signals.

The estimates in Figure 14.4 show that broadband services require the network to handle a wide range of call types, from those with short holding times (e.g., file transfer) to those with long holding times (e.g., distributive services), at a wide range of data rates. Also, it is to be expected that many of these services will show the same busy-hour characteristics of narrowband ISDN services, with peaks during business hours.

14.4 ARCHITECTURE

The B-ISDN will differ from a narrowband ISDN in a number of ways. To meet the requirements for high-resolution video, an upper channel rate of about 150 Mbps will be needed. To support one or more interactive and distributive services simultaneously, a total subscriber line rate of about 600 Mbps is needed. In terms of today's installed telephone plant, this is a stupendous data rate to sustain. The most appropriate technology for widespread support of such data rates is optical fiber. Hence, the introduction of B-ISDN depends on the pace of introduction of fiber subscriber loops.

Internal to the network, there is the issue of the switching technique to be used. The switching facility will have to be capable of handling a wide range of different bit rates and traffic parameters (e.g., burstiness). Despite the increasing power of digital circuit-switching hardware and the increasing use of optical fiber trunking, it may be difficult to handle the large and diverse requirements of B-ISDN with circuit-switching technology. For this reason, there is increasing interest in fast

Table 14.7 Principles of B-ISDN (I.121)

1. Asynchronous transfer mode (ATM) is the transfer mode for implementing B-ISDN and is independent of the means of transport at the physical layer.
2. B-ISDN supports switched, semipermanent, and permanent point-to-point and point-to-multipoint connections, and provides on demand reserved and permanent services. Connections in B-ISDN support both circuit-mode and packet-mode services of a mono- and/or multimedia type and of a connectionless or connection-oriented nature and in a bidirectional or unidirectional configuration.
3. The B-ISDN architecture is detailed in functional terms and is, therefore, technology- and implementation-independent.
4. A B-ISDN will contain intelligent capabilities for the purpose of providing advanced service characteristics and supporting powerful operation and maintenance tools, network control, and management. Further inclusion of additional intelligent features has to be considered in an overall context and may be allocated to different network/terminal elements.
5. Since the B-ISDN is based on overall ISDN concepts, the ISDN access reference configuration is also the basis for the B-ISDN access reference configuration.
6. A layered structure approach, as used in established ISDN protocols, is also appropriate for similar studies in B-ISDN. This approach should be used for studies on other overall aspects of B-ISDN, including information transfer, control, intelligence, and management.
7. Any expression of network capabilities or change in network performance parameters will not degrade the quality of service of existing services.
8. The evolution of B-ISDN should ensure the continued support of existing interfaces and services.
9. New network capabilities will be incorporated into B-ISDN in evolutionary steps to meet new user requirements and accommodate advances in network developments and progress in technology.
10. It is recognized that B-ISDN may be implemented in a variety of ways according to specific national situations.

packet switching as the basic switching technique for B-ISDN. This form of switching readily supports the user–network interface protocol known as asynchronous transfer mode (ATM), which is examined in detail in Part Five.

Table 14.7, taken from recommendation I.121, lists the principles of B-ISDN and is suggestive of its architecture.

Functional Architecture

Figure 14.5 depicts the functional architecture of B-ISDN (compare Figure 5.5). As with narrowband ISDN, control of B-ISDN is based on common-channel signaling. Within the network, an SS7, enhanced to support the expanded capabilities of a higher-speed network, will be used. Similarly, the user–network control signaling protocol will be an enhanced version of Q.931.

B-ISDN must of course support all of the 64-kbps transmission services, both circuit switching and packet switching, that are supported by narrowband ISDN. This protects the user's investment and facilitates migration from narrowband to broadband ISDN. In addition, broadband capabilities are provided for higher-data-rate transmission services. At the user–network interface, these capabilities will be provided with the connection-oriented asynchronous transfer mode (ATM) facility.

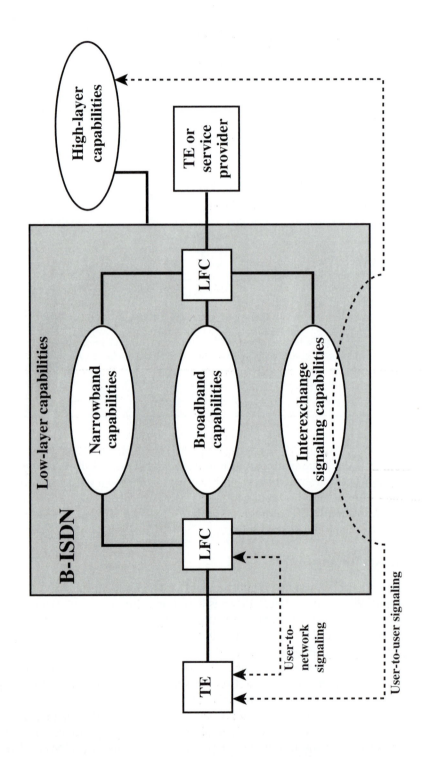

LFC = local function capabilities
TE = terminal equipment

Figure 14.5 B-ISDN Architecture.

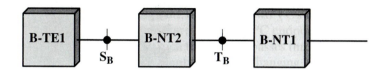

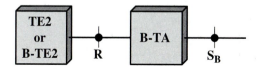

Figure 14.6   B-ISDN Reference Points and Functional Groupings.

User–Network Interface

The reference configuration defined in I.411 is considered general enough to be used for B-ISDN. Figure 14.6, which is almost identical to Figure 6.2, shows the reference configuration for B-ISDN. To illustrate clearly the broadband aspects, the notations for reference points and functional groupings are labeled with the letter B (e.g., B-NT1, T_B). The broadband functional groups are equivalent to the functional groups defined in I.411 and discussed in Section 5.2 of this book. Interfaces at the R reference point may or may not have broadband capabilities.

Figure 14.7 is a general depiction of the B-ISDN user-access architecture. The local exchange to which subscribers attach must be able to handle both B-ISDN and ISDN subscribers. ISDN subscribers can be supported with twisted pair at the basic and primary access rates. For B-ISDN subscribers, optical fiber will be used. The data rate from network to subscriber will need to be on the order of 600 Mbps to handle multiple video distributions, such as might be required in an office environment. The data rate from subscriber to network would normally need to be much less, because the typical subscriber does not initiate distribution services. A rate of about 150 Mbps or less is probably adequate.

Transmission Structure

In terms of data rates available to B-ISDN subscribers, three new transmission services are defined. The first of these consists of a full-duplex 155.52-Mbps service. The second service defined is asymmetrical, providing transmission from the subscriber to the network at 155.52 Mbps and in the other direction at 622.08 Mbps. And the highest-capacity service yet defined is a full-duplex 622.08-Mbps service.

A data rate of 155.52 Mbps can certainly support all of the narrowband ISDN services. That is, it readily supports one or more basic or primary-rate interfaces. In addition, it can support most of the B-ISDN services. At that rate, one or several video channels can be supported, depending on the video resolution and the coding technique used. Thus, the full-duplex 155.52-Mbps service will probably be the most common B-ISDN service.

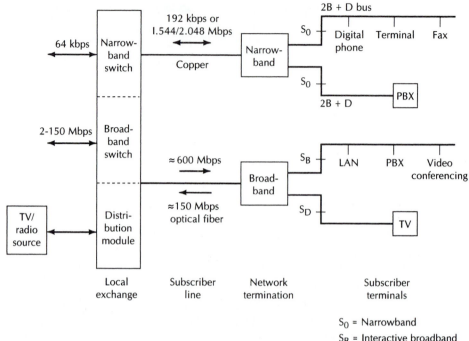

Figure 14.7 Block Diagram of Broadband ISDN User–Network Interface.

The higher data rate of 622.08 Mbps is needed to handle multiple video distribution, such as might be required when a business conducts multiple simultaneous videoconferences. This data rate makes sense in the network-to-subscriber direction. The typical subscriber will not initiate distribution services and thus would still be able to use the lower, 155.52-Mbps service. The full-duplex 622.08-Mbps service would be appropriate for a video distribution provider.

The 1988 document (I.121) discussed the need for a 150-Mbps and 600-Mbps data rate service. The specific rates chosen for the final standards were designed to be compatible with defined digital transmission services.

The 1988 document also included a list of specific channel data rates to be supported within these services. The final standards drop all reference to channel rates. This allows the user and the network to negotiate any channel capacity that can fit in the available capacity provided by the network. Thus, B-ISDN becomes considerably more flexible and can be tailored precisely to a wide variety of applications.

14.5 SUMMARY

Although the development and deployment of ISDN is not yet complete, planners and designers are already looking toward a much more revolutionary change in telecommunications: the broadband ISDN. Advances in terminal technology, optical fiber transmission technology, and switching technology, together with a rising demand for information-rich services, are accelerating the telecommunications environment through ISDN to a B-ISDN before the end of the century. Just as the capacity of B-ISDN is several orders of magnitude greater than ISDN, its impact will also be greater.

14.6 RECOMMENDED READING

[KUMA95] is a useful survey of technologies and applications related to B-ISDN.

KUMA95   Kumar, B. *Broadband Communications: A Professional Guide to ATM, Frame Relay, SMDS, SONET, and B-ISDN.* New York: McGraw-Hill, 1995.

14.7 PROBLEMS

14.1   Is there a need to enhance or otherwise modify Signaling System Number 7 to support broadband ISDN?

14.2   Is there a need to enhance or otherwise modify the Q.931 call control protocol to support broadband ISDN?

14.3   In many developed countries, a substantial investment has been made in coaxial cable installation to support cable TV distribution to home and office. Can this installed plant, rather than optical fiber, become the subscriber loop for B-ISDN? If not, why not maintain this separate network for TV distribution rather than attempting to incorporate all communications services under B-ISDN?

CHAPTER **15**

BROADBAND PROTOCOLS

For B-ISDN, the transfer of information across the user–network interface uses asynchronous transfer mode (ATM). The ATM mechanism is embedded into a protocol reference model that defines the B-ISDN user–network interface. We defer a discussion of the details of ATM to Part Five. This chapter provides an overview of the BISDN protocol reference model and then looks at the underlying physical layer for B-ISDN, referred to as SONET (synchronous optical network) in the United States and as SDH (synchronous digital hierarchy) in ITU-T recommendations.

15.1 B-ISDN PROTOCOL REFERENCE MODEL

The protocol architecture for B-ISDN introduces some new elements not found in the ISDN architecture, as depicted in Figure 15.1. ATM is, in essence, a form of packet transmission across the user–network interface in the same way that X.25 is a form of packet transmission across the user–network interface. One difference between X.25 and ATM is that X.25 includes control signaling on the same channel as data transfer, whereas ATM makes use of common-channel signaling. Another difference is that X.25 packets may be of varying length, whereas ATM packets are of fixed size, referred to as cells.

The decision to use ATM for B-ISDN is a remarkable one. This implies that B-ISDN is a packet-based network, certainly at the interface and almost certainly in terms of its internal switching. Although the recommendation also states that B-ISDN will support circuit-mode applications, this is done over a packet-based transport mechanism. Thus, ISDN, which began as an evolution from the circuit-switching telephone networks, has transformed itself into a packet-switching network as it takes on broadband services.

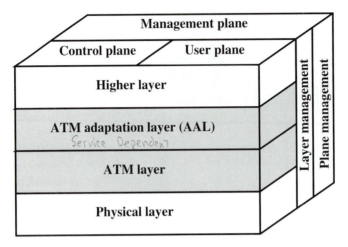

Figure 15.1 ATM Protocol Architecture.

Two layers of the B-ISDN protocol architecture relate to ATM functions. There is an ATM layer common to all services, which provides packet transfer capabilities, and an ATM adaptation layer (AAL), which is service dependent. The AAL maps higher-layer information into ATM cells to be transported over B-ISDN, and collects information from incoming ATM cells for delivery to higher layers. The use of ATM creates the need for an adaptation layer to support information-transfer protocols not based on ATM. Two examples listed in I.121 are PCM voice and LAPD. PCM voice is an application that produces a stream of bits. To employ this application over ATM, it is necessary to assemble PCM bits into cells for transmission and to read them out on reception in such a way as to produce a smooth, constant flow of bits to the receiver. For LAPD, it is necessary to map LAPD frames into ATM packets; this will probably mean segmenting one LAPD frame into a number of packets on transmission and reassembling the frame from packets on reception. By allowing the use of LAPD over ATM, all of the existing ISDN applications and control-signaling protocols can be used on B-ISDN.

The protocol reference model makes reference to three separate planes:

- **User plane:** Provides for user information transfer, along with associated controls (e.g., flow control, error control).
- **Control plane:** Performs call control and connection control functions.
- **Management plane:** Includes plane management, which performs management functions related to a system as a whole and provides coordination between all the planes, and layer management, which performs management functions relating to resources and parameters residing in its protocol entities.

The B-ISDN standards include a description of functions to be performed, as illustrated in Table 15.1. Let us examine each of these briefly.

Physical Layer

The physical layer consists of two sublayers: the physical medium sublayer and the transmission convergence sublayer.

Physical Medium Sublayer

This sublayer includes only physical medium–dependent functions. Its specification will therefore depend on the medium used. One function common to all medium types is bit timing. This sublayer is responsible for transmitting/receiving a continuous flow of bits with associated timing information to synchronize transmission and reception.

Transmission Convergence Sublayer

This sublayer is responsible for the following functions:

- **Transmission frame generation and recovery:** Transmission at the physical layer consists of frames, such as we saw in the basic- and primary-rate interfaces. This function is concerned with generating and maintaining the frame structure appropriate for a given data rate.
- **Transmission frame adaptation:** Information exchange at the ATM layer is a flow of ATM cells. This sublayer is responsible for packaging these cells into a frame. One option is to have no frame structure but simply to transmit and receive a flow of cells.
- **Cell delineation:** For transmission purposes, the bit flow may be scrambled (see Appendix 3A). This sublayer is responsible for maintaining the cell boundaries so that cells may be recovered after descrambling at the destination.

Table 15.1   Functions of the B-ISDN Layers

	Higher-Layer Functions	Higher Layers	
	Convergence	CS	AAL
	Segmentation and reassembly	SAR	
	Generic flow control Cell header generation/extraction Cell VPI/VCI translation Cell multiplex and demultiplex	ATM	
Layer Management	Cell rate decoupling HEC header sequence generation/verification Cell delineation Transmission frame adaptation Transmission frame generation/recovery	TC	Physical layer
	Bit timing Physical medium	PM	

CS   =   Convergence sublayer
SAR =   Segmentation and reassembly sublayer
AAL =   ATM adaptation layer
ATM =   Asynchronous transfer mode
TC   =   Transmission control sublayer
PM   =   Physical medium sublayer

- **HEC sequence generation and cell header verification:** Each cell header is protected by a header error-control (HEC) code. This sublayer is responsible for generating and checking this code.
- **Cell rate decoupling:** This includes insertion and suppression of idle cells to adapt the rate of valid ATM cells to the payload capacity of the transmission system.

ATM Layer

The ATM layer is independent of the physical medium. The details of this layer will be examined in Part Five. Here we give a brief description of its principal functions:

- **Cell multiplexing and demultiplexing:** Multiple logical connections may be maintained across an interface, much like X.25 and frame relay.
- **Virtual path identifier (VPI) and virtual channel identifier (VCI) translation:** The VPI and VCI relate to logical connections and have local significance. Consequently, the values may need to be translated during switching.
- **Cell header generation/extraction:** In the transmit direction, a cell header is appended to user data from the AAL. All of the fields except the HEC code are generated. This function may also include translation from an address to a logical connection number (VPI and VCI).
- **Generic flow control:** This function generates flow-control information for placement in cell headers.

ATM Adaptation Layer

The ATM adaptation layer consists of two sublayers: the segmentation and reassembly sublayer and the convergence sublayer. The details of this layer will be examined in Part Five. Here we give a brief description of its principal functions.

The segmentation and reassembly sublayer is responsible for the segmentation of higher-layer information into a size suitable for the information field of an ATM cell on transmission and the reassembly of the contents of a sequence of ATM cell information fields into higher-layer information on reception.

The convergence sublayer is an interface specification. It defines the services that AAL provides to higher layers.

15.2 B-ISDN PHYSICAL LAYER

The B-ISDN physical layer is specified in I.432. The following options are provided in the standard:

- Full duplex at 155.52 Mbps in each direction
- Subscriber to network at 155.52 Mbps and network to subscriber at 622.08 Mbps
- Full duplex at 622.08 Mbps
- Full duplex at 51.84 Mbps
- Full duplex at 25.6 Mbps

In addition, the primary rates of 1.544 and 2.048 Mbps are supported.

A data rate of 155.52 Mbps can certainly support all of the narrowband ISDN services. That is, it readily supports one or more basic- or primary-rate interfaces. In addition, it can support most of the B-ISDN services. At that rate, one or several video channels can be supported, depending on the video resolution and the coding technique used. Thus, the full-duplex 155.52-Mbps service will probably be the most common B-ISDN service.

The higher data rate of 622.08 Mbps is needed to handle multiple video distribution, such as might be required when a business conducts multiple simultaneous videoconferences. This data rate makes sense in the network-to-subscriber direction. The typical subscriber will not initiate distribution services and thus would still be able to use the lower, 155.52-Mbps, service. The full-duplex 622.08-Mbps service would be appropriate for a video distribution provider.

The lower data rates of 51.84 and 25.6 Mbps were added in 1996 and 1997, respectively. These rates are intended to provide service for users who are not yet ready to move up to SDH data rates and/or do not require the higher speeds.

Table 15.2 summarizes some of the characteristics of the various options. Both electrical (copper) and optical fiber transmission media are considered. For the full-duplex 155.52-Mbps service, either coaxial cable or optical fiber may be used. The coaxial cable is to support connections up to a maximum distance of 100 to 200 m, using one cable for transmission in each direction. The parameters defined in Recommendation G.703 are to be used.

Optical fiber for the full-duplex 155.52-Mbps service supports connections up to a maximum distance of 800 to 2000 m. The transmission medium consists of two single-mode fibers, one for each direction, according to Recommendation G.652.

For a service that includes the 622.08-Mbps rate in one or both directions, only the optical fiber medium has been specified, with the same characteristics as for the lower-speed interface. The use of coaxial cable is for further study.

Both the 51.98-Mbps and the 25.6-Mbps interfaces make use of twisted pair: unshielded twisted pair (UTP) for 51.84 Mbps and either UTP or shielded twisted pair (STP) for 25.6 Mbps. Thus, the interface may be able to take advantage of wiring already installed in the building.

Line Coding

I.432 includes a specification of the line coding technique to be used across the user–network interface for both the electrical and optical media. Keep in mind that this interface is on the customer premises, with relatively short distances between devices across the interface.

Electrical Interface

The line coding for the electrical interface at 155.52 Mbps is coded mark inversion (CMI). CMI uses two different voltage levels and obeys the following rules:

- For binary 0, there is always a positive transition at the midpoint of the binary unit time interval; thus, the signal is at the lower level for the first half of the bit time and at the higher level for the second half of the bit time.

Table 15.2 B-ISDN Physical Layer Characteristics at User–Network Interface

UNI Data Rate	155.52 Mbps		622.08 Mbps*		51.84 Mbps	25.6 Mbps
Interface	Electrical	Optical interface	Electrical	Optical	Electrical	Electrical
Transmission Medium	Two coaxial cables	Two single-mode fibers	For further study	Two single-mode fibers	Two Category 3 UTP	Two Category 3 UTP or two STP
Line Coding	Coded mark inversion (CMI)	Nonreturn to zero (NRZ)	For further study	Nonreturn to zero (NRZ)	16-QAM	4B5B/NRZI
Maximum Distance	200 m	2 km	For further study	2 km	100 m	100 m
ATM Cell Transmission	Cell-based or SDH-based (STM-1)	Cell-based or SDH-based (STM-1)	For further study	Cell-based or SDH-based (STM-4)	Cell-based or SDH-based (STM-1)	Cell-based

*Includes asymmetrical interface with 622.08 Mbps in one direction and 155.52 Mbps in the other direction and symmetrical interface with 622.08 Mbps in both directions.

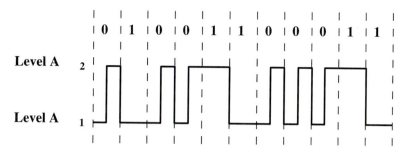

Figure 15.2   Example of Coded Mark Inversion (CMI) Encoding Format.

- For binary 1, there is always a constant signal level for the duration of the bit time. This level alternates between high and low for successive binary 1s.

Figure 15.2 illustrates CMI. CMI has several advantages over a simple NRZ scheme (see Figure 3.9):

1. If the high and low levels are positive and negative voltages of equal amplitude, then the signal has no DC component: Each 0 bit has both a high- and low-level portion, and 1 bits alternate between high and low levels. The lack of DC component improves spectrum characteristics and permits transformer coupling.
2. The frequent transitions make it easier to maintain synchronization between transmitter and receiver.

On the other hand, the signaling rate (baud rate) is higher than the bit rate, which requires greater bandwidth.

At 51.84 Mbps, the line coding scheme is 16-QAM; see Chapter 3 for a description of QAM. At 25.6 Mbps, the line coding scheme is 4B5B/NRZI; this is described in Appendix 15A.

Optical Interface

The line coding for the optical interface is referred to as nonreturn to zero (NRZ). In fact, it is a form of amplitude shift keying with the following rules:

- A binary 1 is represented by the emission of light.
- A binary 0 is represented by no emission of light.

Transmission Structure

A final important issue at the physical layer is the transmission structure to be used to multiplex ATM cells from various logical connections. I.432 specifies two options.

The first of the two options is the use of a continuous stream of cells, with no multiplex frame structure imposed at the interface. Synchronization is on a cell-by-cell basis. That is, the receiver is responsible for assuring that it properly delineates cells on the 53-octet cell boundaries. This task is accomplished using the header error-control (HEC) field. As long as the HEC calculation is indicating no errors, it is assumed that cell alignment is being properly maintained. An occasional error does not change this assumption. However, a string of error detections would indicate that the receiver is out of alignment, at which point it performs a hunting procedure to recover alignment.

The second option is to place the cells in a synchronous time-division multiplex envelope. In this case, the bit stream at the interface has an external frame based on the Synchronous Digital Hierarchy (SDH) defined in Recommendation G.707. In the United States, this frame structure is referred to as SONET (synchronous optical network). The SDH frame may be used exclusively for ATM cells or may also carry other bit streams not yet defined in B-ISDN.

In the remainder of this chapter, we examine the SDH/SONET facility. Its use for carrying ATM cells is discussed in Part Five.

15.3 SONET/SDH

SONET (synchronous optical network) is an optical transmission interface originally proposed by BellCore and standardized by ANSI. A compatible version, referred to as synchronous digital hierarchy (SDH), has been published by ITU-T in the 1996 Recommendation G.707.[1] SONET is intended to provide a specification for taking advantage of the high-speed digital transmission capability of optical fiber.

The SONET standard addresses the following specific issues:

1. Establishes a standard multiplexing format using any number of 51.84-Mbps signals as building blocks. Because each building block can carry a DS3 signal, a standard rate is defined for any high-bandwidth transmission system that might be developed.

2. Establishes an optical signal standard for interconnecting equipment from different suppliers.

3. Establishes extensive operations, administration, and maintenance (OAM) capabilities as part of the standard.

4. Defines a synchronous multiplexing format for carrying lower-level digital signals (DS1, DS2, ITU-T standards). The synchronous structure greatly simplifies the interface to digital switches, digital cross-connect switches, and add–drop multiplexers.

5. Establishes a flexible architecture capable of accommodating future applications, such as broadband ISDN, with a variety of transmission rates.

Three key requirements have driven the development of SONET. First was the need to push multiplexing standards beyond the existing DS-3 (44.736-Mbps) level. With the increasing use of optical transmission systems, a number of vendors have introduced their own proprietary schemes of combining anywhere from 2 to

---

[1]In what follows, we will use the term *SONET* to refer to both specifications. Where differences exist, these will be addressed.

12 DS-3s into an optical signal. In addition, the European schemes, based on the ITU-T hierarchy, are incompatible with North American schemes. SONET provides a standardized hierarchy of multiplexed digital transmission rates that accommodates existing North American and ITU-T rates.

A second requirement was to provide economic access to small amounts of traffic within the bulk payload of an optical signal. For this purpose, SONET introduces a new approach to time-division multiplexing. We address this issue subsequently when we examine the SONET frame format.

A third requirement is to prepare for future sophisticated service offerings, such as virtual private networking, time-of-day bandwidth allocation, and support of the broadband ISDN ATM transmission technique. To meet this requirement, a major increase in network management capabilities within the synchronous time-division signal was needed.

In this section, we provide an overview of SONET/SDH that shows how these requirements have been met.

Signal Hierarchy

The SONET specification defines a hierarchy of standardized digital data rates (Table 15.3). The lowest level, referred to as STS-1 (synchronous transport signal level 1), is 51.84 Mbps. This rate can be used to carry a single DS-3 signal or a group of lower-rate signals, such as DS1, DS1C, DS2, plus ITU-T rates (e.g., 2.048 Mbps).

Multiple STS-1 signals can be combined to form an STS-N signal. The signal is created by interleaving bytes from N STS-1 signals that are mutually synchronized.

For the ITU-T synchronous digital hierarchy, the lowest rate is 155.52 Mbps, which is designated STM-1. This corresponds to SONET STS-3. The reason for the discrepancy is that STM-1 is the lowest-rate signal that can accommodate a ITU-T level 4 signal (139.264 Mbps).

Table 15.3   SONET/SDH Signal Hierarchy

SONET Designation	ITU-T Designation	Data Rate (Mbps)	Payload Rate (Mbps)
STS-1/OC-1		51.84	50.112
STS-3/OC-3	STM-1	155.52	150.336
STS-9/OC-9		466.56	451.008
STS-12/OC-12	STM-4	622.08	601.344
STS-18/OC-18		933.12	902.016
STS-24/OC-24		1244.16	1202.688
STS-36/OC-36		1866.24	1804.032
STS-48/OC-48	STM-16	2488.32	2405.376
STS-96/OC-96		4876.64	4810.752
STS-192/OC-192	STM-64	9953.28	9621.504

STS
Synchronous Transport Signal

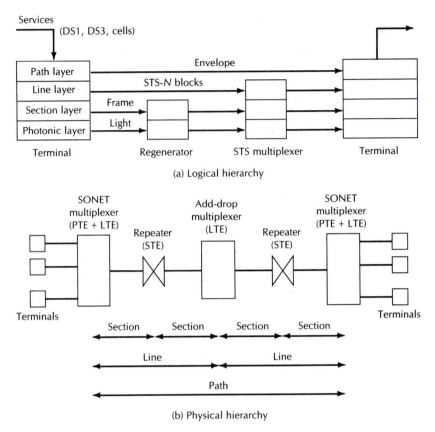

Figure 15.3 SONET System Hierarchy.

System Hierarchy

SONET capabilities have been mapped into a four-layer hierarchy (Figure 15.3a):

- **Photonic:** This is the physical layer. It includes a specification of the type of optical fiber that may be used and details such as the required minimum powers and dispersion characteristics of the transmitting lasers and the required sensitivity of the receivers.
- **Section:** This layer creates the basic SONET frames, converts electronic signals to photonic ones, and has some monitoring capabilities.
- **Line:** This layer is responsible for synchronization, multiplexing of data onto the SONET frames, protection and maintenance functions, and switching.
- **Path:** This layer is responsible for end-to-end transport of data at the appropriate signaling speed.

Figure 15.3b shows the physical realization of the logical layers. A section is the basic physical building block and represents a single run of optical cable between two optical fiber transmitter/receivers. For shorter runs, the cable may run directly between two end units. For longer distances, regenerating repeaters are needed. The repeater is a simple device that accepts a digital stream of data on one side and regenerates and repeats each bit out the other side. Issues of synchronization and timing need to be addressed. A line is a sequence of one or more sections such that the internal signal or channel structure of the signal remains constant. Endpoints and intermediate switches/multiplexers that may add or drop channels terminate a line. Finally, a path connects to end terminals; it corresponds to an end-to-end circuit. Data are assembled at the beginning of a path and are not accessed or modified until they are disassembled at the other end of the path.

Frame Format

The basic SONET building block is the STS-1 frame, which consists of 810 octets and is transmitted once every 125 µs, for an overall data rate of 51.84 Mbps (Figure 15.4a). The frame can logically be viewed as a matrix of 9 rows of 90 octets each, with transmission being one row at a time, from left to right and top to bottom.

The first three columns (3 octets × 9 rows = 27 octets) of the frame are devoted to overhead octets. Nine octets are devoted to section-related overhead, and 18 octets are devoted to line overhead. Figure 15.5a shows the arrangement of overhead octets, and Table 15.4 defines the various fields.

The remainder of the frame is payload, which is provided by the path layer. The payload includes a column of path overhead, which is not necessarily in the first available column position; the line overhead contains a pointer that indicates where the path overhead starts. Figure 15.5b shows the arrangement of path overhead octets, and Table 15.4 defines these.

Figure 15.4b shows the general format for higher-rate frames, using the ITU-T designation.

Pointer Adjustment

In conventional circuit-switched networks, most multiplexers and telephone company channel banks require the demultiplexing and remultiplexing of the entire signal just to access a piece of information that is addressed to a node. For example, consider that T-1 multiplexer B receives data on a single T-1 circuit from T-1 multiplexer A and passes the data on to multiplexer C. In the signal received, a single DS0 channel (64 kbps) is addressed to node B. The rest will pass on to node C and further on into the network. To remove that single DS0 channel, B must demultiplex every bit of the 1.544-Mbps signal, remove the data, and remultiplex every bit. A few proprietary T-1 multiplexers allow for drop-and-insert capability, meaning that only part of the signal has to be demultiplexed and remultiplexed, but this equipment will not communicate with that of other vendors.

SONET offers a standard drop-and-insert capability, and it applies not just to 64-kbps channels but to higher data rates as well. SONET makes use of a set of pointers that locate channels within a payload and the entire payload within a frame, so that information can be accessed, inserted, and removed with a simple adjustment of pointers. Pointer information is contained in the path overhead that refers to the multiplex structure of the channels contained within the payload. A pointer in

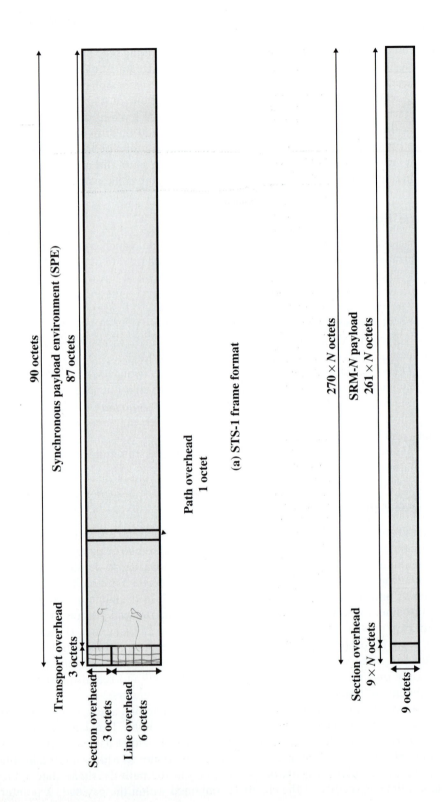

Figure 15.4 SONET/SDH Frame Formats.

90 octets

Synchronous payload environment (SPE)
87 octets

Transport overhead
3 octets

Section overhead
3 octets

Line overhead
6 octets

Path overhead
1 octet

(a) STS-1 frame format

270 × N octets

SRM-N payload
261 × N octets

Section overhead
9 × N octets

9 octets

(b) STM-N frame format

404

Table 15.4 STS-1 Overhead Bits

Section Overhead

A1, A2: Framing bytes = F6,28 hex; used to synchronize the beginning of the frame.

C1: STS-1 ID identifies the STS-1 number (1 to N) for each STS-1 within an STS-N multiplex.

B1: Bit-interleaved parity byte providing even parity over previous STS-N frame after scrambling; the ith bit of this octet contains the even parity value calculated from the ith bit position of all octets in the previous frame.

E1: Section level 64-kbps PCM orderwire; optional 64 kbps voice channel to be used between section terminating equipment, hubs, and remote terminals.

F1: 64-kbps channel set aside for user purposes.

D1-D3: 192-kbps data communications channel for alarms, maintenance, control, and administration between sections.

Line Overhead

H1-H3: Pointer bytes used in frame alignment and frequency adjustment of payload data.

B2: Bit-interleaved parity for line level error monitoring.

K1, K2: Two bytes allocated for signaling between line level automatic protection switching equipment; uses a bit-oriented protocol that provides for error protection and management of the SONET optical link.

D4-D12: 576-kbps data communications channel for alarms, maintenance, control, monitoring, and administration at the line level.

Z1, Z2: Reserved for future use.

E2: 64-kbps PCM voice channel for line level orderwire.

Path Overhead

J1: 64-kbps channel used to repetitively send a 64-octet fixed-length string so a receiving terminal can continuously verify the integrity of a path; the contents of the message are user programmable.

B3: Bit-interleaved parity at the path level, calculated over all bits of the previous SPE.

C2: STS path signal label to designate equipped versus unequipped STS signals. Unequipped means the line connection is complete but there is no path data to send. For equipped signals, the label can indicate the specific STS payload mapping that might be needed in receiving terminals to interpret the payloads.

G1: Status byte sent from path terminating equipment back to path originating equipment to convey status of terminating equipment and path error performance.

F2: 64-kbps channel for path user.

H4: Multiframe indicator for payloads needing frames that are longer than a single STS frame; multiframe indicators are used when packing lower rate channels (virtual tributaries) into the SPE.

Z3-Z5: Reserved for future use.

---

the line overhead serves a similar function for the entire payload. We examine the use of this latter pointer in the remainder of this section.

The synchronous payload environment (SPE) of an STS-1 frame can float with respect to the frame. The actual payload (87 columns × 9 rows) can straddle two frames (Figure 15.6). The H1 and H2 octets in the line overhead indicate the start of the payload.

(text continues on page 408)

	Framing A1	Framing A2	STS-ID C1		Trace J1
Section overhead	BIP-8 B1	Orderwire E1	User F1		BIP-8 B3
	Data Com D1	Data Com D2	Data Com D3		Signal label C2
	Pointer H1	Pointer H2	Pointer action H3		Path status G1
	BIP-8 B2	APS K1	APS K2		User F2
Line overhead	Data Com D4	Data Com D5	Data Com D6		Multiframe H4
	Data Com D7	Data Com D8	Data Com D9		Growth Z3
	Data Com D10	Data Com D11	Data Com D12		Growth Z4
	Growth Z1	Growth Z2	Orderwire E2		Growth Z5

(a) Section overhead   (b) Path overhead

Figure 15.5   SONET STS-1 Overhead Octets.

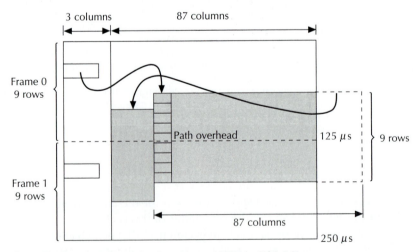

Figure 15.6   Representative Location of SPE in STS-1 Frame.

406

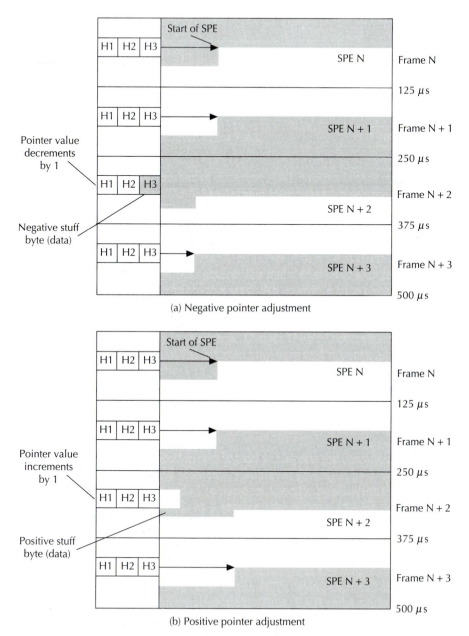

Figure 15.7 STS-1 Pointer Adjustment.

407

Because even the best atomic timing sources can differ by small amounts, SONET is faced with coping with the resulting timing differences. Each node must recalculate the pointer to alert the next receiving node of the exact location of the start of the payload. Thus, the payload is allowed to slip through an STS-1 frame, increasing or decreasing the pointer value at intervals by one byte position.

If the payload rate is higher than the local STS frame rate, the pointer is decreased by one octet position so that the next payload will begin one octet sooner than the earlier payload. To prevent the loss of an octet on the payload that is thus squeezed, the H3 octet is used to hold the extra octet for that one frame (Figure 15.7a). Similarly, if the payload rate lags behind the frame rate, the insertion of the next payload is delayed by one octet. In this case, the octet in the SPE that follows the H3 octet is left empty to allow for the movement of the payload (Figure 15.7b).

15.4 SUMMARY

For B-ISDN, the transfer of information across the user–network interface uses what is referred to as asynchronous transfer mode (ATM). The use of ATM implies that B-ISDN is a packet-based network, certainly at the interface and almost certainly in terms of its internal switching. Although the recommendation also states that B-ISDN will support circuit-mode applications, this is done over a packet-based transport mechanism. Thus, ISDN, which began as an evolution from the circuit-switching telephone networks, has transformed itself into a packet-switching network as it takes on broadband services.

The use of ATM creates the need for an adaptation layer to support information transfer protocols not based on ATM. The ATM adaptation layer (AAL) packages information from the AAL user into 48-octet packages to fit into the ATM cell. This may involve aggregating bits from a bit stream or segmenting a frame into smaller pieces.

Some form of transmission structure must be used to transport ATM cells. Two options are specified. The first is the use of a continuous stream of cells, with no multiplex frame structure imposed at the interface. Synchronization is on a cell-by-cell basis. The second option is to place the cells in a synchronous time-division multiplex envelope. In this case, the bit stream at the interface has an external frame based on the Synchronous Digital Hierarchy (SDH) defined in Recommendation G.707. In the United States, this frame structure is referred to as SONET (synchronous optical network).

15.5 RECOMMENDED READING

[PRYC93] provides an interesting discussion of the B-ISDN protocol reference model and its relationship to OSI. Detailed treatments of SONET/SDH can be found in [GORA97] and [BLAC97b].

BLAC97b Black, U., and Waters, S. *SONET and T1: Architectures for Digital Transport Networks.* Upper Saddle River, NJ: Prentice Hall, 1997.

GORA97 Goralski, W. *SONET: A Guide to Synchronous Optical Networks.* New York: McGraw-Hill, 1997.

PRYC93 Prycker, M.; Peschi, R.; and Van Landegem, R. "B-ISDN and the OSI Protocol Reference Model." *IEEE Network*, March 1993.

Recommended Web sites are as follows:

- **SONET Interoperability Forum:** Discusses current products, technology, and standards.
- **SONET Home Page:** Useful links, tutorials, white papers, FAQ.

15.6 PROBLEMS

15.1 What is the signaling rate for CMI?

15.2 Compare CMI with bipolar AMI, B8ZS, and HDB3 as an encoding technique for the B-ISDN UNI. What, if any, are the advantages of CMI?

15.3 Repeat Problem 3.3 for CMI and NRZI. Assume that the most recent preceding 1 bit had a low voltage.

15.4 Repeat Problem 3.4 for CMI and NRZI. Assume that the most recent preceding 1 bit had a low voltage.

15.5 Show the NRZI waveform for the 15 invalid 4B5B/NRZI codes and comment on the results.

APPENDIX 15A 4B5B/NRZI CODING

I.432.5 specifies the use of the 4B5B/NRZI encoding scheme for transmission over twisted pair at 25.6 Mbps. To understand the significance of this choice, first consider the simple alternative of an NRZ (nonreturn to zero) coding scheme. With NRZ, one signal state represents binary one and one signal state represents binary zero. The disadvantage of this approach is its lack of synchronization. Because transitions on the medium are unpredictable, there is no way for the receiver to synchronize its clock to the transmitter. A solution to this problem is to encode the binary data to guarantee the presence of transitions. An efficient technique for doing this is the 4B5B code. In this scheme, encoding is done four bits at a time; each four bits of data are encoded into a symbol with five *code bits,* such that each code bit contains a single signal element; the block of five code bits are called a *code group*. In effect, each set of four bits is encoded as five bits. The efficiency is thus 80%: 25.6 Mbps is achieved with 32 Mbaud.

To ensure synchronization, there is a second stage of encoding: Each code bit of the 4B5B stream is treated as a binary value and encoded using a variation of NRZ known as **NRZI** (nonreturn to zero, invert on ones). As with NRZ-L, NRZI maintains a constant voltage pulse for the duration of a bit time. The data them-

Table 15.5 4B5B Code Groups

Data Input (4 bits)	Code Group (5 bits)	NRZI pattern	Data Input (4 bits)	Code Group (5 bits)	NRZI pattern
0000	10101		1000	10010	
0001	01001		1001	11001	
0010	01010		1010	11010	
0011	01011		1011	11011	
0100	00111		1100	10111	
0101	01101		1101	11101	
0110	01110		1110	11110	
0111	01111		1111	11111	
			ESC(X)	00010	

selves are encoded as the presence or absence of a signal transition at the beginning of the bit time. A transition (low-to-high or high-to-low) at the beginning of a bit time denotes a binary 1 for that bit time; no transition indicates a binary 0. NRZI is an example of **differential encoding**. In differential encoding, the signal is decoded by comparing the polarity of adjacent signal elements rather than determining the absolute value of a signal element. One benefit of this scheme is that it may be more reliable to detect a transition in the presence of noise than to compare a value to a threshold. Another benefit is that with a complex transmission layout, it is easy to lose the sense of the polarity of the signal. For example, on a multidrop twisted-pair line, if the leads from an attached device to the twisted pair are accidentally inverted, all 1s and 0s for NRZ-L will be inverted. This cannot happen with differential encoding.

Now we are in a position to describe the 4B5B code and to understand the selections that were made. Table 13.8 shows the symbol encoding. Each 5-bit code group pattern is shown, together with its NRZI realization. Because we are encoding 4 bits with a 5-bit pattern, only 16 of the 32 possible patterns are needed for data encoding. The codes selected to represent the 16 4-bit data blocks are such that a transition is present at least twice for each five-code group code. No more than three zeros in a row are allowed across one or more code groups.

The encoding scheme can be summarized as follows:

1. A simple NRZ encoding is rejected because it does not provide synchronization; a string of 1s or 0s will have no transitions.
2. The data to be transmitted must first be encoded to assure transitions. The 4B5B code is chosen over Manchester because it is more efficient.
3. The 4B5B code is further encoded using NRZI so that the resulting differential signal will improve reception reliability.
4. The specific 5-bit patterns for the encoding of the 16 4-bit data patterns are chosen to guarantee no more than three zeros in a row to provide for adequate synchronization.

A seventeenth code is used to represent the escape symbol. This escape symbol has the property (referred to as the *comma property* in I.432.5) of being unique among all possible valid symbol pairs. Those code groups not used to represent data are declared invalid.

PART FIVE

Asynchronous Transfer Mode

The most important technical innovation to come out of the standardization work on broadband ISDN (B-ISDN) is asynchronous transfer mode (ATM). ATM, also known as cell relay, is a transmission technique using fixed-size cells. It has less overhead than frame relay and is designed to operate at significantly higher data rates than frame relay.

Although conceived as a service and switching mechanism for B-ISDN, ATM has gained broad acceptance and is used in a number of networking contexts outside of B-ISDN. Because of its importance, Part Five of this book is devoted to frame relay. ATM

Chapter 16 covers the ATM protocol and the concepts of virtual channel and virtual path. The chapter also describes the way in which ATM cell streams are mapped onto a physical layer transmission scheme. Finally, the chapter examines the ATM adaptation layer (AAL), which serves to map other data transmission protocols onto ATM.

As with frame relay, one of the most difficult technical issues associated with ATM is congestion control. The issues for the ATM case are more complex and difficult than those for frame relay. Chapter 17 examines the nature and importance of the problem and presents a variety of approaches to ATM congestion control.

CHAPTER **16**

ATM PROTOCOLS

J ust as frame relay is the most important technical advance stemming from the work on narrowband ISDN, asynchronous transfer mode (ATM) is the most important contribution of the B-ISDN effort.

We begin this chapter with an examination of the details of the ATM protocol and formats. Next, we look at the manner in which ATM cells are actually packaged for transmission across the user–network interface. Finally, we examine the requirement for mapping various applications onto ATM and consider the ATM adaptation layer (AAL).

16.1 ASYNCHRONOUS TRANSFER MODE

Synchronous versus Asynchronous Transfer

When the standards work on B-ISDN began in the mid-1980s, it was generally assumed by most participants that some form of synchronous time-division multiplexing (TDM) technique would be used, as is the case with the basic- and primary-rate access methods for ISDN. Under this approach, the interface structure that was proposed was

$$j \times H4 + k \times H2 + l \times H1 + m \times H0 + n \times B + D$$

where D, B, H0, and H1 (H11 or H12) are narrowband ISDN channels and H2 and H4 are new B-ISDN fixed-rate channels. H2 would be in the range of 30 to 45 Mbps and H4 in the range of 120 to 140 Mbps.

Although the synchronous TDM approach is a natural extension of narrowband ISDN, it does not provide the best model for B-ISDN. There are two basic disadvantages of the synchronous approach [MINZ89b]. First, it does not provide a flexible interface for meeting a variety of needs. At the high data rates offered by B-ISDN, there could be a wide variety of applications, and many different data rates, that need to be switched. One or two fixed-rate channel types do not provide a structure that can easily accommodate this requirement. Furthermore, many data (as opposed to voice or video) applications are bursty in nature and can be handled more efficiently with some sort of packet-switching approach. A final aspect of the inflexibility of the synchronous approach is that it does not lend itself to rate adaptation. We have seen that rate adaptation within the 64-kbps channel is quite complex. One can imagine the complexity and inefficiency of extending this concept to channels in the tens and hundreds of megabits per second.

The second disadvantage of the synchronous approach for high-speed transmission is that the use of multiple high data rates (e.g., a number of H2 and H4 channels) complicates the switching system. We would require switches that can handle data streams of multiple high data rates. This is in contrast to narrowband ISDN, which has just the 64-kbps data stream to switch.

Thus, synchronous TDM has been rejected. However, it is still possible to multiplex several ATM streams using synchronous TDM techniques to achieve transmission interfaces that exceed the rate of operation of ATM switches and multiplexers. We examine this topic in Section 16.2.

ATM Overview

ATM is similar in concept to frame relay, which we examined in Chapter 12. Both frame relay and ATM take advantage of the reliability and fidelity of modern digital facilities to provide faster packet switching than X.25. ATM, at its higher data rate, is even more streamlined in its functionality than frame relay, as we shall see.

ATM is a packet-oriented transfer mode. Like frame relay and X.25, it allows multiple logical connections to be multiplexed over a single physical interface. The information flow on each logical connection is organized into fixed-size packets, called cells. As with frame relay, there is no link-by-link error control or flow control.

Figure 16.1 shows the overall hierarchy of function in an ATM-based network. This hierarchy is seen from the point of view of the internal network functions needed to support ATM as well as the user–network functions. The ATM layer consists of virtual channel and virtual path levels; these are discussed in the next subsection.

The physical layer can be divided into three functional levels:

- **Transmission path level:** Extends between network elements that assemble and disassemble the payload of a transmission system. For end-to-end communication, the payload is end-user information. For user-to-network communication, the payload may be signaling information. Cell delineation and header error-control functions are required at the endpoints of each transmission path.

- **Digital section:** Extends between network elements that assemble and disassemble a continuous bit or byte stream. This refers to the exchanges or signal transfer points in a network that are involved in switching data streams.

- **Regenerator section level:** A portion of a digital section. An example of this level is a repeater that is used simply to regenerate the digital signal along a transmission path that is too long to be used without such regeneration; no switching is involved.

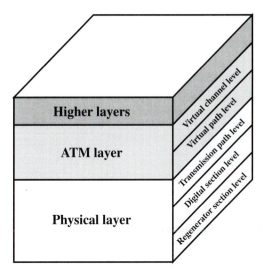

Figure 16.1 ATM Protocol Hierarchy.

Virtual Channels and Virtual Paths

Logical connections in ATM are referred to as virtual channel connections (VCCs). A VCC is analogous to a virtual circuit in X.25 or a frame relay logical connection. It is the basic unit of switching in B-ISDN. A VCC is set up between two end users through the network, and a variable-rate, full-duplex flow of fixed-size cells is exchanged over the connection. VCCs are also used for user–network exchange (control signaling) and network–network exchange (network management and routing).

For ATM, a second sublayer of processing provides for virtual paths (Figure 16.2). A virtual path connection (VPC) is a bundle of VCCs that have the same endpoints. Thus, all of the cells flowing over all of the VCCs in a single VPC are switched along the same route.

The virtual path concept was developed in response to a trend in high-speed networking in which the control cost of the network is becoming an increasingly higher proportion of the overall network cost [BURG91]. The virtual path technique helps contain the control cost by grouping connections sharing common paths through the network into a single unit. Network management actions can then be applied to a small number of groups of connections instead of a large number of individual connections.

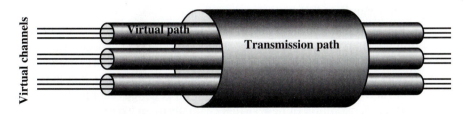

Figure 16.2 ATM Connection Relationships.

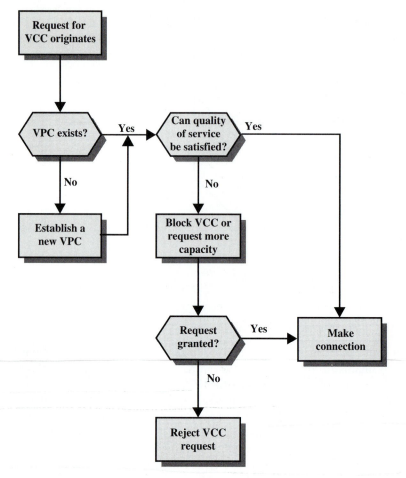

Figure 16.3 Call Establishment Using Virtual Paths.

Several advantages can be listed for the use of virtual paths:

- **Simplified network architecture:** Network transport functions can be separated into those related to an individual logical connection (virtual channel) and those related to a group of logical connections (virtual path).
- **Increased network performance and reliability:** The network deals with fewer, aggregated entities.
- **Reduced processing and short connection setup time:** Much of the work is done when the virtual path is set up. By reserving capacity on a virtual path connection in anticipation of later call arrivals, new virtual channel connections can be established by executing simple control functions at the endpoints of the virtual path connection; no call processing is required at transit nodes. Thus, the addition of new virtual channels to an existing virtual path involves minimal processing.

- **Enhanced network services:** The virtual path is used internal to the network but is also visible to the end user. Thus, the user may define closed user groups or closed networks of virtual channel bundles.

Figure 16.3 suggests in a general way the call establishment process using virtual channels and virtual paths. The process of setting up a virtual path connection is decoupled from the process of setting up an individual virtual channel connection:

- The virtual path control mechanisms include calculating routes, allocating capacity, and storing connection state information.
- For an individual virtual channel setup, control involves checking that there is a virtual path connection to the required destination node with sufficient available capacity to support the virtual channel, with the appropriate quality of service, and then storing the required state information (virtual channel/ virtual path mapping).

The terminology of virtual paths and virtual channels used in the standard is a bit confusing, and it is summarized in Table 16.1. Whereas most of the ISDN and B-ISDN concepts that we deal with in this book relate only to the user–network

Table 16.1   Virtual Path/Virtual Channel Terminology

Virtual Channel (VC)	A generic term used to describe unidirectional transport of ATM cells associated by a common unique identifier value.
Virtual Channel Link	A means of unidirectional transport of ATM cells between a point where a VCI value is assigned and the point where that value is translated or terminated.
Virtual Channel Identifier (VCI)	A unique numerical tag that identifies a particular VC link for a given VPC.
Virtual Channel Connection (VCC)	A concatenation of VC links that extends between two points where ATM service users access the ATM layer. VCCs are provided for the purpose of use--user, user–network, or network–network information transfer. Cell sequence integrity is preserved for cells belonging to the same VCC.
Virtual Path	A generic term used to describe unidirectional transport of ATM cells belonging to virtual channels that are associated by a common unique identifier value.
Virtual Path Link	A group of VC links, identified by a common value of VPI, between a point where a VPI value is assigned and the point where that value is translated or terminated.
Virtual Path Identifier (VPI)	Identifies a particular VP link.
Virtual Path Connection (VPC)	A concatenation of VP links that extends between the point where the VCI values are assigned and the point where those values are translated or removed (i.e., extending the length of a bundle of VC links that share the same VPI). VPCs are provided for the purpose of user–user, user–network, or network–network information transfer.

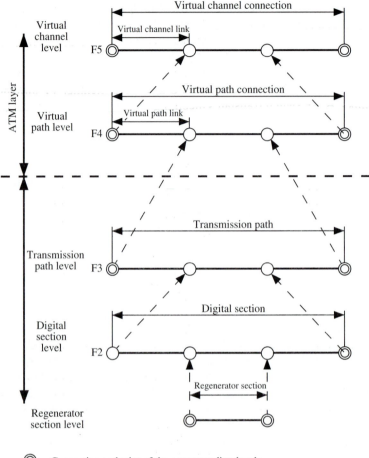

Figure 16.4 Hierarchical Layer-to-Layer Relationship (I.311).

interface, the concepts of virtual path and virtual channel are defined in the ITU-T recommendations with reference to both the user–network interface and the internal network operation.

Figure 16.4 may help to clarify the relationship among the various terms. A VCC provides end-to-end transfer of ATM cells between ATM users (usually the ATM adaptation layer). The endpoints may be end users, network entities, or an end user and a network entity. Each endpoint associates a unique virtual channel identifier (VCI) with each VCC; as with X.25, the two endpoints may employ different VCIs for the same VCC. In addition, within the network, there may be a number of points at which virtual channels are switched, and at those points the VCI may be changed. Thus, a VCC consists of a concatenation of one or more virtual channel links, with the VCI remaining constant for the extent of the VC link and changing at the VC switch points.

Between an endpoint and a VC switch point, or between two VC switch points, a VPC provides a route for all VC links that share the two VPC endpoints. Again, at this level, there may be internal switching, such that a VPC passes through one or more VP switch points, with the virtual path identifier (VPI) changing at each such point. Thus, a VPC consists of a concatenation of one or more virtual path links.

Figure 16.5 shows the concepts of VC and VP switching. VP switches terminate VP links. A VP switch translates incoming VPIs to the corresponding outgoing

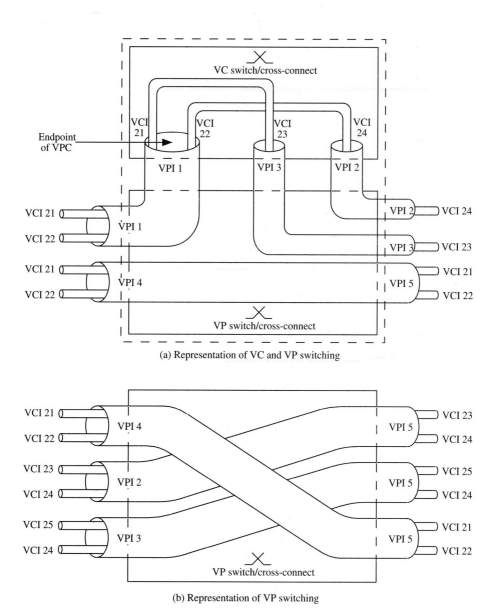

(a) Representation of VC and VP switching

(b) Representation of VP switching

Figure 16.5 Representation of VP and VC Switching Hierarchy.

VPIs according to the destination of the VPC; VCI values remain unchanged. VC switches terminate VC links and necessarily VP links. A VC switch must therefore switch both virtual paths and virtual channels, and so both VPI and VCI translation is performed.

Virtual Channel Connection Uses

The endpoints of a VCC may be end users, network entities, or an end user and a network entity. In all cases, cell sequence integrity is preserved within a VCC: That is, cells are delivered in the same order in which they are sent. Let us consider examples of the three uses of a VCC:

- **Between end users:** Can be used to carry end-to-end user data; can also be used to carry control signaling between end users, as explained later. A VPC between end users provides them with an overall capacity; the VCC organization of the VPC is up to the two end users, provided the set of VCCs does not exceed the VPC capacity.
- **Between an end user and a network entity:** Used for user-to-network control signaling, as discussed later. A user-to-network VPC can be used to aggregate traffic from an end user to a network exchange or network server.
- **Between two network entities:** Used for network traffic management and routing functions. A network-to-network VPC can be used to define a common route for the exchange of network management information.

Virtual Path/Virtual Channel Characteristics

Recommendation I.150 lists the following as characteristics of virtual channel connections:

- **Quality of service:** A user of a virtual channel is provided with a quality of service specified by parameters such as cell loss ratio (ratio of cells lost to cells transmitted) and cell delay variation.
- **Switched and semipermanent virtual channel connections:** Both switched connections, which require call control signaling, and dedicated connections can be provided.
- **Cell sequence integrity:** The sequence of transmitted cells within a virtual channel is preserved.
- **Traffic parameter negotiation and usage monitoring:** Traffic parameters can be negotiated between a user and the network for each virtual channel. The input of cells to the virtual channel is monitored by the network to ensure that the negotiated parameters are not violated.

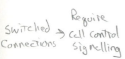
Switched Connections → Require Cell control signalling

The types of traffic parameters that can be negotiated would include average rate, peak rate, burstiness, and peak duration. The network may need a number of strategies to deal with congestion and to manage existing and requested virtual channels. At the crudest level, the network may simply deny new requests for virtual channels to prevent congestion. Additionally, cells may be discarded if negotiated parameters are violated or if congestion becomes severe. In an extreme situation, existing connections might be terminated.

I.150 also lists characteristics of virtual paths. The first four characteristics listed are identical to those for virtual channels. That is, quality of service, switched and semipermanent virtual paths, cell sequence integrity, and traffic parameter negotiation and usage monitoring are also characteristics of a virtual path. There are a number of reasons for this duplication. First, this provides some flexibility in how the network manages the requirements placed upon it. Second, the network service must be concerned with the overall requirements for a virtual path, and within a virtual path may negotiate the establishment of virtual channels with given characteristics. Finally, once a virtual path is set up, it is possible for the end users to negotiate the creation of new virtual channels. The virtual path characteristics impose a discipline on the choices that the end users may make.

In addition, a fifth characteristic is listed for virtual paths:

- **Virtual channel identifier restriction within a VPC:** One or more virtual channel identifiers, or numbers, may not be available to the user of the virtual path, but may be reserved for network use. Examples would be virtual channels used for network management.

Control Signaling

In narrowband ISDN, the D channel is provided for control signaling of calls on B and H channels. In B-ISDN, with its ATM interface, there is no simple fixed-rate structure of H, B, and D channels. Thus, a more flexible arrangement for control signaling is needed. The requirement is further complicated by the need for the establishment and release of two types of entities: virtual channels and virtual paths.

For virtual channels, I.150 specifies four methods for providing an establishment/release facility. One or a combination of these methods will be used in any particular network:

- **Semipermanent VCCs** may be used for user-to-user exchange. In this case, no control signaling is required.
- If there is no preestablished call control signaling channel, then one must be set up. For that purpose, a control-signaling exchange must take place between the user and the network on some channel. Hence we need a permanent channel, probably of low data rate, that can be used to set up a virtual channel that can be used for call control. Such a channel is called a **meta-signaling channel**, because the channel is used to set up signaling channels.
- The meta-signaling channel can be used to set up a virtual channel between the user and the network for call control signaling. This **user-to-network signaling virtual channel** can then be used to set up virtual channels to carry user data.
- The meta-signaling channel can also be used to set up a **user-to-user signaling virtual channel**. Such a channel must be set up within a preestablished virtual path. It can then be used to allow the two end users, without network intervention, to establish and release user-to-user virtual channels to carry user data.

For virtual paths, three methods are defined in I.150:

- A virtual path can be established on a semipermanent basis by prior agreement. In this case, no control signaling is required.
- Virtual path establishment/release may be customer controlled. In this case, the customer uses a signaling virtual channel to request the virtual path from the network.
- Virtual path establishment/release may be network controlled. In this case, the network establishes a virtual path for its own convenience. The path may be network-to-network, user-to-network, or user-to-user.

ATM Cells

The asynchronous transfer mode makes use of fixed-size cells, consisting of a 5-octet header and a 48-octet information field (Figure 16.6).

There are several advantages to the use of small, fixed-size cells. First, the use of small cells may reduce queuing delay for a high-priority cell, because the call waits less if it arrives slightly behind a lower-priority cell that has gained access to a resource (e.g., the transmitter). Second, it appears that fixed-size cells can be

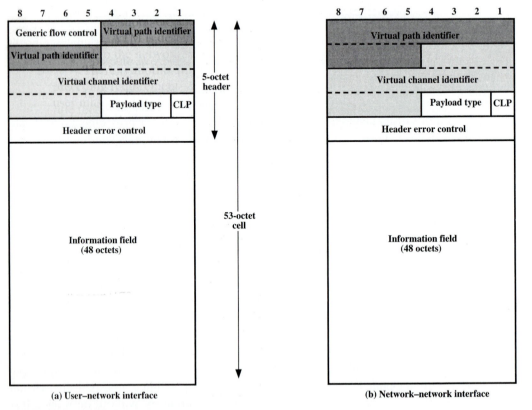

(a) User–network interface

(b) Network–network interface

Figure 16.6 ATM Cell Format.

switched more efficiently, which is important for the very high data rates of ATM. For a discussion of these issues, see [PARE88].

Header Format

Figure 16.6a shows the header format at the user–network interface (S or T reference point). Figure 16.6b shows the cell header format internal to the network. The generic flow-control field, which performs local functions, is not retained inside the network. Instead, the virtual path identifier field is expanded from 8 to 12 bits.

The **generic flow-control** (GFC) field does not appear in the cell header internal to the network, but only at the user–network interface. Hence, it can be used for control of cell flow only at the local user–network interface. The field could be used to assist the customer in controlling the flow of traffic for different qualities of service. In any case, the GFC mechanism is used to alleviate short-term overload conditions in the network.

I.150 lists as a requirement for the GFC mechanism that all terminals be able to get access to their assured capacities. This includes all constant-bit-rate (CBR) terminals as well as the variable-bit-rate (VBR) terminals that have an element of guaranteed capacity. The current GFC mechanism is described in a subsequent subsection.

The **virtual path identifier** (VPI) constitutes a routing field for the network. It is 8 bits at the user–network interface and 12 bits at the network–network interface. The latter allows support for an expanded number of VPCs internal to the network, to include those supporting subscribers and those required for network management. The **virtual channel identifier** (VCI) is used for routing to and from the end user. Thus, it functions much as a service access point.

The **payload type** field indicates the type of information in the information field. Table 16.2 shows the interpretation of the PT bits. A value of 0 in the first bit indicates user information—that is, information from the next higher layer. In this case, the second bit indicates whether congestion has been experienced; the third

Congestion experienced

Table 16.2   Payload Type (PT) Field Coding

PT Coding	Interpretation		
0 0 0	User data cell,	congestion not experienced,	SDU type = 0
0 0 1	User data cell,	congestion not experienced,	SDU type = 1
0 1 0	User data cell,	congestion experienced,	SDU type = 0
0 1 1	User data cell,	congestion experienced,	SDU type = 1
1 0 0	OAM segment associated cell		
1 0 1	OAM end-to-end associated cell		
1 1 0	Resource management cell		
1 1 1	Reserved for future function		

SDU   = Service Data Unit
OAM   = Operations, Administration, and Maintenance

bit, known as the service data unit (SDU)[1] type bit, is a one-bit field that can be used to discriminate two types of ATM SDUs associated with a connection. The term SDU refers to the 48-octet payload of the cell.

A value of 1 in the first bit of the payload type field indicates that this cell carries network management or maintenance information. This indication allows the insertion of network management cells onto a user's VCC without impacting the user's data. Thus, it can provide inband control information.

The **cell loss priority** (CLP) bit is used to provide guidance to the network in the event of congestion. A value of 0 indicates a cell of relatively higher priority, which should not be discarded unless no other alternative is available. A value of 1 indicates that this cell is subject to discard within the network. The user might employ this field so that extra cells (beyond the negotiated rate) may be inserted into the network, with a CLP of 1, and delivered to the destination if the network is not congested. The network may set this field to 1 for any data cell that is in violation of an agreement concerning traffic parameters between the user and the network. In this case, the switch that does the setting realizes that the cell exceeds the agreed traffic parameters but that the switch is capable of handling the cell. At a later point in the network, if congestion is encountered, this cell has been marked for discard in preference to cells that fall within agreed traffic limits.

The **header error-control** field is used for both error control and synchronization, as explained subsequently.

Generic Flow Control

I.150 specifies the use of the GFC field to control traffic flow at the user–network interface (UNI) in order to alleviate short-term overload conditions. The actual flow-control mechanism is defined in I.361. GFC flow control is part of a proposed controlled cell transfer (CCT) capability intended to meet the requirements of non-ATM LANs connected to a wide area ATM network [LUIN97]. In particular, CCT is intended to provide good service for high-volume bursty traffic with variable-length messages. In the remainder of this subsection, we examine the GFC mechanism, which has already been standardized.

When the equipment at the UNI is configured to support the GFC mechanism, two sets of procedures are used: uncontrolled transmission and controlled transmission. In essence, every connection is identified as either subject to flow control or not. Of those subject to flow control, there may be one group of controlled connections (Group A) that is the default, or controlled traffic may be classified into two groups of controlled connections (Group A and Group B); these are known respectively as the 1-queue and 2-queue models. Flow control is exercised in the direction from the subscriber to the network by the NT2 function.

First, we consider the operation of the GFC mechanism when there is only one group of controlled connections. The controlled equipment (TE) initializes two variables: TRANSMIT is a flag initialized to SET (1) and GO_CNTR, which is a credit counter, is initialized to 0. A third variable, GO_VALUE, is either initialized to 1

---

[1]This is the term used in ATM Forum documents. In ITU-T documents, this bit is referred to as the ATM-user-to-ATM-user (AAU) indication bit. The meaning is the same.

or set to some larger value at configuration time. The rules for transmission by the controlled device are as follows:

1. If TRANSMIT = 1, cells on uncontrolled connections may be sent at any time. If TRANSMIT = 0, no cells may be sent on either controlled or uncontrolled connections.

2. If a HALT signal is received from the controlling equipment, TRANSMIT is set to 0 and remains at zero until a NO_HALT signal is received, at which time TRANSMIT is set to 1.

3. If TRANSMIT = 1 and there is no cell to transmit on any uncontrolled connections, then

   ¤ If GO_CNTR > 0, then the TE may send a cell on a controlled connection. The TE marks that cell as a cell on a controlled connection and decrements GO_CNTR.

   ¤ If GO_CNTR = 0, then the TE may not send a cell on a controlled connection.

4. The TE sets GO_CNTR to GO_VALUE upon receiving a SET signal; a null signal has no effect on GO_CNTR.

The HALT signal is used logically to limit the effective ATM data rate and should be cyclic. For example, to reduce the data rate over a link by half, the HALT command is issued by the controlling equipment so as to be in effect 50% of the time. This is done in a predictable, regular pattern over the lifetime of the physical connection.

For the 2-queue model, there are two counters, each with a current counter value and an initialization value: GO_CNTR_A, GO_VALUE_A, GO_CNTR_B, and GO_VALUE_B. This enables the NT2 to control two separate groups of connections.

Table 16.3 summarizes the rules for setting GFC bits.

Header Error Control

In Section A.2 of Appendix A, the use of a code for error detection is discussed. This code is commonly used in data communications protocols, such as LAPD and LAPB. The procedure is as follows:

1. The transmit side calculates an error code value based on the contents of the transmitted data (e.g., an entire frame or the header of the frame).

2. The transmit side inserts the resulting code into the transmitted data as an additional field.

3. The receive side, using the same algorithm, calculates an error code value based on the contents of the received data.

4. The receive side compares the value that it has calculated with the contents of the error code field that is received as part of the transmission. If the codes match, it is assumed that no error has occurred. If there is no match, then an error is detected.

A similar procedure is adopted in ATM, with the use of an 8-bit header error-control field (HEC) that is calculated based on the remaining 32 bits of the header. In this case, the polynomial used to generate the code is $X^8 + X^2 + X + 1$ (see

Table 16.3 Generic Flow-Control (GFC) Field Coding

| | Uncontrolled | Controlling → controlled | | Controlled → controlling | |
		1-queue model	2-queue model	1-queue model	2-queue model
First bit	0	HALT(0)/NO_HALT(1)	HALT(0)/NO_HALT(1)	0	0
Second bit	0	SET(1)/NULL(0)	SET(1)/NULL(0) for Group A	Cell belongs to controlled(1) /uncontrolled(0)	Cell belongs to Group A(1/ or not (0)
Third bit	0	0	SET(1)/NULL(0) for Group B	0	Cell belongs to Group B(1)/ or not (0)
Fourth bit	0	0	0	Equipment is uncontrolled(0)/ controlled(1)	Equipment is uncontrolled(0)/ controlled(1)

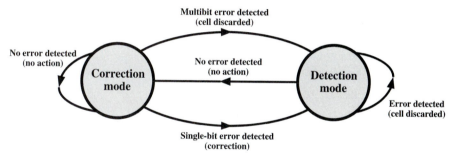

Figure 16.7 HEC Operation at Receiver.

Appendix A for a discussion of the use of polynomials to calculate an error code). There is, however, one significant difference. In the case of most existing protocols, such as LAPD and LAPB, the data that serve as input to the error code calculation are, in general, much longer than the size of the resulting error code. This allows for error detection. In the case of ATM, the input to the calculation is only 32 bits, compared with 8 bits for the code. The fact that this input is relatively short allows the code to be used not only for error detection but, in some cases, for actual error correction. This is because there is sufficient redundancy in the code to recover from certain error patterns.

Figure 16.7 depicts the operation of the HEC algorithm at the receiver. At initialization the receiver's error-correction algorithm is in the default mode for single-bit error correction. As each cell is received, the HEC calculation and comparison are performed. As long as no errors are detected, the receiver remains in error-correction mode. When an error is detected, the receiver will correct the error if it is a single-bit error or will detect that a multibit error has occurred. In either case, the receiver now moves to detection mode. In this mode, no attempt is made to correct errors. The reason for this change is to recognize a noise burst or other event that might cause a sequence of errors. The receiver remains in detection mode as long as errored cells are received. When a header is examined and found not to be in error, the receiver switches back to correction mode. The flowchart of Figure 16.8 shows the consequence of errors in the cell header.

The error-protection function provides both recovery from single-bit header errors and a low probability of the delivery of cells with errored headers under bursty error conditions. The error characteristics of fiber-based transmission systems appear to be a mix of single-bit errors and relatively large burst errors. For some transmission systems, the error-correction capability, which is more time-consuming, might not be invoked.

Figure 16.9, based on a figure in I.432, indicates how random bit errors impact the probability of occurrence of discarded cells and valid cells with errored headers.

Preassigned Cell Header Values

Cells reserved for the use of the physical layer have preassigned values reserved for the whole header; these values are not to be used by the ATM layer. The assigned values cover octets 1 through 4 of the cell header; the HEC field is

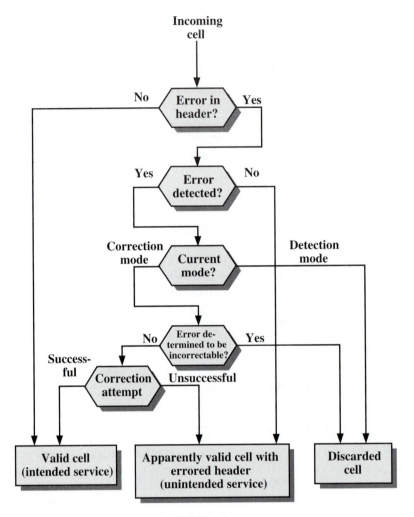

Figure 16.8 Effect of Error in Cell Header.

calculated in the usual fashion because the HEC function is a physical-layer rather than an ATM-layer function.

Figure 16.10 shows the general format of preassigned cell header values. Bits 5 through 28 of the cell header are set to 0; all other header bits can be used by assigned cells. Note that the least significant bit of octet 4 is always set to 1 for physical-layer cells; this bit is therefore not available for use in the cell loss priority (CLP) mechanism. Of course, because the CLP function is an ATM-layer and not a physical-layer function, the CLP bit is not needed for physical-layer cells.

Several specific preassigned physical-layer cell header values have been defined. Some of these relate to operation and maintenance (OAM) functions. Another assignment is for the idle cell. When there are no ATM or OAM cells available for transmission, an idle cell is inserted to adapt the rate of valid ATM cells to the payload capacity of the transmission system. Such cells can be discarded at the

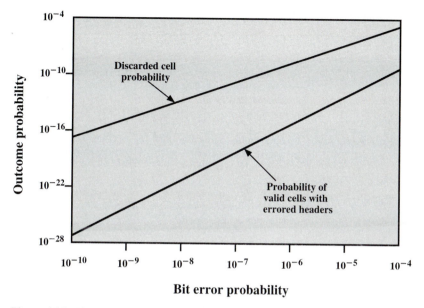

Figure 16.9   Impact of Random Bit Errors on HEC Performance.

receiving end or at some intermediate point for purposes of traffic flow control. Each octet of the information field of an idle cell is filled with 01101010.

Operation and Maintenance Functions

Recommendation I.610 describes functions for maintaining the physical layer and the ATM layer at the user–network interface. Maintenance is defined in Recommendation M.60 as "the combination of all technical and corresponding adminis-

	Octet 1	Octet 2	Octet 3	Octet 4
Idle cell identification	00000000	00000000	00000000	00000001
Physical layer OAM cell identification	00000000	00000000	00000000	00001001
Reserved for use of the physical layer	PPPP0000	00000000	00000000	0000PPP1

Note: P indicates that the bit is available for use by the physical layer. Values assigned to these bits have no meaning with respect to the fields occupying the corresponding bit positions of the ATM layer.

Figure 16.10   Preassigned Cell Header Values at the User–Network Interface (excluding the HEC field).

Table 16.4 OAM Actions (I.610)

Name	Action	Result
Performance monitoring	Normal functioning of the managed entity is monitored by continuous or periodic checking of functions.	Maintenance event information is produced.
Defect and failure detection	Malfunctions or predicted malfunctions are detected by continuous or periodic checking.	Maintenance event information or various alarms are produced.
System protection	Effect of failure of a managed entity is minimized by blocking or changeover to other entities.	The failed entity is excluded from operation.
Failure or performance information	Failure information is given to other management entities.	Alarm indications are given to other management planes. Response to a status report request is also given.
Fault localization	Determination by internal or external test system of a failed entity if failure information is insufficient.	

trative actions, including supervision actions, intended to retain an item in, or restore it to, a state in which it can perform a required function."

Table 16.4 lists the five phases, or types, of actions that are used by ITU-T in specifying an OAM capability. The last phase, fault localization, has not been addressed for B-ISDN and is a subject for further study.

OAM functions are implemented as bidirectional information flows that are defined on five hierarchical levels, associated with the ATM and physical layers. Figure 16.4 shows the relationship between the flows, labeled F1 through F5, and the hierarchical structure of the B-ISDN protocol reference model.[2] As an example of an OAM flow, cited in [HAND91], two endpoints could monitor a VPC by means of a loopback test. During the monitoring phase, each cell received at one endpoint could be repeated back to the sender.

Table 16.5 lists the OAM functions at the ATM layer. Monitoring of availability is done at the virtual path level and monitoring of performance at the virtual path and virtual channel levels. These OAM flows are provided by cells dedicated to ATM-layer OAM functions. The implementation of these cells is for further study. One possibility mentioned in I.610 is that the ATM-layer OAM cells could be identified by the payload type field in the cell header and by VPI/VCI.

OAM functions at the physical layer are examined in the next section.

---

[2]For cell-based transmission, flows F1 through F5 apply; for SDH-based transmission, only flows F3 through F5 apply. These forms of transmission are explained later in this chapter.

Table 16.5   OAM Functions of the ATM Layer

Level	Function	Flow	Defect/Failure Detection	System protection and failure information
Virtual Path	Monitoring of path availability Performance monitoring	F4	Path not available Degraded Performance	For further study
Virtual Channel	Monitoring of channel availability Performance monitoring	F5	Channel not available Degraded Performance	For further study

16.2 TRANSMISSION OF ATM CELLS

I.432 specifies that ATM cells may be transmitted at one of several data rates: 622.08 Mbps, 155.52 Mbps, 51.84 Mbps, or 25.6 Mbps. As with ISDN, we need to specify the transmission structure that will be used to carry this payload. Two approaches are defined in I.432: a cell-based physical layer and an SDH-based physical layer.[3] We examine each of these approaches in turn.

Cell–Based Physical Layer

For the cell-based physical layer, no framing is imposed. The interface structure consists of a continuous stream of 53-octet cells (Figure 16.11).

Synchronization

Because there is no external frame imposed in the cell-based approach, some form of synchronization is needed. Synchronization is achieved on the basis of the

Figure 16.11   Cell-Based Physical Interface for ATM Cell Transmission.

---

[3]The SDH-based approach is not defined for 25.6 Mbps.

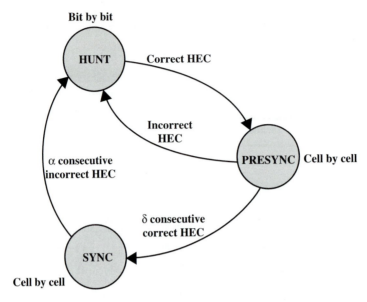

Figure 16.12 Cell Delineation State Diagram.

header error-control (HEC) field in the cell header. The procedure is as follows (Figure 16.12):

1. In the HUNT state, a cell-delineation algorithm is performed bit by bit to determine if the HEC coding law is observed (i.e., match between received HEC and calculated HEC). Once a match is achieved, it is assumed that one header has been found, and the method enters the PRESYNC state.

2. In the PRESYNC state, a cell structure is assumed. The cell-delineation algorithm is performed cell by cell until the encoding law has been confirmed δ times consecutively; then there is a transition to the SYNC state.

3. In the SYNC state, the HEC is used for error detection and correction (see Figure 16.7). Cell delineation is assumed to be lost if the HEC coding law is recognized as incorrect α times consecutively.

The values of α and δ are design parameters. Greater values of δ result in longer delays in establishing synchronization but in greater robustness against false delineation. Greater values of α result in longer delays in recognizing a misalignment but in greater robustness against false misalignment. Figures 16.13 and 16.14 show the impact of random bit errors on cell-delineation performance for various values of α and δ. The first figure shows the average amount of time that the receiver will maintain synchronization in the face of errors, with α as a parameter. The second figure shows the average amount of time to acquire synchronization as a function of error rate, with δ as a parameter.

The advantage of using a cell-based transmission scheme is the simplified interface that results when both transmission- and transfer-mode functions are based on a common structure.

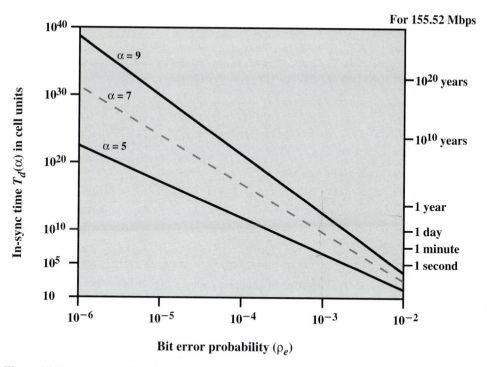

Figure 16.13 Impact of Random Bit Errors on Cell-Delineation Performance.

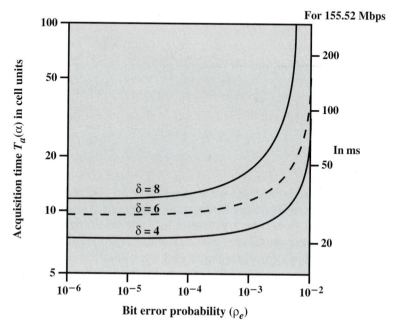

Figure 16.14 Acquisition Time versus Bit Error Probability.

Table 16.6 OAM Functions of the Cell-Based Physical Layer

Level	Function	Defect/Failure Detection
Regenerator Section	Physical layer OAM (PLOAM) cell recognition	Loss of PLOAM cell recognition
Digital Section	PLOAM cell recognition	Loss of PLOAM cell recognition
	Section error monitoring	Degraded error performance
	Section error reporting	Degraded error performance
Transmission Path	Customer network (CN) status monitoring	CN alarm indication signal
	Cell delineation	Loss of cell synchronization
	Header error detection/correction	Uncorrectable header
	Header error performance monitoring	Degraded header error performance
	Cell rate decoupling	Failure of insertion and suppression of idle cells

OAM Functions

Finally, ATM cells are used to convey operations, administration, and maintenance (OAM) information (see Figure 16.10).

Table 16.6 is an overview of OAM functions for the cell-based physical layer. The OAM cells are identified by preassigned cell header values, one for each level of information flow.

SDH–Based Physical Layer

The SDH-based physical layer imposes a structure on the ATM cell stream. In this section, we look at the I.432 specification for 155.52 Mbps; similar structures are used at other data rates.

Framing

For the SDH-based physical layer, framing is imposed using the STM-1 (STS-3) frame. Figure 16.15 shows the payload portion of an STM-1 frame. This payload may be offset from the beginning of the frame, as indicated by the pointer in the section overhead of the frame. As can be seen, the payload consists of a 9-octet path overhead portion and the remainder, which contains ATM cells. Because the payload capacity (2340 octets) is not an integer multiple of the cell length (53 octets), a cell may cross a payload boundary.

The H4 octet in the path overhead is set at the sending side to indicate the next occurrence of a cell boundary. That is, the value in the H4 field indicates the number of octets to the first cell boundary following the H4 octet. The permissible range of values is 0 to 52.

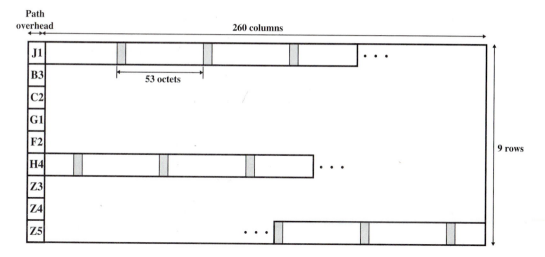

Figure 16.15   STM-1 Payload for SDH-Based ATM Cell Transmission.

The advantages of the SDH-based approach include the following [MINZ89a]:

- It can be used to carry either ATM-based or STM-based (synchronous transfer mode) payloads, making it possible initially to deploy a high-capacity fiber-based transmission infrastructure for a variety of circuit-switched and dedicated applications and then to migrate readily to the support of B-ISDN.

- Some specific connection can be circuit-switched using an SDH channel. For example, a connection carrying constant-bit-rate video traffic can be mapped into its own exclusive payload envelope of the STM-1 signal, which can be circuit switched. This may be more efficient than ATM switching.

- Using SDH synchronous multiplexing techniques, several ATM streams can be combined to build interfaces with higher bit rates than those supported by the ATM layer at a particular site. For example, four separate ATM streams, each with a bit rate of 155 Mbps (STM-1), can be combined to build a 622-Mbps (STM-4) interface. This arrangement may be more cost-effective than one using a single 622-Mbps ATM stream.

OAM Functions

With the SDH frame structure, OAM information is carried in the overhead octets of the frame. Flows F1 and F2 are carried on bytes in the section overhead. Flow F3 is carried in the path overhead. Part of the F3 flow could also be carried in physical-layer OAM cells as part of the ATM cell stream; this is a matter for further study.

Table 16.7 is an overview of OAM functions for the SDH-based physical layer. The VC-4 offset function refers to the placement of the ATM payload within the STM-1 frame.

Table 16.7 OAM Functions of the SDH-Based Physical Layer

Level	Function	Defect/Failure Detection
Regenerator Section	Frame alignment	Loss of frame
	Section error monitoring	Degraded error performance
Digital Section	Frame alignment	Loss of frame
	Section error monitoring	Degraded error performance
	Section error reporting	Degraded error performance
Transmission Path	Customer network (CN) status monitoring	CN alarm indication signal
	Cell delineation	Loss of cell synchronization
	VC-4 offset	Loss of AU-4 pointer
	Path error monitoring	Degraded error performance
	Path error reporting	Degraded error performance
	Cell rate decoupling	Failure of insertion and suppression of idle cells

16.3 ATM ADAPTATION LAYER

[handwritten margin note: Not at intermediate switches - only at Terminal Elements]

The use of ATM creates the need for an adaptation layer to support information-transfer protocols not based on ATM. Two examples are PCM (pulse-code modulation) voice and LAPD. PCM voice is an application that produces a stream of bits from a voice signal. To employ this application over ATM, it is necessary to assemble PCM bits into cells for transmission and to read them out on reception in such a way as to produce a smooth, constant flow of bits to the receiver. LAPD is the standard data link control protocol for ISDN and B-ISDN. It is necessary to map LAPD frames into ATM cells; this will usually mean segmenting one LAPD frame into a number of cells on transmission and reassembling the frame from cells on reception. By allowing the use of LAPD over ATM, all of the existing ISDN applications and control-signaling protocols can be used on B-ISDN.

AAL Services

I.362 lists the following general examples of services provided by AAL:

- Handling of transmission errors
- Segmentation and reassembly, to enable larger blocks of data to be carried in the information field of ATM cells
- Handling of lost and misinserted cell conditions
- Flow control and timing control

CBR | VBR | ABR | UBR

	Class A	Class B _CT VBR_ _NT VBR_	Class C	Class D
Timing relation between source and destination	Required		Not required	
Bit rate	Constant	Variable		
Connection mode	Connection oriented			Connectionless
AAL protocol	Type 1	Type 2	Type 3/4,Type 5	Type 3/4

best effort

Figure 16.16 Service Classification for AAL.

in order and correct

To minimize the number of different AAL protocols that must be specified to meet a variety of needs, ITU-T has defined four classes of service that cover a broad range of requirements (Figure 16.16). The classification is based on whether a timing relationship must be maintained between source and destination, whether the application requires a constant bit rate, and whether the transfer is connection oriented or connectionless. An example of a class A service is circuit emulation. In this case, a constant bit rate, which requires the maintenance of a timing relation, is used, and the transfer is connection-oriented. An example of a class B service is variable-bit-rate video, such as might be used in a teleconference. Here, the application is connection oriented and timing is important, but the bit rate varies depending on the amount of activity in the scene. Classes C and D correspond to data-transfer applications. In both cases, the bit rate may vary and no particular timing relationship is required; differences in data rate are handled by the end systems using buffers. The data transfer may be either connection oriented (class C) or connectionless (class D).

AAL Protocols

The AAL layer is organized in two logical sublayers: the convergence sublayer (CS) and the segmentation and reassembly sublayer (SAR). The convergence sublayer provides the functions needed to support specific applications using AAL. Each application attaches to AAL at a service access point (SAP), which is simply the address of the application (see Appendix B for a discussion of SAPs). This sublayer is thus service dependent.

The segmentation and reassembly sublayer is responsible for packaging information received from CS into cells for transmission and unpacking the information at the other end. As we have seen, at the ATM layer, each cell consists of a 5-octet header and a 48-octet information field. Thus, SAR must pack any SAR headers and trailers plus CS information into 48-octet blocks.

Figure 16.17 indicates the general protocol architecture for ATM and AAL. Typically, a higher-layer block of data is encapsulated in a single protocol data unit (PDU) consisting of the higher-layer data and possibly a header and trailer containing protocol information at the CS level. This CS PDU is then passed down to the SAR layer and segmented into a number of blocks. Each of these blocks is encapsulated in a single 48-octet SAR PDU, which may include a header and a

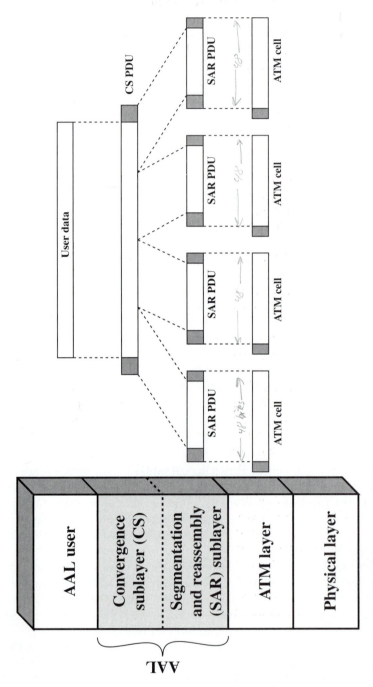

Figure 16.17 AAL Protocols and PDUs.

trailer in addition to the block of data passed down from CS. Finally, each SAR PDU forms the payload of a single ATM cell.

Initially, ITU-T defined one protocol type for each class of service, named type 1 through type 4. Actually, each protocol type consists of two protocols, one at the CS sublayer and one at the SAR sublayer. More recently, types 3 and 4 were merged, with the result being defined as type 3/4, and a new type, type 5, was defined. Figure 16.16 shows which services are supported by which types, and Table 16.8 lists the currently defined functional details of the four types.

Figure 16.18 shows the formats of the PDU at the SAR level except for type 2, which has not yet been defined.

AAL Type 1

For type 1 operation, we are dealing with a constant-bit-rate source. In this case, the only responsibility of the SAR protocol is to pack the bits into cells for transmission and unpack them at reception. Each block is accompanied by a **sequence number** (SN) so that errored PDUs can be tracked. The 4-bit SN field consists of a convergence sublayer indication (CSI) bit and a 3-bit sequence count (SC). On transmission, the CS sublayer provides the SAR sublayer with a CSI value to place in the SN field. On reception, the SAR sublayer passes this value up to the CS sublayer. The CSI bit is used in to communicate information in the following fashion: The 3-bit sequence count defines a frame structure consisting of 8 consecutive ATM cells, numbered 0 through 7. The CSI values in cells 1, 3, 5, and 7 are interpreted as a 4-bit timing value. This value is used to provide a measure of the frequency difference between the network's reference clock and the transmitter's clock. In even-numbered cells, the CSI can be used to support the blocking of information from a higher layer. If the CSI bit is set to one in an even-numbered cell (0, 2, 4, 6), then the first octet of the SAR-PDU payload is a pointer that indicates the start of the next structured block within the payload of this cell and the next cell. That is, two cells (0-1, 2-3, 4-5, 6-7) are treated as containing a one-octet pointer and a 93-octet payload, and the pointer indicates where in that 93-octet payload is the first octet of the next block of data. The offset value 93 is used to indicate that the end of the 93-octet payload coincides with the end of a structured block. The dummy offset value 127 is used when no structure boundary is being indicated.

The 3-bit SC field, as we have just seen, provides an 8-cell frame structure. It also provides a means of detecting lost/misordered cells.

The **sequence number protection** (SNP) field is an error code for error detection and possibly correction on the sequence number field. It consists of a 3-bit cyclic redundancy check (CRC), calculated over the 4-bit SN field, and a parity bit. The parity bit is set so that the parity of the 8-bit SAR header is even.

No CS PDU has been defined for type 1. The functions of the CS sublayer for type 1 primarily have to do with clocking and synchronization, and a separate CS header is not needed.

AAL Type 2

The remainder of the protocol types (2, 3/4, and 5) deal with variable-bit-rate information. Type 2 is intended for analog applications, such as video and audio, that require timing information but do not require a constant bit rate. An initial

(text continues on page 444)

Table 16.8 ATM Adaptation-Layer Protocol Types

	Services Provided	Overall Functions	SAR Functions	CS Functions
Type 1	• Transfer of SDUs with constant bit rate (CBR) • Transfer of timing information between source and destination • Transfer of structure information between source and destination • Indication of lost or errored information not recovered by type 1	• Segmentation and reassembly • Handling of cell delay variation • Handling of cell payload assembly delay • Handling of lost and misinserted cells • Source clock frequency recovery at destination • Recovery of the source data structure at the receiver • Monitoring and handling of PCI bit errors • Monitoring of user information for bit errors and possible corrective action	• Mapping between CS-PDU and SAR-PDU • Indicate existence of CS function • Sequence numbering • Error protection	• Handling of cell delay variation • Handling of lost and misinserted cells • For some services, clock recovery at the receiver • Transfer of structure information • Forward error correction for high-quality video and audio • Report end-to-end performance status
Type 2	• Transfer of SDUs with variable bit rate (VBR) • Transfer of timing information between source and destination • Indication of lost or errored information not recovered by type 2	• Segmentation and reassembly • Handling of cell delay variation • Handling of lost and misinserted cells • Source clock frequency recovery at destination • Recovery of the source data structure at the receiver • Monitoring and handling of header and trailer bit errors • Monitoring of user information for bit errors and possible corrective action	For further study	For further study
Type 3/4	• Message-mode service • Streaming-mode service • Assured operation • Nonassured operation		• Segmentation and reassembly • Error detection • Sequence integrity • Multiplexing	• Error detection and handling • Indication of buffer allocation size
Type 5	• Message-mode service • Streaming-mode service • Assured operation • Nonassured operation		• Segmentation and reassembly • Handling of congestion information • Handling of loss priority information	• Error detection and handling • Padding • Handling of congestion information • Handling of loss priority information

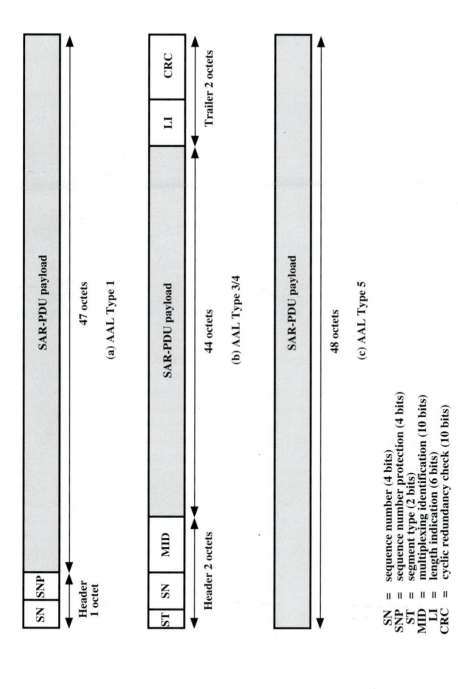

Figure 16.18 Segmentation and Reassembly (SAR) Protocol Data Units (PDUs).

specification for the type 2 protocols (SAR and CS) has been withdrawn, and the current version of I.363 simply lists the services and functions shown in Table 16.8.

AAL Type 3/4

The initial specifications of AAL type 3 and type 4 were very similar in terms of PDU format and functionality. Accordingly, it was decided within ITU-T to combine the two into a single protocol specification at the SAR and CS sublayers, known as type 3/4.

The types of service provided by AAL type 3/4 can be characterized along two dimensions:

1. The service may be connectionless or connection oriented. In the former case, each block of data presented to the SAR layer (SAR service data unit, or SDU) is treated independently. In the latter case, it is possible to define multiple SAR logical connections over a single ATM connection.

2. The service may be message mode or streaming mode. Message-mode service transfers framed data. Thus, any of the OSI-related protocols and applications would fit into this category. In particular, LAPD or frame relay would be message mode. A single block of data from the layer above AAL is transferred in one or more cells. Streaming-mode service supports the transfer of low-speed continuous data with low delay requirements. The data are presented to AAL in fixed-size blocks, which may be as small as one octet. One block is transferred per cell.

The type 3/4 AAL provides its data-transfer service by accepting blocks of data from the next higher layer and transmitting each to a destination AAL user. Because the ATM layer limits data transfer to a cell payload of 48 octets, the AAL layer must provide, at minimum, a segmentation and reassembly function.

The approach taken by type 3/4 AAL is depicted in Figure 16.19. A block of data from a higher layer, such as a PDU, is encapsulated into a PDU at the CS sublayer. In fact, this sublayer is referred to as the common part convergence sublayer (CPCS), leaving open the possibility that additional, specialized functions may be performed at the CS level. The CPCS PDU is then passed to the SAR sublayer, where it is broken up into 44-octet payload blocks. Each payload block can fit into an SAR PDU, which includes a header and a trailer for a total length of 48 octets. Each 48-octet SAR PDU fits into a single ATM cell.

To understand the functioning of the two sublayers within AAL type 3/4, let us look at the respective PDUs. The CPCS PDU is shown in Figure 16.20a. The header consists of three fields:

- **Common part indicator (1 octet):** Indicates the interpretation of the remaining fields in the CPCS PDU header. Currently, only one interpretation is defined: A CPI value of 0 indicates that the BASize field defines the buffer allocation requirement in octets and that the Length field defines the length of the CPCS PDU payload in octets.
- **Beginning tag (1 octet):** A number associated with a particular CPCS PDU. The same value appears in the Btag field in the header and the Etag field in the

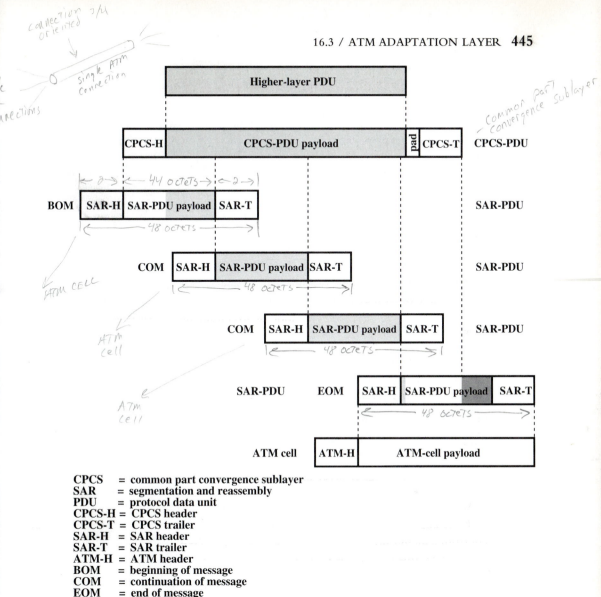

Figure 16.19   Example of AAL 3/4 Transmission.

trailer. The sender changes the value for each successive CPCS PDU, enabling the receiver to associate correctly the header and trailer of each CPCS PDU.

- **Buffer allocation size (2 octets):** Indicates to the receiving peer entity the maximum buffer size required for reassembly of the CPCS SDU (service data unit). For message mode, the value is equal to the CPCS PDU payload length. For streaming mode, the value is greater than or equal to the CPCS PDU payload length.

The payload from the next higher layer is padded out so that the trailer begins on a 32-bit boundary. The CPCS PDU trailer contains these fields:

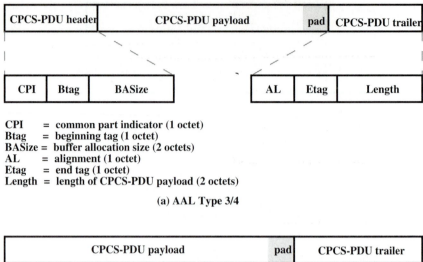

CPI   = common part indicator (1 octet)
Btag   = beginning tag (1 octet)
BASize = buffer allocation size (2 octets)
AL   = alignment (1 octet)
Etag   = end tag (1 octet)
Length = length of CPCS-PDU payload (2 octets)

(a) AAL Type 3/4

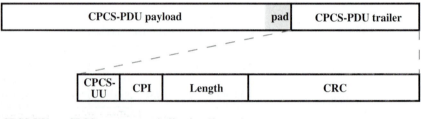

CPCS-UU = CPCS user-to-user indication (1 octet)
CPI   = common part indicator (1 octet)
Length   = length of CPCS-PDU payload (2 octets)
CRC   = cyclic redundancy check (4 octets)

(b) AAL Type 5

Figure 16.20   CPCS PDUs.

- **Alignment (1 octet):** A filler octet whose only purpose is to make the length of the CPCS PDU equal to 32 bits.
- **End tag (1 octet):** Used with the Btag field in the header.
- **Length (2 octets):** Length of the CPCS PDU payload field.

Thus, the purpose of the CPCS layer is to alert the receiver that a block of data is coming in segments and that buffer space must be allocated for the reassembly. This enables the receiving CPCS function to verify the correct reception of the entire CPCS PDU.

Figure 16.18b shows the format for the type 3/4 SAR PDU. Information from the next higher layer, the CS, arrives in blocks referred to as SAR service data units (SDUs). Each SDU is transmitted in one or more SAR PDUs. Each SAR PDU, in turn, is transmitted in a single ATM cell. The SAR PDU header fields are used for the process of segmenting SDUs on transmission and reassembling them on reception:

- **Segment type (2 bits):** There are four types of SAR PDUs. A single sequence message (SSM) contains an entire SAR SDU. If the SAR SDU is segmented into two or more SAR PDUs, the first SAR PDU is the beginning of message (BOM), the last SAR PDU is the end of message (EOM), and any intermediate SAR PDUs are continuation of message (COM).
- **Sequence number (4 bits):** Used in reassembling an SAR SDU to verify that all of the SAR PDUs have been received and concatenated properly. A value of the sequence number is set in the BOM and incremented for each successive COM and the EOM for a single SAR SDU.
- **Multiplexing identification (10 bits):** This is a unique identifier associated with the set of SAR PDUs that carry a single SAR SDU. Again, this number is needed to ensure proper reassembly. In connection-oriented applications, this field allows the multiplexing of multiple SAR connections on a single ATM connection.

The SAR PDU trailer contains the following fields:

- **Length indication (6 bits):** Indicates the number of octets from the SAR SDU that occupy the segmentation unit of the SAR PDU. The number has a value between 4 and 44 octets, in multiples of 4. The value will always be 44 for BOM and COM SAR PDUs. It is a lesser number in an SSM if the SAR SDU is less than 44 octets in length. It is a lesser number in an EOM if the length of the SAR SDU is not an integer multiple of 44 octets in length, necessitating the use of a partially filled EOM. In that case, the remainder of the SAR PDU payload is padded.
- **CRC (10 bits):** This is a 10-bit CRC on the entire SAR PDU.

A distinctive feature of AAL 3/4 is that it can multiplex different streams of data on the same virtual ATM connection (VCI/VPI). For the connection-oriented service, each logical connection between AAL users is assigned a unique MID value. Thus, the cell traffic from up to 210 different AAL connections can be multiplexed and interleaved over a single ATM connection. For the connectionless service, the MID field can be used to communicate a unique identifier associated with each connectionless user and, again, traffic from multiple AAL users may be multiplexed.

AAL Type 5

The most recent addition to the AAL specification is the type 5 protocol. This protocol was introduced to provide a streamlined transport facility for higher-layer protocols that are connection oriented. If it is assumed that the higher layer takes care of connection management and that the ATM layer produces minimal errors, then most of the fields in the SAR and CPCS PDUs are not necessary. For example, with connection-oriented service, the MID field is not necessary: The VCI/VPI is available for cell-by-cell multiplexing, and the higher layer supports message-by-message multiplexing.

Type 5 was introduced to

- Reduce protocol processing overhead.
- Reduce transmission overhead.
- Ensure adaptability to existing transport protocols.

Figures 16.18c and 16.20b show the SAR PDU and CPCS PDU formats for type 5. Compared with type 3/4, we have the following amounts of overhead:

Type 3/4	Type 5
8 octets per AAL SDU	8 octets per AAL SDU
4 octets per ATM cell	0 octets per ATM cell

To understand the operation of type 5, let us begin with the CPCS level. The CPCS PDU includes a trailer with the following fields:

- **CPCS user-to-user indication (1 octet):** Used to transfer user-to-user information transparently.
- **Common part indicator (1 octet):** Indicates the interpretation of the remaining fields in the CPCS PDU trailer. Currently, only one interpretation is defined.
- **Length (2 octets):** Length of the CPCS PDU payload field.
- **Cyclic redundancy check (4 octets):** Used to detect bit errors in the CPCS PDU.

Note that the BASize facility has been eliminated. If it is felt necessary for the receiver to preallocate a buffer to do reassembly, this information must be passed at a higher layer. And, in fact, many higher-layer protocols set or negotiate a maximum PDU size; this information can be used by the receiver to allocate buffers. A 32-bit CRC protects the entire CPCS PDU, whereas for AAL type 3/4, a 10-bit CRC is provided for each SAR PDU. The type 5 CRC provides strong protection against bit errors. In addition, [WANG92] shows that the 32-bit CRC provides robust detection of cell misordering, a fault condition that might be possible under network failure conditions.

The payload from the next higher layer is padded out so that the entire CPCS PDU is a multiple of 48 octets.

The SAR PDU consists simply of 48 octets of payload, carrying a portion of the CPCS PDU. The lack of protocol overhead has several implications:

- Because there is no sequence number, the receiver must assume that all SAR PDUs arrive in the proper order for reassembly. The CRC field in the CPCS PDU is intended to guarantee that.
- The lack of MID field means that it is not possible to interleave cells from different CPCS PDUs. Therefore, each successive SAR PDU carries a portion of the current CPCS PDU or the first block of the next CPCS PDU. To distinguish between these two cases, the SDU type bit in the payload type field of the ATM cell header is used (Figure 16.6). A CPCS PDU consists of zero or

more consecutive SAR PDUs with SDU set to 0 followed immediately by an SAR PDU with SDU set to 1.

- The lack of an LI field means that there is no way for the SAR entity to distinguish between CPCS PDU octets and filler in the last SAR PDU. Therefore, there is no way for the SAR entity to find the CPCS PDU trailer in the last SAR PDU. To avoid this situation, it is required that the CPCS PDU payload be padded out so that the last bit of the CPCS trailer occurs as the last bit of the final SAR PDU.

Figure 16.21 shows an example of AAL 5 transmission. The CPCS PDU, including padding and trailer, is divided into 48-octet blocks. Each block is transmitted in a single ATM cell.

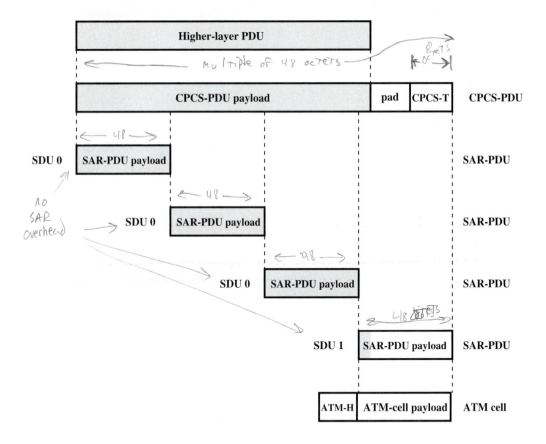

CPCS   = common part convergence sublayer
SAR   = segmentation and reassembly
PDU   = protocol data unit
CPCS-T   = CPCS trailer
ATM-H   = ATM header
SDU   = service data unit type bit

Figure 16.21   Example of AAL 5 Transmission.

16.4 SUMMARY

As with frame relay, <u>ATM is a streamlined packet-transfer interface</u>. ATM makes use of fixed-size packets, called cells. The use of a fixed size and fixed format results in an efficient scheme for transmission over high-speed networks.

Some form of transmission structure must be used to transport ATM cells. One option is the use of a continuous stream of cells, with no multiplex frame structure imposed at the interface. Synchronization is on a cell-by-cell basis. That is, it is the responsibility of the receiver to assure that it properly delineates cells on the 53-octet cell boundaries. The way that this is to be accomplished is by use of the header error-control (HEC) field. As long as the HEC calculation is indicating no errors, it is assumed that cell alignment is being properly maintained. An occasional error does not change this assumption. However, a string of error detections would indicate that the receiver is out of alignment, at which point it performs a hunting procedure to recover alignment.

The second option is to place the cells in a synchronous time-division multiplex envelope. In this case, the bit stream at the interface has an external frame based on the Synchronous Digital Hierarchy (SDH) defined in Recommendation G.709.

The use of ATM creates the need for an adaptation layer to support information-transfer protocols not based on ATM. The ATM adaptation layer (AAL) packages information from the AAL user into 48-octet packages to fit into the ATM cell. This may involve aggregating bits from a bit stream or segmenting a frame into smaller pieces.

16.5 RECOMMENDED READING

[GORA95], [MCDY95], [HAND94], and [PRYC96] provide in-depth coverage of ATM. The virtual path/virtual channel approach of ATM is examined in [SATO90], [SATO91], and [BURG91]. [ARMI93] and [SUZU94] discuss AAL and compare types 3/4 and 5.

ARMI93   Armitage, G., and Adams, K. "Packet Reassembly During Cell Loss." *IEEE Network*, September 1993.

BURG91   Burg, J., and Dorman, D. "Broadband ISDN Resource Management: The Role of Virtual Paths." *IEEE Communications Magazine*, September 1991.

GORA95   Goralski, W. *Introduction to ATM Networking.* New York: McGraw-Hill, 1995.

HAND94   Handel, R.; Huber, N.; and Schroder, S. *ATM Networks: Concepts, Protocols, Applications.* Reading, MA: Addison-Wesley, 1994.

MCDY95   McDysan, D., and Spohn, D. *ATM: Theory and Application.* New York: McGraw-Hill, 1995.

PRYC96   Prycker, M. *Asynchronous Transfer Mode: Solutions for Broadband ISDN.* New York: Ellis Horwood, 1996.

SATO90   Sato, K.; Ohta, S.; and Tokizawa, I. "Broad-band ATM Network Architecture Based on Virtual Paths." *IEEE Transactions on Communications,* August 1990.

SATO91   Sato, K.; Ueda, H.; and Yoshikai, M. "The Role of Virtual Path Crossconnection." *IEEE LTS,* August 1991.

SUZU94   Suzuki, T. "ATM Adaptation Layer Protocol." *IEEE Communications Magazine*, April 1994.

Recommended Web sites are as follows:

- **ATM Forum Web site:** Contains technical specifications, white papers, and online copies of the Forum's publication, *53 Bytes*.
- **Cell Relay Retreat:** Contains archives of the cell-relay mailing list, links to numerous ATM-related documents, and links to many ATM-related Web sites.

16.6 PROBLEMS

16.1 List all 16 possible values of the GFC field and the interpretation of each value (some values are illegal).

16.2 Although ATM does not include any end-to-end error detection and control functions on the user data, it is provided with an HEC field to detect and correct header errors. Let us consider the value of this feature. Suppose that the bit error rate of the transmission system is B. If errors are uniformly distributed, then the probability of an error in the header is

$$\frac{h}{h + i} \times B$$

and the probability of error in the data field is

$$\frac{i}{h + i} \times B$$

where h is the number of bits in the header and i is the number of bits in the data field.

a. Suppose that errors in the header are not detected and not corrected. In that case, a header error may result in a misrouting of the cell to the wrong destination; therefore, i bits will arrive at an incorrect destination, and i bits will not arrive at the correct destination. What is the overall bit error rate $B1$? Find an expression for the multiplication effect on the bit error rate: $M1 = B1/B$.

b. Now suppose that header errors are detected but not corrected. In that case, i bits will not arrive at the correct destination. What is the overall bit error rate $B2$? Find an expression for the multiplication effect on the bit error rate: $M2 = B2/B$.

c. Now suppose that header errors are detected and corrected. What is the overall bit error rate $B3$? Find an expression for the multiplication effect on the bit error rate: $M3 = B3/B$.

d. Plot $M1$, $M2$, and $M3$ as a function of header length, for $i = 48 \times 8 = 384$ bits. Comment on the results.

16.3 One key design decision for ATM was whether to use fixed- or variable-length cells. Let us consider this decision from the point of view of efficiency. We can define transmission efficiency as

$$N = \frac{\text{Number of information octets}}{\text{Number of information octets} + \text{Number of overhead octets}}$$

a. Consider the use of fixed-length packets. In this case the overhead consists of the header octets. Define:

L = Data field size of the cell in octets

H = Header size of the cell in octets

X = Number of information octets to be transmitted as a single message

Derive an expression for N. *Hint*: the expression will need to use the operator $\lceil \bullet \rceil$, where $\lceil Y \rceil$ = the smallest integer greater than or equal to Y.

b. If cells have variable length, then overhead is determined by the header, plus the flags to delimit the cells or an additional length field in the header. Let Hv = additional overhead octets required to enable the use of variable-length cells. Derive an expression for N in terms of X, H, and Hv.

c. Let $L = 48$, $H = 5$, and $Hv = 2$. Plot N versus message size for fixed- and variable-length cells. Comment on the results.

16.4 Another key design decision for ATM is the size of the data field for fixed-size cells. Let us consider this decision from the point of view of efficiency and delay.

a. Assume that an extended transmission takes place, so that all cells are completely filled. Derive an expression for the efficiency N as a function of H and L.

b. Packetization delay is the delay introduced into a transmission stream by the need to buffer bits until an entire packet is filled before transmission. Derive an expression for this delay as a function of L and the data rate R of the source.

c. Common data rates for voice coding are 32 kbps and 64 kbps. Plot packetization delay as a function of L for these two data rates; use a left-hand y axis with a maximum value of 2 ms. On the same graph, plot transmission efficiency as a function of L; use a right-hand y axis with a maximum value of 100%. Comment on the results.

16.5 Suppose that AAL 3/4 is being used and that the receiver is in an idle state (no incoming cells). Then a block of user data is transmitted as a sequence of SAR-PDUs.

a. Suppose that the BOM SAR-PDU is lost. What happens at the receiving end?

b. Suppose that one of the COM SAR-PDUs is lost. What happens at the receiving end?

c. Suppose that 16 consecutive COM SAR-PDUs are lost. What happens at the receiving end?

d. Suppose that a multiple of 16 consecutive COM SAR-PDUs are lost. What happens at the receiving end?

16.6 Again using AAL 3/4, suppose that the receiver is in an idle state and that two blocks of user data are transmitted as two separate sequences of SAR-PDUs.

a. Suppose that the EOM SAR-PDU of the first sequence is lost. What happens at the receiving end?

b. Suppose that the EOM SAR-PDU of the first sequence and the BOM SAR-PDU of the second sequence are both lost. What happens at the receiving end?

16.7 Suppose that AAL 5 is being used and that the receiver is in an idle state (no incoming cells). Then a block of user data is transmitted as a sequence of SAR-PDUs.

a. Suppose that a single bit error in one of the SAR-PDUs occurs. What happens at the receiving end?

b. Suppose that one of the cells with SDU type bit = 0 is lost. What happens at the receiving end?

c. Suppose that one of the cells with SDU type bit = 1 is lost. What happens at the receiving end?

CHAPTER 17

ATM TRAFFIC AND CONGESTION CONTROL

As is the case with frame relay networks, traffic and congestion control techniques are vital to the successful operation of ATM-based networks. Without such techniques, traffic from user nodes can exceed the capacity of the network, causing memory buffers of ATM switches to overflow and leading to data losses.

Congestion control in ATM networks presents difficulties not found in other types of networks, including frame relay networks. The complexity of the problem is compounded by the limited number of overhead bits available for exerting control over the flow of user cells. This area is currently the subject of intense research. ITU-T has defined an initial set of traffic and congestion control capabilities aiming at simple mechanisms and realistic network efficiency; these are specified in I.371. The ATM Forum has published a somewhat more advanced version of this set in the Traffic Management Specification Version 4.0 [ATM96]. This chapter focuses on the ATM Forum specifications.

We begin with an overview of the congestion problem and the framework adopted by ITU-T and the ATM Forum. Then we look at the types of traffic ATM is intended to support and the traffic-related attributes used to characterize traffic performance. The next section examines traffic management, which includes actions taken by the network to avoid congestion and actions taken by the network to minimize the intensity, spread, and duration of congestion once congestion has already occurred. Finally, we look at the congestion control schemes developed for dealing with bursty traffic, which have been adopted as part of the available bit rate (ABR) service.

17.1 REQUIREMENTS FOR ATM TRAFFIC AND CONGESTION CONTROL

The types of traffic patterns imposed on ATM networks, as well as the transmission characteristics of those networks, differ markedly from those of other switching networks. Most packet-switching and frame relay networks carry non-real-time data traffic. Typically, the traffic on individual virtual circuits or frame relay connections is bursty in nature, and the receiving system expects to receive incoming traffic on each connection in a bursty fashion. As a result,

1. The network does not need to replicate the exact timing pattern of incoming traffic at the exit node.
2. Simple statistical multiplexing can be used to accommodate multiple logical connections over the physical interface between user and network. The average data rate required by each connection is less than the burst rate for that connection, and the user–network interface (UNI) need only be designed for a capacity somewhat greater than the sum of the average data rates for all connections.

A number of tools have been developed for control of congestion in packet-switched and frame relay networks, as we have seen. These types of congestion control schemes are inadequate for ATM networks. [GERS91] cites the following reasons:

1. Much of the traffic is not amenable to flow control. For example, voice and video traffic sources cannot stop generating cells even when the network is congested.
2. Feedback is slow due to the drastically reduced cell transmission time compared to propagation delays across the network.
3. ATM networks typically support a wide range of applications requiring capacity ranging from a few kbps to several hundred Mbps. Relatively simple-minded congestion control schemes generally end up penalizing one end or the other of that spectrum.
4. Applications on ATM networks may generate very different traffic patterns (e.g., constant-bit-rate versus variable-bit-rate sources). Again, it is difficult for conventional congestion control techniques to handle fairly such variety.
5. Different applications on ATM networks require different network services (e.g., delay-sensitive service for voice and video, and loss-sensitive service for data).
6. The very high speeds in switching and transmission make ATM networks more volatile in terms of congestion and traffic control. A scheme that relies heavily on reacting to changing conditions will produce extreme and wasteful fluctuations in routing policy and flow control.

Two key performance issues that relate to the preceding points are latency/speed effects and cell delay variation, topics to which we now turn.

Latency/Speed Effects

Consider the transfer of ATM cells over a network at a data rate of 150 Mbps. At that rate, it takes $(53 \times 8 \text{ bits})/(150 \times 10^6 \text{ bps}) \approx 3 \times 10^{-6}$ seconds to insert a single cell onto the network. The time it takes to transfer the cell from the source to the destination user will depend on the number of intermediate ATM switches, the switching time at each switch, and the propagation time along all links in the path from source to destination. For simplicity, ignore ATM switching delays and assume propagation at the speed of light. Then, if source and destination are on opposite coasts of the United States, the round-trip propagation delay is about 30×10^{-3} seconds.

With these conditions in place, suppose that source A is performing a long file transfer to destination B and that implicit congestion control is being used (i.e., there are no explicit congestion notifications; the source deduces the presence of congestion by the loss of data). If the network drops a cell due to congestion, B can return a reject message to A, which must then retransmit the dropped cell and possibly all subsequent cells. But by the time the notification gets back to A, it has transmitted an additional N cells, where

$$N = \frac{30 \times 10^{-3} \text{ seconds}}{3 \times 10^{-6} \text{ seconds/cell}} = 10^4 \text{ cells} = 4.24 \times 10^6 \text{ bits}$$

Over 4 megabits of data have been transmitted before A can react to the congestion indication.

This calculation helps to explain why techniques that are satisfactory for more traditional networks break down when dealing with ATM WANs.

We can get a better grasp at the implications of this example by considering a parameter that is commonly used in characterizing network performance, generally designated as a, and defined as

$$a = \frac{\text{Propagation time}}{\text{Insertion time}}$$

The insertion time is equal to the length of the cell L divided by the data rate R, so for a propagation time P

$$a = \frac{P}{L/R} = \frac{P \times R}{L}$$

One useful way of looking at a is that it represents the length of the network path in bits $(P \times R)$ compared to the length of the cell in bits (L), or the number of cells that can be in the pipeline from source to destination at one time. From our example, we can conclude that the smaller the value of a, the more responsive end systems will be to feedback concerning congestion.

Table 17.1 shows values of a for some representative networks, assuming a cell size of 53 octets. Because the value of a increases with an increase in either data rate or distance, the range of values is enormous. From a typical local area network (LAN) with an extent of about 1000 m, to a continent-wide ATM wide area network (WAN), there is a range of over 5 orders of magnitude for this critical parameter. This helps to explain why the techniques that are satisfactory for more traditional networks break down when dealing with ATM WANs.

Table 17.1 Representative Values of *a*

	Data Rate (Mbps)	Propagation Delay (ms)	*a*
Ethernet	10	0.005	0.1
Fiber LAN (FDDI)	100	0.01	2.4
Metropolitan area network	45	0.1	10.6
Wide area packet-switching network	0.06	15	2.1
Satellite link	0.06	270	38
Frame relay WAN	1.5	15	53
ATM WAN	150	15	5,300
ATM WAN	600	15	21,200

Cell Delay Variation

For an ATM network, voice and video signals can be digitized and transmitted as a stream of cells. A key requirement, especially for voice, is that the delay across the network be short. Generally, this will be the case for ATM networks. As we have discussed, ATM is designed to minimize the processing and transmission overhead internal to the network so that very fast cell switching and routing is possible.

There is another important requirement that to some extent conflicts with the preceding requirement—namely, that the rate of delivery of cells to the destination user must be constant. It is inevitable that there will be some variability in the rate of delivery of cells due both to effects within the network and at the source UNI; we summarize these effects presently. First, let us consider how the destination user might cope with variations in the delay of cells as the transit from source user to destination user.

A general procedure for achieving a constant bit rate (CBR) is illustrated in Figure 17.1. Let $D(i)$ represent the end-to-end delay experienced by the ith cell. The destination system does not know the exact amount of this delay: There is no time-stamp information associated with each cell and, even if there were, it is impossible to keep source and destination clocks perfectly synchronized. When the first cell on a connection arrives at time $t(0)$, the target user delays the cell an additional amount $V(0)$ prior to delivery to the application. $V(0)$ is an estimate of the amount of cell delay variation that this application can tolerate and that is likely to be produced by the network.

Subsequent cells are delayed so that they are delivered to the user at a constant rate of R cells per second. The time between delivery of cells to the target application (time between the start of delivery of one cell and the start of delivery of the next cell) is therefore $\delta = 1/R$. To achieve a constant rate, the next cell is delayed a variable amount $V(1)$ to satisfy

$$t(1) + V(1) = t(0) + V(0) + \delta$$

So

$$V(1) = V(0) - [t(1) - (t(0) + \delta)]$$

In general,

$$V(i) = V(0) - [t(i) - (t(0) + i \times \delta)]$$

which can also be expressed as

$$V(i) = V(i - 1) - [t(i) - (t(i-1) + \delta)]$$

If the computed value of $V(i)$ is negative, then that cell is discarded. The result is that data are delivered to the higher layer at a constant bit rate, with occasional gaps due to dropped cells.

The amount of the initial delay $V(0)$, which is also the average delay applied to all incoming cells, is a function of the anticipated cell delay variation. To minimize this delay, a subscriber will therefore request a minimal cell delay variation from the network provider. This leads to a tradeoff: Cell delay variation can be reduced by increasing the data rate at the UNI relative to the load and by increasing resources within the network.

Network Contribution to Cell Delay Variation

One component of cell delay variation is due to events within the network. For packet-switching networks, packet delay variation can be considerable due to queuing effects at each of the intermediate switching nodes and the processing time

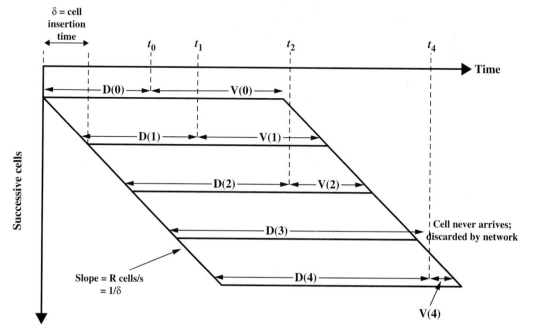

Figure 17.1 Time Reassembly of CBR Cells.

required to analyze packet headers and perform routing. To a much lesser extent, this is also true of frame delay variation in frame relay networks. In the case of ATM networks, cell delay variations due to network effects are likely to be even less than for frame relay. The principal reasons for this are the following:

- The ATM protocol is designed to minimize processing overhead at intermediate switching nodes. The cells are fixed size with fixed header formats, and there is no flow-control or error-control processing required.
- To accommodate the high speeds of ATM networks, ATM switches have had to be designed to provide extremely high throughput. Thus, the processing time for an individual cell at a node is negligible.

The only factor that could lead to noticeable cell delay variation within the network is congestion. If the network begins to become congested, either cells must be discarded or there will be a buildup of queuing delays at affected switches. Thus, it is important that the total load accepted by the network at any time not be such as to cause congestion.

Cell Delay Variation at the UNI

Even if an application generates data for transmission at a constant bit rate, cell delay variation can occur at the source due to the processing that takes place at the three layers of the ATM model.

Figure 17.2 illustrates the potential causes of cell delay variation. In this example, ATM connections A and B support user data rates of X and Y Mbps, respectively ($X > Y$). At the AAL level, data are segmented into 48-octet blocks. Note that on a time diagram, the blocks appear to be of different sizes for the two connections; specifically, the time required to generate a 48-octet block of data, in microseconds, is

$$\text{Connection A: } \frac{48 \times 8}{X}$$

$$\text{Connection B: } \frac{48 \times 8}{Y}$$

The ATM layer encapsulates each segment into a 53-octet cell. These cells must be interleaved and delivered to the physical layer to be transmitted at the data rate of the physical link. Delay is introduced into this interleaving process: If two cells from different connections arrive at the ATM layer at overlapping times, one of the cells must be delayed by the amount of the overlap. In addition, the ATM layer is generating OAM (operation and maintenance) cells that must also be interleaved with user cells.

At the physical layer, there is opportunity for the introduction of further cell delays. For example, if cells are transmitted in SDH (synchronous digital hierarchy) frames, overhead bits for those frames will be inserted onto the physical link, delaying bits from the ATM layer.

None of the delays just listed can be predicted in any detail, and none follow any repetitive pattern. Accordingly, there is a random element to the time interval between reception of data at the ATM layer from the AAL and the transmission of that data in a cell across the UNI.

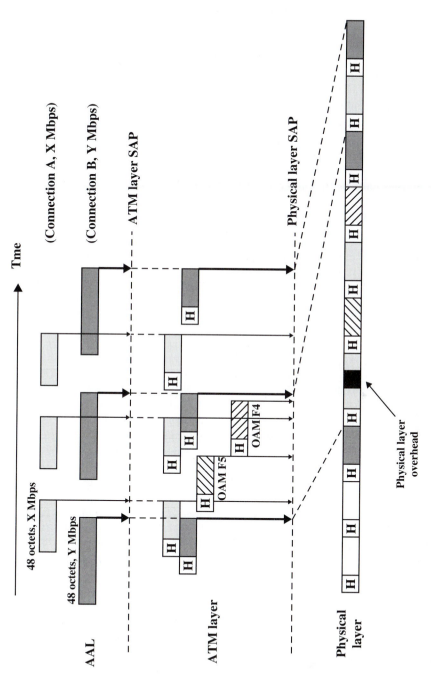

Figure 17.2 Origins of Cell Delay Variation (I.371).

459

17.2 ATM SERVICE CATEGORIES

Before examining the mix of techniques developed for ATM traffic management, we need to understand the types of traffic ATM is intended to carry. An ATM network is designed to be able to transfer many different types of traffic simultaneously, including real-time flows such as voice, video, and bursty TCP flows. Although each such traffic flow is handled as a stream of 53-octet cells traveling through a virtual channel, the way in which each data flow is handled within the network depends on the characteristics of the traffic flow and the requirements of the application. For example, real-time video traffic must be delivered within minimum variation in delay. In this section, we summarize ATM service categories, which are used by an end system to identify the type of service required. The following service categories have been defined by the ATM Forum:

- **Real-Time Services**
  - ◻ Constant Bit Rate (CBR)
  - ◻ Real-Time Variable Bit Rate (rt-VBR)
- **Non-Real-Time Services**
  - ◻ Non-Real-Time Variable Bit Rate (nrt-VBR)
  - ◻ Available Bit Rate (ABR)
  - ◻ Unspecified Bit Rate (UBR)

Real–Time Services

The most important distinction among applications concerns the amount of delay and the variability of delay, referred to as jitter, that the application can tolerate. Real-time applications typically involve a flow of information to a user that is intended to reproduce that flow at a source. For example, a user expects a flow of audio or video information to be presented in a continuous, smooth fashion. A lack of continuity or excessive loss results in significant loss of quality. Applications that involve interaction between people have tight constraints on delay. Typically, any delay above a few hundred milliseconds becomes noticeable and annoying. Accordingly, the demands in the ATM network for switching and delivery of real-time data are high.

Constant Bit Rate

The CBR service is perhaps the simplest service to define. It is used by applications that require a fixed data rate that is continuously available during the connection lifetime and a relatively tight upper bound on transfer delay. CBR is commonly used for uncompressed audio and video information. Example of CBR applications include

- Videoconferencing
- Interactive audio (e.g., telephony)
- Audio/video distribution (e.g., television, distance learning, pay-per-view)
- Audio/video retrieval (e.g., video-on-demand, audio library)

Real-Time Variable Bit Rate

The rt-VBR category is intended for time-sensitive applications; that is, those requiring tightly constrained delay and delay variation. The principal difference between applications appropriate for rt-VBR and those appropriate for CBR is that rt-VBR applications transmit at a rate that varies with time. Equivalently, an rt-VBR source can be characterized as somewhat bursty. For example, the standard approach to video compression results in a sequence of image frames of varying sizes. Because real-time video requires a uniform frame transmission rate, the actual data rate varies.

The rt-VBR service allows the network more flexibility than CBR. The network is able to statistically multiplex a number of connections over the same dedicated capacity and still provide the required service to each connection.

Non–Real–Time Services

Non-real-time services are intended for applications that have bursty traffic characteristics and do not have tight constraints on delay and delay variation. Accordingly, the network has greater flexibility in handling such traffic flows and can make greater use of statistical multiplexing to increase network efficiency.

Non-Real-Time Variable Bit Rate

For some non-real-time applications, it is possible to characterize the expected traffic flow so that the network can provide substantially improved quality of service (QoS) in the areas of loss and delay. Such applications can use the nrt-VBR service. With this service, the end system specifies a peak cell rate, a sustainable or average cell rate, and a measure of how bursty or clumped the cells may be. With this information, the network can allocate resources to provide relatively low delay and minimal cell loss.

The nrt-VBR service can be used for data transfers that have critical response-time requirements. Examples include airline reservations, banking transactions, and process monitoring.

Unspecified Bit Rate

At any given time, a certain amount of the capacity of an ATM network is consumed in carrying CBR and the two types of VBR traffic. Additional capacity is available for one or both of the following reasons: (1) Not all of the total resources have been committed to CBR and VBR traffic, and (2) the bursty nature of VBR traffic means that at some times less than the committed capacity is being used. All of this unused capacity could be made available for the UBR service. This service is suitable for applications that can tolerate variable delays and some cell losses, which is typically true of TCP-based traffic. With UBR, cells are forwarded on a first-in-first-out (FIFO) basis using the capacity not consumed by other services; both delays and variable losses are possible. No initial commitment is made to a UBR source and no feedback concerning congestion is provided; this is referred to as a **best-effort service**. Examples of UBR applications include

- Text/data/image transfer, messaging, distribution, retrieval
- Remote terminal (e.g., telecommuting)

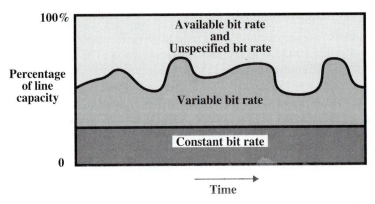

Figure 17.3 ATM Bit Rate Services.

Available Bit Rate

Bursty applications that use a reliable end-to-end protocol such as TCP can detect congestion in a network by means of increased round-trip delays and packet discarding. However, TCP has no mechanism for causing the resources within the network to be shared fairly among many TCP connections. Further, TCP does not minimize congestion as efficiently as is possible using explicit information from congested nodes within the network.

To improve the service provided to bursty sources that would otherwise use UBR, the ABR service has been defined. An application using ABR specifies a peak cell rate (PCR) that it will use and a minimum cell rate (MCR) that it requires. The network allocates resources so that all ABR applications receive at least their MCR capacity. Any unused capacity is then shared in a fair and controlled fashion among all ABR sources. The ABR mechanism uses explicit feedback to sources to assure that capacity is fairly allocated. Any capacity not used by ABR sources remains available for UBR traffic.

An example of an application using ABR is LAN interconnection. In this case, the end systems attached to the ATM network are routers.

Figure 17.3 suggests how a network allocates resources during a steady-state period of time (no additions or deletions of virtual channels).

17.3 ATM TRAFFIC-RELATED ATTRIBUTES

The service categories outlined in the preceding section are characterized by a number of ATM attributes that fall into three categories:

- **Traffic descriptors:** Describe the traffic characteristics of a source and of a connection. A network will establish a connection for this source only if sufficient resources are available to support this traffic volume.

Table 17.2 ATM Service Category Attributes

Attribute	ATM Layer Service Category				
	CBR	**rt-VBR**	**nrt-VBR**	**UBR**	**ABR**
Traffic Parameters					
PCR and CDVT(4,5)	Specified			Specified(2)	Specified(3)
SCR, MBS, CDVT(4,5)	N/A	Specified		N/A	
MCR(4)	N/A				Specified
QoS Parameters					
peak-to-peak CDV	Specified		Unspecified		
maxCTD	Specified		Unspecified		
CLR(4)	Specified			Unspecified	(1)
Other Attributes					
Feedback	Unspecified				Specified

1. CLR is low for sources that adjust cell flow in response to control information. Whether a quantitative value for CLR is specified is network specific.
2. May not be subject to CAC and UPC procedures.
3. Represents the maximum rate at which ABR source may ever send. The actual rate is subject to the control information.
4. These parameters are either explicitly or implicitly specified for PVCs or SVCs.
5. CDVT is not signaled. In general, CDVT need not have a unique value for a connection. Different values may apply at each interface along the path of a connection.

- **QoS parameters:** Characterize the performance of an ATM connection in terms of the quality of service (QoS) that it provides. For a given connection, a user will request a particular QoS.
- **Other:** The only other attribute defined so far is a feedback attribute for ABR.

Table 17.2 lists the ATM attributes and indicates their applicability to each service category.

Traffic Descriptors

The ATM Forum has defined a number of descriptors that characterize the traffic pattern of a flow of cells over an ATM connection. This traffic pattern must be viewed from two different perspectives. First, there is the intrinsic nature of the traffic generated by the source and submitted to the network across the user–network interface (UNI). Second, this flow of cells will be modified inside the network, along the ATM connection, by the variability in delays suffered and by the treatment of cells that do not conform to the source traffic pattern.

The source characteristics of an ATM flow are captured in a **source traffic descriptor**, which includes the following: peak cell rate (PCR), sustainable cell rate

(SCR), maximum burst size (MBS), and minimum cell rate (MCR). Not all of these descriptors are used to characterize all flows (see Table 17.2). The characteristics of an ATM flow over an ATM connection are captured in a **connection traffic descriptor**, which includes the following: the source traffic descriptor, a cell delay variation tolerance (CDVT), and a conformance definition that unambiguously specifies a test for determining whether a given cell on this connection conforms to the source traffic descriptor.

Thus, the structure of the connection traffic descriptor is of this form:

Connection Traffic Descriptor

Source traffic descriptor
—Peak cell rate (PCR)
—Sustainable cell rate (SCR)
—Maximum burst size (MBS)
—Minimum cell rate (MCR)
Cell delay variation tolerance (CDVT)
Conformance definition

The PCR, SCR, MBS, and MCR descriptors characterize the traffic submitted to the network and are sufficient for the network to make resource allocation decisions. As we have seen, at least a portion of the cell delay variation is caused by the network and therefore cannot be specified by the source, but must be supplied by the network. We now define each of these descriptors in turn.

Source Traffic Descriptor

The **peak cell rate** defines an upper bound on the traffic that can be submitted by a source on an ATM connection. The PCR is defined in terms of the variable T, the minimum spacing between cells, so that the $PCR = 1/T$. The PCR descriptor is mandatory for CBR and VBR services.

The **sustainable cell rate** defines an upper bound on the average rate of an ATM connection, calculated over a time scale that is large relative to T. SCR is needed to specify a VBR source. It enables the network to allocate resources efficiently among a number of VBR sources without dedicating the amount of resources required to support a constant PCR rate. The SCR descriptor is only useful if SCR < PCR.

The **maximum burst size** is the maximum number of cells that can be sent continuously at the peak cell rate. If cells are presented to the network in clumps equal to the MBS, then the idle gap between clumps must be sufficient so that the overall rate does not exceed the SCR. The SCR and MBS must both be specified for VBR sources.

The **minimum cell rate** is used with the ABR service. It defines the minimum commitment requested of the network; a value of zero can be used. The goal of the ABR service is to provide rapid access to unused network capacity at up to PCR, whenever the capacity is available. The quantity (PCR − MCR) represents an elastic component of data flow for which the network provides only the assurance that this capacity will be shared fairly among the ABR flows.

Connection Traffic Descriptor

In addition to the source traffic descriptor, the connection traffic descriptor includes the CDVT and a conformance definition. The **cell delay variation tolerance** is a measure of the amount of variation in cell delay that is introduced by the network interface (e.g., SDH) and at the UNI. CDVT represents a bound on the delay variability due to the slotted nature of ATM, the physical layer overhead, and ATM layer functions such as cell multiplexing. CDVT is expressed as time variable τ. The interpretation of τ is discussed in Section 17.5. The **conformance definition** is used to specify unambiguously the conforming cells of a connection at the UNI. The network may enforce conformance by dropping or marking cells that exceed the conformance definition. The generic cell rate algorithm (GCRA), described in Section 17.5, is used to define conformance.

QoS Parameters

The following ATM QoS parameters are defined by the ATM Forum:

- Peak-to-peak cell delay variation
- Maximum cell transfer delay (maxCTD)
- Cell loss ratio (CLR)

We need first to define cell transfer delay (CTD), which is the elapsed time between two cell events. Typically, CTD refers to the time between transmission of the last bit of a cell at the source UNI and the receipt of the first bit of a cell at the destination UNI. In general terms, CTD is a variable that typically has a probability density function that looks like that of Figure 17.4. As indicated, there is a minimum delay, called the fixed delay, which includes propagation delay through the physical media, delays induced by the transmission system, and fixed components of switch processing delay. The variable portion of the delay (CDV) is due to buffering and cell scheduling.

With reference to this figure, **maxCTD** defines the maximum requested delay for this connection. A fraction α of all cells will exceed this threshold and must either be discarded or delivered late. The remaining $(1 - \alpha)$ portion is within the requested QoS. The amount of delay experienced by such cells is within the range between the fixed delay and maxCTD; this range is referred to as the **peak-to-peak CDV**.

The QoS parameter CDV should not be confused with the traffic contract CDVT. CDV is usually negotiated during connection establishment (for switched virtual connections), whereas CDVT is normally explicitly set at the UNI and is not negotiated. The source traffic has to conform to the CDVT value to be eligible for QoS guarantees; this is checked and enforced by usage parameter control, described in Section 17.5. The delay variation addressed by CDVT is the variation introduced by the source traffic itself. The network tries to provide the negotiated CDV to the compliant source traffic. This CDV is the difference between the best- and worst-case expected end-to-end cell transfer delay. The best case is equal to the fixed

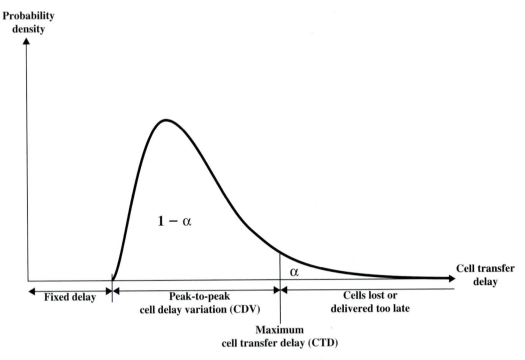

Figure 17.4 Cell Transfer Delay Probability Density Function (for real-time service categories).

delay. The worst case is equal to maxCTD, incurred as a result of buffering and cell switching. Therefore, CDVT is an upper bound on CDV at the UNI, the latter being only one of several contributing factors to CDV.

Finally, the **cell loss ratio** is simply the ratio of lost cells to total transmitted cells on a connection.

17.4 TRAFFIC MANAGEMENT FRAMEWORK

I.371 lists the following objectives of ATM layer traffic and congestion control:

- ATM layer traffic and congestion control should support a set of ATM layer QoS classes sufficient for all foreseeable network services; the specification of these QoS classes should be consistent with network performance parameters currently under study.
- ATM layer traffic and congestion control should not rely on AAL protocols that are network service specific, nor on higher-layer protocols that are application specific. Protocol layers above the ATM layer may make use of information provided by the ATM layer to improve the utility they can derive from the network.

Table17.3 Traffic Control and Congestion Control Functions

Response Time	Traffic Control Functions	Congestion Control Functions
Long Term	• Resource management using virtual paths	
Connection Duration	• Connection admission control (CAC)	
Round-Trip Propagation Time	• Fast resource management	• Explicit forward congestion indication (EFCI) • ABR flow control
Cell Insertion Time	• Usage parameter control (UPC) • Priority control • Traffic shaping	• Selective cell discard • Frame discard

- The design of an optimum set of ATM-layer traffic controls and congestion controls should minimize network and end-system complexity while maximizing network utilization.

To meet these objectives, ITU-T has defined a collection of traffic and congestion control functions that operate across a spectrum of timing intervals. Table 17.3 lists these functions with respect to the response times within which they operate. Four levels of timing are considered:

- **Cell insertion time:** Functions at this level react immediately to cells as they are transmitted.
- **Round-trip propagation time:** At this level, the network responds within the lifetime of a cell in the network and may provide feedback indications to the source.
- **Connection duration:** At this level, the network determines whether a new connection at a given QoS can be accommodated and what performance levels will be agreed to.
- **Long term:** These are controls that affect more than one ATM connection and are established for long-term use.

The essence of the traffic control strategy is based on (1) determining whether a given new ATM connection can be accommodated and (2) agreeing with the subscriber on the performance parameters that will be supported. In effect, the subscriber and the network enter into a traffic contract: The network agrees to support traffic at a certain level on this connection, and the subscriber agrees not to exceed performance limits. Traffic control functions are concerned with establishing these traffic parameters and enforcing them. Thus, they are concerned with congestion avoidance. If traffic control fails in certain instances, then congestion may occur. At this point, congestion control functions are invoked to respond to and recover from the congestion.

17.5 TRAFFIC MANAGEMENT

ITU-T and the ATM Forum have defined a range of traffic management functions to maintain the QoS of ATM connections. ATM traffic management function refers to the set of actions taken by the network to avoid congestion conditions or to minimize congestion effects. The following functions have been defined:

- Resource management using virtual paths
- Connection admission control
- Usage parameter control
- Selective cell discard
- Traffic shaping
- Explicit forward congestion indication

We examine each of these in turn.

Resource Management Using Virtual Paths

The essential concept behind network resource management is to allocate network resources in such a way as to separate traffic flows according to service characteristics. So far, the only specific traffic control function based on network resource management defined by the ATM Forum deals with the use of virtual paths.

As discussed in Chapter 16, a virtual path connection (VPC) provides a convenient means of grouping similar virtual channel connections (VCCs). The network provides aggregate capacity and performance characteristics on the virtual path, and these are shared by the virtual connections. There are three cases to consider:

- **User-to-user application:** The VPC extends between a pair of UNIs. In this case the network has no knowledge of the QoS of the individual VCCs within a VPC. It is the user's responsibility to assure that the aggregate demand from the VCCs can be accommodated by the VPC.
- **User-to-network application:** The VPC extends between a UNI and a network node. In this case, the network is aware of the QoS of the VCCs within the VPC and has to accommodate them.
- **Network-to-network application:** The VPC extends between two network nodes. Again, in this case, the network is aware of the QoS of the VCCs within the VPC and has to accommodate them.

The QoS parameters that are of primary concern for network resource management are cell loss ratio, maximum cell transfer delay, and peak-to-peak cell delay variation, all of which are affected by the amount of resources devoted to the VPC by the network. If a VCC extends through multiple VPCs, then the performance of that VCC depends on the performances of the consecutive VPCs and on how the connection is handled at any node that performs VCC-related functions. Such a node may be a switch, concentrator, or other network equipment. The performance of each VPC depends on the capacity of that VPC and the traffic characteristics of

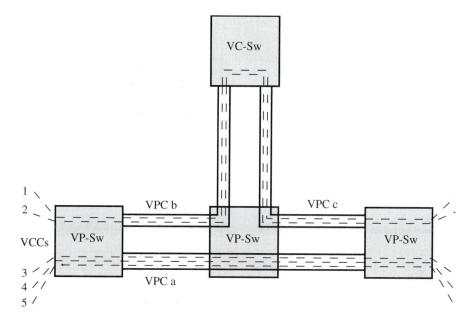

VPC	=	Virtual path connection
VCC	=	Virtual channel connection
VP-Sw	=	Virtual path switching function
VC-Sw	=	Virtual channel switching function

Figure 17.5 Configuration of VCCs and VPCs.

the VCCs contained within the VPC. The performance of each VCC-related function depends on the switching/processing speed at the node and on the relative priority with which various cells are handled.

Figure 17.5 gives an example. VCCs 1 and 2 experience a performance that depends on VPCs b and c and on how these VCCs are handled by the intermediate nodes. This may differ from the performance experienced by VCCs 3, 4, and 5.

There are a number of alternatives for the way in which VCCs are grouped and the type of performance they experience. If all of the VCCs within a VPC are handled similarly, then they should experience similar expected network performance, in terms of cell loss ratio, cell transfer delay, and cell delay variation. Alternatively, when different VCCs within the same VPC require different QoS, the VPC performance objectives agreed by network and subscriber should be set suitably for the most demanding VCC requirement.

In either case, with multiple VCCs within the same VPC, the network has two general options for allocating capacity to the VPC:

- **Aggregate peak demand:** The network may set the capacity (data rate) of the VPC equal to the total of the peak data rates of all of the VCCs within the VPC. The advantage of this approach is that each VCC can be given a QoS that accommodates its peak demand. The disadvantage is that most of the time, the

VPC capacity will not be fully utilized and therefore the network will have underutilized resources.

- **Statistical multiplexing:** If the network sets the capacity of the VPC to be greater than or equal to the average data rates of all the VCCs but less than the aggregate peak demand, then a statistical multiplexing service is supplied. With statistical multiplexing, VCCs experience greater cell delay variation and greater cell-transfer delay. Depending on the size of buffers used to queue cells for transmission, VCCs may also experience greater cell loss ratio. This approach has the advantage of more efficient utilization of capacity and is attractive if the VCCs can tolerate the lower QoS.

When statistical multiplexing is used, it is preferable to group VCCs into VPCs on the basis of similar traffic characteristics and similar QoS requirements. If dissimilar VCCs share the same VPC and statistical multiplexing is used, it is difficult to provide fair access to both high-demand and low-demand traffic streams.

Connection Admission Control

Connection admission control (CAC) is the first line of defense for the network in protecting itself from excessive loads. In essence, when a user requests a new VPC or VCC, the user must specify (implicitly or explicitly) the service required in both directions for that connection. The request consists of the following:

- Service category (CBR, rt-VBR, nrt-vBR, ABR, UBR)
- Connection traffic descriptor, consisting of
  - Source traffic descriptor (PCR, SCR, MBS, MCR)
  - CDVT
  - Requested conformance definition
- Requested and acceptable value of each QoS parameter (peak-to-peak CDV, maxCTD, CLR)

The network accepts the connection only if it can commit the resources necessary to support that traffic level while at the same time maintaining the agreed QoS of existing connections. By accepting the connection, the network forms a *traffic contract* with the user. Once the connection is accepted, the network continues to provide the agreed QoS as long as the user complies with the traffic contract.

For a given connection (VPC or VCC) the traffic contract parameters may be specified in several ways, as illustrated in Table 17.4. Parameter values may be implicitly defined by default rules set by the network operator. In this case, all connections are assigned the same values, or all connections of a given class are assigned the same values for that class. The network operator may also associate parameter values with a given subscriber and assign these at the time of subscription. Finally, parameter values tailored to a particular connection may be assigned at connection time. In the case of a permanent virtual connection, these values are assigned by the network when the connection is set up. For a switched virtual connection, the parameters are negotiated between the user and the network via a signaling protocol.

Table 17.4 Procedures Used to Set Values of Traffic Contract Parameters

	Explicitly Specified Parameters		Implicitly Specified Parameters
	Parameter values set at connection-setup time	**Parameter values specified at subscription time**	**Parameter values set using default rules**
	Requested by user/NMS	**assigned by network operator**	
SVC	Signaling	By subscription	Network-operator default rules
PVC	NMS	By subscription	Network-operator default rules

SVC = switched virtual connection
PVC = permanent virtual connection
NMS = network management system

Another aspect of the traffic contract that may be requested or assigned for a connection is cell loss priority. A user may request two levels of cell loss priority for an ATM connection; the priority of an individual cell is indicated by the user through the CLP bit in the cell header (Figure 16.6). When two priority levels are used, the traffic parameters for both cell flows must be specified. Typically, this is done by specifying a set of traffic parameters for high-priority traffic (CLP = 0) and a set of traffic parameters for all traffic (CLP = 0 + 1). Based on this break-down, the network may be able to allocate resources more efficiently.

Usage Parameter Control

Once a connection has been accepted by the connection admission control function, the usage parameter control (UPC) function of the network monitors the connection to determine whether the traffic conforms to the traffic contract. The main purpose of usage parameter control is to protect network resources from an overload on one connection that would adversely affect the QoS on other connections by detecting violations of assigned parameters and taking appropriate actions.

UPC Location

Usage parameter control can be done at both the virtual path and virtual channel levels. Of these, the more important is VPC-level control, because network resources are, in general, initially allocated on the basis of virtual paths, with the virtual path capacity shared among the member virtual channels.

The place at which usage parameter control can be exercised depends on the configuration, as illustrated in Figure 17.6. If the first point of termination of a VCC is a node within the network that performs virtual channel connection-related functions (case A), then UPC is performed on incoming cells before the VCC switching function is executed. If a VCC passes through one or more VPC switching points before connection to a VCC switching point within the network (case B), then

1. Usage parameter control is performed on incoming cells on a virtual path basis at the VPC switching points.
2. Usage parameter control is performed on a virtual channel basis at the first point where VCC-related functions are performed.

Finally, if a VCC is connected to a user or another network provider (case C), then this network provides usage parameter control only at the virtual path level.

Peak Cell Rate Algorithm

So far, we have discussed usage parameter control in general terms, without specifying how the UPC function determines whether the user is complying with the traffic contract. There are two separate functions encompassed by UPC:

- Control of peak cell rate and the associated CDVT
- Control of sustainable cell rate and the associated burst tolerance

Let us first consider the peak cell rate and the associated CDVT. In simple terms, a traffic flow is compliant if the peak rate of cell transmission does not exceed the agreed peak cell rate, subject to the possibility of cell delay variation within the agreed bound.

I.371 and the ATM Traffic Management Specification provide an algorithm that (1) serves as an operational definition of the relationship between peak cell rate

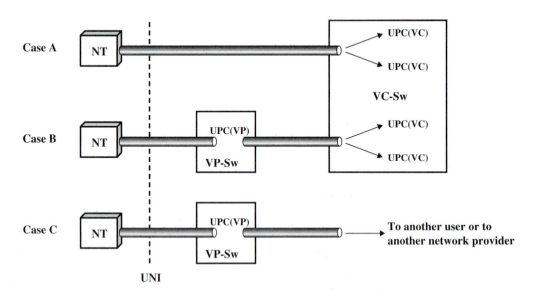

Figure 17.6 Location of the Usage Parameter Control Function.

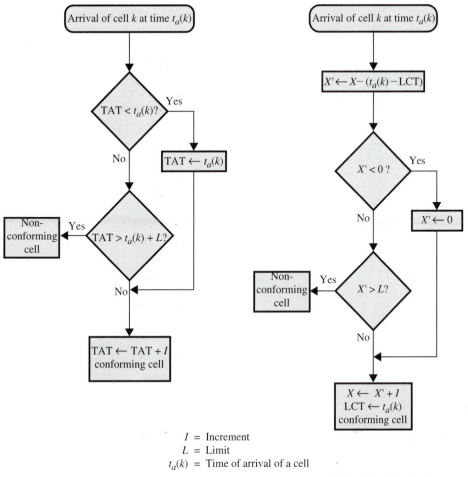

I = Increment
L = Limit
$t_a(k)$ = Time of arrival of a cell

X = Value of the leaky bucket counter
X' = Auxiliary variable
LCT = Last compliance time

TAT= Theoretical arrival time

At the time of arrival $t_a(1)$ of the first cell
of the connection, TAT = $t_a(1)$

At the time of arrival $t_a(1)$ of the first cell
of the connection, $X = 0$ and LCT = $t_a(1)$

(a) Virtual scheduling algorithm

(b) Continuous-state leaky bucket algorithm

Figure 17.7 Equivalent Versions of the Generic Cell Rate Algorithm—GCRA(I,L).

and CDVT, and (2) can be used for usage parameter control to monitor compliance
with the traffic contract.

Figure 17.7 shows two equivalent versions of the algorithm. The algorithm is
referred to as the generic cell rate algorithm because it is also used for the sustainable cell rate, as explained later. The algorithm takes two arguments, an increment
I and a limit L, and is expressed as GCRA(I,L).

It is useful to examine both versions to gain greater insight into the relationship between the two parameters. Suppose that we have specified a peak cell rate R

and a CDVT limit of τ. Then $T = 1/R$ is the interarrival time between cells if there were no CDVT. With CDVT, T is the average interarrival time at the peak rate. The peak cell rate algorithm is therefore expressed as GCRA(T,τ).

Consider the **virtual scheduling algorithm**. The algorithm is initialized with the arrival of the first cell on a connection at time $t_a(1)$. The algorithm updates a theoretical arrival time (TAT), which is a target time for the next cell arrival. If the cell arrives later than the TAT, then it is compliant and the TAT is updated to the arrival time plus T. If the cell arrives earlier than TAT but within τ time units of TAT, then the cell is still considered compliant and TAT is incremented by T. In this latter case, it is permissible for the cell to arrive early because it does so within the CDVT. Finally, if the cell arrives too early (before TAT $- \tau$), then it is outside the CDVT bound and is declared noncompliant; in this case TAT remains unchanged. Figure 17.8a illustrates these three zones.

An example of this algorithm is shown in Figure 17.9. For this figure, the time to insert a single 53-octet cell is δ, and $T = 4.5\delta$. Thus, the peak cell rate is equal to the data rate at the UNI divided by 4.5. For example, if the data rate is 150 Mbps, then the peak cell rate is $150/4.5 = 33.33$ Mbps. Part (a) of the figure allows the min-

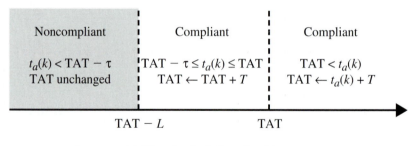

(a) Virtual scheduling algorithm

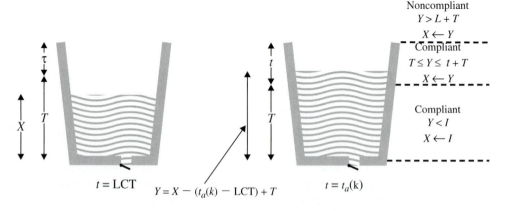

(b) Continuous-state leaky bucket algorithm

Figure 17.8 Depiction of GCRA(T, τ).

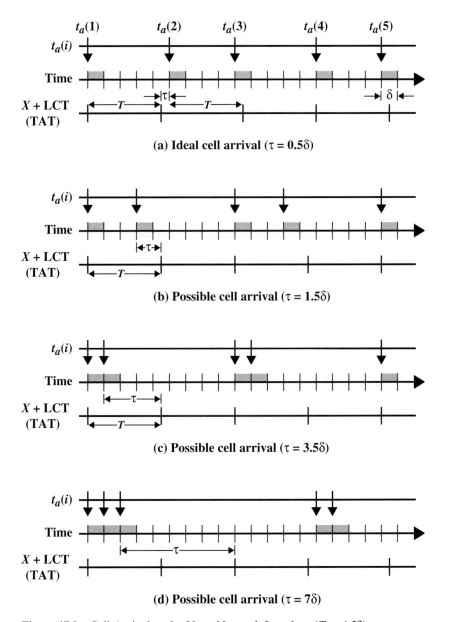

Figure 17.9 Cell Arrival at the User–Network Interface ($T = 4.5\delta$).

imum CDVT ($\tau = \delta/2$), just enough to accommodate the fact that data are transmitted in cells and therefore each arrival time will be an integer multiple of δ, whereas the increment value is on a 0.5 mark. Because of the tight tolerance, the cell arrival time can never drift very far from the TAT.

As the CDVT, τ, increases, cell arrivals can drift increasingly far from the TAT. More significantly, the potential for cell clumping, which is the phenomenon that will stress network resources, increases. The greatest degree of clumping occurs when it is possible for a source to transmit multiple cells back to back (i.e., at the full link rate). This condition is possible when τ exceeds $T - \delta$. Specifically, for $\tau > T - \delta$, the maximum number N of conforming back-to-back cells equals

$$N = \left\lfloor 1 + \frac{\tau}{T - \delta} \right\rfloor \qquad (17.1)$$

where $\lfloor x \rfloor$ stands for the integer part of x. Back-to-back cell clumping is illustrated in parts (c) and (d) of Figure 17.8.

Returning to the flowchart in Figure 17.7a, note that it is not possible to build up credit. If a cell arrives late, meaning that there has been an idle period on this connection, the next value of TAT is set relative to the current arrival, rather than the current value of TAT. If this rule were not followed and TAT were simply incremented by T after every cell arrival, then the occurrence of a long idle period would enable a source to send a long string of cells at the full link rate. This would create a surge not accounted for in the network resource allocation.

The GCRA can also be expressed as a **leaky bucket algorithm** (Figure 13.7). The algorithm maintains a running count of the cumulative amount of data sent in a counter X. The counter is decremented at a constant rate of one unit per time unit to a minimum value of zero; this is equivalent to a bucket that leaks at a rate of 1. The counter is incremented by I for each arriving cell, subject to the restriction that the maximum counter value is $I + L$. Any arriving cell that would cause the counter to exceed its maximum is defined as nonconforming; this is equivalent to a bucket with a capacity of $I + L$.

Figure 17.7b shows a leaky bucket algorithm that is equivalent to the virtual scheduling algorithm of Figure 17.7a. The algorithm defines a finite-capacity bucket that drains at a continuous rate of 1 unit per time unit and whose content is increased by T for each compliant cell. The total capacity of the bucket is $T + \tau$. After the arrival of the kth cell, at $t_a(k)$, the algorithm checks to see if the bucket has overflowed. If so, the cell is nonconforming. If not, the bucket is incremented. The amount of the increment depends on whether the bucket was fully drained between cell arrivals. Figure 17.8b illustrates the algorithm; the left part shows the state of the bucket after a cell has been processed, and the right part shows the state of the bucket after a new cell arrives. A review of Figure 17.9 shows that this algorithm is equivalent to that of Figure 17.7a.

Sustainable Cell Rate Algorithm

The sustainable cell rate algorithm (1) serves as an operational definition of the relationship between sustainable cell rate and burst tolerance, and (2) can be used for usage parameter control to monitor compliance with the traffic contract.

The same algorithm that is used to define peak cell rate monitoring is also used to define sustainable cell rate monitoring. In this case, for a sustainable cell rate R_s, $T_s = 1/R_s$ is the interarrival time between cells at that rate if there is no burstiness. The burst tolerance is represented as τ_s. Thus the sustainable cell rate algorithm is expressed as GCRA(T_s, τ_s).

Unlike the CDVT, the burst tolerance is not selected directly. Rather, it is derived from an understanding of the burstiness of the traffic stream. In particular, let T be the time between cells at the peak rate. If the traffic stream is constrained by both a peak cell rate using GCRA(T,τ) and a sustainable cell rate GCRA(T_s,τ_s), then the maximum burst size, *MBS*, that may be transmitted at the peak rate is given by

$$MBS = \left\lfloor 1 + \frac{\tau_s}{T_s - T} \right\rfloor \qquad (17.2)$$

In the signaling message, the burst tolerance is conveyed using *MBS*, which is coded in number of cells. The *MBS* is then used to derive τ_s, which in turn is used in the GCRA algorithm to monitor the sustainable cell rate. Given the *MBS*, T, and T_s, then τ_s can be any value in the interval

$$[(MBS - 1)(T_s - T), MBS(T_s - T)] \qquad (17.3)$$

For uniformity, the minimum value is used:

$$\tau_s = (MBS - 1)(T_s - T)$$

UPC Actions

The GCRA algorithm, or some similar algorithm, is used by the network to ensure compliance with the negotiated traffic contract. The simplest strategy is that compliant cells are passed along and noncompliant cells are discarded at the point of the UPC function.

When no additional network resource has been allocated to CLP = 1 traffic flow, CLP = 0 cells identified as nonconforming are discarded. If the user has negotiated two levels of cell loss priority for a network, then the situation is more complex. The following rules apply:

1. A cell with CLP = 0 that conforms to the traffic contract for CLP = 0 passes.
2. A cell with CLP = 0 that is noncompliant for (CLP = 0) traffic but compliant for (CLP = 0 + 1) traffic is tagged and passed.
3. A cell with CLP = 0 that is noncompliant for (CLP = 0) traffic and noncompliant for (CLP = 0 + 1) traffic is discarded.
4. A cell with CLP = 1 that is compliant for (CLP = 0 + 1) traffic is passed.
5. A cell with CLP = 1 that is noncompliant for (CLP = 0 + 1) traffic is discarded.

Figure 17.10 illustrates the relationship between the UPC function and the CLP bit. The UPC function first tests the (CLP = 0) flow for compliance and then the combined (CLP = 0 + 1) flow. If the tagging option is used, a noncompliant (CLP = 0) cell is tagged but still considered part of the (CLP = 0 + 1) flow and subjected to the second test.

Selective Cell Discard

Selective cell discard comes into play when the network, at some point beyond the UPC function, discards (CLP = 1) cells. The objective is to discard lower-priority cells to protect the performance for higher-priority cells. Note that the network has

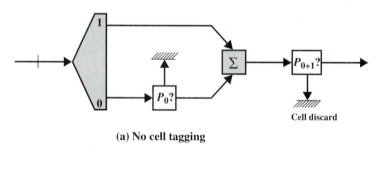

(a) No cell tagging

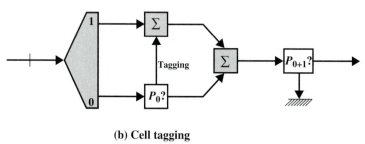

(b) Cell tagging

P? = Compliance test for parameter P

Figure 17.10 Possible Actions of the UPC Function.

no way to discriminate between cells that were labeled as lower priority by the source and cells that were tagged by the UPC function.

Traffic Shaping

The GCRA algorithm is referred to as a form of **traffic policing**. Traffic policing occurs when a flow of data is regulated so that cells (or frames or packets) that exceed a certain performance level are discarded or tagged. It may be desirable to supplement a traffic policing policy with a **traffic shaping** policy. Traffic shaping is used to smooth out a traffic flow and reduce cell clumping. This can result in a fairer allocation of resources and a reduced average delay time.

A simple approach to traffic shaping is to use a form of the leaky bucket algorithm known as token bucket. In contrast to the GCRA leaky bucket, which simply monitors the traffic and rejects or discards noncompliant cells, a traffic shaping leaky bucket controls the flow of compliant cells.

Figure 17.11 illustrates the basic principle of the token bucket. A token generator produces tokens at a rate of ρ tokens per second and places these in the token bucket, which has a maximum capacity of β tokens. Cells arriving from the source are placed in a buffer with a maximum capacity of K cells. To transmit a cell through the server, one token must be removed from the bucket. If the token bucket is empty, the cell is queued waiting for the next token. The result of this scheme is that if there is a backlog of cells and an empty bucket, then cells are emitted at a smooth flow of ρ cells per second with no cell delay variation until the backlog is cleared. Thus, the token bucket smoothes out bursts of cells.

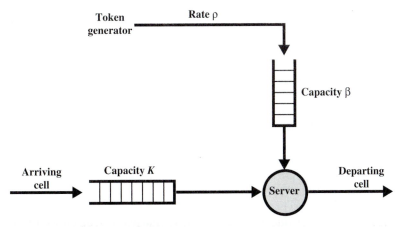

Figure 17.11   Token Bucket for Traffic Shaping.

Explicit Forward Congestion Indication

Explicit forward congestion notification for ATM network works in essentially the same manner as for frame relay networks. Any ATM network node that is experiencing congestion may set an explicit forward congestion indication in the cell header of cells on connections passing through the node. The indication notifies the user that congestion avoidance procedures should be initiated for traffic in the same direction as the received cell. It indicates that this cell on this ATM connection has encountered congested resources. The user may then invoke actions in higher-layer protocols to lower adaptively the cell rate of the connection.

The network issues the indication by setting the first two bits of the payload type field in the cell header to 01 (Table 16.2). Once this value is set by any node, it may not be altered by other network nodes along the path to the destination user.

Note that the generic flow control (GFC) field (Figure 16.6) is not involved. The GFC field has only local significance and cannot be communicated across the network.

17.6 ABR TRAFFIC MANAGEMENT

The QoS provided for CBR, rt-VBR, and nrt-VBR is based on (1) a traffic contract that specifies the characteristics of the cell flow and (2) UPC performed by the network to enforce the flow. During the connection admission process, the network uses the proposed traffic contract to determine if resources are available for this new connection. If so, and once the connection is established, UPC may discard or tag as lower priority any cell that exceeds the parameters of the traffic contract. There is no feedback to the source concerning congestion. The approach just described is referred to as **open-loop control** because of its lack of feedback.

The open-loop approach is not suited to many data applications. Typical non-real-time applications, such as file transfer, Web access, remote procedure calls, distributed file service, and so on, do not have well-defined traffic characteristics, other than perhaps a peak cell rate. The PCR by itself is not sufficient for the network to allocate resources effectively. Furthermore, such applications can generally tolerate unpredictable delays and time-varying throughput.

Such applications can be handled in one of two ways. One possibility is to allow these applications to share the unused capacity in a relatively uncontrolled fashion. As congestion rises, cells will be lost, and the various sources will back off and reduce their data rate; this style of transmission fits will with TCP's congestion control techniques, and this is the mode of operation for the UBR service. This approach is referred to as **best effort**. The disadvantage of the best-effort approach is its inefficiency: Cells are dropped, causing retransmissions.

The other way is to allow a number of sources to share the capacity not used by CBR and VBR but to provide feedback to sources to adjust the load dynamically and thus avoid cell loss and share the capacity fairly. This is referred to as **closed-loop control** because of its use of feedback. This approach is used for ABR.

In this section, we provide an overview of the ABR service and look in some detail at the feedback mechanism used to control cell flow.

ABR Rate Control

[CHEN96] lists the following as the chief characteristics of the ABR service:

1. ABR connections share available capacity. ABR connections have access to the instantaneous capacity unused by CBR/VBR connections. Thus, ABR can increase network utilization without affecting the QoS of CBR/VBR connections.

2. The share of available capacity used by a single ABR connection is dynamic and varies between an agreed MCR and PCR. The MCR assigned to a particular connection may be zero. With a nonzero MCR, the network provides an assurance of minimum throughput; however, a source may transmit at less than a nonzero MCR over any period of time.

3. The network provides feedback to ABR sources so that ABR flow is limited to available capacity. The time delays inherent in providing feedback dictate the use of buffers along a connection's path; the buffers absorb excess traffic generated prior to the arrival of the feedback at the source. Because of the large data rate and relatively large propagation delay through a network, these buffers may be substantial, leading to large delays. Accordingly, the ABR service is appropriate for applications that can tolerate adjustments to their transmission rates and unpredictable cell delays.

4. For ABR sources that adapt their transmission rate to the provided feedback, a low cell loss ratio is guaranteed. This is a major distinction between ABR and UBR.

Feedback Mechanisms

The rate of transmission of cells from a source on an ABR connection is characterized by four parameters:

- **Allowed cell rate (ACR):** The current rate at which the source is permitted to transmit cells. The source may transmit at any rate between zero and ACR.
- **Minimum cell rate (MCR):** The minimum value that ACR may take (i.e., the network will not restrict a source's flow to less than MCR). MCR may, however, be set to zero for a given connection.
- **Peak cell rate (PCR):** The maximum value that ACR may take.
- **Initial cell rate (ICR):** The initial value assigned to ACR.

A source starts out with ACR = ICR and dynamically adjusts ACR based on feedback from the network. Feedback is provided periodically in the form of a sequence of resource management (RM) cells. Each cell contains three fields that provide feedback to the source: a *congestion indication* (CI) bit, a *no increase* (NI) bit, and an *explicit cell rate* (ER) field. The source reacts according to the following rules:

if CI = 1
    reduce ACR by an amount proportional to the current ACR but not
    less than MCR
else if NI = 0 increase ACR by an amount proportional to PCR but not
    more than PCR
if ACR > ER set ACR ← max [ER, MCR]

Thus, the source first checks the two feedback bits. If an increase is called for, it is a fixed-size increment equal to RIF × PCR, where RIF is a *fixed-rate increase* factor. If a decrease is called for, the decrease is exponential by an amount RDF × ACR, where RDF is a *fixed-rate decrease* factor. Finally, if ER is smaller than ACR, the source reduces ACR to ER. All of these adjustments are subject to the constraint that ACR varies between the limits of MCR and PCR. The following table summarizes these rules:

NI	CI	Action
0	0	ACR ← max[MCR, min[ER, PCR, ACR + RIF × PCR]]
0	1	ACR ← max[MCR, min[ER, ACR(1 − RDF)]]
1	0	ACR ← max[MCR, min[ER, ACR]]
1	1	ACR ← max[MCR, min[ER, ACR(1 − RDF)]]

Figure 17.12 illustrates the effect of feedback on ACR. For this example an RIF of 1/16 is used, which is the default value; as can be seen, each increase is by a constant amount. The default value for RDF is also 1/16, but a value of 1/4 is used in Figure 17.12 to highlight the exponential effect of RDF: The amount of the decrease is proportional to the current value of ACR. With linear increase and exponential decrease, the source will slowly increase its rate when there is no evidence of congestion, but at high rates will rapidly decrease its rate when there is indication of congestion.

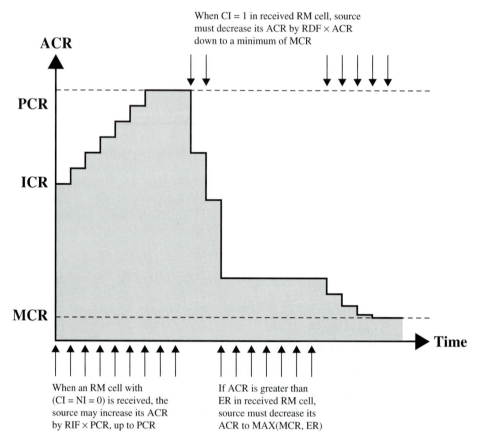

Figure 17.12 Variations in Allowed Cell Rate (based on [SAIT96]).

Cell Flow

Having looked at the way in which a source reacts to feedback, we now describe the way in which feedback is provided. Figure 17.13 illustrates the mechanism. This figure depicts a flow of data in one direction over an ATM connection; a similar flow occurs in the opposite sense for two-way data communication.

Two types of ATM cells flow on an ABR connection: data cells and resource management (RM) cells. A source receives a regular sequence of RM cells that provide feedback to enable it to adjust its rate of cell transmission. The bulk of the RM cells are initiated by the source, which transmits one **forward RM (FRM) cell** for every (Nrm − 1) data cells, where Nrm is a preset parameter (usually equal to 32). As each FRM is received at the destination, it is turned around and transmitted back to the source as a **backward RM (BRM) cell**.

Each FRM contains the CI, NI, and ER fields. The source typically sets CI = 0, NI = 0 or 1, and ER equal to some desired transmission rate in the range ICR ≤ ER ≤ PCR. Any of these fields may be changed by an ATM switch or the destination system before the corresponding BRM returns to the source.

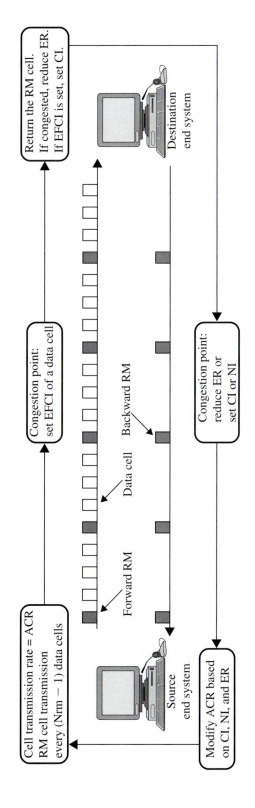

Figure 17.13 Flow of Data and RM Cells on an ABR Connection (based on [SAIT96]).

483

An ATM switch has a number of ways to provide rate control feedback to a source:

- **EFCI marking:** The switch may set the EFCI (explicit forward congestion indication) condition in an ATM data cell header (using the payload type field) as it passes in the forward direction. This will cause the destination end system to set the CI bit in a BRM cell.
- **Relative rate marking:** The switch may directly set the CI or NI bit of a passing RM. If the bit is set in an FRM, then that bit will remain set in the corresponding BRM when the turnaround occurs at the destination. More rapid results are achieved by setting one of these bits in a passing BRM. To achieve the most rapid result, a switch may generate a BRM with CI or NI set rather than wait for a passing BRM.
- **Explicit rate marking:** The switch may reduce the value of the ER field of an FRM or BRM.

These actions enable an ATM switch to signal a source that congestion is occurring and to reduce its cell rate. The destination system can also signal congestion. Under normal conditions, a destination system simply converts each incoming FRM to a BRM without changing the NI, CI, or ER fields, except that the CI bit is set if an EFCI signal has been received on the previous data cell. However, if the destination is experiencing congestion, it may set the CI or NI bit or reduce the ER value when converting an FRM to a BRM.

The first ATM switches to support ABR use the EFCI, NI, and CI bits, providing a simple relative-rate-control mechanism. The more complex controls associated with the use of explicit rate constitute a second generation of ABR service.

RM Cell Format

Figure 17.14 shows the format of an RM cell. It includes the following elements:

- **Header (5 octets):** The ATM header has PT = 110 to indicate an RM cell. For rate control on a virtual channel, the VPI and VCI are identical to those of data cells on that connection. For rate control on a virtual path, the same VPI is used and VCI = 6.
- **Protocol Identifier (1 octet):** Identifies service using this RM cell. For ABR, ID = 1.
- **Message Type (1 octet):** Contains the following 1-bit indicators:
  - ¤ **Direction (DIR):** FRM (DIR = 0) or BRM (DIR = 1)
  - ¤ **BECN Cell (BN):** Indicates cell initially generated by source (BN = 0) or by a switch or destination (BN = 1).
  - ¤ **Congestion Indication (CI):** (CI = 1) indicates congestion.
  - ¤ **No Increase (NI):** (NI = 1) indicates no additive increase allowed.
  - ¤ **Request/Acknowledge (RA):** Defined in I.371; not used in ATM Forum ABR.
- **Explicit Cell Rate (2 octets):** Used to limit the source ACR to a specified value.

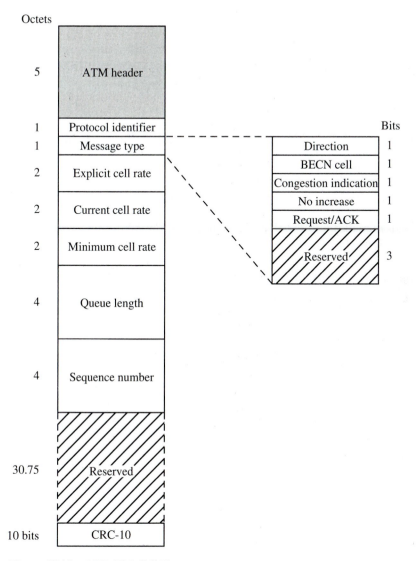

Figure 17.14   ABR RM Cell Format.

- **Current Cell Rate (2 octets):** Set by source to its current ACR. This may be useful to network elements in determining a value for ER.
- **Minimum Cell Rate (2 octets):** Set by source. May be useful to network elements in allocating capacity among connections.
- **Queue Length (4 octets):** Defined in I.371; not used in ATM Forum ABR.
- **Sequence Number (4 octets):** Defined in I.371; not used in ATM Forum ABR.
- **CRC-10 (10 bits):** An error-detection code that covers the RM payload (entire cell except for header).

Table 17.5   Initial Values of RM Cell Fields

Field	If source generated	If switch generated or destination generated
Direction (DIR)	0	1
BECN Cell (BN)	0	1
Congestion Indication (CI)	0	0 or 1
No Increase (NI)	0 or 1	0 or 1
Explicit Cell Rate (ECR)	≤PCR parameter	Any rate value
Current Cell Rate (CCR)	ACR parameter	0
Minimum Cell Rate (MCR)	MCR parameter	0

Table 17.5 shows the initial values assigned to an RM cell when it is first generated. In addition to the RM fields, there are a number of parameters that control the ABR mechanism; these are defined in Table 17.6.

ABR Capacity Allocation

In support of the ABR service, ATM switches must perform two functions:

- **Congestion control:** Because the ABR service is to provide for minimal cell loss, the rate control mechanisms of ABR must be used by switches to limit the rate of arriving packets to that which can be handled by the network. For this purpose, a switch must monitor queue lengths and begin to throttle back rates as the buffers approach capacity.
- **Fair capacity allocation:** An ATM switch should allocate a fair share of its capacity among all connections that pass through this switch point. Therefore, when congestion arises, the switch should throttle back on those connections that are using more than their fair share of the capacity.

Switch algorithms for congestion control and fair capacity allocation fall into two broad categories: binary feedback schemes that use only the EFCI, CI and NI bits, and explicit rate feedback schemes that use the ER field. This is an area of active ongoing research. Here we survey some of the most important schemes proposed in the two categories.

Binary Feedback Schemes

All binary feedback schemes have the same general structure. An ATM switch monitors its buffer utilization on each output port. When congestion approaches, the switch performs a binary notification either by setting the EFCI on a forward data cell or by setting CI or NI on a forward or backward RM. The distinction among different schemes is in the determination of which connection to notify first. We summarize three approaches: single FIFO queue, multiple queues, and fair share notification.

The simplest approach is to dedicate the buffer at each output port to a **single FIFO queue**. When buffer occupancy exceeds a threshold (e.g., 80% of buffer size), the switch begins to issue binary notifications and continues to do so until buffer

Table 17.6   ABR Parameters

Label	Name	Description	Default
PCR	Peak cell rate	Fixed upper limit on source rate	—
MCR	Minimum cell rate	Lower limit on source rate guaranteed by network	0
ICR	Initial cell rate	Initial value of ACR; rate at which source should send initially and after an idle period	PCR
RIF	Rate increase factor	Amount by which cell transmission rate may increase upon receipt of an RM cell	1/16
Nrm		Maximum number of cells a source may send for each forward RM cell	32
Mrm		Controls allocation of bandwidth between forward RM cells, backward RM cells, and data cells	2
RDF	Rate decrease factor	Multiplicative factor that controls the decrease of cell transmission rate	1/16
ACR	Allowed cell rate	Current upper limit on source rate; adjusted by feedback within the range of MCR to PCR	—
CRM		Number of forward RM cells that may be sent in the absence of received backward RM cells	$2^{19}-1$
ADTF	ACR decrease time factor	Time allowed between sending RM cells before the rate is decreased to ICR	0.5 ms
Trm		Upper bound on the time between consecutive forward RM cells for an active source	100 ms
FRTT	Fixed round-trip time	Sum of the fixed and propagation delays from source to destination and back	—
TBE	Transient buffer exposure	Negotiated number of cells that source can send initially before first RM cell returns	$2^{24}-1$
CDF	Cutoff decrease factor	Controls decrease in ACR in combination with CRM	1/16
TCR	Tagged cell rate	Upper limit on rate at which a source may send out-of-rate forward RM cells	10 cells/s

occupancy falls below the threshold. Notification could be issued by marking the EFCI in each incoming data cell or by setting CI or NI on each passing RM cell. A minor refinement is the use of two thresholds. When queue length increases sufficiently to cross the upper threshold, binary notification begins. Binary notification ceases only when the queue decreases below the lower threshold. This is similar to the operation of a thermostat and prevents frequent on/off transitions.

On the face of it, this approach seems fair, because a connection that has relatively more cells passing through a switch has a greater probability of receiving a binary notification. However, the single FIFO queue may unfairly penalize connections that pass through a number of switches. Suppose that a number of switches in the network are congested. In that case, connections that pass through more switches have a greater probability of receiving a binary notification than connections with comparable traffic but a shorter path.

Fairness can be improved by allocating a **separate queue** to each virtual connection (VC) or to each group of VCs. A separate threshold is used on each queue so that at any time, binary notification is provided only to VCs with long queues. In addition to being more fair, this approach has two other advantages. First, because each queue is isolated from the others, a misbehaving source will not affect other VCs. Second, the delay and loss behavior of individual VCs are decoupled, resulting in the potential of giving different QoS to different VCs.

More sophisticated is a technique referred to as selective feedback or intelligent marking. This technique is based on trying to allocate a **fair share** of the capacity dynamically. For example, we can define

$$Fairshare = \frac{\text{Target rate}}{\text{Number of connections}}$$

When congestion occurs, the switch marks cells on any VC that satisfies CCR > fairshare.

Explicit Rate Feedback Schemes

All explicit rate feedback schemes share the following general functions:

- Compute the fair share of the capacity for each VC that can be supported.
- Determine the current load, or degree of congestion.
- Compute an explicit rate (ER) for each connection and send that ER to the source.

In the remainder of this section, we describe the following examples of explicit rate feedback:

- Enhanced proportional rate control algorithm (EPRCA)
- Explicit rate indication for congestion avoidance (ERICA)
- Congestion avoidance using proportional control (CAPC)

For the **EPRCA** scheme, a switch keeps track of the average value of the current load on each connection, which is termed the mean allowed cell rate (MACR):

$$MACR(I) = (1 - \alpha) \times MACR(I - 1) + \alpha \times CCR(I)$$

where $CCR(I)$ is the value of the CCR field in the Ith arriving FRM. This is an exponential average of the kind we have seen a number of times in this book. Typically, $\alpha = 1/16$, so that more weight is given to past values of CCR than the current value. Thus, MACR represents an estimate of the average load passing through the switch at the current time. The objective is this: If congestion occurs, the switch reduces each VC to no more than DPF × MACR, where DPF is a *down pressure factor*. Because all VCs are reduced to the same ER, the throttling is performed fairly. Specifically, when the queue length at an output port exceeds a threshold, all RMs for connections that pass through that port are updated as follows:

$$ER \leftarrow \min[ER, DPF \times MACR]$$

A typical value for DPF is 7/8.

The EPRCA scheme reacts to congestion by lowering the ERs of VCs that are consuming more than their fair share of capacity. The next two schemes are congestion avoidance schemes that attempt to manage the ERs of all connections to avoid the onset of severe congestion. Schemes in this category make adjustments based on a load factor, LF, defined as follows:

$$LF = \frac{\text{Input rate}}{\text{Target rate}} \tag{17.4}$$

The input rate is measured over a fixed averaging interval, and the target rate is set slightly below the link bandwidth (e.g., 85–90%). When LF > 1, congestion is threatened, and many VCs will have their rates reduced. When LF < 1, there is no congestion and rate reduction is not necessary. Both the ERICA and CAPC schemes make use of LF, and in both cases the objective is to maintain the network at a load LF close to 1.

The **ERICA algorithm** defines the fair share for each connection as follows:

$$Fairshare = \frac{\text{Target rate}}{\text{Number of connections}}$$

The current share used by a particular VC is defined as

$$VCshare = \frac{\text{CCR}}{\text{LF}}$$

This may seem a strange way to calculate share. To clarify, we expand using Equation 17.4:

$$VCshare = \frac{\text{CCR}}{\text{Input rate}} \times \text{Target rate}$$

The first term on the right-hand side says what fraction of the current load passing through this output port is due to this VC. Multiplying this by the target rate indicates the relative amount of the target rate that would be assigned to this VC if we simply adjusted all VC rates up or down so that the total input rate equals the target rate. Rather than adjust all VC rates up or down, ERICA selectively adjusts VC rates so that the total ER allocated to connections equals the target rate and is allocated fairly. This is achieved by using the following allocation:

$$ER = \max[Fairshare, VCshare] \tag{17.5}$$

The effect of this is the following. Under low loads (LF < 1), each VC is assigned an ER greater than its current CCR, with those VCs whose *VCshare* is less than their *Fairshare* receiving a proportionately greater increase. Under high loads (LF > 1), some VCs are assigned an ER greater than their current CCR, and some are assigned a lower ER, done in such a way as to benefit those VCs with the lesser shares.

To get some insight into the behavior of ERICA, consider a case in which congestion is currently low and all connections begin to send at high rates of CCR. ERICA allows all VCs to change their rate to *VCshare*, which aims at bringing the system to an efficient operating point (LF = 1). At this load, if some VCs drop their rate (reduce CCR), then LF drops and individual *VCshare* values increase. However, regardless of load, sources are allowed to send at a rate of at least *Fairshare*. The effect of these rules is that ERICA improves fairness at every step, even under overload conditions [JAIN96b].

Equation 17.5 does not take into account any restrictions placed on a flow by other switches upstream from this switch. No switch is allowed to increase the ER value in an RM, so that we must revise the allocation as follows:

$$\text{newER} = \min[\text{oldER}, \max[\textit{Fairshare}, \textit{VCshare}]] \qquad (17.6)$$

where oldER is the value in an incoming RM and newER is the value in the corresponding outgoing RM.

The CAPC algorithm also uses the load factor LF to determine ER assignments. The fair share for each VC is initialized at (target rate)/(number of connections), as in ERICA. Then, with each arriving RM, *Fairshare* is updated as follows:

if $LF < 1$ $\textit{Fairshare} \leftarrow \textit{Fairshare} \times \min[ERU, 1 + (1 - LF) \times Rup)$

if $LF > 1$ $\textit{Fairshare} \leftarrow \textit{Fairshare} \times \max[ERF, 1 - (LF - 1) \times Rdn)$

where

ERU = determines the maximum increase allowed in the allotment of fair share; $ERU > 1$
Rup = a slope parameter between 0.025 and 0.1
ERF = determines the maximum decrease allowed in the allotment of fair share; typically set to 0.5
Rdn = a slope parameter between 0.2 and 0.8

If the calculated value of *Fairshare* is lower than the ER value in the RM cell, then the ER field in the RM cell is set to *Fairshare*.

The CAPC algorithm is simpler to implement than ERICA. However, the algorithm has been shown to exhibit very large rate oscillations if RIF (rate increase factor) is set too high and can sometimes lead to unfairness [ARUL96].

17.7 RECOMMENDED READING

[GARR96] provides a rationale for the ATM service categories and discusses the traffic management implications of each. [MCDY95] contains a thorough discussion of ATM traffic control for CBR and VBR. Two excellent treatments of ATM traffic characteristics and performance are [SCHW96] and [PITT96].

[CHEN96] is a good overview of ABR that contrasts this service with CBR and VBR and summarizes the traffic control mechanism. [JAIN96] provides a detailed explanation of the behavior of source and destination systems in transmitting data and RM cells. [ARUL96] is a broad survey of capacity allocation schemes for ABR service. [SAIT96] is a useful discussion of the performance implications of the various elements of the ABR traffic control mechanism. Two other helpful performance analyses are found in [BONO95] and [OSHA95].

ARUL96   Arulambalam, A.; Chen, X.; and Ansari, N. "Allocating Fair Rates for Available Bit Rate Service in ATM Networks." *IEEE Communications Magazine*, November 1996.

BONO95   Bonomi, F., and Fendick, K. "The Rate-Based Flow Control Framework for the Available Bit Rate ATM Service." *IEEE Network*, March/April 1995.

CHEN96   Chen, T.; Liu, S.; and Samalam, V. "The Available Bit Rate Service for Data in ATM Networks." *IEEE Communications Magazine*, May 1996.

GARR96   Garrett, M. "A Service Architecture for ATM: From Applications to Scheduling." *IEEE Network*, May/June 1996.

JAIN96   Jain, R., et al. "Source Behavior for ATM ABR Traffic Management: An Explanation. *IEEE Communications Magazine*, November 1996.

MCDY95   McDysan, D., and Spohn, D. *ATM: Theory and Application.* New York: McGraw-Hill, 1995.

OSHA95   Oshaki, H., et al. "Rate-Based Congestion Control for ATM Networks." *Computer Communication Review*, April 1995.

PITT96   Pitts, J., and Schormans, J. *Introduction to ATM Design and Performance.* New York: Wiley, 1996.

SAIT96   Saito, J., et al. "Performance Issues in Public ABR Service." *IEEE Communications Magazine*, November 1996.

SCHW96   Schwartz, M. *Broadband Integrated Networks.* Upper Saddle River, NJ: Prentice Hall PTR, 1996.

17.8 PROBLEMS

17.1   **a.** Demonstrate that Equation 17.1 is correct.
   b. Demonstrate that Equation 17.2 is correct.
   c. Demonstrate that Equation 17.3 is correct.

17.2   Show that over any closed interval of length t, the number of cells, $N(t)$, that can be emitted with spacing no less than T and still be in conformance with $GCRA(T_s, \tau_s)$ is bounded by

$$N(t) \leq \min\left(\left\lfloor 1 + \frac{t + \tau_s}{T_s} \right\rfloor, \left\lfloor 1 + \frac{t}{T} \right\rfloor\right)$$

17.3   For the ERICA algorithm, consider the action at a switch in which each incoming ER value is greater than or equal to the incoming CCR value, so that we may use Equation 17.5 rather than Equation 17.6; this corresponds to a case in which other switches are not restricting flow. List the conditions (e.g., in terms of LF, *Fairshare*, and *VCshare*) under which the ER assigned to a VC is greater than the current CCR and the conditions under which ER < CCR.

APPENDIX A

FLOW CONTROL, ERROR DETECTION, AND ERROR CONTROL

Fundamental to the operation of a data communications facility are the mechanisms of flow control, error control, and error detection. These mechanisms are found in levels 2 and 3 of X.25, in the signaling link level of Signaling System Number 7, and in LAPD. They are also found in a number of other protocols, such as HDLC. This appendix examines the basic principles of these mechanisms. Their application in X.25, SS7, and ISDN is presented at the appropriate points in the main part of this book.

A.1 FLOW CONTROL

Flow control is a technique for assuring that a transmitting entity does not overwhelm a receiving entity with data. The receiver will typically allocate a data buffer of some maximum length. When data are received, the receiver must do a certain amount of processing (e.g., examine the header and remove it) before passing the data to a higher-level user. In the absence of flow control, the receiver's buffer may fill up and overflow while it is processing old data.

In this section, we examine mechanisms for flow control in the absence of errors. The model we will use is depicted in Figure A.1a. Data are sent as a sequence of blocks. We will refer to the block as a *protocol data unit* (PDU) to emphasize that the exact nature of the block depends on the protocol involved. In X.25 level 2 and in LAPD, the term *frame* is used; in the signaling link level of Signaling System Number 7, the term *signal unit* is used; and in X.25 level 3, the term *packet* is used. In any case, for now we assume that all PDUs that are transmitted are successfully received; no PDUs are lost and none arrive with errors. Furthermore, PDUs arrive in the same order in which they are sent. However, each transmitted PDU suffers an arbitrary and variable amount of delay before reception.

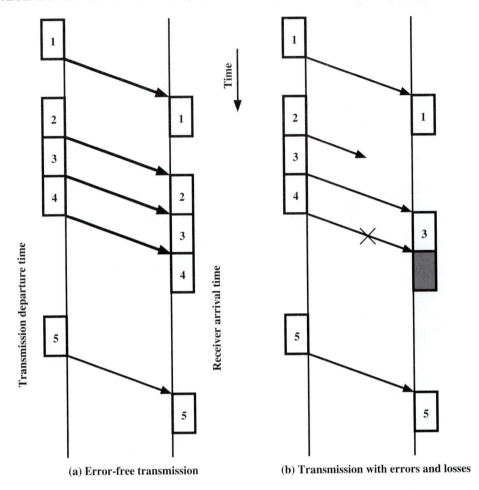

(a) Error-free transmission   (b) Transmission with errors and losses

Figure A.1   Model of Frame Transmission.

The simplest form of flow control, known as **stop-and-wait flow control**, works as follows. A source entity transmits a PDU. After reception, the destination entity indicates its willingness to accept another PDU by sending back an acknowledgment to the PDU just received. The source must wait until it receives the acknowledgment before sending the next PDU. The destination can thus stop the flow of data by simply withholding acknowledgment. This procedure works fine and, indeed, can hardly be improved upon when a message is sent as one continuous block of data. However, it is often the case that a source will break up a large block of data into smaller blocks and send these one at a time. This is done for one or more of the following reasons:

- The buffer size of the receiver may be limited.
- On a multipoint line (such as may be found using LAPD), it is usually desirable not to permit one station to occupy the line for very long, thus causing long delays at the other stations.
- On a shared network (such as an X.25 packet-switching network), the network may impose a maximum packet size.

- The longer the transmission, the more likely it is that there will be an error, necessitating retransmission of the entire block. With smaller blocks, errors are detected sooner, and a smaller amount of data needs to be retransmitted.

With the use of multiple PDUs for a single message, the stop-and-wait proce-dure may be inadequate. The essence of the problem is that only one PDU at a time can be in transit. In situations where the bit length of the link is greater than the PDU length, serious inefficiencies result. This is illustrated in Figure A.2; in the fig-ure, the transmission time (the time it takes for a station to transmit a PDU) is nor-malized to one, and the propagation delay (the time it takes for a bit to propagate from sender to receiver) is expressed as the variable a. Note that most of the time, most of the line is idle.

Efficiency can be greatly improved by allowing multiple PDUs to be in transit at the same time. Let us examine how this might work for two stations, A and B, con-nected via a full-duplex link. Station B allocates buffer space for n PDUs instead of the one just discussed. Thus, B can accept n PDUs, and A is allowed to send n PDUs without waiting for an acknowledgment. To keep track of which PDUs have been acknowledged, each is labeled with a sequence number. B acknowledges a PDU by sending an acknowledgment that includes the sequence number of the next PDU expected. This acknowledgment also implicitly announces that B is prepared to receive

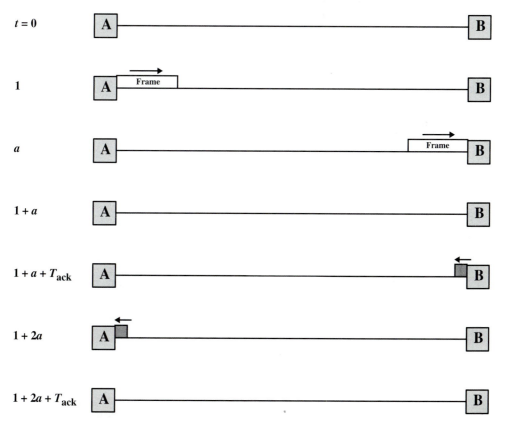

Figure A.2 Stop-and-Wait Link Utilization.

the next n PDUs, beginning with the number specified. This scheme can also be used to acknowledge multiple PDUs. For example, B could receive PDUs 2, 3, and 4, but withhold acknowledgment until PDU 4 has arrived. By then returning an acknowledgment with sequence number 5, B acknowledges PDUs 2, 3, and 4 at one time. A maintains a list of sequence numbers that it is allowed to send and B maintains a list of sequence numbers that it is prepared to receive. Each of these lists can be thought of as a *window* of PDUs. The operation is referred to as **sliding-window flow control**.

Several additional comments need to be made. First, because the sequence number to be used occupies a field in the PDU, it is clearly of bounded size. For a k-bit field, the sequence number can range from 0 to $2^k - 1$. Accordingly, PDUs are numbered modulo 2^k; that is, after sequence number $2^k - 1$, the next number is zero. Second, the maximum size of the window is some number $n \leq 2^k - 1$. The limitation to $2^k - 1$ rather than 2^k has to do with the error-control mechanism and will be justified in due course.

Figure A.3 is a useful way of depicting the sliding-window process. It assumes the use of a 3-bit sequence number, so that PDUs are numbered sequentially from 0 through 7, and then the same numbers are reused for subsequent PDUs. The shaded rectangle indicates that the sender may transmit seven PDUs, beginning with PDU 6. Each time a PDU is sent, the shaded window shrinks; each time an acknowledgment is received, the shaded window grows.

An example is shown in Figure A.4. The example assumes a 3-bit sequence number field and a maximum window size of seven frames. Initially, A and B have windows indicating that A may transmit seven frames, beginning with frame 0 (F0). After transmitting three frames (F0, F1, F2) without acknowledgment, A has shrunk its window to four frames and maintains a copy of the three transmitted frames. The window indicates that A may transmit four frames, beginning with frame number 3. B then transmits an RR (receive ready) 3, which means,[1] "I have received all frames up through frame number 2 and am ready to receive frame number 3; in fact, I am prepared to receive seven frames, beginning with frame number 3." With this acknowledgment, A is back up to permission to transmit seven frames, still beginning with frame 3; also A may discard the buffered frames that have now been acknowledged. A proceeds to transmit frames 3, 4, 5, and 6. B returns RR 4, which acknowledges F3, and allows transmission of F4 through F2. By the time this RR reaches A, it has already transmitted F4, F5, and F6, and therefore A may only open its window to permit sending four frames beginning with F7.

Figure A.5, which shows the efficiency implications of this mechanism, is to be contrasted with the stop-and-wait mechanism illustrated in Figure A.2. If the maximum window size, n, is a little greater than twice the round-trip propagation delay ($n > 2a + 1$), then it is possible to utilize the link to the fullest.[2] Even for smaller window sizes, the utilization of the link is clearly superior to that of stop-and-wait.

The mechanism so far described does indeed provide a form of flow control: The receiver must only be able to accommodate n PDUs beyond the one it has last

---

[1]The RR is a separate control frame. Most data link control protocols also allow for *piggybacked acknowledgments*. Each data frame includes not only a sequence number for that frame but also an acknowledgment sequence number that serves the same function as the RR frame. Thus, in a full-duplex exchange of data frames, separate RR frames are rarely used.

[2]Recall that the time to transmit one PDU is normalized to one time unit, and the propagation time is the variable a. Hence, the time to transmit n PDUs in succession is n time units.

(text continues on page 500)

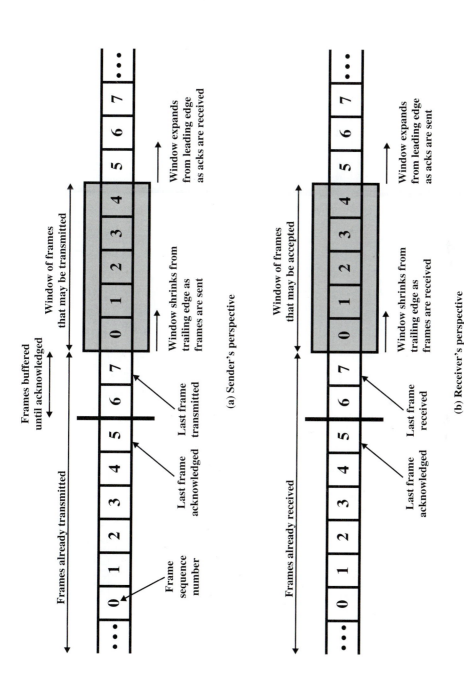

Figure A.3 Sliding-Window Depiction.

497

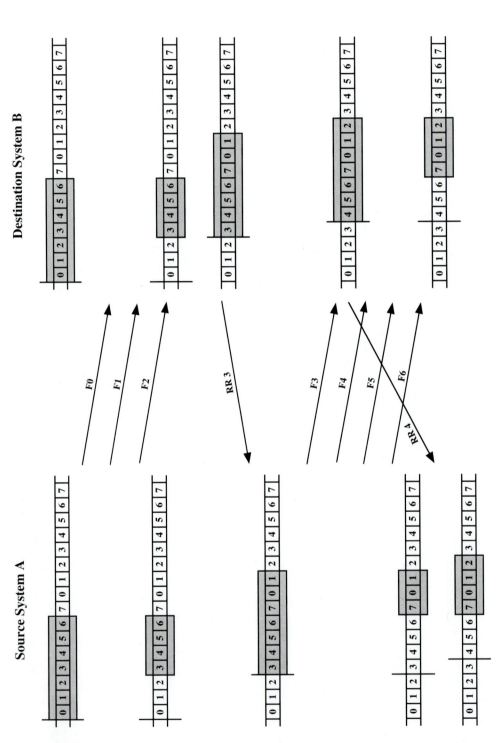

Figure A.4 Example of a Sliding-Window Protocol.

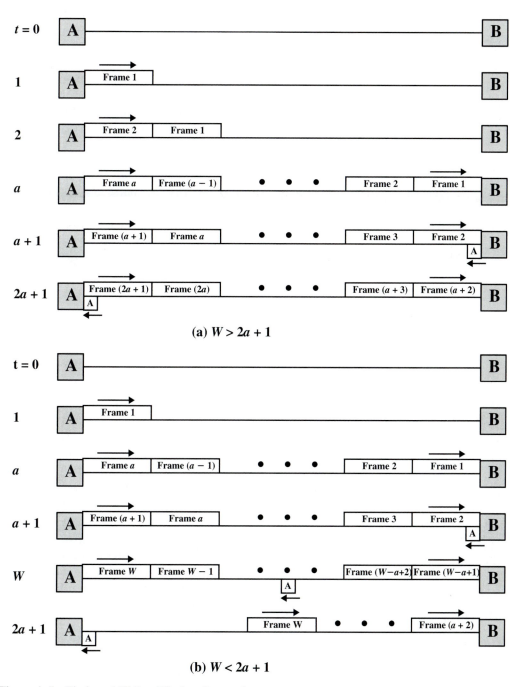

Figure A.5   Timing of Sliding-Window Protocol.

acknowledged. To supplement this, most protocols also allow a station to cut off completely the flow of PDUs from the other side by sending a receive not ready (RNR) message, which acknowledges former PDUs but forbids transfer of future PDUs. Thus, RNR 5 means, "I have received all PDUs up through number 4 but am unable to accept any more." At some subsequent point, the station must send a normal acknowledgment to reopen the window.

So far, we have discussed transmission in one direction only. If two stations exchange data, each needs to maintain two windows: one for transmit and one for receive, and each side needs to send the data and acknowledgments to the other. To provide efficient support for this requirement, a feature known as *piggybacking* is typically provided. Each *data PDU* includes a field that holds the sequence number of that PDU plus a field that holds the sequence number used for acknowledgment. Thus, if a station has data to send and an acknowledgment to send, it sends both together in one PDU, saving communication capacity. Of course, if a station has an acknowledgment but no data to send, it sends a separate *acknowledgment PDU.* If a station has data to send but no new acknowledgment to send, it must repeat the last acknowledgment that it sent. This is because the data PDU includes a field for the acknowledgment number, and some value must be put into that field. When a station receives a duplicate ACK, it simply ignores it.

A.2 ERROR DETECTION

The Error-Detection Process

Any data transmission is subject to errors. In transmitting across a data link, signal impairments, such as the following, may alter the contents of a unit of data [STAL97]:

- **Attenuation:** The strength of the signal decreases with distance over any transmission medium. With sufficient attenuation, it becomes difficult for the receiver to recover the data from the received signal.
- **Attenuation distortion:** Attenuation is an increasing function of frequency. Thus, frequency components of a signal are differentially affected, which introduces distortion into the signal.
- **Delay distortion:** The velocity of propagation of a signal through a wire medium varies with frequency; the velocity tends to be highest near the center frequency of the signal and fall off toward the two edges of the signal's bandwidth. This causes the signal energy from one bit time to spill into the time slots of neighboring bits, a phenomenon known as intersymbol interference.
- **Noise:** Noise is any unwanted signal that combines with, and hence distorts, the signal intended for reception. Varieties include thermal noise, intermodulation noise, crosstalk, and impulse noise.
- **Collisions:** In a multipoint link, if two stations transmit at the same time, their signals overlap and neither signal can be successfully received.

Because of these impairments, a protocol entity (e.g., LAPD, X.25 level 2, SS7 signaling link level) may receive a PDU from the other side in which some bits have

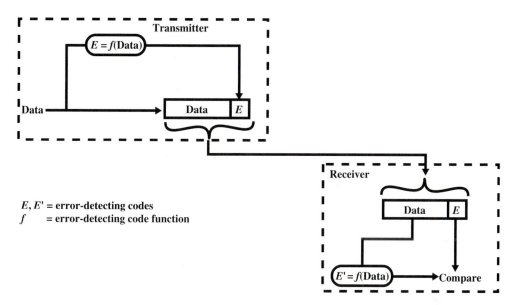

Figure A.6   Error Detection.

changed value. Accordingly, some form of error detection is needed to avoid delivering incorrect data to the user.

The error-detection process is illustrated in Figure A.6. On transmission, a calculation is performed on the bits of the PDU to be transmitted; the result, called an **error-detecting code**, is inserted as an additional field in the frame. On reception, the same calculation is performed on the received bits and the calculated result is compared with the value stored in the incoming frame. If there is a discrepancy, the receiver assumes that an error has occurred and discards the PDU.

The Cyclic Redundancy Check

One of the most common, and one of the most powerful, of the error-detecting codes is the cyclic redundancy check (CRC). It is used in X.25 level 2, SS7 signaling link level, and LAPD. We first examine the operation of this code and then look at its effectiveness.

CRC Operation

Given a k-bit block of data, the transmitter generates an n-bit sequence, known as a *frame-check sequence* (FCS), so that the resulting frame, consisting of $k + n$ bits, is exactly divisible by some predetermined number. The receiver then divides the incoming frame by the same number and, if there is no remainder, assumes that there was no error.

To clarify the preceding, we present the procedure in several ways:

- Modulo 2 arithmetic
- Polynomials
- Shift registers and exclusive-or gates

First, we work with binary numbers and modulo 2 arithmetic. Modulo 2 arithmetic uses binary addition with no carries, which is just the exclusive-or operation.

Examples

```
  1111        11001
+ 1010        ×  11
  0101        11001
             11001
            101011
```

Now define:

$T = (k + n)$-bit PDU to be transmitted, with $n < k$
$M = k$-bit message, the first k bits of T
$F = n$-bit FCS, the last n bits of T
$P =$ pattern of $n + 1$ bits; this is the predetermined divisor mentioned previously

We would like T/P to have no remainder. It should be clear that

$$T = 2^n M + F$$

That is, by multiplying M by 2^n, we have in effect shifted it to the left by n bits and padded out the result with 0s. Adding F gives us the concatenation of M and F, which is T. Now we want T to be exactly divisible by P. Suppose that we divided $2^n M$ by P:

$$\frac{2^n M}{P} = Q + \frac{R}{P} \tag{A.1}$$

There is a quotient and a remainder. Because division is binary, the remainder is always one bit less than the divisor. We will use this remainder as our FCS. Then

$$T = 2^n M + R$$

Does this R satisfy our condition? To see that it does, consider

$$\frac{T}{P} = \frac{2^n M + R}{P}$$

Substituting Equation (A.1), we have

$$\frac{T}{P} = Q + \frac{R}{P} + \frac{R}{P}$$

However, any binary number added to itself modulo 2 yields zero. Thus,

$$\frac{T}{P} = Q + \frac{R + R}{P} = Q$$

There is no remainder, and therefore T is exactly divisible by P. Thus, the FCS is easily generated. Simply divide $2^n M$ by P and use the remainder as the FCS. On reception, the receiver will divide T by P and will get no remainder if there have been no errors.

A simple example of the procedure is now presented:

1. Given

   $$\begin{aligned}
   \text{Message } M &= 1010001101 \text{ (10 bits)} \\
   \text{Pattern } P &= 110101 \text{ (6 bits)} \\
   \text{FCS } R &= \text{to be calculated (5 bits)}
   \end{aligned}$$

2. The message is multiplied by 2^5, yielding 101000110100000.
3. This product is divided by P:

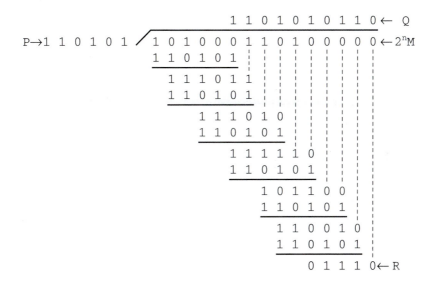

4. The remainder is added to $2^n M$ to give $T = 101000110101110$, which is transmitted.
5. If there are no errors, the receiver receives T intact. The received PDU is divided by P:

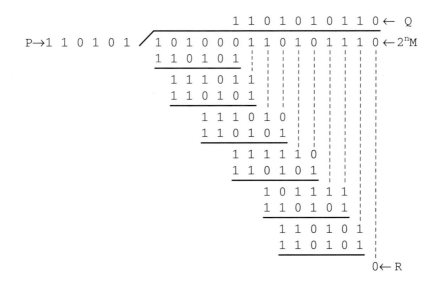

Because there is no remainder, it is assumed that there have been no errors.

The pattern P is chosen to be one bit longer than the desired FCS, and the exact bit pattern chosen depends on the type of errors expected. At minimum, both the high- and low-order bits of P must be 1.

The occurrence of an error is easily expressed. An error results in the reversal of a bit. Mathematically, this is equivalent to taking the exclusive-or of the bit and one: $0 + 1 = 1; 1 + 1 = 0$. Thus, the errors in an $(n + k)$-bit PDU can be represented by an $(n + k)$-bit field with 1s in each error position. The resulting frame T_r can be expressed as

$$T_r = T + E$$

where

T = transmitted frame
E = error pattern with 1s in positions where errors occur
T_r = received frame

The receiver will fail to detect an error if and only if T_r is divisible by P—that is, if and only if E is divisible by P. Intuitively, this seems an unlikely occurrence.

A second way of viewing the CRC process is to express all values as polynomials in a dummy variable X with binary coefficients. The coefficients correspond to the bits in the binary number. Thus, for $M = 110011$, we have $M(X) = X^5 + X^4 + X + 1$, and for $P = 11001$, we have $P(X) = X^4 + X^3 + 1$. Arithmetic operations are again modulo 2. The CRC process can now be described as

$$1. \quad \frac{X^n M(X)}{P(X)} = Q(X) + \frac{R(X)}{P(X)}$$

$$2. \quad T(X) = X^n M(X) + R(X)$$

Four versions of $P(X)$ are widely used:

$$
\begin{aligned}
\text{CRC-12} &= X^{12} + X^{11} + X^3 + X^2 + X + 1 \\
\text{CRC-16} &= X^{16} + X^{15} + X^2 + 1 \\
\text{CRC-CCITT} &= X^{16} + X^{12} + X^5 + 1 \\
\text{CRC-32} &= X^{32} + X^{26} + X^{23} + X^{22} + X^{16} + X^{12} + X^{11} \\
&\quad + X^{10} + X^8 + X^7 + X^5 + X^4 + X^2 + X + 1
\end{aligned}
$$

The CRC-12 system is used for transmission of streams of 6-bit characters and generates a 12-bit FCS. Both CRC-16 and CRC-CCITT are popular for 8-bit characters, in the United States and Europe, respectively, and both result in a 16-bit FCS. This would seem adequate for most applications, although CRC-32 is specified as an option in some point-to-point synchronous transmission standards.

As a final representation, Figure A.7 shows that the CRC process can easily be implemented as a dividing circuit consisting of exclusive-or gates and a shift register. The circuit is implemented as follows:

1. The register contains n bits, equal to the length of the FCS.

2. There are up to n exclusive-or gates.

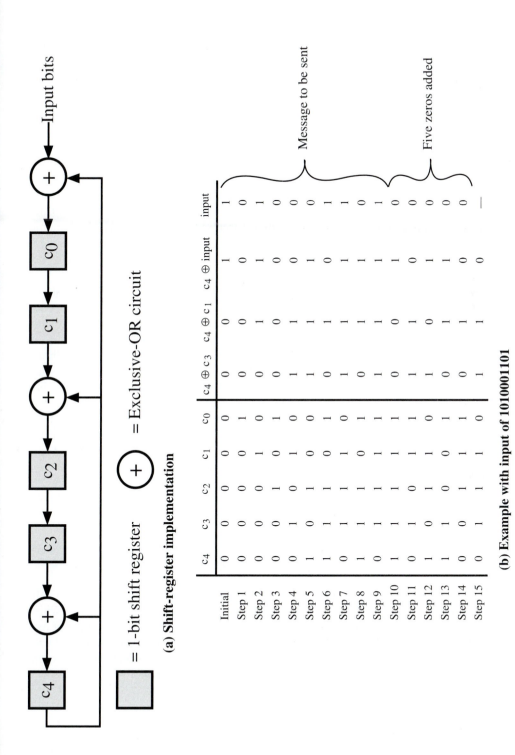

(a) Shift-register implementation

(b) Example with input of 1010001101

Figure A.7 Circuit with Shift Registers for Dividing by the Polynomial $X^5 + X^4 + X^2 + 1$.

3. The presence or absence of a gate corresponds to the presence or absence of a term in the divisor polynomial, $P(X)$.

In this example, we use

$$\text{Message } M = 1010001101; M(X) = X^9 + X^7 + X^3 + X^2 + 1$$

$$\text{Divisor } P = 110101; P(X) = X^5 + X^4 + X^2 + 1$$

which were used earlier in the discussion.

Part (a) of the figure shows the shift register implementation. The process begins with the shift register cleared (all zeros). The message, or dividend, is then entered, one bit at a time, starting with the most significant bit. Part (b) is a table that shows the step-by-step operation as the input is applied one bit at a time. Each row of the table shows the values currently stored in the five shift-register elements. In addition, the row shows the values that appear at the outputs of the three exclusive-or circuits. Finally, the row shows the value of the next input bit, which is available for the operation of the next step.

Because no feedback occurs until a 1 dividend bit arrives at the most significant end of the register, the first five operations are simple shifts. Whenever a 1 bit arrives at the left end of the register (c_4), a 1 is subtracted (exclusive-or) from the second (c_3), fourth (c_1), and sixth (input) bits on the next shift. This is identical to the binary long division process illustrated earlier. The process continues through all the bits of the message, plus five zero bits. These latter bits account for shifting M to the left five position to accommodate the FCS. After the last bit is processed, the shift register contains the remainder (FCS), which can then be transmitted.

At the receiver, the same logic is used. As each bit of M arrives, it is inserted into the shift register at A. If there have been no errors, the shift register should contain the bit pattern for R at the conclusion of M. The transmitted bits of R now begin to arrive, and the effect is to zero out the register so that, at the conclusion of reception, the register contains all 0s.

A.3 ERROR CONTROL

Error control refers to mechanisms to detect and correct errors that occur in the transmission of protocol data units (PDUs). The model that we will use, which covers the typical case, is illustrated in Figure A.1b. As before, data are sent as a sequence of PDUs; PDUs arrive in the same order in which they are sent, and each transmitted PDU suffers an arbitrary and variable amount of delay before reception. In addition, we admit the possibility of two types of errors:

- **Lost PDU:** A PDU fails to arrive at the other side. In the case of a network, the network may simply fail to deliver a packet. In the case of a direct point-to-point data link, a noise burst may damage a frame to the extent that the receiver is not aware that a frame has been transmitted.

- **Damaged PDU:** A recognizable PDU does arrive, but some of the bits are in error (have been altered during transmission).

The most common techniques for error control are based on some or all of the following ingredients:

- **Error detection:** The destination detects and discards PDUs that are in error, using the techniques described in the preceding section.
- **Positive acknowledgment:** The destination returns a positive acknowledgment to successfully received, error-free PDUs.
- **Retransmission after timeout:** The source retransmits a PDU that has not been acknowledged after a predetermined amount of time.
- **Negative acknowledgment and retransmission:** The destination returns a negative acknowledgment to PDUs in which an error is detected. The source retransmits such PDUs.

Collectively, these mechanisms are all referred to as **automatic repeat request** (ARQ). The most common form of ARQ is go-back-N ARQ.

In go-back-N ARQ, a station may send a series of PDUs sequentially numbered modulo some maximum value. The number of unacknowledged PDUs outstanding is determined by window size, using the sliding-window flow-control technique. While no errors occur, the destination will acknowledge (ACK) incoming PDUs as usual. If the destination station detects an error in a PDU, it sends a negative acknowledgment (NAK) for that PDU. The destination station will discard that PDU and all future incoming PDUs until the PDU in error is correctly received. Thus, the source station, when it receives a NAK, must retransmit the PDU in error plus all succeeding PDUs that had been transmitted in the interim.

Consider that station A is sending PDUs to station B. After each transmission, A sets an acknowledgment timer for the PDU just transmitted. The go-back-N technique takes into account the following contingencies:

1. Damaged PDU. There are three subcases:
   - A transmits PDU i. B detects an error and has previously successfully received PDU $(i - 1)$. B sends a NAK i, indicating that frame i is rejected. When A receives this NAK, it must retransmit PDU i and all subsequent PDUs that it has transmitted.
   - PDU i is lost in transit. A subsequently sends PDU $(i + 1)$. B receives PDU $(i + 1)$ out of order and sends a NAK i.
   - PDU i is lost in transit and A does not soon send additional PDUs. B receives nothing and returns neither an ACK nor a NAK. A will time out and retransmit PDU i.

2. Damaged ACK. There are two subcases:
   - B receives PDU i and sends ACK $(i + 1)$, which is lost in transit. Because ACKs are cumulative (e.g., ACK 6 means that all PDUs through 5 are acknowledged), it may be that A will receive a subsequent ACK to a

subsequent PDU that will do the job of the lost ACK before the associated timer expires.

◻ If *A*'s timer expires, *A* retransmits PDU *i* and all subsequent PDUs.

3. Damaged NAK. If a NAK is lost, *A* will eventually time out on the associated PDU and retransmit that PDU and all subsequent PDUs.

Figure A.8 shows the PDU flow for go-back-N ARQ on a full-duplex line, assuming a 3-bit sequence number.

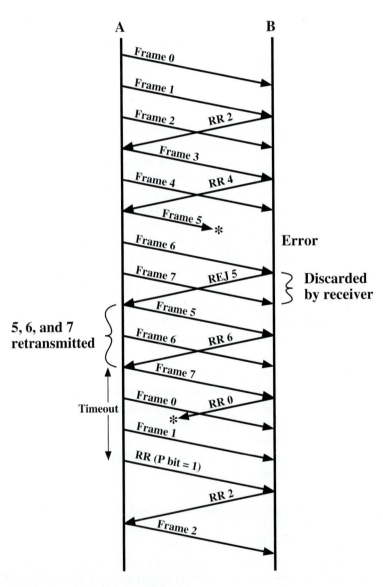

Figure A.8 Go-back-N ARQ.

In the section on flow control, we mentioned that for a k-bit sequence number field, which provides a sequence number range of 2^k, the maximum window size is limited to $2^k - 1$. This has to do with the interaction between error control and acknowledgment. Consider that if data are being exchanged in both directions, station B must send a piggybacked acknowledgment to station A's PDUs in the data PDUs being transmitted by B, even if the acknowledgment has already been sent. As we have mentioned, this is because B must put some number in the acknowledgment field of its data PDUs. As an example, assume a 3-bit sequence number size. Suppose a station sends PDU 0 and gets back an ACK 1, and then sends PDUs 1, 2, 3, 4, 5, 6, 7, 0 and gets another ACK 1. This could mean that all eight PDUs were received correctly and the ACK 1 is a cumulative acknowledgment. It could also mean that all eight PDUs were damaged in transit, and the receiving station is repeating its previous ACK 1. The problem is avoided if the maximum window size is limited to $7 = (2^3 - 1)$.

APPENDIX B

THE OSI REFERENCE MODEL

One of the most important concepts in data communications is the open systems interconnection (OSI) reference model. This model serves as a framework within which communication protocol standards are developed. It also serves as a frame of reference for talking about data communications. Although the ISDN recommendations represent a separate effort from OSI and OSI-related standards, the ISDN protocols do fit within the OSI framework. This appendix provides an overview of the OSI model.

B.1 MOTIVATION

When work is done that involves more than one computer, additional elements must be added to the system: the hardware and software to support the communication between or among the systems. Communications hardware is reasonably standard and generally presents few problems. However, when communication is desired among heterogeneous (different vendors, different models of same vendor) machines, the software development effort can be a nightmare. Different vendors use different data formats and data exchange conventions. Even within one vendor's product line, different models of computers may communicate in unique ways.

As the use of computer communications and computer networking proliferates, a one-at-a-time special-purpose approach to communications software development is too costly to be acceptable. The only alternative is for computer vendors to adopt and implement a common set of conventions. For this to happen, a set of international or at least national standards must be promulgated by appropriate organizations. Such standards have two effects:

- Vendors feel encouraged to implement the standards because of an expectation that, because of wide usage of the standards, their products would be less marketable without them.
- Customers are in a position to require that the standards be implemented by any vendor wishing to propose equipment to them.

Table B.1   Purpose of the OSI Model (ISO 7498)

The purpose of this International Standard Reference Model of Open Systems Interconnection is to provide a common basis for the coordination of standards development for the purpose of systems interconnection, while allowing existing standards to be placed into perspective within the overall Reference Model.

The term Open Systems Interconnection (OSI) qualifies standards for the exchange of information among systems that are "open" to one another for this purpose by virtue of their mutual use of the applicable standards.

The fact that a system is open does not imply any particular systems implementation, technology, or means of interconnection, but refers to the mutual recognition and support of the applicable standards.

It is also the purpose of this International Standard to identify areas for developing or improving standards and to provide a common reference for maintaining consistency of all related standards. It is not the intent of this International Standard either to serve as an implementation specification or to be a basis for appraising the conformance of actual implementations or to provide a sufficient level of detail to define precisely the services and protocols of the interconnection architecture. Rather, this International Standard provides a conceptual and functional framework which allows international teams of experts to work productively and independently on the development of standards for each layer of the Reference Model of OSI.

It should become clear from the ensuing discussion that no single standard will suffice. The task of communication in a truly cooperative way between applications on different computers is too complex to be handled as a unit. The problem must be decomposed into manageable parts. Hence, before one can develop standards, there should be a structure or *architecture* that defines the communications tasks.

This line of reasoning led the International Organization for Standardization (ISO) in 1977 to establish a subcommittee to develop such an architecture. The result was the *Open Systems Interconnection* reference model, which is a framework for defining standards for linking heterogeneous computers. The OSI model provides the basis for connecting open systems for distributed applications processing. The term *open* denotes the ability of any two systems conforming to the reference model and the associated standards to connect.

Table B.1, extracted from the basic OSI document (ISO 7498), summarizes the purpose of the model.

B.2   CONCEPTS

A widely accepted structuring technique, and the one chosen by ISO, is layering. The communications functions are partitioned into a hierarchical set of layers. Each layer performs a related subset of the functions required to communicate with another system. It relies on the next lower layer to perform more primitive functions and to conceal the details of those functions. It provides services to the next higher layer. Ideally, the layers should be defined so that changes in one layer do not require changes in the other layers. Thus, we have decomposed one problem into a number of more manageable subproblems.

The task of ISO was to define a set of layers and the services performed by each layer. The partitioning should group functions logically and should have enough layers to make each layer manageably small, but should not have so many layers that the processing overhead imposed by the collection of layers is burden-some. The principles that guided the design effort are summarized in Table B.2. The resulting reference model has seven layers, which are listed with a brief definition in Figure B.1. Table B.3 provides ISO's justification for the selection of these layers.

Table B.1 defines, in general terms, the functions that must be performed in a system for it to communicate. Of course, it takes two to communicate, and so the same set of layered functions must exist in two systems. Communication is achieved by having the corresponding (*peer*) layers in two systems communicate. The peer layers communicate by means of a set of rules or conventions known as a *protocol*. The key elements of a protocol are as follows:

- **Syntax:** Includes such things as data format and signal levels.
- **Semantics:** Includes control information for coordination and error handling.
- **Timing:** Includes speed matching and sequencing.

Figure B.2 illustrates the OSI architecture. Each system contains the seven layers. Communication is between applications in the two computers, labeled appli-

Table B.2   Principles Used in Defining the OSI Layers (ISO 7498)

---

1. Do not create so many layers as to make the system engineering task of describing and integrating the layers more difficult than necessary.

2. Create a boundary at a point where the description of services can be small and the number of interactions across the boundary are minimized.

3. Create separate layers to handle functions that are manifestly different in the process performed or the technology involved.

4. Collect similar functions into the same layer.

5. Select boundaries at a point which past experience has demonstrated to be successful.

6. Create a layer of easily localized functions so that the layer could be totally redesigned and its protocols changed in a major way to take advantage of new advances in architecture, hardware or software technology without changing the services expected from and provided to the adjacent layers.

7. Create a boundary where it may be useful at some point in time to have the corresponding interface standardized.

8. Create a layer where there is a need for a different level of abstraction in the handling of data, for example morphology, syntax, semantic.

9. Allow changes of functions or protocols to be made within a layer without affecting other layers.

10. Create for each layer boundaries with its upper and lower layer only.

Similar principles have been applied to sublayering:

11. Create further subgrouping and organization of functions to form sublayers within a layer in cases where distinct communication services need it.

12. Create, where needed, two or more sublayers with a common, and therefore minimal, functionality to allow interface operation with adjacent layers.

13. Allow by-passing of sublayers.

cation X and application Y in the figure. If application X wishes to send a message to application Y, it invokes the application layer (layer 7). Layer 7 establishes a peer relationship with layer 7 of the target computer, using a layer-7 protocol (application protocol). This protocol requires services from layer 6, so the two layer-6 entities use a protocol of their own, and so on down to the physical layer, which actually transmits bits over a transmission medium.

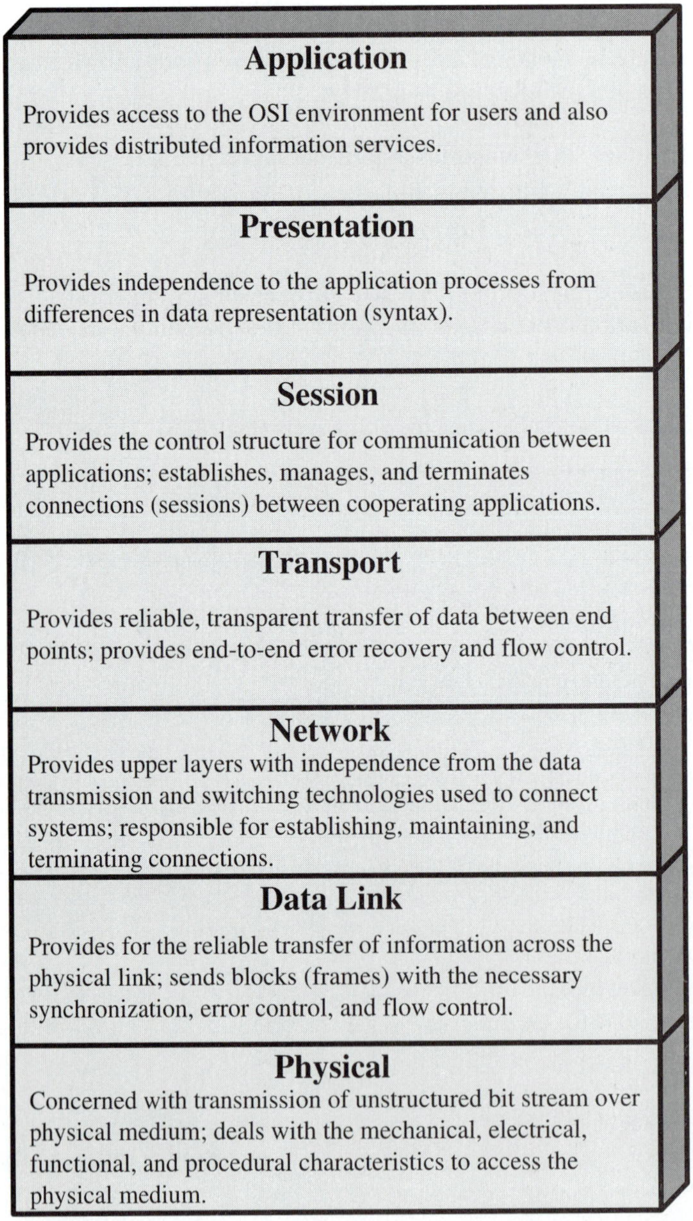

Application
Provides access to the OSI environment for users and also provides distributed information services.

Presentation
Provides independence to the application processes from differences in data representation (syntax).

Session
Provides the control structure for communication between applications; establishes, manages, and terminates connections (sessions) between cooperating applications.

Transport
Provides reliable, transparent transfer of data between end points; provides end-to-end error recovery and flow control.

Network
Provides upper layers with independence from the data transmission and switching technologies used to connect systems; responsible for establishing, maintaining, and terminating connections.

Data Link
Provides for the reliable transfer of information across the physical link; sends blocks (frames) with the necessary synchronization, error control, and flow control.

Physical
Concerned with transmission of unstructured bit stream over physical medium; deals with the mechanical, electrical, functional, and procedural characteristics to access the physical medium.

Figure B.1 The OSI Layers.

Table B.3 Justification of the OSI Layers (ISO 7498)

1. It is essential that the architecture permits usage of a realistic variety of physical media for inter-connection with different control procedures (for example V.24, V.25, etc. ...). Application of principles 3, 5, and 8 (Table 15.2) leads to identification of a **Physical Layer** as the lowest layer in the architecture.

2. Some physical communication media (for example telephone line) require specific techniques to be used in order to transmit data between systems despite a relatively high error rate (i.e., an error rate not acceptable for the great majority of applications). These specific techniques are used in data-link control procedures which have been studied and standardized for a number of years. It must also be recognized that new physical communication media (for example fiber optics) will require different data-link control procedures. Application of principles 3, 5, and 8 leads to identification of a **Data Link Layer** on top of the Physical Layer in the architecture.

3. In the open systems architecture, some open systems will act as the final destination of data. Some open systems may act only as intermediate nodes (forwarding data to other systems). Application of principles 3, 5, and 7 leads to identification of a **Network Layer** on top of the data link layer. Network oriented protocols such as routing, for example, will be grouped in this layer. Thus, the Network Layer will provide a connection path (network-connection) between a pair of transport entities, including the case where intermediate nodes are involved.

4. Control of data transportation from source end open system to destination end open system (which is not performed in intermediate nodes) is the last function to be performed in order to provide the totality of the transport service. Thus, the upper layer in the transport service part of the architecture is the **Transport Layer**, on top of the Network Layer. This Transport Layer relieves higher layer entities from any concern with the transportation of data between them.

5. There is a need to organize and synchronize dialogue, and to manage the exchange of data. Application of principles 3 and 4 leads to the identification of a **Session Layer** on top of the Transport Layer.

6. The remaining set of general interest functions are those related to representation and manipulation of structured data for the benefit of application programs. Application of principles 3 and 4 leads to the identification of a **Presentation Layer** on top of the Session Layer.

7. Finally, there are applications consisting of application processes which perform information processing. An aspect of these application processes and the protocols by which they communicate comprise the **Application Layer** as the highest layer of the architecture.

Note that there is no direct communication between peer layers except at the physical layer. That is, above the physical layer, each protocol entity sends data down to the next lower layer to get the data across to its peer entity. Even at the physical layer, the OSI model does not stipulate that two systems be directly connected. For example, a packet-switched or circuit-switched network may be used to provide the communication link.

Figure B.2 also highlights the use of protocol data units (PDUs) within the OSI architecture. First, consider the most common way in which protocols are realized. When application X has a message to send to application Y, it transfers those data to an application entity in the application layer. A header is appended to the data that contains the required information for the peer layer 7 protocol (encapsulation). The original data, plus the header, is now passed as a unit to layer 6. The presentation entity treats the whole unit as data and appends its own header (a second encapsulation). This process continues down through layer 2, which generally adds both a header and a trailer (e.g., HDLC). This layer 2 unit, called a frame, is then

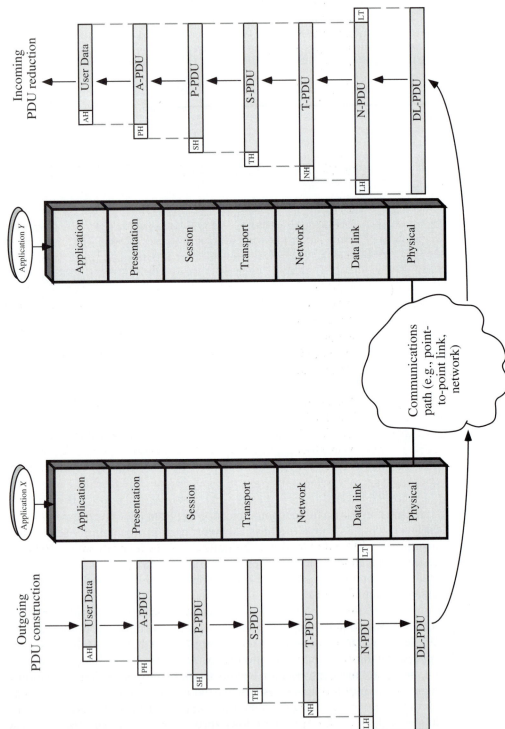

Figure B.2 The OSI Environment.

passed by the physical layer onto the transmission medium. When the frame is received by the target system, the reverse process occurs. As the data ascend, each layer strips off the outermost header, acts on the protocol information contained therein, and passes the remainder up to the next layer.

At each stage of the process, a layer may fragment the data unit it receives from the next higher layer into several parts, to accommodate its own requirements. These data units must then be reassembled by the corresponding peer layer before being passed up.

B.3 STANDARDIZATION WITHIN THE OSI FRAMEWORK

The principal motivation for the development of the OSI model was to provide a framework for standardization. Within the model, one or more protocol standards can be developed at each layer. The model defines in general terms the functions to be performed at that layer and facilitates the standards-making process in two ways:

- Because the functions of each layer are well defined, standards can be developed independently and simultaneously for each layer. This speeds up the standards-making process.
- Because the boundaries between layers are well defined, changes in standards in one layer need not affect already existing software in another layer. This makes it easier to introduce new standards.

Figure B.3 illustrates the use of the OSI model as such a framework. The overall communications function is decomposed into seven distinct layers, using the principles outlined in Table B.2. These principles essentially amount to using modular design. That is, the overall function is broken up into a number of modules, making the interfaces between modules as simple as possible. In addition, the design principle of information hiding is used: Lower layers are concerned with greater levels of detail; upper layers are independent of these details. Within each layer, both the service provided to the next higher layer and the protocol to the peer layer in other systems is provided.

Figure B.4 shows more specifically the nature of the standardization required at each layer. Three elements are key:

- **Protocol specification:** Two entities at the same layer in different systems cooperate and interact by means of a protocol. Because two different open systems are involved, the protocol must be specified precisely. This includes the format of the protocol data units exchanged, the semantics of all fields, and the allowable sequence of PDUs.
- **Service definition:** In addition to the protocol or protocols that operate at a given layer, standards are needed for the services that each layer provides to the next higher layer. Typically, the definition of services is equivalent to a functional description that defines what services are provided, but not how the services are to be provided.

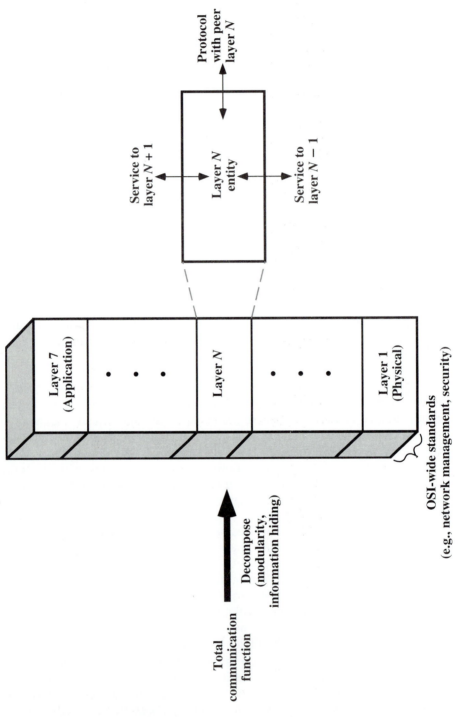

Figure B.3 The OSI Architecture as a Framework for Standardization.

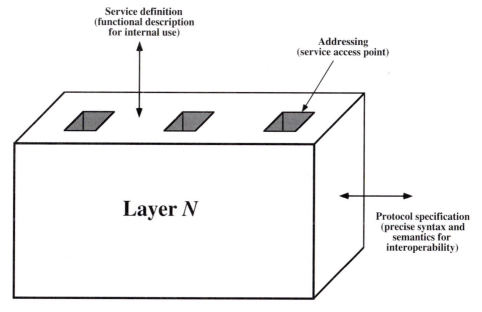

Figure B.4 Layer-Specific Standards.

- **Addressing:** Each layer provides services to entities at the next higher layer. These entities are referenced by means of a service access point (SAP). Thus, a network service access point (NSAP) indicates a transport entity that is a user of the network service.

The need to provide a precise protocol specification for open systems is self-evident. The other two items listed warrant further comment. With respect to service definitions, the motivation for providing only a functional definition is as follows. First, the interaction between two adjacent layers takes places within the confines of a single open system and is not the concern of any other open system. Thus, as long as peer layers in different systems provide the same services to their next higher layers, the details of how the services are provided may differ from one system to another without loss of interoperability. Second, it will usually be the case that adjacent layers are implemented on the same processor. In that case, we would like to leave the system programmer free to exploit the hardware and operating system to provide an interface that is as efficient as possible.

B.4 LAYERS

Physical Layer

The *physical layer* covers the physical interface between devices and the rules by which bits are passed from one to another. The physical layer has four important characteristics:

- Mechanical
- Electrical
- Functional
- Procedural

Examples of standards at this layer are EIA-232-E, as well as portion of ISDN and LAN standards.

Data Link Layer

Although the physical layer provides only a raw bit stream service, the *data link layer* attempts to make the physical link reliable and provides the means to activate, maintain, and deactivate the link. The principal service provided by the link layer to the higher layers is that of error detection and control. Thus, with a fully functional data link layer protocol, the next higher layer may assume virtually error-free transmission over the link. If communication is between two systems that are not directly connected, however, the connection will comprise a number of data links in tandem, each functioning independently. Thus, the higher layers are not relieved of an error-control responsibility.

Examples of standards at this layer are HDLC, LAPB, LAPD, and LLC.

Network Layer

The basic service of the *network layer* is to provide for the transparent transfer of data between transport entities. It relieves the transport layer of the need to know anything about the underlying data transmission and switching technologies used to connect systems. The network service is responsible for establishing, maintaining, and terminating connections across the intervening communications facility.

There is a spectrum of possibilities for intervening communications facilities to be managed by the network layer. At one extreme, the simplest, there is a direct link between stations. In this case, there may be little or no need for a network layer, because the data link layer can perform the necessary functions of managing the link. Between extremes, the most common use of layer 3 is to handle the details of using a communication network. In this case, the network entity in the station must provide the network with sufficient information to switch and route data to another station. At the other extreme, two stations might wish to communicate but are not even connected to the same network. Rather, they are connected to networks that, directly or indirectly, are connected to each other. One approach to providing for data transfer in such a case is to use an internet protocol (IP), which sits on top of a network protocol and is used by a transport protocol. IP is responsible for internetwork routing and delivery and relies on a layer 3 at each network for intranetwork services. IP is sometimes referred to as "layer 3.5."

The best-known example of layer 3 is the X.25 layer 3 standard.

Transport Layer

The purpose of layer 4 is to provide a reliable mechanism for the exchange of data between processes in different systems. The *transport layer* ensures that data units are delivered error free, in sequence, with no losses or duplications. The transport layer may also be concerned with optimizing the use of network services and providing a requested quality of service to session entities. For example, the session entity might specify acceptable error rates, maximum delay, priority, and security. In effect, the transport layer serves as the user's liaison with the communications facility.

The size and complexity of a transport protocol depend on the type of service it can get from layer 3. For a reliable layer 3 with a virtual circuit capability, a minimal layer 4 is required. If layer 3 is unreliable, the layer 4 protocol should include extensive error detection and recovery. Accordingly, ISO has defined five classes of transport protocol, each oriented toward a different underlying service.

Session Layer

The *session layer* provides the mechanism for controlling the dialogue between presentation entities. At a minimum, the session layer provides a means for two presentation entities to establish and use a connection, called a *session*. In addition, it may provide some of the following services:

- **Dialogue type:** This can be two-way simultaneous, two-way alternate, or one-way.
- **Recovery:** The session layer can provide a checkpointing mechanism, so that if a failure of some sort occurs between checkpoints, the session entity can retransmit all data since the last checkpoint.

Presentation Layer

The presentation layer offers application programs and terminal-handler programs a set of data transformation services. Services that this layer would typically provide include the following:

- **Data translation:** code and character set translation
- **Formatting:** modification of data layout
- **Syntax selection:** initial selection and subsequent modification of the transformation used

Examples of presentation protocols are data compression, encryption, and virtual terminal protocol. A virtual terminal protocol converts between specific terminal characteristics and a generic or virtual model used by application programs.

Application Layer

The *application layer* provides a means for application processes to access the OSI environment. This layer contains management functions and generally useful mechanisms to support distributed applications. Examples of protocols at this level are virtual file protocol and job transfer and manipulation protocol.

GLOSSARY

Analog Data   Data represented by a physical quantity that is considered to be continuously variable and whose magnitude is made directly proportional to the data or to a suitable function of the data.

Analog Signal   A continuously varying electromagnetic wave that may be propagated over a variety of media.

Analog Transmission   The transmission of analog signals without regard to content. The signal may be amplified, but there is no intermediate attempt to recover the data from the signal.

Application Layer   Layer 7 of the OSI model. This layer determines the interface of the system with the user and provides useful application-oriented services.

Asynchronous Transfer Mode (ATM)   A form of packet transmission using fixed-size packets, called cells. ATM is the data transfer interface for B-ISDN. Unlike X.25, ATM does not provide error-control and flow-control mechanisms.

ATM Adaptation Layer (AAL)   The layer that maps information transfer protocols onto ATM.

Automatic Repeat Request (ARQ)   A feature that automatically initiates a request for retransmission when an error in transmission is detected.

Basic Access   A term used to describe a simple standardized combination of access channels that constitute the access arrangements for the majority of ISDN users.

Bell Operating Company (BOC)   Before the divestiture of AT&T, the 22 Bell Operating Companies were AT&T subsidiaries that built, operated, and maintained the local and intrastate networks and provided most of the day-to-day service for customers. After divestiture, the BOCs retain their identity within seven regional companies (RBOCs) and are responsible for local service as defined by local access and transport areas (LATAs).

Bit Stuffing   The insertion of extra bits into a data stream to avoid the appearance of unintended control sequences.

Broadband ISDN (B-ISDN)   A second generation of ISDN. The key characteristic of broadband ISDN is that it provides transmission channels capable of supporting rates greater than the primary ISDN rate.

Cell Relay   The packet-switching mechanism used for the fixed-size packets called cells. ATM is based on cell relay technology.

Circuit Switching   A method of communicating in which a dedicated communications path is established between two devices through one or more intermediate switching nodes. Unlike packet switching, digital data are sent as a continuous stream of bits. Data rate is guaranteed, and delay is essentially limited to propagation time.

Codec   Coder-decoder. Transforms analog data into a digital bit stream (coder), and digital signals into analog data (decoder).

Common Carrier   In the United States, companies that furnish long-distance telecommunication services to the public. Common carriers are subject to regulation by federal and state regulatory commissions.

Common-Channel Signaling   A method of signaling in which signaling information relating to a multiplicity of circuits, or relating to a function for network management, is conveyed over a single channel by addressed messages.

Communications Architecture   The hardware and software structure that implements the communications function.

Cyclic Redundancy Check (CRC)   An error-detecting code in which the code is the remainder resulting from dividing the bits to be checked by a predetermined binary number.

Data Circuit-Terminating Equipment (DCE)   In a data station, the equipment that provides the signal conversion and coding between the data terminal equipment (DTE) and the line. The DCE may be separate equipment or an integral part of the DTE or of intermediate equipment. The DCE may perform other functions that are normally performed at the network end of the line.

Datagram   In packet switching, a self-contained packet, independent of other packets, that does not require acknowledgment and that carries information sufficient for routing from the originating data terminal equipment (DTE), without relying on earlier exchanges between the DTEs and the network.

Data Link Layer   Layer 2 of the OSI model. Converts an unreliable transmission channel into a reliable one.

Data Terminal Equipment (DTE)   Equipment consisting of digital end instruments that convert the user information into data signals for transmission or reconvert the received data signals into user information.

Digital Data   Data represented by discrete values or conditions.

Digital PBX   A private branch exchange (PBX) that operates internally on digital signals. Thus, voice signals must be digitized for use in the PBX.

Digital Signal   A discrete or discontinuous signal, such as a sequence of voltage pulses.

Digital Subscriber Signaling System 1   The collective term to define the D channel signaling capabilities across the ISDN user–network interface. Includes physical (I.430/I.431), data link (Q.921) and network-layer (Q.931) protocols.

Digital Transmission   The transmission of digital data or analog data that have been digitized, using either an analog or digital signal, in which the digital content is recovered and repeated at intermediate points to reduce the effects of impairments, such as noise, distortion, and attenuation.

Digitize   To convert an analog signal to a digital signal.

Encapsulation   The addition of control information by a protocol entity to data obtained from a protocol user.

Error-Detecting Code   A code in which each data signal conforms to specific rules of construction, so that departures from this construction in the received signal can be automatically detected.

Error Rate   The ratio of the number of data units in error to the total number of data units.

Exchange Area   A geographical area within which there is a single uniform set of charges for telephone service. A call between any two points within an exchange area is a local call.

Flow Control   A function performed by a receiving entity to limit the amount or rate of data sent by a transmitting entity.

Frame-Check Sequence   An error-detecting code inserted as a field in a block of data to be transmitted. The code serves to check for errors upon reception of the data.

Frame-Mode Bearer Service (FMBS)   A service by which data are transferred in variable-size packets, called frames, at the data link layer. This service is provided in ISDN as an alternative to X.25. Unlike X.25, FMBS does not provide error-control and flow-control mechanisms.

Frame Relay   The packet-switching mechanism used for the frames of the frame-mode bearer service.

Frequency-Division Multiplexing (FDM)   Division of a transmission facility into two or more channels by splitting the frequency band transmitted by the facility into narrower bands, each of which is used to constitute a distinct channel.

Full-Duplex Transmission   Transmission of data in both directions at the same time.

Functional Group   A set of functions that may be performed by a single piece of equipment.

Half-Duplex Transmission   Data transmitted in either direction, one direction at a time.

Header   System-defined control information that precedes user data.

Inchannel Signaling   A technique in which the same channel is used to carry network control signals as is used to carry the call to which the control signals relate.

Integrated Digital Network (IDN)   The integration of transmission and switching functions using digital technology in a circuit-switched telecommunications network.

Integrated Services Digital Network (ISDN)   Planned worldwide telecommunication service that will use digital transmission and switching technology to support voice and digital data communications.

Layer A conceptual region that embodies one or more functions between an upper and a lower logical boundary.

Local Access and Transport Areas (LATA) A geographic area generally equivalent to a standard metropolitan statistical area. The territory served by the Bell System was divided into approximately 160 LATAs at divestiture. Intra-LATA services are provided by the Bell Operating Companies.

Local Loop A transmission path, generally twisted pair, between the individual subscriber and the nearest switching center of a public telecommunications network. Also referred to as a subscriber loop.

Modem Modulator-demodulator. Transforms a digital bit stream into an analog signal (modulator) and vice versa (demodulator).

Multiplexing In data transmission, a function that permits two or more data sources to share a common transmission medium such that each data source has its own channel.

Network Layer Layer 3 of the OSI model. Responsible for routing data through a communication network.

Network Terminating Equipment (NTE) A grouping of ISDN functions at the boundary between the ISDN and the subscriber.

Open Systems Interconnection (OSI) Reference Model A model of communications between cooperating devices. It defines a seven-layer architecture of communication functions.

Packet Switching A method of transmitting messages through a communications network, in which long messages are subdivided into short packets. Each packet is passed from source to destination through intermediate nodes. At each node, the entire message is received, stored briefly, and then passed on to the next node.

Physical Layer Layer 1 of the OSI model. Concerned with the electrical, mechanical, and timing aspects of signal transmission over a medium.

Piggybacking The inclusion of an acknowledgment of a previously received protocol data unit in an outgoing protocol data unit.

Ping-Pong Transmission Technique See *Time-Compression Multiplexing.*

Postal, Telegraph, and Telephone (PTT) A government organization that operates a nationalized public telecommunications network.

Presentation Layer Layer 6 of the OSI model. Concerned with data format and display.

Private Branch Exchange (PBX) A telephone exchange on the user's premises. Provides a circuit-switching facility for telephones on extension lines within the building and access to the public telephone network.

Private Network A facility in which the customer leases circuits and sometimes switching capacity for the customer's exclusive use. Access may be provided to a public switched telecommunication service.

Protocol A formal statement of the procedures that are adopted to ensure communication between two or more functions within the same layer of a hierarchy of functions.

Protocol Data Unit (PDU)   Information that is delivered as a unit between peer entities of a network and may contain control information, address information, or data.

Pseudoternary Coding   A form of digital signaling in which three signal levels are used to encode binary data. In ISDN, the form of pseudoternary is one in which binary one is represented by no line signal and binary zero is represented, alternately, by positive and negative voltage pulses.

Public Data Network (PDN)   A packet-switched network that is publicly available to subscribers. Usually, the term connotes government control or national monopoly.

Pulse-Code Modulation (PCM)   A process in which a signal is sampled, and the magnitude of each sample with respect to a fixed reference is quantized and converted by coding to a digital signal.

Recognized Private Operating Agency (RPOA)   A private or government-controlled corporation that provides telecommunications services (e.g., AT&T). RPOAs participate as nonvoting members of ITU-T.

Reference Configuration   A combination of functional groups and reference points that shows possible network arrangements.

Reference Point   A conceptual point at the conjunction of two nonoverlapping functional groupings.

Service Access Point (SAP)   A means of identifying a user of the services of a protocol entity. A protocol entity provides one or more SAPs, for use by higher-level entities.

Session Layer   Layer 5 of the OSI model. Manages a logical connection (session) between two communicating processes or applications.

Signaling   The exchange of information specifically concerned with the establishment and control of connections, and with management, in a telecommunication network.

Sliding-Window Technique   A method of flow control in which a transmitting station may send numbered protocol data units (PDUs) within a window of numbers. The window changes dynamically to allow additional PDUs to be sent.

Specialized Common Carrier   In the United States, a telecommunications common carrier other than AT&T and the Bell Operating Companies, authorized to provide a variety of transmission services.

Subscriber Loop   See *Local Loop.*

Synchronous Digital Hierarchy (SDH)   A hierarchy of high-speed synchronous time-division multiplexing (TDM) facilities defined by a ITU-T specification of frame structure and data rates.

Synchronous Optical Network (SONET)   An American National Standards Institute (ANSI) specification that is compatible with SDH. SONET covers one more data rate than does SDH.

Synchronous Time-Division Multiplexing   A method of TDM in which time slots on a shared transmission line are assigned to devices on a fixed, predetermined basis.

Teleaction Service   Telemetry service. A type of telecommunication service that uses short messages, requiring a very low transmission rate, between the user and the network.

Telecommunication Service   That which is offered by an administration or RPOA to its customers in order to satisfy a specific telecommunications requirement. Bearer service, teleservice, and teleaction service are types of telecommunication service.

Telematics   User-oriented information-transfer services, including teletex, videotex, and facsimile.

Teleservice   A type of telecommunication service that provides the complete capability, including terminal equipment functions, for communication between users according to protocols established by agreement between administrations and/or RPOAs.

Teletex   A text communications service that provides message preparation and transmission facilities.

Teletext   A one-way information retrieval service. A fixed number of information pages are repetitively broadcast on unused portions of a TV channel bandwidth. A decoder at the TV set is used to select and display pages.

Time-Compression Multiplexing   A means for providing full-duplex digital data transmission over a single twisted pair. Data are buffered at each end and are sent across the line at approximately double the subscriber data rate, with the two ends taking turns.

Time-Division Multiplexing (TDM)   The division of a transmission facility into multiple channels by allotting the facility to different channels, one at a time.

Transport Layer   Layer 4 of the OSI model. Provides reliable, sequenced transfer of data between endpoints.

User–User Protocol   A protocol that is adopted between two or more users in order to ensure communication between them.

Videotex   A two-way information retrieval service accessible to terminals and TV sets equipped with a special decoder. Pages of information at a central resource are retrieved interactively over a switched telephone line connection.

Virtual Circuit   A packet-switching mechanism in which a logical connection (virtual circuit) is established between two stations at the start of transmission. All packets follow the same route, need not carry a complete address, and arrive in sequence.

REFERENCES

ACKL93   Ackland, B., et al. "A Video-Codec Chip Set for Multimedia Applications." *AT&T Technical Journal,* January/February 1993.

ARMB87   Armbruster, H. "Broadband Communications and Its Realization with Broadband ISDN." *IEEE Communications Magazine*, November 1987.

ARMI93   Armitage, G., and Adams, K. "Packet Reassembly During Cell Loss." *IEEE Network,* September 1993.

ARUL96   Arulambalam, A.; Chen, X.; and Ansari, N. "Allocating Fair Rates for Available Bit Rate Service in ATM Networks." *IEEE Communications Magazine*, November 1996.

ASH90   Ash, G. "Design and Control of Networks with Dynamic Nonhierarchical Routing." *IEEE Communications Magazine,* October 1990.

ATM96   ATM Forum. *Traffic Management Specification Version 4.0.* April 1996.

BELL82   Bell Telephone Laboratories. *Transmission Systems for Communications.* Murray Hill, NJ, 1982.

BELL90   Bell Communication Research. *Telecommunication Transmission Engineering,* 3rd edition, 1990.

BELL91   Bellamy, J. *Digital Telephony.* New York: Wiley, 1991.

BERG91   Bergman, W. "Narrowband Frame Relay Congestion Control." *Proceedings of the Tenth Annual Phoenix Conference of Computers and Communications,* March 1991.

BERG96   Bergmans, J. *Digital Baseband Transmission and Recording.* Boston: Kluwer, 1996.

BERT92   Bertsekas, D., and Gallager, R. *Data Networks.* Englewood Cliffs, NJ: Prentice Hall, 1992.

BHAT97   Bhatnagar, P. *Engineering Networks for Synchronization, CCS 7 and ISDN.* New York: IEEE Press, 1997.

BLAC95   Black, U. *The V Series Recommendations.* New York: McGraw-Hill, 1995.

529

BLAC96   Black, U. *Frame Relay Networks: Specifications and Implementations.* New York: McGraw-Hill, 1996.

BLAC97a   Black, U. *ISDN and SS7: Architectures for Digital Signaling Networks.* Upper Saddle River, NJ: Prentice Hall, 1997.

BLAC97b   Black, U., and Waters, S. *SONET and T1: Architectures for Digital Transport Networks.* Upper Saddle River, NJ: Prentice Hall, 1997.

BONO95   Bonomi, F., and Fendick, K. "The Rate-Based Flow Control Framework for the Available Bit Rate ATM Service." *IEEE Network*, March/April 1995.

BURG91   Burg, J., and Dorman, D. "Broadband ISDN Resource Management: The Role of Virtual Paths." *IEEE Communications Magazine,* September 1991.

BUSH89   Bush, J. "Frame-Relay Services Promise WAN Bandwidth on Demand." *Data Communications*, July 1989.

CERN84   Cerni, D. *Standards in Process: Foundations and Profiles of ISDN and OSI Studies.* National Telecommunications and Information Administration, Report 84–170. December 1984.

CHEN89a   Chen, K., and Rege, K. "A Comparative Performance Study of Various Congestion Controls for ISDN Frame-Relay Networks." *Proceedings, IEEE INFOCOM '89,* April 1989.

CHEN89b   Chen, K., Ho, K., and Saksena, V. "Analysis and Design of a Highly Reliable Transport Architecture for ISDN Frame-Relay Networks." *IEEE Journal on Selected Areas in Communications,* October 1989.

CHEN96   Chen, T.; Liu, S.; and Samalam, V. "The Available Bit Rate Service for Data in ATM Networks." *IEEE Communications Magazine*, May 1996.

CIOF97   Cioffi, J. "Asymmetric Digital Subscriber Lines." In [GIBS97].

COUC97   Couch, L. *Digital and Analog Communication Systems.* Upper Saddle River, NJ: Prentice Hall, 1997.

DEMA93   DeMaio, M., and Kafka, H. "Broadband Applications and Services Prospectus." *AT&T Technical Journal,* November/December 1993.

DONO86   Donohoe, D.; Johannessen, G.; and Stone, R. "Realization of a Signaling System No. 7 Network for AT&T." *IEEE Journal on Selected Areas in Communications,* November 1986.

DORL96   Dorling, B.; Pieters, P.; and Valenzuela, E. IBM Frame Relay Guide. IBM Publication SG24-4463-01, 1996. Available at www.redbooks.ibm.com.

DOSH88   Doshi, B., and Nguyen, H. "Congestion Control in ISDN Frame-Relay Networks." *AT&T Technical Journal,* November/December 1988.

DUBO92   DuBose, K., and Sim, H. "An Effective Bit Rate/Table Lookup Based Admission Control Algorithm for the ATM B-ISDN." *Proceedings, 17th Conference on Local Computer Networks,* September 1992.

FALC82   Falconer, D. "Adaptive Reference Echo Cancellation." *IEEE Transactions on Communications,* September 1982.

FREE94   Freeman, R. *Reference Manual for Telecommunications Engineering.* New York: Wiley, 1994.

FREE96   Freeman, R. *Telecommunication System Engineering.* New York: Wiley, 1996.

FUJI90   Fujioka, M., Ikeda, Y., and Norigoe, M. "Error Control Criteria in the Message Transfer Part of CCITT Signaling System No. 7." *IEEE Transactions on Communications,* September 1990.

GARR96   Garrett, M. "A Service Architecture for ATM: From Applications to Scheduling." *IEEE Network*, May/June 1996.

GERS91   Gersht, A., and Lee, K. "A Congestion Control Framework for ATM Networks." *IEEE Journal on Selected Areas in Communications*, September 1991.

GERW84   Gerwen, P.; Verhoeckx, N.; and Claasen, T. "Design Considerations for a 144 kbit/s Digital Transmission Unit for the Local Telephone Network." *IEEE Journal on Selected Areas in Communications,* March 1984.

GIBS97   Gibson, J., ed. *The Communications Handbook.* Boca Raton, FL: CRC Press, 1997.

GIFF86   Gifford, W. "ISDN User–Network Interfaces." *IEEE Journal on Selected Areas in Communications,* May 1986.

GOLD91   Goldstein, F. "Congestion Control in Frame Relay Networks Using Explicit Binary Feedback." *Proceedings, Tenth Annual Phoenix Conference on Computers and Communications,* March 1991.

GORA95   Goralski, W. *Introduction to ATM Networking.* New York: McGraw-Hill, 1995.

GORA97   Goralski, W. *SONET: A Guide to Synchronous Optical Networks.* New York: McGraw-Hill, 1997.

HAND91   Handel, R., and Huber, M. *Integrated Broadband Networks.* Reading, MA: Addison-Wesley, 1991.

HAND94   Handel, R.; Huber, N.; and Schroder, S. *ATM Networks: Concepts, Protocols, Applications.* Reading, MA: Addison-Wesley, 1994.

HARM89   Harman, W., and Newman, C. "ISDN Protocols for Connection Control." *IEEE Journal on Selected Areas in Communications,* September 1989.

HASK87   Haskell, B.; Pearson, D.; and Yamamoto, H., editors. *Low Bit-Rate Coding of Moving Images.* Special issue of *IEEE Journal on Selected Areas in Communications,* August 1987.

HAWL97   Hawley, G. "Systems Considerations for the Use of xDSL Technology for Data Access." *IEEE Communications Magazine*, March 1997.

HUAN91   Huang, D., and Valenti, D. "Digital Subscriber Lines: Network Considerations for ISDN Basic Access." *Proceedings of the IEEE*, February 1991.

HUMP97   Humphrey, M., and Freeman, J. "How xDSL Supports Broadband Services to the Home." *IEEE Network*, January/March 1997.

JABB91   Jabbari, B. "Common Channel Signaling System Number 7 for ISDN and Intelligent Networks." *Proceedings of the IEEE,* February 1991.

JAIN91   Jain, R. *The Art of Computer Systems Performance Analysis: Techniques for Experimental Design, Measurement, Simulation, and Modeling.* New York: Wiley, 1991.

JAIN96a   Jain, R., et al. "Source Behavior for ATM ABR Traffic Management: An Explanation." *IEEE Communications Magazine,* November 1996.

JAIN96b   Jain, R., et al. *ERICA Switch Algorithm: A Complete Description.* ATM Forum Contribution 96-1172, August 1996. Available at http://www.cis.ohio-state.edu/~jain.

KADE81   Kaderali, F., and Weston, J. "Digital Subscriber Loops." *Electrical Communication*, Vol. 56, No. 1, 1981.

KESS97   Kessler, G. *ISDN: Concepts, Facilities, and Services.* New York: McGraw-Hill, 1997.

KOVA94   Kovarik, K., and Maveddat, P. "Multi-Rate ISDN." *IEEE Communications Magazine,* April 1994.

KUMA95   Kumar, B. *Broadband Communications: A Professional Guide to ATM, Frame Relay, SMDS, SONET, and B-ISDN.* New York: McGraw-Hill, 1995.

LAI88   Lai, W. "Packet Forwarding." *IEEE Communications Magazine,* July 1988.

LECH86   Lechleider, J. "Loop Transmission Aspects of ISDN Basic Access." *IEEE Journal on Selected Areas in Communications,* November 1986.

LECH89   Lechleider, J. "Line Codes for Digital Subscriber Lines." *IEEE Communications Magazine,* September 1989.

LEE89   Lee, K., and Lim, Y. "Performance Analysis of the Congestion Control Scheme in Signaling System No. 7." *Proceedings, INFOCOM '89,* April 1989.

LIN90   Lin, D. "Minimum Mean-Squared Error Echo Cancellation and Equalization for Digital Subscriber Line Transmission." *IEEE Transactions on Communications,* January 1990.

LUIN97   Luinen, S.; Budrikis, Z.; and Cantoni, A. "The Controlled Cell Transfer Capability." *Computer Communications Review*, January 1997.

MANF93   Manfield, D.; Millsteed, G.; and Zukerman, M. "Congestion Controls in SS7 Signaling Networks." *IEEE Communications Magazine,* June 1993.

MART90   Martin, J. *Telecommunications and the Computer.* Englewood Cliffs, NJ: Prentice Hall, 1990.

MAXW96   Maxwell, K. "Asymmetric Digital Subscriber Line: Interim Technology for the Next Forty Years." *IEEE Communications Magazine*, October 1996.

MCDY95   McDysan, D., and Spohn, D. *ATM: Theory and Application.* New York: McGraw-Hill, 1995.

MESS86   Messerschmitt, D. "Design Issues in the ISDN U-Interface Transceiver." *IEEE Journal on Selected Areas in Communications,* November 1986.

MINZ89a Minzer, S., and Spears, D. "New Directions in Signaling for Broadband ISDN." *IEEE Communications Magazine*, February 1989.

MINZ89b Minzer, S., and Spears, D. "Broadband ISDN and Asynchronous Transfer Mode." *IEEE Communications Magazine*, September 1989.

MOCH94 Mochida, Y. "Technologies for Local-Access Fibering." *IEEE Communications Magazine*, February 1994.

NSPA79 National Standards Policy Advisory Committee. *National Policy on Standards for the United States.* 1979. Reprinted in [CERN84].

OKAD92 Okada, K., and Shinohara, H. "Fiber Optic Subscriber Systems." *IEEE LTS*, November 1992.

OSHA95 Oshaki, H., et al. "Rate-Based Congestion Control for ATM Networks." *Computer Communication Review*, April 1995.

PAND90 Pandya, R., and Cullum, M. "Planning for Circuit-Switched Data Services in the ISDN Era: Interworking Solutions and Standards." *Computer Networks and ISDN Systems,* December 1990.

PARE88 Parekh, S., and Sohraby, K. "Some Performance Trade-Offs Associated with ATM Fixed-Length Vs. Variable-Length Cell Formats." *Proceedings, GlobeCom,* November 1988.

PHEL86 Phelan, J. "Signaling System 7." *Telecommunications,* September 1986.

PITT96 Pitts, J., and Schormans, J. *Introduction to ATM Design and Performance.* New York: Wiley, 1996.

PRAS93 Prasanna, P.; Levy, R.; and Swenson, J. "Principles and Standards for Broadband ISDN." *AT&T Technical Journal,* November/December 1993.

PRYC93 Prycker, M.; Peschi, R.; and Van Landegem, R. "B-ISDN and the OSI Protocol Reference Model." *IEEE Network,* March 1993.

PRYC96 Prycker, M. *Asynchronous Transfer Mode: Solutions for Broadband ISDN.* New York: Ellis Horwood, 1996.

RAMA93 Ramaswami, V., and Wang, J. "Analysis of the Link Error Monitoring Protocols in the Common Channel Signaling Network." *IEEE Transactions on Networking,* February 1993.

REEV95 Reeve, W. *Subscriber Loop Signaling and Transmission Handbook.* Piscataway, NJ: IEEE Press, 1995.

REY83 Rey, R., editor. *Engineering and Operations in the Bell System,* 2nd edition. Murray Hill, NJ: AT&T Bell Laboratories, 1983.

RUMS95 Rumsewicz, M., and Smith, D. "A Comparison of SS7 Congestion Control Options During Mass Call-In Situations." *IEEE/ACM Transactions on Networking*, February 1995.

RUSS95 Russell, R. *Signaling System #7.* New York: McGraw-Hill, 1995.

SAIT96 Saito, J., et al. "Performance Issues in Public ABR Service." *IEEE Communications Magazine*, November 1996.

SATO90   Sato, K.; Ohta, S.; and Tokizawa, I. "Broad-band ATM Network Architecture Based on Virtual Paths." *IEEE Transactions on Communications,* August 1990.

SATO91   Sato, K.; Ueda, H.; and Yoshikai, M. "The Role of Virtual Path Crossconnection." *IEEE LTS,* August 1991.

SCHW96   Schwartz, M. *Broadband Integrated Networks.* Upper Saddle River, NJ: Prentice Hall PTR, 1996.

SKLA88   Sklar, B. *Digital Communications: Fundamentals and Applications.* Englewood Cliffs, NJ: Prentice Hall, 1988.

SPOH97   Spohn, D. *Data Network Design.* New York: McGraw-Hill, 1997.

SPRA91   Spragins, J,; Hammond, J.; and Pawlikowski, K. *Telecommunications Protocols and Design.* Reading, MA.: Addison-Wesley, 1991.

STAL97   Stallings, W. *Data and Computer Communications,* 5th edition. Upper Saddle River, NJ: Prentice Hall, 1997.

SUGI88   Sugimoto, M.; Taniguchi, M.; Yokoi, S.; and Hata, H. "Videotex: Advancing to Higher Bandwidth." *IEEE Communications Magazine,* February 1988.

SUZU94   Suzuki, T. "ATM Adaptation Layer Protocol." *IEEE Communications Magazine,* April 1994.

SZEC86   Szechenyi, K.; Zapf, F.; and Sallaerts, D. "Integrated Full Digital U-Interface Circuit for ISDN Subscriber Loops." *IEEE Journal on Selected Areas in Communications,* November 1986.

VAUG59   Vaughan, H. "Research Model for Time Separation Integrated Communication." *Bell System Technical Journal,* July 1959.

VERM90   Verma, P., editor. *ISDN Systems: Architecture, Technology, and Applications.* Englewood Cliffs, NJ: Prentice Hall, 1990.

WANG92   Wang, Z., and Crowcroft, J. "SEAL Detects Cell Misordering." *IEEE Network,* July 1992.

WEIS89   Weisberger, A. "The Evolving Versions of ISDN's Terminal Adapter." *Data Communications,* August 1989.

INDEX

ACRONYMS

AAL	ATM Adaptation Layer
ADSL	Asymmetric Digital Subscriber Line
AMI	Alternate Mark Inversion
ANSI	American National Standards Institute
ASK	Amplitude Shift Keying
ATM	Asynchronous Transfer Mode
B-ISDN	Broadband ISDN
CBR	Constant Bit Rate
CCITT	Consultative Committee on International Telegraphy and Telephony
CIR	Committed Information Rate
CMI	Coded Mark Inversion
CRC	Cyclic Redundancy Check
CLP	Cell Loss Priority
CSPDN	Circuit-Switched Public Data Network
DCE	Data Circuit-Terminating Equipment
DLCI	Data Link Connection Identifier
DMT	Discrete Multitone
DSS 1	Digital Subscriber Signaling System 1
DTE	Data Terminal Equipment
FCS	Frame Check Sequence
FDM	Frequency-Division Multiplexing
FMBS	Frame-Mode Bearer Service
FSK	Frequency Shift Keying
HDLC	High-Level Data Link Control
IDN	Integrated Digital Network
ISDN	Integrated Services Digital Network
ISO	International Organization for Standardization
ITU	International Telecommunication Union
ITU-T	ITU Telecommunication Standardization Sector
LAPB	Link Access Procedures—Balanced
LAPD	Link Access Procedure on the D Channel
LAPF	Link Access Procedure for Frame-Mode Bearer Services
NNI	Network–Network Interface
OSI	Open Systems Interconnection
PCM	Pulse-Code Modulation
PDU	Protocol Data Unit
POTS	Plain Old Telephone Service
PSK	Phase Shift Keying
PSPDN	Packet-Switched Public Data Network
QAM	Quadrature Amplitude Modulation
QOS	Quality of Service
SDH	Synchronous Digital Hierarchy
SDU	Service Data Unit
SONET	Synchronous Optical Network
TDM	Time-Division Multiplexing
UNI	User–Network Interface
VBR	Variable Bit Rate
WDM	Wavelength-Division Multiplexing
2B1Q	Two Binary, One Quaternary